200 Best Jobs Through Apprenticeships

Second Edition

Part of JIST's Best Jobs® Series

Michael Farr and Laurence Shatkin, Ph.D.

Also in JIST's Best Jobs Series

- ✳ Best Jobs for the 21st Century
- ✳ 200 Best Jobs for College Graduates
- ✳ 300 Best Jobs Without a Four-Year Degree
- ✳ 50 Best Jobs for Your Personality
- ✳ 40 Best Fields for Your Career
- ✳ 225 Best Jobs for Baby Boomers
- ✳ 250 Best-Paying Jobs
- ✳ 150 Best Jobs for Your Skills

- ✳ 150 Best Jobs Through Military Training
- ✳ 150 Best Recession-Proof Jobs
- ✳ 175 Best Jobs Not Behind a Desk
- ✳ 150 Best Jobs for a Better World
- ✳ 200 Best Jobs for Introverts
- ✳ 150 Best Low-Stress Jobs
- ✳ 10 Best College Majors for Your Personality

JIST Works
America's Career Publisher®

200 Best Jobs Through Apprenticeships, Second Edition

© 2009 by JIST Publishing

Published by JIST Works, an imprint of JIST Publishing
7321 Shadeland Station, Suite 200
Indianapolis, IN 46256-3923

Phone: 800-648-JIST   Fax: 877-454-7839
E-mail: info@jist.com   Web site: www.jist.com

Some Other Books by the Authors

Michael Farr

The Quick Resume & Cover Letter Book

Same-Day Resume

Top 100 Careers Without a Four-Year Degree

Overnight Career Choice

100 Fastest-Growing Careers

Laurence Shatkin

90-Minute College Major Matcher

Quick Guide to College Majors and Careers

Your $100,000 Career Plan

New Guide for Occupational Exploration

150 Best Recession-Proof Jobs

Quantity discounts are available for JIST products. Have future editions of JIST books automatically delivered to you on publication through our convenient standing order program. Please call 800-648-JIST or visit www.jist.com for a free catalog and more information.

Visit www.jist.com for information on JIST, free job search information, tables of contents and sample pages, and ordering information on our many products.

Acquisitions Editor: Susan Pines
Development Editor: Stephanie Koutek
Cover and Interior Designer: Aleata Halbig
Cover Photography: Image Source, Getty Images

Interior Layout: Toi Davis
Proofreaders: Jeanne Clark, Paula Lowell
Indexer: Cheryl Lenser

Printed in the United States of America

14 13 12 11 10 09 08   9 8 7 6 5 4 3 2 1

Library of Congress Cataloging-in-Publication Data

Farr, J. Michael.
  200 best jobs through apprenticeships / Michael Farr and Laurence Shatkin.
    p. cm. -- (JIST's best jobs series)
  Rev. ed. of: 250 best jobs through apprenticeships. c2005.
  Includes index.
  ISBN 978-1-59357-537-3 (alk. paper)
  1. Apprenticeship programs--United States. 2. Vocational guidance--United States. 3. Occupations--United States. I. Shatkin, Laurence. II.
  Farr, J. Michael. 250 best jobs through apprenticeships. III. Title. IV. Title: Two hundred best jobs through apprenticeships.
  HD4885.U5F37 2009
  331.25'9220973--dc22

                              2008046427

We have been careful to provide accurate information throughout this book, but it is possible that errors and omissions have been introduced. Please consider this in making any career plans or other important decisions. Trust your own judgment above all else and in all things.

Trademarks: All brand names and product names used in this book are trade names, service marks, trademarks, or registered trademarks of their respective owners.

ISBN 978-1-59357-537-3

This Is a Big Book, But It Is Very Easy to Use

For your whole life, you've been hearing people tell you that education is the key to a good career. But the best-kept secret about careers is that most job skills are learned on the job. Still, young people face a chicken-and-egg problem: How do you get the job where you can learn the skills if you don't have the skills that qualify you for the job? A lot of young people solve this problem by getting a college degree that serves as a ticket to get them into the job.

But wouldn't it be marvelous if there were another formal entry route to careers besides college—an entry route that consisted mostly of on-the-job training, with only as much book learning mixed in as needed? Good news: This entry route already exists, and it's called apprenticeship. But so many people think apprenticeship is old-fashioned or it's only for "grease monkeys" and construction trades.

This book is designed to open your eyes. It will alert you to the many career possibilities that are open to you through apprenticeships. In fact, more than 1,000 apprenticeships are registered with the U.S. Department of Labor, and they are linked to over 350 occupations.

Because there are so many apprenticeable jobs to choose from, this book is also designed to narrow your thinking. The easy-to-browse lists of the best apprenticeable jobs will help you focus on the career opportunities that combine high rewards (good income, many job openings) with other features that matter to you, such as your interests.

Of course, a list goes only so far. To make a good career choice, you need to dig down into the details of what a job is like—what the tasks are, what skills are required, what the work environment is like, and so forth. This book provides a wealth of information on apprenticeable jobs, based on the most current data available from the U.S. Department of Labor and the Census Bureau.

After you've opened your eyes, narrowed your thinking, and dug into the details about an apprenticeable job, you may be ready to make your career move. So this book also tells you how to find out about apprenticeship programs in your area and how to become informed about the actual requirements of the programs that you find.

You may face a lot of competition to get into the apprenticeship program that appeals most to you. But in some industries and in some parts of the U.S., apprenticeships are begging for qualified applicants. Maybe a rewarding career is waiting for you to take the initiative—and the best part of all is that you will be paid to be an apprentice.

So get started in this book and learn about a route to career entry that doesn't require you to shell out tens of thousands of dollars in tuition or endure grueling basic training in a distant boot camp.

Table of Contents

Summary of Major Sections

Introduction. A short overview to help you better understand and use the book. *Starts on page 1.*

Part I—Overview of Apprenticeships. Part I is an overview of apprenticeship—what it is, where the opportunities are, what the requirements are, what the pros and cons are, and where to find out more. This section may clear up some misunderstandings you have about apprenticeship, and it will help you appreciate what apprenticeship has to offer you. *Starts on page 17.*

Part II—Master List of Nationally Registered Apprenticeships. This part lists all 1,052 apprenticeships that are currently registered with the U.S. Department of Labor. The apprenticeships are grouped according to interest fields, so you can easily find those in industries that appeal to you. *Starts on page 29.*

Part III—The Best Jobs Lists: Jobs You Can Enter Through Apprenticeship. The 43 lists in Part III show you the best apprenticeable jobs in terms of high salaries, fast growth, and plentiful job openings. You can also see which jobs are best when these factors are combined. Further lists classify the jobs according to their interest fields and several other features, such as jobs with the highest percentage of women and of men. Although there are a lot of lists, they are easy to understand because they have clear titles and are organized into groupings of related lists. *Starts on page 75.*

Part IV—Descriptions of the 200 Best Apprenticeable Jobs. This part provides a brief information-packed description of each of the 200 apprenticeable jobs that met our criteria for high pay, fast growth, or many openings. Each description contains information on earnings, projected growth, years of apprenticeship required, job duties, skills, related job titles, related knowledge and courses, and many other details. The descriptions are in alphabetical order. This structure makes it easy to look up a job that you've identified from Part II or Part III and that you want to learn more about. *Starts on page 139.*

Part V—Appendixes. This part contains five appendixes. Appendix A describes the parts of an apprenticeship standards document and explains its contents. Appendix B contains excerpts from apprenticeship standards documents. Appendix C lists contact information for state apprenticeship offices. Appendix D explains the various skills listed in the job descriptions in Part IV, and Appendix E lists the GOE interest areas and work groups. *Starts on page 409.*

Detailed Table of Contents

Introduction

Apprenticeship: "The Other Four-Year Degree"

Apprenticeship is a system of job training in which trainees become highly skilled workers through a combination of worksite learning and classroom learning. It is sometimes called "the other four-year degree" because it often takes four years and it results in a nationally recognized credential that can open the door to income and job security that can be as good as or better than what college graduates enjoy.

Where the Information Came From

The information we used in creating this book came mostly from databases created by the U.S. Department of Labor:

❋ We started with the 1,052 apprenticeship programs presently included in the Department of Labor's Registered Apprenticeship Partners Information Data System (RAPIDS) database.

❋ The RAPIDS database links these jobs to occupations in the Department of Labor's O*NET (Occupational Information Network) database, which is now the primary source of detailed information on occupations. The Department of Labor updates the O*NET on a regular basis, and we used the most recent one available—O*NET release 13.

❋ Because we wanted to include data on earnings, growth, and number of openings—information not included in the O*NET—we used sources at the U.S. Department of Labor's Bureau of Labor Statistics (BLS). The Occupational Employment Statistics survey provided the most reliable figures on earnings we could obtain, and the Employment Projections program provided the nation's best figures on job growth and openings. These two BLS programs use a slightly different system of job titles than the O*NET does, but we were able to link the BLS data to most of the O*NET job titles we used to develop this book.

- To get figures on the percentage of women in occupations, we cross-referenced data from Current Population Survey (CPS), conducted by the U.S. Census Bureau. As with the BLS data, we had to match slightly different sets of job titles, but we were able to identify CPS data for almost all the O*NET jobs.

Of course, information in a database format can be boring and even confusing, so we did many things to help make the data useful and present it to you in a form that is easy to understand.

How the Best Apprenticeable Jobs in This Book Were Selected

Here is the procedure we followed to select the 200 jobs we included in this book:

1. We began by obtaining from the U.S. Department of Labor the most up-to-date list of the apprenticeships registered with them. This list totaled 1,052 (an increase of almost 20% since 2004).
2. The government database that lists the apprenticeships matches them to jobs in the O*NET database. Often multiple apprenticeships are linked to a single O*NET job. For example, there are apprenticeships for nine kinds of electricians. Thus, the number of apprenticeable *jobs* came to only 353.
3. The Department of Labor also identifies the educational and/or training requirements for all the O*NET jobs. We eliminated all jobs that normally require a bachelor's degree or higher. For example, there is a registered apprenticeship program for Computer Systems Analysts, but this career normally requires a bachelor's degree. There are also apprenticeships for Historians, who usually need a master's degree. We decided *not* to eliminate jobs that normally require an associate degree, because the classroom learning component of apprenticeship programs sometimes includes this degree or is accepted as a substitute for the degree. Once we had eliminated occupations that commonly require four or more years of college, 306 apprenticeable jobs remained.
4. We eliminated one more job, Commercial Pilots, because the related apprenticeship program (Air Transport Pilot) requires that applicants already have a commercial pilot's license and considerable flight experience.
5. Of the remaining 305 jobs, 292 could be linked to a reasonably complete set of data from the Department of Labor: annual earnings, projected growth through 2016, number of job openings projected per year, work tasks, and skills.
6. Next, we removed 15 jobs because they have annual earnings of less than $20,920, which means that 75% of workers earn more than the workers in these jobs. We also removed eight jobs that are expected to employ fewer than 500 workers per year and to shrink rather than grow in workforce size.

7. We ranked the remaining 269 apprenticeable jobs three times, based on these important criteria: annual earnings, projected growth, and number of job openings projected per year.

8. We then added the three numerical rankings for each job to calculate its overall score.

9. To emphasize jobs that tend to pay more, are likely to grow more rapidly, and have more job openings, we selected the 200 job titles with the best total overall scores. These jobs are the focus of this book.

For example, the apprenticeable job with the best combined score for earnings, growth, and number of job openings is Paralegals and Legal Assistants, so this job is listed first even though it is not the best-paying apprenticeable job (which is Air Traffic Controllers), the fastest-growing job (which is Medical Assistants), or the job with the most openings (which is Office Clerks, General).

Understand the Limits of the Data in This Book

In this book we use the most reliable and up-to-date information available on earnings, projected growth, number of openings, and other topics. The data came from the U.S. Department of Labor source known as Occupation and Employment Statistics. As you look at the data, keep in mind that the figures are estimates. They give you a general idea about the number of workers employed, annual earnings, rate of job growth, and annual job openings.

Understand that a problem with such data is that it is true only on the average. Just as there is no precisely average person, there is no such thing as a statistically average example of a particular job. We say this because data, while helpful, can also be misleading.

Take, for example, the yearly earnings information in this book. This is highly reliable data obtained from a very large U.S. working population sample by the Bureau of Labor Statistics. It tells us the average annual pay received as of May 2007 by people in various job titles (actually, it is the median annual pay, which means that half earned more and half less).

This sounds great, except that half of all people in that occupation earned less than that amount. For example, people who are new to the occupation or with only a few years of work experience often earn much less than the average amount. People who live in rural areas or who work for smaller employers typically earn less than those who do similar work in cities (where the cost of living is higher) or for bigger employers. People in certain areas of the country earn less than those in others. Other factors also influence how much you are likely to earn in a given job in your area. For example,

Aircraft Mechanics and Service Technicians in the Detroit–Warren–Livonia, Michigan, metropolitan area have median earnings of $56,740, probably because Northwest Airlines has a hub in Detroit and its mechanics are unionized. By comparison, the Allentown–Bethlehem–Easton, Pennsylvania, metropolitan area has no major airline hub and only a small aircraft service facility with nonunionized workers. Aircraft Mechanics and Service Technicians there earn a median of only $31,540.

What's especially relevant to this book is the fact that people who are working in trades for which they have completed an apprenticeship, especially those who are union members, tend to earn considerably more than workers who have learned informally or are not unionized. For example, in 2007 a national sample of workers paid under union contracts earned 25% more than nonunion workers. Of course, not all former apprentices are union members, but someone who has completed an apprenticeship can expect to command a higher wage in that trade (especially at the beginning of a career) than someone whose skills are not documented. Keep this in mind when you look at the wage figures in this book.

Also keep in mind that the figures for job growth and number of openings are projections by labor economists—their best guesses about what we can expect between now and 2016. Those projections are not guarantees. A major economic downturn, war, or technological breakthrough could change the actual outcome. These figures represent job growth and job openings for *all* workers, not just for apprentices.

Finally, don't forget that the job market consists of both job openings and job *seekers*. The Department of Labor does not publish figures on the supply of job candidates, so we are unable to tell you about the level of competition you can expect—either for entry to an apprenticeship program or for job openings once you are a journey worker. Competition is an important issue that you should research for any tentative career goal. The *Occupational Outlook Handbook* provides informative statements for many occupations. You should speak to people who train tomorrow's workers; they probably have a good idea of how many applicants get enrolled in apprenticeships and how quickly, plus how quickly journey workers are able to find employment after completing their apprenticeship. People in the workforce can provide insights into these issues as well. Use your critical thinking skills to evaluate what people tell you. For example, trainers may be trying to recruit you, whereas people in the workforce may be trying to discourage you from competing. Get a variety of opinions to balance out possible biases.

So, in reviewing the information in this book, please understand the limitations of data. You need to use common sense in career decision making as in most other things in life. We hope that, using that approach, you find the information helpful and interesting.

The Data Complexities

For those of you who like details, we present some of the complexities inherent in our sources of information and what we did to make sense of them here. You don't need to know these things to use the book, so jump to the next section of the introduction if details bore you.

We selected the jobs on the basis of economic data, and we include information on earnings, projected growth, and number of job openings for each job throughout this book.

Education or Training Required

The 200 jobs selected for this book were chosen partly on the basis of the amount of education or training that they typically require for entry: For all 200 jobs, a registered apprenticeship is available somewhere in the United States, and for workers who instead prepare by going to college or a vocational-technical school, the minimum education required is less than a four-year degree. We base the educational requirement on ratings supplied by the Bureau of Labor Statistics.

You should keep in mind that some people working in these jobs may have credentials that differ considerably from the level listed here. For example, Air Traffic Controllers is included in this book because the minimum requirement for entry is long-term on-the-job training and an apprenticeship is available through the armed forces. However, almost one-third of Air Traffic Controllers have a bachelor's degree.

Some workers who have more than the minimum required education for their job have earned a higher degree *after* being hired, but others entered the job with this educational credential, and the more advanced degree may have given them an advantage over other job seekers with less education. Some workers with *less* than the normal minimum requirement may have been hired on the basis of their work experience in a similar job. So don't assume that apprenticeship is always the best way to prepare for the job or that the simple statement of "Education/Training Required (Nonapprenticeship Route)" in the Part IV job description gives a complete picture of the background of the other job seekers you will be competing against. If you're considering the job seriously, you need to investigate this topic in greater detail.

Earnings

The employment security agency of each state gathers information on earnings for various jobs and forwards it to the U.S. Bureau of Labor Statistics. This information is organized in standardized ways by a BLS program called Occupational Employment Statistics, or OES. To keep the earnings for the various jobs and regions comparable, the OES screens out certain types of earnings and includes others, so the OES earnings we use in this book represent straight-time gross pay exclusive of premium pay. More specifically, the OES earnings include each job's base rate; cost-of-living allowances; guaranteed pay; hazardous-duty pay; incentive pay, including commissions and production bonuses; on-call pay; and tips. The OES earnings do not include back pay, jury duty pay, overtime pay, severance pay, shift differentials, nonproduction bonuses, or tuition reimbursements. Also, self-employed workers are not included in the estimates, and they can be a significant segment in certain occupations. (For example, slightly more than half of all Photographers, Jewelers, and Animal Trainers are self-employed.)

The Annual Earnings figure for the job shows the median earnings (half earn more, half earn less). Journey workers typically earn more than the median, but we don't have accurate data to supply a figure.

The median earnings for all workers in all occupations were $31,410 in May 2007. The 200 apprenticeable jobs in this book were chosen partly on the basis of good earnings, so their average is a little higher, $32,559. (This is a weighted average, which means that jobs with larger workforces are given greater weight in the computation.)

Projected Growth and Number of Job Openings

This information comes from the Office of Occupational Statistics and Employment Projections, a program within the Bureau of Labor Statistics that develops information about projected trends in the nation's labor market for the next ten years. The most recent projections available cover the years from 2006 to 2016. The projections are based on information about people moving into and out of occupations. The BLS uses data from various sources in projecting the growth and number of openings for each job title—some data comes from the Census Bureau's Current Population Survey and some comes from an OES survey. The BLS economists assume a steady economy unaffected by a major war, depression, or other upheaval. They also assume that recessions may occur during the decade covered by projections, as would be consistent with the pattern of business cycles we have experienced for several decades. However, because their projections cover 10 years, the figures for job growth and openings are intended to provide an average of both the good times and the bad times.

Like the earnings figures, the figures on projected growth and job openings are reported according to the SOC classification. So, again, you will find that some of the available information applies to more than one O*NET job. For example, the Department of Labor reports job growth (12.1%) and openings (18,887) for one SOC occupation called Fire Fighters, so we report the same figures for both Forest Fire Fighters and Municipal Fire Fighters (the two related O*NET occupations). When you see that Forest Fire Fighters is described as having 12.1% projected growth and 18,887 projected job openings and Municipal Fire Fighters is described with the same two numbers, you should realize that the 12.1% rate of projected growth represents the *average* of these two occupations—one may actually experience higher growth than the other—and that these two occupations will *share* the 18,887 projected openings.

While salary figures are fairly straightforward, you may not know what to make of job-growth figures. For example, is projected growth of 15% good or bad? Keep in mind that the average (mean) growth projected for all occupations by the Bureau of Labor Statistics is 10.4%. One-quarter of the SOC occupations have a growth projection of 3.2% or lower. Growth of 11.6% is the median, meaning that half of the occupations have more, half less. Only one-quarter of the occupations have growth projected at more than 17.4%.

Although the jobs in this book were selected as "best" partly on the basis of job growth, their mean growth is 9.6%, which is lower than the mean for all jobs. Among these 200 jobs, the job ranked 50th by projected growth has a figure of 13.5%, the job ranked 100th (the median) has a projected growth of 10.0%, and the job ranked 150th has a projected growth of 4.1%.

The average number of job openings for the 200 best apprenticeable jobs is slightly higher than the national average for all occupations. The Bureau of Labor Statistics projects an average of about 35,000 job openings per year for the 750 occupations that it studies, but for the 200 occupations included in this book, the average is about 39,500 openings. The job ranked 50th for job openings has a figure of about 31,400 annual openings, the job ranked 100th (the median) has about 9,800 openings projected, and the job ranked 150th has about 3,800 openings projected.

However, keep in mind that figures for job openings depend on how BLS defines an occupation. For example, consider the occupation Jewelers and Precious Stone and Metal Workers, which employs a workforce of about 52,000 people and is expected to provide almost 7,400 job openings each year. The BLS regards this as one occupation when it reports figures for earnings and job projections, but O*NET divides it into three separate occupations: Gem and Diamond Workers; Jewelers; and Precious Metal Workers. If the BLS employment-projection tables were to list these as three separate occupations and divide the 7,400 openings among them, the average number of openings for all occupations would be smaller. So it follows that because the way BLS defines occupations is somewhat arbitrary, any "average" figure for job openings is also somewhat arbitrary.

Perhaps you're wondering why we present figures on both job growth *and* number of openings. Aren't these two ways of saying the same thing? Actually, you need to know both. Consider the occupation Locksmiths and Safe Repairers, which is projected to grow at the impressive rate of 22.1%. There should be lots of opportunities in such a fast-growing job, right? Not exactly. This is a small occupation, with only about 26,000 people currently employed, so even though it is growing rapidly, it will not create many new jobs (about 3,500 per year). Now consider Team Assemblers. Because of automation and the loss of manufacturing jobs to Asia, this occupation is hardly growing at all—it's growing at the glacial rate of 0.1%. Nevertheless, this is a huge occupation that employs more than one million workers. So, even though its growth is stalled, it is expected to take on more than 250,000 new workers each year as existing workers retire, die, or move on to other jobs. That's why we base our selection of the best jobs on both of these economic indicators and why you should pay attention to both when you scan our lists of best jobs.

Other Job Characteristics

Like the figures for earnings, some of the other figures that describe jobs in this book are shared by more than one job title. Usually this is the case for occupations that are so small that BLS does not release separate statistics for them. For example, the occupation Tree Trimmers and Pruners has a total workforce of only about 40,000 workers, so BLS does not report a specific figure for the percentage of women workers. In this case, we had to use the figure that BLS reports for a group of occupations it calls Grounds Maintenance Workers. We relied on this same figure for two other jobs: Pesticide Handlers, Sprayers, and Applicators, Vegetation and Landscaping and Groundskeeping Workers.

How This Book Is Organized

The information about apprenticeships and careers in this book moves from the general to the highly specific.

Part I. Overview of Apprenticeships

Part I is an overview of apprenticeship—what it is, where the opportunities are, what the requirements are, what the pros and cons are, and where to find out more. This section may clear up some misunderstandings you have about apprenticeship, and it will help you appreciate what apprenticeship has to offer you.

Part II. Master List of Nationally Registered Apprenticeships

Part II lists all 1,052 apprenticeships that currently are registered with the U.S. Department of Labor. You may be surprised at some of the titles that appear here. For each apprenticeship, you can see how many years it takes and what career it is related to.

The apprenticeships are grouped according to interest fields, so you can easily find those that belong to industries that appeal to you.

Part III. The Best Jobs Lists: Jobs You Can Enter Through Apprenticeship

For many people, the 43 lists in Part III are the most interesting section of the book. Here you can see which apprenticeable jobs are best in terms of high salaries, fast growth, and plentiful job openings. You can also see which jobs are best when these factors are combined, and that list is broken out further according to the interest fields and several other features of the jobs. Look in the table of contents for a complete list of the lists. The lists are not difficult to understand because they have clear titles and are organized into groupings of related lists.

People who prefer to think about careers in terms of personality types will want to browse the lists that show the best jobs for the Artistic, Conventional, Enterprising, Investigative, Realistic, and Social personality types. On the other hand, some people think first in terms of interest fields, and these people will prefer the lists that show the best jobs using the interest categories of the Guide for Occupational Exploration, which you may also know as career clusters.

We suggest that you use the lists that make the most sense for you. Following are the names of each group of lists along with short comments on each group. You will find additional information in a brief introduction provided at the beginning of each group of lists in Part III.

Best Jobs Overall: Apprenticeable Jobs with the Highest Pay, Fastest Growth, and Most Openings

This group has four lists, and they are the ones that most people want to see first. The first list presents all 200 apprenticeable jobs that are included in this book in order of their total scores for earnings, growth, and number of job openings. These jobs are used in the more-specialized lists that follow and in the descriptions in Part IV. Three more lists in this group present the 100 best-paying apprenticeable jobs, the 100 fastest-growing apprenticeable jobs, and the 100 apprenticeable jobs with the most openings.

Apprenticeable Jobs with the Highest Percentage of Women and Men

This group includes four lists that extract from the 200 best jobs only those that have a workforce with 70% or more women or men. One pair of lists orders these jobs by the percentage of women or men; the other pair orders the corresponding jobs by their total combined score for earnings, growth, and number of openings.

Best Apprenticeable Jobs Based on Personality Types

This group provides lists of apprenticeable jobs for six personality types, based on a system that is used in a variety of popular career exploration inventories. The lists present the jobs in order of their total combined scores for earnings, growth, and number of openings. We explain the personality types in the introduction to these lists.

Best Apprenticeable Jobs Based on Interests (Career Clusters)

There are 16 lists in this group, and they contain all of the apprenticeable jobs from our 200 best jobs that fall within the 16 major areas of interest (also known as career clusters). The number of jobs varies by list, and the lists are organized in order of their total combined scores for earnings, growth, and number of openings.

Best Apprenticeable Jobs Based on Number of Years Required

Apprenticeships generally vary in duration from less than one to up to five years. Each of the seven lists in this group presents jobs for which it takes a specific amount of time to complete the related apprenticeship. The number of jobs varies by list. Within each list, the jobs are ordered by their total combined scores for earnings, growth, and number of openings.

Most Popular Apprenticeships

This group contains a list of the 25 most popular apprenticeships and a list of the 23 jobs linked to these apprenticeships, ordered by their total combined score for earnings, growth, and number of openings.

Bonus List: The 50 Best Apprenticeable Jobs at Any Educational or Training Level

Unlike the core list of 200 best apprenticeable jobs, this list was not restricted to jobs that normally do not require a bachelor's degree or higher. We selected and ordered the 50 best jobs based on their total combined scores for earnings, growth, and number of openings.

Part IV. Descriptions of the 200 Best Apprenticeable Jobs

This part of the book provides a brief but information-packed description of each of the 200 best apprenticeable jobs that met our criteria for this book. The descriptions are presented in alphabetical order by job title. This structure makes it easy to look up any job that you've found in Part II or Part III that you want to learn more about.

We used the most current information from a variety of government sources to create the descriptions. Although we've tried to make the descriptions easy to understand, the sample job description that follows—and the explanation of each of its parts—may help you better understand and use the descriptions.

Here are some details on each of the major parts of the job descriptions you will find in Part IV:

* **Job Title:** This is the job title for the job as defined by the U.S. Department of Labor and used in its O*NET database. (If you are wondering why this is the title of a job, not an apprenticeship, see the explanation in the following section, "Why We Describe Apprenticeable Jobs, Not Apprenticeships.")

* **Data Elements:** The information on earnings, growth, annual openings, and percentage of women comes from various government databases, as we explained earlier in this introduction. Keep in mind that journey workers usually have **above-average** earnings.

* **Related Apprenticeships:** This is a listing of registered apprenticeships in the RAPIDS database that prepare for the occupation. For each program, the required number of hours of on-the-job learning is identified in parentheses. In competency-based or hybrid programs, this time requirement is flexible, and such programs are identified.

* **Summary Description and Tasks:** The first part of each job description provides a summary of the occupation in bold type. It is followed by a listing of tasks that are generally performed by people who work in the job. This information comes from the O*NET database; where necessary, we edited the tasks to keep them from exceeding 2,200 characters.

Job Title →

Ambulance Drivers and Attendants, Except Emergency Medical Technicians

Data Elements →

* Annual Earnings: $21,140
* Growth: 21.7%
* Annual Job Openings: 3,703
* Percentage of Women: 28.0%

Related Apprenticeships →

Related Apprenticeship—Ambulance Attendant (EMT) (2000 hrs.).

Summary Description and Tasks →

Drive ambulance or assist ambulance driver in transporting sick, injured, or convalescent persons. Assist in lifting patients. Drive ambulances or assist ambulance drivers in transporting sick, injured, or convalescent persons. Remove and replace soiled linens and equipment to maintain sanitary conditions. Accompany and assist emergency medical technicians on calls. Place patients on stretchers and load stretchers into ambulances, usually with assistance from other attendants. Earn and maintain appropriate certifications. Replace supplies and disposable items on ambulances. Report facts concerning accidents or emergencies to hospital personnel or law enforcement officials. Administer first aid such as bandaging, splinting, and administering oxygen. Restrain or shackle violent patients.

GOE Information →

GOE—Career Cluster/Interest Area: 16. Transportation, Distribution, and Logistics. **Work Group:** 16.06. Other Services Requiring Driving. **Other Apprenticeable Jobs in This Work Group:** No others in group. **Personality**

Personality Type →

Type: Realistic. These occupations frequently involve work activities that include practical, hands-on problems and solutions. They often deal with plants; animals; and real-world materials such as wood, tools, and machinery. Many

of the occupations require working outside and don't involve a lot of paperwork or working closely with others.

Skills—Equipment Maintenance; Operation Monitoring; Operation and Control; Repairing; Technology Design; Equipment Selection; Troubleshooting; Service Orientation. ← **Skills**

Education/Training Required (Nonapprenticeship Route): Moderate-term on-the-job training. **Related Knowledge/Courses—Transportation:** Principles and methods for moving people or goods by air, rail, sea, or road, including their relative costs, advantages, and limitations. **Psychology:** Human behavior and performance, mental processes, psychological research methods, and the assessment and treatment of behavioral and affective disorders. **Medicine and Dentistry:** The information and techniques needed to diagnose and treat injuries, diseases, and deformities. This includes symptoms, treatment alternatives, drug properties and interactions, and preventive health-care measures. **Customer and Personal Service:** Principles and processes for providing customer and personal services, including needs assessment techniques, quality service standards, alternative delivery systems, and customer satisfaction evaluation techniques. **Telecommunications:** Transmission, broadcasting, switching, control, and operation of telecommunications systems. **Public Safety and Security:** Weaponry; public safety; security operations, rules, regulations, precautions, and prevention; and the protection of people, data, and property.

← **Education/Training Required (Nonapprenticeship Route)**

← **Related Knowledge/Courses**

Work Environment: Outdoors; noisy; very hot or cold; disease or infections; sitting; using hands on objects, tools, or controls. ← **Work Environment**

❈ **GOE Information:** This information cross-references the Guide for Occupational Exploration (or the GOE), a system developed by the U.S. Department of Labor that organizes jobs based on interests. We use the groups from the *New Guide for Occupational Exploration*, Fourth Edition, as published by JIST. That book uses a set of interest areas based on the 16 career clusters developed by the U.S. Department of Education and used in a variety of career information systems. Here we include the major interest area/cluster the job fits into, its more specific work group, and a list of apprenticeable O*NET job titles that are in this same GOE work group. (All of these jobs are related to apprenticeships in the RAPIDS database. None of them requires a bachelor's degree or higher. Not all of them are included in this book.) This information will help you identify other job titles that have similar interests or require similar skills. You can find more information on the GOE and its interest areas in Appendix D.

❈ **Personality Type:** This part gives the name of the personality type that most closely matches each job, according to O*NET, as well as a brief definition of this personality type. You can find more information on the personality types in the introduction to the lists of jobs based on personality types in Part III.

❈ **Skills:** The O*NET database provides data on 35 skills, so we decided to list only those that were most important for each job rather than list pages of unhelpful details. For each job, we identified any skill with a rating for level of mastery that was higher than the average rating for this skill for all jobs and a rating for importance that was higher than very low. We ordered the skills by the amount by which their ratings exceeded the average rating for all occupations, from highest to lowest. If there were more than eight such skills, we included only those eight with the highest ratings. If no skill had a rating higher than the average for all jobs, we said "None met the criteria." You can find definitions of the skills in Appendix D.

❈ **Education/Training Required (Nonapprenticeship Route):** This item tells the typical amount of education or training you would need for this job if you did not enter through an apprenticeship.

❈ **Related Knowledge/Courses:** This entry can help you understand the most important knowledge areas that are required for a job and the types of courses or programs you will likely need to take during (or possibly before) your apprenticeship. For each job, we identified the highest-rated knowledge area in the O*NET database, so every job has at least one listed. We identified any additional knowledge area with a rating that was higher than the average rating for that knowledge area for all jobs. We listed as many as six knowledge areas in descending order.

❈ **Work Environment:** We included any work condition with a rating that exceeded the midpoint of the rating scale. The order does not indicate any condition's frequency on the job. Consider whether you like these conditions and whether any of these conditions would make you uncomfortable. Keep in mind that when hazards are present (for example, contaminants), protective equipment and procedures are provided to keep you safe.

✸ **Further Information:** Some descriptions contain contact information for unions or other organizations.

Getting all the information we used in the job descriptions was not a simple process, and it is not always perfect. Even so, we used the best and most recent sources of data we could find, and we think that our efforts will be helpful to many people.

Why We Describe Apprenticeable Jobs, Not Apprenticeships

When you look over the "best apprenticeable jobs" lists in this book or read the descriptions of jobs, keep in mind that these are lists and descriptions of *occupations* that you can enter through apprenticeship—they are not lists and descriptions of *apprenticeships*. Why did we do this?

First of all, apprenticeships are usually sponsored and administered at the local level, and although some states gather data about these programs, the states share only a limited amount of data with the Office of Apprenticeship at the U.S. Department of Labor. In the absence of nationally applicable statistics about apprenticeships, it is impossible to create a useful list of best apprenticeships. For example, nobody can tell you how many electrician apprenticeships there are throughout the United States, what the apprentice electricians are earning, how fast the programs are growing, or how many openings there are each year. On the other hand, we can readily obtain such figures for the *occupation* of Electricians and see how it stacks up against other jobs.

For this same reason—limited summary data about locally sponsored apprenticeship programs—it would be impossible for us to describe your locally available apprenticeships accurately. The work tasks you learn and the subjects you study in night classes may or may not be guided by national standards. (For examples of national standards, see Appendix B.)

Finally, it helps to remember that apprenticeship is only the front door to an occupation. It lasts only a few years, but the career it leads to may keep you employed for many years. Therefore, it would be a mistake for you to focus primarily on what lies immediately ahead. Take the long view. Consider what the jobs have to offer, and when you have found one that looks promising, investigate your local apprenticeship opportunities to decide whether you want to use this entry route to prepare for that goal.

There is one exception to this book's focus on jobs rather than on apprenticeships: That is the list of the "Most Popular Apprenticeships" in Part III. But even here we take care to point out the limitations of the available data, which is derived from only 31 states.

How to Use This Book

This is a book that you can dive right into:

* **If you are uncertain about exactly what apprenticeship is,** you'll want to read Part I, which is an overview of this method of training. You'll learn about the typical requirements of an apprenticeship and the pluses and minuses of starting a career this way.

* **If you like lists and want an easy way to compare jobs,** turn to Part III. Here you can browse the apprenticeable jobs with the best pay, the fastest growth, and the most job openings. You can see these best jobs broken down in various ways, such as by interest field. The list in Part II, which includes every registered apprenticeship, will give you an idea of the variety of careers you can enter through this route.

* **For detailed information about apprenticeable jobs,** turn to Part IV and read the profiles of the jobs. We include 200 apprenticeable jobs and itemize their major tasks, their top skills, the main features of their work environment, and other factors you won't learn from the lists in Part III.

On the other hand, if you like to do things in a methodical way, you may want to read the sections in order:

* Part I will give you useful background on what apprenticeship is. This will help you decide whether this is the way you might want to start your career.

* The complete listing of registered apprenticeships in Part II will give you a sense of how varied the opportunities are.

* As you browse the lists of best jobs in Part III, you can take notes on the jobs that have the greatest appeal for you.

* Then you can look up the descriptions of these jobs in Part IV and narrow down your list. Ask yourself, Do the work tasks interest me? Does the work environment discourage me?

* When you have a short list of jobs you might like to apprentice for, you can consult Appendix C to identify the state office where you can learn about apprenticeship opportunities in your area.

* If you obtain the national apprenticeship standards for a program in your area, Appendix A can help you understand how to read the document—what to look for and what to look out for.

Credits and Acknowledgments: While the authors created this book, it is based on the work of many others. The occupational information is based on data obtained from the U.S. Department of Labor and the U.S. Census Bureau. These sources provide the most authoritative occupational information available. The job titles and their related descriptions are from the O*NET database, which was developed by researchers and developers under the direction of the U.S. Department of Labor. They, in turn, were assisted by thousands of employers who provided details on the nature of work in the many thousands of job samplings used in the database's development. We used the most recent version of the O*NET database, release 13.0. We appreciate and thank the staff of the U.S. Department of Labor for their efforts and expertise in providing such a rich source of data.

Overview of Apprenticeships

This part provides general information about apprenticeships: what they are, how they're funded, which industries use them, their entry and completion requirements, pros and cons, and how to find and evaluate an apprenticeship program.

What Is an Apprenticeship?

Apprenticeship is a form of job training that has been in use for centuries. The stonemasons who built the pyramids of Egypt learned their skills through an apprenticeship. So did the medieval scribes who copied the Bible by hand; the shipwrights who constructed the Niña, the Pinta, and the Santa María; the midwives who delivered the 20 children of Johann Sebastian Bach; the gunsmiths who supplied Napoleon's army with firepower; and the wheelwrights who worked on the Conestoga wagons that carried American pioneers westward.

But apprenticeship is not a relic of another era. It has stayed up to date with changes in the economy and in technology. Nowadays apprentices may learn jobs such as Internetworking Technician, Sound Mixer, or Photogrammetric Technician. Apprenticeship is an essential part of our modern economy, and about 470,000 Americans are presently registered as apprentices.

Even some of the terms used to describe apprenticeship have changed. In olden times, a person who completed an apprenticeship and became a fully qualified worker was called a "journeyman." The French word *journée* means the span of a day, so a journeyman was someone who could charge a fee for a day's work. Nowadays the term "journeyman" is still sometimes used, but it is being replaced by "journey worker" or "journeyperson." (In this book we use "journey worker.") Apprenticeship is definitely not all-male. In Part III you can find a list of the apprenticeable jobs with the greatest proportion of women workers.

Worksite learning has always been at the core of apprenticeship. Apprentices are supervised and taught by experienced workers who can pass on skills, work habits, strategies for problem solving, and obscure lore that often cannot be learned anywhere else. To learn all this, apprentices need to do more than just watch experienced workers or act as "helpers." They perform real work tasks at higher and higher levels of skill, and they are rotated through all aspects of the job so that they learn the full range of skills.

Because modern jobs involve technology and take place in a complex business world, modern apprentices have to learn theory as well as practical skills. They need to master concepts that cannot be taught well at the worksite—for example, technical math, principles of mechanics, electronic circuits, business law, or human anatomy. So apprenticeships now include a component of classroom learning. These classes usually meet after working hours and may be held at a community college or a vocational school, by correspondence, or even on the Web.

Most forms of learning cost money, and college tuition is getting more expensive at an alarming rate. But apprentices earn while they learn. They start out at a rate of pay that is often only half the hourly rate of a journey worker, but as they gain work experience they get regular increases in pay. Of course, these increases depend on satisfactory performance at the worksite and in classes. During the last phase of the apprenticeship, they typically earn 90 percent of a journey worker's hourly rate. (When you see salary figures elsewhere in this book, keep in mind that these are based on the earnings of *everyone* working in the occupation—the apprentices, the journey workers, and the workers who entered through some route other than apprenticeship. Thus these figures are likely to be lower than the average journey worker's pay.) Apprentices may also receive health insurance or retirement benefits.

How Are Apprenticeships Administered and Funded?

Small employers may create informal apprenticeships, but the kinds of apprenticeships discussed in this book are formal apprenticeships that are registered with the state and, most often, with the U.S. Department of Labor. (For a listing of state offices that register apprenticeships, see Appendix C.) These registered apprenticeships are created and funded by apprenticeship committees, which may be formed by employers, employer associations, labor unions, or some combination of these parties (or by a branch of the military that offers apprenticeship as part of military training). To be registered, the apprenticeships must meet certain standards for safety, fairness, and training. When an apprentice completes the program, the committee issues a certificate that confers journey worker status and that usually is recognized anywhere in the U.S.

What Industries Use Apprenticeships?

Apprenticeships have been created in a wide range of industries, and each year from 6 to 20 new apprenticeships are registered with the U.S. Department of Labor. The following diagram shows the number of people in apprenticeships within certain major industry groups in 2007. The diagram is based on figures from 31 states and does not represent the entire nation exactly, but it is probably a rough approximation of the actual breakdown. Although the construction industry clearly dominates, the whole pie represents one-quarter of a million people, so even the small slices represent a large number of apprentices. Furthermore, apprenticeship is growing as an entry route to other industries.

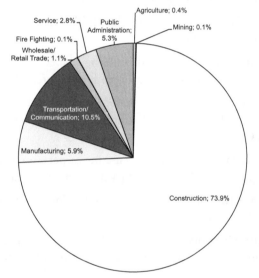

Figure 1: Percentage of people in apprenticeships by industry group, 2007.

Here are some examples, from a variety of industry sectors, of apprenticeable jobs that are described in Part IV of this book. **(Those industries that are starred have been targeted as special areas of growth under the President's High Growth Job Training Initiative; they are expected to fuel the U.S. economy in the years ahead and to need a good supply of trained workers.)**

- ❋ **Automotive*:** Automotive Body and Related Repairers; Automotive Master Mechanics; Automotive Specialty Technicians

- ❋ **Construction*:** Construction Carpenters; Electricians; Insulation Workers, Floor, Ceiling, and Wall; Plasterers and Stucco Masons; Plumbers

- ❋ **Energy*:** Petroleum Pump System Operators, Refinery Operators, and Gaugers; Rotary Drill Operators, Oil and Gas

- **Financial Services*:** Payroll and Timekeeping Clerks; Tellers
- **Geospatial*:** Mapping Technicians; Surveying Technicians
- **Health Care*:** Dental Assistants; Medical Secretaries; Pharmacy Technicians; Surgical Technologists
- **Hospitality*:** Bartenders; Butchers and Meat Cutters; Chefs and Head Cooks; Hotel, Motel, and Resort Desk Clerks
- **Information Technology/Networking*:** Computer Operators; Computer, Automated Teller, and Office Machine Repairers
- **Manufacturing*:** Computer-Controlled Machine Tool Operators, Metal and Plastic; Food Batchmakers; Industrial Machinery Mechanics; Industrial Production Managers; Model Makers, Metal and Plastic
- **Military:** Air Traffic Controllers; Avionics Technicians; Equal Opportunity Representatives and Officers
- **Public Sector:** Construction and Building Inspectors; Government Property Inspectors and Investigators; Municipal Fire Fighters; Postal Service Clerks
- **Public Utilities:** Electrical Power-Line Installers and Repairers; Power Distributors and Dispatchers; Power Plant Operators; Water and Liquid Waste Treatment Plant and System Operators
- **Service and Retail Industries*:** First-Line Supervisors/Managers of Retail Sales Workers; Food Service Managers; Private Detectives and Investigators
- **Telecommunications:** Telecommunications Equipment Installers and Repairers, Except Line Installers
- **Transportation*:** Pilots, Ship; Truck Drivers, Heavy and Tractor-Trailer; Transportation Vehicle, Equipment and Systems Inspectors, Except Aviation

What Are the Entry Requirements of Apprenticeships?

Requirements vary, but they are usually related to the demands of the job.

Age. Usually the minimum age for entry is 18. In some cases it may be as low as 16, but not if the job is at all hazardous. There rarely is a maximum age. The average age of new apprentices is probably somewhere in the upper 20s.

Education. Usually a high school diploma or G.E.D. is required. Sometimes you need to have specific classes on your transcript, or having taken these classes may improve your chances of being accepted. These classes may be closely related to work tasks, such as blueprint reading or metal shop, or they may be fundamental subjects, such as algebra, that you need to know to succeed in the classes required by the apprenticeship. In highly technical fields or fields where there's a lot of competition for entry to apprenticeships, a college degree or certificate may help. Related training in the military may also improve your chances of entry.

Fitness. You probably need a statement from a doctor that you are physically capable of doing the job. Keep in mind that the 1990 Americans with Disabilities Act (ADA) forbids employers from discriminating against people who have disabilities and who can perform the work tasks if provided with reasonable accommodations. This law applies to apprentices just as much as it applies to any other kind of worker. Therefore, if you have a disability, your doctor should specify what accommodations would allow you to perform the kind of job you are aiming for. A few jobs, such as Municipal Fire Fighter, require you to pass a specific fitness test—for example, you may need to be able to lift and carry a certain weight.

Residency status. You may be required to be a citizen of the United States, but in some cases you need to demonstrate only that your residency status allows you to work here. Programs having trouble finding recruits have been known to overlook residency requirements.

Transportation. You need to demonstrate that you have a way of getting to the worksite. In jobs where the worksite may shift locations frequently or may be in out-of-the-way locations (for example, in many construction jobs), you may be required to have a valid driver's license and access to a car.

Aptitude. You may need to pass a test of your aptitude for the work tasks. For example, if the job involves a lot of delicate work with your hands, you may need to demonstrate fine motor coordination. For some construction jobs, you may be required to have no unbearable fear of heights. For a health-care job, you may need to provide evidence of people skills.

Interview. Like most jobs, apprenticeships usually require you to be interviewed. Keep in mind that you are asking the apprenticeship committee to invest in you (the apprenticeship is like an "industry scholarship" that may be worth $40,000–$150,000), so you need to convince the interviewers that you are genuinely interested in the job and that you are determined to complete the requirements. The interviewers may mention some of the difficult or unpleasant aspects of the job to judge whether you are easily discouraged. You should be informed about the nature of the job so that you can point out the aspects of the job that attract you. The interviewers may want additional clarification of some of the requirements mentioned previously (for example, your academic background) and probably will require the names, addresses, and phone numbers of at least three people not related to you who can comment on your character and ability.

The point system. Most often, there are more candidates for an apprenticeship than there are openings in the program, and the apprenticeship committee is required to follow a fair procedure for selecting the top contenders. The committee may award candidates a certain number of points for their ability to meet some of the requirements listed above. For example, a candidate may receive x points for education, y points for aptitude, and z points for the interview. The candidates with the greatest number of points are the first to be taken on as apprentices when openings become available.

Waiting period. If there is a lot of competition, the industry is in a slump, or your point score is not among the highest, you may have to wait for weeks, months, or even years to be admitted to an apprenticeship. You probably can improve your chances by taking related courses or by working at related jobs and then re-applying. With these activities on your resume, you are likely to have a better point score for education and give a more impressive interview. At the very least, your experiences will give you a clearer picture of whether the job you are aiming for is a good choice for you.

What Are the Requirements for Completing an Apprenticeship?

When you begin an apprenticeship, you and the sponsor sign an apprenticeship agreement, and this brief document (typically one page) references a longer document called the apprenticeship standards. You should examine this standards document even before you apply for the apprenticeship because it spells out all the requirements for the apprenticeship and tells you what to expect. (Appendix A provides tips for how to read a standards document by explaining what is typically included, and Appendix B contains excerpts from actual standards documents.)

Worksite learning. Most apprenticeships require you to complete a certain number of hours of worksite learning, typically 2,000 hours per year. That may seem like a lot of time, but it represents an eight-hour day, a five-day week, and a work year that gives you two weeks off for vacation and holidays. Most apprenticeships require a total of four years. A smaller number of apprenticeships require two or three years. Some require as little as one year or as much as six years. (See Part II for the years required for each nationally registered apprenticeship.)

Classroom learning. Typically you are required to complete 144 hours of classroom learning per year, which is equivalent to taking two classes during each academic session. Keep in mind that you will have to take these classes and do your studying in the evening, not during the workday. You will not be paid for your time in class. You may be excused from some courses if you have acquired relevant classroom training in college or in the military. In some apprenticeship programs, you enroll in an associate degree program and receive your degree at the same time you become a journey worker. This is particularly common in fields where you need to be licensed and the license requires the degree.

Competency-based and hybrid programs. A small but growing number of apprenticeships require you to achieve *competency* rather than log a specific number of hours of worksite and classroom learning. They use assessments that measure how far you have progressed toward mastering the work or academic subjects and determine when you are fully qualified. Often the program is outlined as a "career lattice"—a set of different work roles that can be combined in various sequences. You receive a certificate of training as you demonstrate mastery of each role, and when you have completed one of the permitted sequences of roles, you are awarded a certification of completion that grants you journey worker status.

If you are a quick learner, you can complete a competency-based program faster than other apprentices. If you enter the program with some experience and skills from work, military training, or a partially completed apprenticeship in another trade, you may be able to skip some of the entry-level learning. Likewise, your required hours in the classroom may be reduced or even eliminated if you have relevant prior learning, either formal or informal. The credential you receive from a competency-based program assures employers that you have demonstrated all the required skills and mastered all the relevant concepts and have not simply "paid your dues."

Still other apprenticeships are called "hybrid," because they require a certain minimum number of hours of worksite and classroom learning but use assessments to determine when you have attained full competency.

Things you may pay for. Although apprentices earn pay at the worksite, they may have to pay certain apprenticeship-related expenses out of their own pockets. For example, they may have to buy a set of basic tools for the job. They may have to buy protective clothing, work boots, gloves, goggles, or other necessary gear. Sometimes they must pay for the night classes that they are required to take, although all or part of these costs may be waived by the local community college or covered by veterans' benefits, the program sponsor, or the state. Apprentices usually have to pay for their textbooks. If the worksite is unionized, apprentices are likely to have to pay union dues, although often at a reduced rate. You should investigate these requirements before you sign up for the apprenticeship.

Why Might Apprenticeship Be a Good Choice?

One of the most important reasons for apprenticing has been mentioned already: You earn as you learn. Of course, in some industries you could simply take a low-level job and acquire skills by watching what the more advanced workers do. But in a registered apprenticeship, you are taken through several job rotations so that you learn the full range of skills for the job. You get personal attention as you learn—the average number of apprentices per program is about eight. When you consider that these eight people would be in different stages of apprenticeship and therefore would probably not be working at the same worksite or on the same kind of task, you can appreciate the individual attention that you can get in this form of learning. (Compare this to a classroom in a trade school.)

Furthermore, your work performance in an apprenticeship is documented—you have a written record of all the work tasks you have performed and all the skills you have mastered. This documentation is portable, which means that any employer in the U.S. will accept it as proof of your status as a fully qualified worker. An apprenticeship also plugs you into a network of journey workers and employers. These personal contacts can help you find jobs when you complete the apprenticeship and for years to come.

Finally, consider how useful apprenticeship may be as part of your long-term career path. For many people, the apprenticeship and the job it leads to as a journey worker are only the first steps in a career path with unlimited potential. The president of the ironworkers union for western Washington state, who started out as an apprentice, likes to point out that when he speaks to a high school class, he's the highest-paid person in the building. Others who started in construction trades are now managing contracting businesses, selling building supplies, or teaching vocational education. Likewise, in other industries where people apprentice, there are countless opportunities for ambitious and resourceful people, especially those who have a knack for acquiring new skills on the job.

What Can Go Wrong in an Apprenticeship?

Although some apprenticeship programs have more openings than applicants, others have many applicants competing for only a few openings. In competitive situations, applicants with good personal connections sometimes have an advantage over other applicants; women and minority-group members have experienced incidents of discrimination. The point system used by most registered apprenticeship programs is supposed to create a level playing field, but if you suspect favoritism or prejudice, look at the section of the apprenticeship standards document that covers complaint procedures. (This is discussed in Appendix A.)

During the first few months of an apprenticeship, some apprentices become discouraged when they compare their status to that of the journey workers. Their wages are so much lower, and the work tasks they do may seem menial by comparison.

In addition, a few apprentices may find that they cannot handle the demands of the workplace or of the classroom—or perhaps they do not care enough about the job to try. Most apprenticeships begin with a probationary period of a few months during which the program sponsor can terminate someone's participation in the program without having to show cause. After the probationary period, apprentices still need to perform their work satisfactorily and maintain a certain minimum grade-point average in the classes.

If the industry is in a slump, apprentices are often the first workers to be laid off. When that happens, they usually have a guarantee that they can resume their apprenticeship when there is work for them, but the layoff pushes back the date when they become a journey worker. It also leaves them without wages, and they may have trouble finding some other job if it is known that they will quit that new job as soon as they have a chance to resume their apprenticeship.

During the last year of an apprenticeship, apprentices have enough work experience and skills that outside employers may tempt them with job offers and cause them to consider quitting the program before completion. In such cases, the apprentices would do well to remember that the job being offered may be temporary, whereas journey worker status is permanent.

How Can I Find an Apprenticeship?

Some apprenticeships are advertised in the "help wanted" section of the newspaper. But when there is enough competition for openings, there may be no need to advertise. Instead, it's up to you to identify the available apprenticeship and apply for it. Here are some places to investigate:

* Union locals in your community
* Medium- to large-sized employers in your community
* Your state's Job Service (see the blue pages of your telephone book or www.jobbankinfo.org)
* A local One-Stop Career Center (see the blue pages of your telephone book)
* A school or college career counseling office
* A military recruitment office (see the blue pages of your telephone book), because some apprenticeships are offered as part of military training
* For people in the military (including the Reserves and the National Guard), the Transition Assistance Office or the Helmets to Hardhats program (http://helmetstohardhats.org)

❈ Your state's office that registers apprenticeships. In some states, this is the State Apprenticeship Council (see the blue pages of your telephone book or www.doleta. gov/OA/stateagencies.cfm). In other states, it is the Bureau of Apprenticeship and Training (see the blue pages of your telephone book or www.doleta.gov/ OA/stateoffices.cfm). Many states offer Web sites with searchable databases of apprenticeship programs. For a full listing of contacts, see Appendix C.

❈ The searchable database of sponsors (who may or may not have apprenticeships open at present) at the Apprenticeship Training, Employer and Labor Services Sponsors Web site (http://oa.doleta.gov/bat.cfm). Note that not all states are covered here and that listings on your state's own Web site may be more comprehensive or more current.

You may also find it useful to ask journey workers in the field that interests you, especially those who have recently completed an apprenticeship. This is particularly important if you are looking for an unusual apprenticeship—for example, Fur Finisher, Harpsichord Maker, Horseshoer, or Wine Maker—one that is available in only a limited number of places.

Note that this book covers only nationally registered apprenticeships and the occupations they train for. These apprenticeships meet certain basic requirements and are recognized everywhere. Other apprenticeships are available, with varying degrees of formality. Some may have considerable local prestige, but they may not carry as much weight elsewhere, and their standards document may not protect the apprentices' rights as well as one for a nationally registered program.

How Can I Investigate an Apprenticeship Program?

The single best way to learn about the good and bad aspects of an apprenticeship program is to speak to apprentices who are enrolled in it and to journey workers who have completed it. Any apprenticeship program that you are considering should be willing to provide you with names and phone numbers of people to contact. Talk to several people, not just one or two. Ask them how thorough the training was and how much personal attention they received. Also ask for their impressions of future job openings in the field—is this an industry that is growing in your community?

Give a careful reading to the apprenticeship standards document, which specifies the obligations that both you and the sponsor agree to. Appendix A shows the major headings of a typical standards document and points out what you should expect to find, and Appendix B contains excerpts from sample standards documents.

Perhaps you're wondering whether union apprenticeship programs (about one-third of existing programs) have any advantage over nonunion programs. This can vary, but a study of the construction industry in Kentucky found that union programs had a completion rate that was almost twice that of nonunion programs, had twice as many male minority and female apprentices enrolled, and had twice as many male minority and female apprentices achieving journey worker status. Similar benefits from union programs were found by a study in Michigan that covered the construction industry and another study in Maryland that covered all industries with apprenticeships.

PART II

Master List of Nationally Registered Apprenticeships

Apprenticeship is being introduced to more industries each year. It is truly impressive to see all the available apprenticeships listed in one place, which is what this section of the book does. But keep in mind that not every apprenticeship is presently available within your geographic area; in fact, a few apprenticeships are offered at only one location in the United States. For detailed information about programs available in your area, see the "How Can I Find an Apprenticeship?" section in Part I.

The following table contains the list of apprenticeships in the Registered Apprenticeship Partners Information Data System (RAPIDS), updated as of mid-2008. The apprenticeships are ordered alphabetically within the interest areas/clusters of the *New Guide for Occupational Exploration* (for more about these GOE interest fields, see Appendix E). For each apprenticeship, you may see the following information:

❋ RAPIDS code number and title. Codes ending in "CB" indicate competency-based programs; "HY" indicates hybrid; all others are time-based.

❋ Number of hours for completion; 2,000 hours is the equivalent of one year.

❋ The title of the job that is linked to it in the Department of Labor's O*NET database.

You can find detailed information about the related O*NET jobs in Part IV, where the jobs are arranged alphabetically. Exceptions:

❋ O*NET jobs linked to apprenticeships that are marked with * usually require a bachelor's degree or higher, so apprenticeship is not considered the normal entry route. These jobs therefore were not considered for inclusion among the top 200 apprenticeable jobs and are not described in Part IV.

❋ O*NET jobs linked to apprenticeships that are marked with ‡ met all the criteria for inclusion in this book except that they lacked important data elements or were ranked 201 or lower. They also are not described in Part IV.

If you are interested in a job whose apprenticeship is marked with * or ‡, you can look it up in JIST's *O*NET Dictionary of Occupational Titles*.

Interest Area/Cluster: 01 Agriculture and Natural Resources

RAPIDS Code	RAPIDS Apprenticeship Title	Hours	Title of Related O*NET Job
0703	Agricultural Service Worker	4000	Pesticide Handlers, Sprayers, and Applicators, Vegetation
0886	Beekeeper	8000	Farmers and Ranchers
0957	Dragline Operator	2000	Excavating and Loading Machine and Dragline Operators
0125	Drilling-Machine Operator	6000	Mine Cutting and Channeling Machine Operators
1000	Exterminator, Termite	4000	Pest Control Workers
0177	Farmer, General (Agriculture)	8000	Farmers and Ranchers
0981	Farmworker, General I	2000	Agricultural Equipment Operators
1024	Fish Hatchery Worker‡	2000	Farmworkers, Farm and Ranch Animals
0934	Greenskeeper II	4000	Landscaping and Groundskeeping Workers
0236	Horticulturist*	6000	Soil and Plant Scientists
0267	Laboratory Assistant	6000	Environmental Science and Protection Technicians, Including Health
0271	Landscape Gardener	8000	Landscaping and Groundskeeping Workers
0574	Landscape Management Technician	2000	Landscaping and Groundskeeping Workers
0571	Landscape Technician	4000	Landscaping and Groundskeeping Workers
0900	Logger, All-Around	4000	Fallers
1029	Mine Inspector (Government), Coal*	8000	Mining and Geological Engineers, Including Mining Safety Engineers
1028	Mine Inspector (Government), Metal—Nonmetal*	8000	Mining and Geological Engineers, Including Mining Safety Engineers
0354	Miner I (Mine and Quarry)	2000	Helpers—Extraction Workers
1071CB	Munitions Systems	2000	Explosives Workers, Ordnance Handling Experts, and Blasters
0416	Prospecting Driller (Petroleum)	4000	Rotary Drill Operators, Oil and Gas
0450	Soil Conservation Technician*	6000	Soil and Water Conservationists
0482	Test Engine Operator	4000	Geological Sample Test Technicians
0956	Tester (Petroleum Refining)	6000	Geological Sample Test Technicians
0595	Tree Surgeon	6000	Tree Trimmers and Pruners
0607	Tree Trimmer (Line Clear)	4000	Tree Trimmers and Pruners
0629	Well Drill Operator (Construction)	8000	Earth Drillers, Except Oil and Gas

*Jobs linked to apprenticeships marked with * usually require college and are not included in Parts III and IV. Jobs linked to apprenticeships marked with ‡ were ranked 201 or lower and are not included in Parts III and IV.*

Interest Area/Cluster: 02 Architecture and Construction

RAPIDS Code	RAPIDS Apprenticeship Title	Hours	Title of Related O*NET Job
0861	Acoustical Carpenter	8000	Drywall and Ceiling Tile Installers
0990	Air and Hydronic Balancing Technician	6000	Heating and Air Conditioning Mechanics and Installers
0105	Architectural, Coatings Finisher	6000	Painters, Construction and Maintenance
0872	Asphalt Paving Machine Operator	6000	Paving, Surfacing, and Tamping Equipment Operators
0877	Assembler, Metal Building	4000	Structural Iron and Steel Workers
0021	Automatic-Equipment Technician	8000	Telecommunications Equipment Installers and Repairers, Except Line Installers
0605	Aviation Safety Equipment Technician‡	8000	Installation, Maintenance, and Repair Workers, All Other
0036	Boatbuilder, Wood	8000	Construction Carpenters
0038	Boilerhouse Mechanic	6000	Boilermakers
0039	Boilermaker Fitter	8000	Boilermakers
0040	Boilermaker I	6000	Boilermakers
0041	Boilermaker II	6000	Boilermakers
0052HY	Bricklayer	4500–8000	Brickmasons and Blockmasons
0051	Bricklayer (Brick and Tile)	8000	Brickmasons and Blockmasons
0052	Bricklayer (Construction)	6000	Brickmasons and Blockmasons
0706	Bricklayer, Firebrick and Refractory Tile	8000	Brickmasons and Blockmasons
0051HY	Bricklayer/Mason	4500–6000	Brickmasons and Blockmasons
0056	Cable Installer-Repairer	6000	Electrical Power-Line Installers and Repairers
0058	Cable Splicer	8000	Electrical Power-Line Installers and Repairers
0566	Cable Television Installer	2000	Telecommunications Line Installers and Repairers
0067	Carpenter	8000	Construction Carpenters
0067HY	Carpenter	5200–8000	Construction Carpenters
0861HY	Carpenter, Acoustical Specialist	3900–6000	Drywall and Ceiling Tile Installers
0653	Carpenter, Interior Systems	8000	Construction Carpenters
0653HY	Carpenter, Interior Systems	5200–8000	Construction Carpenters
0068	Carpenter, Maintenance	8000	Construction Carpenters
0762	Carpenter, Mold	2000	Construction Carpenters
1009	Carpenter, Piledriver	8000	Rough Carpenters

*Jobs linked to apprenticeships marked with * usually require college and are not included in Parts III and IV. Jobs linked to apprenticeships marked with ‡ were ranked 201 or lower and are not included in Parts III and IV.*

(continued)

(continued)

Interest Area/Cluster: 02 Architecture and Construction

RAPIDS Code	RAPIDS Apprenticeship Title	Hours	Title of Related O*NET Job
0069	Carpenter, Rough	8000	Rough Carpenters
0070	Carpenter, Ship	8000	Construction Carpenters
0071	Carpet Layer	6000	Carpet Installers
0073	Casket Assembler	6000	Construction Carpenters
0075	Cement Mason	4000	Cement Masons and Concrete Finishers
0076	Central-Office Installer	8000	Telecommunications Equipment Installers and Repairers, Except Line Installers
0077	Central-Office Repairer	8000	Telecommunications Equipment Installers and Repairers, Except Line Installers
0849	Chimney Repairer	2000	Brickmasons and Blockmasons
0661	Construction Craft Laborer	4000	Construction Laborers
0661HY	Construction Craft Laborer	8200–10200	Construction Laborers
0091	Coppersmith (Ship and Boat)	8000	Pipe Fitters and Steamfitters
0095	Cork Insulator, Refrigeration Plant	8000	Insulation Workers, Floor, Ceiling, and Wall
0920	Corrosion-Control Fitter	8000	Electrical and Electronics Repairers, Powerhouse, Substation, and Relay
0126	Drafter, Architectural	8000	Architectural Drafters
0128	Drafter, Civil	8000	Civil Drafters
0129	Drafter, Commercial	8000	Architectural Drafters
0133	Drafter, Heating and Ventilation	8000	Architectural Drafters
0134	Drafter, Landscape	8000	Architectural Drafters
0135	Drafter, Marine	8000	Architectural Drafters
0111	Drafter, Plumbing	8000	Architectural Drafters
0139	Drafter, Structural	6000	Architectural Drafters
0145	Dry-Wall Applicator	4000	Drywall and Ceiling Tile Installers
0159	Electrician	8000	Electricians
0771	Electrician (Ship and Boat)	8000	Electricians
0158	Electrician (Water Transportation)	8000	Electricians
0643	Electrician, Maintenance	8000	Electricians
0163	Electrician, Powerhouse	8000	Electrical and Electronics Repairers, Powerhouse, Substation, and Relay
0166	Electrician, Substation	6000	Electrical and Electronics Repairers, Powerhouse, Substation, and Relay
1041	Electronic Systems Technician	8000	Telecommunications Equipment Installers and Repairers, Except Line Installers
0138	Elevating-Grader Operator	4000	Operating Engineers and Other Construction Equipment Operators
0173	Elevator Constructor	8000	Elevator Installers and Repairers

Interest Area/Cluster: 02 Architecture and Construction

RAPIDS Code	RAPIDS Apprenticeship Title	Hours	Title of Related O*NET Job
0174	Elevator Repairer	8000	Elevator Installers and Repairers
0165	Equipment Installer (Telephone and Telegraph)	8000	Telecommunications Equipment Installers and Repairers, Except Line Installers
0672	Facilities Locator	4000	Helpers—Installation, Maintenance, and Repair Workers
0711	Fence Erector	6000	Fence Erectors
0201	Floor Cover Layer (RR Equipment)	6000	Floor Layers, Except Carpet, Wood, and Hard Tiles
0199	Floor Layer	6000	Floor Layers, Except Carpet, Wood, and Hard Tiles
0199HY	Floor Layer	5200–8000	Floor Layers, Except Carpet, Wood, and Hard Tiles
0206	Form Builder (Construction)	4000	Rough Carpenters
0206HY	Form Builder (Construction)	3350–4600	Rough Carpenters
0794	Furnace Installer	6000	Heating and Air Conditioning Mechanics and Installers
0678	Furnace Installer and Repairer	8000	Heating and Air Conditioning Mechanics and Installers
0964	Gas-Main Fitter	8000	Pipe Fitters and Steamfitters
0221	Glazier	6000	Glaziers
0222	Glazier, Stained Glass	8000	Glaziers
0591	Hazardous-Waste Material Technician‡	4000	Construction and Related Workers, All Other
0637	Heating and Air-Conditioning Instrument Servicer	6000	Heating and Air Conditioning Mechanics and Installers
0909	Insulation Worker	8000	Insulation Workers, Floor, Ceiling, and Wall
0264	Joiner (Ship and Boat Building)	8000	Construction Carpenters
0272	Lather	6000	Construction Carpenters
0272HY	Lathing Specialist	3900–6000	Construction Carpenters
0281	Line Erector	6000	Electrical Power-Line Installers and Repairers
0282	Line Installer-Repairer	8000	Telecommunications Line Installers and Repairers
0283	Line Maintainer	8000	Electrical Power-Line Installers and Repairers

*Jobs linked to apprenticeships marked with * usually require college and are not included in Parts III and IV. Jobs linked to apprenticeships marked with ‡ were ranked 201 or lower and are not included in Parts III and IV.*

(continued)

(continued)

Interest Area/Cluster: 02 Architecture and Construction

RAPIDS Code	RAPIDS Apprenticeship Title	Hours	Title of Related O*NET Job
0284	Line Repairer	6000	Electrical Power-Line Installers and Repairers
1050	Lubrication Servicer/Materials Disposal Technician‡	4000	Installation, Maintenance, and Repair Workers, All Other
0309	Maintenance Mechanic, Telephone	6000	Telecommunications Equipment Installers and Repairers, Except Line Installers
0310	Maintenance Repairer, Buildings	4000	Maintenance and Repair Workers, General
0311	Maintenance Repairer, Industrial	8000	Maintenance and Repair Workers, General
1049	Maintenance Technician, Municipal	4000	Construction Laborers
0973	Marble Finisher	4000	Helpers—Brickmasons, Blockmasons, Stonemasons, and Tile and Marble Setters
0973HY	Marble Finisher	3500–4000	Helpers—Brickmasons, Blockmasons, Stonemasons, and Tile and Marble Setters
0313	Marble Setter	6000	Stonemasons
0313HY	Marble Setter	4500–8000	Stonemasons
0946	Marine Services Technician	6000	Maintenance and Repair Workers, General
0352	Monument Setter (Construction)	8000	Stonemasons
0353	Mosaic Worker	6000	Tile and Marble Setters
0353HY	Mosaic Worker	4500–8000	Tile and Marble Setters
0932	Motor-Grader Operator	6000	Operating Engineers and Other Construction Equipment Operators
0692	Neon-Sign Servicer	8000	Electricians
0966	Oil Burner Servicer and Installer	4000	Heating and Air Conditioning Mechanics and Installers
0365	Operating Engineer	6000	Operating Engineers and Other Construction Equipment Operators
0365HY	Operating Engineer (Grade and Paving Equipment Operator)	4000–6000	Operating Engineers and Other Construction Equipment Operators
0365HY	Operating Engineer (Heavy Duty Repairer)	4000–6000	Operating Engineers and Other Construction Equipment Operators
0365HY	Operating Engineer (Plant Equipment Operator)	4000–6000	Operating Engineers and Other Construction Equipment Operators
0365HY	Operating Engineer (Universal-Equipment Operator)	4000–6000	Operating Engineers and Other Construction Equipment Operators
0373	Ornamental Iron Worker‡	6000	Construction and Related Workers, All Other
0373HY	Ornamental Ironworker /Architect‡	6000–8000	Construction and Related Workers, All Other

Interest Area/Cluster: 02 Architecture and Construction

RAPIDS Code	RAPIDS Apprenticeship Title	Hours	Title of Related O*NET Job
0379	Painter (Construction)	6000	Painters, Construction and Maintenance
0385	Painter, Shipyard	6000	Painters, Construction and Maintenance
0390	Paperhanger	4000	Paperhangers
1042	Pavement Striper	4000	Painters, Construction and Maintenance
0411	Pipe Coverer and Insulator	8000	Insulation Workers, Mechanical
0414S	Pipe Fitter—Sprinkler Fitter	8000	Pipe Fitters and Steamfitters
0414	Pipe Fitter (Construction)	8000	Pipe Fitters and Steamfitters
0412	Pipe Fitter (Ship and Boat)	8000	Pipe Fitters and Steamfitters
0423	Plasterer	4000	Plasterers and Stucco Masons
0423HY	Plasterer	4500–8000	Plasterers and Stucco Masons
0432	Plumber	8000	Plumbers
0061HY	Pointer-Cleaner-Caulker	4500–8000	Construction Laborers
0646	Private-Branch-Exchange Installer	8000	Telecommunications Equipment Installers and Repairers, Except Line Installers
1006	Private-Branch-Exchange Repairer	8000	Telecommunications Equipment Installers and Repairers, Except Line Installers
0455	Prop Maker (Amusement and Recreation)	8000	Construction Carpenters
0459	Protective-Signal Installer	8000	Electricians
0006	Protective-Signal Repairer	6000	Electricians
0666	Refrigeration Mechanic (Any Industry)	6000	Refrigeration Mechanics and Installers
0918	Refrigeration Unit Repairer	6000	Refrigeration Mechanics and Installers
0471HY	Reinforcing Ironworker, Concrete	6000–8000	Reinforcing Iron and Rebar Workers
0471	Reinforcing Metal Worker	6000	Reinforcing Iron and Rebar Workers
0975	Relay Technician	4000	Electrical and Electronics Repairers, Powerhouse, Substation, and Relay
0564	Residential Carpenter	4000	Construction Carpenters
0564HY	Residential Carpenter Specialist	3900–6000	Construction Carpenters
1022	Residential Wireman	4800	Electricians
0474	Rigger	6000	Riggers
0473	Rigger (Ship and Boat Building)	4000	Riggers
0480	Roofer	4000	Roofers
0493	Sandblaster, Stone	6000	Stone Cutters and Carvers, Manufacturing
0615	Service Planner (Light, Heating)	8000	Helpers—Installation, Maintenance, and Repair Workers

*Jobs linked to apprenticeships marked with * usually require college and are not included in Parts III and IV. Jobs linked to apprenticeships marked with ‡ were ranked 201 or lower and are not included in Parts III and IV.*

(continued)

(continued)

Interest Area/Cluster: 02 Architecture and Construction

RAPIDS Code	RAPIDS Apprenticeship Title	Hours	Title of Related O*NET Job
0615HY	Service Planner (Light, Heating)	7500–8000	Helpers—Installation, Maintenance, and Repair Workers
0510	Sheet Metal Worker	8000	Sheet Metal Workers
0510HY	Sheet Metal Worker	8000–10000	Sheet Metal Workers
0979	Shipwright (Ship and Boat)	8000	Construction Carpenters
0517	Sign Erector I‡	6000	Construction and Related Workers, All Other
0449	Soft Tile Setter (Construction)	6000	Floor Layers, Except Carpet, Wood, and Hard Tiles
0528	Sound Technician	6000	Telecommunications Equipment Installers and Repairers, Except Line Installers
0647	Station Installer and Repairer	8000	Telecommunications Equipment Installers and Repairers, Except Line Installers
0460	Steam Service Inspector	8000	Pipe Fitters and Steamfitters
0539	Stone Carver	6000	Stone Cutters and Carvers, Manufacturing
0542	Stonecutter, Hand	6000	Stone Cutters and Carvers, Manufacturing
0540	Stonemason	6000	Stonemasons
0540HY	Stonemason	4500–8000	Stonemasons
0545	Street-Light Servicer	8000	Electricians
0669HY	Structural Ironworker	6000–8000	Structural Iron and Steel Workers
0669HY	Structural Steel/Ironworker	6000–8000	Structural Iron and Steel Workers
0669	Structural-Steel Worker	6000	Structural Iron and Steel Workers
0558	Tank Setter (Petroleum Products)	4000	Structural Iron and Steel Workers
0561	Taper	4000	Tapers
0552	Technician, Submarine Cable	4000	Telecommunications Equipment Installers and Repairers, Except Line Installers
0618	Telecommunications Technician	8000	Telecommunications Equipment Installers and Repairers, Except Line Installers
0972	Terrazzo Finisher	4000	Terrazzo Workers and Finishers
0972HY	Terrazzo Finisher	3500–4000	Terrazzo Workers and Finishers
0568	Terrazzo Worker	6000	Terrazzo Workers and Finishers
0568HY	Terrazzo Worker	4500–8000	Terrazzo Workers and Finishers
0971	Tile Finisher	4000	Helpers—Brickmasons, Blockmasons, Stonemasons, and Tile and Marble Setters
0971HY	Tile Finisher	3500–4000	Helpers—Brickmasons, Blockmasons, Stonemasons, and Tile and Marble Setters
0573	Tile Setter	6000	Tile and Marble Setters
0573HY	Tile Setter	4500–8000	Tile and Marble Setters

Interest Area/Cluster: 02 Architecture and Construction

RAPIDS Code	RAPIDS Apprenticeship Title	Hours	Title of Related O*NET Job
0069HY	Timber Framer	5000–7000	Rough Carpenters
0858	Trouble Shooter II	6000	Electrical Power-Line Installers and Repairers
0014	Truck Crane Operator	6000	Crane and Tower Operators
0680	Tuckpointer, Cleaner, Caulker	6000	Construction Laborers

*Jobs linked to apprenticeships marked with * usually require college and are not included in Parts III and IV. Jobs linked to apprenticeships marked with ‡ were ranked 201 or lower and are not included in Parts III and IV.*

Interest Area/Cluster: 03 Arts and Communication

RAPIDS Code	RAPIDS Apprenticeship Title	Hours	Title of Related O*NET Job
0862	Actor‡	4000	Actors
1101CB	Air Traffic Controller (Military Only)	2500	Air Traffic Controllers
1063CB	Airfield Management	2500	Airfield Operations Specialists
0870	Alarm Operator (Government Service)	2000	Police, Fire, and Ambulance Dispatchers
0879	Audio Operator	4000	Broadcast Technicians
0640	Bank-Note Designer*	10000	Commercial and Industrial Designers
0955	Camera Operator	6000	Camera Operators, Television, Video, and Motion Picture
0037	Cartoonist, Motion Picture*	6000	Multi-Media Artists and Animators
0081	Cloth Designer*	8000	Commercial and Industrial Designers
0013	Commercial Designer*	8000	Commercial and Industrial Designers
0082	Decorator (Any Industry)	8000	Merchandise Displayers and Window Trimmers
0970	Director, Television*	4000	Directors—Stage, Motion Pictures, Television, and Radio
0681	Dispatcher, Service	4000	Dispatchers, Except Police, Fire, and Ambulance
0098	Display Designer (Professional and Kindred)*	8000	Set and Exhibit Designers
0324	Displayer, Merchandise	2000	Merchandise Displayers and Window Trimmers
0960	Field Engineer (Radio and TV)	8000	Broadcast Technicians
0127	Film or Videotape Editor*	8000	Film and Video Editors
0202	Floral Designer	2000	Floral Designers
0215	Fretted Instrument Repairer	6000	Musical Instrument Repairers and Tuners

(continued)

(continued)

Interest Area/Cluster: 03 Arts and Communication

RAPIDS Code	RAPIDS Apprenticeship Title	Hours	Title of Related O*NET Job
0224	Fur Designer	8000	Fashion Designers
0225	Furniture Designer*	8000	Commercial and Industrial Designers
0010	Graphic Designer*	3000	Graphic Designers
0240	Illustrator (Professional and Kindred)	8000	Fine Artists, Including Painters, Sculptors, and Illustrators
0016	Industrial Designer*	8000	Commercial and Industrial Designers
0265	Interior Designer	4000	Interior Designers
0276	Light Technician	8000	Audio and Video Equipment Technicians
0340	Model Maker (Pottery and Porcelain)	4000	Potters, Manufacturing
1064CB	Operations Resource Flight/Jump Management	2500	Airfield Operations Specialists
0626	Painter (Professional and Kindred)	2000	Fine Artists, Including Painters, Sculptors, and Illustrators
0403	Photographer, Still	6000	Photographers
0408	Piano Technician	8000	Musical Instrument Repairers and Tuners
0793	Piano Tuner	6000	Musical Instrument Repairers and Tuners
0388	Pipe Organ Tuner and Repairer	8000	Musical Instrument Repairers and Tuners
0439	Pottery Machine Operator	6000	Potters, Manufacturing
0913	Program Assistant*	6000	Producers
0952	Radio Station Operator	8000	Radio Operators
0926	Recording Engineer	4000	Sound Engineering Technicians
1075CB	Services (Base Facilities)*	2500	Public Relations Specialists
0527	Sound Mixer	8000	Sound Engineering Technicians
0521	Stage Technician	6000	Audio and Video Equipment Technicians
0382	Stained Glass Artist*	8000	Commercial and Industrial Designers
0562	Taxidermist (Professional and Kindred)	6000	Craft Artists
1002	Telecommunicator	8000	Police, Fire, and Ambulance Dispatchers
0494	Wardrobe Supervisor	4000	Costume Attendants
0357	Wind Instrument Repairer	8000	Musical Instrument Repairers and Tuners

*Jobs linked to apprenticeships marked with * usually require college and are not included in Parts III and IV. Jobs linked to apprenticeships marked with ‡ were ranked 201 or lower and are not included in Parts III and IV.*

Interest Area/Cluster: 04 Business and Administration

RAPIDS Code	RAPIDS Apprenticeship Title	Hours	Title of Related O*NET Job
1125HY	Accounting Technician	4000–5000	Bookkeeping, Accounting, and Auditing Clerks
1057CB	Career Development Technician*	4500	Employment Interviewers
1079CB	Education and Training*	2500	Training and Development Specialists
1083CB	Financial Management	2000	Payroll and Timekeeping Clerks
1087	Fire Department Training Officer*	4000	Training and Development Specialists
1084	Health Unit Coordinator	2000	Office Clerks, General
0259	Industrial Engineering Technician	8000	Industrial Engineering Technicians
1073CB	Information Management (Word Processing)	2000	Word Processors and Typists
1072CB	Information Management Specialist	2000	Word Processors and Typists
0800	Legal Secretary	2000	Legal Secretaries
0304	Mailer	8000	Mail Clerks and Mail Machine Operators, Except Postal Service
1061	Manager, Household (Private Residence)	4000	First-Line Supervisors/Managers of Housekeeping and Janitorial Workers
0856	Material Coordinator	4000	Production, Planning, and Expediting Clerks
0751	Medical Secretary	2000	Medical Secretaries
1033	Office Manager, Administrative Services*	4000	Administrative Services Managers
1077CB	Personnel Systems Management	2000	Human Resources Assistants, Except Payroll and Timekeeping
0285	Photocomposing-Perforation-Maker	4000	Data Entry Keyers
0596	Post Office Clerk	4000	Postal Service Clerks
0462	Quality Control Technician	4000	Industrial Engineering Technicians
0445	Script Supervisor	2000	Secretaries, Except Legal, Medical, and Executive
0366	Supercargo (Water Transportation)	4000	Production, Planning, and Expediting Clerks
0951	Telegraphic-Typewriter Operator	6000	Word Processors and Typists
1039	Youth Development Practitioner*	4000	Employment Interviewers
1039HY	Youth Development Practitioner*	3000–4000	Employment Interviewers

*Jobs linked to apprenticeships marked with * usually require college and are not included in Parts III and IV. Jobs linked to apprenticeships marked with ‡ were ranked 201 or lower and are not included in Parts III and IV.*

Interest Area/Cluster: 05 Education and Training

RAPIDS Code	RAPIDS Apprenticeship Title	Hours	Title of Related O*NET Job
0569	Counselor*	4000	Educational, Vocational, and School Counselors
0657	Teacher Aide I	4000	Teacher Assistants

Jobs linked to apprenticeships marked with * usually require college and are not included in Parts III and IV. Jobs linked to apprenticeships marked with ‡ were ranked 201 or lower and are not included in Parts III and IV.

Interest Area/Cluster: 06 Finance and Insurance

RAPIDS Code	RAPIDS Apprenticeship Title	Hours	Title of Related O*NET Job
1055	Teller (Financial)	2000	Tellers

Jobs linked to apprenticeships marked with * usually require college and are not included in Parts III and IV. Jobs linked to apprenticeships marked with ‡ were ranked 201 or lower and are not included in Parts III and IV.

Interest Area/Cluster: 07 Government and Public Administration

RAPIDS Code	RAPIDS Apprenticeship Title	Hours	Title of Related O*NET Job
1119	Boiler Pressure Vessel Inspector‡	2000	Compliance Officers, Except Agriculture, Construction, Health and Safety, and Transportation
1121	Field Technician, Concrete/Masonry Inspector	3000–6000	Construction and Building Inspectors
1121HY	Field Technician, Concrete/Masonry Inspector	3000–6000	Construction and Building Inspectors
1122	Field Technician, Soil/Asphalt Inspector	2400–6000	Construction and Building Inspectors
1122HY	Field Technician, Soil/Asphalt Inspector	2400–6000	Construction and Building Inspectors
1123	Field Technician, Steel/Welding/Fireproofing Inspector	3000–6000	Construction and Building Inspectors
1123HY	Field Technician, Steel/Welding/Fireproofing Inspector	3000–6000	Construction and Building Inspectors
0516	Fire Inspector	8000	Fire Inspectors
0902	Fish and Game Warden (Government Service)	4000	Fish and Game Wardens
0941	Inspector, Building	6000	Construction and Building Inspectors

Interest Area/Cluster: 07 Government and Public Administration

RAPIDS Code	RAPIDS Apprenticeship Title	Hours	Title of Related O*NET Job
0581	Inspector, Motor Vehicles	4000	Transportation Vehicle, Equipment, and Systems Inspectors, Except Aviation
0992	Inspector, Quality Assurance	6000	Government Property Inspectors and Investigators
1078CB	Military Equal Opportunity (MEO)	2000	Equal Opportunity Representatives and Officers
1080CB	Public Health*	2500	Occupational Health and Safety Technicians
1007	Radiation Monitor	8000	Nuclear Monitoring Technicians
0707	Safety Inspector/Technician*	6000	Occupational Health and Safety Specialists

*Jobs linked to apprenticeships marked with * usually require college and are not included in Parts III and IV. Jobs linked to apprenticeships marked with ‡ were ranked 201 or lower and are not included in Parts III and IV.*

Interest Area/Cluster: 08 Health Science

RAPIDS Code	RAPIDS Apprenticeship Title	Hours	Title of Related O*NET Job
0871	Animal Trainer	4000	Animal Trainers
1103CB	Bio-Manufacturing Technician (Downstream)*	2000	Biological Technicians
1102CB	Bio-Manufacturing Technician (Upstream)*	2000	Biological Technicians
1133	Central Sterile Processing Technician	2000	Medical Equipment Preparers
0824MA	Certified Nursing Assistant (Medication Aide Specialty)	700–1200	Nursing Aides, Orderlies, and Attendants
1116	Computed Tomography (CT) Technologist	1838	Radiologic Technologists
0630	Dairy Technologist*	8000	Biological Technicians
0101	Dental Assistant	2000	Dental Assistants
1081CB	Diagnostic Imaging Specialty	2500	Radiologic Technologists
0665	Embalmer (Personal Services)	4000	Embalmers
0602	Health Care Sanitary Technician‡	2000	Health Technologists and Technicians, All Other
1086AA	Health Support Specialist‡	2500–5000	Home Health Aides
1086AA (HY)	Health Support Specialist‡	2500–5000	Home Health Aides

(continued)

(continued)

Interest Area/Cluster: 08 Health Science

RAPIDS Code	RAPIDS Apprenticeship Title	Hours	Title of Related O*NET Job
1086AA (HY)	Health Support Specialist (ACT Director)‡	250–500	Home Health Aides
1086AA (HY)	Health Support Specialist (CNA)‡	500–1000	Home Health Aides
1086AA (HY)	Health Support Specialist (CRT Medical Aide)‡	750–1500	Home Health Aides
1086AA (HY)	Health Support Specialist (DIN Services)‡	540–1080	Home Health Aides
1086AA (HY)	Health Support Specialist (Environmental Services)‡	510–1020	Home Health Aides
1086AA (HY)	Health Support Specialist (Home Health Aide)‡	250–500	Home Health Aides
1086AA (HY)	Health Support Specialist (Rehabilitation Aide)‡	200–400	Home Health Aides
1086CB	Home Health Aide‡	2000	Home Health Aides
1108CB	Home Health Director*	2000	Medical and Health Services Managers
1001	Horse Trainer	2000	Animal Trainers
0235	Horseshoer‡	4000	Nonfarm Animal Caretakers
1105CB	Long-Term Care (LTC) Nurse Management*	2000–3000	Medical and Health Services Managers
1115	Magnetic Resonance Imaging (MRI) Technologist	1856	Radiologic Technologists
1117	Mammography Technologist	1856	Radiologic Technologists
1085	Medical Assistant	4000	Medical Assistants
1114	Medical Coder	2712	Medical Records and Health Information Technicians
1111	Medical Transcriptionist	4000	Medical Transcriptionists
1111HY	Medical Transcriptionist	4000	Medical Transcriptionists
0323	Medical-Laboratory Technician	4000	Medical and Clinical Laboratory Technicians
0824	Nurse Assistant	2000	Nursing Aides, Orderlies, and Attendants
0824CB	Nurse Assistant, Certified/CNA/ Level 1	300–600	Nursing Aides, Orderlies, and Attendants
0824CB	Nurse Assistant, Certified/CNA/ Level 2 (Advanced)	300–600	Nursing Aides, Orderlies, and Attendants
0824CB	Nurse Assistant, Certified/CNA/ Level 3 (Dementia Specialty)	1000	Nursing Aides, Orderlies, and Attendants
0824CB	Nurse Assistant, Certified/CNA/ Level 3 (Geriatric Specialty)	1000	Nursing Aides, Orderlies, and Attendants

Interest Area/Cluster: 08 Health Science

RAPIDS Code	RAPIDS Apprenticeship Title	Hours	Title of Related O*NET Job
0824CB	Nurse Assistant, Certified/CNA/Level 3 (Restorative Specialty)	1000	Nursing Aides, Orderlies, and Attendants
0824CB	Nurse Assistant, Certified/CNA/Level 4 (Mentor Specialty)	1000	Nursing Aides, Orderlies, and Attendants
0837	Nurse, Licensed Practical	2000	Licensed Practical and Licensed Vocational Nurses
0824CB	Nursing Assistant, Certified	6000	Nursing Aides, Orderlies, and Attendants
0089HY	Ophthalmic Dispenser/Optician, Contact Lens	6000+	Opticians, Dispensing
0089	Optician, Dispensing	4000	Opticians, Dispensing
0458	Orthotist*	8000	Orthotists and Prosthetists
0844	Pharmacist Assistant	2000	Pharmacy Technicians
0844CB	Pharmacy Technician	2000–2500	Pharmacy Technicians
0406	Podiatric Assistant	4000	Medical Assistants
0418	Prosthetist (Medical Services)*	8000	Orthotists and Prosthetists
1109CB	Senior Housing Manager*	2000	Medical and Health Services Managers
1051CB	Surgical Technologist	4000	Surgical Technologists
1004	Tumor Registrar	4000	Medical Records and Health Information Technicians
1112CB	Veterinary/Lab Animal Technician‡	2000	Veterinary Assistants and Laboratory Animal Caretakers

Jobs linked to apprenticeships marked with * usually require college and are not included in Parts III and IV. Jobs linked to apprenticeships marked with ‡ were ranked 201 or lower and are not included in Parts III and IV.

Interest Area/Cluster: 09 Hospitality, Tourism, and Recreation

RAPIDS Code	RAPIDS Apprenticeship Title	Hours	Title of Related O*NET Job
0776	Baker (Hotel and Restaurant)	6000	Chefs and Head Cooks
0883	Baker, Pizza (Hotel and Restaurant)‡	2000	Cooks, Fast Food
0030	Barber	2000	Barbers
0608	Bartender‡	2000	Bartenders
0894	Butcher, Meat (Hotel and Restaurant)	6000	Butchers and Meat Cutters
1053	Chief Cook (Water Transportation)	4000.5	Chefs and Head Cooks
1053CB	Chief Cook (Water Transportation)‡	1000–2080	Dining Room and Cafeteria Attendants and Bartender Helpers

(continued)

(continued)

Interest Area/Cluster: 09 Hospitality, Tourism, and Recreation

RAPIDS Code	RAPIDS Apprenticeship Title	Hours	Title of Related O*NET Job
0090	Cook (Any Industry)	4000	Cooks, Institution and Cafeteria
0663	Cook (Hotel and Restaurant)	6000	Cooks, Restaurant
0663HY	Cook (Hotel and Restaurant)	4000–6000	Cooks, Restaurant
0722	Cook, Pastry (Hotel and Restaurant)	6000	Chefs and Head Cooks
0096	Cosmetologist	2000	Hairdressers, Hairstylists, and Cosmetologists
0096A	Hair Stylist	2000	Hairdressers, Hairstylists, and Cosmetologists
1035	Hotel Associate‡	4000	Hotel, Motel, and Resort Desk Clerks
0943	Housekeeper, Commercial/Residential/Industrial‡	2000	Maids and Housekeeping Cleaners
0593	Manager, Food Service	6000	Food Service Managers
0316	Meat Cutter	6000	Butchers and Meat Cutters
0688	Multi-Story Window Builder‡	6000	Janitors and Cleaners, Except Maids and Housekeeping Cleaners
0433	Rug Cleaner, Hand‡	2000	Building Cleaning Workers, All Other
0838	Swimming-Pool Servicer‡	4000	Janitors and Cleaners, Except Maids and Housekeeping Cleaners

*Jobs linked to apprenticeships marked with * usually require college and are not included in Parts III and IV. Jobs linked to apprenticeships marked with ‡ were ranked 201 or lower and are not included in Parts III and IV.*

Interest Area/Cluster: 10 Human Service

RAPIDS Code	RAPIDS Apprenticeship Title	Hours	Title of Related O*NET Job
1082CB	Chaplain Service Support*	2000	Directors, Religious Activities and Education
0840	Child Care Development Specialist‡	4000	Child Care Workers
1040CB	Direct Support Specialist	3000	Social and Human Service Assistants
1076CB	Public Affairs	2500	Residential Advisors

*Jobs linked to apprenticeships marked with * usually require college and are not included in Parts III and IV. Jobs linked to apprenticeships marked with ‡ were ranked 201 or lower and are not included in Parts III and IV.*

Interest Area/Cluster: 11 Information Technology

RAPIDS Code	RAPIDS Apprenticeship Title	Hours	Title of Related O*NET Job
1129CB	Application Developer*	2000	Computer Software Engineers, Applications
0878	Assembly Technician	4000	Computer, Automated Teller, and Office Machine Repairers
0072	Cash-Register Servicer	6000	Computer, Automated Teller, and Office Machine Repairers
0609	Coin-Machine-Service Repairer	6000	Coin, Vending, and Amusement Machine Servicers and Repairers
1073CB	Communications—Computer Systems Planning and Implementation*	2500	Computer Systems Analysts
0676	Computer Operator	6000	Computer Operators
0817	Computer Peripheral Equipment Operator	2000	Computer Operators
0811	Computer Programmer*	4000	Computer Programmers
1130CB	Database Technician*	2000	Database Administrators
0085	Dictating-Transcription-Machine Servicer	6000	Computer, Automated Teller, and Office Machine Repairers
1054CB	E-commerce Specialist	6000	Web Developers
0170	Electronics Mechanic	8000	Computer, Automated Teller, and Office Machine Repairers
1131CB	Help Desk Technician	2000	Computer Support Specialists
1060	Information Assurance Specialist*	6000	Computer Security Specialists
1060CB	Information Assurance Specialist*	6000	Computer Security Specialists
1038	Internetworking Technician*	5000	Network Systems and Data Communications Analysts
1059	IT Generalist‡	2880	Computer Specialists, All Other
1059CB	IT Generalist‡	2880	Computer Specialists, All Other
1048CB	IT Project Manager*	6000	Computer and Information Systems Managers
1132CB	Network Support Technician*	2000	Network and Computer Systems Administrators
0359	Office-Machine Servicer	6000	Computer, Automated Teller, and Office Machine Repairers
0949	Programmer, Engineering and Scientific*	8000	Computer Programmers

*Jobs linked to apprenticeships marked with * usually require college and are not included in Parts III and IV. Jobs linked to apprenticeships marked with ‡ were ranked 201 or lower and are not included in Parts III and IV.*

Interest Area/Cluster: 12 Law and Public Safety

RAPIDS Code	RAPIDS Apprenticeship Title	Hours	Title of Related O*NET Job
0863	Aircraft Mechanic, Armament	8000	Artillery and Missile Crew Members
0531	Arson and Bomb Investigator	4000	Fire Investigators
1065CB	Command Post Specialty	2500	Command and Control Center Specialists
0851	Correction Officer	2000	Correctional Officers and Jailers
1113CB	Crime Scene Technician*	4000	Forensic Science Technicians
0730	Emergency Medical Technician	6000	Emergency Medical Technicians and Paramedics
0535	Fire Apparatus Engineer	6000	Municipal Fire Fighters
0576	Fire Captain	6000	Municipal Fire Fighting and Prevention Supervisors
0541	Fire Engineer	2000	Municipal Fire Fighters
0195	Fire Fighter	6000	Municipal Fire Fighters
1092	Fire Fighter Diver	7000	Municipal Fire Fighters
1091	Fire Fighter Paramedic	8000	Municipal Fire Fighters
0192	Fire Fighter, Crash, Fire	2000	Municipal Fire Fighters
1090	Fire Marshall	4000	Fire Investigators
0754	Fire Medic	6000	Municipal Fire Fighters
1089	Fire Prevention Officer	4000	Municipal Fire Fighting and Prevention Supervisors
1088	Fire Suppression Technician	4000	Forest Fire Fighters
0193	Fire-Control Mechanic	4000	Artillery and Missile Crew Members
0695HY	Guard, Security	3000–6000	Security Guards
0579	Investigator, Private	2000	Private Detectives and Investigators
1120	Medicaid Disability Claims Adjudicator*	6000	Administrative Law Judges, Adjudicators, and Hearing Officers
1066CB	Operations Intelligence	2000	Command and Control Center Specialists
0372	Ordnance Artificer (Government Service)	6000	Artillery and Missile Crew Members
1003	Paralegal	6000	Paralegals and Legal Assistants
0543	Paramedic	4000	Emergency Medical Technicians and Paramedics
0437	Police Officer I	4000	Police Patrol Officers
1058CB	Production Controller	4000	Emergency Management Specialists
0544	Wildland Fire Fighter Specialist	2000	Forest Fire Fighters

*Jobs linked to apprenticeships marked with * usually require college and are not included in Parts III and IV. Jobs linked to apprenticeships marked with ‡ were ranked 201 or lower and are not included in Parts III and IV.*

Interest Area/Cluster: 13 Manufacturing

RAPIDS Code	RAPIDS Apprenticeship Title	Hours	Title of Related O*NET Job
0860	Accordion Maker	8000	Cabinetmakers and Bench Carpenters
1067CB	Aerospace Propulsion Jet Engine Mechanic	2500	Aircraft Mechanics and Service Technicians
0002	Air Conditioner Installer, Window	6000	Home Appliance Repairers
0686	Air Conditioning Mechanic (Auto Service)	2000	Automotive Specialty Technicians
0865	Aircraft Mechanic, Armament	8000	Aircraft Structure, Surfaces, Rigging, and Systems Assemblers
0003	Aircraft Mechanic, Electrical	8000	Avionics Technicians
0867	Aircraft Mechanic, Photographic Equipment	8000	Camera and Photographic Equipment Repairers
0866	Aircraft Mechanic, Plumbing and Hydraulic	8000	Aircraft Structure, Surfaces, Rigging, and Systems Assemblers
1068CB	Aircraft Metals Technology (Machinist/CNC/Welder)	2500	Computer-Controlled Machine Tool Operators, Metal and Plastic
0005	Airframe and Powerplant Mechanic	8000	Aircraft Mechanics and Service Technicians
1044	Airframe Mechanic	3100	Aircraft Mechanics and Service Technicians
0868	Airplane Coverer‡	8000	Production Workers, All Other
0004	Airplane Inspector	6000	Inspectors, Testers, Sorters, Samplers, and Weighers
0007	Alteration Tailor	4000	Tailors, Dressmakers, and Custom Sewers
0011	Artificial Glass Eye Maker	10000	Glass Blowers, Molders, Benders, and Finishers
0012	Artificial Plastic Eye Maker	10000	Medical Appliance Technicians
0873	Assembler, Aircraft Powerplant	4000	Engine and Other Machine Assemblers
0874	Assembler, Aircraft Structures	8000	Aircraft Structure, Surfaces, Rigging, and Systems Assemblers
0876	Assembler-Installer, General	4000	Aircraft Structure, Surfaces, Rigging, and Systems Assemblers
0903	Assistant Press Operator	4000	Printing Machine Operators
0880	Audio-Video Repairer	4000	Electronic Home Entertainment Equipment Installers and Repairers

*Jobs linked to apprenticeships marked with * usually require college and are not included in Parts III and IV. Jobs linked to apprenticeships marked with ‡ were ranked 201 or lower and are not included in Parts III and IV.*

(continued)

(continued)

Interest Area/Cluster: 13 Manufacturing

RAPIDS Code	RAPIDS Apprenticeship Title	Hours	Title of Related O*NET Job
0779	Auger Press Operator, Manual Controlled	4000	Extruding, Forming, Pressing, and Compacting Machine Setters, Operators, and Tenders
0836	Auto Cooling System Diagnostic Technician	4000	Automotive Specialty Technicians
0027	Auto-Maintenance-Equipment Servicer	8000	Industrial Machinery Mechanics
1128	Automated Access Systems Technician	3520	Mechanical Door Repairers
0821	Automated Equipment Engineer—Technician	8000	Millwrights
0024	Automobile Body Repairer	8000	Automotive Body and Related Repairers
0023	Automobile Mechanic	8000	Automotive Master Mechanics
0881	Automobile Tester	8000	Inspectors, Testers, Sorters, Samplers, and Weighers
0639	Automobile Upholsterer	6000	Upholsterers
0638	Automobile-Repair-Service Estimator	8000	Inspectors, Testers, Sorters, Samplers, and Weighers
1034CB	Automotive Technician Specialist	2000–4000	Automotive Specialty Technicians
1034CB	Automotive Technician Specialist (Entry Level 1, Experienced)	650–1000	Automotive Specialty Technicians
1034CB	Automotive Technician Specialist (Entry Level 1, Nonexperienced)	650–1000	Automotive Specialty Technicians
1034CB	Automotive Technician Specialist (Lead Technician A, Level 4)	4000–8000	Automotive Specialty Technicians
1034CB	Automotive Technician Specialist (Senior Technician B, Level 3)	4000–8000	Automotive Specialty Technicians
1034CB	Automotive Technician Specialist (Technician C, Level 2)	2000–4000	Automotive Specialty Technicians
0882	Automotive-Generator-Starter Repairer	4000	Electric Motor, Power Tool, and Related Repairers
0784	Auto-Radiator Mechanic	4000	Automotive Specialty Technicians
0599	Aviation Support Equipment Repairer	8000	Industrial Machinery Mechanics
0464	Avionics Technician	8000	Electrical and Electronics Repairers, Commercial and Industrial Equipment
0028	Baker (Bake Produce)	6000	Bakers
0029	Bakery-Machine Mechanic	6000	Industrial Machinery Mechanics

Interest Area/Cluster: 13 Manufacturing

RAPIDS Code	RAPIDS Apprenticeship Title	Hours	Title of Related O*NET Job
0884	Batch-and-Furnace Operator	8000	Furnace, Kiln, Oven, Drier, and Kettle Operators and Tenders
0885	Battery Repairer	4000	Electric Motor, Power Tool, and Related Repairers
0031	Bench Hand (Jewelry—Silver)	4000	Jewelers
0887	Ben-Day Artist	12000	Printing Machine Operators
0033	Bindery Worker	8000	Bindery Workers
0026	Bindery-Machine Setter	8000	Bindery Workers
0888	Biomedical Equipment Technician	8000	Medical Equipment Repairers
0035	Blacksmith‡	8000	Metal Workers and Plastic Workers, All Other
0889	Blocker and Cutter, Contact Lens	2000	Ophthalmic Laboratory Technicians
0815	Boiler Operator	8000	Stationary Engineers and Boiler Operators
0047	Bookbinder	10000	Bookbinders
0890	Bootmaker, Hand	2000	Shoe and Leather Workers and Repairers
0891	Bracelet and Brooch Maker	8000	Jewelers
0892	Brake Repairer (Auto Service)	4000	Automotive Specialty Technicians
0893	Brilliandeer-Lopper	6000	Gem and Diamond Workers
0662	Butcher, All-Around	6000	Slaughterers and Meat Packers
0054	Buttermaker	4000	Separating, Filtering, Clarifying, Precipitating, and Still Machine Setters, Operators, and Tenders
0055	Cabinetmaker	8000	Cabinetmakers and Bench Carpenters
0055HY	Cabinetmaker	5200–8000	Cabinetmakers and Bench Carpenters
0059	Cable Tester (Telephone and Telegraph)	8000	Inspectors, Testers, Sorters, Samplers, and Weighers
1031	Calibrator (Military)	4000	Inspectors, Testers, Sorters, Samplers, and Weighers
0062	Camera Repairer	4000	Camera and Photographic Equipment Repairers
0790	Canal Equipment Mechanic	4000	Industrial Machinery Mechanics
0065	Candy Maker	6000	Food Batchmakers
0641	Canvas Worker‡	6000	Production Workers, All Other
0642	Car Repairer (Railroad Equipment)	8000	Rail Car Repairers
0896	Carburetor Mechanic	8000	Automotive Specialty Technicians

*Jobs linked to apprenticeships marked with * usually require college and are not included in Parts III and IV. Jobs linked to apprenticeships marked with ‡ were ranked 201 or lower and are not included in Parts III and IV.*

(continued)

(continued)

	Interest Area/Cluster: 13 Manufacturing		
RAPIDS Code	RAPIDS Apprenticeship Title	Hours	Title of Related O*NET Job
0897	Card Cutter, Jacquard‡	8000	Textile, Apparel, and Furnishings Workers, All Other
0898	Card Grinder	8000	Tool Grinders, Filers, and Sharpeners
0899	Carpet Cutter (Retail Trade)	2000	Cutters and Trimmers, Hand
0042	Carver, Hand	8000	Cabinetmakers and Bench Carpenters
0043	Casing-In-Line Setter	8000	Bindery Workers
0074	Caster (Jewelry—Silver)	4000	Jewelers
0044	Caster (Nonferrous Metal)	4000	Molding, Coremaking, and Casting Machine Setters, Operators, and Tenders, Metal and Plastic
0046	Cell Maker	2000	Molding and Casting Workers
1124	Cellar Worker (Wine)	2136	Separating, Filtering, Clarifying, Precipitating, and Still Machine Setters, Operators, and Tenders
0049	Chaser (Jewelry—Silver)	8000	Precious Metal Workers
0078	Cheesemaker	4000	Food Batchmakers
0791	Chemical Operator III	6000	Chemical Equipment Operators and Tenders
0057	Chief Operator (Chemicals)	6000	Chemical Plant and System Operators
0060	Clarifying-Plant Operator (Text)	2000	Water and Liquid Waste Treatment Plant and System Operators
1099CB	CNC Set-Up Programmer—Milling	5000	Numerical Tool and Process Control Programmers
1100CB	CNC Set-Up Programmer—Milling and Turning	6400	Numerical Tool and Process Control Programmers
1095CB	CNC Set-Up Programmer—Turning	4800	Numerical Tool and Process Control Programmers
1025	Coating Machine Operator I	2000	Coating, Painting, and Spraying Machine Setters, Operators, and Tenders
0084	Colorist, Photography	4000	Photographic Process Workers
0061	Complaint Inspector	8000	Inspectors, Testers, Sorters, Samplers, and Weighers
0086	Composing-Room Machinist	12000	Industrial Machinery Mechanics
1118	Composite Fitter Mechanic	4000	Fiberglass Laminators and Fabricators
0087	Compositor	8000	Prepress Technicians and Workers
0336	Construction Equipment Mechanic	8000	Mobile Heavy Equipment Mechanics, Except Engines
0904	Contour Wire Specialist, Denture	8000	Dental Laboratory Technicians

Interest Area/Cluster: 13 Manufacturing

RAPIDS Code	RAPIDS Apprenticeship Title	Hours	Title of Related O*NET Job
0693	Control Equipment Electronics Technician	10000	Electrical and Electronics Repairers, Commercial and Industrial Equipment
0066	Conveyor Maintenance Mechanic	4000	Industrial Machinery Mechanics
0557	Conveyor System Operator	8000	Conveyor Operators and Tenders
0722HY	Cook, Pastry (Hotel and Restaurant)	4000–6000	Bakers
0634	Cooling Tower Technician	4000	Industrial Machinery Mechanics
0094	Coremaker	8000	Foundry Mold and Coremakers
0991	Cupola Tender	6000	Metal-Refining Furnace Operators and Tenders
0314	Custom Tailor (Garment)	8000	Tailors, Dressmakers, and Custom Sewers
1008	Customer Service Representative	6000	Home Appliance Repairers
0613	Cutter, Machine I	6000	Cutters and Trimmers, Hand
0080	Cylinder Grinder (Printing and Publishing)	10000	Tool Grinders, Filers, and Sharpeners
0677	Cylinder Press Operator	8000	Printing Machine Operators
0099	Dairy Equipment Repairer	6000	Farm Equipment Mechanics
0100	Decorator (Glass Manufacturing)	8000	Painting, Coating, and Decorating Workers
0102	Dental Ceramist	4000	Dental Laboratory Technicians
0103	Dental Laboratory Technician	6000	Dental Laboratory Technicians
0650	Dental-Equipment Installer and Servicer	6000	Medical Equipment Repairers
0107	Design and Patternmaker, Shoe	4000	Fabric and Apparel Patternmakers
0083	Diamond Selector (Jewelry)	8000	Gem and Diamond Workers
0114	Die Finisher	8000	Tool and Die Makers
0115	Die Maker (Jewelry—Silver)	8000	Tool and Die Makers
0654	Die Maker (Paper Goods)	8000	Tool and Die Makers
0668	Die Maker, Bench, Stamping	8000	Tool and Die Makers
0118	Die Maker, Stamping	6000	Tool and Die Makers
0119	Die Maker, Trim	8000	Tool and Die Makers
0939	Die Maker, Wire Drawing	6000	Tool and Die Makers
0120	Die Polisher (Nonferrous Metal)	2000	Tool Grinders, Filers, and Sharpeners
0121	Die Setter (Forging)	4000	Forging Machine Setters, Operators, and Tenders, Metal and Plastic
0122	Die Sinker	8000	Tool and Die Makers

*Jobs linked to apprenticeships marked with * usually require college and are not included in Parts III and IV. Jobs linked to apprenticeships marked with ‡ were ranked 201 or lower and are not included in Parts III and IV.*

(continued)

(continued)

Interest Area/Cluster: 13 Manufacturing

RAPIDS Code	RAPIDS Apprenticeship Title	Hours	Title of Related O*NET Job
0093	Diesel Engine Tester	8000	Inspectors, Testers, Sorters, Samplers, and Weighers
0124	Diesel Mechanic	8000	Bus and Truck Mechanics and Diesel Engine Specialists
0104	Door-Closer Mechanic	6000	Mechanical Door Repairers
0679	Dot Etcher	10000	Prepress Technicians and Workers
0144	Dressmaker	8000	Tailors, Dressmakers, and Custom Sewers
0649	Dry Cleaner‡	6000	Laundry and Dry-Cleaning Workers
0330	Electric Meter Installer I	8000	Control and Valve Installers and Repairers, Except Mechanical Door
0151	Electric Meter Repairer	8000	Control and Valve Installers and Repairers, Except Mechanical Door
0792	Electric Meter Tester	8000	Inspectors, Testers, Sorters, Samplers, and Weighers
0927	Electric Motor and Generator Assembler	4000	Engine and Other Machine Assemblers
0829	Electric Motor Assembler and Tester	4000	Electric Motor, Power Tool, and Related Repairers
0149	Electric Motor Repairer	8000	Electric Motor, Power Tool, and Related Repairers
0652	Electric Sign Assembler	8000	Electrical and Electronic Equipment Assemblers
0150	Electric Tool Repairer	8000	Home Appliance Repairers
0154	Electrical Appliance Repairer	6000	Home Appliance Repairers
0156	Electrical Appliance Servicer	6000	Home Appliance Repairers
0905	Electric-Distribution Checker	4000	Inspectors, Testers, Sorters, Samplers, and Weighers
0160	Electrician, Aircraft	8000	Avionics Technicians
0161	Electrician, Automotive	4000	Electronic Equipment Installers and Repairers, Motor Vehicles
0162	Electrician, Locomotive	8000	Electrical and Electronics Installers and Repairers, Transportation Equipment
0164	Electrician, Radio	8000	Radio Mechanics
0829	Electric-Motor Assembler and Tester	8000	Electric Motor, Power Tool, and Related Repairers
0171	Electric-Product-Line Maintenance Mechanic	2000	Industrial Machinery Mechanics
0132	Electric-Track-Switch Maintenance Mechanic	8000	Signal and Track Switch Repairers

Interest Area/Cluster: 13 Manufacturing

RAPIDS Code	RAPIDS Apprenticeship Title	Hours	Title of Related O*NET Job
0168	Electromedical Equipment Repairer	4000	Medical Equipment Repairers
0617	Electronic Prepress System Operator	10000	Desktop Publishers
0137	Electronic-Organ Technician	4000	Electronic Home Entertainment Equipment Installers and Repairers
0570	Electronics Tester	6000	Inspectors, Testers, Sorters, Samplers, and Weighers
0967	Electronics Utility Worker‡	8000	Production Workers, All Other
0906	Electronic-Sales-and-Service Technician	8000	Electrical and Electronics Repairers, Commercial and Industrial Equipment
1036	Electrostatic Powder Coating Technician	8000	Coating, Painting, and Spraying Machine Setters, Operators, and Tenders
0172	Electrotyper	10000	Prepress Technicians and Workers
0704	Embosser	4000	Printing Machine Operators
0684	Embossing-Press Operator	8000	Printing Machine Operators
0176	Engine Repairer, Service	8000	Outdoor Power Equipment and Other Small Engine Mechanics
0143	Engine Turner (Jewelry)	4000	Jewelers
0249	Engineering Model Maker (Instrumentation and Applications)	8000	Model Makers, Metal and Plastic
0142	Engine-Lathe Set-Up Operator	4000	Lathe and Turning Machine Tool Setters, Operators, and Tenders, Metal and Plastic
0782	Engine-Lathe Set-Up Operator, Tool	4000	Lathe and Turning Machine Tool Setters, Operators, and Tenders, Metal and Plastic
0178	Engraver (Glass Products)	4000	Etchers and Engravers
0705	Engraver I	10000	Etchers and Engravers
0146	Engraver, Block (Printing and Publishing)	8000	Etchers and Engravers
0806	Engraver, Hand, Hard Metal	8000	Etchers and Engravers
0147	Engraver, Hand, Soft Metal	8000	Etchers and Engravers
0963	Engraver, Machine	8000	Printing Machine Operators
0179	Engraver, Pantograph I	8000	Etchers and Engravers
0148	Engraver, Picture (Printing and Publishing)	2000	Etchers and Engravers
0915	Engraving Press Operator	6000	Printing Machine Operators
0180	Envelope-Folding-Machine Adjuster	6000	Paper Goods Machine Setters, Operators, and Tenders
0175	Etcher, Hand (Printing and Publishing)	10000	Prepress Technicians and Workers

*Jobs linked to apprenticeships marked with * usually require college and are not included in Parts III and IV. Jobs linked to apprenticeships marked with ‡ were ranked 201 or lower and are not included in Parts III and IV.*

(continued)

(continued)

Interest Area/Cluster: 13 Manufacturing			
RAPIDS Code	RAPIDS Apprenticeship Title	Hours	Title of Related O*NET Job
0182	Etcher, Photoengraving	8000	Prepress Technicians and Workers
0183	Experimental Assembler	4000	Inspectors, Testers, Sorters, Samplers, and Weighers
0184	Experimental Mechanic, Motor and Bikes	8000	Model Makers, Metal and Plastic
0185	Extruder Operator (Plastics)	2000	Extruding and Drawing Machine Setters, Operators, and Tenders, Metal and Plastic
0833	Fabricator-Assembler, Metal Products	8000	Structural Metal Fabricators and Fitters
0187	Farm Equipment Mechanic I	6000	Farm Equipment Mechanics
0789	Farm Equipment Mechanic II	8000	Farm Equipment Mechanics
0808	Fastener Technologist	6000	Forging Machine Setters, Operators, and Tenders, Metal and Plastic
0916	Field Service Engineer	4000	Electrical and Electronics Repairers, Commercial and Industrial Equipment
0921	Film Developer‡	6000	Photographic Processing Machine Operators
0907	Film Lab Technician‡	6000	Photographic Processing Machine Operators
0908	Film Lab Technician I	6000	Photographic Process Workers
0181	Finisher, Denture	2000	Dental Laboratory Technicians
0188	Firer, Kiln (Pottery and Porcelain)	6000	Furnace, Kiln, Oven, Drier, and Kettle Operators and Tenders
1052	Firer, Marine	2115.5	Stationary Engineers and Boiler Operators
0197	Fitter (Machine Shop)	4000	Structural Metal Fabricators and Fitters
0189	Fitter I (Any Industry)	6000	Structural Metal Fabricators and Fitters
0198	Fixture Maker (Light Fixtures)	4000	Machinists
0194	Folding Machine Operator	4000	Bindery Workers
0203	Forge-Shop-Machine Repairer	6000	Industrial Machinery Mechanics
0196	Forging-Press Operator I	2000	Forging Machine Setters, Operators, and Tenders, Metal and Plastic
0200	Former, Hand (Any Industry)	4000	Structural Metal Fabricators and Fitters
0048	Forming-Machine Operator	8000	Extruding, Forming, Pressing, and Compacting Machine Setters, Operators, and Tenders
0204	Fourdrinier-Machine Operator	6000	Separating, Filtering, Clarifying, Precipitating, and Still Machine Setters, Operators, and Tenders

Interest Area/Cluster: 13 Manufacturing

RAPIDS Code	RAPIDS Apprenticeship Title	Hours	Title of Related O*NET Job
0208	Four-Slide-Machine Setter	4000	Multiple Machine Tool Setters, Operators, and Tenders, Metal and Plastic
0211	Freezer Operator (Dairy)	2000	Cooling and Freezing Equipment Operators and Tenders
0209	Front-End Mechanic	8000	Automotive Specialty Technicians
0922	Fuel Injection Servicer	8000	Automotive Specialty Technicians
0610	Fuel System Maintenance Worker	4000	Industrial Machinery Mechanics
0220	Fur Cutter	4000	Cutters and Trimmers, Hand
0210	Fur Finisher‡	4000	Sewing Machine Operators
0944	Furnace Operator	8000	Metal-Refining Furnace Operators and Tenders
0212	Furniture Finisher	6000	Furniture Finishers
0213	Furniture Upholsterer	8000	Upholsterers
0214	Furrier	8000	Tailors, Dressmakers, and Custom Sewers
0228	Gang Sawyer, Stone	4000	Cutting and Slicing Machine Setters, Operators, and Tenders
0917	Gas Appliance Servicer	6000	Home Appliance Repairers
0594	Gas Utility Worker	4000	Control and Valve Installers and Repairers, Except Mechanical Door
0230	Gas-Engine Repairer	8000	Outdoor Power Equipment and Other Small Engine Mechanics
0331	Gas-Meter Mechanic I	6000	Control and Valve Installers and Repairers, Except Mechanical Door
0232	Gas-Regulator Repairer	6000	Control and Valve Installers and Repairers, Except Mechanical Door
0226	Gauger (Petroleum Products)	4000	Petroleum Pump System Operators, Refinery Operators, and Gaugers
0241	Gear Hobber Setup Operator	8000	Multiple Machine Tool Setters, Operators, and Tenders, Metal and Plastic
0664	Gearcut-Machine Set-Up Operator and Tool Setter	6000	Multiple Machine Tool Setters, Operators, and Tenders, Metal and Plastic
0234	Gear-Cutting-Machine Setup Operator	6000	Multiple Machine Tool Setters, Operators, and Tenders, Metal and Plastic
0242	Gem Cutter (Jewelry)	6000	Gem and Diamond Workers
0218	Glass Bender (Fabrication, not elsewhere classified)	8000	Glass Blowers, Molders, Benders, and Finishers

*Jobs linked to apprenticeships marked with * usually require college and are not included in Parts III and IV. Jobs linked to apprenticeships marked with ‡ were ranked 201 or lower and are not included in Parts III and IV.*

(continued)

(continued)

Interest Area/Cluster: 13 Manufacturing

RAPIDS Code	RAPIDS Apprenticeship Title	Hours	Title of Related O*NET Job
0219	Glass Blower	6000	Glass Blowers, Molders, Benders, and Finishers
0768	Glass Blower, Lab Apparatus	8000	Glass Blowers, Molders, Benders, and Finishers
0714	Glass Installer (Auto Service)	4000	Automotive Glass Installers and Repairers
0243	Glass-Blowing-Lathe Operator	8000	Glass Blowers, Molders, Benders, and Finishers
0984	Grader (Woodworking)	8000	Inspectors, Testers, Sorters, Samplers, and Weighers
0244	Grinder I (Clock and Watch)	8000	Grinding, Lapping, Polishing, and Buffing Machine Tool Setters, Operators, and Tenders, Metal and Plastic
0671	Grinder Operator, Tool (Precision)	8000	Tool Grinders, Filers, and Sharpeners
0635	Grinder Set-Up Operator, Jig	8000	Grinding, Lapping, Polishing, and Buffing Machine Tool Setters, Operators, and Tenders, Metal and Plastic
0974	Grinder Set-Up Operator, Universal	8000	Tool Grinders, Filers, and Sharpeners
0229	Gunsmith	8000	Multiple Machine Tool Setters, Operators, and Tenders, Metal and Plastic
0245	Harness Maker	6000	Shoe and Leather Workers and Repairers
0248	Harpsichord Maker	4000	Cabinetmakers and Bench Carpenters
0253	Hat-Block Maker (Woodwork)	6000	Cabinetmakers and Bench Carpenters
0831	Head Sawyer	6000	Sawing Machine Setters, Operators, and Tenders, Wood
0233	Heat Treater I	8000	Heat Treating Equipment Setters, Operators, and Tenders, Metal and Plastic
0947	Heavy Forger	8000	Forging Machine Setters, Operators, and Tenders, Metal and Plastic
0651	Hydraulic Repairer	8000	Industrial Machinery Mechanics
0783	Hydraulic-Press Servicer (Ordinance)	4000	Industrial Machinery Mechanics
0237	Hydroelectric-Machinery Mechanic	6000	Industrial Machinery Mechanics
0238	Hydroelectric-Station Operator	6000	Power Plant Operators
0239	Hydrometer Calibrator	4000	Inspectors, Testers, Sorters, Samplers, and Weighers
1037	Industrial Machinery Systems Technician	4000	Industrial Machinery Mechanics
0246	Injection-Molding-Machine Operator	2000	Molding, Coremaking, and Casting Machine Setters, Operators, and Tenders, Metal and Plastic

Interest Area/Cluster: 13 Manufacturing

RAPIDS Code	RAPIDS Apprenticeship Title	Hours	Title of Related O*NET Job
0968	Inspector, Electromechanic	8000	Inspectors, Testers, Sorters, Samplers, and Weighers
0697	Inspector, Metal Fabricating	8000	Inspectors, Testers, Sorters, Samplers, and Weighers
0380	Inspector, Outside Product	8000	Inspectors, Testers, Sorters, Samplers, and Weighers
0424	Inspector, Precision	4000	Inspectors, Testers, Sorters, Samplers, and Weighers
0636	Inspector, Set-Up and Lay-Out	8000	Inspectors, Testers, Sorters, Samplers, and Weighers
0251	Instrument Maker	8000	Machinists
0254	Instrument Maker and Repairer	10000	Machinists
0270	Jacquard-Loom Weaver	8000	Textile Knitting and Weaving Machine Setters, Operators, and Tenders
0258	Jacquard-Plate Maker	2000	Textile Knitting and Weaving Machine Setters, Operators, and Tenders
0260	Jeweler	4000	Jewelers
0261	Jig Builder (Wood Containers)	4000	Model Makers, Wood
0262	Job Printer	8000	Job Printers
0266	Kiln Operator (Woodworking)	6000	Furnace, Kiln, Oven, Drier, and Kettle Operators and Tenders
0273	Knitter Mechanic	8000	Textile Knitting and Weaving Machine Setters, Operators, and Tenders
0850	Knitting Machine Fixer	8000	Textile Knitting and Weaving Machine Setters, Operators, and Tenders
0275	Last-Model Maker	8000	Cabinetmakers and Bench Carpenters
0691	Laundry-Machine Mechanic	6000	Industrial Machinery Mechanics
0554	Lay-Out Technician	8000	Ophthalmic Laboratory Technicians
0825	Lay-Out Worker I (Any Industry)	8000	Lay-Out Workers, Metal and Plastic
0274	Lead Burner	8000	Welders, Cutters, and Welder Fitters
0935	Leather Stamper	2000	Shoe and Leather Workers and Repairers
0280	Letterer (Professional and Kindred)	4000	Printing Machine Operators
0279	Liner (Pottery and Porcelain)	6000	Painting, Coating, and Decorating Workers
0286	Linotype Operator (Printing and Publishing)	10000	Prepress Technicians and Workers
0683CB	Lithograph Press Operator	1000–4000	Printing Machine Operators
0063	Lithographic Platemaker	8000	Prepress Technicians and Workers

*Jobs linked to apprenticeships marked with * usually require college and are not included in Parts III and IV. Jobs linked to apprenticeships marked with ‡ were ranked 201 or lower and are not included in Parts III and IV.*

(continued)

(continued)

| \multicolumn{4}{c}{**Interest Area/Cluster: 13 Manufacturing**} |
RAPIDS Code	RAPIDS Apprenticeship Title	Hours	Title of Related O*NET Job
0683	Lithograph-Press Operator, Tin	8000	Printing Machine Operators
1047	Load Dispatcher	8000	Power Distributors and Dispatchers
0289	Locksmith	8000	Locksmiths and Safe Repairers
0290	Loft Worker (Ship and Boat)	8000	Model Makers, Wood
0299	Logging-Equipment Mechanic	8000	Mobile Heavy Equipment Mechanics, Except Engines
0841	Loom Fixer	6000	Textile Knitting and Weaving Machine Setters, Operators, and Tenders
0301	Machine Assembler	4000	Engine and Other Machine Assemblers
0291	Machine Builder	4000	Engine and Other Machine Assemblers
0291CB	Machine Builder	9200	Engine and Other Machine Assemblers
0293	Machine Erector	8000	Millwrights
0302	Machine Fixer (Carpet and Rug)	8000	Industrial Machinery Mechanics
0305	Machine Fixer (Textile)	6000	Textile Winding, Twisting, and Drawing Out Machine Setters, Operators, and Tenders
0511	Machine Operator I	2000	Multiple Machine Tool Setters, Operators, and Tenders, Metal and Plastic
0292	Machine Repairer, Maintenance	8000	Industrial Machinery Mechanics
0938	Machine Setter (Any Industry)	8000	Multiple Machine Tool Setters, Operators, and Tenders, Metal and Plastic
0317	Machine Setter (Clock)	8000	Multiple Machine Tool Setters, Operators, and Tenders, Metal and Plastic
0263	Machine Setter (Machine Shop)	6000	Multiple Machine Tool Setters, Operators, and Tenders, Metal and Plastic
0321	Machine Setter (Woodwork)	8000	Woodworking Machine Setters, Operators, and Tenders, Except Sawing
0958	Machine Set-Up Operator	4000	Multiple Machine Tool Setters, Operators, and Tenders, Metal and Plastic
0327	Machine Set-Up Operator, Paper	8000	Paper Goods Machine Setters, Operators, and Tenders
0659	Machine Tryout Setter	8000	Multiple Machine Tool Setters, Operators, and Tenders, Metal and Plastic
0296	Machinist	8000	Machinists
0294	Machinist, Automotive	8000	Machinists
0295	Machinist, Experimental	8000	Machinists
0297	Machinist, Linotype	8000	Industrial Machinery Mechanics

Interest Area/Cluster: 13 Manufacturing

RAPIDS Code	RAPIDS Apprenticeship Title	Hours	Title of Related O*NET Job
0298	Machinist, Marine Engine	8000	Bus and Truck Mechanics and Diesel Engine Specialists
0191	Machinist, Motion Picture Equipment	4000	Camera and Photographic Equipment Repairers
0300	Machinist, Outside (Ship)	8000	Machinists
0303	Machinist, Wood	8000	Cabinetmakers and Bench Carpenters
0306	Maintenance Machinist	8000	Machinists
0308	Maintenance Mechanic (Any Industry)	8000	Industrial Machinery Mechanics
0022	Maintenance Mechanic (Construction; Petroleum)	8000	Bus and Truck Mechanics and Diesel Engine Specialists
0307	Maintenance Mechanic (Grain and Feed)	4000	Industrial Machinery Mechanics
0020	Maintenance Mechanic, Compgas	8000	Industrial Machinery Mechanics
0319	Mechanic, Endless Track Vehicle	8000	Mobile Heavy Equipment Mechanics, Except Engines
0153	Mechanic, Industrial Truck	8000	Bus and Truck Mechanics and Diesel Engine Specialists
0337	Mechanical-Unit Repairer	8000	Rail Car Repairers
0325	Metal Fabricator	8000	Structural Metal Fabricators and Fitters
0329	Meteorological Equipment Repairer	8000	Electrical and Electronics Repairers, Commercial and Industrial Equipment
0332	Meter Repairer (Any Industry)	6000	Control and Valve Installers and Repairers, Except Mechanical Door
0333	Miller, Wet Process	6000	Crushing, Grinding, and Polishing Machine Setters, Operators, and Tenders
0334	Milling Machine Set-Up Operator	4000	Milling and Planing Machine Setters, Operators, and Tenders, Metal and Plastic
0335	Millwright	8000	Millwrights
0335HY	Millwright	5200–8000	Millwrights
0350	Mine-Car Repairer	4000	Rail Car Repairers
0358	Mockup Builder (Aircraft)	8000	Model Makers, Metal and Plastic
0343	Model and Mold Maker (Brick)‡	4000	Production Workers, All Other
0344	Model and Mold Maker (Plaster)‡	8000	Production Workers, All Other
0339	Model Builder (Furniture)	4000	Model Makers, Metal and Plastic
0341	Model Maker (Aircraft)	8000	Model Makers, Wood
0491	Model Maker (Auto Manufacturing)	8000	Model Makers, Metal and Plastic
0363	Model Maker (Clock and Watch)	8000	Model Makers, Metal and Plastic

*Jobs linked to apprenticeships marked with * usually require college and are not included in Parts III and IV. Jobs linked to apprenticeships marked with ‡ were ranked 201 or lower and are not included in Parts III and IV.*

(continued)

(continued)

Interest Area/Cluster: 13 Manufacturing

RAPIDS Code	RAPIDS Apprenticeship Title	Hours	Title of Related O*NET Job
0773	Model Maker II (Jewelry)	8000	Jewelers
0780	Model Maker, Firearms	8000	Model Makers, Metal and Plastic
0342	Model Maker, Wood	8000	Model Makers, Wood
0345	Mold Maker (Pottery and Porcelain)	6000	Molding and Casting Workers
0346	Mold Maker I (Jewelry)	8000	Jewelers
0347	Mold Maker II (Jewelry)	4000	Jewelers
0116	Mold Maker, Die-Cast and Plastic	8000	Tool and Die Makers
0348	Mold Setter	2000	Molding, Coremaking, and Casting Machine Setters, Operators, and Tenders, Metal and Plastic
0349	Molder	8000	Foundry Mold and Coremakers
0351	Molder, Pattern (Foundry)	8000	Molding, Coremaking, and Casting Machine Setters, Operators, and Tenders, Metal and Plastic
0367	Monotype-Keyboard Operator	6000	Prepress Technicians and Workers
0355	Motorboat Mechanic	6000	Motorboat Mechanics
0356	Motorcycle Repairer	6000	Motorcycle Mechanics
0371	Multi-Operation-Machine Operator	6000	Forging Machine Setters, Operators, and Tenders, Metal and Plastic
0931	Multo-Per Form Machine Setter‡	8000	Metal Workers and Plastic Workers, All Other
0296CB	NIMS Certified Machinist	5600	Machinists
0845	Numerical Control Machine Operator	8000	Computer-Controlled Machine Tool Operators, Metal and Plastic
0361	Offset-Press Operator I	8000	Printing Machine Operators
0364	Oil Field Equipment Mechanic	4000	Bus and Truck Mechanics and Diesel Engine Specialists
0364CB	Oil Field Equipment Mechanic (Operator I Frac/Acid)	2000	Bus and Truck Mechanics and Diesel Engine Specialists
0959	Operational Test Mechanic	6000	Inspectors, Testers, Sorters, Samplers, and Weighers
0250	Optical Instrument Assembler	4000	Ophthalmic Laboratory Technicians
0377	Optician (Optical Goods)	8000	Ophthalmic Laboratory Technicians
0032	Optician (Optical Goods; Retail Trade)	10000	Ophthalmic Laboratory Technicians
0374	Ornamental Metal Worker	8000	Multiple Machine Tool Setters, Operators, and Tenders, Metal and Plastic
0375	Orthodontic Technician	4000	Dental Laboratory Technicians
0910	Orthopedic Boot/Shoe Designer	10000	Shoe and Leather Workers and Repairers

Interest Area/Cluster: 13 Manufacturing

RAPIDS Code	RAPIDS Apprenticeship Title	Hours	Title of Related O*NET Job
0911	Orthotics Technician	2000	Medical Appliance Technicians
0378	Outboard-Motor Mechanic	4000	Motorboat Mechanics
0384	Overhauler (Textile)	4000	Industrial Machinery Mechanics
0383	Painter, Hand (Any Industry)	6000	Painting, Coating, and Decorating Workers
0386	Painter, Sign‡	8000	Production Workers, All Other
0381	Painter, Transportation Equipment	6000	Painters, Transportation Equipment
0389	Pantograph-Machine Set-Up Operator	4000	Milling and Planing Machine Setters, Operators, and Tenders, Metal and Plastic
0392	Paste-Up Artist	6000	Prepress Technicians and Workers
0394	Patternmaker (Metal Products)	8000	Patternmakers, Metal and Plastic
0796	Patternmaker (Stonework)	8000	Patternmakers, Metal and Plastic
0710	Patternmaker (Textiles)	6000	Fabric and Apparel Patternmakers
0857	Patternmaker, All-Around	10000	Patternmakers, Metal and Plastic
0395	Patternmaker, Metal	10000	Patternmakers, Metal and Plastic
0396	Patternmaker, Metal, Bench	10000	Patternmakers, Metal and Plastic
0397	Patternmaker, Plaster‡	6000	Production Workers, All Other
0923	Patternmaker, Plastics	6000	Patternmakers, Metal and Plastic
0398	Patternmaker, Wood	10000	Patternmakers, Wood
0982	Pewter Caster	6000	Precious Metal Workers
0986	Pewter Fabricator	8000	Precious Metal Workers
0983	Pewter Finisher	4000	Precious Metal Workers
0988	Pewterer	4000	Precious Metal Workers
0399	Photoengraver	10000	Prepress Technicians and Workers
0400	Photoengraving Finisher	10000	Prepress Technicians and Workers
0401	Photoengraving Printer	10000	Prepress Technicians and Workers
0402	Photoengraving Proofer	10000	Prepress Technicians and Workers
0912	Photograph Retoucher	6000	Photographic Process Workers
0685	Photographer, Lithographic	10000	Prepress Technicians and Workers
0405	Photographer, Photoengraving	12000	Prepress Technicians and Workers
0563	Photographic Equipment Maintenance	6000	Camera and Photographic Equipment Repairers
0924	Photographic Equipment Technician	6000	Camera and Photographic Equipment Repairers
0407	Photographic-Plate Maker	8000	Prepress Technicians and Workers
0387	Pinsetter Adjuster, Automatic	6000	Industrial Machinery Mechanics
0985	Pinsetter Mechanic, Automatic	4000	Maintenance Workers, Machinery

*Jobs linked to apprenticeships marked with * usually require college and are not included in Parts III and IV. Jobs linked to apprenticeships marked with ‡ were ranked 201 or lower and are not included in Parts III and IV.*

(continued)

(continued)

Interest Area/Cluster: 13 Manufacturing

RAPIDS Code	RAPIDS Apprenticeship Title	Hours	Title of Related O*NET Job
0417	Pipe Organ Builder	6000	Cabinetmakers and Bench Carpenters
0961	Plant Operator	6000	Crushing, Grinding, and Polishing Machine Setters, Operators, and Tenders
0393	Plant Operator, Furnace Process	8000	Chemical Plant and System Operators
0404	Plaster Pattern Caster	10000	Molding and Casting Workers
0843	Plastic Fixture Builder	8000	Tool and Die Makers
0660	Plastic Process Technician	8000	Molding, Coremaking, and Casting Machine Setters, Operators, and Tenders, Metal and Plastic
0426	Plastic Tool Maker	8000	Tool and Die Makers
0186	Plastics Fabricator‡	4000	Production Workers, All Other
0427	Plate Finisher (Printing and Publishing)	12000	Prepress Technicians and Workers
0430	Platen-Press Operator	8000	Printing Machine Operators
0431	Plater	6000	Plating and Coating Machine Setters, Operators, and Tenders, Metal and Plastic
1107	Pneudraulic Systems Mechanic	4800	Aircraft Mechanics and Service Technicians
0434	Pneumatic Tool Repairer	8000	Industrial Machinery Mechanics
0435	Pneumatic Tube Repairer	4000	Industrial Machinery Mechanics
0901	Pony Edger (Sawmill)	4000	Sawing Machine Setters, Operators, and Tenders, Wood
0443	Powerhouse Mechanic	8000	Industrial Machinery Mechanics
1045	Powerplant Mechanic	3000	Aircraft Mechanics and Service Technicians
0440	Power-Plant Operator	8000	Power Plant Operators
0441	Power-Saw Mechanic	6000	Outdoor Power Equipment and Other Small Engine Mechanics
0442	Power-Transformer Repairer	8000	Electric Motor, Power Tool, and Related Repairers
0410	Precision Assembler	6000	Aircraft Structure, Surfaces, Rigging, and Systems Assemblers
0962	Precision Assembler, Bench	4000	Electromechanical Equipment Assemblers
0277	Precision-Lens Grinder	8000	Ophthalmic Laboratory Technicians
0928	Press Operator, Heavy Duty	8000	Cutting, Punching, and Press Machine Setters, Operators, and Tenders, Metal and Plastic
0928CB	Press Setup Operator, Stamping	3900	Cutting, Punching, and Press Machine Setters, Operators, and Tenders, Metal and Plastic

Interest Area/Cluster: 13 Manufacturing

RAPIDS Code	RAPIDS Apprenticeship Title	Hours	Title of Related O*NET Job
0452	Printer, Plastic	8000	Printing Machine Operators
0451	Printer-Slotter Operator	8000	Printing Machine Operators
1023	Production Finisher	4000	Coating, Painting, and Spraying Machine Setters, Operators, and Tenders
1027CB	Production Technologist	competency	Team Assemblers
0413	Projection Printer	8000	Photographic Process Workers
0288	Proof-Press Operator	10000	Printing Machine Operators
0415	Proofsheet Corrector (Printing)	8000	Prepress Technicians and Workers
0456	Propulsion Motor and Generator Repairer	8000	Electric Motor, Power Tool, and Related Repairers
0376	Prosthetics Technician	8000	Medical Appliance Technicians
0846	Prototype Model Maker	8000	Model Makers, Metal and Plastic
0419	Pump Erector (Construction)	4000	Industrial Machinery Mechanics
0933	Pump Servicer	6000	Industrial Machinery Mechanics
0950	Pumper—Gauger	6000	Tank Car, Truck, and Ship Loaders
0461	Purification Operator II	8000	Separating, Filtering, Clarifying, Precipitating, and Still Machine Setters, Operators, and Tenders
0936	Quality Control Inspector	4000	Inspectors, Testers, Sorters, Samplers, and Weighers
0465	Radio Mechanic (Any Industry)	6000	Radio Mechanics
0466	Radio Repairer (Any Industry)	8000	Electronic Home Entertainment Equipment Installers and Repairers
0468	Radiographer	8000	Inspectors, Testers, Sorters, Samplers, and Weighers
0420	Recovery Operator (Paper)	2000	Separating, Filtering, Clarifying, Precipitating, and Still Machine Setters, Operators, and Tenders
0852	Refinery Operator	6000	Petroleum Pump System Operators, Refinery Operators, and Gaugers
0666HY	Refrigeration and Air Conditioning Mechanic‡	7480–8800	Heating, Air Conditioning, and Refrigeration Mechanics and Installers
0687	Relay Tester	8000	Inspectors, Testers, Sorters, Samplers, and Weighers
0674	Repairer I (Chemicals)	8000	Industrial Machinery Mechanics
0421	Repairer, Handtools	6000	Electric Motor, Power Tool, and Related Repairers

*Jobs linked to apprenticeships marked with * usually require college and are not included in Parts III and IV. Jobs linked to apprenticeships marked with ‡ were ranked 201 or lower and are not included in Parts III and IV.*

(continued)

(continued)

Interest Area/Cluster: 13 Manufacturing

RAPIDS Code	RAPIDS Apprenticeship Title	Hours	Title of Related O*NET Job
0997	Repairer, Heavy	4000	Automotive Master Mechanics
0807	Repairer, Recreational Vehicles	8000	Recreational Vehicle Service Technicians
0422	Repairer, Welding Equipment	4000	Industrial Machinery Mechanics
1005	Repairer, Welding Systems and Equipment	6000	Industrial Machinery Mechanics
0092	Reproduction Technician	2000	Photographic Process Workers
0472	Retoucher, Photoengraving	10000	Prepress Technicians and Workers
0475	Rocket Motor Mechanic	8000	Machinists
0425	Rocket-Engine-Component Mechanic	8000	Aircraft Mechanics and Service Technicians
0428	Roll Threader Operator	2000	Rolling Machine Setters, Operators, and Tenders, Metal and Plastic
0795	Roller Engraver, Hand	4000	Etchers and Engravers
0481	Rotogravure-Press Operator	8000	Printing Machine Operators
0429	Rubber Tester	8000	Inspectors, Testers, Sorters, Samplers, and Weighers
0485	Rubberizing Mechanic	8000	Industrial Machinery Mechanics
0484	Rubber-Stamp Maker	8000	Molding and Casting Workers
0487	Saddle Maker	4000	Shoe and Leather Workers and Repairers
0488	Safe and Vault Service Mechanic	8000	Locksmiths and Safe Repairers
0490	Sample Maker, Appliances	8000	Model Makers, Metal and Plastic
0436	Sample Stitcher (Garment)	8000	Tailors, Dressmakers, and Custom Sewers
0495	Saw Filer (Any Industry)	8000	Tool Grinders, Filers, and Sharpeners
0496	Saw Maker (Cutlery and Tools)	6000	Tool and Die Makers
0497	Scale Mechanic	8000	Industrial Machinery Mechanics
0855	Scanner Operator	4000	Prepress Technicians and Workers
0520	Screen Printer	4000	Painting, Coating, and Decorating Workers
0500	Screw-Machine Operator, Multiple Spindle	8000	Lathe and Turning Machine Tool Setters, Operators, and Tenders, Metal and Plastic
0444	Screw-Machine Operator, Single Spindle	6000	Lathe and Turning Machine Tool Setters, Operators, and Tenders, Metal and Plastic
0502	Screw-Machine Set-Up Operator	8000	Lathe and Turning Machine Tool Setters, Operators, and Tenders, Metal and Plastic
0506	Screw-Machine Set-Up Operator, Single Spindle	6000	Lathe and Turning Machine Tool Setters, Operators, and Tenders, Metal and Plastic
0446	Service Mechanic (Auto Manufacturing)	4000	Automotive Body and Related Repairers

Interest Area/Cluster: 13 Manufacturing

RAPIDS Code	RAPIDS Apprenticeship Title	Hours	Title of Related O*NET Job
0508	Sewing Machine Repairer	6000	Industrial Machinery Mechanics
0611	Ship Propeller Finisher	6000	Structural Metal Fabricators and Fitters
0513	Shipfitter (Ship and Boat)	8000	Lay-Out Workers, Metal and Plastic
0514	Shoe Repairer	6000	Shoe and Leather Workers and Repairers
0812	Shoemaker, Custom	6000	Shoe and Leather Workers and Repairers
0524	Shop Optician, Benchroom	8000	Ophthalmic Laboratory Technicians
0526	Shop Optician, Surface Room	8000	Ophthalmic Laboratory Technicians
0515	Shop Tailor	8000	Tailors, Dressmakers, and Custom Sewers
0447	Siderographer (Printing and Publishing)	10000	Etchers and Engravers
0518	Sign Writer, Hand‡	2000	Production Workers, All Other
0942	Signal Maintainer (Railroad Transportation)	8000	Signal and Track Switch Repairers
0519	Silkscreen Cutter	6000	Cutters and Trimmers, Hand
0522	Silversmith II	6000	Precious Metal Workers
0448	Sketch Maker I (Printing and Publishing)	10000	Printing Machine Operators
0523	Sketch Maker II (Printing and Publishing)	8000	Etchers and Engravers
0525	Small Engine Mechanic	4000	Outdoor Power Equipment and Other Small Engine Mechanics
0453	Solderer (Jewelry)	6000	Jewelers
0530	Spinner, Hand	6000	Lathe and Turning Machine Tool Setters, Operators, and Tenders, Metal and Plastic
0457	Spring Coiling Machine Set	8000	Cutting, Punching, and Press Machine Setters, Operators, and Tenders, Metal and Plastic
0532	Spring Maker	8000	Multiple Machine Tool Setters, Operators, and Tenders, Metal and Plastic
0533	Spring Repairer, Hand	8000	Automotive Specialty Technicians
0534	Spring-Manufacturing Set-Up Technician	8000	Multiple Machine Tool Setters, Operators, and Tenders, Metal and Plastic
0536	Stationary Engineer	8000	Stationary Engineers and Boiler Operators
0785	Steel-Die Printer	8000	Printing Machine Operators
0463	Stencil Cutter‡	4000	Production Workers, All Other
0538	Stereotyper	2000	Prepress Technicians and Workers

*Jobs linked to apprenticeships marked with * usually require college and are not included in Parts III and IV. Jobs linked to apprenticeships marked with ‡ were ranked 201 or lower and are not included in Parts III and IV.*

(continued)

(continued)

Interest Area/Cluster: 13 Manufacturing

RAPIDS Code	RAPIDS Apprenticeship Title	Hours	Title of Related O*NET Job
0467	Stoker Erector and Servicer	8000	Industrial Machinery Mechanics
0017	Stone Polisher	6000	Grinding, Lapping, Polishing, and Buffing Machine Tool Setters, Operators, and Tenders, Metal and Plastic
0312	Stone Setter (Jewelry)	8000	Jewelers
0470	Stone-Lathe Operator	6000	Cutting and Slicing Machine Setters, Operators, and Tenders
0726	Stripper (Printing and Publishing)	10000	Prepress Technicians and Workers
0064	Stripper, Lithographic II	8000	Prepress Technicians and Workers
0553	Substation Operator	8000	Power Distributors and Dispatchers
1106	Supervisory Control and Data Acquisition Technician (SCADA)	8000	Electrical and Electronics Repairers, Commercial and Industrial Equipment
0478	Surface-Plate Finisher	4000	Crushing, Grinding, and Polishing Machine Setters, Operators, and Tenders
1069CB	Survival Equipment (Parachute Repair)	2500	Fabric Menders, Except Garment
0801	Switchboard Operator (Utility)	6000	Power Distributors and Dispatchers
0559	Tap and Die Maker Technician	8000	Tool and Die Makers
0560	Tape-Recorder Repairer	8000	Electronic Home Entertainment Equipment Installers and Repairers
0565	Television and Radio Repairer	8000	Electronic Home Entertainment Equipment Installers and Repairers
0567	Template Maker	8000	Patternmakers, Metal and Plastic
0123	Template Maker, Extrusion Die	8000	Patternmakers, Metal and Plastic
0483	Test Technician (Professional and Kindred)	10000	Machinists
0572	Testing and Regulating Technician	8000	Inspectors, Testers, Sorters, Samplers, and Weighers
0489	Thermometer Tester	2000	Inspectors, Testers, Sorters, Samplers, and Weighers
0575	Tinter (Paint and Varnish)	4000	Mixing and Blending Machine Setters, Operators, and Tenders
0586	Tool and Die Maker	8000	Tool and Die Makers
0205	Tool Builder	8000	Model Makers, Metal and Plastic
0582	Tool Grinder I	6000	Tool Grinders, Filers, and Sharpeners
0765	Tool Grinder Operator	8000	Tool Grinders, Filers, and Sharpeners
0588	Tool Machine Set-Up Operator	6000	Multiple Machine Tool Setters, Operators, and Tenders, Metal and Plastic
0584	Tool Maker	8000	Tool and Die Makers

Interest Area/Cluster: 13 Manufacturing

RAPIDS Code	RAPIDS Apprenticeship Title	Hours	Title of Related O*NET Job
0585	Tool Maker, Bench	8000	Tool and Die Makers
0690	Tool Programmer, Numerical	6000	Numerical Tool and Process Control Programmers
0589	Tractor Mechanic	8000	Bus and Truck Mechanics and Diesel Engine Specialists
0590	Transformer Repairer	8000	Electric Motor, Power Tool, and Related Repairers
0592	Transmission Mechanic	4000	Automotive Master Mechanics
0847	Treatment Plant Mechanic	6000	Industrial Machinery Mechanics
0805	Trouble Locator, Test Desk	4000	Inspectors, Testers, Sorters, Samplers, and Weighers
0598	Truck Body Builder	8000	Automotive Body and Related Repairers
0600	Tune-Up Mechanic	4000	Automotive Specialty Technicians
0601	Turbine Operator	8000	Power Plant Operators
1021	Turret Lathe Set-Up Operator	8000	Lathe and Turning Machine Tool Setters, Operators, and Tenders, Metal and Plastic
1034	Undercar Specialist	4000	Automotive Specialty Technicians
0097	Upholsterer	4000	Upholsterers
0606	Upholsterer, Inside	6000	Upholsterers
0492	Violin Maker, Hand	8000	Cabinetmakers and Bench Carpenters
1070CB	Visual Imagery Intrusion Detection Systems (Maintenance)	2500	Electrical and Electronics Repairers, Commercial and Industrial Equipment
0612	Wallpaper Printer I	8000	Printing Machine Operators
0614	Waste Treatment Operator	4000	Water and Liquid Waste Treatment Plant and System Operators
0507	Wastewater-Treatment-Plant Operator	4000	Water and Liquid Waste Treatment Plant and System Operators
0616	Watch Repairer	8000	Watch Repairers
0619	Water Treatment Plant Operator	6000	Water and Liquid Waste Treatment Plant and System Operators
0667	Webpress Operator	8000	Printing Machine Operators
0620	Welder, Arc	8000	Welders, Cutters, and Welder Fitters
0622	Welder, Combination	6000	Welders, Cutters, and Welder Fitters
0627	Welder-Fitter	8000	Welders, Cutters, and Welder Fitters
0945	Welding Machine Operator, Arc	6000	Welding, Soldering, and Brazing Machine Setters, Operators, and Tenders

*Jobs linked to apprenticeships marked with * usually require college and are not included in Parts III and IV. Jobs linked to apprenticeships marked with ‡ were ranked 201 or lower and are not included in Parts III and IV.*

(continued)

(continued)

Interest Area/Cluster: 13 Manufacturing

RAPIDS Code	RAPIDS Apprenticeship Title	Hours	Title of Related O*NET Job
0034	Wine Maker (Vinous Liquor)	4000	Industrial Production Managers
0501	Wire Sawyer (Stonework)	4000	Cutting and Slicing Machine Setters, Operators, and Tenders
0504	Wire Weaver, Cloth	8000	Textile Knitting and Weaving Machine Setters, Operators, and Tenders
0633	Wirer (Office Machines)	4000	Electrical and Electronic Equipment Assemblers
0505	Wood-turning Lathe Operator	2000	Woodworking Machine Setters, Operators, and Tenders, Except Sawing
0919	X-ray Equipment Tester	4000	Inspectors, Testers, Sorters, Samplers, and Weighers

*Jobs linked to apprenticeships marked with * usually require college and are not included in Parts III and IV. Jobs linked to apprenticeships marked with ‡ were ranked 201 or lower and are not included in Parts III and IV.*

Interest Area/Cluster: 14 Retail and Wholesale Sales and Service

RAPIDS Code	RAPIDS Apprenticeship Title	Hours	Title of Related O*NET Job
0820	Director, Funeral	4000	Funeral Directors
1056CB	Facility Manager*	4000	Property, Real Estate, and Community Association Managers
0578	Manager, Retail Store	6000	First-Line Supervisors/Managers of Retail Sales Workers
0948	Purchasing Agent	8000	Purchasing Agents, Except Wholesale, Retail, and Farm Products
0753	Salesperson, Parts	4000	Parts Salespersons
1126CB	Subcontract Administrator	4000	Purchasing Agents, Except Wholesale, Retail, and Farm Products
1127CB	Subcontract Administrator Associate	4000	Purchasing Agents, Except Wholesale, Retail, and Farm Products

*Jobs linked to apprenticeships marked with * usually require college and are not included in Parts III and IV. Jobs linked to apprenticeships marked with ‡ were ranked 201 or lower and are not included in Parts III and IV.included in Parts III and IV.*

Interest Area/Cluster: 15 Scientific Research, Engineering, and Mathematics

RAPIDS Code	RAPIDS Apprenticeship Title	Hours	Title of Related O*NET Job
0875	Assembler, Electromechanical	8000	Electro-Mechanical Technicians
0895	Calibration Laboratory Technician	8000	Electronics Engineering Technicians
0969	Chemical Engineering Technician	8000	Chemical Technicians
0050	Chemical Laboratory Technician	8000	Chemical Technicians
0053	Chief of Party (Professional and Kindred)‡	8000	Surveying and Mapping Technicians
0106	Design Drafter, Electromechanical	8000	Electronic Drafters
0108	Detailer	8000	Mechanical Drafters
0113	Die Designer	8000	Mechanical Drafters
0019	Drafter, Auto Design Layout	8000	Mechanical Drafters
0018	Drafter, Automotive Design	8000	Mechanical Drafters
0109	Drafter, Cartographic*	8000	Cartographers and Photogrammetrists
0130	Drafter, Detail	8000	Mechanical Drafters
0131	Drafter, Electrical	8000	Electrical Drafters
0995	Drafter, Electronic	8000	Electronic Drafters
0136	Drafter, Mechanical	8000	Mechanical Drafters
0140	Drafter, Tool Design	8000	Mechanical Drafters
0157	Electrical Instrument Repairer	6000	Electronics Engineering Technicians
0155	Electrical Technician	8000	Electrical Engineering Technicians
0167	Electromechanical Technician	6000	Electro-Mechanical Technicians
0169	Electronics Technician	8000	Electronics Engineering Technicians
0764	Engineering Assistant, Mechanical Equipment	8000	Mechanical Drafters
0648	Environmental Analyst*	7000	Environmental Scientists and Specialists, Including Health
0965	Estimator and Drafter	8000	Electrical Drafters
0207	Foundry Metallurgist*	8000	Materials Engineers
0217	Geodetic Computator	4000	Mapping Technicians
1062	Geospatial Specialist*	4000	Cartographers and Photogrammetrists
1062CB	Geospatial Specialist*	2000–4000	Cartographers and Photogrammetrists
0257	Heat Transfer Technician	8000	Mechanical Engineering Technicians
1074CB	Historian*	2500	Historians
0644	Instrument Mechanic (Any Industry)	8000	Electronics Engineering Technicians

*Jobs linked to apprenticeships marked with * usually require college and are not included in Parts III and IV. Jobs linked to apprenticeships marked with ‡ were ranked 201 or lower and are not included in Parts III and IV.*

(continued)

(continued)

Interest Area/Cluster: 15 Scientific Research, Engineering, and Mathematics

RAPIDS Code	RAPIDS Apprenticeship Title	Hours	Title of Related O*NET Job
0996	Instrument Mechanic, Weapons Systems	8000	Electronics Engineering Technicians
0775	Instrument Repairer (Any Industry)	8000	Electronics Engineering Technicians
0252	Instrument Technician (Utilities)	8000	Electronics Engineering Technicians
0255	Instrumentation Technician	8000	Electronics Engineering Technicians
0621	Laboratory Assistant, Metallurgical‡	4000	Engineering Technicians, Except Drafters, All Other
0268	Laboratory Technician	2000	Chemical Technicians
0269	Laboratory Tester	4000	Chemical Technicians
0632	Logistics Engineer*	8000	Industrial Engineers
0328	Materials Engineer*	10000	Materials Engineers
0777	Mechanical Engineering Technician	8000	Mechanical Engineering Technicians
0940	Meteorologist*	6000	Atmospheric and Space Scientists
1030	Mold Designer (Plastics Industry)	4000	Mechanical Drafters
1010	Non-Destructive Tester‡	2000	Engineering Technicians, Except Drafters, All Other
1010CB	Non-Destructive Tester‡	4000	Engineering Technicians, Except Drafters, All Other
1010CB	Non-Destructive Tester/Acoustic Emmitance Technician/Level I‡	500	Engineering Technicians, Except Drafters, All Other
1010CB	Non-Destructive Tester/Acoustic Emmittance Technician/Level II‡	1500	Engineering Technicians, Except Drafters, All Other
1010CB	Non-Destructive Tester/Eddy Current Technician/Level I‡	500	Engineering Technicians, Except Drafters, All Other
1010CB	Non-Destructive Tester/Eddy Current Technician/Level II‡	1500	Engineering Technicians, Except Drafters, All Other
1010CB	Non-Destructive Tester/Leak Test Bubble Technician/Level I‡	2	Engineering Technicians, Except Drafters, All Other
1010CB	Non-Destructive Tester/Leak Test Bubble Technician/Level II‡	83	Engineering Technicians, Except Drafters, All Other
1010CB	Non-Destructive Tester/Leak Test Halogen Diode/Level I‡	250	Engineering Technicians, Except Drafters, All Other
1010CB	Non-Destructive Tester/Leak Test Halogen Diode/Level II‡	665	Engineering Technicians, Except Drafters, All Other
1010CB	Non-Destructive Tester/Leak Test Mass Spectrometry Technician/ Level I‡	665	Engineering Technicians, Except Drafters, All Other

Interest Area/Cluster: 15 Scientific Research, Engineering, and Mathematics

RAPIDS Code	RAPIDS Apprenticeship Title	Hours	Title of Related O*NET Job
1010CB	Non-Destructive Tester/Leak Test Mass Spectrometry Technician/Level II‡	1000	Engineering Technicians, Except Drafters, All Other
1010CB	Non-Destructive Tester/Leak Test Pressure Change Technician/Level I‡	250	Engineering Technicians, Except Drafters, All Other
1010CB	Non-Destructive Tester/Leak Test Pressure Change Technician/Level II‡	655	Engineering Technicians, Except Drafters, All Other
1010CB	Non-Destructive Tester/Magnetic Particle Technician/Level I‡	166	Engineering Technicians, Except Drafters, All Other
1010CB	Non-Destructive Tester/Magnetic Particle Technician/Level II‡	500	Engineering Technicians, Except Drafters, All Other
1010CB	Non-Destructive Tester/Penetrant Technician/Level I‡	166	Engineering Technicians, Except Drafters, All Other
1010CB	Non-Destructive Tester/Penetrant Technician/Level II Limited‡	332	Engineering Technicians, Except Drafters, All Other
1010CB	Non-Destructive Tester/Penetrant Technician/Level II‡	332	Engineering Technicians, Except Drafters, All Other
1010CB	Non-Destructive Tester/Radiographic Technician/Level I‡	500	Engineering Technicians, Except Drafters, All Other
1010CB	Non-Destructive Tester/Radiographic Technician/Level II Limited‡	1500	Engineering Technicians, Except Drafters, All Other
1010CB	Non-Destructive Tester/Radiographic Technician/Level II‡	1500	Engineering Technicians, Except Drafters, All Other
1010CB	Non-Destructive Tester/Thermal Infrared Technician/Level I‡	166	Engineering Technicians, Except Drafters, All Other
1010CB	Non-Destructive Tester/Thermal Infrared Technician/Level II‡	332	Engineering Technicians, Except Drafters, All Other
1010CB	Non-Destructive Tester/Ultrasonic Technician/Level I‡	500	Engineering Technicians, Except Drafters, All Other
1010CB	Non-Destructive Tester/Ultrasonic Technician/Level II‡	1500	Engineering Technicians, Except Drafters, All Other
1010CB	Non-Destructive Tester/Ultrasound Technician/Level II Limited‡	1000	Engineering Technicians, Except Drafters, All Other
1010CB	Non-Destructive Tester/Visual Technician/Level I‡	166	Engineering Technicians, Except Drafters, All Other
1010CB	Non-Destructive Tester/Visual Technician/Level II‡	332	Engineering Technicians, Except Drafters, All Other

Jobs linked to apprenticeships marked with * usually require college and are not included in Parts III and IV. Jobs linked to apprenticeships marked with ‡ were ranked 201 or lower and are not included in Parts III and IV.

(continued)

(continued)

Interest Area/Cluster: 15 Scientific Research, Engineering, and Mathematics

RAPIDS Code	RAPIDS Apprenticeship Title	Hours	Title of Related O*NET Job
0368	Optomechanical Technician	8000	Mechanical Engineering Technicians
0546	Photogrammetric Technician	6000	Mapping Technicians
0788	Research Mechanic (Aircraft)	8000	Aerospace Engineering and Operations Technicians
0551	Surveyor Assistant, Instruments	4000	Surveying Technicians
0190	Test Equipment Mechanic	10000	Aerospace Engineering and Operations Technicians
0587	Tool Design Checker	8000	Mechanical Engineering Technicians
0580	Tool Designer*	8000	Mechanical Engineers
0001	Weather Observer‡	4000	Life, Physical, and Social Science Technicians, All Other
0498	Welding Technician‡	8000	Engineering Technicians, Except Drafters, All Other
0499	Wind Tunnel Mechanic	8000	Aerospace Engineering and Operations Technicians

*Jobs linked to apprenticeships marked with * usually require college and are not included in Parts III and IV. Jobs linked to apprenticeships marked with ‡ were ranked 201 or lower and are not included in Parts III and IV.*

Interest Area/Cluster: 16 Transportation, Distribution, and Logistics

RAPIDS Code	RAPIDS Apprenticeship Title	Hours	Title of Related O*NET Job
1043	Able Seaman	2760	Sailors and Marine Oilers
1046CB	Air Transport Pilot	6780	Commercial Pilots
0724	Ambulance Attendant (EMT)	2000	Ambulance Drivers and Attendants, Except Emergency Medical Technicians
1032	Construction Driver	2400	Truck Drivers, Heavy and Tractor-Trailer
0117	Dredge Operator	2000	Dredge Operators
1110	Hydro Blaster/Vacuum Technician‡	4000	Cleaners of Vehicles and Equipment
0287	Locomotive Engineer	8000	Locomotive Engineers
1104	Officer In Charge of Navigational Watch (OICNW)	3000	Mates—Ship, Boat, and Barge
0623	Pilot, Ship	3000	Pilots, Ship
0655	Transportation Clerk	3000	Cargo and Freight Agents

Interest Area/Cluster: 16 Transportation, Distribution, and Logistics

RAPIDS Code	RAPIDS Apprenticeship Title	Hours	Title of Related O*NET Job
0980	Truck Driver, Heavy	2000	Truck Drivers, Heavy and Tractor-Trailer
0980HY	Truck Driver, Heavy	3000–4560	Truck Drivers, Heavy and Tractor-Trailer

*Jobs linked to apprenticeships marked with * usually require college and are not included in Parts III and IV. Jobs linked to apprenticeships marked with ‡ were ranked 201 or lower and are not included in Parts III and IV.*

PART III

The Best Jobs Lists: Jobs You Can Enter Through Apprenticeship

This part contains a lot of interesting lists, and it's a good place for you to start using the book. Here are some suggestions for using the lists to explore career options:

✵ The table of contents at the beginning of this book presents a complete listing of the list titles in this section. You can browse the lists or use the table of contents to find those that interest you most.

✵ We gave the lists clear titles, so most require little explanation. We provide comments for each group of lists.

✵ As you review the lists of jobs, one or more of the jobs may appeal to you enough that you want to seek additional information. As this happens, mark that job (or, if someone else will be using this book, write it on a separate sheet of paper) so that you can look up the description of the job in Part IV.

✵ Keep in mind that all jobs in these lists meet our basic criteria for being included in this book, as explained in the introduction. All lists, therefore, contain jobs that have high pay, high growth, or large numbers of openings. These measures are easily quantified and are often presented in lists of best jobs in the newspapers and other media. Although earnings, growth, and openings are important, you also should consider other factors in your career planning, such as liking the people you work with, having an opportunity to serve others, and having opportunities to be creative. These factors and many others that may help define the ideal job for you are difficult or impossible to quantify and thus aren't used in this book, so you will need to consider the importance of these issues yourself.

✵ All data used to create these lists comes from the U.S. Department of Labor and the Census Bureau. The earnings figures are based on the average annual pay received by full-time workers. Because the earnings represent the national averages, actual pay rates can vary greatly by location, amount of previous work experience, and other factors, including journey worker status. (Journey workers tend to earn more than the national average.)

Some Details on the Lists

The sources of the information we used in constructing these lists are presented in this book's introduction. Here are some additional details on how we created the lists:

✳ Some jobs have the same scores for one or more data elements. For example, in the category of best-paying, two jobs (Architectural Drafters and Civil Drafters) have the same income, $43,310, because the salary survey used by the Department of Labor considers these to be two specializations within one occupation, Drafters. Therefore we ordered these two jobs alphabetically, and their order in relation to each other has no other significance. Avoiding these ties was impossible, so understand that the difference of several positions on a list may not mean as much as it seems.

✳ Likewise, it is unwise to place too much emphasis on small differences in outlook information (projections for job growth and job openings): For example, Police Patrol Officers are projected to have 37,842 job openings per year, whereas 37,469 openings are projected for Automotive Body and Related Repairers. This is a difference of only 373 jobs spread over the entire United States, and of course, it is only a projection. Before 2007, the Bureau of Labor Statistics rounded these projections to the nearest 1,000 and would have assigned these two occupations the same figure (37,000), which would have given Automotive Body and Related Repairers the higher rank on the basis of alphabetical ordering. So, again, keep in mind that small differences of position on a list aren't very significant.

Best Jobs Overall: Apprenticeable Jobs with the Highest Pay, Fastest Growth, and Most Openings

The four lists that follow are the most important lists in this book. The first list presents the apprenticeable jobs with the highest combined scores for pay, growth, and number of openings. This is a very appealing list because it represents jobs with the very highest quantifiable measures from our labor market. Three additional lists present apprenticeable jobs with the highest scores on each of three measures: annual earnings, projected percentage growth, and largest number of openings. As you review these lists, keep in mind that the lists include jobs with the highest measures from a database of jobs that included all major jobs that are linked to registered apprenticeships and don't usually require a four-year college degree. Jobs that did not make it onto the list of 200 best apprenticeable jobs are not included in the descriptions in Part IV, although they are named in the list of all registered apprenticeships in Part II, and some of them are named in a bonus list.

The 200 Best Apprenticeable Jobs

This is the list that most people want to see first. It includes the 200 jobs you can enter through apprenticeship that have the highest overall combined ratings for earnings, projected growth through 2016, and number of openings. (The section in the introduction called "How the Best Apprenticeable Jobs in This Book Were Selected" explains in detail how we rated jobs to assemble this list.)

You'll notice a wide variety of jobs on the list. Among the top 20 are jobs in protective services, construction, high tech, business services, transportation, and health care.

Paralegals and Legal Assistants was the occupation with the best total score, and it is on the top of the list. The other occupations follow in descending order based on their total scores. Many jobs had tied scores and are simply listed one after another, so there are often only very small or even no differences between the scores of jobs that are near each other on the list. All other jobs lists in this part of the book (except the jobs in the bonus list) use these jobs as their source list. You can find a description for each of these jobs in Part IV, beginning on page 139.

The 200 Best Apprenticeable Jobs

Job	Annual Earnings	Percent Growth	Annual Openings
1. Paralegals and Legal Assistants	$44,990	22.2%	22,756
2. Computer Support Specialists	$42,400	12.9%	97,334
3. Construction and Building Inspectors	$48,330	18.2%	12,606
4. Radiologic Technologists	$50,260	15.1%	12,836
5. Police Patrol Officers	$49,630	10.8%	37,842
6. Correctional Officers and Jailers	$36,970	16.9%	56,579
7. Licensed Practical and Licensed Vocational Nurses	$37,940	14.0%	70,610
8. Pipe Fitters and Steamfitters	$44,090	10.6%	68,643
9. Plumbers	$44,090	10.6%	68,643
10. Surgical Technologists	$37,540	24.5%	15,365
11. Automotive Master Mechanics	$34,170	14.3%	97,350
12. Automotive Specialty Technicians	$34,170	14.3%	97,350
13. Interior Designers	$43,970	19.5%	8,434
14. Forest Fire Fighters	$43,170	12.1%	18,887
15. Municipal Fire Fighters	$43,170	12.1%	18,887
16. Legal Secretaries	$38,810	11.7%	38,682
17. Construction Carpenters	$37,660	10.3%	223,225
18. Rough Carpenters	$37,660	10.3%	223,225
19. Electricians	$44,780	7.4%	79,083

(continued)

(continued)

The 200 Best Apprenticeable Jobs

Job	Annual Earnings	Percent Growth	Annual Openings
20. Environmental Science and Protection Technicians, Including Health	$39,370	28.0%	8,404
21. Truck Drivers, Heavy and Tractor-Trailer	$36,220	10.4%	279,032
22. Bus and Truck Mechanics and Diesel Engine Specialists	$38,640	11.5%	25,428
23. Bookkeeping, Accounting, and Auditing Clerks	$31,560	12.5%	286,854
24. Roofers	$33,240	14.3%	38,398
25. Dental Assistants	$31,550	29.2%	29,482
26. Aircraft Mechanics and Service Technicians	$49,010	10.6%	9,708
27. Automotive Body and Related Repairers	$35,690	11.6%	37,469
28. Tile and Marble Setters	$38,720	15.4%	9,066
29. Food Service Managers	$44,570	5.0%	59,302
30. Mobile Heavy Equipment Mechanics, Except Engines	$41,450	12.3%	11,037
31. Cargo and Freight Agents	$37,060	16.5%	9,967
32. Industrial Machinery Mechanics	$42,350	9.0%	23,361
33. Brickmasons and Blockmasons	$44,070	9.7%	17,569
34. Mates—Ship, Boat, and Barge	$57,210	17.9%	2,665
35. Medical Assistants	$27,430	35.4%	92,977
36. Pilots, Ship	$57,210	17.9%	2,665
37. Operating Engineers and Other Construction Equipment Operators	$38,130	8.4%	55,468
38. Aircraft Structure, Surfaces, Rigging, and Systems Assemblers	$45,420	12.8%	6,550
39. Painters, Construction and Maintenance	$32,080	11.8%	101,140
40. Private Detectives and Investigators	$37,640	18.2%	7,329
41. Social and Human Service Assistants	$26,630	33.6%	80,142
42. First-Line Supervisors/Managers of Housekeeping and Janitorial Workers	$32,850	12.7%	30,613
43. Heating and Air Conditioning Mechanics and Installers	$38,360	8.7%	29,719
44. Refrigeration Mechanics and Installers	$38,360	8.7%	29,719
45. Water and Liquid Waste Treatment Plant and System Operators	$37,090	13.8%	9,575
46. Medical Secretaries	$28,950	16.7%	60,659
47. Cement Masons and Concrete Finishers	$33,840	11.4%	34,625
48. Municipal Fire Fighting and Prevention Supervisors	$65,040	11.5%	3,771
49. Medical Records and Health Information Technicians	$29,290	17.8%	39,048
50. Pharmacy Technicians	$26,720	32.0%	54,453
51. Funeral Directors	$50,370	12.5%	3,939
52. Sheet Metal Workers	$39,210	6.7%	31,677

The 200 Best Apprenticeable Jobs

Job	Annual Earnings	Percent Growth	Annual Openings
53. Equal Opportunity Representatives and Officers	$48,400	4.9%	15,841
54. Government Property Inspectors and Investigators	$48,400	4.9%	15,841
55. Maintenance and Repair Workers, General	$32,570	10.1%	165,502
56. Medical and Clinical Laboratory Technicians	$34,270	15.0%	10,866
57. Human Resources Assistants, Except Payroll and Timekeeping	$34,970	11.3%	18,647
58. Production, Planning, and Expediting Clerks	$39,690	4.2%	52,735
59. Mapping Technicians	$33,640	19.4%	8,299
60. Police, Fire, and Ambulance Dispatchers	$32,660	13.6%	17,628
61. Purchasing Agents, Except Wholesale, Retail, and Farm Products	$52,460	0.1%	22,349
62. Surveying Technicians	$33,640	19.4%	8,299
63. Transportation Vehicle, Equipment, and Systems Inspectors, Except Aviation	$51,440	16.4%	2,122
64. Electrical Engineering Technicians	$52,140	3.6%	12,583
65. Electronics Engineering Technicians	$52,140	3.6%	12,583
66. Nursing Aides, Orderlies, and Attendants	$23,160	18.2%	321,036
67. Architectural Drafters	$43,310	6.1%	16,238
68. Civil Drafters	$43,310	6.1%	16,238
69. Telecommunications Equipment Installers and Repairers, Except Line Installers	$54,070	2.5%	13,541
70. Telecommunications Line Installers and Repairers	$47,220	4.6%	14,719
71. Drywall and Ceiling Tile Installers	$36,520	7.3%	30,945
72. Audio and Video Equipment Technicians	$36,050	24.2%	4,681
73. Boilermakers	$50,700	14.0%	2,333
74. Emergency Medical Technicians and Paramedics	$28,400	19.2%	19,513
75. Landscaping and Groundskeeping Workers	$22,240	18.1%	307,138
76. Electrical Power-Line Installers and Repairers	$52,570	7.2%	6,401
77. Industrial Engineering Technicians	$47,490	9.9%	6,172
78. First-Line Supervisors/Managers of Retail Sales Workers	$34,470	4.2%	221,241
79. Medical Transcriptionists	$31,250	13.5%	18,080
80. Mechanical Drafters	$44,740	5.2%	10,902
81. Security Guards	$22,570	16.9%	222,085
82. Office Clerks, General	$24,460	12.6%	765,803
83. Medical Equipment Repairers	$40,320	21.7%	2,351
84. Sailors and Marine Oilers	$32,570	15.7%	8,600

(continued)

(continued)

The 200 Best Apprenticeable Jobs

Job	Annual Earnings	Percent Growth	Annual Openings
85. Construction Laborers	$27,310	10.9%	257,407
86. Industrial Production Managers	$80,560	–5.9%	14,889
87. Electrical and Electronics Repairers, Commercial and Industrial Equipment	$47,110	6.8%	6,607
88. Tapers	$42,050	7.1%	9,026
89. Elevator Installers and Repairers	$68,000	8.8%	2,850
90. Motorboat Mechanics	$34,210	19.0%	4,326
91. Tellers	$22,920	13.5%	146,077
92. Computer, Automated Teller, and Office Machine Repairers	$37,100	3.0%	22,330
93. Glaziers	$35,230	11.9%	6,416
94. Camera Operators, Television, Video, and Motion Picture	$41,850	11.5%	3,496
95. Chefs and Head Cooks	$37,160	7.6%	9,401
96. Welders, Cutters, and Welder Fitters	$32,270	5.1%	61,125
97. Reinforcing Iron and Rebar Workers	$37,890	11.5%	4,502
98. Emergency Management Specialists	$48,380	12.3%	1,538
99. Locksmiths and Safe Repairers	$33,230	22.1%	3,545
100. Structural Iron and Steel Workers	$42,130	6.0%	6,969
101. Air Traffic Controllers	$112,930	10.2%	1,213
102. Cooks, Restaurant	$21,220	11.5%	238,542
103. Electrical Drafters	$49,250	4.1%	4,786
104. Electronic Drafters	$49,250	4.1%	4,786
105. Hairdressers, Hairstylists, and Cosmetologists	$22,210	12.4%	73,030
106. Fine Artists, Including Painters, Sculptors, and Illustrators	$42,070	9.9%	3,830
107. Millwrights	$46,090	5.8%	4,758
108. Mechanical Engineering Technicians	$47,280	6.4%	3,710
109. Geological Sample Test Technicians	$50,950	8.6%	1,895
110. Helpers—Installation, Maintenance, and Repair Workers	$22,920	11.8%	52,058
111. Fire Inspectors	$50,830	11.0%	644
112. Fire Investigators	$50,830	11.0%	644
113. Locomotive Engineers	$57,520	2.9%	3,548
114. Machinists	$35,230	–3.1%	39,505
115. Aerospace Engineering and Operations Technicians	$54,930	10.4%	707
116. Cooks, Institution and Cafeteria	$21,340	10.8%	111,898
117. Teacher Assistants	$21,580	10.4%	193,986
118. Insulation Workers, Mechanical	$36,570	8.6%	5,787
119. Payroll and Timekeeping Clerks	$33,810	3.1%	18,544

The 200 Best Apprenticeable Jobs

Job	Annual Earnings	Percent Growth	Annual Openings
120. Pesticide Handlers, Sprayers, and Applicators, Vegetation	$28,560	14.0%	7,443
121. Dispatchers, Except Police, Fire, and Ambulance	$33,140	1.5%	29,793
122. Automotive Glass Installers and Repairers	$31,470	18.7%	3,457
123. Helpers—Brickmasons, Blockmasons, Stonemasons, and Tile and Marble Setters	$26,260	11.0%	22,500
124. Fashion Designers	$62,810	5.0%	1,968
125. Pest Control Workers	$29,030	15.5%	6,006
126. Tree Trimmers and Pruners	$29,800	11.1%	9,621
127. Embalmers	$36,800	14.3%	1,660
128. Animal Trainers	$26,190	22.7%	6,713
129. Medical Equipment Preparers	$27,040	14.2%	8,363
130. Farmers and Ranchers	$33,360	−8.5%	129,552
131. Nuclear Monitoring Technicians	$66,140	6.7%	1,021
132. Photographers	$27,720	10.3%	16,100
133. Chemical Technicians	$40,740	5.8%	4,010
134. Excavating and Loading Machine and Dragline Operators	$34,050	8.3%	6,562
135. Plasterers and Stucco Masons	$36,430	8.1%	4,509
136. Recreational Vehicle Service Technicians	$31,760	18.2%	2,442
137. Secretaries, Except Legal, Medical, and Executive	$28,220	1.2%	239,630
138. Residential Advisors	$23,050	18.5%	8,053
139. Sound Engineering Technicians	$46,550	9.1%	1,194
140. Maintenance Workers, Machinery	$35,590	−1.1%	15,055
141. Slaughterers and Meat Packers	$22,500	12.7%	15,511
142. Avionics Technicians	$48,100	8.1%	1,193
143. Bakers	$22,590	10.0%	31,442
144. Stonemasons	$36,950	10.0%	2,657
145. Control and Valve Installers and Repairers, Except Mechanical Door	$46,140	0.3%	3,855
146. Food Batchmakers	$23,730	10.9%	15,704
147. Power Plant Operators	$56,640	2.7%	1,796
148. Broadcast Technicians	$32,230	12.1%	2,955
149. Postal Service Clerks	$45,050	1.2%	3,703
150. Rail Car Repairers	$44,970	5.1%	1,989
151. Tank Car, Truck, and Ship Loaders	$33,140	9.2%	4,519
152. Painters, Transportation Equipment	$36,000	8.4%	3,268
153. Airfield Operations Specialists	$38,320	11.8%	245
154. Chemical Plant and System Operators	$50,860	−15.3%	5,620

(continued)

(continued)

The 200 Best Apprenticeable Jobs

Job	Annual Earnings	Percent Growth	Annual Openings
155. Insulation Workers, Floor, Ceiling, and Wall	$31,280	8.4%	6,580
156. Motorcycle Mechanics	$30,300	12.5%	3,564
157. Stationary Engineers and Boiler Operators	$47,640	3.4%	1,892
158. Petroleum Pump System Operators, Refinery Operators, and Gaugers	$53,010	−13.4%	4,477
159. Inspectors, Testers, Sorters, Samplers, and Weighers	$30,310	−7.0%	75,361
160. Mechanical Door Repairers	$31,880	14.9%	1,706
161. Structural Metal Fabricators and Fitters	$31,030	−0.2%	20,746
162. Team Assemblers	$24,630	0.1%	264,135
163. Merchandise Displayers and Window Trimmers	$24,830	10.7%	9,103
164. Parts Salespersons	$28,130	−2.2%	52,414
165. Tool and Die Makers	$45,090	−9.6%	5,286
166. Carpet Installers	$36,040	−1.2%	6,692
167. Electrical and Electronics Installers and Repairers, Transportation Equipment	$43,940	4.3%	1,663
168. Computer-Controlled Machine Tool Operators, Metal and Plastic	$32,550	−3.0%	12,997
169. Desktop Publishers	$35,510	1.0%	6,420
170. Earth Drillers, Except Oil and Gas	$36,310	6.5%	2,619
171. Paving, Surfacing, and Tamping Equipment Operators	$32,360	9.0%	3,471
172. Crane and Tower Operators	$40,260	2.8%	2,626
173. Multiple Machine Tool Setters, Operators, and Tenders, Metal and Plastic	$30,390	0.3%	15,709
174. Electrical and Electronics Repairers, Powerhouse, Substation, and Relay	$58,970	−4.7%	1,591
175. Computer Operators	$34,610	−24.7%	17,842
176. Terrazzo Workers and Finishers	$34,390	10.9%	1,052
177. Ambulance Drivers and Attendants, Except Emergency Medical Technicians	$21,140	21.7%	3,703
178. Electro-Mechanical Technicians	$46,610	2.6%	1,142
179. Mixing and Blending Machine Setters, Operators, and Tenders	$30,340	−5.1%	18,661
180. Word Processors and Typists	$30,380	−11.6%	32,279
181. Welding, Soldering, and Brazing Machine Setters, Operators, and Tenders	$30,980	3.0%	7,707
182. Data Entry Keyers	$25,370	−4.7%	79,166
183. Opticians, Dispensing	$31,430	8.7%	3,143

The 200 Best Apprenticeable Jobs

Job	Annual Earnings	Percent Growth	Annual Openings
184. Woodworking Machine Setters, Operators, and Tenders, Except Sawing	$24,190	6.4%	11,860
185. Butchers and Meat Cutters	$27,480	1.9%	14,503
186. Printing Machine Operators	$31,490	–5.7%	12,274
187. Cabinetmakers and Bench Carpenters	$27,970	2.8%	9,780
188. Dental Laboratory Technicians	$33,480	3.7%	3,479
189. Home Appliance Repairers	$33,560	1.5%	4,243
190. Mine Cutting and Channeling Machine Operators	$39,930	3.8%	923
191. Fish and Game Wardens	$47,830	–0.2%	576
192. Rotary Drill Operators, Oil and Gas	$43,480	–5.4%	2,145
193. Prepress Technicians and Workers	$33,990	–21.1%	10,002
194. Fiberglass Laminators and Fabricators	$26,630	6.2%	7,315
195. Gem and Diamond Workers	$31,200	–2.2%	7,375
196. Jewelers	$31,200	–2.2%	7,375
197. Precious Metal Workers	$31,200	–2.2%	7,375
198. Fence Erectors	$26,720	10.6%	2,812
199. Medical Appliance Technicians	$32,640	9.4%	895
200. Chemical Equipment Operators and Tenders	$44,050	–3.9%	1,469

Job 4 shares 12,836 openings with another job not included in this list. Job 5 shares 37,842 openings with another job not included in this list. Jobs 8 and 9 share 68,643 openings. Jobs 11 and 12 share 97,350 openings. Jobs 14 and 15 share 18,887 openings. Jobs 17 and 18 share 223,225 openings. Jobs 34 and 36 share 2,665 openings with each other and with another job not included in this list. Jobs 43 and 44 share 29,719 openings. Job 48 shares 3,771 openings with another job not included in this list. Jobs 53 and 54 share 15,841 openings with each other and with three other jobs not included in this list. Jobs 59 and 62 share 8,299 openings. Job 63 shares 2,122 openings with another job not included in this list. Jobs 64 and 65 share 12,583 openings. Jobs 67 and 68 share 16,238 openings. Job 96 shares 61,125 openings with another job not included in this list. Jobs 103 and 104 share 4,786 openings. Job 109 shares 1,895 openings with another job not included in this list. Jobs 111 and 112 share 644 openings. Job 113 shares 3,548 openings with two other jobs not included in this list. Job 131 shares 1,021 openings with another job not included in this list. Jobs 195, 196, and 197 share 7,375 openings.

The 100 Best-Paying Apprenticeable Jobs

Of the 200 jobs that met our criteria for this book, this list shows the 100 with the highest median earnings. (*Median earnings* means that half of all workers in each of these jobs earn more than that amount and half earn less.) This is a popular list, for obvious reasons.

If you look at the descriptions of these jobs in Part IV, you'll notice that the number of years required to complete the apprenticeship varies quite a lot. There is not a very strong link between the number of years of apprenticeship and the amount of pay. But note that one of the highest-paying jobs on the list, Municipal Fire Fighting and Prevention Supervisors, requires more than just the three-year apprenticeship called Fire Captain; to qualify for the

Fire Captain apprenticeship, you must previously have logged some years of experience as a Municipal Fire Fighter, which itself requires a three-year apprenticeship.

Among the top 25, technology is a common factor: Several of the jobs are in the energy industry, communications, or transportation.

As you review this list, keep in mind what we said earlier about how earnings can vary by region of the country, amount of experience, and many other factors. For example, when you have journey worker status in an occupation, you are likely to be paid more than the average amount listed here because this amount is based on the earnings of *everyone* working in the job, including apprentices and those who learned informally.

The 100 Best-Paying Apprenticeable Jobs

Job	Annual Earnings
1. Air Traffic Controllers	$112,930
2. Industrial Production Managers	$80,560
3. Elevator Installers and Repairers	$68,000
4. Nuclear Monitoring Technicians	$66,140
5. Municipal Fire Fighting and Prevention Supervisors	$65,040
6. Fashion Designers	$62,810
7. Electrical and Electronics Repairers, Powerhouse, Substation, and Relay	$58,970
8. Locomotive Engineers	$57,520
9. Mates—Ship, Boat, and Barge	$57,210
10. Pilots, Ship	$57,210
11. Power Plant Operators	$56,640
12. Aerospace Engineering and Operations Technicians	$54,930
13. Telecommunications Equipment Installers and Repairers, Except Line Installers	$54,070
14. Petroleum Pump System Operators, Refinery Operators, and Gaugers	$53,010
15. Electrical Power-Line Installers and Repairers	$52,570
16. Purchasing Agents, Except Wholesale, Retail, and Farm Products	$52,460
17. Electrical Engineering Technicians	$52,140
18. Electronics Engineering Technicians	$52,140
19. Transportation Vehicle, Equipment, and Systems Inspectors, Except Aviation	$51,440
20. Geological Sample Test Technicians	$50,950
21. Chemical Plant and System Operators	$50,860
22. Fire Inspectors	$50,830
23. Fire Investigators	$50,830
24. Boilermakers	$50,700
25. Funeral Directors	$50,370
26. Radiologic Technologists	$50,260
27. Police Patrol Officers	$49,630

The 100 Best-Paying Apprenticeable Jobs

Job	Annual Earnings
28. Electrical Drafters	$49,250
29. Electronic Drafters	$49,250
30. Aircraft Mechanics and Service Technicians	$49,010
31. Equal Opportunity Representatives and Officers	$48,400
32. Government Property Inspectors and Investigators	$48,400
33. Emergency Management Specialists	$48,380
34. Construction and Building Inspectors	$48,330
35. Avionics Technicians	$48,100
36. Fish and Game Wardens	$47,830
37. Stationary Engineers and Boiler Operators	$47,640
38. Industrial Engineering Technicians	$47,490
39. Mechanical Engineering Technicians	$47,280
40. Telecommunications Line Installers and Repairers	$47,220
41. Electrical and Electronics Repairers, Commercial and Industrial Equipment	$47,110
42. Electro-Mechanical Technicians	$46,610
43. Sound Engineering Technicians	$46,550
44. Control and Valve Installers and Repairers, Except Mechanical Door	$46,140
45. Millwrights	$46,090
46. Aircraft Structure, Surfaces, Rigging, and Systems Assemblers	$45,420
47. Tool and Die Makers	$45,090
48. Postal Service Clerks	$45,050
49. Paralegals and Legal Assistants	$44,990
50. Rail Car Repairers	$44,970
51. Electricians	$44,780
52. Mechanical Drafters	$44,740
53. Food Service Managers	$44,570
54. Pipe Fitters and Steamfitters	$44,090
55. Plumbers	$44,090
56. Brickmasons and Blockmasons	$44,070
57. Chemical Equipment Operators and Tenders	$44,050
58. Interior Designers	$43,970
59. Electrical and Electronics Installers and Repairers, Transportation Equipment	$43,940
60. Rotary Drill Operators, Oil and Gas	$43,480
61. Architectural Drafters	$43,310
62. Civil Drafters	$43,310
63. Forest Fire Fighters	$43,170
64. Municipal Fire Fighters	$43,170

(continued)

(continued)

The 100 Best-Paying Apprenticeable Jobs

Job	Annual Earnings
65. Computer Support Specialists	$42,400
66. Industrial Machinery Mechanics	$42,350
67. Structural Iron and Steel Workers	$42,130
68. Fine Artists, Including Painters, Sculptors, and Illustrators	$42,070
69. Tapers	$42,050
70. Camera Operators, Television, Video, and Motion Picture	$41,850
71. Mobile Heavy Equipment Mechanics, Except Engines	$41,450
72. Chemical Technicians	$40,740
73. Medical Equipment Repairers	$40,320
74. Crane and Tower Operators	$40,260
75. Mine Cutting and Channeling Machine Operators	$39,930
76. Production, Planning, and Expediting Clerks	$39,690
77. Environmental Science and Protection Technicians, Including Health	$39,370
78. Sheet Metal Workers	$39,210
79. Legal Secretaries	$38,810
80. Tile and Marble Setters	$38,720
81. Bus and Truck Mechanics and Diesel Engine Specialists	$38,640
82. Heating and Air Conditioning Mechanics and Installers	$38,360
83. Refrigeration Mechanics and Installers	$38,360
84. Airfield Operations Specialists	$38,320
85. Operating Engineers and Other Construction Equipment Operators	$38,130
86. Licensed Practical and Licensed Vocational Nurses	$37,940
87. Reinforcing Iron and Rebar Workers	$37,890
88. Construction Carpenters	$37,660
89. Rough Carpenters	$37,660
90. Private Detectives and Investigators	$37,640
91. Surgical Technologists	$37,540
92. Chefs and Head Cooks	$37,160
93. Computer, Automated Teller, and Office Machine Repairers	$37,100
94. Water and Liquid Waste Treatment Plant and System Operators	$37,090
95. Cargo and Freight Agents	$37,060
96. Correctional Officers and Jailers	$36,970
97. Stonemasons	$36,950
98. Embalmers	$36,800
99. Insulation Workers, Mechanical	$36,570
100. Drywall and Ceiling Tile Installers	$36,520

The 100 Fastest-Growing Apprenticeable Jobs

Of the 200 jobs that met our criteria for this book, this list shows the 100 that are projected to have the highest percentage increase in the number of people employed through 2016. Growth rates are one measure to consider in exploring career options, as jobs with higher growth rates tend to provide more job opportunities.

Note that eight of the top 25 jobs are in the health-care field, an industry that is growing quickly and that will provide many opportunities. A large number of the highest-ranked jobs, even in other fields, involve the human touch—providing services to people directly and in person. These jobs are growing so fast partly because they can't be done by computers or by overseas workers.

The 100 Fastest-Growing Apprenticeable Jobs

Job	Percent Growth
1. Medical Assistants	35.4%
2. Social and Human Service Assistants	33.6%
3. Pharmacy Technicians	32.0%
4. Dental Assistants	29.2%
5. Environmental Science and Protection Technicians, Including Health	28.0%
6. Surgical Technologists	24.5%
7. Audio and Video Equipment Technicians	24.2%
8. Animal Trainers	22.7%
9. Paralegals and Legal Assistants	22.2%
10. Locksmiths and Safe Repairers	22.1%
11. Medical Equipment Repairers	21.7%
12. Ambulance Drivers and Attendants, Except Emergency Medical Technicians	21.7%
13. Interior Designers	19.5%
14. Mapping Technicians	19.4%
15. Surveying Technicians	19.4%
16. Emergency Medical Technicians and Paramedics	19.2%
17. Motorboat Mechanics	19.0%
18. Automotive Glass Installers and Repairers	18.7%
19. Residential Advisors	18.5%
20. Construction and Building Inspectors	18.2%
21. Nursing Aides, Orderlies, and Attendants	18.2%
22. Private Detectives and Investigators	18.2%
23. Recreational Vehicle Service Technicians	18.2%
24. Landscaping and Groundskeeping Workers	18.1%
25. Mates—Ship, Boat, and Barge	17.9%

(continued)

(continued)

The 100 Fastest-Growing Apprenticeable Jobs

Job	Percent Growth
26. Pilots, Ship	17.9%
27. Medical Records and Health Information Technicians	17.8%
28. Correctional Officers and Jailers	16.9%
29. Security Guards	16.9%
30. Medical Secretaries	16.7%
31. Cargo and Freight Agents	16.5%
32. Transportation Vehicle, Equipment, and Systems Inspectors, Except Aviation	16.4%
33. Sailors and Marine Oilers	15.7%
34. Pest Control Workers	15.5%
35. Tile and Marble Setters	15.4%
36. Radiologic Technologists	15.1%
37. Medical and Clinical Laboratory Technicians	15.0%
38. Mechanical Door Repairers	14.9%
39. Automotive Master Mechanics	14.3%
40. Automotive Specialty Technicians	14.3%
41. Embalmers	14.3%
42. Roofers	14.3%
43. Medical Equipment Preparers	14.2%
44. Boilermakers	14.0%
45. Licensed Practical and Licensed Vocational Nurses	14.0%
46. Pesticide Handlers, Sprayers, and Applicators, Vegetation	14.0%
47. Water and Liquid Waste Treatment Plant and System Operators	13.8%
48. Police, Fire, and Ambulance Dispatchers	13.6%
49. Medical Transcriptionists	13.5%
50. Tellers	13.5%
51. Computer Support Specialists	12.9%
52. Aircraft Structure, Surfaces, Rigging, and Systems Assemblers	12.8%
53. First-Line Supervisors/Managers of Housekeeping and Janitorial Workers	12.7%
54. Slaughterers and Meat Packers	12.7%
55. Office Clerks, General	12.6%
56. Bookkeeping, Accounting, and Auditing Clerks	12.5%
57. Funeral Directors	12.5%
58. Motorcycle Mechanics	12.5%
59. Hairdressers, Hairstylists, and Cosmetologists	12.4%
60. Emergency Management Specialists	12.3%
61. Mobile Heavy Equipment Mechanics, Except Engines	12.3%

The 100 Fastest-Growing Apprenticeable Jobs

Job	Percent Growth
62. Broadcast Technicians	12.1%
63. Forest Fire Fighters	12.1%
64. Municipal Fire Fighters	12.1%
65. Glaziers	11.9%
66. Airfield Operations Specialists	11.8%
67. Helpers—Installation, Maintenance, and Repair Workers	11.8%
68. Painters, Construction and Maintenance	11.8%
69. Legal Secretaries	11.7%
70. Automotive Body and Related Repairers	11.6%
71. Bus and Truck Mechanics and Diesel Engine Specialists	11.5%
72. Camera Operators, Television, Video, and Motion Picture	11.5%
73. Cooks, Restaurant	11.5%
74. Municipal Fire Fighting and Prevention Supervisors	11.5%
75. Reinforcing Iron and Rebar Workers	11.5%
76. Cement Masons and Concrete Finishers	11.4%
77. Human Resources Assistants, Except Payroll and Timekeeping	11.3%
78. Tree Trimmers and Pruners	11.1%
79. Fire Inspectors	11.0%
80. Fire Investigators	11.0%
81. Helpers—Brickmasons, Blockmasons, Stonemasons, and Tile and Marble Setters	11.0%
82. Construction Laborers	10.9%
83. Food Batchmakers	10.9%
84. Terrazzo Workers and Finishers	10.9%
85. Cooks, Institution and Cafeteria	10.8%
86. Police Patrol Officers	10.8%
87. Merchandise Displayers and Window Trimmers	10.7%
88. Aircraft Mechanics and Service Technicians	10.6%
89. Fence Erectors	10.6%
90. Pipe Fitters and Steamfitters	10.6%
91. Plumbers	10.6%
92. Aerospace Engineering and Operations Technicians	10.4%
93. Teacher Assistants	10.4%
94. Truck Drivers, Heavy and Tractor-Trailer	10.4%
95. Construction Carpenters	10.3%
96. Photographers	10.3%
97. Rough Carpenters	10.3%

(continued)

(continued)

The 100 Fastest-Growing Apprenticeable Jobs

Job	Percent Growth
98. Air Traffic Controllers	10.2%
99. Maintenance and Repair Workers, General	10.1%
100. Stonemasons	10.0%

The 100 Apprenticeable Jobs with the Most Openings

Of the 200 jobs that met our criteria for this book, this list shows the 100 jobs that are projected to have the largest number of job openings per year.

Jobs with many openings present several advantages that may be attractive to you. Because there are many openings, these jobs can be easier to obtain, particularly for those just entering the job market. These jobs may also offer more opportunities to move from one employer to another with relative ease. Though some of these jobs have average or below-average pay, some also pay quite well and can provide good long-term career opportunities or the ability to move up to more responsible roles.

It is interesting to note that high technology does not play a large role among most of the top 25 jobs on this list. Therefore it is not really true that nowadays you must master high-tech skills to be employable. In fact, most of these jobs have so many openings precisely because they require hands-on work and the workers cannot be replaced by technology. Most of these jobs also require on-site work, sometimes in-person work, and therefore cannot be exported overseas.

The 100 Apprenticeable Jobs with the Most Openings

Job	Annual Openings
1. Office Clerks, General	765,803
2. Nursing Aides, Orderlies, and Attendants	321,036
3. Landscaping and Groundskeeping Workers	307,138
4. Bookkeeping, Accounting, and Auditing Clerks	286,854
5. Truck Drivers, Heavy and Tractor-Trailer	279,032
6. Team Assemblers	264,135
7. Construction Laborers	257,407
8. Secretaries, Except Legal, Medical, and Executive	239,630

The 100 Apprenticeable Jobs with the Most Openings

Job	Annual Openings
9. Cooks, Restaurant	238,542
10. Construction Carpenters	223,225
11. Rough Carpenters	223,225
12. Security Guards	222,085
13. First-Line Supervisors/Managers of Retail Sales Workers	221,241
14. Teacher Assistants	193,986
15. Maintenance and Repair Workers, General	165,502
16. Tellers	146,077
17. Farmers and Ranchers	129,552
18. Cooks, Institution and Cafeteria	111,898
19. Painters, Construction and Maintenance	101,140
20. Automotive Master Mechanics	97,350
21. Automotive Specialty Technicians	97,350
22. Computer Support Specialists	97,334
23. Medical Assistants	92,977
24. Social and Human Service Assistants	80,142
25. Data Entry Keyers	79,166
26. Electricians	79,083
27. Inspectors, Testers, Sorters, Samplers, and Weighers	75,361
28. Hairdressers, Hairstylists, and Cosmetologists	73,030
29. Licensed Practical and Licensed Vocational Nurses	70,610
30. Pipe Fitters and Steamfitters	68,643
31. Plumbers	68,643
32. Welders, Cutters, and Welder Fitters	61,125
33. Medical Secretaries	60,659
34. Food Service Managers	59,302
35. Correctional Officers and Jailers	56,579
36. Operating Engineers and Other Construction Equipment Operators	55,468
37. Pharmacy Technicians	54,453
38. Production, Planning, and Expediting Clerks	52,735
39. Parts Salespersons	52,414
40. Helpers—Installation, Maintenance, and Repair Workers	52,058
41. Machinists	39,505
42. Medical Records and Health Information Technicians	39,048
43. Legal Secretaries	38,682
44. Roofers	38,398
45. Police Patrol Officers	37,842

(continued)

(continued)

The 100 Apprenticeable Jobs with the Most Openings

Job	Annual Openings
46. Automotive Body and Related Repairers	37,469
47. Cement Masons and Concrete Finishers	34,625
48. Word Processors and Typists	32,279
49. Sheet Metal Workers	31,677
50. Bakers	31,442
51. Drywall and Ceiling Tile Installers	30,945
52. First-Line Supervisors/Managers of Housekeeping and Janitorial Workers	30,613
53. Dispatchers, Except Police, Fire, and Ambulance	29,793
54. Heating and Air Conditioning Mechanics and Installers	29,719
55. Refrigeration Mechanics and Installers	29,719
56. Dental Assistants	29,482
57. Bus and Truck Mechanics and Diesel Engine Specialists	25,428
58. Industrial Machinery Mechanics	23,361
59. Paralegals and Legal Assistants	22,756
60. Helpers—Brickmasons, Blockmasons, Stonemasons, and Tile and Marble Setters	22,500
61. Purchasing Agents, Except Wholesale, Retail, and Farm Products	22,349
62. Computer, Automated Teller, and Office Machine Repairers	22,330
63. Structural Metal Fabricators and Fitters	20,746
64. Emergency Medical Technicians and Paramedics	19,513
65. Forest Fire Fighters	18,887
66. Municipal Fire Fighters	18,887
67. Mixing and Blending Machine Setters, Operators, and Tenders	18,661
68. Human Resources Assistants, Except Payroll and Timekeeping	18,647
69. Payroll and Timekeeping Clerks	18,544
70. Medical Transcriptionists	18,080
71. Computer Operators	17,842
72. Police, Fire, and Ambulance Dispatchers	17,628
73. Brickmasons and Blockmasons	17,569
74. Architectural Drafters	16,238
75. Civil Drafters	16,238
76. Photographers	16,100
77. Equal Opportunity Representatives and Officers	15,841
78. Government Property Inspectors and Investigators	15,841
79. Multiple Machine Tool Setters, Operators, and Tenders, Metal and Plastic	15,709
80. Food Batchmakers	15,704
81. Slaughterers and Meat Packers	15,511

The 100 Apprenticeable Jobs with the Most Openings

Job	Annual Openings
82. Surgical Technologists	15,365
83. Maintenance Workers, Machinery	15,055
84. Industrial Production Managers	14,889
85. Telecommunications Line Installers and Repairers	14,719
86. Butchers and Meat Cutters	14,503
87. Telecommunications Equipment Installers and Repairers, Except Line Installers	13,541
88. Computer-Controlled Machine Tool Operators, Metal and Plastic	12,997
89. Radiologic Technologists	12,836
90. Construction and Building Inspectors	12,606
91. Electrical Engineering Technicians	12,583
92. Electronics Engineering Technicians	12,583
93. Printing Machine Operators	12,274
94. Woodworking Machine Setters, Operators, and Tenders, Except Sawing	11,860
95. Mobile Heavy Equipment Mechanics, Except Engines	11,037
96. Mechanical Drafters	10,902
97. Medical and Clinical Laboratory Technicians	10,866
98. Prepress Technicians and Workers	10,002
99. Cargo and Freight Agents	9,967
100. Cabinetmakers and Bench Carpenters	9,780

Jobs 10 and 11 share 223,225 openings. Jobs 20 and 21 share 97,350 openings. Jobs 30 and 31 share 68,643 openings. Job 32 shares 61,125 openings with another job not included in this list. Job 45 shares 37,842 openings with another job not included in this list. Jobs 54 and 55 share 29,719 openings. Jobs 65 and 66 share 18,887 openings. Jobs 74 and 75 share 16,238 openings. Jobs 77 and 78 share 15,841 openings with each other and with three other jobs not included in this list. Job 89 shares 12,836 openings with another job not included in this list. Jobs 91 and 92 share 12,583 openings.

Apprenticeable Jobs with the Highest Percentage of Women and Men

Apprenticeship is often mistakenly thought of as an all-male preserve. The continuing use (in some places—not in this book) of the term "journeyman" has not helped. It is true that less than 10 percent of apprentices are women. On the other hand, it is not clear whether this low turnout of women means that women are being discouraged or that women are not interested. Where there is interest, there sometimes is opportunity—some employers and unions have been moving aggressively for inclusion of women in apprenticeships. (Union-based apprenticeships are known for having a better representation of women who are recruited and also who achieve journey worker status.)

Therefore, as you look over the following lists of apprenticeable jobs with a high percentage of women and men, you should not regard the lists as intended to restrict women or men from considering apprenticeship options. In fact, one reason for including these lists is exactly the opposite. We hope the lists help people see possibilities that they might not otherwise have considered. For example, we suggest that women browse the lists of apprenticeable jobs that employ high percentages of men. Many of these occupations pay quite well, and women who want to do them and are willing to undertake the necessary apprenticeships should consider them.

We created the lists by sorting the jobs that met the criteria for this book and including only those employing 70 percent or more of women or men. Of the 200 best apprenticeable jobs, 27 met this criterion for women and 124 for men.

In the following lists, if you compare the apprenticeable occupations employing a high percentage of women with those employing a high percentage of men, you may notice some distinct differences beyond the obvious. For example, you may notice that the jobs with the highest percentage of women tend to cluster into certain industries. The following chart, based on 2007 data for registered apprentices in 31 states, shows an estimation of how the distribution varies among different industries:

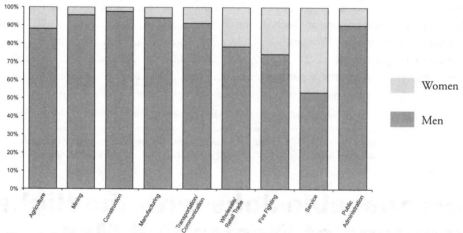

Figure 2: Gender distribution of apprentices among industries, 2007.

You may also notice in the following lists that the jobs with a high percentage of women are growing somewhat faster than those with a high percentage of men. We've done the math and discovered that the difference is an average growth rate of 12.9 percent for the jobs that employ mostly women versus an average rate of 9.0 percent for the jobs that employ mostly men. The number of annual job openings shows a similar pattern. Occupations with a high percentage of men average 28,324 openings per year, while more than three times that number of openings, 101,501, are projected on average for occupations with a high percentage of women.

This discrepancy might explain why men have had more problems than women in adapting to an economy dominated by service and information-based jobs. Many women may simply be better prepared for these jobs, possessing more appropriate skills for the jobs that are now growing rapidly and have more job openings.

On the other hand, you may notice that on average the jobs with a high percentage of men have higher wages (an average of $36,660) than do the jobs with a high percentage of women ($28,056). This suggests that women interested in improving their earnings may want to consider jobs traditionally dominated by men. Remember that a time-honored gender imbalance is not always a barrier to women. As noted earlier, some apprenticeship programs are seeking female recruits to counterbalance a traditional male dominance.

Best Apprenticeable Jobs with the Highest Percentage of Women

Job	Percent Women
1. Legal Secretaries	96.9%
2. Medical Secretaries	96.9%
3. Secretaries, Except Legal, Medical, and Executive	96.9%
4. Dental Assistants	95.4%
5. Licensed Practical and Licensed Vocational Nurses	94.2%
6. Hairdressers, Hairstylists, and Cosmetologists	93.4%
7. Payroll and Timekeeping Clerks	92.4%
8. Teacher Assistants	92.3%
9. Medical Records and Health Information Technicians	92.0%
10. Human Resources Assistants, Except Payroll and Timekeeping	91.9%
11. Desktop Publishers	91.2%
12. Word Processors and Typists	91.2%
13. Medical Assistants	90.4%
14. Medical Transcriptionists	90.4%
15. Bookkeeping, Accounting, and Auditing Clerks	90.3%
16. Paralegals and Legal Assistants	89.1%
17. Nursing Aides, Orderlies, and Attendants	88.9%
18. Tellers	84.8%
19. Office Clerks, General	81.9%
20. Data Entry Keyers	81.6%
21. Surgical Technologists	80.1%
22. Pharmacy Technicians	80.1%
23. Medical and Clinical Laboratory Technicians	78.1%
24. Cargo and Freight Agents	75.4%
25. Opticians, Dispensing	73.4%
26. Radiologic Technologists	72.9%
27. Social and Human Service Assistants	70.5%

Best 25 Apprenticeable Jobs Overall with a High Percentage of Women

Job	Percent Women	Annual Earnings	Percent Growth	Annual Openings
1. Paralegals and Legal Assistants	89.1%	$44,990	22.2%	22,756
2. Medical Assistants	90.4%	$27,430	35.4%	92,977
3. Licensed Practical and Licensed Vocational Nurses	94.2%	$37,940	14.0%	70,610
4. Bookkeeping, Accounting, and Auditing Clerks	90.3%	$31,560	12.5%	286,854
5. Social and Human Service Assistants	70.5%	$26,630	33.6%	80,142
6. Surgical Technologists	80.1%	$37,540	24.5%	15,365
7. Dental Assistants	95.4%	$31,550	29.2%	29,482
8. Nursing Aides, Orderlies, and Attendants	88.9%	$23,160	18.2%	321,036
9. Radiologic Technologists	72.9%	$50,260	15.1%	12,836
10. Pharmacy Technicians	80.1%	$26,720	32.0%	54,453
11. Legal Secretaries	96.9%	$38,810	11.7%	38,682
12. Medical Records and Health Information Technicians	92.0%	$29,290	17.8%	39,048
13. Medical Secretaries	96.9%	$28,950	16.7%	60,659
14. Office Clerks, General	81.9%	$24,460	12.6%	765,803
15. Cargo and Freight Agents	75.4%	$37,060	16.5%	9,967
16. Medical and Clinical Laboratory Technicians	78.1%	$34,270	15.0%	10,866
17. Tellers	84.8%	$22,920	13.5%	146,077
18. Secretaries, Except Legal, Medical, and Executive	96.9%	$28,220	1.2%	239,630
19. Human Resources Assistants, Except Payroll and Timekeeping	91.9%	$34,970	11.3%	18,647
20. Medical Transcriptionists	90.4%	$31,250	13.5%	18,080
21. Payroll and Timekeeping Clerks	92.4%	$33,810	3.1%	18,544
22. Teacher Assistants	92.3%	$21,580	10.4%	193,986
23. Hairdressers, Hairstylists, and Cosmetologists	93.4%	$22,210	12.4%	73,030
24. Data Entry Keyers	81.6%	$25,370	–4.7%	79,166
25. Desktop Publishers	91.2%	$35,510	1.0%	6,420

Job 9 shares 12,836 openings with another job not included in this list.

Best Apprenticeable Jobs with the Highest Percentage of Men

Job	Percent Men
1. Automotive Body and Related Repairers	99.4%
2. Automotive Glass Installers and Repairers	99.4%
3. Cement Masons and Concrete Finishers	99.3%
4. Terrazzo Workers and Finishers	99.3%

Best Apprenticeable Jobs with the Highest Percentage of Men

Job	Percent Men
5. Bus and Truck Mechanics and Diesel Engine Specialists	99.1%
6. Electrical Power-Line Installers and Repairers	99.1%
7. Tool and Die Makers	99.1%
8. Roofers	98.9%
9. Mobile Heavy Equipment Mechanics, Except Engines	98.6%
10. Rail Car Repairers	98.6%
11. Crane and Tower Operators	98.5%
12. Excavating and Loading Machine and Dragline Operators	98.5%
13. Home Appliance Repairers	98.5%
14. Automotive Master Mechanics	98.4%
15. Automotive Specialty Technicians	98.4%
16. Brickmasons and Blockmasons	98.4%
17. Stonemasons	98.4%
18. Operating Engineers and Other Construction Equipment Operators	98.3%
19. Paving, Surfacing, and Tamping Equipment Operators	98.3%
20. Pipe Fitters and Steamfitters	98.2%
21. Plumbers	98.2%
22. Electricians	98.1%
23. Pest Control Workers	97.8%
24. Reinforcing Iron and Rebar Workers	97.8%
25. Structural Iron and Steel Workers	97.8%
26. Power Plant Operators	97.7%
27. Stationary Engineers and Boiler Operators	97.7%
28. Carpet Installers	97.6%
29. Construction Carpenters	97.6%
30. Rough Carpenters	97.6%
31. Tile and Marble Setters	97.6%
32. Heating and Air Conditioning Mechanics and Installers	97.3%
33. Refrigeration Mechanics and Installers	97.3%
34. Drywall and Ceiling Tile Installers	97.1%
35. Millwrights	97.1%
36. Tapers	97.1%
37. Sheet Metal Workers	96.9%
38. Boilermakers	96.9%
39. Earth Drillers, Except Oil and Gas	96.9%
40. Elevator Installers and Repairers	96.9%
41. Fence Erectors	96.9%

(continued)

(continued)

Best Apprenticeable Jobs with the Highest Percentage of Men

Job	Percent Men
42. Glaziers	96.9%
43. Insulation Workers, Floor, Ceiling, and Wall	96.9%
44. Insulation Workers, Mechanical	96.9%
45. Mine Cutting and Channeling Machine Operators	96.9%
46. Plasterers and Stucco Masons	96.9%
47. Rotary Drill Operators, Oil and Gas	96.9%
48. Motorboat Mechanics	96.6%
49. Motorcycle Mechanics	96.6%
50. Forest Fire Fighters	96.5%
51. Municipal Fire Fighters	96.5%
52. Construction Laborers	96.3%
53. Industrial Machinery Mechanics	96.2%
54. Maintenance Workers, Machinery	96.2%
55. Maintenance and Repair Workers, General	96.0%
56. Water and Liquid Waste Treatment Plant and System Operators	96.0%
57. Cabinetmakers and Bench Carpenters	95.6%
58. Control and Valve Installers and Repairers, Except Mechanical Door	95.4%
59. Electrical and Electronics Installers and Repairers, Transportation Equipment	95.4%
60. Electrical and Electronics Repairers, Powerhouse, Substation, and Relay	95.4%
61. Helpers—Installation, Maintenance, and Repair Workers	95.4%
62. Mechanical Door Repairers	95.4%
63. Recreational Vehicle Service Technicians	95.4%
64. Truck Drivers, Heavy and Tractor-Trailer	94.8%
65. Aircraft Mechanics and Service Technicians	94.7%
66. Welders, Cutters, and Welder Fitters	94.1%
67. Welding, Soldering, and Brazing Machine Setters, Operators, and Tenders	94.1%
68. Helpers—Brickmasons, Blockmasons, Stonemasons, and Tile and Marble Setters	93.8%
69. Landscaping and Groundskeeping Workers	93.8%
70. Pesticide Handlers, Sprayers, and Applicators, Vegetation	93.8%
71. Tree Trimmers and Pruners	93.8%
72. Locomotive Engineers	93.5%
73. Machinists	93.3%
74. Municipal Fire Fighting and Prevention Supervisors	92.8%
75. Painters, Construction and Maintenance	92.3%
76. Computer-Controlled Machine Tool Operators, Metal and Plastic	91.8%

Best Apprenticeable Jobs with the Highest Percentage of Men

Job	Percent Men
77. Telecommunications Line Installers and Repairers	91.4%
78. Construction and Building Inspectors	91.2%
79. Computer, Automated Teller, and Office Machine Repairers	90.3%
80. Mapping Technicians	90.1%
81. Surveying Technicians	90.1%
82. Mixing and Blending Machine Setters, Operators, and Tenders	88.8%
83. Police Patrol Officers	87.2%
84. Air Traffic Controllers	87.0%
85. Chemical Equipment Operators and Tenders	87.0%
86. Locksmiths and Safe Repairers	86.1%
87. Medical Equipment Repairers	86.1%
88. Airfield Operations Specialists	85.2%
89. Mates—Ship, Boat, and Barge	85.2%
90. Pilots, Ship	85.2%
91. Sailors and Marine Oilers	85.2%
92. Transportation Vehicle, Equipment, and Systems Inspectors, Except Aviation	85.2%
93. Avionics Technicians	84.8%
94. Electrical and Electronics Repairers, Commercial and Industrial Equipment	84.8%
95. Telecommunications Equipment Installers and Repairers, Except Line Installers	84.8%
96. Audio and Video Equipment Technicians	84.4%
97. Broadcast Technicians	84.4%
98. Camera Operators, Television, Video, and Motion Picture	84.4%
99. Sound Engineering Technicians	84.4%
100. Parts Salespersons	83.7%
101. Industrial Production Managers	83.6%
102. Painters, Transportation Equipment	83.4%
103. Tank Car, Truck, and Ship Loaders	83.1%
104. Aerospace Engineering and Operations Technicians	79.4%
105. Electrical Engineering Technicians	79.4%
106. Electro-Mechanical Technicians	79.4%
107. Electronics Engineering Technicians	79.4%
108. Industrial Engineering Technicians	79.4%
109. Mechanical Engineering Technicians	79.4%
110. Architectural Drafters	78.2%
111. Civil Drafters	78.2%

(continued)

(continued)

Best Apprenticeable Jobs with the Highest Percentage of Men

Job	Percent Men
112. Electrical Drafters	78.2%
113. Electronic Drafters	78.2%
114. Mechanical Drafters	78.2%
115. Printing Machine Operators	77.8%
116. Fire Inspectors	77.7%
117. Fire Investigators	77.7%
118. Fish and Game Wardens	77.7%
119. Security Guards	77.0%
120. Chefs and Head Cooks	76.1%
121. Farmers and Ranchers	75.0%
122. Ambulance Drivers and Attendants, Except Emergency Medical Technicians	72.0%
123. Correctional Officers and Jailers	71.8%
124. Computer Support Specialists	71.1%

Best 25 Apprenticeable Jobs Overall with a High Percentage of Men

Job	Percent Men	Annual Earnings	Percent Growth	Annual Openings
1. Construction and Building Inspectors	91.2%	$48,330	18.2%	12,606
2. Computer Support Specialists	71.1%	$42,400	12.9%	97,334
3. Police Patrol Officers	87.2%	$49,630	10.8%	37,842
4. Correctional Officers and Jailers	71.8%	$36,970	16.9%	56,579
5. Pipe Fitters and Steamfitters	98.2%	$44,090	10.6%	68,643
6. Plumbers	98.2%	$44,090	10.6%	68,643
7. Forest Fire Fighters	96.5%	$43,170	12.1%	18,887
8. Municipal Fire Fighters	96.5%	$43,170	12.1%	18,887
9. Mates—Ship, Boat, and Barge	85.2%	$57,210	17.9%	2,665
10. Pilots, Ship	85.2%	$57,210	17.9%	2,665
11. Automotive Master Mechanics	98.4%	$34,170	14.3%	97,350
12. Automotive Specialty Technicians	98.4%	$34,170	14.3%	97,350
13. Aircraft Mechanics and Service Technicians	94.7%	$49,010	10.6%	9,708
14. Construction Carpenters	97.6%	$37,660	10.3%	223,225
15. Municipal Fire Fighting and Prevention Supervisors	92.8%	$65,040	11.5%	3,771
16. Rough Carpenters	97.6%	$37,660	10.3%	223,225

Best 25 Apprenticeable Jobs Overall with a High Percentage of Men

Job	Percent Men	Annual Earnings	Percent Growth	Annual Openings
17. Bus and Truck Mechanics and Diesel Engine Specialists	99.1%	$38,640	11.5%	25,428
18. Electricians	98.1%	$44,780	7.4%	79,083
19. Mobile Heavy Equipment Mechanics, Except Engines	98.6%	$41,450	12.3%	11,037
20. Truck Drivers, Heavy and Tractor-Trailer	94.8%	$36,220	10.4%	279,032
21. Tile and Marble Setters	97.6%	$38,720	15.4%	9,066
22. Landscaping and Groundskeeping Workers	93.8%	$22,240	18.1%	307,138
23. Transportation Vehicle, Equipment, and Systems Inspectors, Except Aviation	85.2%	$51,440	16.4%	2,122
24. Roofers	98.9%	$33,240	14.3%	38,398
25. Brickmasons and Blockmasons	98.4%	$44,070	9.7%	17,569

Job 3 shares 37,842 openings with another job not included in this list. Jobs 5 and 6 share 68,643 openings. Jobs 7 and 8 share 18,887 openings. Jobs 9 and 10 share 2,665 openings with each other and with another job not included in this list. Jobs 11 and 12 share 97,350 openings. Jobs 14 and 16 share 223,225 openings. Job 15 shares 3,771 openings with another job not included in this list. Job 23 shares 2,122 openings with two other jobs not included in this list.

Best Apprenticeable Jobs Based on Personality Types

Several popular career assessment inventories organize jobs into groupings based on personality types. The most-used system is one that presents six personality types: Realistic, Investigative, Artistic, Social, Enterprising, and Conventional. This system is used in the *Self-Directed Search (SDS)*, developed by John Holland, and many other inventories.

Here are brief descriptions of the kinds of jobs that suit each of the six personality types:

※ **Realistic.** These occupations frequently involve work activities that include practical, hands-on problems and solutions. They often deal with plants; animals; and real-world materials such as wood, tools, and machinery. Many of the occupations require working outside and don't involve a lot of paperwork or working closely with others.

※ **Investigative.** These occupations frequently involve working with ideas and require an extensive amount of thinking. They can involve searching for facts and figuring out problems mentally. Note that only four of the best 200 apprenticeable jobs are associated with this personality type. A college education is usually needed to acquire the research skills required for investigative work.

※ **Artistic.** These occupations frequently involve working with forms, designs, and patterns. They often require self-expression, and the work can be done without following a clear set of rules.

⊛ **Social.** These occupations frequently involve working with, communicating with, and teaching people and often involve helping or providing service to others.

⊛ **Enterprising.** These occupations frequently involve starting up and carrying out projects and can involve leading people and making many decisions. They sometimes require risk taking and often deal with business.

⊛ **Conventional.** These occupations frequently involve following set procedures and routines and can include working with data and details more than with ideas. Usually there is a clear line of authority to follow.

If you have used one of the career exploration systems based on these six personality types, the following lists may help. Even if you have not, you may find the concept of personality types—and the jobs that are related to them—helpful to you. We've broken down the list of 200 top apprenticeable jobs into the six personality types and ranked the jobs within each grouping based on their total combined scores for earnings, growth, and annual openings. Each job is listed in its primary personality type, but you should be aware that most also are linked to one or two secondary personality types. Consider reviewing the jobs for more than one personality type so you don't overlook possible jobs that would interest you.

Best Apprenticeable Jobs for People with a Realistic Personality Type

Job	Annual Earnings	Percent Growth	Annual Openings
1. Construction and Building Inspectors	$48,330	18.2%	12,606
2. Radiologic Technologists	$50,260	15.1%	12,836
3. Computer Support Specialists	$42,400	12.9%	97,334
4. Police Patrol Officers	$49,630	10.8%	37,842
5. Correctional Officers and Jailers	$36,970	16.9%	56,579
6. Pipe Fitters and Steamfitters	$44,090	10.6%	68,643
7. Plumbers	$44,090	10.6%	68,643
8. Surgical Technologists	$37,540	24.5%	15,365
9. Forest Fire Fighters	$43,170	12.1%	18,887
10. Municipal Fire Fighters	$43,170	12.1%	18,887
11. Automotive Master Mechanics	$34,170	14.3%	97,350
12. Automotive Specialty Technicians	$34,170	14.3%	97,350
13. Construction Carpenters	$37,660	10.3%	223,225
14. Rough Carpenters	$37,660	10.3%	223,225
15. Pilots, Ship	$57,210	17.9%	2,665
16. Bus and Truck Mechanics and Diesel Engine Specialists	$38,640	11.5%	25,428
17. Electricians	$44,780	7.4%	79,083
18. Truck Drivers, Heavy and Tractor-Trailer	$36,220	10.4%	279,032
19. Aircraft Mechanics and Service Technicians	$49,010	10.6%	9,708
20. Roofers	$33,240	14.3%	38,398

Best Apprenticeable Jobs for People with a Realistic Personality Type

Job	Annual Earnings	Percent Growth	Annual Openings
21. Tile and Marble Setters	$38,720	15.4%	9,066
22. Mobile Heavy Equipment Mechanics, Except Engines	$41,450	12.3%	11,037
23. Automotive Body and Related Repairers	$35,690	11.6%	37,469
24. Brickmasons and Blockmasons	$44,070	9.7%	17,569
25. Aircraft Structure, Surfaces, Rigging, and Systems Assemblers	$45,420	12.8%	6,550
26. Landscaping and Groundskeeping Workers	$22,240	18.1%	307,138
27. Transportation Vehicle, Equipment, and Systems Inspectors, Except Aviation	$51,440	16.4%	2,122
28. Industrial Machinery Mechanics	$42,350	9.0%	23,361
29. Painters, Construction and Maintenance	$32,080	11.8%	101,140
30. Security Guards	$22,570	16.9%	222,085
31. Operating Engineers and Other Construction Equipment Operators	$38,130	8.4%	55,468
32. Water and Liquid Waste Treatment Plant and System Operators	$37,090	13.8%	9,575
33. Heating and Air Conditioning Mechanics and Installers	$38,360	8.7%	29,719
34. Refrigeration Mechanics and Installers	$38,360	8.7%	29,719
35. Boilermakers	$50,700	14.0%	2,333
36. Cement Masons and Concrete Finishers	$33,840	11.4%	34,625
37. Medical and Clinical Laboratory Technicians	$34,270	15.0%	10,866
38. Surveying Technicians	$33,640	19.4%	8,299
39. Audio and Video Equipment Technicians	$36,050	24.2%	4,681
40. Electrical Engineering Technicians	$52,140	3.6%	12,583
41. Electronics Engineering Technicians	$52,140	3.6%	12,583
42. Maintenance and Repair Workers, General	$32,570	10.1%	165,502
43. Sheet Metal Workers	$39,210	6.7%	31,677
44. Telecommunications Equipment Installers and Repairers, Except Line Installers	$54,070	2.5%	13,541
45. Telecommunications Line Installers and Repairers	$47,220	4.6%	14,719
46. Medical Equipment Repairers	$40,320	21.7%	2,351
47. Construction Laborers	$27,310	10.9%	257,407
48. Civil Drafters	$43,310	6.1%	16,238
49. Electrical Power-Line Installers and Repairers	$52,570	7.2%	6,401
50. Sailors and Marine Oilers	$32,570	15.7%	8,600
51. Elevator Installers and Repairers	$68,000	8.8%	2,850
52. Drywall and Ceiling Tile Installers	$36,520	7.3%	30,945
53. Cooks, Restaurant	$21,220	11.5%	238,542

(continued)

(continued)

Best Apprenticeable Jobs for People with a Realistic Personality Type

Job	Annual Earnings	Percent Growth	Annual Openings
54. Motorboat Mechanics	$34,210	19.0%	4,326
55. Mechanical Drafters	$44,740	5.2%	10,902
56. Electrical and Electronics Repairers, Commercial and Industrial Equipment	$47,110	6.8%	6,607
57. Helpers—Installation, Maintenance, and Repair Workers	$22,920	11.8%	52,058
58. Camera Operators, Television, Video, and Motion Picture	$41,850	11.5%	3,496
59. Reinforcing Iron and Rebar Workers	$37,890	11.5%	4,502
60. Cooks, Institution and Cafeteria	$21,340	10.8%	111,898
61. Tapers	$42,050	7.1%	9,026
62. Glaziers	$35,230	11.9%	6,416
63. Locksmiths and Safe Repairers	$33,230	22.1%	3,545
64. Aerospace Engineering and Operations Technicians	$54,930	10.4%	707
65. Animal Trainers	$26,190	22.7%	6,713
66. Computer, Automated Teller, and Office Machine Repairers	$37,100	3.0%	22,330
67. Electrical Drafters	$49,250	4.1%	4,786
68. Helpers—Brickmasons, Blockmasons, Stonemasons, and Tile and Marble Setters	$26,260	11.0%	22,500
69. Geological Sample Test Technicians	$50,950	8.6%	1,895
70. Slaughterers and Meat Packers	$22,500	12.7%	15,511
71. Mechanical Engineering Technicians	$47,280	6.4%	3,710
72. Locomotive Engineers	$57,520	2.9%	3,548
73. Millwrights	$46,090	5.8%	4,758
74. Welders, Cutters, and Welder Fitters	$32,270	5.1%	61,125
75. Embalmers	$36,800	14.3%	1,660
76. Medical Equipment Preparers	$27,040	14.2%	8,363
77. Pesticide Handlers, Sprayers, and Applicators, Vegetation	$28,560	14.0%	7,443
78. Structural Iron and Steel Workers	$42,130	6.0%	6,969
79. Pest Control Workers	$29,030	15.5%	6,006
80. Automotive Glass Installers and Repairers	$31,470	18.7%	3,457
81. Food Batchmakers	$23,730	10.9%	15,704
82. Nuclear Monitoring Technicians	$66,140	6.7%	1,021
83. Bakers	$22,590	10.0%	31,442
84. Sound Engineering Technicians	$46,550	9.1%	1,194
85. Tree Trimmers and Pruners	$29,800	11.1%	9,621
86. Insulation Workers, Mechanical	$36,570	8.6%	5,787
87. Machinists	$35,230	–3.1%	39,505
88. Recreational Vehicle Service Technicians	$31,760	18.2%	2,442

Best Apprenticeable Jobs for People with a Realistic Personality Type

Job	Annual Earnings	Percent Growth	Annual Openings
89. Avionics Technicians	$48,100	8.1%	1,193
90. Farmers and Ranchers	$33,360	–8.5%	129,552
91. Chemical Plant and System Operators	$50,860	–15.3%	5,620
92. Petroleum Pump System Operators, Refinery Operators, and Gaugers	$53,010	–13.4%	4,477
93. Power Plant Operators	$56,640	2.7%	1,796
94. Ambulance Drivers and Attendants, Except Emergency Medical Technicians	$21,140	21.7%	3,703
95. Stonemasons	$36,950	10.0%	2,657
96. Control and Valve Installers and Repairers, Except Mechanical Door	$46,140	0.3%	3,855
97. Plasterers and Stucco Masons	$36,430	8.1%	4,509
98. Broadcast Technicians	$32,230	12.1%	2,955
99. Excavating and Loading Machine and Dragline Operators	$34,050	8.3%	6,562
100. Maintenance Workers, Machinery	$35,590	–1.1%	15,055
101. Team Assemblers	$24,630	0.1%	264,135
102. Mechanical Door Repairers	$31,880	14.9%	1,706
103. Motorcycle Mechanics	$30,300	12.5%	3,564
104. Rail Car Repairers	$44,970	5.1%	1,989
105. Stationary Engineers and Boiler Operators	$47,640	3.4%	1,892
106. Tank Car, Truck, and Ship Loaders	$33,140	9.2%	4,519
107. Tool and Die Makers	$45,090	–9.6%	5,286
108. Electrical and Electronics Repairers, Powerhouse, Substation, and Relay	$58,970	–4.7%	1,591
109. Painters, Transportation Equipment	$36,000	8.4%	3,268
110. Terrazzo Workers and Finishers	$34,390	10.9%	1,052
111. Insulation Workers, Floor, Ceiling, and Wall	$31,280	8.4%	6,580
112. Electrical and Electronics Installers and Repairers, Transportation Equipment	$43,940	4.3%	1,663
113. Structural Metal Fabricators and Fitters	$31,030	–0.2%	20,746
114. Electro-Mechanical Technicians	$46,610	2.6%	1,142
115. Multiple Machine Tool Setters, Operators, and Tenders, Metal and Plastic	$30,390	0.3%	15,709
116. Paving, Surfacing, and Tamping Equipment Operators	$32,360	9.0%	3,471
117. Woodworking Machine Setters, Operators, and Tenders, Except Sawing	$24,190	6.4%	11,860
118. Carpet Installers	$36,040	–1.2%	6,692

(continued)

(continued)

Best Apprenticeable Jobs for People with a Realistic Personality Type

Job	Annual Earnings	Percent Growth	Annual Openings
119. Computer-Controlled Machine Tool Operators, Metal and Plastic	$32,550	–3.0%	12,997
120. Crane and Tower Operators	$40,260	2.8%	2,626
121. Earth Drillers, Except Oil and Gas	$36,310	6.5%	2,619
122. Fish and Game Wardens	$47,830	–0.2%	576
123. Butchers and Meat Cutters	$27,480	1.9%	14,503
124. Mixing and Blending Machine Setters, Operators, and Tenders	$30,340	–5.1%	18,661
125. Prepress Technicians and Workers	$33,990	–21.1%	10,002
126. Fence Erectors	$26,720	10.6%	2,812
127. Mine Cutting and Channeling Machine Operators	$39,930	3.8%	923
128. Welding, Soldering, and Brazing Machine Setters, Operators, and Tenders	$30,980	3.0%	7,707
129. Cabinetmakers and Bench Carpenters	$27,970	2.8%	9,780
130. Fiberglass Laminators and Fabricators	$26,630	6.2%	7,315
131. Rotary Drill Operators, Oil and Gas	$43,480	–5.4%	2,145
132. Printing Machine Operators	$31,490	–5.7%	12,274
133. Chemical Equipment Operators and Tenders	$44,050	–3.9%	1,469
134. Medical Appliance Technicians	$32,640	9.4%	895
135. Dental Laboratory Technicians	$33,480	3.7%	3,479
136. Home Appliance Repairers	$33,560	1.5%	4,243
137. Gem and Diamond Workers	$31,200	–2.2%	7,375
138. Jewelers	$31,200	–2.2%	7,375
139. Precious Metal Workers	$31,200	–2.2%	7,375

Job 2 shares 12,836 openings with another job not included in this list. Job 4 shares 37,842 openings with another job not included in this list. Jobs 6 and 7 share 68,643 openings. Jobs 9 and 10 share 18,887 openings. Jobs 11 and 12 share 97,350 openings. Jobs 13 and 14 share 223,225 openings. Job 15 shares 2,665 openings with two other jobs not included in this list. Job 27 shares 2,122 openings with two other jobs not included in this list. Jobs 33 and 34 share 29,719 openings. Job 38 shares 8,299 openings with another job not included in this list. Jobs 40 and 41 share 12,583 openings. Job 48 shares 16,238 openings with another job not included in this list. Job 67 shares 4,786 openings with another job not included in this list. Job 69 shares 1,895 openings with another job not included in this list. Job 72 shares 3,548 openings with two other jobs not included in this list. Job 74 shares 61,125 openings with another job not included in this list. Jobs 137, 138, and 139 share 7,375 openings.

Best Apprenticeable Jobs for People with an Investigative Personality Type

Job	Annual Earnings	Percent Growth	Annual Openings
1. Environmental Science and Protection Technicians, Including Health	$39,370	28.0%	8,404
2. Fire Investigators	$50,830	11.0%	644
3. Industrial Engineering Technicians	$47,490	9.9%	6,172
4. Chemical Technicians	$40,740	5.8%	4,010

Job 2 shares 644 openings with another job not included in this list.

Best Apprenticeable Jobs for People with an Artistic Personality Type

Job	Annual Earnings	Percent Growth	Annual Openings
1. Interior Designers	$43,970	19.5%	8,434
2. Architectural Drafters	$43,310	6.1%	16,238
3. Hairdressers, Hairstylists, and Cosmetologists	$22,210	12.4%	73,030
4. Photographers	$27,720	10.3%	16,100
5. Merchandise Displayers and Window Trimmers	$24,830	10.7%	9,103
6. Fashion Designers	$62,810	5.0%	1,968
7. Fine Artists, Including Painters, Sculptors, and Illustrators	$42,070	9.9%	3,830
8. Desktop Publishers	$35,510	1.0%	6,420

Job 2 shares 16,238 openings with another job not included in this list.

Best Apprenticeable Jobs for People with a Social Personality Type

Job	Annual Earnings	Percent Growth	Annual Openings
1. Medical Assistants	$27,430	35.4%	92,977
2. Emergency Medical Technicians and Paramedics	$28,400	19.2%	19,513
3. Nursing Aides, Orderlies, and Attendants	$23,160	18.2%	321,036
4. Licensed Practical and Licensed Vocational Nurses	$37,940	14.0%	70,610
5. Equal Opportunity Representatives and Officers	$48,400	4.9%	15,841
6. Emergency Management Specialists	$48,380	12.3%	1,538
7. Residential Advisors	$23,050	18.5%	8,053
8. Teacher Assistants	$21,580	10.4%	193,986

Job 5 shares 15,841 openings with four other jobs not included in this list.

Best Apprenticeable Jobs for People with an Enterprising Personality Type

Job	Annual Earnings	Percent Growth	Annual Openings
1. Private Detectives and Investigators	$37,640	18.2%	7,329
2. Funeral Directors	$50,370	12.5%	3,939
3. Mates—Ship, Boat, and Barge	$57,210	17.9%	2,665
4. First-Line Supervisors/Managers of Housekeeping and Janitorial Workers	$32,850	12.7%	30,613
5. Food Service Managers	$44,570	5.0%	59,302
6. Municipal Fire Fighting and Prevention Supervisors	$65,040	11.5%	3,771
7. Air Traffic Controllers	$112,930	10.2%	1,213
8. Industrial Production Managers	$80,560	–5.9%	14,889
9. First-Line Supervisors/Managers of Retail Sales Workers	$34,470	4.2%	221,241
10. Chefs and Head Cooks	$37,160	7.6%	9,401
11. Airfield Operations Specialists	$38,320	11.8%	245
12. Parts Salespersons	$28,130	–2.2%	52,414
13. Opticians, Dispensing	$31,430	8.7%	3,143

Job 3 shares 2,665 openings with two other jobs not included in this list. Job 6 shares 3,771 openings with another job not included in this list.

Best Apprenticeable Jobs for People with a Conventional Personality Type

Job	Annual Earnings	Percent Growth	Annual Openings
1. Paralegals and Legal Assistants	$44,990	22.2%	22,756
2. Bookkeeping, Accounting, and Auditing Clerks	$31,560	12.5%	286,854
3. Social and Human Service Assistants	$26,630	33.6%	80,142
4. Legal Secretaries	$38,810	11.7%	38,682
5. Dental Assistants	$31,550	29.2%	29,482
6. Pharmacy Technicians	$26,720	32.0%	54,453
7. Production, Planning, and Expediting Clerks	$39,690	4.2%	52,735
8. Medical Secretaries	$28,950	16.7%	60,659
9. Medical Records and Health Information Technicians	$29,290	17.8%	39,048
10. Office Clerks, General	$24,460	12.6%	765,803
11. Cargo and Freight Agents	$37,060	16.5%	9,967
12. Purchasing Agents, Except Wholesale, Retail, and Farm Products	$52,460	0.1%	22,349
13. Tellers	$22,920	13.5%	146,077

Best Apprenticeable Jobs for People with a Conventional Personality Type

Job	Annual Earnings	Percent Growth	Annual Openings
14. Human Resources Assistants, Except Payroll and Timekeeping	$34,970	11.3%	18,647
15. Mapping Technicians	$33,640	19.4%	8,299
16. Government Property Inspectors and Investigators	$48,400	4.9%	15,841
17. Fire Inspectors	$50,830	11.0%	644
18. Police, Fire, and Ambulance Dispatchers	$32,660	13.6%	17,628
19. Electronic Drafters	$49,250	4.1%	4,786
20. Medical Transcriptionists	$31,250	13.5%	18,080
21. Secretaries, Except Legal, Medical, and Executive	$28,220	1.2%	239,630
22. Dispatchers, Except Police, Fire, and Ambulance	$33,140	1.5%	29,793
23. Payroll and Timekeeping Clerks	$33,810	3.1%	18,544
24. Inspectors, Testers, Sorters, Samplers, and Weighers	$30,310	−7.0%	75,361
25. Postal Service Clerks	$45,050	1.2%	3,703
26. Data Entry Keyers	$25,370	−4.7%	79,166
27. Word Processors and Typists	$30,380	−11.6%	32,279
28. Computer Operators	$34,610	−24.7%	17,842

Job 15 shares 8,299 openings with another job not included in this list. Job 16 shares 15,841 openings with four other jobs not included in this list. Job 17 shares 644 openings with another job not included in this list. Job 19 shares 4,786 openings with another job not included in this list.

Best Apprenticeable Jobs Based on Interests

This group of lists organizes the 200 best apprenticeable jobs into 16 interest areas (also called career clusters). You can use these lists to identify jobs quickly based on your interests. Within each interest area, jobs are listed in order of each combined score for earnings, job growth, and job openings, from highest to lowest.

Find the interest area or areas that appeal to you most and review the jobs in those areas. When you find jobs you want to explore in more detail, look up their descriptions in Part IV. You can also review interest areas in which you've had past experience, education, or training to see whether other jobs in those areas would meet your current requirements.

Note: The 16 interest areas used in these lists are those used in the *New Guide for Occupational Exploration*, Fourth Edition, published by JIST. The original GOE was developed by the U.S. Department of Labor as an intuitive way to assist in career exploration. The 16 interest areas used in the *New GOE* are based on the 16 career clusters that the U.S.

Department of Education's Office of Vocational and Adult Education developed around 1999 and that many states now use to organize their career-oriented programs and career information.

Descriptions for the 16 Interest Areas

Brief descriptions follow for the 16 interest areas we use in the lists. The descriptions are from the *New Guide for Occupational Exploration,* Fourth Edition. Some of them refer to jobs (as examples) that aren't included in this book.

Also note that in most cases we put each of the 200 best jobs into only one interest area list, the one its related O*NET job fits into best. However, many jobs could be included in more than one list, so consider reviewing a variety of these interest areas to find jobs that you might otherwise overlook.

For a detailed outline that shows the work groups classified into each interest area, see Appendix E.

❋ **Agriculture and Natural Resources:** *An interest in working with plants, animals, forests, or mineral resources for agriculture, horticulture, conservation, extraction, and other purposes.* You can satisfy this interest by working in farming, landscaping, forestry, fishing, mining, and related fields. You may like doing physical work outdoors, such as on a farm or ranch, in a forest, or on a drilling rig. If you have a scientific curiosity, you could study plants and animals or analyze biological or rock samples in a lab. If you have management ability, you could own, operate, or manage a fish hatchery, a landscaping business, or a greenhouse.

❋ **Architecture and Construction:** *An interest in designing, assembling, and maintaining components of buildings and other structures.* You may want to be part of the team of architects, drafters, and others who design buildings and render plans. If construction interests you, you might find fulfillment in the many building projects being undertaken at all times. If you like to organize and plan, you can find careers in managing these projects. Or you can play a more direct role in putting up and finishing buildings by doing jobs such as plumbing, carpentry, masonry, painting, or roofing, either as a skilled craftsworker or as a helper. You can prepare the building site by operating heavy equipment or installing, maintaining, and repairing vital building equipment and systems such as electricity and heating.

❋ **Arts and Communication:** *An interest in creatively expressing feelings or ideas, in communicating news or information, or in performing.* You can satisfy this interest in creative, verbal, or performing activities. For example, if you enjoy literature, perhaps writing or editing would appeal to you. Journalism and public relations are other fields for people who like to use their writing or speaking skills. Do you prefer to work in the performing arts? If so, you could direct or perform in drama, music, or dance. If you especially enjoy the visual arts, you could create paintings, sculpture, or ceramics or design products or visual displays. A flair for technology might lead you to specialize in photography, broadcast production, or dispatching.

❋ **Business and Administration:** *An interest in making a business organization or function run smoothly.* You can satisfy this interest by working in a position of leadership or by specializing in a function that contributes to the overall effort in a business, a nonprofit organization, or a government agency. If you especially enjoy working with people, you may find fulfillment from working in human resources. An interest in numbers may lead you to consider accounting, finance, budgeting, billing, or financial record-keeping. A job as an administrative assistant may interest you if you like a variety of tasks in a busy environment. If you are good with details and word processing, you may enjoy a job as a secretary or data-entry clerk. Or perhaps you would do well as the manager of a business.

❋ **Education and Training:** *An interest in helping people learn.* You can satisfy this interest by teaching students, who may be preschoolers, retirees, or any age in between. You may specialize in a particular academic field or work with learners of a particular age, with a particular interest, or with a particular learning problem. Working in a library or museum may give you an opportunity to expand people's understanding of the world.

❋ **Finance and Insurance:** *An interest in helping businesses and people be assured of a financially secure future.* You can satisfy this interest by working in a financial or insurance business in a leadership or support role. If you like gathering and analyzing information, you may find fulfillment as an insurance adjuster or financial analyst. Or you may deal with information at the clerical level as a banking or insurance clerk or in person-to-person situations providing customer service. Another way to interact with people is to sell financial or insurance services that will meet their needs.

❋ **Government and Public Administration:** *An interest in helping a government agency serve the needs of the public.* You can satisfy this interest by working in a position of leadership or by specializing in a function that contributes to the role of government. You may help protect the public by working as an inspector or examiner to enforce standards. If you enjoy using clerical skills, you could work as a clerk in a law court or government office. Or perhaps you prefer the top-down perspective of a government executive or urban planner.

❋ **Health Science:** *An interest in helping people and animals be healthy.* You can satisfy this interest by working on a health-care team as a doctor, therapist, or nurse. You might specialize in one of the many different parts of the body (such as the teeth or eyes) or in one of the many different types of care. Or you may want to be a generalist who deals with the whole patient. If you like technology, you might find satisfaction working with X rays or new diagnostic methods. You might work with relatively healthy people, helping them to eat better. If you enjoy working with animals, you might care for them and keep them healthy.

❋ **Hospitality, Tourism, and Recreation:** *An interest in catering to the personal wishes and needs of others so that they can enjoy a clean environment, good food and drink, comfortable lodging away from home, and recreation.* You can satisfy this interest by providing services for the convenience, care, and pampering of others in hotels, restaurants, airplanes, beauty parlors, and so on. You may want to use your love of cooking as a chef. If you like working with people, you may want to provide personal services by being a travel guide, a flight attendant, a concierge, a hairdresser, or a waiter. You may want to work in cleaning and building services if you like a clean environment. If you enjoy sports or games, you could work for an athletic team or casino.

✱ **Human Service:** *An interest in improving people's social, mental, emotional, or spiritual well-being.* You can satisfy this interest as a counselor, social worker, or religious worker who helps people sort out their complicated lives or solve personal problems. You may work as a caretaker for very young people or the elderly. Or you may interview people to help identify the social services they need.

✱ **Information Technology:** *An interest in designing, developing, managing, and supporting information systems.* You can satisfy this interest by working with hardware, software, multimedia, or integrated systems. If you like to use your organizational skills, you might work as a systems or database administrator. Or you can solve complex problems as a software engineer or systems analyst. If you enjoy getting your hands on hardware, you might find work servicing computers, peripherals, and information-intense machines such as cash registers and ATMs.

✱ **Law and Public Safety:** *An interest in upholding people's rights or in protecting people and property by using authority, inspecting, or investigating.* You can satisfy this interest by working in law, law enforcement, fire fighting, the military, and related fields. For example, if you enjoy mental challenge and intrigue, you could investigate crimes or fires for a living. If you enjoy working with verbal skills and research skills, you may want to defend citizens in court or research deeds, wills, and other legal documents. If you want to help people in critical situations, you may want to fight fires, work as a police officer, or become a paramedic. Or, if you want more routine work in public safety, perhaps a job in guarding, patrolling, or inspecting would appeal to you. If you have management ability, you could seek a leadership position in law enforcement and the protective services. Work in the military gives you a chance to use technical and leadership skills while serving your country.

✱ **Manufacturing:** *An interest in processing materials into intermediate or final products or maintaining and repairing products by using machines or hand tools.* You can satisfy this interest by working in one of many industries that mass-produce goods or by working for a utility that distributes electrical power or other resources. You might enjoy manual work, using your hands or hand tools in highly skilled jobs such as assembling engines or electronic equipment. If you enjoy making machines run efficiently or fixing them when they break down, you could seek a job installing or repairing such devices as copiers, aircraft engines, cars, or watches. Perhaps you prefer to set up or operate machines used to manufacture products made of food, glass, or paper. You could enjoy cutting and grinding metal and plastic parts to desired shapes and measurements. Or you may want to operate equipment in systems that provide water and process wastewater. You may like inspecting, sorting, counting, or weighing products. Another option is to work with your hands and machinery to move boxes and freight in a warehouse. If leadership appeals to you, you could manage people engaged in production and repair.

❋ **Retail and Wholesale Sales and Service:** *An interest in bringing others to a particular point of view by personal persuasion and by sales and promotional techniques.* You can satisfy this interest in various jobs that involve persuasion and selling. If you like using knowledge of science, you may enjoy selling pharmaceutical, medical, or electronic products or services. Real estate offers several kinds of sales jobs as well. If you like speaking on the phone, you could work as a telemarketer. Or you may enjoy selling apparel and other merchandise in a retail setting. If you prefer to help people, you may want a job in customer service.

❋ **Scientific Research, Engineering, and Mathematics:** *An interest in discovering, collecting, and analyzing information about the natural world; in applying scientific research findings to problems in medicine, the life sciences, human behavior, and the natural sciences; in imagining and manipulating quantitative data; and in applying technology to manufacturing, transportation, and other economic activities.* You can satisfy this interest by working with the knowledge and processes of the sciences. You may enjoy researching and developing new knowledge in mathematics, or perhaps solving problems in the physical, life, or social sciences would appeal to you. You may want to study engineering and help create new machines, processes, and structures. If you want to work with scientific equipment and procedures, you could seek a job in a research or testing laboratory.

❋ **Transportation, Distribution, and Logistics:** *An interest in operations that move people or materials.* You can satisfy this interest by managing a transportation service, by helping vehicles keep on their assigned schedules and routes, or by driving or piloting a vehicle. If you enjoy taking responsibility, perhaps managing a rail line would appeal to you. If you work well with details and can take pressure on the job, you might consider being an air traffic controller. Or would you rather get out on the highway, on the water, or up in the air? If so, you could drive a truck from state to state, be employed on a ship, or fly a crop duster over a cornfield. If you prefer to stay closer to home, you could drive a delivery van, taxi, or school bus. You can use your physical strength to load freight and arrange it so that it gets to its destination in one piece.

Best Jobs for People Interested in Agriculture and Natural Resources

Job	Annual Earnings	Percent Growth	Annual Openings
1. Environmental Science and Protection Technicians, Including Health	$39,370	28.0%	8,404
2. Landscaping and Groundskeeping Workers	$22,240	18.1%	307,138
3. Tree Trimmers and Pruners	$29,800	11.1%	9,621
4. Geological Sample Test Technicians	$50,950	8.6%	1,895
5. Excavating and Loading Machine and Dragline Operators	$34,050	8.3%	6,562
6. Pest Control Workers	$29,030	15.5%	6,006
7. Pesticide Handlers, Sprayers, and Applicators, Vegetation	$28,560	14.0%	7,443

(continued)

(continued)

Best Jobs for People Interested in Agriculture and Natural Resources

Job	Annual Earnings	Percent Growth	Annual Openings
8. Farmers and Ranchers	$33,360	–8.5%	129,552
9. Earth Drillers, Except Oil and Gas	$36,310	6.5%	2,619
10. Rotary Drill Operators, Oil and Gas	$43,480	–5.4%	2,145
11. Mine Cutting and Channeling Machine Operators	$39,930	3.8%	923

Job 4 shares 1,895 openings with another job not included in this list.

Best Jobs for People Interested in Architecture and Construction

Job	Annual Earnings	Percent Growth	Annual Openings
1. Pipe Fitters and Steamfitters	$44,090	10.6%	68,643
2. Plumbers	$44,090	10.6%	68,643
3. Construction Carpenters	$37,660	10.3%	223,225
4. Rough Carpenters	$37,660	10.3%	223,225
5. Electricians	$44,780	7.4%	79,083
6. Tile and Marble Setters	$38,720	15.4%	9,066
7. Roofers	$33,240	14.3%	38,398
8. Boilermakers	$50,700	14.0%	2,333
9. Painters, Construction and Maintenance	$32,080	11.8%	101,140
10. Brickmasons and Blockmasons	$44,070	9.7%	17,569
11. Construction Laborers	$27,310	10.9%	257,407
12. Cement Masons and Concrete Finishers	$33,840	11.4%	34,625
13. Maintenance and Repair Workers, General	$32,570	10.1%	165,502
14. Heating and Air Conditioning Mechanics and Installers	$38,360	8.7%	29,719
15. Helpers—Installation, Maintenance, and Repair Workers	$22,920	11.8%	52,058
16. Operating Engineers and Other Construction Equipment Operators	$38,130	8.4%	55,468
17. Elevator Installers and Repairers	$68,000	8.8%	2,850
18. Refrigeration Mechanics and Installers	$38,360	8.7%	29,719
19. Reinforcing Iron and Rebar Workers	$37,890	11.5%	4,502
20. Glaziers	$35,230	11.9%	6,416
21. Sheet Metal Workers	$39,210	6.7%	31,677
22. Architectural Drafters	$43,310	6.1%	16,238
23. Electrical Power-Line Installers and Repairers	$52,570	7.2%	6,401
24. Telecommunications Equipment Installers and Repairers, Except Line Installers	$54,070	2.5%	13,541

Best Jobs for People Interested in Architecture and Construction

Job	Annual Earnings	Percent Growth	Annual Openings
25. Telecommunications Line Installers and Repairers	$47,220	4.6%	14,719
26. Civil Drafters	$43,310	6.1%	16,238
27. Helpers—Brickmasons, Blockmasons, Stonemasons, and Tile and Marble Setters	$26,260	11.0%	22,500
28. Drywall and Ceiling Tile Installers	$36,520	7.3%	30,945
29. Tapers	$42,050	7.1%	9,026
30. Structural Iron and Steel Workers	$42,130	6.0%	6,969
31. Stonemasons	$36,950	10.0%	2,657
32. Insulation Workers, Mechanical	$36,570	8.6%	5,787
33. Electrical and Electronics Repairers, Powerhouse, Substation, and Relay	$58,970	–4.7%	1,591
34. Terrazzo Workers and Finishers	$34,390	10.9%	1,052
35. Fence Erectors	$26,720	10.6%	2,812
36. Plasterers and Stucco Masons	$36,430	8.1%	4,509
37. Paving, Surfacing, and Tamping Equipment Operators	$32,360	9.0%	3,471
38. Insulation Workers, Floor, Ceiling, and Wall	$31,280	8.4%	6,580
39. Crane and Tower Operators	$40,260	2.8%	2,626
40. Carpet Installers	$36,040	–1.2%	6,692

Jobs 1 and 2 share 68,643 openings. Jobs 3 and 4 share 223,225 openings. Jobs 14 and 18 share 29,719 openings. Jobs 22 and 26 share 16,238 openings.

Best Jobs for People Interested in Arts and Communication

Job	Annual Earnings	Percent Growth	Annual Openings
1. Interior Designers	$43,970	19.5%	8,434
2. Audio and Video Equipment Technicians	$36,050	24.2%	4,681
3. Police, Fire, and Ambulance Dispatchers	$32,660	13.6%	17,628
4. Camera Operators, Television, Video, and Motion Picture	$41,850	11.5%	3,496
5. Air Traffic Controllers	$112,930	10.2%	1,213
6. Fine Artists, Including Painters, Sculptors, and Illustrators	$42,070	9.9%	3,830
7. Dispatchers, Except Police, Fire, and Ambulance	$33,140	1.5%	29,793
8. Photographers	$27,720	10.3%	16,100
9. Broadcast Technicians	$32,230	12.1%	2,955
10. Fashion Designers	$62,810	5.0%	1,968
11. Merchandise Displayers and Window Trimmers	$24,830	10.7%	9,103
12. Airfield Operations Specialists	$38,320	11.8%	245
13. Sound Engineering Technicians	$46,550	9.1%	1,194

Best Jobs for People Interested in Business and Administration

Job	Annual Earnings	Percent Growth	Annual Openings
1. Bookkeeping, Accounting, and Auditing Clerks	$31,560	12.5%	286,854
2. Legal Secretaries	$38,810	11.7%	38,682
3. Medical Secretaries	$28,950	16.7%	60,659
4. Office Clerks, General	$24,460	12.6%	765,803
5. Production, Planning, and Expediting Clerks	$39,690	4.2%	52,735
6. First-Line Supervisors/Managers of Housekeeping and Janitorial Workers	$32,850	12.7%	30,613
7. Industrial Engineering Technicians	$47,490	9.9%	6,172
8. Human Resources Assistants, Except Payroll and Timekeeping	$34,970	11.3%	18,647
9. Postal Service Clerks	$45,050	1.2%	3,703
10. Secretaries, Except Legal, Medical, and Executive	$28,220	1.2%	239,630
11. Payroll and Timekeeping Clerks	$33,810	3.1%	18,544
12. Data Entry Keyers	$25,370	–4.7%	79,166
13. Word Processors and Typists	$30,380	–11.6%	32,279

Best Jobs for People Interested in Education and Training

Job	Annual Earnings	Percent Growth	Annual Openings
1. Teacher Assistants	$21,580	10.4%	193,986

Best Jobs for People Interested in Finance and Insurance

Job	Annual Earnings	Percent Growth	Annual Openings
1. Tellers	$22,920	13.5%	146,077

Best Jobs for People Interested in Government and Public Administration

Job	Annual Earnings	Percent Growth	Annual Openings
1. Transportation Vehicle, Equipment, and Systems Inspectors, Except Aviation	$51,440	16.4%	2,122
2. Construction and Building Inspectors	$48,330	18.2%	12,606
3. Equal Opportunity Representatives and Officers	$48,400	4.9%	15,841

Best Jobs for People Interested in Government and Public Administration

Job	Annual Earnings	Percent Growth	Annual Openings
4. Nuclear Monitoring Technicians	$66,140	6.7%	1,021
5. Government Property Inspectors and Investigators	$48,400	4.9%	15,841
6. Fire Inspectors	$50,830	11.0%	644
7. Fish and Game Wardens	$47,830	–0.2%	576

Job 1 shares 2,122 openings with two other jobs not included in this list. Jobs 3 and 5 share 15,841 openings with three other jobs not included in this list. Job 4 shares 1,021 openings with another job not included in this list. Job 6 shares 644 openings with another job not included in this list.

Best Jobs for People Interested in Health Science

Job	Annual Earnings	Percent Growth	Annual Openings
1. Medical Assistants	$27,430	35.4%	92,977
2. Dental Assistants	$31,550	29.2%	29,482
3. Surgical Technologists	$37,540	24.5%	15,365
4. Licensed Practical and Licensed Vocational Nurses	$37,940	14.0%	70,610
5. Pharmacy Technicians	$26,720	32.0%	54,453
6. Radiologic Technologists	$50,260	15.1%	12,836
7. Medical Records and Health Information Technicians	$29,290	17.8%	39,048
8. Nursing Aides, Orderlies, and Attendants	$23,160	18.2%	321,036
9. Medical and Clinical Laboratory Technicians	$34,270	15.0%	10,866
10. Embalmers	$36,800	14.3%	1,660
11. Medical Transcriptionists	$31,250	13.5%	18,080
12. Animal Trainers	$26,190	22.7%	6,713
13. Medical Equipment Preparers	$27,040	14.2%	8,363
14. Opticians, Dispensing	$31,430	8.7%	3,143

Job 6 shares 12,836 openings with another job not included in this list.

Best Jobs for People Interested in Hospitality, Tourism, and Recreation

Job	Annual Earnings	Percent Growth	Annual Openings
1. Hairdressers, Hairstylists, and Cosmetologists	$22,210	12.4%	73,030
2. Cooks, Restaurant	$21,220	11.5%	238,542
3. Cooks, Institution and Cafeteria	$21,340	10.8%	111,898
4. Food Service Managers	$44,570	5.0%	59,302

(continued)

(continued)

Best Jobs for People Interested in Hospitality, Tourism, and Recreation

Job	Annual Earnings	Percent Growth	Annual Openings
5. Chefs and Head Cooks	$37,160	7.6%	9,401
6. Butchers and Meat Cutters	$27,480	1.9%	14,503

Best Jobs for People Interested in Human Service

Job	Annual Earnings	Percent Growth	Annual Openings
1. Social and Human Service Assistants	$26,630	33.6%	80,142
2. Residential Advisors	$23,050	18.5%	8,053

Best Jobs for People Interested in Information Technology

Job	Annual Earnings	Percent Growth	Annual Openings
1. Computer Support Specialists	$42,400	12.9%	97,334
2. Computer, Automated Teller, and Office Machine Repairers	$37,100	3.0%	22,330
3. Computer Operators	$34,610	–24.7%	17,842

Best Jobs for People Interested in Law and Public Safety

Job	Annual Earnings	Percent Growth	Annual Openings
1. Paralegals and Legal Assistants	$44,990	22.2%	22,756
2. Correctional Officers and Jailers	$36,970	16.9%	56,579
3. Emergency Medical Technicians and Paramedics	$28,400	19.2%	19,513
4. Police Patrol Officers	$49,630	10.8%	37,842
5. Security Guards	$22,570	16.9%	222,085
6. Forest Fire Fighters	$43,170	12.1%	18,887
7. Municipal Fire Fighting and Prevention Supervisors	$65,040	11.5%	3,771
8. Private Detectives and Investigators	$37,640	18.2%	7,329
9. Emergency Management Specialists	$48,380	12.3%	1,538
10. Municipal Fire Fighters	$43,170	12.1%	18,887
11. Fire Investigators	$50,830	11.0%	644

Job 4 shares 37,842 openings with another job not included in this list. Jobs 6 and 10 share 18,887 openings. Job 7 shares 3,771 openings with another job not included in this list. Job 11 shares 644 openings with another job not included in this list.

Best Jobs for People Interested in Manufacturing

Job	Annual Earnings	Percent Growth	Annual Openings
1. Automotive Master Mechanics	$34,170	14.3%	97,350
2. Automotive Specialty Technicians	$34,170	14.3%	97,350
3. Automotive Body and Related Repairers	$35,690	11.6%	37,469
4. Bus and Truck Mechanics and Diesel Engine Specialists	$38,640	11.5%	25,428
5. Aircraft Mechanics and Service Technicians	$49,010	10.6%	9,708
6. Industrial Machinery Mechanics	$42,350	9.0%	23,361
7. Mobile Heavy Equipment Mechanics, Except Engines	$41,450	12.3%	11,037
8. Aircraft Structure, Surfaces, Rigging, and Systems Assemblers	$45,420	12.8%	6,550
9. Water and Liquid Waste Treatment Plant and System Operators	$37,090	13.8%	9,575
10. Electrical and Electronics Repairers, Commercial and Industrial Equipment	$47,110	6.8%	6,607
11. Medical Equipment Repairers	$40,320	21.7%	2,351
12. Motorboat Mechanics	$34,210	19.0%	4,326
13. Industrial Production Managers	$80,560	–5.9%	14,889
14. Welders, Cutters, and Welder Fitters	$32,270	5.1%	61,125
15. Millwrights	$46,090	5.8%	4,758
16. Locksmiths and Safe Repairers	$33,230	22.1%	3,545
17. Machinists	$35,230	–3.1%	39,505
18. Bakers	$22,590	10.0%	31,442
19. Maintenance Workers, Machinery	$35,590	–1.1%	15,055
20. Slaughterers and Meat Packers	$22,500	12.7%	15,511
21. Avionics Technicians	$48,100	8.1%	1,193
22. Food Batchmakers	$23,730	10.9%	15,704
23. Control and Valve Installers and Repairers, Except Mechanical Door	$46,140	0.3%	3,855
24. Power Plant Operators	$56,640	2.7%	1,796
25. Automotive Glass Installers and Repairers	$31,470	18.7%	3,457
26. Painters, Transportation Equipment	$36,000	8.4%	3,268
27. Stationary Engineers and Boiler Operators	$47,640	3.4%	1,892
28. Rail Car Repairers	$44,970	5.1%	1,989
29. Recreational Vehicle Service Technicians	$31,760	18.2%	2,442
30. Tank Car, Truck, and Ship Loaders	$33,140	9.2%	4,519
31. Chemical Plant and System Operators	$50,860	–15.3%	5,620
32. Team Assemblers	$24,630	0.1%	264,135
33. Desktop Publishers	$35,510	1.0%	6,420
34. Mechanical Door Repairers	$31,880	14.9%	1,706

(continued)

(continued)

Best Jobs for People Interested in Manufacturing

Job	Annual Earnings	Percent Growth	Annual Openings
35. Petroleum Pump System Operators, Refinery Operators, and Gaugers	$53,010	−13.4%	4,477
36. Structural Metal Fabricators and Fitters	$31,030	−0.2%	20,746
37. Electrical and Electronics Installers and Repairers, Transportation Equipment	$43,940	4.3%	1,663
38. Multiple Machine Tool Setters, Operators, and Tenders, Metal and Plastic	$30,390	0.3%	15,709
39. Woodworking Machine Setters, Operators, and Tenders, Except Sawing	$24,190	6.4%	11,860
40. Computer-Controlled Machine Tool Operators, Metal and Plastic	$32,550	−3.0%	12,997
41. Tool and Die Makers	$45,090	−9.6%	5,286
42. Motorcycle Mechanics	$30,300	12.5%	3,564
43. Inspectors, Testers, Sorters, Samplers, and Weighers	$30,310	−7.0%	75,361
44. Welding, Soldering, and Brazing Machine Setters, Operators, and Tenders	$30,980	3.0%	7,707
45. Dental Laboratory Technicians	$33,480	3.7%	3,479
46. Home Appliance Repairers	$33,560	1.5%	4,243
47. Cabinetmakers and Bench Carpenters	$27,970	2.8%	9,780
48. Fiberglass Laminators and Fabricators	$26,630	6.2%	7,315
49. Prepress Technicians and Workers	$33,990	−21.1%	10,002
50. Mixing and Blending Machine Setters, Operators, and Tenders	$30,340	−5.1%	18,661
51. Printing Machine Operators	$31,490	−5.7%	12,274
52. Medical Appliance Technicians	$32,640	9.4%	895
53. Gem and Diamond Workers	$31,200	−2.2%	7,375
54. Jewelers	$31,200	−2.2%	7,375
55. Precious Metal Workers	$31,200	−2.2%	7,375
56. Chemical Equipment Operators and Tenders	$44,050	−3.9%	1,469

Jobs 1 and 2 share 97,350 openings. Job 14 shares 61,125 openings with another job not included in this list. Jobs 53, 54, and 55 share 7,375 openings.

Best Jobs for People Interested in Retail and Wholesale Sales and Service

Job	Annual Earnings	Percent Growth	Annual Openings
1. First-Line Supervisors/Managers of Retail Sales Workers	$34,470	4.2%	221,241
2. Funeral Directors	$50,370	12.5%	3,939
3. Purchasing Agents, Except Wholesale, Retail, and Farm Products	$52,460	0.1%	22,349
4. Parts Salespersons	$28,130	–2.2%	52,414

Best Jobs for People Interested in Scientific Research, Engineering, and Mathematics

Job	Annual Earnings	Percent Growth	Annual Openings
1. Electrical Engineering Technicians	$52,140	3.6%	12,583
2. Electronics Engineering Technicians	$52,140	3.6%	12,583
3. Aerospace Engineering and Operations Technicians	$54,930	10.4%	707
4. Mapping Technicians	$33,640	19.4%	8,299
5. Surveying Technicians	$33,640	19.4%	8,299
6. Electrical Drafters	$49,250	4.1%	4,786
7. Electronic Drafters	$49,250	4.1%	4,786
8. Mechanical Drafters	$44,740	5.2%	10,902
9. Mechanical Engineering Technicians	$47,280	6.4%	3,710
10. Chemical Technicians	$40,740	5.8%	4,010
11. Electro-Mechanical Technicians	$46,610	2.6%	1,142

Jobs 1 and 2 share 12,583 openings. Jobs 4 and 5 share 8,299 openings. Jobs 6 and 7 share 4,786 openings.

Best Jobs for People Interested in Transportation, Distribution, and Logistics

Job	Annual Earnings	Percent Growth	Annual Openings
1. Cargo and Freight Agents	$37,060	16.5%	9,967
2. Mates—Ship, Boat, and Barge	$57,210	17.9%	2,665
3. Pilots, Ship	$57,210	17.9%	2,665
4. Ambulance Drivers and Attendants, Except Emergency Medical Technicians	$21,140	21.7%	3,703

(continued)

(continued)

Best Jobs for People Interested in Transportation, Distribution, and Logistics			
Job	Annual Earnings	Percent Growth	Annual Openings
5. Locomotive Engineers	$57,520	2.9%	3,548
6. Sailors and Marine Oilers	$32,570	15.7%	8,600
7. Truck Drivers, Heavy and Tractor-Trailer	$36,220	10.4%	279,032

Jobs 2 and 3 share 2,665 openings with each other and with another job not included in this list. Job 5 shares 3,548 openings with two other jobs not included in this list.

Best Apprenticeable Jobs Based on Number of Years Required

The lists that follow organize the 200 apprenticeable jobs that met the criteria for this book according to how many years are required to reach journey worker status. To create the lists, we considered one year equivalent to 2,000 hours of on-the-job learning and we rounded the number of years down to the nearest whole year. For example, the apprenticeship for Cargo and Freight Agents requires 3,000 hours, or 1.5 years, which rounds down to 1 year, so this job appears in the list of "Best Jobs with Apprenticeships that Take as Little as One Year." Figures in the "Years Required" column are rounded to the nearest half-year, so you'll find the figure 1.5 there for this job.

In some cases, the number of years required is expressed as a number plus a letter, such as "0.5C" or "1H." The C stands for "competency" and the H stands for "hybrid." As Part I explains, these apprenticeships define achievement in terms of competency rather than hours spent, and the specified amount of time required is a *minimum;* an apprenticeship labeled 1H may actually require you spend two or three years acquiring competency, depending on your previous experience and your aptitude for the work.

Note that for many occupations, more than one apprenticeship program is available as an entry route, and sometimes the different programs have different durations. For example, Water and Liquid Waste Treatment Plant and System Operators may learn their skills in any of the following apprenticeship programs: Clarifying-Plant Operator (requiring one year), Wastewater-Treatment-Plant Operator (two years), Waste-Treatment Operator (two years), or Water-Treatment-Plant Operator (three years). Therefore, this job is listed below among "Best Jobs with Apprenticeships that Take as Little as One Year," and the "Years Required" column lists "1, 2, or 3."

Within each list, we order the jobs by the same three economic measures we use in the other best jobs lists: earnings, job growth, and job openings.

Best Jobs with Apprenticeships that Can Take Less than One Year

Job	Annual Earnings	Percent Growth	Annual Openings	Years Required
1. Nursing Aides, Orderlies, and Attendants	$23,160	18.2%	321,036	0C, 0.5C, 1, or 3C
2. Team Assemblers	$24,630	0.1%	264,135	0C
3. Printing Machine Operators	$31,490	–5.7%	12,274	0.5C, 2, 3, 4.5, or 6

Best Jobs with Apprenticeships that Take as Little as One Year

Job	Annual Earnings	Percent Growth	Annual Openings	Years Required
1. Computer Support Specialists	$42,400	12.9%	97,334	1
2. Construction and Building Inspectors	$48,330	18.2%	12,606	1H, 1.5H, or 3
3. Correctional Officers and Jailers	$36,970	16.9%	56,579	1
4. Licensed Practical and Licensed Vocational Nurses	$37,940	14.0%	70,610	1
5. Radiologic Technologists	$50,260	15.1%	12,836	1 or 1C
6. Automotive Specialty Technicians	$34,170	14.3%	97,350	0.5C, 1, 1C, 2, or 4
7. Forest Fire Fighters	$43,170	12.1%	18,887	1 or 2
8. Municipal Fire Fighters	$43,170	12.1%	18,887	1, 3, 3.5, or 4
9. Dental Assistants	$31,550	29.2%	29,482	1
10. Construction Carpenters	$37,660	10.3%	223,225	1, 2, 2H, 2.5H, 3, or 4
11. Legal Secretaries	$38,810	11.7%	38,682	1
12. Truck Drivers, Heavy and Tractor-Trailer	$36,220	10.4%	279,032	1 or 1.5H
13. Pharmacy Technicians	$26,720	32.0%	54,453	1 or 1C
14. Landscaping and Groundskeeping Workers	$22,240	18.1%	307,138	1, 2, or 4
15. Bus and Truck Mechanics and Diesel Engine Specialists	$38,640	11.5%	25,428	1C, 2, or 4
16. Medical Records and Health Information Technicians	$29,290	17.8%	39,048	1.5 or 2
17. Medical Secretaries	$28,950	16.7%	60,659	1
18. Aircraft Mechanics and Service Technicians	$49,010	10.6%	9,708	1C, 1.5, 2, or 4
19. Office Clerks, General	$24,460	12.6%	765,803	1
20. Private Detectives and Investigators	$37,640	18.2%	7,329	1

(continued)

(continued)

Best Jobs with Apprenticeships that Take as Little as One Year

Job	Annual Earnings	Percent Growth	Annual Openings	Years Required
21. Industrial Machinery Mechanics	$42,350	9.0%	23,361	1, 2, 3, 4, or 6
22. Brickmasons and Blockmasons	$44,070	9.7%	17,569	1, 2H, 3, or 4
23. Equal Opportunity Representatives and Officers	$48,400	4.9%	15,841	1C
24. Tellers	$22,920	13.5%	146,077	1
25. Human Resources Assistants, Except Payroll and Timekeeping	$34,970	11.3%	18,647	1
26. Police, Fire, and Ambulance Dispatchers	$32,660	13.6%	17,628	1 or 4
27. Water and Liquid Waste Treatment Plant and System Operators	$37,090	13.8%	9,575	1, 2, or 3
28. Telecommunications Line Installers and Repairers	$47,220	4.6%	14,719	1 or 4
29. Hairdressers, Hairstylists, and Cosmetologists	$22,210	12.4%	73,030	1
30. Air Traffic Controllers	$112,930	10.2%	1,213	1.2
31. Sailors and Marine Oilers	$32,570	15.7%	8,600	1.4
32. Animal Trainers	$26,190	22.7%	6,713	1 or 2
33. Electrical and Electronics Repairers, Commercial and Industrial Equipment	$47,110	6.8%	6,607	1C, 2, 4, or 5
34. Secretaries, Except Legal, Medical, and Executive	$28,220	1.2%	239,630	1
35. Fine Artists, Including Painters, Sculptors, and Illustrators	$42,070	9.9%	3,830	1 or 4
36. Residential Advisors	$23,050	18.5%	8,053	1.2
37. Airfield Operations Specialists	$38,320	11.8%	245	1.2
38. Inspectors, Testers, Sorters, Samplers, and Weighers	$30,310	−7.0%	75,361	1, 2, 3, or 4
39. Medical Equipment Preparers	$27,040	14.2%	8,363	1
40. Payroll and Timekeeping Clerks	$33,810	3.1%	18,544	1
41. Stationary Engineers and Boiler Operators	$47,640	3.4%	1,892	1 or 4
42. Chemical Technicians	$40,740	5.8%	4,010	1, 2, or 4
43. Computer Operators	$34,610	−24.7%	17,842	1 or 3
44. Ambulance Drivers and Attendants, Except Emergency Medical Technicians	$21,140	21.7%	3,703	1
45. Word Processors and Typists	$30,380	−11.6%	32,279	1C or 3
46. Excavating and Loading Machine and Dragline Operators	$34,050	8.3%	6,562	1
47. Merchandise Displayers and Window Trimmers	$24,830	10.7%	9,103	1 or 4

Best Jobs with Apprenticeships that Take as Little as One Year

Job	Annual Earnings	Percent Growth	Annual Openings	Years Required
48. Multiple Machine Tool Setters, Operators, and Tenders, Metal and Plastic	$30,390	0.3%	15,709	1, 2, 3, or 4
49. Computer-Controlled Machine Tool Operators, Metal and Plastic	$32,550	–3.0%	12,997	1C or 4
50. Prepress Technicians and Workers	$33,990	–21.1%	10,002	1, 2, 3, 4, 5, or 6
51. Medical Appliance Technicians	$32,640	9.4%	895	1, 4, or 5
52. Woodworking Machine Setters, Operators, and Tenders, Except Sawing	$24,190	6.4%	11,860	1 or 4
53. Dental Laboratory Technicians	$33,480	3.7%	3,479	1, 2, 3, or 4

Job 5 shares 12,836 openings with another job not included in this list. Job 6 shares 97,350 openings with another job not included in this list. Jobs 7 and 8 share 18,887 openings. Job 10 shares 223,225 openings with another job not included in this list. Job 23 shares 15,841 openings with four other jobs not included in this list.

Best Jobs with Apprenticeships that Take as Little as Two Years

Job	Annual Earnings	Percent Growth	Annual Openings	Years Required
1. Surgical Technologists	$37,540	24.5%	15,365	2
2. Police Patrol Officers	$49,630	10.8%	37,842	2
3. Automotive Master Mechanics	$34,170	14.3%	97,350	2 or 4
4. Interior Designers	$43,970	19.5%	8,434	2
5. Rough Carpenters	$37,660	10.3%	223,225	1.5H, 2, 2.5, or 4
6. Mates—Ship, Boat, and Barge	$57,210	17.9%	2,665	1.5
7. Medical Assistants	$27,430	35.4%	92,977	2
8. Pilots, Ship	$57,210	17.9%	2,665	1.5
9. Bookkeeping, Accounting, and Auditing Clerks	$31,560	12.5%	286,854	2
10. Social and Human Service Assistants	$26,630	33.6%	80,142	1.5C
11. Roofers	$33,240	14.3%	38,398	2
12. Cargo and Freight Agents	$37,060	16.5%	9,967	1.5
13. Electricians	$44,780	7.4%	79,083	2.5, 3, or 4
14. Tile and Marble Setters	$38,720	15.4%	9,066	2H or 3
15. Automotive Body and Related Repairers	$35,690	11.6%	37,469	2 or 4
16. Painters, Construction and Maintenance	$32,080	11.8%	101,140	2 or 3

(continued)

(continued)

Best Jobs with Apprenticeships that Take as Little as Two Years

Job	Annual Earnings	Percent Growth	Annual Openings	Years Required
17. Transportation Vehicle, Equipment, and Systems Inspectors, Except Aviation	$51,440	16.4%	2,122	2
18. Security Guards	$22,570	16.9%	222,085	1.5
19. Aircraft Structure, Surfaces, Rigging, and Systems Assemblers	$45,420	12.8%	6,550	2, 3, or 4
20. Municipal Fire Fighting and Prevention Supervisors	$65,040	11.5%	3,771	2 or 3
21. Funeral Directors	$50,370	12.5%	3,939	2
22. Operating Engineers and Other Construction Equipment Operators	$38,130	8.4%	55,468	2, 2H, or 3
23. Medical Equipment Repairers	$40,320	21.7%	2,351	2, 3, or 4
24. First-Line Supervisors/Managers of Housekeeping and Janitorial Workers	$32,850	12.7%	30,613	2
25. Mapping Technicians	$33,640	19.4%	8,299	2 or 3
26. Medical and Clinical Laboratory Technicians	$34,270	15.0%	10,866	2
27. Surveying Technicians	$33,640	19.4%	8,299	2
28. Cement Masons and Concrete Finishers	$33,840	11.4%	34,625	2
29. Maintenance and Repair Workers, General	$32,570	10.1%	165,502	2, 3, or 4
30. Production, Planning, and Expediting Clerks	$39,690	4.2%	52,735	2
31. Purchasing Agents, Except Wholesale, Retail, and Farm Products	$52,460	0.1%	22,349	2C or 4
32. Emergency Medical Technicians and Paramedics	$28,400	19.2%	19,513	2 or 3
33. Heating and Air Conditioning Mechanics and Installers	$38,360	8.7%	29,719	2, 3, or 4
34. Telecommunications Equipment Installers and Repairers, Except Line Installers	$54,070	2.5%	13,541	2, 3, or 4
35. Construction Laborers	$27,310	10.9%	257,407	2, 2H, 3, or 4H
36. Motorboat Mechanics	$34,210	19.0%	4,326	2 or 3
37. Medical Transcriptionists	$31,250	13.5%	18,080	2
38. Cooks, Restaurant	$21,220	11.5%	238,542	2H or 3
39. Drywall and Ceiling Tile Installers	$36,520	7.3%	30,945	2, 2H, or 4
40. Emergency Management Specialists	$48,380	12.3%	1,538	2C
41. Industrial Engineering Technicians	$47,490	9.9%	6,172	2 or 4
42. Industrial Production Managers	$80,560	–5.9%	14,889	2
43. Mechanical Drafters	$44,740	5.2%	10,902	2 or 4
44. Helpers—Installation, Maintenance, and Repair Workers	$22,920	11.8%	52,058	2, 4, or 4H

Best Jobs with Apprenticeships that Take as Little as Two Years

Job	Annual Earnings	Percent Growth	Annual Openings	Years Required
45. Computer, Automated Teller, and Office Machine Repairers	$37,100	3.0%	22,330	2, 3, or 4
46. Fire Investigators	$50,830	11.0%	644	2
47. Teacher Assistants	$21,580	10.4%	193,986	2
48. Cooks, Institution and Cafeteria	$21,340	10.8%	111,898	2
49. Tapers	$42,050	7.1%	9,026	2
50. Automotive Glass Installers and Repairers	$31,470	18.7%	3,457	2
51. Chefs and Head Cooks	$37,160	7.6%	9,401	2 or 3
52. Embalmers	$36,800	14.3%	1,660	2
53. Geological Sample Test Technicians	$50,950	8.6%	1,895	2 or 3
54. Machinists	$35,230	–3.1%	39,505	2, 2.5C, 4, or 5
55. Pest Control Workers	$29,030	15.5%	6,006	2
56. Helpers—Brickmasons, Blockmasons, Stonemasons, and Tile and Marble Setters	$26,260	11.0%	22,500	2 or 2H
57. Pesticide Handlers, Sprayers, and Applicators, Vegetation	$28,560	14.0%	7,443	2
58. Structural Iron and Steel Workers	$42,130	6.0%	6,969	2, 3, or 3H
59. Dispatchers, Except Police, Fire, and Ambulance	$33,140	1.5%	29,793	2
60. Tree Trimmers and Pruners	$29,800	11.1%	9,621	2 or 3
61. Sound Engineering Technicians	$46,550	9.1%	1,194	2 or 4
62. Bakers	$22,590	10.0%	31,442	2H or 3
63. Control and Valve Installers and Repairers, Except Mechanical Door	$46,140	0.3%	3,855	2, 3, or 4
64. Petroleum Pump System Operators, Refinery Operators, and Gaugers	$53,010	–13.4%	4,477	2 or 3
65. Broadcast Technicians	$32,230	12.1%	2,955	2 or 4
66. Food Batchmakers	$23,730	10.9%	15,704	2 or 3
67. Mechanical Door Repairers	$31,880	14.9%	1,706	2 or 3
68. Maintenance Workers, Machinery	$35,590	–1.1%	15,055	2
69. Postal Service Clerks	$45,050	1.2%	3,703	2
70. Plasterers and Stucco Masons	$36,430	8.1%	4,509	2 or 2H
71. Stonemasons	$36,950	10.0%	2,657	2H, 3, or 4
72. Rail Car Repairers	$44,970	5.1%	1,989	2 or 4
73. Electrical and Electronics Repairers, Powerhouse, Substation, and Relay	$58,970	–4.7%	1,591	2, 3, or 4
74. Parts Salespersons	$28,130	–2.2%	52,414	2
75. Terrazzo Workers and Finishers	$34,390	10.9%	1,052	2, 2H, or 3

(continued)

(continued)

Best Jobs with Apprenticeships that Take as Little as Two Years

Job	Annual Earnings	Percent Growth	Annual Openings	Years Required
76. Structural Metal Fabricators and Fitters	$31,030	–0.2%	20,746	2, 3, or 4
77. Data Entry Keyers	$25,370	–4.7%	79,166	2
78. Fish and Game Wardens	$47,830	–0.2%	576	2
79. Opticians, Dispensing	$31,430	8.7%	3,143	2 or 3H
80. Mixing and Blending Machine Setters, Operators, and Tenders	$30,340	–5.1%	18,661	2
81. Rotary Drill Operators, Oil and Gas	$43,480	–5.4%	2,145	2
82. Cabinetmakers and Bench Carpenters	$27,970	2.8%	9,780	2, 2.5H, 3, or 4
83. Fiberglass Laminators and Fabricators	$26,630	6.2%	7,315	2
84. Jewelers	$31,200	–2.2%	7,375	2, 3, or 4
85. Precious Metal Workers	$31,200	–2.2%	7,375	2, 3, or 4

Job 2 shares 37,842 openings with another job not included in this list. Job 3 shares 97,350 openings with another job not included in this list. Job 5 shares 223,225 openings with another job not included in this list. Jobs 6 and 8 share 2,665 openings with each other and with another job not included in this list. Job 17 shares 2,122 openings with another job not included in this list. Job 20 shares 3,771 openings with another job not included in this list. Jobs 25 and 27 share 8,299 openings. Job 33 shares 29,719 openings with another job not included in this list. Job 46 shares 644 openings with another job not included in this list. Job 53 shares 1,895 openings with another job not included in this list. Jobs 84 and 85 share 7,375 openings with another job not included in this list.

Best Jobs with Apprenticeships that Take as Little as Three Years

Job	Annual Earnings	Percent Growth	Annual Openings	Years Required
1. Paralegals and Legal Assistants	$44,990	22.2%	22,756	3
2. Environmental Science and Protection Technicians, Including Health	$39,370	28.0%	8,404	3
3. Food Service Managers	$44,570	5.0%	59,302	3
4. Electrical Power-Line Installers and Repairers	$52,570	7.2%	6,401	3 or 4
5. Government Property Inspectors and Investigators	$48,400	4.9%	15,841	3
6. Architectural Drafters	$43,310	6.1%	16,238	3 or 4
7. Refrigeration Mechanics and Installers	$38,360	8.7%	29,719	3
8. Electronics Engineering Technicians	$52,140	3.6%	12,583	3 or 4
9. Boilermakers	$50,700	14.0%	2,333	3 or 4
10. Audio and Video Equipment Technicians	$36,050	24.2%	4,681	3 or 4
11. Glaziers	$35,230	11.9%	6,416	3 or 4
12. Millwrights	$46,090	5.8%	4,758	3H or 4

Best Jobs with Apprenticeships that Take as Little as Three Years

Job	Annual Earnings	Percent Growth	Annual Openings	Years Required
13. First-Line Supervisors/Managers of Retail Sales Workers	$34,470	4.2%	221,241	3
14. Camera Operators, Television, Video, and Motion Picture	$41,850	11.5%	3,496	3
15. Slaughterers and Meat Packers	$22,500	12.7%	15,511	3
16. Welders, Cutters, and Welder Fitters	$32,270	5.1%	61,125	3 or 4
17. Photographers	$27,720	10.3%	16,100	3
18. Reinforcing Iron and Rebar Workers	$37,890	11.5%	4,502	3 or 3H
19. Chemical Plant and System Operators	$50,860	−15.3%	5,620	3 or 4
20. Power Plant Operators	$56,640	2.7%	1,796	3 or 4
21. Tank Car, Truck, and Ship Loaders	$33,140	9.2%	4,519	3
22. Motorcycle Mechanics	$30,300	12.5%	3,564	3
23. Tool and Die Makers	$45,090	−9.6%	5,286	3 or 4
24. Painters, Transportation Equipment	$36,000	8.4%	3,268	3
25. Carpet Installers	$36,040	−1.2%	6,692	3
26. Paving, Surfacing, and Tamping Equipment Operators	$32,360	9.0%	3,471	3
27. Welding, Soldering, and Brazing Machine Setters, Operators, and Tenders	$30,980	3.0%	7,707	3
28. Electro-Mechanical Technicians	$46,610	2.6%	1,142	3 or 4
29. Crane and Tower Operators	$40,260	2.8%	2,626	3
30. Butchers and Meat Cutters	$27,480	1.9%	14,503	3
31. Fence Erectors	$26,720	10.6%	2,812	3
32. Mine Cutting and Channeling Machine Operators	$39,930	3.8%	923	3
33. Gem and Diamond Workers	$31,200	−2.2%	7,375	3 or 4
34. Chemical Equipment Operators and Tenders	$44,050	−3.9%	1,469	3
35. Home Appliance Repairers	$33,560	1.5%	4,243	3 or 4

Job 5 shares 15,841 openings with four other jobs not included in this list. Job 6 shares 16,238 openings with another job not included in this list. Job 7 shares 29,719 openings with another job not included in this list. Job 8 shares 12,583 openings with another job not included in this list. Job 16 shares 61,125 openings with another job not included in this list. Job 33 shares 7,375 openings with two other jobs not included in this list.

Best Jobs with Apprenticeships that Take as Little as Four Years

Job	Annual Earnings	Percent Growth	Annual Openings	Years Required
1. Pipe Fitters and Steamfitters	$44,090	10.6%	68,643	4
2. Plumbers	$44,090	10.6%	68,643	4
3. Elevator Installers and Repairers	$68,000	8.8%	2,850	4
4. Mobile Heavy Equipment Mechanics, Except Engines	$41,450	12.3%	11,037	4
5. Electrical Engineering Technicians	$52,140	3.6%	12,583	4
6. Sheet Metal Workers	$39,210	6.7%	31,677	4 or 4H
7. Aerospace Engineering and Operations Technicians	$54,930	10.4%	707	4 or 5
8. Fire Inspectors	$50,830	11.0%	644	4
9. Nuclear Monitoring Technicians	$66,140	6.7%	1,021	4
10. Civil Drafters	$43,310	6.1%	16,238	4
11. Insulation Workers, Mechanical	$36,570	8.6%	5,787	4
12. Locksmiths and Safe Repairers	$33,230	22.1%	3,545	4
13. Electrical Drafters	$49,250	4.1%	4,786	4
14. Electronic Drafters	$49,250	4.1%	4,786	4
15. Fashion Designers	$62,810	5.0%	1,968	4
16. Mechanical Engineering Technicians	$47,280	6.4%	3,710	4
17. Locomotive Engineers	$57,520	2.9%	3,548	4
18. Avionics Technicians	$48,100	8.1%	1,193	4
19. Insulation Workers, Floor, Ceiling, and Wall	$31,280	8.4%	6,580	4
20. Recreational Vehicle Service Technicians	$31,760	18.2%	2,442	4
21. Farmers and Ranchers	$33,360	–8.5%	129,552	4
22. Earth Drillers, Except Oil and Gas	$36,310	6.5%	2,619	4
23. Electrical and Electronics Installers and Repairers, Transportation Equipment	$43,940	4.3%	1,663	4

Jobs 1 and 2 share 68,643 openings. Job 5 shares 12,583 openings with another job not included in this list. Job 8 shares 644 openings with another job not included in this list. Job 9 shares 1,021 openings with another job not included in this list. Job 10 shares 16,238 openings with another job not included in this list. Jobs 13 and 14 share 4,786 openings. Job 17 shares 3,548 openings with two other jobs not included in this list.

Best Jobs with Apprenticeships that Take as Little as Five Years

Job	Annual Earnings	Percent Growth	Annual Openings	Years Required
1. Desktop Publishers	$35,510	1.0%	6,420	5

Most Popular Apprenticeships

As you scan the following lists, keep in mind that they are based on somewhat limited information (collected in 2007). The statistics on the most popular apprenticeships are derived from the Registered Apprenticeship Information System, which gets input from only 31 states. Thus it does not represent the entire country and may not be a good reflection of conditions in your state and locality. In addition, some apprenticeship titles in the list represent a combination of two or more apprenticeships and may not exactly match apprenticeship titles available in your area or listed elsewhere in this book.

The list with the "Best 23 Jobs Linked to the 25 Most Popular Apprenticeships" contains only 23 jobs because two pairs of occupations among the top 25 apprenticeships (jobs 6 and 12 and jobs 19 and 20) are each linked to one O*NET occupation. One of the jobs on these lists, Child Care Workers, has low earnings that caused it to be eliminated from the 200 best jobs, so it is not described in Part IV of this book.

The 25 Most Popular Apprenticeships

Apprenticeship	Job	Total Active Apprentices Enrolled	Number of Active Programs	Average Enrollment per Program
1. Electrician	Electricians	45,609	3,209	14.2
2. Truck Driver, Heavy	Truck Drivers, Heavy and Tractor-Trailer	37,805	39	969.4
3. Carpenter	Construction Carpenters	33,027	446	74.1
4. Plumber	Plumbers	18,578	2644	7.0
5. Construction Craft Laborer	Construction Laborers	9,836	94	104.6
6. Pipe Fitter (Construction)	Pipe Fitters and Steamfitters	9,542	722	13.2
7. Sheet Metal Worker	Sheet Metal Workers	8,754	518	16.9
8. Structural-Steel Worker	Structural-Steel Workers	8,659	131	66.1
9. Roofer	Roofers	5,943	139	42.8
10. Elevator Constructor	Elevator Installers and Repairers	5,746	62	92.7
11. Dry-Wall Applicator	Drywall and Ceiling Tile Installers	5,541	44	125.9
12. Sprinkler Fitter	Pipe Fitters and Steamfitters	5,433	124	43.8
13. Operating Engineer	Operating Engineers and Other Construction Equipment Operators	4,837	131	36.9
14. Painter (Construction)	Painters, Construction and Maintenance	4,795	248	19.3
15. Boilermaker	Boilermakers	4,089	32	127.8
16. Bricklayer (Construction)	Brickmasons and Blockmasons	3,729	194	19.2
17. Millwright	Millwrights	3,185	381	8.4

(continued)

The 25 Most Popular Apprenticeships

Apprenticeship	Job	Total Active Apprentices Enrolled	Number of Active Programs	Average Enrollment per Program
18. Heating/Air-Conditioner Installer	Heating and Air Conditioning Mechanics and Installers	3,099	601	5.2
19. Powerline Maintainer	Electrical Power-Line Installers and Repairers	3,087	297	10.4
20. Powerline Installer and Repairer	Electrical Power-Line Installers and Repairers	2,886	92	31.4
21. Insulation Worker	Insulation Workers, Floor, Ceiling, and Wall	2,328	101	23.0
22. Correction Officer	Correctional Officers and Jailers	2,290	58	39.5
23. Child Care Development Specialist	Child Care Workers	2,282	971	2.4
24. Cook (Hospitality and Cruise Ship)	Cooks (Hotel and Restaurant)	2,259	1	2,259.0
25. Cement Mason	Cement Masons and Concrete Finishers	2,240	127	17.6

The Best 23 Jobs Linked to the 25 Most Popular Apprenticeships

Job	Annual Earnings	Percent Growth	Annual Openings
1. Pipe Fitters and Steamfitters	$44,090	10.6%	68,643
2. Plumbers	$44,090	10.6%	68,643
3. Child Care Workers	$18,350	17.8%	471,956
4. Correctional Officers and Jailers	$36,970	16.9%	56,579
5. Truck Drivers, Heavy and Tractor-Trailer	$36,220	10.4%	279,032
6. Boilermakers	$50,700	14.0%	2,333
7. Construction Carpenters	$37,660	10.3%	223,225
8. Electricians	$44,780	7.4%	79,083
9. Painters, Construction and Maintenance	$32,080	11.8%	101,140
10. Construction Laborers	$27,310	10.9%	257,407
11. Cooks, Restaurant	$21,220	11.5%	238,542
12. Roofers	$33,240	14.3%	38,398
13. Cement Masons and Concrete Finishers	$33,840	11.4%	34,625
14. Elevator Installers and Repairers	$68,000	8.8%	2,850
15. Brickmasons and Blockmasons	$44,070	9.7%	17,569

The Best 23 Jobs Linked to the 25 Most Popular Apprenticeships

Job	Annual Earnings	Percent Growth	Annual Openings
16. Operating Engineers and Other Construction Equipment Operators	$38,130	8.4%	55,468
17. Electrical Power-Line Installers and Repairers	$52,570	7.2%	6,401
18. Heating and Air Conditioning Mechanics and Installers	$38,360	8.7%	29,719
19. Sheet Metal Workers	$39,210	6.7%	31,677
20. Millwrights	$46,090	5.8%	4,758
21. Drywall and Ceiling Tile Installers	$36,520	7.3%	30,945
22. Structural Iron and Steel Workers	$42,130	6.0%	6,969
23. Insulation Workers, Floor, Ceiling, and Wall	$31,280	8.4%	6,580

Jobs 1 and 2 share 68,643 openings. Job 3 shares 471,956 openings with another job not included in this list. Job 7 shares 223,225 openings with another job not included in this list. Job 18 shares 29,719 openings with another job not included in this list.

Bonus List: The 50 Best Apprenticeable Jobs at Any Educational or Training Level

As one of the steps in selecting the 200 best jobs that are the basis of this book, we eliminated all jobs that normally require a four-year (or higher) college degree. However, we thought you might be interested in seeing a list of the best apprenticeable jobs without this restriction. This bonus list includes 22 jobs that are not described in this book; if any of these jobs interests you, you may learn more about it from JIST's *O*NET Dictionary of Occupational Titles.*

The rightmost column of the list indicates how much education or training is normally required. Note that the list includes 22 jobs that normally require a bachelor's or master's degree. Six of those 22 jobs require work experience in addition to the degree, and although an apprenticeship is one way to gain that experience, it normally is not a substitute for the degree. For example, about three-quarters of Computer and Information Systems Managers have a bachelor's degree, and almost all those without the degree have completed some college, so you are unlikely to qualify for this job simply by completing an apprenticeship; more likely, you will need to have some college background or a degree to *enter* the apprenticeship.

On the other hand, remember that apprenticeships include classroom learning, often at the college level, and a few programs lead to an associate degree along with journey worker status. So even if an apprenticeship can't substitute for a bachelor's degree, it may help you make progress toward that degree—while you are earning a paycheck.

It's interesting to note that 28 of these 50 jobs *are* included in the 200 best jobs described in this book. Although they don't require a bachelor's (or higher) degree, they have such good economic rewards that they earn a place in this list alongside jobs that do.

The 50 Best Apprenticeable Jobs at Any Educational or Training Level

Job	Annual Earnings	Percent Growth	Annual Openings	Educational or Training Level
1. Computer Software Engineers, Applications	$83,130	44.6%	58,690	Bachelor's degree
2. Computer Systems Analysts	$73,090	29.0%	63,166	Bachelor's degree
3. Network Systems and Data Communications Analysts	$68,220	53.4%	35,086	Bachelor's degree
4. Computer Security Specialists	$64,690	27.0%	37,010	Bachelor's degree
5. Network and Computer Systems Administrators	$64,690	27.0%	37,010	Bachelor's degree
6. Computer and Information Systems Managers	$108,070	16.4%	30,887	Work experience plus degree
7. Medical and Health Services Managers	$76,990	16.4%	31,877	Work experience plus degree
8. Public Relations Specialists	$49,800	17.6%	51,216	Bachelor's degree
9. Training and Development Specialists	$49,630	18.3%	35,862	Work experience plus degree
10. Industrial Engineers	$71,430	20.3%	11,272	Bachelor's degree
11. Multi-Media Artists and Animators	$54,550	25.8%	13,182	Bachelor's degree
12. Database Administrators	$67,250	28.6%	8,258	Bachelor's degree
13. Educational, Vocational, and School Counselors	$49,450	12.6%	54,025	Master's degree
14. Employment Interviewers	$44,380	18.4%	33,588	Bachelor's degree

The 50 Best Apprenticeable Jobs at Any Educational or Training Level

Job	Annual Earnings	Percent Growth	Annual Openings	Educational or Training Level
15. Paralegals and Legal Assistants	$44,990	22.2%	22,756	Associate degree
16. Administrative Services Managers	$70,990	11.7%	19,513	Work experience plus degree
17. Property, Real Estate, and Community Association Managers	$43,670	15.1%	49,916	Bachelor's degree
18. Computer Support Specialists	$42,400	12.9%	97,334	Associate degree
19. Environmental Scientists and Specialists, Including Health	$58,380	25.1%	6,961	Master's degree
20. Construction and Building Inspectors	$48,330	18.2%	12,606	Work experience in a related occupation
21. Police Patrol Officers	$49,630	10.8%	37,842	Long-term on-the-job training
22. Radiologic Technologists	$50,260	15.1%	12,836	Associate degree
23. Correctional Officers and Jailers	$36,970	16.9%	56,579	Moderate-term on-the-job training
24. Licensed Practical and Licensed Vocational Nurses	$37,940	14.0%	70,610	Postsecondary vocational training
25. Pipe Fitters and Steamfitters	$44,090	10.6%	68,643	Long-term the-job training
26. Plumbers	$44,090	10.6%	68,643	Long-term on-the-job training
27. Automotive Master Mechanics	$34,170	14.3%	97,350	Postsecondary vocational training
28. Automotive Specialty Technicians	$34,170	14.3%	97,350	Postsecondary vocational training

(continued)

(continued)

The 50 Best Apprenticeable Jobs at Any Educational or Training Level

Job	Annual Earnings	Percent Growth	Annual Openings	Educational or Training Level
29. Surgical Technologists	$37,540	24.5%	15,365	Postsecondary vocational training
30. Interior Designers	$43,970	19.5%	8,434	Associate degree
31. Directors—Stage, Motion Pictures, Television, and Radio	$61,090	11.1%	8,992	Work experience plus degree
32. Producers	$61,090	11.1%	8,992	Work experience plus degree
33. Legal Secretaries	$38,810	11.7%	38,682	Associate degree
34. Construction Carpenters	$37,660	10.3%	223,225	Long-term on-the-job training
35. Rough Carpenters	$37,660	10.3%	223,225	Long-term on-the-job training
36. Electricians	$44,780	7.4%	79,083	Long-term on-the-job training
37. Forest Fire Fighters	$43,170	12.1%	18,887	Long-term on-the-job training
38. Municipal Fire Fighters	$43,170	12.1%	18,887	Long-term on-the-job training
39. Environmental Science and Protection Technicians, Including Health	$39,370	28.0%	8,404	Associate degree
40. Truck Drivers, Heavy and Tractor-Trailer	$36,220	10.4%	279,032	Moderate-term on-the-job training
41. Biological Technicians	$37,810	16.0%	15,374	Bachelor's degree
42. Dental Assistants	$31,550	29.2%	29,482	Moderate-term on-the-job training
43. Medical Assistants	$27,430	35.4%	92,977	Moderate-term on-the-job training

The 50 Best Apprenticeable Jobs at Any Educational or Training Level

Job	Annual Earnings	Percent Growth	Annual Openings	Educational or Training Level
44. Bookkeeping, Accounting, and Auditing Clerks	$31,560	12.5%	286,854	Moderate-term on-the-job training
45. Roofers	$33,240	14.3%	38,398	Moderate-term on-the-job training
46. Bus and Truck Mechanics and Diesel Engine Specialists	$38,640	11.5%	25,428	Postsecondary vocational training
47. Forensic Science Technicians	$47,680	30.7%	3,074	Bachelor's degree
48. Social and Human Service Assistants	$26,630	33.6%	80,142	Moderate-term on-the-job training
49. Automotive Body and Related Repairers	$35,690	11.6%	37,469	Long-term on-the-job training
50. Directors, Religious Activities and Education	$35,370	19.7%	11,463	Bachelor's degree

Jobs 4 and 5 share 37,010 openings. Job 14 shares 33,588 openings with another job not included in this list. Job 21 shares 37,842 openings with another job not included in this list. Job 22 shares 12,836 openings with another job not included in this list. Jobs 25 and 26 share 68,643 openings. Jobs 27 and 28 share 97,350 openings. Jobs 31 and 32 share 8,992 openings with each other and with three other jobs not included in this list. Jobs 34 and 35 share 223,225 openings. Jobs 37 and 38 share 18,887 openings.

PART IV

Descriptions of the 200 Best Apprenticeable Jobs

This part provides descriptions for all the jobs included in one or more of the lists in Part III. The book's introduction gives more details on how to use and interpret the job descriptions, but here are the highlights, along with some additional information.

- ✹ The job descriptions that follow meet our criteria for inclusion in this book, as we describe in the introduction. The jobs in this book can be entered via a registered apprenticeship and score among the 200 highest for earnings, projected growth, and number of job openings. Many good jobs do not meet one or more of these criteria, but we think the jobs that do are the best ones to consider in your career planning.

- ✹ Keep in mind that although every job in this book can be entered via a registered apprenticeship *somewhere* in the United States, it is not likely that apprenticeships for *all* of these jobs are available in your area. For example, where you live, Police Patrol Officers may be required to get a college degree. Follow the suggestions under "How Can I Find an Apprenticeship?" in Part I to investigate what apprenticeships are available in your area.

- ✹ The job descriptions are arranged in alphabetical order by job title. This approach allows you to find a description quickly if you know its title from one of the lists in Part III. If you have not browsed the lists in Part III, consider spending some time there. The lists are interesting and will help you identify job titles that you can look up in the descriptions that follow.

- ✹ Refer to the introduction, beginning on page 1, for details on interpreting the contents of the job descriptions.

- ✹ The section about GOE includes a subsection titled Other Apprenticeable Jobs in This Work Group to help you identify similar jobs. Not all of the jobs listed here are among the top 200.

- ✹ When reviewing the descriptions, keep in mind that the jobs meet our criteria for being among the top 200 jobs based on their total scores for earnings, growth, and number of openings—but one or more of these measures may not be among the highest. For example, an occupation that has high pay may be included, even though growth rate and number of job openings are below average.

"Well," you might ask, "doesn't this mean that at least some 'bad' jobs are described in this part?" Our answer is yes and no. Some jobs with high scores for all measures, such as Paralegals and Legal Assistants—the apprenticeable job with the highest total for pay, growth, and number of openings—would be a very bad job for people who dislike or are not good at that sort of work. On the other hand, many people love working as Jewelers even though that job has lower earnings, a lower projected growth rate, and fewer openings. Descriptions for both jobs are included in this book.

It's entirely possible that somewhere an ex-paralegal works as a jeweler and loves it. Some who do so may even have figured out how to make more money (say, by running their own business successfully), have a more flexible schedule, have more fun, or have other advantages not available to paralegals.

The point is that each job is right for somebody, perhaps at a certain time in their lives. We are all likely to change careers and jobs several times, and it's not always money that motivates us. So browse the job descriptions that follow and know that somewhere there is a good place for you. We hope you find it.

Aerospace Engineering and Operations Technicians

- ❊ Annual Earnings: $54,930
- ❊ Growth: 10.4%
- ❊ Annual Job Openings: 707
- ❊ Percentage of Women: 20.6%

Related Apprenticeships—Research Mechanic (Aircraft) (8000 hrs.); Test Equipment Mechanic (10000 hrs.); Wind Tunnel Mechanic (8000 hrs.).

Operate, install, calibrate, and maintain integrated computer/communications systems consoles; simulators; and other data acquisition, test, and measurement instruments and equipment to launch, track, position, and evaluate air and space vehicles. May record and interpret test data. Inspect, diagnose, maintain, and operate test setups and equipment to detect malfunctions. Record and interpret test data on parts, assemblies, and mechanisms. Confer with engineering personnel regarding details and implications of test procedures and results. Adjust, repair, or replace faulty components of test setups and equipment. Identify required data, data acquisition plans, and test parameters, setting up equipment to conform to these specifications. Construct and maintain test facilities for aircraft parts and systems according to specifications. Operate and calibrate computer systems and devices to comply with test requirements and to perform data acquisition and analysis. Test aircraft systems under simulated operational conditions, performing systems readiness tests and pre- and post-operational checkouts, to establish design or fabrication parameters. Fabricate and install parts and systems to be tested in test equipment, using hand tools, power tools, and test instruments. Finish

vehicle instrumentation and deinstrumentation. Exchange cooling system components in various vehicles.

GOE—Career Cluster/Interest Area: 15. Scientific Research, Engineering, and Mathematics. **Work Group:** 15.09. Engineering Technology. **Other Apprenticeable Jobs in This Work Group:** Electrical Drafters; Electrical Engineering Technicians; Electro-Mechanical Technicians; Electronic Drafters; Electronics Engineering Technicians; Mapping Technicians; Mechanical Drafters; Mechanical Engineering Technicians; Surveying and Mapping Technicians; Surveying Technicians. **Personality Type:** Realistic. These occupations frequently involve work activities that include practical, hands-on problems and solutions. They often deal with plants; animals; and real-world materials such as wood, tools, and machinery. Many of the occupations require working outside and don't involve a lot of paperwork or working closely with others.

Skills—Installation; Technology Design; Operation Monitoring; Science; Troubleshooting; Repairing; Operations Analysis; Operation and Control.

Education/Training Required (Nonapprenticeship Route): Associate degree. **Related Knowledge/Courses—Engineering and Technology:** Equipment, tools, and mechanical devices and their uses to produce motion, light, power, technology, and other applications. **Mechanical Devices:** Machines and tools, including their designs, uses, benefits, repair, and maintenance. **Computers and Electronics:** Electric circuit boards, processors, chips, and computer hardware and software, including applications and programming. **Production and Processing:** Inputs, outputs, raw materials, waste, quality control, costs, and techniques for maximizing the manufacture and distribution of goods. **Public Safety and Security:** Weaponry; public safety; security operations, rules, regulations, precautions, and prevention; and the protection of people, data, and property. **Design:** Design techniques, principles, tools, and instruments involved in the production and use of precision technical plans, blueprints, drawings, and models.

Work Environment: Indoors; noisy; sitting; using hands on objects, tools, or controls; repetitive motions.

Air Traffic Controllers

- ❋ Annual Earnings: $112,930
- ❋ Growth: 10.2%
- ❋ Annual Job Openings: 1,213
- ❋ Percentage of Women: 13.0%

Related Apprenticeship—Air Traffic Controller (Military Only) (2500 hrs. or competency).

Control air traffic on and within vicinity of airport and movement of air traffic between altitude sectors and control centers according to established procedures and policies. Authorize, regulate, and control commercial airline flights according to government or company regulations to expedite and ensure flight safety. Issue landing and take-off authorizations and instructions. Monitor and direct the movement of aircraft within an assigned airspace and on the ground at airports to minimize delays and maximize safety. Monitor aircraft within a specific airspace, using radar, computer equipment, and visual references. Inform pilots about nearby planes as well as potentially hazardous conditions such as weather, speed and direction of wind, and visibility problems. Provide flight path changes or directions to emergency landing fields for pilots traveling in bad weather or in emergency situations. Alert airport emergency services in cases of emergency and when aircraft experience difficulties. Direct pilots to runways when space is available or direct them to maintain a traffic pattern until there is space for them to land. Transfer control of departing flights to traffic control centers and accept control of arriving flights. Direct ground traffic, including taxiing aircraft, maintenance and baggage vehicles, and airport workers. Determine the timing and procedures for flight vector changes. Maintain radio and telephone contact with adjacent control towers, terminal control units, and other area control centers in order to coordinate aircraft movement. Contact pilots by radio to provide meteorological, navigational, and other information. Initiate and coordinate searches for missing aircraft. Check conditions and traffic at different altitudes in response to pilots' requests for altitude changes. Relay to control centers air traffic information such as courses, altitudes, and expected arrival times. Compile information about flights from flight plans, pilot reports, radar, and observations. Inspect, adjust, and control radio equipment and airport lights. Conduct preflight briefings on weather conditions, suggested routes, altitudes, indications of turbulence, and other flight safety information. Analyze factors such as weather reports, fuel requirements, and maps in order to determine air routes. Organize flight plans and traffic management plans to prepare for planes about to enter assigned airspace.

GOE—Career Cluster/Interest Area: 03. Arts and Communication. **Work Group:** 03.10. Communications Technology. **Other Apprenticeable Jobs in This Work Group:** Airfield Operations Specialists; Dispatchers, Except Police, Fire, and

Ambulance; Police, Fire, and Ambulance Dispatchers. **Personality Type:** Enterprising. These occupations frequently involve starting up and carrying out projects and can involve leading people and making many decisions. They sometimes require risk taking and often deal with business.

Skills—Operation and Control; Operation Monitoring; Coordination; Complex Problem Solving; Active Listening; Instructing; Judgment and Decision Making; Monitoring.

Education/Training Required (Nonapprenticeship Route): Long-term on-the-job training. **Related Knowledge/Courses—Transportation:** Principles and methods for moving people or goods by air, rail, sea, or road, including their relative costs, advantages, and limitations. **Geography:** Various methods for describing the location and distribution of land, sea, and air masses, including their physical locations, relationships, and characteristics. **Telecommunications:** Transmission, broadcasting, switching, control, and operation of telecommunications systems. **Public Safety and Security:** Weaponry; public safety; security operations, rules, regulations, precautions, and prevention; and the protection of people, data, and property. **Physics:** Physical principles, laws, and applications, including air, water, material dynamics, light, atomic principles, heat, electric theory, earth formations, and meteorological and related natural phenomena. **Education and Training:** Instructional methods and training techniques, including curriculum design principles, learning theory, group and individual teaching techniques, design of individual development plans, and test design principles.

Work Environment: Indoors; noisy; sitting; using hands on objects, tools, or controls; repetitive motions.

Aircraft Mechanics and Service Technicians

* Annual Earnings: $49,010
* Growth: 10.6%
* Annual Job Openings: 9,708
* Percentage of Women: 5.3%

Related Apprenticeships—Aerospace Propulsion Jet Engine Mechanic (2500 hrs. or competency); Airframe and Powerplant Mechanic (8000 hrs.); Airframe Mechanic (3100 hrs.); Pneudraulic Systems Mechanic (4800 hrs.); Powerplant Mechanic (3000 hrs.); Rocket-Engine-Component Mechanic (8000 hrs.).

Diagnose, adjust, repair, or overhaul aircraft engines and assemblies, such as hydraulic and pneumatic systems. Read and interpret maintenance manuals, service bulletins, and other specifications to determine the feasibility and method of repairing or replacing malfunctioning or damaged components. Inspect completed work to certify that maintenance meets standards and that aircraft are ready for operation. Maintain repair logs, documenting all preventive and corrective aircraft maintenance. Conduct routine and special inspections as required by regulations. Examine and inspect aircraft components, including landing gear, hydraulic systems, and de-icers, to locate cracks, breaks, leaks, or other problem. Inspect airframes for wear or other defects. Maintain, repair, and rebuild aircraft structures; functional components; and parts such as wings and fuselage, rigging, hydraulic units, oxygen systems, fuel systems, electrical systems, gaskets, and seals. Measure the tension of control cables. Replace or repair worn, defective, or damaged components, using hand tools, gauges, and testing equipment. Measure parts for wear, using precision instruments. Assemble and install electrical, plumbing, mechanical, hydraulic, and structural components and accessories, using hand tools and power tools. Test operation of engines and other systems, using test equipment such as ignition analyzers, compression checkers, distributor timers, and ammeters. Obtain fuel and oil samples and check them for contamination. Reassemble engines following repair or inspection and re-install engines in aircraft. Read and interpret pilots' descriptions of problems to diagnose causes. Modify aircraft structures, space vehicles, systems, or components, following drawings, schematics, charts, engineering orders, and technical publications. Install and align repaired or replacement parts for subsequent riveting or welding, using clamps and wrenches. Locate and mark dimensions and reference lines on defective or replacement parts, using templates, scribes, compasses, and steel rules. Clean, strip, prime, and sand structural surfaces and materials to prepare them for bonding. Service and maintain aircraft and related apparatus by performing activities such as flushing crankcases, cleaning screens, and lubricating moving parts.

GOE—Career Cluster/Interest Area: 13. Manufacturing. **Work Group:** 13.14. Vehicle and Facility Mechanical Work. **Other Apprenticeable Jobs in This Work Group:** Aircraft Structure, Surfaces, Rigging, and Systems Assemblers; Automotive Body and Related Repairers; Automotive Glass Installers and Repairers; Automotive Master Mechanics; Automotive Specialty Technicians; Bus and Truck Mechanics and Diesel Engine Specialists; Farm Equipment Mechanics; Fiberglass Laminators and Fabricators; Mobile Heavy Equipment Mechanics, Except Engines; Motorboat Mechanics; Motorcycle Mechanics; Outdoor Power Equipment and Other Small Engine Mechanics; Rail Car Repairers; Recreational Vehicle Service Technicians. **Personality Type:** Realistic. These occupations frequently involve work activities that include practical, hands-on problems and solutions. They often deal with plants; animals; and real-world materials such as wood, tools, and machinery. Many of the occupations require working outside and don't involve a lot of paperwork or working closely with others.

Skills—Repairing; Equipment Maintenance; Installation; Operation Monitoring; Troubleshooting; Operation and Control; Quality Control Analysis; Complex Problem Solving.

Education/Training Required (Nonapprenticeship Route): Postsecondary vocational training. **Related Knowledge/Courses—Mechanical Devices:** Machines and tools, including their designs, uses, benefits, repair, and maintenance. **Design:** Design techniques, principles, tools, and instruments involved in the production and use of precision technical plans, blueprints, drawings, and models. **Physics:** Physical principles, laws, and applications, including air, water, material dynamics, light, atomic principles, heat, electric theory, earth formations, and meteorological and related natural phenomena. **Chemistry:** The composition, structure, and properties of substances and of the chemical processes and transformations that they undergo. This includes uses of chemicals and their interactions, danger signs, production techniques, and disposal methods. **Engineering and Technology:** Equipment, tools, and mechanical devices and their uses to produce motion, light, power, technology, and other applications. **Transportation:** Principles and methods for moving people or goods by air, rail, sea, or road, including their relative costs, advantages, and limitations.

Work Environment: Noisy; contaminants; cramped work space, awkward positions; standing; using hands on objects, tools, or controls; bending or twisting the body.

Aircraft Structure, Surfaces, Rigging, and Systems Assemblers

❋ Annual Earnings: $45,420
❋ Growth: 12.8%
❋ Annual Job Openings: 6,550
❋ Percentage of Women: 30.4%

Related Apprenticeships—Aircraft Mechanic, Armament (8000 hrs.); Aircraft Mechanic, Plumbing and Hydraulic (8000 hrs.); Assembler, Aircraft Structures (8000 hrs.); Assembler-Installer, General (4000 hrs.); Precision Assembler (6000 hrs.).

Assemble, fit, fasten, and install parts of airplanes, space vehicles, or missiles, such as tails, wings, fuselage, bulkheads, stabilizers, landing gear, rigging and control equipment, or heating and ventilating systems. Form loops or splices in cables, using clamps and fittings, or reweave cable strands. Align and fit structural assemblies manually or signal crane operators to position assemblies for joining. Align, fit, assemble, connect, and install system components, using jigs, fixtures, measuring instruments, hand tools, and power tools. Assemble and fit prefabricated parts to form subassemblies. Assemble, install, and connect parts, fittings, and assemblies on aircraft, using layout tools; hand tools; power tools; and fasteners such as bolts, screws, rivets, and clamps. Attach brackets, hinges, or clips to secure or support components and subassemblies, using bolts, screws, rivets, chemical

bonding, or welding. Select and install accessories in swaging machines, using hand tools. Fit and fasten sheet metal coverings to surface areas and other sections of aircraft prior to welding or riveting. Lay out and mark reference points and locations for installation of parts and components, using jigs, templates, and measuring and marking instruments. Inspect and test installed units, parts, systems, and assemblies for fit, alignment, performance, defects, and compliance with standards, using measuring instruments and test equipment. Install mechanical linkages and actuators and verify tension of cables, using tensiometers. Join structural assemblies such as wings, tails, and fuselage. Measure and cut cables and tubing, using master templates, measuring instruments, and cable cutters or saws. Read and interpret blueprints, illustrations, and specifications to determine layouts, sequences of operations, or identities and relationships of parts. Prepare and load live ammunition, missiles, and bombs onto aircraft according to established procedures. Adjust, repair, rework, or replace parts and assemblies to eliminate malfunctions and to ensure proper operation. Cut, trim, file, bend, and smooth parts and verify sizes and fitting tolerances in order to ensure proper fit and clearance of parts. Install and connect control cables to electronically controlled units, using hand tools, ring locks, cotter keys, threaded connectors, turnbuckles, and related devices.

GOE—Career Cluster/Interest Area: 13. Manufacturing. **Work Group:** 13.14. Vehicle and Facility Mechanical Work. **Other Apprenticeable Jobs in This Work Group:** Aircraft Mechanics and Service Technicians; Automotive Body and Related Repairers; Automotive Glass Installers and Repairers; Automotive Master Mechanics; Automotive Specialty Technicians; Bus and Truck Mechanics and Diesel Engine

Specialists; Farm Equipment Mechanics; Fiberglass Laminators and Fabricators; Mobile Heavy Equipment Mechanics, Except Engines; Motorboat Mechanics; Motorcycle Mechanics; Outdoor Power Equipment and Other Small Engine Mechanics; Rail Car Repairers; Recreational Vehicle Service Technicians. **Personality Type:** Realistic. These occupations frequently involve work activities that include practical, hands-on problems and solutions. They often deal with plants; animals; and real-world materials such as wood, tools, and machinery. Many of the occupations require working outside and don't involve a lot of paperwork or working closely with others.

Skills—Installation; Equipment Maintenance; Repairing; Quality Control Analysis; Equipment Selection; Operation Monitoring; Mathematics; Troubleshooting.

Education/Training Required (Nonapprenticeship Route): Moderate-term on-the-job training. **Related Knowledge/Courses—Mechanical Devices:** Machines and tools, including their designs, uses, benefits, repair, and maintenance. **Design:** Design techniques, principles, tools, and instruments involved in the production and use of precision technical plans, blueprints, drawings, and models. **Chemistry:** The composition, structure, and properties of substances and of the chemical processes and transformations that they undergo. This includes uses of chemicals and their interactions, danger signs, production techniques, and disposal methods. **Public Safety and Security:** Weaponry; public safety; security operations, rules, regulations, precautions, and prevention; and the protection of people, data, and property. **Production and Processing:** Inputs, outputs, raw materials, waste, quality control, costs, and

techniques for maximizing the manufacture and distribution of goods.

Work Environment: More often indoors than outdoors; hazardous equipment; standing; using hands on objects, tools, or controls; repetitive motions.

Airfield Operations Specialists

* Annual Earnings: $38,320
* Growth: 11.8%
* Annual Job Openings: 245
* Percentage of Women: 14.8%

Related Apprenticeships—Airfield Management (2500 hrs. or competency); Operations Resource Flight/Jump Management (2500 hrs. or competency).

Ensure the safe takeoff and landing of commercial and military aircraft. Duties include coordination between air traffic control and maintenance personnel; dispatching; using airfield landing and navigational aids; implementing airfield safety procedures; monitoring and maintaining flight records; and applying knowledge of weather information. Implement airfield safety procedures to ensure a safe operating environment for personnel and aircraft operation. Plan and coordinate airfield construction. Coordinate with agencies such as air traffic control, civil engineers, and command posts to ensure support of airfield management activities. Monitor the arrival, parking, refueling, loading, and departure of all aircraft. Maintain air-to-ground and point-to-point radio contact with aircraft commanders. Train operations staff. Relay departure, arrival, delay, aircraft and airfield status, and other pertinent information to upline controlling agencies. Procure, produce, and provide information on the safe operation of aircraft, such as flight-planning publications, operations publications, charts and maps, and weather information. Coordinate communications between air traffic control and maintenance personnel. Perform and supervise airfield management activities, which may include mobile airfield management functions. Receive, transmit, and control message traffic. Receive and post weather information and flight plan data such as air routes and arrival and departure times. Maintain flight and events logs, air crew flying records, and flight operations records of incoming and outgoing flights. Coordinate with agencies to meet aircrew requirements for billeting, messing, refueling, ground transportation, and transient aircraft maintenance. Collaborate with others to plan flight schedules and air crew assignments. Coordinate changes to flight itineraries with appropriate Air Traffic Control (ATC) agencies. Anticipate aircraft equipment needs for air evacuation and cargo flights. Provide air crews with information and services needed for airfield management and flight planning. Conduct departure and arrival briefings. Use airfield landing and navigational aids and digital data terminal communications equipment to perform duties. Post visual display boards and status boards. Check military flight plans with civilian agencies.

GOE—Career Cluster/Interest Area: 03. Arts and Communication. **Work Group:** 03.10. Communications Technology. **Other Apprenticeable Jobs in This Work Group:** Air Traffic Controllers; Dispatchers, Except Police, Fire, and Ambulance; Police, Fire, and Ambulance Dispatchers. **Personality Type:** Enterprising. These occupations frequently involve starting up and carrying out projects and can involve leading people and making many decisions. They sometimes require risk taking and often deal with business.

Skills—Operation Monitoring; Operations Analysis; Science; Instructing; Writing; Active Learning; Management of Personnel Resources; Operation and Control.

Education/Training Required (Nonapprenticeship Route): Long-term on-the-job training. **Related Knowledge/Courses—Transportation:** Principles and methods for moving people or goods by air, rail, sea, or road, including their relative costs, advantages, and limitations. **Geography:** Various methods for describing the location and distribution of land, sea, and air masses, including their physical locations, relationships, and characteristics. **Telecommunications:** Transmission, broadcasting, switching, control, and operation of telecommunications systems. **Customer and Personal Service:** Principles and processes for providing customer and personal services, including needs assessment techniques, quality service standards, alternative delivery systems, and customer satisfaction evaluation techniques. **Physics:** Physical principles, laws, and applications, including air, water, material dynamics, light, atomic principles, heat, electric theory, earth formations, and meteorological and related natural phenomena. **Computers and Electronics:** Electric circuit boards, processors, chips, and computer hardware and software, including applications and programming.

Work Environment: More often indoors than outdoors; noisy; very hot or cold; contaminants; sitting.

Ambulance Drivers and Attendants, Except Emergency Medical Technicians

- ❋ Annual Earnings: $21,140
- ❋ Growth: 21.7%
- ❋ Annual Job Openings: 3,703
- ❋ Percentage of Women: 28.0%

Related Apprenticeship—Ambulance Attendant (EMT) (2000 hrs.).

Drive ambulance or assist ambulance driver in transporting sick, injured, or convalescent persons. Assist in lifting patients. Drive ambulances or assist ambulance drivers in transporting sick, injured, or convalescent persons. Remove and replace soiled linens and equipment to maintain sanitary conditions. Accompany and assist emergency medical technicians on calls. Place patients on stretchers and load stretchers into ambulances, usually with assistance from other attendants. Earn and maintain appropriate certifications. Replace supplies and disposable items on ambulances. Report facts concerning accidents or emergencies to hospital personnel or law enforcement officials. Administer first aid such as bandaging, splinting, and administering oxygen. Restrain or shackle violent patients.

GOE—Career Cluster/Interest Area: 16. Transportation, Distribution, and Logistics. **Work Group:** 16.06. Other Services Requiring Driving. **Other Apprenticeable Jobs in This Work Group:** No others in group. **Personality Type:** Realistic. These occupations frequently involve work activities that include practical, hands-on problems and solutions. They often deal with plants; animals; and real-world materials such as wood, tools, and machinery. Many of the occupations require working outside and don't involve a lot of paperwork or working closely with others.

Skills—Equipment Maintenance; Operation Monitoring; Operation and Control; Repairing; Technology Design; Equipment Selection; Troubleshooting; Service Orientation.

Education/Training Required (Nonapprenticeship Route): Moderate-term on-the-job training. **Related Knowledge/Courses—Transportation:** Principles and methods for moving people or goods by air, rail, sea, or road, including their relative costs, advantages, and limitations. **Psychology:** Human behavior and performance, mental processes, psychological research methods, and the assessment and treatment of behavioral and affective disorders. **Medicine and Dentistry:** The information and techniques needed to diagnose and treat injuries, diseases, and deformities. This includes symptoms, treatment alternatives, drug properties and interactions, and preventive health-care measures. **Customer and Personal Service:** Principles and processes for providing customer and personal services, including needs assessment techniques, quality service standards, alternative delivery systems, and customer satisfaction evaluation techniques. **Telecommunications:** Transmission, broadcasting, switching, control, and operation of telecommunications systems. **Public Safety and Security:** Weaponry; public safety; security operations, rules, regulations, precautions, and prevention; and the protection of people, data, and property.

Work Environment: Outdoors; noisy; very hot or cold; disease or infections; sitting; using hands on objects, tools, or controls.

Animal Trainers

- ❋ Annual Earnings: $26,190
- ❋ Growth: 22.7%
- ❋ Annual Job Openings: 6,713
- ❋ Percentage of Women: 57.3%

Related Apprenticeships—Animal Trainer (4000 hrs.); Horse Trainer (2000 hrs.).

Train animals for riding, harness, security, performance, or obedience or assisting persons with disabilities. Accustom animals to human voice and contact and condition animals to respond to commands. Train animals according to prescribed standards for show or competition. May train animals to carry pack loads or work as part of pack team. Observe animals' physical conditions to detect illness or unhealthy conditions requiring medical care. Cue or signal animals during performances. Administer prescribed medications to animals. Evaluate animals to determine their temperaments, abilities, and aptitude for training. Feed and exercise animals and provide other general care such as cleaning and maintaining holding and performance areas. Talk to and interact with animals in order to familiarize them to human voices and contact. Conduct training programs to develop and maintain desired animal behaviors for competition, entertainment, obedience, security, riding, and related areas. Keep records documenting animal health, diet, and behavior. Advise animal owners regarding the purchase of specific animals. Instruct jockeys in handling specific horses during races. Train horses or other equines for riding, harness, show, racing, or other work, using knowledge of breed characteristics, training methods, performance standards, and the peculiarities of each animal. Use oral, spur, rein, and hand commands to condition horses to carry riders or to pull horse-drawn equipment. Place tack or harnesses on horses to accustom horses to the feel of equipment. Train dogs in human-assistance or property protection duties. Retrain horses to break bad habits, such as kicking, bolting, and resisting bridling and grooming. Train and rehearse animals, according to scripts, for motion picture, television, film, stage, or circus performances. Organize and conduct animal shows. Arrange for mating of stallions and mares and assist mares during foaling.

GOE—Career Cluster/Interest Area: 08. Health Science. **Work Group:** 08.05. Animal Care. **Other Apprenticeable Jobs in This Work Group:** Nonfarm Animal Caretakers; Veterinary Assistants and Laboratory Animal Caretakers. **Personality Type:** Realistic. These occupations frequently involve work activities that include practical, hands-on problems and solutions. They often deal with plants; animals; and real-world materials such as wood, tools, and machinery. Many of the occupations require working outside and don't involve a lot of paperwork or working closely with others.

Skills—Management of Financial Resources; Persuasion; Service Orientation; Instructing; Learning Strategies; Monitoring; Management of Material Resources; Social Perceptiveness.

Education/Training Required (Nonapprenticeship Route): Moderate-term on-the-job training. **Related Knowledge/Courses—Sales and Marketing:** Principles and methods involved in showing, promoting, and selling products or services. This includes marketing strategies and tactics, product demonstration and sales techniques, and sales control systems. **Biology:** Plant and animal living tissue, cells, organisms, and entities, including their functions, interdependencies, and interactions with each other and the environment. **Economics and Accounting:** Economic and accounting principles and practices, the financial markets, banking, and the analysis and reporting of financial data. **Communications and Media:** Media production, communication, and dissemination techniques and methods, including alternative ways to inform and entertain via written, oral, and visual media. **Customer and Personal Service:** Principles and processes for providing customer and personal services, including needs assessment techniques, quality service standards, alternative delivery systems, and customer satisfaction evaluation techniques. **Clerical Practices:** Administrative and clerical procedures and systems such as word-processing systems, filing and records management systems, stenography and transcription, forms, design principles, and other office procedures and terminology.

Work Environment: Outdoors; noisy; standing; walking and running; using hands on objects, tools, or controls; repetitive motions.

Architectural Drafters

- ❊ Annual Earnings: $43,310
- ❊ Growth: 6.1%
- ❊ Annual Job Openings: 16,238
- ❊ Percentage of Women: 21.8%

Our sources did not provide separate job openings data for this occupation. The job openings listed here are shared with Civil Drafters.

Related Apprenticeships—Drafter, Architectural (8000 hrs.); Drafter, Commercial (8000 hrs.); Drafter, Heating and Ventilation (8000 hrs.); Drafter, Landscape (8000 hrs.); Drafter, Marine (8000 hrs.); Drafter, Plumbing (8000 hrs.); Drafter, Structural (6000 hrs.).

Prepare detailed drawings of architectural designs and plans for buildings and structures according to specifications provided by architect. Analyze building codes, by-laws, space and site requirements, and other technical documents and reports to determine their effect on architectural designs. Operate computer-aided drafting (CAD) equipment or conventional drafting station to produce designs, working drawings, charts, forms, and records. Coordinate structural, electrical, and mechanical designs and determine a method of presentation to graphically represent building plans. Obtain and assemble data to complete architectural designs, visiting job sites to compile measurements as necessary. Lay out and plan interior room arrangements for commercial buildings, using computer-assisted drafting (CAD) equipment and software. Draw rough and detailed scale plans for foundations, buildings, and structures based on preliminary concepts, sketches, engineering calculations, specification sheets, and other data. Supervise, coordinate, and inspect the work of draftspersons, technicians, and technologists on construction projects. Represent architect on construction site, ensuring builder compliance with design specifications and advising on design corrections under architect's supervision. Check dimensions of materials to be used and assign numbers to lists of materials. Determine procedures and instructions to be followed according to design specifications and quantity of required materials. Analyze technical implications of architect's design concept, calculating weights, volumes, and stress factors. Create freehand drawings and lettering to accompany drawings. Prepare colored drawings of landscape and interior designs for presentation to client. Reproduce drawings on copy machines or trace copies of plans and drawings, using transparent paper or cloth, ink, pencil, and standard drafting instruments. Prepare cost estimates, contracts, bidding documents, and technical reports for specific projects under an architect's supervision. Calculate heat loss and gain of buildings and structures to determine required equipment specifications, following standard procedures. Build landscape, architectural, and display models.

GOE—Career Cluster/Interest Area: 02. Architecture and Construction. **Work Group:** 02.03. Architecture/Construction Engineering Technologies. **Other Apprenticeable Jobs in This Work Group:** Civil Drafters. **Personality Type:** Artistic. These occupations frequently involve working with forms, designs, and patterns. They often require self-expression, and the work can be done without following a clear set of rules.

Skills—Operations Analysis; Coordination; Active Learning; Technology Design; Mathematics; Complex Problem Solving; Science; Monitoring.

Education/Training Required (Nonapprenticeship Route): Postsecondary vocational training. **Related Knowledge/Courses—Design:** Design techniques, principles, tools, and instruments involved in the production and use of precision technical plans, blueprints, drawings, and models. **Building and Construction:** Materials, methods, and the appropriate tools to construct objects, structures, and buildings. **Engineering and Technology:** Equipment, tools, and mechanical devices and their uses to produce motion, light, power, technology, and other applications. **Computers and Electronics:** Electric circuit boards, processors, chips, and computer hardware and software, including applications and programming. **Mathematics:** Numbers and their operations and interrelationships, including arithmetic, algebra, geometry, calculus, and statistics and their applications. **Physics:** Physical principles, laws, and applications, including air, water, material dynamics, light, atomic principles, heat, electric theory, earth formations, and meteorological and related natural phenomena.

Work Environment: Indoors; noisy; sitting; using hands on objects, tools, or controls; repetitive motions.

Audio and Video Equipment Technicians

- ❋ Annual Earnings: $36,050
- ❋ Growth: 24.2%
- ❋ Annual Job Openings: 4,681
- ❋ Percentage of Women: 15.6%

Related Apprenticeships—Light Technician (8000 hrs.); Stage Technician (6000 hrs.).

Set up or set up and operate audio and video equipment, including microphones, sound speakers, video screens, projectors, video monitors, recording equipment, connecting wires and cables, sound and mixing boards, and related electronic equipment for concerts, sports events, meetings and conventions, presentations, and news conferences. May also set up and operate associated spotlights and other custom lighting systems. Notify supervisors when major equipment repairs are needed. Monitor incoming and outgoing pictures and sound feeds to ensure quality; notify directors of any possible problems. Mix and regulate sound inputs and feeds or coordinate audio feeds with television pictures. Install, adjust, and operate electronic equipment used to record, edit, and transmit radio and television programs, cable programs, and motion pictures. Design layouts of audio and video equipment and perform upgrades and maintenance. Perform minor repairs and routine cleaning of audio and video equipment. Diagnose and resolve media system problems in classrooms. Switch sources of video input from one camera or studio to another, from film to live programming, or from network to local programming. Meet with directors and senior members of camera crews to discuss assignments and determine filming sequences, camera movements, and picture composition. Construct and position properties, sets, lighting equipment, and other equipment. Compress, digitize, duplicate, and store audio and video data. Obtain, set up, and load videotapes for scheduled productions or broadcasts. Edit videotapes by erasing and removing portions of programs and adding video or sound as required. Direct and coordinate activities of assistants and other personnel during production. Plan and develop pre-production ideas into outlines, scripts, storyboards, and graphics, using own ideas or specifications of assignments. Maintain inventories of audiotapes and videotapes and related supplies. Determine formats, approaches, content, levels, and media to effectively meet objectives within budgetary constraints, utilizing research, knowledge, and training. Record and edit audio material such as movie soundtracks, using audio recording and editing equipment. Inform users of audiotaping and videotaping service policies and procedures. Obtain and preview musical performance programs prior to events to become familiar with the order and approximate times of pieces. Produce rough and finished graphics and graphic designs. Locate and secure settings, properties, effects, and other production necessities.

GOE—Career Cluster/Interest Area: 03. Arts and Communication. **Work Group:** 03.09.

Media Technology. **Other Apprenticeable Jobs in This Work Group:** Broadcast Technicians; Camera Operators, Television, Video, and Motion Picture; Photographers; Radio Operators; Sound Engineering Technicians. **Personality Type:** Realistic. These occupations frequently involve work activities that include practical, hands-on problems and solutions. They often deal with plants; animals; and real-world materials such as wood, tools, and machinery. Many of the occupations require working outside and don't involve a lot of paperwork or working closely with others.

Skills—Installation; Operation and Control; Equipment Maintenance; Troubleshooting; Operation Monitoring; Repairing; Equipment Selection; Technology Design.

Education/Training Required (Nonapprenticeship Route): Long-term on-the-job training. **Related Knowledge/Courses—Computers and Electronics:** Electric circuit boards, processors, chips, and computer hardware and software, including applications and programming. **Telecommunications:** Transmission, broadcasting, switching, control, and operation of telecommunications systems. **Engineering and Technology:** Equipment, tools, and mechanical devices and their uses to produce motion, light, power, technology, and other applications. **Communications and Media:** Media production, communication, and dissemination techniques and methods, including alternative ways to inform and entertain via written, oral, and visual media. **Mechanical Devices:** Machines and tools, including their designs, uses, benefits, repair, and maintenance. **Physics:** Physical principles, laws, and applications, including air, water, material dynamics, light, atomic principles, heat, electric theory, earth formations, and meteorological and related natural phenomena.

Work Environment: Indoors; standing; using hands on objects, tools, or controls.

Automotive Body and Related Repairers

- ❋ Annual Earnings: $35,690
- ❋ Growth: 11.6%
- ❋ Annual Job Openings: 37,469
- ❋ Percentage of Women: 0.6%

Related Apprenticeships—Automobile Body Repairer (8000 hrs.); Service Mechanic (Auto Manufacturing) (4000 hrs.); Truck Body Builder (8000 hrs.).

Repair and refinish automotive vehicle bodies and straighten vehicle frames. File, grind, sand, and smooth filled or repaired surfaces, using power tools and hand tools. Sand body areas to be painted and cover bumpers, windows, and trim with masking tape or paper to protect them from the paint. Follow supervisors' instructions as to which parts to restore or replace and how much time a job should take. Remove damaged sections of vehicles, using metal-cutting guns, air grinders, and wrenches, and install replacement parts, using wrenches or welding equipment. Cut and tape plastic separating film to outside repair areas to avoid damaging surrounding surfaces during repair procedure and remove tape and wash surfaces after repairs are complete. Prime and paint repaired surfaces, using paint spray guns and motorized sanders. Inspect repaired vehicles for dimensional accuracy and test-drive them to ensure proper alignment and handling. Mix polyester resins and hardeners to be used in restoring damaged areas. Chain or clamp frames and sections to alignment machines that use hydraulic pressure to align damaged components. Fill small dents that cannot be worked out with plastic or solder. Fit and weld replacement parts into place, using wrenches and welding equipment, and grind down welds to smooth them, using power grinders and other tools. Position dolly blocks against surfaces of dented areas and beat opposite surfaces to remove dents, using hammers. Remove damaged panels and identify the family and properties of the plastic used on a vehicle. Review damage reports, prepare or review repair cost estimates, and plan work to be performed. Remove small pits and dimples in body metal, using pick hammers and punches. Remove upholstery, accessories, electrical window- and seat-operating equipment, and trim to gain access to vehicle bodies and fenders. Clean work areas, using air hoses, to remove damaged material and discarded fiberglass strips used in repair procedures. Adjust or align headlights, wheels, and brake systems. Apply heat to plastic panels, using hot-air welding guns or immersion in hot water, and press the softened panels back into shape by hand. Soak fiberglass matting in resin mixtures and apply layers of matting over repair areas to specified thicknesses.

GOE—Career Cluster/Interest Area: 13. Manufacturing. **Work Group:** 13.14. Vehicle and Facility Mechanical Work. **Other Apprenticeable Jobs in This Work Group:** Aircraft Mechanics and Service Technicians; Aircraft Structure, Surfaces, Rigging, and Systems Assemblers; Automotive Glass Installers and Repairers; Automotive Master Mechanics; Automotive Specialty Technicians; Bus and Truck Mechanics and Diesel Engine Specialists; Farm Equipment Mechanics; Fiberglass Laminators and Fabricators; Mobile Heavy Equipment Mechanics, Except Engines; Motorboat Mechanics; Motorcycle Mechanics; Outdoor Power Equipment and Other Small Engine Mechanics; Rail Car Repairers; Recreational Vehicle Service

Technicians. **Personality Type:** Realistic. These occupations frequently involve work activities that include practical, hands-on problems and solutions. They often deal with plants; animals; and real-world materials such as wood, tools, and machinery. Many of the occupations require working outside and don't involve a lot of paperwork or working closely with others.

Skills—Repairing; Installation; Equipment Maintenance; Troubleshooting; Equipment Selection; Management of Financial Resources.

Education/Training Required (Nonapprenticeship Route): Long-term on-the-job training. **Related Knowledge/Courses—Mechanical Devices:** Machines and tools, including their designs, uses, benefits, repair, and maintenance. **Building and Construction:** Materials, methods, and the appropriate tools to construct objects, structures, and buildings. **Chemistry:** The composition, structure, and properties of substances and of the chemical processes and transformations that they undergo. This includes uses of chemicals and their interactions, danger signs, production techniques, and disposal methods. **Production and Processing:** Inputs, outputs, raw materials, waste, quality control, costs, and techniques for maximizing the manufacture and distribution of goods. **Administration and Management:** Principles and processes involved in business and organizational planning, coordination, and execution. This includes strategic planning, resource allocation, manpower modeling, leadership techniques, and production methods. **Transportation:** Principles and methods for moving people or goods by air, rail, sea, or road, including their relative costs, advantages, and limitations.

Work Environment: Noisy; contaminants; hazardous equipment; standing; using hands on objects, tools, or controls; repetitive motions.

Automotive Glass Installers and Repairers

* Annual Earnings: $31,470
* Growth: 18.7%
* Annual Job Openings: 3,457
* Percentage of Women: 0.6%

Related Apprenticeship—Glass Installer (Auto Service) (4000 hrs.).

Replace or repair broken windshields and window glass in motor vehicles. Remove all dirt, foreign matter, and loose glass from damaged areas; then apply primer along windshield or window edges and allow it to dry. Install replacement glass in vehicles after old glass has been removed and all necessary preparations have been made. Allow all glass parts installed with urethane ample time to cure, taking temperature and humidity into account. Prime all scratches on pinch welds with primer and allow primed scratches to dry. Obtain windshields or windows for specific automobile makes and models from stock and examine them for defects before installation. Apply a bead of urethane around the perimeter of each pinch weld and dress the remaining urethane on the pinch welds so that it is of uniform level and thickness all the way around. Check for moisture or contamination in damaged areas, dry out any moisture before making repairs, and keep damaged areas dry until repairs are complete. Select appropriate tools, safety equipment, and parts according to job requirements. Remove broken or damaged glass windshields or window glass from motor vehicles, using hand tools to remove screws from frames holding glass. Remove all moldings, clips, windshield wipers, screws, bolts, and inside A-pillar moldings; then lower headliners before beginning installation or repair work. Install, repair, and replace safety glass and related materials, such as back glass heating elements, on vehicles and equipment. Install rubber channeling strips around edges of glass or frames to weatherproof windows or to prevent rattling. Hold cut or uneven edges of glass against automated abrasive belts to shape or smooth edges. Cut flat safety glass according to specified patterns or perform precision pattern-making and glass-cutting to custom-fit replacement windows. Replace or adjust motorized or manual window-raising mechanisms. Install new foam dams on pinch welds if required. Cool or warm glass in the event of temperature extremes. Replace all moldings, clips, windshield wipers, and other parts that were removed before glass replacement or repair.

GOE—Career Cluster/Interest Area: 13. Manufacturing. **Work Group:** 13.14. Vehicle and Facility Mechanical Work. **Other Apprenticeable Jobs in This Work Group:** Aircraft Mechanics and Service Technicians; Aircraft Structure, Surfaces, Rigging, and Systems Assemblers; Automotive Body and Related Repairers; Automotive Master Mechanics; Automotive Specialty Technicians; Bus and Truck Mechanics and Diesel Engine Specialists; Farm Equipment Mechanics; Fiberglass Laminators and Fabricators; Mobile Heavy Equipment Mechanics, Except Engines; Motorboat Mechanics; Motorcycle Mechanics; Outdoor Power Equipment and Other Small Engine Mechanics; Rail Car Repairers; Recreational Vehicle Service Technicians. **Personality Type:** Realistic. These occupations frequently involve work activities that include practical, hands-on problems and

solutions. They often deal with plants; animals; and real-world materials such as wood, tools, and machinery. Many of the occupations require working outside and don't involve a lot of paperwork or working closely with others.

Skills—Installation; Equipment Maintenance; Repairing; Equipment Selection; Management of Material Resources; Quality Control Analysis; Operation and Control.

Education/Training Required (Nonapprenticeship Route): Long-term on-the-job training. **Related Knowledge/Courses—Mechanical Devices:** Machines and tools, including their designs, uses, benefits, repair, and maintenance. **Production and Processing:** Inputs, outputs, raw materials, waste, quality control, costs, and techniques for maximizing the manufacture and distribution of goods. **Customer and Personal Service:** Principles and processes for providing customer and personal services, including needs assessment techniques, quality service standards, alternative delivery systems, and customer satisfaction evaluation techniques. **Administration and Management:** Principles and processes involved in business and organizational planning, coordination, and execution. This includes strategic planning, resource allocation, manpower modeling, leadership techniques, and production methods. **Sales and Marketing:** Principles and methods involved in showing, promoting, and selling products or services. This includes marketing strategies and tactics, product demonstration and sales techniques, and sales control systems. **Transportation:** Principles and methods for moving people or goods by air, rail, sea, or road, including their relative costs, advantages, and limitations.

Work Environment: Outdoors; very hot or cold; contaminants; cramped work space, awkward positions; standing; using hands on objects, tools, or controls.

Automotive Master Mechanics

❋ Annual Earnings: $34,170
❋ Growth: 14.3%
❋ Annual Job Openings: 97,350
❋ Percentage of Women: 1.6%

Our sources did not provide separate job openings data for this occupation. The job openings listed here are shared with Automotive Specialty Technicians.

Related Apprenticeships—Automobile Mechanic (8000 hrs.); Repairer, Heavy (4000 hrs.); Transmission Mechanic (4000 hrs.).

Repair automobiles, trucks, buses, and other vehicles. Master mechanics repair virtually any part on the vehicle or specialize in the transmission system. Examine vehicles to determine extent of damage or malfunctions. Test-drive vehicles and test components and systems, using equipment such as infrared engine analyzers, compression gauges, and computerized diagnostic devices. Repair, reline, replace, and adjust brakes. Review work orders and discuss work with supervisors. Follow checklists to ensure all important parts are examined, including belts, hoses, steering systems, spark plugs, brake and fuel systems, wheel bearings, and other potentially troublesome areas. Plan work procedures, using charts, technical manuals, and experience. Test and adjust repaired systems to meet manufacturers' performance specifications. Confer with customers to obtain descriptions of vehicle problems and to discuss work to be performed and future repair requirements. Perform routine and scheduled maintenance services such as oil changes, lubrications, and tune-ups. Disassemble units and inspect parts for wear, using micrometers, calipers, and gauges. Overhaul or replace carburetors, blowers, generators, distributors, starters, and pumps. Repair and service air conditioning, heating, engine-cooling, and electrical systems. Repair or replace parts such as pistons, rods, gears, valves, and bearings. Tear down, repair, and rebuild faulty assemblies such as power systems, steering systems, and linkages. Rewire ignition systems, lights, and instrument panels. Repair radiator leaks. Install and repair accessories such as radios, heaters, mirrors, and windshield wipers. Repair manual and automatic transmissions. Repair or replace shock absorbers. Align vehicles' front ends. Rebuild parts such as crankshafts and cylinder blocks. Repair damaged automobile bodies. Replace and adjust headlights.

GOE—Career Cluster/Interest Area: 13. Manufacturing. **Work Group:** 13.14. Vehicle and Facility Mechanical Work. **Other Apprenticeable Jobs in This Work Group:** Aircraft Mechanics and Service Technicians; Aircraft Structure, Surfaces, Rigging, and Systems Assemblers; Automotive Body and Related Repairers; Automotive Glass Installers and Repairers; Automotive Specialty Technicians; Bus and Truck Mechanics and Diesel Engine Specialists; Farm Equipment Mechanics; Fiberglass Laminators and Fabricators; Mobile Heavy Equipment Mechanics, Except Engines; Motorboat Mechanics; Motorcycle Mechanics; Outdoor Power Equipment and Other Small Engine Mechanics; Rail Car Repairers; Recreational Vehicle Service Technicians. **Personality Type:** Realistic. These occupations frequently involve work activities that include practical, hands-on problems and solutions. They often deal with plants; animals; and real-world materials such as wood, tools, and machinery. Many of the occupations require working outside and don't involve a lot of paperwork or working closely with others.

Skills—Repairing; Troubleshooting; Installation; Equipment Maintenance; Equipment Selection; Operation Monitoring; Complex Problem Solving; Technology Design.

Education/Training Required (Nonapprenticeship Route): Postsecondary vocational training. **Related Knowledge/Courses— Mechanical Devices:** Machines and tools, including their designs, uses, benefits, repair, and maintenance. **Physics:** Physical principles, laws, and applications, including air, water, material dynamics, light, atomic principles, heat, electric theory, earth formations, and meteorological and related natural phenomena. **Computers and Electronics:** Electric circuit boards, processors, chips, and computer hardware and software, including applications and programming. **Engineering and Technology:** Equipment, tools, and mechanical devices and their uses to produce motion, light, power, technology, and other applications. **Chemistry:** The composition, structure, and properties of substances and of the chemical processes and transformations that they undergo. This includes uses of chemicals and their interactions, danger signs, production techniques, and disposal methods. **Public Safety and Security:** Weaponry; public safety; security operations, rules, regulations, precautions, and prevention; and the protection of people, data, and property.

Work Environment: Noisy; contaminants; hazardous equipment; minor burns, cuts, bites, or stings; standing; using hands on objects, tools, or controls.

Automotive Specialty Technicians

- Annual Earnings: $34,170
- Growth: 14.3%
- Annual Job Openings: 97,350
- Percentage of Women: 1.6%

Our sources did not provide separate job openings data for this occupation. The job openings listed here are shared with Automotive Master Mechanics.

Related Apprenticeships—Air Conditioning Mechanic (Auto Service) (2000 hrs.); Auto Cooling System Diagnostic Technician (4000 hrs.); Automotive Technician Specialist (2000–4000 hrs. or competency); Automotive Technician Specialist (Entry Level 1, Experienced) (650–1000 hrs.); Automotive Technician Specialist (Entry Level 1, Nonexperienced) (650–1000 hrs.); Automotive Technician Specialist (Lead Technician A, Level 4) (4000–8000 hrs. or competency); Automotive Technician Specialist (Senior Technician B, Level 3) (4000–8000 hrs. or competency); Automotive Technician Specialist (Technician C, Level 2) (2000–4000 hrs. or competency); Auto-Radiator Mechanic (4000 hrs.); Brake Repairer (Auto Service) (4000 hrs.); Carburetor Mechanic (8000 hrs.); Front-End Mechanic (8000 hrs.); Fuel Injection Servicer (8000 hrs.); Spring Repairer, Hand (8000 hrs.); Tune-Up Mechanic (4000 hrs.); Undercar Specialist (4000 hrs.).

Repair only one system or component on a vehicle, such as brakes, suspension, or radiator. Examine vehicles, compile estimates of repair costs, and secure customers' approval to perform repairs. Repair, overhaul, and adjust automobile brake systems. Use electronic test equipment to locate and correct malfunctions in fuel, ignition, and emissions control systems. Repair and replace defective ball joint suspensions, brake shoes, and wheel bearings. Inspect and test new vehicles for damage; then record findings so that necessary repairs can be made. Test electronic computer components in automobiles to ensure that they are working properly. Tune automobile engines to ensure proper and efficient functioning. Install and repair air conditioners and service components such as compressors, condensers, and controls. Repair, replace, and adjust defective carburetor parts and gasoline filters. Remove and replace defective mufflers and tailpipes. Repair and replace automobile leaf springs. Rebuild, repair, and test automotive fuel injection units. Align and repair wheels, axles, frames, torsion bars, and steering mechanisms of automobiles, using special alignment equipment and wheel-balancing machines. Repair, install, and adjust hydraulic and electromagnetic automatic lift mechanisms used to raise and lower automobile windows, seats, and tops. Repair and rebuild clutch systems. Convert vehicle fuel systems from gasoline to butane gas operations and repair and service operating butane fuel units.

GOE—Career Cluster/Interest Area: 13. Manufacturing. **Work Group:** 13.14. Vehicle and Facility Mechanical Work. **Other Apprenticeable Jobs in This Work Group:** Aircraft Mechanics and Service Technicians; Aircraft Structure, Surfaces, Rigging, and Systems Assemblers; Automotive Body and Related Repairers; Automotive Glass Installers and Repairers; Automotive Master Mechanics; Bus and Truck Mechanics and Diesel Engine Specialists; Farm Equipment Mechanics; Fiberglass Laminators and Fabricators; Mobile Heavy Equipment Mechanics, Except Engines; Motorboat Mechanics; Motorcycle Mechanics; Outdoor Power Equipment and Other Small Engine Mechanics; Rail Car Repairers; Recreational Vehicle Service Technicians. **Personality Type:**

Realistic. These occupations frequently involve work activities that include practical, hands-on problems and solutions. They often deal with plants; animals; and real-world materials such as wood, tools, and machinery. Many of the occupations require working outside and don't involve a lot of paperwork or working closely with others.

Skills—Repairing; Troubleshooting; Operation Monitoring; Equipment Maintenance; Installation; Equipment Selection; Active Learning; Operation and Control.

Education/Training Required (Nonapprenticeship Route): Postsecondary vocational training. **Related Knowledge/Courses— Mechanical Devices:** Machines and tools, including their designs, uses, benefits, repair, and maintenance. **Physics:** Physical principles, laws, and applications, including air, water, material dynamics, light, atomic principles, heat, electric theory, earth formations, and meteorological and related natural phenomena. **Engineering and Technology:** Equipment, tools, and mechanical devices and their uses to produce motion, light, power, technology, and other applications. **Customer and Personal Service:** Principles and processes for providing customer and personal services, including needs assessment techniques, quality service standards, alternative delivery systems, and customer satisfaction evaluation techniques. **Sales and Marketing:** Principles and methods involved in showing, promoting, and selling products or services. This includes marketing strategies and tactics, product demonstration and sales techniques, and sales control systems. **Administration and Management:** Principles and processes involved in business and organizational planning, coordination, and execution. This includes strategic planning, resource allocation, manpower modeling, leadership techniques, and production methods.

Work Environment: Contaminants; cramped work space, awkward positions; minor burns, cuts, bites, or stings; standing; using hands on objects, tools, or controls; bending or twisting the body.

Avionics Technicians

❀ Annual Earnings: $48,100
❀ Growth: 8.1%
❀ Annual Job Openings: 1,193
❀ Percentage of Women: 15.2%

Related Apprenticeships—Aircraft Mechanic, Electrical (8000 hrs.); Electrician, Aircraft (8000 hrs.).

Install, inspect, test, adjust, or repair avionics equipment, such as radar, radio, navigation, and missile control systems in aircraft or space vehicles. Set up and operate ground support and test equipment to perform functional flight tests of electrical and electronic systems. Test and troubleshoot instruments, components, and assemblies, using circuit testers, oscilloscopes, and voltmeters. Keep records of maintenance and repair work. Coordinate work with that of engineers, technicians, and other aircraft maintenance personnel. Interpret flight test data to diagnose malfunctions and systemic performance problems. Install electrical and electronic components, assemblies, and systems in aircraft, using hand tools, power tools, and soldering irons. Adjust, repair, or replace malfunctioning components or assemblies, using hand tools and soldering irons. Connect components to assemblies such as radio systems, instruments, magnetos, inverters, and in-flight refueling systems,

using hand tools and soldering irons. Assemble components such as switches, electrical controls, and junction boxes, using hand tools and soldering irons. Fabricate parts and test aids as required. Lay out installation of aircraft assemblies and systems, following documentation such as blueprints, manuals, and wiring diagrams. Assemble prototypes or models of circuits, instruments, and systems so that they can be used for testing. Operate computer-aided drafting and design applications to design avionics system modifications.

GOE—Career Cluster/Interest Area: 13. Manufacturing. **Work Group:** 13.12. Electrical and Electronic Repair. **Other Apprenticeable Jobs in This Work Group:** Electric Motor, Power Tool, and Related Repairers; Electrical and Electronics Installers and Repairers, Transportation Equipment; Electrical and Electronics Repairers, Commercial and Industrial Equipment; Electronic Equipment Installers and Repairers, Motor Vehicles; Electronic Home Entertainment Equipment Installers and Repairers; Radio Mechanics. **Personality Type:** Realistic. These occupations frequently involve work activities that include practical, hands-on problems and solutions. They often deal with plants; animals; and real-world materials such as wood, tools, and machinery. Many of the occupations require working outside and don't involve a lot of paperwork or working closely with others.

Skills—Installation; Repairing; Equipment Maintenance; Troubleshooting; Operation and Control; Operation Monitoring; Quality Control Analysis; Science.

Education/Training Required (Nonapprenticeship Route): Postsecondary vocational training. **Related Knowledge/Courses—Engineering and Technology:** Equipment, tools, and mechanical devices and their uses to produce motion, light, power, technology, and other applications. **Mechanical Devices:** Machines and tools, including their designs, uses, benefits, repair, and maintenance. **Computers and Electronics:** Electric circuit boards, processors, chips, and computer hardware and software, including applications and programming. **Telecommunications:** Transmission, broadcasting, switching, control, and operation of telecommunications systems. **Production and Processing:** Inputs, outputs, raw materials, waste, quality control, costs, and techniques for maximizing the manufacture and distribution of goods. **Design:** Design techniques, principles, tools, and instruments involved in the production and use of precision technical plans, blueprints, drawings, and models.

Work Environment: Indoors; noisy; contaminants; hazardous conditions; sitting; using hands on objects, tools, or controls.

Bakers

* Annual Earnings: $22,590
* Growth: 10.0%
* Annual Job Openings: 31,442
* Percentage of Women: 57.9%

Related Apprenticeships—Baker (Bake Produce) (6000 hrs.); Cook, Pastry (Hotel and Restaurant) (4000–6000 hrs., hybrid).

Mix and bake ingredients according to recipes to produce breads, rolls, cookies, cakes, pies, pastries, or other baked goods. Observe color of products being baked and adjust oven temperatures, humidity, and conveyor speeds accordingly. Set oven temperatures and place items into hot ovens for baking. Combine measured ingredients in bowls of mixing, blending, or cooking machinery. Measure and weigh flour and other ingredients to prepare batters, doughs, fillings, and icings, using scales and graduated containers. Roll, knead, cut, and shape dough to form sweet rolls, pie crusts, tarts, cookies, and other products. Place dough in pans, in molds, or on sheets and bake in production ovens or on grills. Adapt the quantity of ingredients to match the amount of items to be baked. Check the quality of raw materials to ensure that standards and specifications are met. Apply glazes, icings, or other toppings to baked goods, using spatulas or brushes. Check equipment to ensure that it meets health and safety regulations and perform maintenance or cleaning as necessary. Decorate baked goods such as cakes and pastries. Set time and speed controls for mixing machines, blending machines, or steam kettles so that ingredients will be mixed or cooked according to instructions. Prepare and maintain inventory and production records. Direct and coordinate bakery deliveries. Order and receive supplies and equipment. Operate slicing and wrapping machines. Develop new recipes for baked goods.

GOE—Career Cluster/Interest Area: 13. Manufacturing. **Work Group:** 13.03. Production Work, Assorted Materials Processing. **Other Apprenticeable Jobs in This Work Group:** Chemical Equipment Operators and Tenders; Coating, Painting, and Spraying Machine Setters, Operators, and Tenders; Cooling and Freezing Equipment Operators and Tenders; Cutting and Slicing Machine Setters, Operators, and Tenders; Extruding, Forming, Pressing, and Compacting Machine Setters, Operators, and Tenders; Food Batchmakers; Furnace, Kiln, Oven, Drier, and Kettle Operators and Tenders; Heat Treating Equipment Setters, Operators, and Tenders, Metal and Plastic; Metal-Refining Furnace Operators and Tenders; Mixing and Blending Machine Setters, Operators, and Tenders; Plating and Coating Machine Setters, Operators, and Tenders, Metal and Plastic; Sawing Machine Setters, Operators, and Tenders, Wood; Separating, Filtering, Clarifying, Precipitating, and Still Machine Setters, Operators, and Tenders; Sewing Machine Operators; Slaughterers and Meat Packers; Team Assemblers; Woodworking Machine Setters, Operators, and Tenders, Except Sawing. **Personality Type:** Realistic. These occupations frequently involve work activities that include practical, hands-on problems and solutions. They often deal with plants; animals; and real-world materials such as wood, tools, and machinery. Many of the occupations require working outside and don't involve a lot of paperwork or working closely with others.

Skills—Quality Control Analysis; Systems Evaluation; Equipment Maintenance; Operation and Control; Troubleshooting; Systems Analysis; Management of Personnel Resources; Operation Monitoring.

Education/Training Required (Nonapprenticeship Route): Long-term on-the-job training. **Related Knowledge/Courses**—**Food Production:** Techniques and equipment for planting, growing, and harvesting of food for consumption, including crop-rotation methods, animal husbandry, and food storage/handling techniques. **Production and Processing:** Inputs, outputs, raw materials, waste, quality control, costs, and techniques for maximizing the manufacture and distribution of goods. **Personnel and Human Resources:** Principles and procedures for personnel recruitment; selection; training; compensation and benefits; labor relations and negotiation; and personnel information systems. **Mathematics:** Numbers and their operations and interrelationships, including arithmetic,

algebra, geometry, calculus, and statistics and their applications. **Sales and Marketing:** Principles and methods involved in showing, promoting, and selling products or services. This includes marketing strategies and tactics, product demonstration and sales techniques, and sales control systems. **Administration and Management:** Principles and processes involved in business and organizational planning, coordination, and execution. This includes strategic planning, resource allocation, manpower modeling, leadership techniques, and production methods.

Work Environment: Indoors; very hot or cold; minor burns, cuts, bites, or stings; standing; walking and running; using hands on objects, tools, or controls.

Boilermakers

- ✹ Annual Earnings: $50,700
- ✹ Growth: 14.0%
- ✹ Annual Job Openings: 2,333
- ✹ Percentage of Women: 3.1%

Related Apprenticeships—Boilerhouse Mechanic (6000 hrs.); Boilermaker Fitter (8000 hrs.); Boilermaker I (6000 hrs.); Boilermaker II (6000 hrs.).

Construct, assemble, maintain, and repair stationary steam boilers and boiler house auxiliaries. Align structures or plate sections to assemble boiler frame tanks or vats, following blueprints. Work involves use of hand and power tools, plumb bobs, levels, wedges, dogs, or turnbuckles. Assist in testing assembled vessels. Direct cleaning of boilers and boiler furnaces. Inspect and repair boiler fittings, such as safety valves, regulators, automatic-control mechanisms, water columns, and auxiliary machines. Examine boilers, pressure vessels, tanks, and vats to locate defects such as leaks, weak spots, and defective sections so that they can be repaired. Bolt or arc-weld pressure vessel structures and parts together, using wrenches and welding equipment. Inspect assembled vessels and individual components, such as tubes, fittings, valves, controls, and auxiliary mechanisms, to locate any defects. Repair or replace defective pressure vessel parts, such as safety valves and regulators, using torches, jacks, caulking hammers, power saws, threading dies, welding equipment, and metalworking machinery. Attach rigging and signal crane or hoist operators to lift heavy frame and plate sections and other parts into place. Bell, bead with power hammers, or weld pressure vessel tube ends in order to ensure leakproof joints. Lay out plate, sheet steel, or other heavy metal and locate and mark bending and cutting lines, using protractors, compasses, and drawing instruments or templates. Install manholes, handholes, taps, tubes, valves, gauges, and feedwater connections in drums of water tube boilers, using hand tools. Study blueprints to determine locations, relationships, and dimensions of parts. Straighten or reshape bent pressure vessel plates and structure parts, using hammers, jacks, and torches. Shape seams, joints, and irregular edges of pressure vessel sections and structural parts in order to attain specified fit of parts, using cutting torches, hammers, files, and metalworking machines. Position, align, and secure structural parts and related assemblies to boiler frames, tanks, or vats of pressure vessels, following blueprints. Locate and mark reference points for columns or plates on boiler foundations, following blueprints and using straightedges, squares, transits, and measuring instruments. Shape and fabricate parts, such as stacks, uptakes, and chutes, in order to adapt pressure vessels, heat exchangers, and piping to premises, using heavy-metalworking

machines such as brakes, rolls, and drill presses. Clean pressure vessel equipment, using scrapers, wire brushes, and cleaning solvents.

GOE—Career Cluster/Interest Area: 02. Architecture and Construction. **Work Group:** 02.04. Construction Crafts. **Other Apprenticeable Jobs in This Work Group:** Brickmasons and Blockmasons; Carpet Installers; Cement Masons and Concrete Finishers; Construction Carpenters; Crane and Tower Operators; Drywall and Ceiling Tile Installers; Electricians; Fence Erectors; Floor Layers, Except Carpet, Wood, and Hard Tiles; Glaziers; Insulation Workers, Floor, Ceiling, and Wall; Insulation Workers, Mechanical; Operating Engineers and Other Construction Equipment Operators; Painters, Construction and Maintenance; Paperhangers; Paving, Surfacing, and Tamping Equipment Operators; Pipe Fitters and Steamfitters; Plasterers and Stucco Masons; Plumbers; Reinforcing Iron and Rebar Workers; Riggers; Roofers; Rough Carpenters; Sheet Metal Workers; Stone Cutters and Carvers, Manufacturing; Stonemasons; Structural Iron and Steel Workers; Tapers; Terrazzo Workers and Finishers; Tile and Marble Setters. **Personality Type:** Realistic. These occupations frequently involve work activities that include practical, hands-on problems and solutions. They often deal with plants; animals; and real-world materials such as wood, tools, and machinery. Many of the occupations require working outside and don't involve a lot of paperwork or working closely with others.

Skills—Repairing; Installation; Equipment Maintenance; Operation Monitoring; Mathematics; Troubleshooting; Operation and Control; Equipment Selection.

Education/Training Required (Nonapprenticeship Route): Long-term on-the-job training.

Related Knowledge/Courses—Building and Construction: Materials, methods, and the appropriate tools to construct objects, structures, and buildings. **Mechanical Devices:** Machines and tools, including their designs, uses, benefits, repair, and maintenance. **Engineering and Technology:** Equipment, tools, and mechanical devices and their uses to produce motion, light, power, technology, and other applications. **Design:** Design techniques, principles, tools, and instruments involved in the production and use of precision technical plans, blueprints, drawings, and models. **Physics:** Physical principles, laws, and applications, including air, water, material dynamics, light, atomic principles, heat, electric theory, earth formations, and meteorological and related natural phenomena. **Transportation:** Principles and methods for moving people or goods by air, rail, sea, or road, including their relative costs, advantages, and limitations.

Work Environment: Noisy; very hot or cold; contaminants; minor burns, cuts, bites, or stings; standing; using hands on objects, tools, or controls.

Further Information: Contact a local joint union-management apprenticeship committee or the nearest office of your state employment service or apprenticeship agency (see Appendix C). To identify the local union office, contact International Brotherhood of Boilermakers, Iron Ship Builders, Blacksmiths, Forgers, and Helpers, 753 State Ave., Suite 570, Kansas City, KS 66101. Internet: www.bnap.com

Bookkeeping, Accounting, and Auditing Clerks

* Annual Earnings: $31,560
* Growth: 12.5%
* Annual Job Openings: 286,854
* Percentage of Women: 90.3%

Related Apprenticeship—Accounting Technician (4000–5000 hrs., hybrid).

Compute, classify, and record numerical data to keep financial records complete. Perform any combination of routine calculating, posting, and verifying duties to obtain primary financial data for use in maintaining accounting records. May also check the accuracy of figures, calculations, and postings pertaining to business transactions recorded by other workers. Operate computers programmed with accounting software to record, store, and analyze information. Check figures, postings, and documents for correct entry, mathematical accuracy, and proper codes. Comply with federal, state, and company policies, procedures, and regulations. Debit, credit, and total accounts on computer spreadsheets and databases, using specialized accounting software. Classify, record, and summarize numerical and financial data to compile and keep financial records, using journals and ledgers or computers. Calculate, prepare, and issue bills, invoices, account statements, and other financial statements according to established procedures. Code documents according to company procedures. Compile statistical, financial, accounting, or auditing reports and tables pertaining to such matters as cash receipts, expenditures, accounts payable and receivable, and profits and losses. Operate 10-key calculators, typewriters, and copy machines to perform calculations and produce documents. Access computerized financial information to answer general questions as well as those related to specific accounts. Reconcile or note and report discrepancies found in records. Perform financial calculations such as amounts due, interest charges, balances, discounts, equity, and principal. Perform general office duties such as filing, answering telephones, and handling routine correspondence. Prepare bank deposits by compiling data from cashiers; verifying and balancing receipts; and sending cash, checks, or other forms of payment to banks. Receive, record, and bank cash, checks, and vouchers. Calculate and prepare checks for utilities, taxes, and other payments. Compare computer printouts to manually maintained journals to determine if they match. Reconcile records of bank transactions. Prepare trial balances of books. Monitor status of loans and accounts to ensure that payments are up to date. Transfer details from separate journals to general ledgers or data-processing sheets. Compile budget data and documents based on estimated revenues and expenses and previous budgets. Calculate costs of materials, overhead, and other expenses, based on estimates, quotations, and price lists.

GOE—Career Cluster/Interest Area: 04. Business and Administration. **Work Group:** 04.06. Mathematical Clerical Support. **Other Apprenticeable Jobs in This Work Group:** Payroll and Timekeeping Clerks. **Personality Type:** Conventional. These occupations frequently involve following set procedures and routines and can include working with data and details more than with ideas. Usually there is a clear line of authority to follow.

Skills—Management of Financial Resources; Mathematics; Time Management.

Education/Training Required (Nonapprenticeship Route): Moderate-term on-the-job training. **Related Knowledge/Courses—Clerical Practices:** Administrative and clerical procedures and systems such as word-processing systems, filing and records management systems, stenography and transcription, forms, design principles, and other office procedures and terminology. **Economics and Accounting:** Economic and accounting principles and practices, the financial markets, banking, and the analysis and reporting of financial data. **Mathematics:** Numbers and their operations and interrelationships, including arithmetic, algebra, geometry, calculus, and statistics and their applications. **Computers and Electronics:** Electric circuit boards, processors, chips, and computer hardware and software, including applications and programming.

Work Environment: Indoors; sitting; repetitive motions.

Brickmasons and Blockmasons

- ❋ Annual Earnings: $44,070
- ❋ Growth: 9.7%
- ❋ Annual Job Openings: 17,569
- ❋ Percentage of Women: 1.6%

Related Apprenticeships—Bricklayer (4500–8000 hrs., hybrid); Bricklayer (Brick and Tile) (8000 hrs.); Bricklayer (Construction) (6000 hrs.); Bricklayer, Firebrick and Refractory Tile (8000 hrs.); Bricklayer/Mason (4500–6000 hrs., hybrid); Chimney Repairer (2000 hrs.).

Lay and bind building materials, such as brick, structural tile, concrete block, cinderblock, glass block, and terra-cotta block, with mortar and other substances to construct or repair walls, partitions, arches, sewers, and

other structures. Construct corners by fastening in plumb position a corner pole or building a corner pyramid of bricks and filling in between the corners, using a line from corner to corner to guide each course, or layer, of brick. Measure distance from reference points and mark guidelines to lay out work, using plumb bobs and levels. Fasten or fuse brick or other building material to structure with wire clamps, anchor holes, torch, or cement. Calculate angles and courses and determine vertical and horizontal alignment of courses. Break or cut bricks, tiles, or blocks to size, using trowel edge, hammer, or power saw. Remove excess mortar with trowels and hand tools and finish mortar joints with jointing tools for a sealed, uniform appearance. Interpret blueprints and drawings to determine specifications and to calculate the materials required. Apply and smooth mortar or other mixture over work surface. Mix specified amounts of sand, clay, dirt, or mortar powder with water to form refractory mixtures. Examine brickwork or structure to determine need for repair. Clean working surface to remove scale, dust, soot, or chips of brick and mortar, using broom, wire brush, or scraper. Lay and align bricks, blocks, or tiles to build or repair structures or high-temperature equipment, such as cupola, kilns, ovens, or furnaces. Remove burned or damaged brick or mortar, using sledgehammer, crowbar, chipping gun, or chisel. Spray or spread refractory material over brickwork to protect against deterioration.

GOE—Career Cluster/Interest Area: 02. Architecture and Construction. **Work Group:** 02.04. Construction Crafts. **Other Apprenticeable Jobs in This Work Group:** Boilermakers; Carpet Installers; Cement Masons and Concrete Finishers; Construction Carpenters; Crane and Tower Operators; Drywall and Ceiling Tile Installers; Electricians; Fence Erectors; Floor Layers, Except Carpet, Wood, and Hard Tiles; Glaziers; Insulation Workers, Floor, Ceiling, and Wall; Insulation Workers, Mechanical; Operating Engineers and Other Construction Equipment Operators; Painters, Construction and Maintenance; Paperhangers; Paving, Surfacing, and Tamping Equipment Operators; Pipe Fitters and Steamfitters; Plasterers and Stucco Masons; Plumbers; Reinforcing Iron and Rebar Workers; Riggers; Roofers; Rough Carpenters; Sheet Metal Workers; Stone Cutters and Carvers, Manufacturing; Stonemasons; Structural Iron and Steel Workers; Tapers; Terrazzo Workers and Finishers; Tile and Marble Setters. **Personality Type:** Realistic. These occupations frequently involve work activities that include practical, hands-on problems and solutions. They often deal with plants; animals; and real-world materials such as wood, tools, and machinery. Many of the occupations require working outside and don't involve a lot of paperwork or working closely with others.

Skills—Equipment Maintenance; Mathematics; Installation; Repairing; Technology Design.

Education/Training Required (Nonapprenticeship Route): Long-term on-the-job training. **Related Knowledge/Courses—Building and Construction:** Materials, methods, and the appropriate tools to construct objects, structures, and buildings. **Design:** Design techniques, principles, tools, and instruments involved in the production and use of precision technical plans, blueprints, drawings, and models. **Mechanical Devices:** Machines and tools, including their designs, uses, benefits, repair, and maintenance. **Production and Processing:** Inputs, outputs, raw materials, waste, quality control, costs, and techniques for maximizing the manufacture and distribution of goods. **Public Safety and Security:** Weaponry; public safety; security operations, rules, regulations, precautions, and prevention; and the protection of people, data, and property. **Mathematics:** Numbers and their operations and interrelationships, including arithmetic, algebra, geometry, calculus, and statistics and their applications.

Work Environment: Outdoors; very hot or cold; hazardous equipment; standing; using hands on objects, tools, or controls; bending or twisting the body.

Further Information: Contact a local joint union-management apprenticeship committee or the nearest office of your state employment service or apprenticeship agency (see Appendix C). To identify the local union office, contact International Union of Bricklayers and Allied Craftworkers, International Masonry Institute, The James Brice House, 42 East St., Annapolis, MD 21401. Internet: www.imiweb.org

Broadcast Technicians

* Annual Earnings: $32,230
* Growth: 12.1%
* Annual Job Openings: 2,955
* Percentage of Women: 15.6%

Related Apprenticeships—Audio Operator (4000 hrs.); Field Engineer (Radio and TV) (8000 hrs.).

Set up, operate, and maintain the electronic equipment used to transmit radio and television programs. Control audio equipment to regulate volume level and quality of sound during radio and television broadcasts. Operate radio transmitter to broadcast radio and television programs. Maintain programming logs as required by station management and the Federal Communications Commission.

Control audio equipment to regulate the volume and sound quality during radio and television broadcasts. Monitor strength, clarity, and reliability of incoming and outgoing signals and adjust equipment as necessary to maintain quality broadcasts. Regulate the fidelity, brightness, and contrast of video transmissions, using video console control panels. Observe monitors and converse with station personnel to determine audio and video levels and to ascertain that programs are airing. Preview scheduled programs to ensure that signals are functioning and programs are ready for transmission. Select sources from which programming will be received or through which programming will be transmitted. Report equipment problems, ensure that repairs are made; make emergency repairs to equipment when necessary and possible. Record sound onto tape or film for radio or television, checking its quality and making adjustments where necessary. Align antennae with receiving dishes to obtain the clearest signal for transmission of broadcasts from field locations. Substitute programs in cases where signals fail. Organize recording sessions and prepare areas such as radio booths and television stations for recording. Perform preventive and minor equipment maintenance, using hand tools. Instruct trainees in how to use television production equipment, how to film events, and how to copy and edit graphics or sound onto videotape. Schedule programming or read television programming logs to determine which programs are to be recorded or aired. Edit broadcast material electronically, using computers. Give technical directions to other personnel during filming. Set up and operate portable field transmission equipment outside the studio. Determine the number, type, and approximate location of microphones needed for best sound recording or transmission quality and position them appropriately. Design and modify equipment to employer specifications. Prepare reports outlining past and future programs, including content.

GOE—Career Cluster/Interest Area: 03. Arts and Communication. **Work Group:** 03.09. Media Technology. **Other Apprenticeable Jobs in This Work Group:** Audio and Video Equipment Technicians; Camera Operators, Television, Video, and Motion Picture; Photographers; Radio Operators; Sound Engineering Technicians. **Personality Type:** Realistic. These occupations frequently involve work activities that include practical, hands-on problems and solutions. They often deal with plants; animals; and real-world materials such as wood, tools, and machinery. Many of the occupations require working outside and don't involve a lot of paperwork or working closely with others.

Skills—Operation Monitoring; Operation and Control; Installation; Troubleshooting; Equipment Maintenance; Repairing; Operations Analysis; Technology Design.

Education/Training Required (Nonapprenticeship Route): Associate degree. **Related Knowledge/Courses—Telecommunications:** Transmission, broadcasting, switching, control, and operation of telecommunications systems. **Communications and Media:** Media production, communication, and dissemination techniques and methods, including alternative ways to inform and entertain via written, oral, and visual media. **Engineering and Technology:** Equipment, tools, and mechanical devices and their uses to produce motion, light, power, technology, and other applications. **Computers and Electronics:** Electric circuit boards, processors, chips, and computer hardware and software, including applications and programming.

Mechanical Devices: Machines and tools, including their designs, uses, benefits, repair, and maintenance. **Production and Processing:** Inputs, outputs, raw materials, waste, quality control, costs, and techniques for maximizing the manufacture and distribution of goods.

Work Environment: Indoors; noisy; sitting; using hands on objects, tools, or controls.

Bus and Truck Mechanics and Diesel Engine Specialists

- ❋ Annual Earnings: $38,640
- ❋ Growth: 11.5%
- ❋ Annual Job Openings: 25,428
- ❋ Percentage of Women: 0.9%

Related Apprenticeships—Diesel Mechanic (8000 hrs.); Machinist, Marine Engine (8000 hrs.); Maintenance Mechanic (Construction; Petroleum) (8000 hrs.); Mechanic, Industrial Truck (8000 hrs.); Oil Field Equipment Mechanic (4000 hrs.); Oil Field Equipment Mechanic (Operator I Frac/Acid) (2000 hrs. or competency); Tractor Mechanic (8000 hrs.).

Diagnose, adjust, repair, or overhaul trucks, buses, and all types of diesel engines. Includes mechanics working primarily with automobile diesel engines. Use hand tools such as screwdrivers, pliers, wrenches, pressure gauges, and precision instruments, as well as power tools such as pneumatic wrenches, lathes, welding equipment, and jacks and hoists. Inspect brake systems, steering mechanisms, wheel bearings, and other important parts to ensure that they are in proper operating condition. Perform routine maintenance such as changing oil, checking batteries, and lubricating equipment and machinery. Adjust and reline brakes, align wheels, tighten bolts and screws, and reassemble equipment.

Raise trucks, buses, and heavy parts or equipment, using hydraulic jacks or hoists. Test drive trucks and buses to diagnose malfunctions or to ensure that they are working properly. Inspect, test, and listen to defective equipment to diagnose malfunctions, using test instruments such as handheld computers, motor analyzers, chassis charts, and pressure gauges. Examine and adjust protective guards, loose bolts, and specified safety devices. Inspect and verify dimensions and clearances of parts to ensure conformance to factory specifications. Specialize in repairing and maintaining parts of the engine, such as fuel injection systems. Attach test instruments to equipment and read dials and gauges to diagnose malfunctions. Rewire ignition systems, lights, and instrument panels. Recondition and replace parts, pistons, bearings, gears, and valves. Repair and adjust seats, doors, and windows and install and repair accessories. Inspect, repair, and maintain automotive and mechanical equipment and machinery such as pumps and compressors. Disassemble and overhaul internal combustion engines, pumps, generators, transmissions, clutches, and differential units. Rebuild gas or diesel engines. Align front ends and suspension systems. Operate valve-grinding machines to grind and reset valves.

GOE—Career Cluster/Interest Area: 13. Manufacturing. **Work Group:** 13.14. Vehicle and Facility Mechanical Work. **Other Apprenticeable Jobs in This Work Group:** Aircraft Mechanics and Service Technicians; Aircraft Structure, Surfaces, Rigging, and Systems Assemblers; Automotive Body and Related Repairers; Automotive Glass Installers and Repairers; Automotive Master Mechanics; Automotive Specialty Technicians; Farm Equipment Mechanics; Fiberglass Laminators and Fabricators; Mobile Heavy Equipment Mechanics, Except Engines; Motorboat Mechanics; Motorcycle Mechanics; Outdoor Power Equipment and Other Small Engine Mechanics; Rail Car Repairers; Recreational Vehicle Service Technicians. **Personality Type:** Realistic. These occupations frequently involve work activities that include practical, hands-on problems and solutions. They often deal with plants; animals; and real-world materials such as wood, tools, and machinery. Many of the occupations require working outside and don't involve a lot of paperwork or working closely with others.

Skills—Repairing; Equipment Maintenance; Troubleshooting; Installation; Science; Technology Design; Equipment Selection.

Education/Training Required (Nonapprenticeship Route): Postsecondary vocational training. **Related Knowledge/Courses—Mechanical Devices:** Machines and tools, including their designs, uses, benefits, repair, and maintenance. **Transportation:** Principles and methods for moving people or goods by air, rail, sea, or road, including their relative costs, advantages, and limitations. **Public Safety and Security:** Weaponry; public safety; security operations, rules, regulations, precautions, and prevention; and the protection of people, data, and property. **Physics:** Physical principles, laws, and applications, including air, water, material dynamics, light, atomic principles, heat, electric theory, earth formations, and meteorological and related natural phenomena. **Engineering and Technology:** Equipment, tools, and mechanical devices and their uses to produce motion, light, power, technology, and other applications. **Law and Government:** Laws, legal codes, court procedures, precedents, government regulations, executive orders, agency rules, and the democratic political process.

Work Environment: Noisy; very bright or dim lighting; contaminants; hazardous equipment; standing; using hands on objects, tools, or controls.

Butchers and Meat Cutters

- ❋ Annual Earnings: $27,480
- ❋ Growth: 1.9%
- ❋ Annual Job Openings: 14,503
- ❋ Percentage of Women: 30.4%

Related Apprenticeships—Butcher, Meat (Hotel and Restaurant) (6000 hrs.); Meat Cutter (6000 hrs.).

Cut, trim, or prepare consumer-sized portions of meat for use or sale in retail establishments. Wrap, weigh, label, and price cuts of meat. Prepare and place meat cuts and products in display counter so they will appear attractive and catch the shopper's eye. Prepare special cuts of meat ordered by customers. Cut, trim, bone, tie, and grind meats, such as beef, pork, poultry, and fish, to prepare meat in cooking form. Receive, inspect, and store meat upon delivery to ensure meat quality. Shape, lace, and tie roasts, using boning knife, skewer, and twine. Estimate requirements and order or requisition meat supplies to maintain inventories. Supervise other butchers or meat cutters. Record quantity of meat received and issued to cooks and keep records of meat sales. Negotiate with representatives from supply companies to determine order details. Cure, smoke, tenderize, and preserve meat. Total sales and collect money from customers.

GOE—Career Cluster/Interest Area: 09. Hospitality, Tourism, and Recreation. **Work Group:** 09.04. Food and Beverage Preparation. **Other**

Apprenticeable Jobs in This Work Group: Chefs and Head Cooks; Cooks, Fast Food; Cooks, Institution and Cafeteria; Cooks, Restaurant. **Personality Type:** Realistic. These occupations frequently involve work activities that include practical, hands-on problems and solutions. They often deal with plants; animals; and real-world materials such as wood, tools, and machinery. Many of the occupations require working outside and don't involve a lot of paperwork or working closely with others.

Skill—Equipment Maintenance.

Education/Training Required (Nonapprenticeship Route): Long-term on-the-job training. **Related Knowledge/Courses—Food Production:** Techniques and equipment for planting, growing, and harvesting of food for consumption, including crop-rotation methods, animal husbandry, and food storage/handling techniques. **Production and Processing:** Inputs, outputs, raw materials, waste, quality control, costs, and techniques for maximizing the manufacture and distribution of goods. **Mechanical Devices:** Machines and tools, including their designs, uses, benefits, repair, and maintenance. **Sales and Marketing:** Principles and methods involved in showing, promoting, and selling products or services. This includes marketing strategies and tactics, product demonstration and sales techniques, and sales control systems.

Work Environment: Indoors; very hot or cold; hazardous equipment; standing; using hands on objects, tools, or controls; repetitive motions.

Cabinetmakers and Bench Carpenters

❋ Annual Earnings: $27,970
❋ Growth: 2.8%
❋ Annual Job Openings: 9,780
❋ Percentage of Women: 4.4%

Related Apprenticeships—Accordion Maker (8000 hrs.); Cabinetmaker (5200–8000 hrs., hybrid); Cabinetmaker (8000 hrs.); Carver, Hand (8000 hrs.); Harpsichord Maker (4000 hrs.); Hat-Block Maker (Woodwork) (6000 hrs.); Last-Model Maker (8000 hrs.); Machinist, Wood (8000 hrs.); Pipe Organ Builder (6000 hrs.); Violin Maker, Hand (8000 hrs.).

Cut, shape, and assemble wooden articles or set up and operate a variety of woodworking machines such as power saws, jointers, and mortisers to surface, cut, or shape lumber or to fabricate parts for wood products. Produce and assemble components of articles such as store fixtures, office equipment, cabinets, and high-grade furniture. Verify dimensions and check the quality and fit of pieces to ensure adherence to specifications. Set up and operate machines, including power saws, jointers, mortisers, tenoners, molders, and shapers, to cut, mold, and shape woodstock and wood substitutes. Measure and mark dimensions of parts on paper or lumber stock prior to cutting, following blueprints, to ensure a tight fit and quality product. Reinforce joints with nails or other fasteners to prepare articles for finishing. Attach parts and subassemblies together to form completed units, using glue, dowels, nails, screws, or clamps. Establish the specifications of articles to be constructed or repaired and plan the methods and operations for shaping and assembling parts, based on blueprints, drawings, diagrams, or oral or written instructions. Cut timber to the right size and shape and trim parts of joints to ensure a snug fit, using hand tools such as planes, chisels, or wood files. Trim, sand, and scrape surfaces and joints to prepare articles for finishing. Match materials for color, grain, and texture, giving attention to knots and other features of the wood. Bore holes for insertion of screws or dowels by hand or using boring machines. Program computers to operate machinery. Estimate the amounts, types, and costs of needed materials. Perform final touch-ups with sandpaper and steel wool. Install hardware such as hinges, handles, catches, and drawer pulls, using hand tools. Discuss projects with customers and draw up detailed specifications. Repair or alter wooden furniture, cabinetry, fixtures, paneling, and other pieces. Apply Masonite, formica, and vinyl surfacing materials. Design furniture, using computer-aided drawing programs. Dip, brush, or spray assembled articles with protective or decorative finishes such as stain, varnish, paint, or lacquer.

GOE—Career Cluster/Interest Area: 13. Manufacturing. **Work Group:** 13.10. Woodworking Technology. **Other Apprenticeable Jobs in This Work Group:** Furniture Finishers; Model Makers, Wood; Patternmakers, Wood. **Personality Type:** Realistic. These occupations frequently involve work activities that include practical, hands-on problems and solutions. They often deal with plants; animals; and real-world materials such as wood, tools, and machinery. Many of the occupations require working outside and don't involve a lot of paperwork or working closely with others.

Skills—Installation; Quality Control Analysis; Mathematics; Instructing; Equipment Selection.

Education/Training Required (Nonapprenticeship Route): Long-term on-the-job training. **Related Knowledge/Courses—Design:** Design techniques, principles, tools, and instruments involved in the production and use of precision technical plans, blueprints, drawings, and models. **Production and Processing:** Inputs, outputs, raw materials, waste, quality control, costs, and techniques for maximizing the manufacture and distribution of goods. **Mechanical Devices:** Machines and tools, including their designs, uses, benefits, repair, and maintenance. **Building and Construction:** Materials, methods, and the appropriate tools to construct objects, structures, and buildings. **Engineering and Technology:** Equipment, tools, and mechanical devices and their uses to produce motion, light, power, technology, and other applications.

Work Environment: Noisy; contaminants; hazardous equipment; standing; walking and running; using hands on objects, tools, or controls.

Further Information: Contact a local joint union-management apprenticeship committee or the nearest office of your state employment service or apprenticeship agency (see Appendix C). To identify the local union office, contact United Brotherhood of Carpenters and Joiners of America, 101 Constitution Ave. NW, Washington, DC 20001. Internet: www. carpenters.org

Camera Operators, Television, Video, and Motion Picture

* Annual Earnings: $41,850
* Growth: 11.5%
* Annual Job Openings: 3,496
* Percentage of Women: 15.6%

Related Apprenticeship—Camera Operator (6000 hrs.).

Operate television, video, or motion picture camera to photograph images or scenes for various purposes, such as TV broadcasts, advertising, video production, or motion pictures. Operate television or motion picture cameras to record scenes for television broadcasts, advertising, or motion pictures. Compose and frame each shot, applying the technical aspects of light, lenses, film, filters, and camera settings to achieve the effects sought by directors. Operate zoom lenses, changing images according to specifications and rehearsal instructions. Use cameras in any of several different camera mounts, such as stationary, track-mounted, or crane-mounted. Test, clean, and maintain equipment to ensure proper working condition. Adjust positions and controls of cameras, printers, and related equipment to change focus, exposure, and lighting. Gather and edit raw footage on location to send to television affiliates for broadcast, using electronic news-gathering or film-production equipment. Confer with directors, sound and lighting technicians, electricians, and other crew members to discuss assignments and determine filming sequences, desired effects, camera movements, and lighting requirements. Observe sets or locations for potential problems and to determine filming and lighting requirements. Instruct camera operators regarding camera setups, angles, distances, movement, and variables and cues for starting and stopping filming. Select and assemble cameras, accessories, equipment, and film stock to be used during filming, using knowledge of filming techniques, requirements, and computations. Label and record contents of exposed film and note details on report forms. Read charts and compute ratios to determine variables such as lighting, shutter angles, filter factors, and camera distances. Set up cameras, optical printers, and related equipment to produce photographs and special effects. View films to resolve problems of exposure control, subject and camera movement, changes in subject distance, and related variables. Reload camera magazines with fresh raw film stock. Read and analyze work orders and specifications to determine locations of subject material, work procedures, sequences of operations, and machine setups. Receive raw film stock and maintain film inventories.

GOE—Career Cluster/Interest Area: 03. Arts and Communication. **Work Group:** 03.09. Media Technology. **Other Apprenticeable Jobs in This Work Group:** Audio and Video Equipment Technicians; Broadcast Technicians; Photographers; Radio Operators; Sound Engineering Technicians. **Personality Type:** Realistic. These occupations frequently involve work activities that include practical, hands-on problems and solutions. They often deal with plants; animals; and real-world materials such as wood, tools, and machinery. Many of the occupations require working outside and don't involve a lot of paperwork or working closely with others.

Skills—Operation Monitoring; Operation and Control; Equipment Maintenance; Troubleshooting; Equipment Selection; Operations Analysis; Active Listening; Installation.

Education/Training Required (Nonapprenticeship Route): Postsecondary vocational training. **Related Knowledge/Courses— Communications and Media:** Media production, communication, and dissemination techniques and methods, including alternative ways to inform and entertain via written, oral, and visual media. **Telecommunications:** Transmission, broadcasting, switching, control, and operation of telecommunications systems. **Computers and Electronics:** Electric circuit boards, processors, chips, and computer hardware and software, including applications and programming. **Engineering and Technology:** Equipment, tools, and mechanical devices and their uses to produce motion, light, power, technology, and other applications.

Work Environment: More often indoors than outdoors; very bright or dim lighting; standing; using hands on objects, tools, or controls.

Cargo and Freight Agents

* Annual Earnings: $37,060
* Growth: 16.5%
* Annual Job Openings: 9,967
* Percentage of Women: 75.4%

Related Apprenticeship—Transportation Clerk (3000 hrs.).

Expedite and route movement of incoming and outgoing cargo and freight shipments in airline, train, and trucking terminals and shipping docks. Take orders from customers and arrange pickup of freight and cargo for delivery to loading platform. Prepare and examine bills of lading to determine shipping charges and tariffs. Negotiate and arrange transport of goods with shipping or freight companies. Notify consignees, passengers, or customers of the arrival of freight or baggage and arrange for delivery. Advise clients on transportation and payment methods. Prepare manifests showing baggage, mail, and freight weights and number of passengers on airplanes and transmit data to destinations. Determine method of shipment and prepare bills of lading, invoices, and other shipping documents. Check import/export documentation to determine cargo contents and classify goods into different fee or tariff groups, using a tariff coding system. Estimate freight or postal rates and record shipment costs and weights. Enter shipping information into a computer by hand or by using a hand-held scanner that reads bar codes on goods. Retrieve stored items and trace lost shipments as necessary. Pack goods for shipping, using tools such as staplers, strapping machines, and hammers. Direct delivery trucks to shipping doors or designated marshalling areas and help load and unload goods safely. Inspect and count items received and check them against invoices or other documents, recording shortages and rejecting damaged goods. Install straps, braces, and padding to loads to prevent shifting or damage during shipment. Keep records of all goods shipped, received, and stored. Coordinate and supervise activities of workers engaged in packing and shipping merchandise. Arrange insurance coverage for goods. Direct or participate in cargo loading to ensure completeness of load and even distribution of weight. Open cargo containers and unwrap contents, using steel cutters, crowbars, or other hand tools. Attach address labels, identification codes, and shipping instructions to containers. Contact vendors or claims adjustment departments to resolve problems with shipments or contact service depots to arrange for repairs. Route received goods to first available flight or to appropriate storage areas or departments, using forklifts, handtrucks, or other equipment. Maintain a supply of packing materials.

GOE—Career Cluster/Interest Area: 16. Transportation, Distribution, and Logistics. **Work Group:** 16.07. Transportation Support Work. **Other Apprenticeable Jobs in This Work Group:** Cleaners of Vehicles and Equipment. **Personality Type:** Conventional. These occupations frequently involve following set procedures and routines and can include working with data and details more than with ideas. Usually there is a clear line of authority to follow.

Skills—Negotiation; Instructing; Writing; Service Orientation; Monitoring; Speaking; Learning Strategies.

Education/Training Required (Nonapprenticeship Route): Moderate-term on-the-job training. **Related Knowledge/Courses—Transportation:** Principles and methods for moving people or goods by air, rail, sea, or road, including their relative costs, advantages, and limitations. **Geography:** Various methods for describing the location and distribution of land, sea, and air masses, including their physical locations, relationships, and characteristics. **Customer and Personal Service:** Principles and processes for providing customer and personal services, including needs assessment techniques, quality service standards, alternative delivery systems, and customer satisfaction evaluation techniques. **Clerical Practices:** Administrative and clerical procedures and systems such as word-processing systems, filing and records management systems, stenography and transcription, forms, design principles, and other office procedures and terminology. **Computers and Electronics:** Electric circuit boards, processors, chips, and computer hardware and software, including applications and programming. **Administration and Management:** Principles and processes involved in business and organizational planning, coordination, and execution. This includes strategic planning, resource allocation, manpower modeling, leadership techniques, and production methods.

Work Environment: Indoors; sitting; repetitive motions.

Carpet Installers

- ❊ Annual Earnings: $36,040
- ❊ Growth: –1.2%
- ❊ Annual Job Openings: 6,692
- ❊ Percentage of Women: 2.4%

Related Apprenticeship—Carpet Layer (6000 hrs.).

Lay and install carpet from rolls or blocks on floors. Install padding and trim flooring materials. Join edges of carpet and seam edges where necessary by sewing or by using tape with glue and heated carpet iron. Cut and trim carpet to fit along wall edges, openings, and projections, finishing the edges with a wall trimmer. Roll out, measure, mark, and cut carpeting to size with a carpet knife, following floor sketches and allowing extra carpet for final fitting. Inspect the surface to be covered to determine its condition and correct any imperfections that might show through carpet or cause carpet to wear unevenly. Plan the layout of the carpet, allowing for expected traffic patterns and placing seams for best appearance and longest wear. Stretch carpet to align with walls and ensure a smooth surface and press carpet in place over tack strips or use staples, tape, tacks, or glue to hold carpet in place. Take measurements and study floor sketches to calculate the area to be carpeted and the amount of material needed. Cut carpet padding to size and install padding, following prescribed method. Install carpet on some floors by using adhesive, following prescribed method. Nail tack strips around area to be carpeted or use old strips to attach edges of new carpet. Fasten metal treads across door openings or where carpet meets flooring to hold carpet in place. Measure, cut, and install tackless strips along the baseboard or wall. Draw building diagrams and record dimensions. Move furniture from area to be carpeted and remove old carpet and padding. Cut and bind material.

GOE—Career Cluster/Interest Area: 02. Architecture and Construction. **Work Group:** 02.04. Construction Crafts. **Other Apprenticeable Jobs in This Work Group:** Boilermakers; Brickmasons and Blockmasons; Cement Masons and Concrete Finishers; Construction Carpenters; Crane and Tower Operators; Drywall and Ceiling Tile Installers; Electricians; Fence Erectors; Floor Layers, Except Carpet, Wood, and Hard Tiles; Glaziers; Insulation Workers, Floor, Ceiling, and Wall; Insulation Workers, Mechanical; Operating Engineers and Other Construction Equipment Operators; Painters, Construction and Maintenance; Paperhangers; Paving, Surfacing, and Tamping Equipment Operators; Pipe Fitters and Steamfitters; Plasterers and Stucco Masons; Plumbers; Reinforcing Iron and Rebar Workers; Riggers; Roofers; Rough Carpenters; Sheet Metal Workers; Stone Cutters and Carvers, Manufacturing; Stonemasons; Structural Iron and Steel Workers; Tapers; Terrazzo Workers and Finishers; Tile and Marble Setters. **Personality Type:** Realistic. These occupations frequently involve work activities that include practical, hands-on problems and solutions. They often deal with plants; animals; and real-world materials such as wood, tools, and machinery. Many of the occupations require working outside and don't involve a lot of paperwork or working closely with others.

Skills—Installation; Equipment Selection; Repairing; Management of Personnel Resources; Mathematics; Equipment Maintenance; Complex Problem Solving; Coordination.

Education/Training Required (Nonapprenticeship Route): Moderate-term on-the-job training. **Related Knowledge/Courses—Building and Construction:** Materials, methods, and the appropriate tools to construct objects, structures, and buildings. **Public Safety and Security:** Weaponry; public safety; security operations, rules, regulations, precautions, and prevention; and the protection of people, data, and property. **Sales and Marketing:** Principles and methods involved in showing, promoting, and selling products or services. This includes marketing strategies and tactics, product demonstration and sales techniques, and sales control systems. **Transportation:** Principles and methods for moving people or goods by air, rail, sea, or road, including their relative costs, advantages, and limitations. **Mechanical Devices:** Machines and tools, including their designs, uses, benefits, repair, and maintenance. **Design:** Design techniques, principles, tools, and instruments involved in the production and use of precision technical plans, blueprints, drawings, and models.

Work Environment: Minor burns, cuts, bites, or stings; standing; walking and running; kneeling, crouching, stooping, or crawling; using hands on objects, tools, or controls; bending or twisting the body.

Cement Masons and Concrete Finishers

- ❀ Annual Earnings: $33,840
- ❀ Growth: 11.4%
- ❀ Annual Job Openings: 34,625
- ❀ Percentage of Women: 0.7%

Related Apprenticeship—Cement Mason (4000 hrs.).

Smooth and finish surfaces of poured concrete, such as floors, walks, sidewalks, roads, or curbs, using a variety of hand and power tools. Align forms for sidewalks, curbs, or gutters; patch voids; and use saws to cut expansion joints. Check the forms that hold the concrete to see that they are properly constructed. Set the forms that hold concrete to the desired pitch and depth and align them. Spread, level, and smooth concrete, using rake, shovel, hand or power trowel, hand or power screed, and float. Mold expansion joints and edges, using edging tools, jointers, and straightedge. Monitor how the wind, heat, or cold affect the curing of the concrete throughout the entire process. Signal truck driver to position truck to facilitate pouring concrete and move chute to direct concrete on forms. Produce rough concrete surface, using broom. Operate power vibrator to compact concrete. Direct the casting of the concrete and supervise laborers who use shovels or special tools to spread it. Mix cement, sand, and water to produce concrete, grout, or slurry, using hoe, trowel, tamper, scraper, or concrete-mixing machine. Cut out damaged areas, drill holes for reinforcing rods, and position reinforcing rods to repair concrete, using power saw and drill. Wet surface to prepare for bonding, fill holes and cracks with grout or slurry, and smooth, using trowel. Wet concrete surface and rub with stone to smooth surface and obtain specified finish. Clean chipped area, using wire brush, and feel and observe surface to determine if it is rough or uneven. Apply hardening and sealing compounds to cure surface of concrete and waterproof or restore surface. Chip, scrape, and grind high spots, ridges, and rough projections to finish concrete, using pneumatic chisels, power grinders, or hand tools. Spread roofing paper on surface of foundation and spread concrete onto roofing paper with trowel to form terrazzo base. Build wooden molds and clamp molds around area to be repaired, using hand tools. Sprinkle colored marble or stone chips, powdered steel, or coloring powder over surface to produce prescribed finish. Cut metal division strips and press them into terrazzo base so that top edges form desired design or pattern. Fabricate concrete beams, columns, and panels. Waterproof or restore concrete surfaces, using appropriate compounds.

GOE—Career Cluster/Interest Area: 02. Architecture and Construction. **Work Group:** 02.04. Construction Crafts. **Other Apprenticeable Jobs in This Work Group:** Boilermakers; Brickmasons and Blockmasons; Carpet Installers; Construction Carpenters; Crane and Tower Operators; Drywall and Ceiling Tile Installers; Electricians; Fence Erectors; Floor Layers, Except Carpet, Wood, and Hard Tiles; Glaziers; Insulation Workers, Floor, Ceiling, and Wall; Insulation Workers, Mechanical; Operating Engineers and Other Construction Equipment Operators; Painters, Construction and Maintenance; Paperhangers; Paving, Surfacing, and Tamping Equipment Operators; Pipe Fitters and Steamfitters; Plasterers and Stucco Masons; Plumbers; Reinforcing Iron and Rebar Workers; Riggers; Roofers; Rough Carpenters; Sheet Metal Workers; Stone Cutters and Carvers, Manufacturing; Stonemasons; Structural Iron and Steel Workers; Tapers; Terrazzo Workers and Finishers; Tile and Marble Setters. **Personality Type:** Realistic. These occupations frequently involve work activities that include practical, hands-on problems and solutions. They often deal with plants; animals; and real-world materials such as wood, tools, and machinery. Many of the occupations require working outside and don't involve a lot of paperwork or working closely with others.

Skills—Mathematics; Installation; Repairing; Equipment Maintenance; Equipment Selection; Coordination.

Education/Training Required (Nonapprenticeship Route): Moderate-term on-the-job training. **Related Knowledge/Courses—Building and Construction:** Materials, methods, and the appropriate tools to construct objects, structures, and buildings. **Public Safety and Security:** Weaponry; public safety; security operations, rules, regulations, precautions, and prevention; and the protection of people, data, and property. **Mechanical Devices:** Machines and tools, including their designs, uses, benefits, repair, and maintenance. **Design:** Design techniques, principles, tools, and instruments involved in the production and use of precision technical plans, blueprints, drawings, and models. **Engineering and Technology:** Equipment, tools, and mechanical devices and their uses to produce motion, light, power, technology, and other applications.

Work Environment: Outdoors; noisy; hazardous equipment; standing; using hands on objects, tools, or controls; bending or twisting the body.

Chefs and Head Cooks

- ❋ Annual Earnings: $37,160
- ❋ Growth: 7.6%
- ❋ Annual Job Openings: 9,401
- ❋ Percentage of Women: 23.9%

Related Apprenticeships—Baker (Hotel and Restaurant) (6000 hrs.); Chief Cook (Water Transportation) (4000.5 hrs.); Cook, Pastry (Hotel and Restaurant) (6000 hrs.).

Direct the preparation, seasoning, and cooking of salads, soups, fish, meats, vegetables, desserts, or other foods. May plan and price menu items, order supplies, and keep records and accounts. May participate in cooking.

Check the quality of raw and cooked food products to ensure that standards are met. Monitor sanitation practices to ensure that employees follow standards and regulations. Check the quantity and quality of received products. Order or requisition food and other supplies needed to ensure efficient operation. Inspect supplies, equipment, and work areas to ensure conformance to established standards. Supervise and coordinate activities of cooks and workers engaged in food preparation. Determine how food should be presented and create decorative food displays. Instruct cooks and other workers in the preparation, cooking, garnishing, and presentation of food. Estimate amounts and costs of required supplies, such as food and ingredients. Collaborate with other personnel to plan and develop recipes and menus, taking into account such factors as seasonal availability of ingredients and the likely number of customers. Analyze recipes to assign prices to menu items, based on food, labor, and overhead costs. Prepare and cook foods of all types, either on a regular basis or for special guests or functions. Determine production schedules and staff requirements necessary to ensure timely delivery of services. Recruit and hire staff, including cooks and other kitchen workers. Meet with customers to discuss menus for special occasions such as weddings, parties, and banquets. Demonstrate new cooking techniques and equipment to staff. Meet with sales representatives in order to negotiate prices and order supplies. Arrange for equipment purchases and repairs. Record production and operational data on specified forms. Plan, direct, and supervise the food preparation and cooking activities of multiple kitchens or restaurants in an establishment such as a restaurant chain, hospital, or hotel. Coordinate planning, budgeting, and purchasing for all the food operations within establishments such as clubs, hotels, or restaurant chains.

GOE—Career Cluster/Interest Area: 09. Hospitality, Tourism, and Recreation. **Work Group:** 09.04. Food and Beverage Preparation. **Other Apprenticeable Jobs in This Work Group:** Butchers and Meat Cutters; Cooks, Fast Food; Cooks, Institution and Cafeteria; Cooks, Restaurant. **Personality Type:** Enterprising. These occupations frequently involve starting up and carrying out projects and can involve leading people and making many decisions. They sometimes require risk taking and often deal with business.

Skills—Equipment Maintenance; Management of Financial Resources; Repairing; Management of Personnel Resources; Service Orientation; Negotiation; Quality Control Analysis; Systems Analysis.

Education/Training Required (Nonapprenticeship Route): Work experience in a related occupation. **Related Knowledge/Courses— Food Production:** Techniques and equipment for planting, growing, and harvesting of food for consumption, including crop-rotation methods, animal husbandry, and food storage/handling techniques. **Production and Processing:** Inputs, outputs, raw materials, waste, quality control, costs, and techniques for maximizing the manufacture and distribution of goods. **Administration and Management:** Principles and processes involved in business and organizational planning, coordination, and execution. This includes strategic planning, resource allocation, manpower modeling, leadership techniques, and production methods. **Chemistry:** The composition, structure, and properties of substances and of the chemical processes and transformations that they undergo. This includes uses of chemicals and their interactions, danger signs, production techniques, and disposal methods. **Education and Training:** Instructional methods and training techniques, including curriculum design principles, learning theory, group and individual teaching techniques, design of individual development plans, and test design principles. **Personnel and Human Resources:** Principles and procedures for personnel recruitment; selection; training; compensation and benefits; labor relations and negotiation; and personnel information systems.

Work Environment: Minor burns, cuts, bites, or stings; standing; walking and running; using hands on objects, tools, or controls; bending or twisting the body; repetitive motions.

Chemical Equipment Operators and Tenders

* Annual Earnings: $44,050
* Growth: –3.9%
* Annual Job Openings: 1,469
* Percentage of Women: 13.0%

Related Apprenticeship—Chemical Operator III (6000 hrs.).

Operate or tend equipment to control chemical changes or reactions in processing of industrial or consumer products. Equipment used includes devulcanizers, steam-jacketed kettles, and reactor vessels. Adjust controls to regulate temperature, pressure, feed, and flow of liquids and gases and times of prescribed reactions according to knowledge of equipment and processes. Observe safety precautions to prevent fires and explosions. Monitor gauges, recording instruments, flowmeters, or products to ensure that specified conditions are maintained. Control and operate equipment in which chemical changes or reactions take place during processing of industrial or consumer products. Measure, weigh, and mix chemical ingredients according to specifications. Inspect equipment or units to detect leaks and malfunctions, shutting equipment down if necessary. Patrol work areas to detect leaks and equipment malfunctions and to monitor operating conditions. Test product samples for specific gravity, chemical characteristics, pH levels, and concentrations or viscosities or send them to laboratories for testing. Draw samples of products at specified stages so that analyses can be performed. Record operational data such as temperatures, pressures, ingredients used, processing times, or test results. Notify maintenance engineers of equipment malfunctions. Add treating or neutralizing agents to products and pump products through filters or centrifuges to remove impurities or to precipitate products. Open valves or start pumps, agitators, reactors, blowers, or automatic feed of materials. Read plant specifications to determine products, ingredients, and prescribed modifications of plant procedures. Drain equipment and pump water or other solutions through to flush and clean tanks and equipment. Use hand tools to make minor repairs and lubricate and maintain equipment. Flush or clean equipment with steam hoses or mechanical reamers. Observe colors and consistencies of products and compare them to instrument readings and to laboratory and standard test results. Implement appropriate industrial emergency response procedures. Dump or scoop prescribed solid, granular, or powdered materials into equipment. Estimate materials required for production and manufacturing of products.

GOE—Career Cluster/Interest Area: 13. Manufacturing. **Work Group:** 13.03. Production Work, Assorted Materials Processing.

Other Apprenticeable Jobs in This Work Group: Bakers; Coating, Painting, and Spraying Machine Setters, Operators, and Tenders; Cooling and Freezing Equipment Operators and Tenders; Cutting and Slicing Machine Setters, Operators, and Tenders; Extruding, Forming, Pressing, and Compacting Machine Setters, Operators, and Tenders; Food Batchmakers; Furnace, Kiln, Oven, Drier, and Kettle Operators and Tenders; Heat Treating Equipment Setters, Operators, and Tenders, Metal and Plastic; Metal-Refining Furnace Operators and Tenders; Mixing and Blending Machine Setters, Operators, and Tenders; Plating and Coating Machine Setters, Operators, and Tenders, Metal and Plastic; Sawing Machine Setters, Operators, and Tenders, Wood; Separating, Filtering, Clarifying, Precipitating, and Still Machine Setters, Operators, and Tenders; Sewing Machine Operators; Slaughterers and Meat Packers; Team Assemblers; Woodworking Machine Setters, Operators, and Tenders, Except Sawing. **Personality Type:** Realistic. These occupations frequently involve work activities that include practical, hands-on problems and solutions. They often deal with plants; animals; and real-world materials such as wood, tools, and machinery. Many of the occupations require working outside and don't involve a lot of paperwork or working closely with others.

Skills—Operation Monitoring; Operation and Control; Troubleshooting; Equipment Maintenance; Science; Repairing; Operations Analysis; Quality Control Analysis.

Education/Training Required (Nonapprenticeship Route): Moderate-term on-the-job training. **Related Knowledge/ Courses**—**Chemistry:** The composition, structure, and properties of substances and of the chemical processes and transformations that they undergo. This includes uses of chemicals and their interactions, danger signs, production techniques, and disposal methods. **Mechanical Devices:** Machines and tools, including their designs, uses, benefits, repair, and maintenance. **Production and Processing:** Inputs, outputs, raw materials, waste, quality control, costs, and techniques for maximizing the manufacture and distribution of goods. **Public Safety and Security:** Weaponry; public safety; security operations, rules, regulations, precautions, and prevention; and the protection of people, data, and property.

Work Environment: More often outdoors than indoors; noisy; very hot or cold; contaminants; hazardous conditions.

Chemical Plant and System Operators

- ❀ Annual Earnings: $50,860
- ❀ Growth: –15.3%
- ❀ Annual Job Openings: 5,620
- ❀ Percentage of Women: 30.4%

Related Apprenticeships—Chief Operator (Chemicals) (6000 hrs.); Plant Operator, Furnace Process (8000 hrs.).

Control or operate an entire chemical process or system of machines. Move control settings to make necessary adjustments on equipment units affecting speeds of chemical reactions, quality, and yields. Monitor recording instruments, flowmeters, panel lights, and other indicators and listen for warning signals to verify conformity of process conditions. Control or operate chemical processes or systems of machines, using panelboards, control boards, or semi-automatic equipment. Record operating data such as process conditions, test results, and instrument readings. Confer with technical and supervisory personnel to report or resolve conditions affecting safety, efficiency, and product quality. Draw samples of products and conduct quality control tests to monitor processing and to ensure that standards are met. Regulate or shut down equipment during emergency situations as directed by supervisory personnel. Start pumps to wash and rinse reactor vessels; to exhaust gases and vapors; to regulate the flow of oil, steam, air, and perfume to towers; and to add products to converter or blending vessels. Interpret chemical reactions visible through sight glasses or on television monitors and review laboratory test reports for process adjustments. Patrol work areas to ensure that solutions in tanks and troughs are not in danger of overflowing. Notify maintenance, stationary-engineering, and other auxiliary personnel to correct equipment malfunctions and to adjust power, steam, water, or air supplies. Direct workers engaged in operating machinery that regulates the flow of materials and products. Inspect operating units such as towers, soap-spray storage tanks, scrubbers, collectors, and driers to ensure that all are functioning and to maintain maximum efficiency. Turn valves to regulate flow of products or byproducts through agitator tanks, storage drums, or neutralizer tanks. Calculate material requirements or yields according to formulas. Gauge tank levels, using calibrated rods. Repair and replace damaged equipment. Defrost frozen valves, using steam hoses. Supervise the cleaning of towers, strainers, and spray tips.

GOE—Career Cluster/Interest Area: 13. Manufacturing. **Work Group:** 13.16. Utility Operation and Energy Distribution. **Other Apprenticeable Jobs in This Work Group:** Petroleum Pump System Operators, Refinery Operators, and Gaugers; Power Distributors and Dispatchers; Power Plant Operators; Stationary Engineers and Boiler Operators; Water and Liquid Waste Treatment Plant and System Operators. **Personality Type:** Realistic. These occupations frequently involve work activities that include practical, hands-on problems and solutions. They often deal with plants; animals; and real-world materials such as wood, tools, and machinery. Many of the occupations require working outside and don't involve a lot of paperwork or working closely with others.

Skills—Operation Monitoring; Operation and Control; Troubleshooting; Science; Equipment Maintenance; Operations Analysis; Systems Analysis; Quality Control Analysis.

Education/Training Required (Nonapprenticeship Route): Long-term on-the-job training. **Related Knowledge/Courses—Production and Processing:** Inputs, outputs, raw materials, waste, quality control, costs, and techniques for maximizing the manufacture and distribution of goods. **Chemistry:** The composition, structure, and properties of substances and of the chemical processes and transformations that they undergo. This includes uses of chemicals and their interactions, danger signs, production techniques, and disposal methods. **Mechanical Devices:** Machines and tools, including their designs, uses, benefits, repair, and maintenance. **Physics:** Physical principles, laws, and applications, including air, water, material dynamics, light, atomic principles, heat, electric theory, earth formations, and meteorological and related natural phenomena. **Engineering and Technology:** Equipment, tools, and mechanical devices and their uses to produce motion, light, power, technology, and other applications. **Public Safety and Security:** Weaponry; public safety; security operations, rules, regulations, precautions, and prevention; and the protection of people, data, and property.

Work Environment: More often indoors than outdoors; noisy; very hot or cold; contaminants; hazardous conditions.

Chemical Technicians

* Annual Earnings: $40,740
* Growth: 5.8%
* Annual Job Openings: 4,010
* Percentage of Women: 35.9%

Related Apprenticeships—Chemical Engineering Technician (8000 hrs.); Chemical Laboratory Technician (8000 hrs.); Laboratory Technician (2000 hrs.); Laboratory Tester (4000 hrs.).

Conduct chemical and physical laboratory tests to assist scientists in making qualitative and quantitative analyses of solids, liquids, and gaseous materials for purposes such as research and development of new products or processes; quality control; maintenance of environmental standards; and other work involving experimental, theoretical, or practical application of chemistry and related sciences. Monitor product quality to ensure compliance to standards and specifications. Set up and conduct chemical experiments, tests, and analyses using techniques such as chromatography, spectroscopy, physical and chemical separation techniques, and microscopy. Conduct chemical and physical laboratory tests to assist scientists in making qualitative and quantitative analyses of solids, liquids, and gaseous materials. Compile and interpret results of tests and analyses. Provide technical support and assistance to chemists and engineers. Prepare chemical solutions for products and processes following standardized formulas or create experimental formulas. Maintain, clean, and sterilize laboratory instruments and equipment. Write technical reports or prepare graphs and charts to document experimental results. Order and inventory materials to maintain supplies. Develop and conduct programs of sampling and analysis to maintain quality standards of raw materials, chemical intermediates, and products. Direct or monitor other workers producing chemical products. Operate experimental pilot plants, assisting with experimental design. Develop new chemical engineering processes or production techniques. Design and fabricate experimental apparatus to develop new products and processes.

GOE—Career Cluster/Interest Area: 15. Scientific Research, Engineering, and Mathematics. **Work Group:** 15.05. Physical Science Laboratory Technology. **Other Apprenticeable Jobs in This Work Group:** No others in group. **Personality Type:** Investigative. These occupations frequently involve working with ideas and require an extensive amount of thinking. They can involve searching for facts and figuring out problems mentally.

Skills—Science; Operation Monitoring; Quality Control Analysis; Equipment Maintenance; Operation and Control; Repairing; Mathematics; Troubleshooting.

Education/Training Required (Nonapprenticeship Route): Associate degree. **Related Knowledge/Courses—Chemistry:** The composition, structure, and properties of substances and of the chemical processes and transformations that they undergo. This includes uses of chemicals and their interactions, danger signs, production techniques, and disposal methods. **Mechanical Devices:** Machines and tools, including their designs, uses, benefits, repair, and maintenance. **Computers and Electronics:** Electric circuit boards, processors, chips, and computer hardware and software, including applications and programming. **Mathematics:** Numbers and their operations and interrelationships, including arithmetic, algebra, geometry, calculus, and statistics and their applications.

Work Environment: Indoors; noisy; contaminants; hazardous conditions; standing.

Civil Drafters

❋ Annual Earnings: $43,310
❋ Growth: 6.1%
❋ Annual Job Openings: 16,238
❋ Percentage of Women: 21.8%

Our sources did not provide separate job openings data for this occupation. The job openings listed here are shared with Architectural Drafters.

Related Apprenticeship—Drafter, Civil (8000 hrs.).

Prepare drawings and topographical and relief maps used in civil engineering projects such as highways, bridges, pipelines, flood control projects, and water and sewerage control systems. Produce drawings by using computer-assisted drafting systems (CAD) or drafting machines or by hand, using compasses, dividers, protractors, triangles, and other drafting devices. Draw maps, diagrams, and profiles, using cross-sections and surveys, to represent elevations, topographical contours, subsurface formations, and structures. Draft plans and detailed drawings for structures, installations, and construction projects such as highways, sewage disposal systems, and dikes, working from sketches or notes. Determine the order of work and method of presentation such as orthographic or isometric drawing. Finish and duplicate drawings and

documentation packages according to required mediums and specifications for reproduction, using blueprinting, photography, or other duplication methods. Review rough sketches, drawings, specifications, and other engineering data received from civil engineers to ensure that they conform to design concepts. Calculate excavation tonnage and prepare graphs and fill-hauling diagrams for use in earth-moving operations. Supervise and train other technologists, technicians, and drafters. Correlate, interpret, and modify data obtained from topographical surveys, well logs, and geophysical prospecting reports. Determine quality, cost, strength, and quantity of required materials and enter figures on materials lists. Locate and identify symbols located on topographical surveys to denote geological and geophysical formations or oil field installations. Calculate weights, volumes, and stress factors and their implications for technical aspects of designs. Supervise or conduct field surveys, inspections, or technical investigations to obtain data required to revise construction drawings. Explain drawings to production or construction teams and provide adjustments as necessary. Plot characteristics of boreholes for oil and gas wells from photographic subsurface survey recordings and other data, representing depth, degree, and direction of inclination.

GOE—Career Cluster/Interest Area: 02. Architecture and Construction. **Work Group:** 02.03. Architecture/Construction Engineering Technologies. **Other Apprenticeable Jobs in This Work Group:** Architectural Drafters. **Personality Type:** Realistic. These occupations frequently involve work activities that include practical, hands-on problems and solutions. They often deal with plants; animals; and real-world materials such as wood, tools, and machinery. Many of the occupations require working outside and don't involve a lot of paperwork or working closely with others.

Skills—Programming; Systems Analysis; Mathematics; Quality Control Analysis; Systems Evaluation.

Education/Training Required (Nonapprenticeship Route): Postsecondary vocational training. **Related Knowledge/Courses—Design:** Design techniques, principles, tools, and instruments involved in the production and use of precision technical plans, blueprints, drawings, and models. **Engineering and Technology:** Equipment, tools, and mechanical devices and their uses to produce motion, light, power, technology, and other applications. **Building and Construction:** Materials, methods, and the appropriate tools to construct objects, structures, and buildings. **Geography:** Various methods for describing the location and distribution of land, sea, and air masses, including their physical locations, relationships, and characteristics. **Mathematics:** Numbers and their operations and interrelationships, including arithmetic, algebra, geometry, calculus, and statistics and their applications. **Physics:** Physical principles, laws, and applications, including air, water, material dynamics, light, atomic principles, heat, electric theory, earth formations, and meteorological and related natural phenomena.

Work Environment: Indoors; sitting; repetitive motions.

Computer Operators

- ❋ Annual Earnings: $34,610
- ❋ Growth: –24.7%
- ❋ Annual Job Openings: 17,842
- ❋ Percentage of Women: 49.6%

Related Apprenticeships—Computer Operator (6000 hrs.); Computer Peripheral Equipment Operator (2000 hrs.).

Monitor and control electronic computer and peripheral electronic data processing equipment to process business, scientific, engineering, and other data according to operating instructions. May enter commands at a computer terminal and set controls on computer and peripheral devices. Monitor and respond to operating and error messages. Enter commands, using computer terminal, and activate controls on computer and peripheral equipment to integrate and operate equipment. Monitor the system for equipment failure or errors in performance. Notify supervisor or computer maintenance technicians of equipment malfunctions. Respond to program error messages by finding and correcting problems or terminating the program. Read job setup instructions to determine equipment to be used, order of use, material such as disks and paper to be loaded, and control settings. Operate spreadsheet programs and other types of software to load and manipulate data and to produce reports. Retrieve, separate, and sort program output as needed and send data to specified users. Load peripheral equipment with selected materials for operating runs or oversee loading of peripheral equipment by peripheral equipment operators. Answer telephone calls to assist computer users encountering problems. Record information such as computer operating time, problems that occurred, and actions taken. Oversee the operation of computer hardware systems, including coordinating and scheduling the use of computer terminals and networks to ensure efficient use. Clear equipment at end of operating run and review schedule to determine next assignment. Type command on keyboard to transfer encoded data from memory unit to magnetic tape and assist in labeling, classifying, cataloging, and maintaining tapes. Supervise and train peripheral equipment operators and computer operator trainees. Help programmers and systems analysts test and debug new programs.

GOE—Career Cluster/Interest Area: 11. Information Technology. **Work Group:** 11.02. Information Technology Specialties. **Other Apprenticeable Jobs in This Work Group:** Computer Support Specialists. **Personality Type:** Conventional. These occupations frequently involve following set procedures and routines and can include working with data and details more than with ideas. Usually there is a clear line of authority to follow.

Skills—Troubleshooting; Systems Evaluation; Critical Thinking; Service Orientation; Operation and Control; Instructing; Mathematics; Management of Financial Resources.

Education/Training Required (Nonapprenticeship Route): Moderate-term on-the-job training. **Related Knowledge/Courses—Computers and Electronics:** Electric circuit boards, processors, chips, and computer hardware and software, including applications and programming. **Sales and Marketing:** Principles and methods involved in showing, promoting, and selling products or services. This includes marketing strategies and tactics, product demonstration and sales techniques, and sales control systems. **Clerical Practices:** Administrative and clerical procedures and systems such as word-processing systems, filing and records management systems, stenography and transcription, forms, design principles, and other office procedures and terminology. **Telecommunications:** Transmission, broadcasting, switching, control, and operation of telecommunications systems.

Administration and Management: Principles and processes involved in business and organizational planning, coordination, and execution. This includes strategic planning, resource allocation, manpower modeling, leadership techniques, and production methods.

Work Environment: Indoors; sitting; using hands on objects, tools, or controls; repetitive motions.

Computer Support Specialists

* Annual Earnings: $42,400
* Growth: 12.9%
* Annual Job Openings: 97,334
* Percentage of Women: 28.9%

Related Apprenticeship—Help Desk Technician (2000 hrs. or competency).

Provide technical assistance to computer system users. Answer questions or resolve computer problems for clients in person, via telephone, or from remote locations. May provide assistance concerning the use of computer hardware and software, including printing, installation, word processing, e-mail, and operating systems. Oversee the daily performance of computer systems. Answer user inquiries regarding computer software or hardware operation to resolve problems. Enter commands and observe system functioning to verify correct operations and detect errors. Set up equipment for employee use, performing or ensuring proper installation of cables, operating systems, or appropriate software. Install and perform minor repairs to hardware, software, or peripheral equipment, following design or installation specifications. Maintain records of daily data communication transactions, problems and remedial actions taken, or installation activities. Read technical manuals, confer with users, or conduct computer diagnostics to investigate and resolve problems or to provide technical assistance and support. Refer major hardware or software problems or defective products to vendors or technicians for service. Develop training materials and procedures or train users in the proper use of hardware or software. Confer with staff, users, and management to establish requirements for new systems or modifications. Prepare evaluations of software or hardware and recommend improvements or upgrades. Read trade magazines and technical manuals or attend conferences and seminars to maintain knowledge of hardware and software. Hire, supervise, and direct workers engaged in special project work, problem solving, monitoring, and installing data communication equipment and software. Inspect equipment and read order sheets to prepare for delivery to users. Modify and customize commercial programs for internal needs. Conduct office automation feasibility studies, including workflow analysis, space design, or cost comparison analysis.

GOE—Career Cluster/Interest Area: 11. Information Technology. **Work Group:** 11.02. Information Technology Specialties. **Other Apprenticeable Jobs in This Work Group:** Computer Operators. **Personality Type:** Realistic. These occupations frequently involve work activities that include practical, hands-on problems and solutions. They often deal with plants; animals; and real-world materials such as wood, tools, and machinery. Many of the occupations require working outside and don't involve a lot of paperwork or working closely with others.

Skills—Programming; Installation; Systems Analysis; Operation Monitoring; Repairing; Systems Evaluation; Troubleshooting; Operation and Control.

Education/Training Required (Nonapprenticeship Route): Associate degree. **Related Knowledge/Courses—Computers and Electronics:** Electric circuit boards, processors, chips, and computer hardware and software, including applications and programming. **Telecommunications:** Transmission, broadcasting, switching, control, and operation of telecommunications systems. **Engineering and Technology:** Equipment, tools, and mechanical devices and their uses to produce motion, light, power, technology, and other applications. **Clerical Practices:** Administrative and clerical procedures and systems such as word-processing systems, filing and records management systems, stenography and transcription, forms, design principles, and other office procedures and terminology. **Customer and Personal Service:** Principles and processes for providing customer and personal services, including needs assessment techniques, quality service standards, alternative delivery systems, and customer satisfaction evaluation techniques. **Communications and Media:** Media production, communication, and dissemination techniques and methods, including alternative ways to inform and entertain via written, oral, and visual media.

Work Environment: Indoors; noisy; sitting; repetitive motions.

Computer, Automated Teller, and Office Machine Repairers

- Annual Earnings: $37,100
- Growth: 3.0%
- Annual Job Openings: 22,330
- Percentage of Women: 9.7%

Related Apprenticeships—Assembly Technician (4000 hrs.); Cash-Register Servicer (6000 hrs.); Dictating-Transcription-Machine Servicer (6000 hrs.); Electronics Mechanic (8000 hrs.); Office-Machine Servicer (6000 hrs.).

Repair, maintain, or install computers, word-processing systems, automated teller machines, and electronic office machines such as duplicating and fax machines. Converse with customers in order to determine details of equipment problems. Reassemble machines after making repairs or replacing parts. Travel to customers' stores or offices to service machines or to provide emergency repair service. Reinstall software programs or adjust settings on existing software in order to fix machine malfunctions. Advise customers concerning equipment operation, maintenance, and programming. Assemble machines according to specifications, using hand tools, power tools, and measuring devices. Test new systems in order to ensure that they are in working order. Operate machines in order to test functioning of parts and mechanisms. Maintain records of equipment maintenance work and repairs. Install and configure new equipment, including operating software and peripheral equipment. Maintain parts inventories and order any additional parts needed for repairs. Update existing equipment, performing tasks such as installing updated circuit boards or additional memory. Test components and circuits of faulty equipment in order to locate defects, using oscilloscopes, signal generators, ammeters, voltmeters, or special diagnostic software programs. Align, adjust, and calibrate equipment according to specifications. Repair, adjust, or replace electrical and mechanical components and parts, using hand tools, power tools, and soldering or welding equipment. Complete repair bills, shop records, time cards, and expense reports. Disassemble machine to examine parts such as wires, gears, and bearings for wear and defects, using

hand tools, power tools, and measuring devices. Clean, oil, and adjust mechanical parts to maintain machines' operating efficiency and to prevent breakdowns. Read specifications such as blueprints, charts, and schematics in order to determine machine settings and adjustments. Enter information into computers to copy programs from one electronic component to another or to draw, modify, or store schematics. Lay cable and hook up electrical connections between machines, power sources, and phone lines. Analyze equipment performance records in order to assess equipment functioning.

GOE—Career Cluster/Interest Area: 11. Information Technology. **Work Group:** 11.03. Digital Equipment Repair. **Other Apprenticeable Jobs in This Work Group:** Coin, Vending, and Amusement Machine Servicers and Repairers. **Personality Type:** Realistic. These occupations frequently involve work activities that include practical, hands-on problems and solutions. They often deal with plants; animals; and real-world materials such as wood, tools, and machinery. Many of the occupations require working outside and don't involve a lot of paperwork or working closely with others.

Skills—Installation; Repairing; Troubleshooting; Equipment Maintenance; Management of Material Resources; Programming; Technology Design; Systems Evaluation.

Education/Training Required (Nonapprenticeship Route): Postsecondary vocational training. **Related Knowledge/Courses—Computers and Electronics:** Electric circuit boards, processors, chips, and computer hardware and software, including applications and programming. **Telecommunications:** Transmission, broadcasting, switching, control, and operation of telecommunications systems. **Mechanical**

Devices: Machines and tools, including their designs, uses, benefits, repair, and maintenance. **Customer and Personal Service:** Principles and processes for providing customer and personal services, including needs assessment techniques, quality service standards, alternative delivery systems, and customer satisfaction evaluation techniques. **Engineering and Technology:** Equipment, tools, and mechanical devices and their uses to produce motion, light, power, technology, and other applications. **Sales and Marketing:** Principles and methods involved in showing, promoting, and selling products or services. This includes marketing strategies and tactics, product demonstration and sales techniques, and sales control systems.

Work Environment: Indoors; sitting; using hands on objects, tools, or controls; repetitive motions.

Computer-Controlled Machine Tool Operators, Metal and Plastic

- ❊ Annual Earnings: $32,550
- ❊ Growth: –3.0%
- ❊ Annual Job Openings: 12,997
- ❊ Percentage of Women: 8.2%

Related Apprenticeships—Aircraft Metals Technology (Machinist/CNC/Welder) (2500 hrs. or competency); Numerical Control Machine Operator (8000 hrs.).

Operate computer-controlled machines or robots to perform one or more machine functions on metal or plastic workpieces. Measure dimensions of finished workpieces to ensure conformance to specifications, using precision measuring instruments, templates, and fixtures. Remove and replace dull cutting tools. Mount, install, align, and secure tools, attachments, fixtures, and workpieces on machines, using hand tools and precision measuring instruments. Listen to machines during operation to detect sounds such as those made by dull cutting tools or excessive vibration and adjust machines to compensate for problems. Adjust machine feed and speed, change cutting tools, or adjust machine controls when automatic programming is faulty or if machines malfunction. Stop machines to remove finished workpieces or to change tooling, setup, or workpiece placement according to required machining sequences. Lift workpieces to machines manually or with hoists or cranes. Modify cutting programs to account for problems encountered during operation and save modified programs. Calculate machine speed and feed ratios and the size and position of cuts. Insert control instructions into machine control units to start operation. Check to ensure that workpieces are properly lubricated and cooled during machine operation. Input initial part dimensions into machine control panels. Set up and operate computer-controlled machines or robots to perform one or more machine functions on metal or plastic workpieces. Confer with supervisors or programmers to resolve machine malfunctions and production errors and to obtain approval to continue production. Review program specifications or blueprints to determine and set machine operations and sequencing, finished workpiece dimensions, or numerical control sequences. Monitor machine operation and control panel displays and compare readings to specifications to detect malfunctions. Control coolant systems. Maintain machines and remove and replace broken or worn machine tools, using hand tools. Stack or load finished items or place items on conveyor systems. Clean machines, tooling, and parts, using solvents or solutions and rags. Enter commands or load control media such as tapes, cards, or disks into machine controllers to retrieve programmed instructions.

GOE—Career Cluster/Interest Area: 13. Manufacturing. **Work Group:** 13.05. Production Machining Technology. **Other Apprenticeable Jobs in This Work Group:** Foundry Mold and Coremakers; Lay-Out Workers, Metal and Plastic; Machinists; Model Makers, Metal and Plastic; Numerical Tool and Process Control Programmers; Patternmakers, Metal and Plastic; Tool and Die Makers; Tool Grinders, Filers, and Sharpeners. **Personality Type:** Realistic. These occupations frequently involve work activities that include practical, hands-on problems and solutions. They often deal with plants; animals; and real-world materials such as wood, tools, and machinery. Many of the occupations require working outside and don't involve a lot of paperwork or working closely with others.

Skills—Operation Monitoring; Operation and Control; Equipment Maintenance; Quality Control Analysis; Programming; Troubleshooting; Mathematics; Repairing.

Education/Training Required (Nonapprenticeship Route): Moderate-term on-the-job training. **Related Knowledge/ Courses—Mechanical Devices:** Machines and tools, including their designs, uses, benefits, repair, and maintenance. **Production and Processing:** Inputs, outputs, raw materials, waste, quality control, costs, and techniques for maximizing the manufacture and distribution of goods. **Engineering and Technology:** Equipment, tools, and mechanical devices and their uses to produce motion, light, power, technology, and other applications. **Design:** Design techniques, principles, tools, and instruments involved in the production and use of precision technical plans, blueprints, drawings, and models. **Mathematics:** Numbers and their operations and interrelationships, including arithmetic, algebra, geometry, calculus, and statistics and their applications. **Computers and Electronics:** Electric circuit boards, processors, chips, and computer hardware and software, including applications and programming.

Work Environment: Noisy; contaminants; hazardous equipment; standing; using hands on objects, tools, or controls; repetitive motions.

Further Information: Contact a local joint union-management apprenticeship committee or the nearest office of your state employment service or apprenticeship agency (see Appendix C). Information about apprenticeships is available from the National Tooling and Metalworking Association, 9300 Livingston Rd., Fort Washington, MD 20744 or The National Institute for Metalworking Skills, 10565 Fairfax Blvd., Suite 203, Fairfax, VA 22030. Internet: www.nims-skills.org

Construction and Building Inspectors

- ✹ Annual Earnings: $48,330
- ✹ Growth: 18.2%
- ✹ Annual Job Openings: 12,606
- ✹ Percentage of Women: 8.8%

Related Apprenticeships—Field Technician, Concrete/Masonry Inspector (3000–6000 hrs.); Field Technician, Concrete/Masonry Inspector (3000–6000 hrs., hybrid); Field Technician, Soil/Asphalt Inspector (2400–6000 hrs.); Field Technician, Soil/Asphalt Inspector (2400–6000 hrs., hybrid); Field Technician, Steel/Welding/ Fireproofing Inspector (3000–6000 hrs.); Field Technician, Steel/Welding/Fireproofing Inspector (3000–6000 hrs., hybrid); Inspector, Building (6000 hrs.).

Inspect structures, using engineering skills to determine structural soundness and compliance with specifications, building codes, and other regulations. Inspections may be general in nature or may be limited to a specific area, such as electrical systems or plumbing. Issue violation notices and stop-work orders, conferring with owners, violators, and authorities to explain regulations and recommend rectifications. Inspect bridges, dams, highways, buildings, wiring, plumbing, electrical circuits, sewers, heating systems, and foundations during and after construction for structural quality, general safety, and conformance to specifications and codes. Approve and sign plans that meet required specifications. Review and interpret plans, blueprints, site layouts, specifications, and construction methods to ensure compliance with legal requirements and safety regulations. Monitor installation of plumbing, wiring, equipment, and appliances to ensure that installation is performed properly and is in compliance with applicable regulations. Inspect and monitor construction sites to ensure adherence to safety standards, building codes, and specifications. Measure dimensions and verify level, alignment, and elevation of structures and fixtures to ensure compliance with building plans and codes. Maintain daily logs and supplement inspection records with photographs. Use survey instruments, metering devices, tape measures, and test equipment such as concrete strength measurers to perform inspections. Train, direct, and supervise other construction inspectors. Issue permits for construction, relocation, demolition, and occupancy. Examine lifting and conveying devices such as elevators, escalators, moving sidewalks, lifts and hoists, inclined railways, ski lifts, and amusement rides to ensure safety and proper functioning. Compute estimates of work completed or of needed renovations or upgrades and approve payment for contractors. Evaluate premises for cleanliness, including proper garbage disposal and lack of vermin infestation.

GOE—Career Cluster/Interest Area: 07. Government and Public Administration. **Work Group:** 07.03. Regulations Enforcement. **Other Apprenticeable Jobs in This Work Group:** Compliance Officers, Except Agriculture, Construction, Health and Safety, and Transportation; Equal Opportunity Representatives and Officers; Fire Inspectors; Fish and Game Wardens; Government Property Inspectors and Investigators; Nuclear Monitoring Technicians; Transportation Vehicle, Equipment and Systems Inspectors, Except Aviation. **Personality Type:** Realistic. These occupations frequently involve work activities that include practical, hands-on problems and solutions. They often deal with plants; animals; and real-world materials such as wood, tools, and machinery. Many of the occupations require working outside and don't involve a lot of paperwork or working closely with others.

Skills—Quality Control Analysis; Systems Analysis; Systems Evaluation; Management of Personnel Resources; Operation Monitoring.

Education/Training Required (Nonapprenticeship Route): Work experience in a related occupation. **Related Knowledge/Courses— Building and Construction:** Materials, methods, and the appropriate tools to construct objects, structures, and buildings. **Engineering and Technology:** Equipment, tools, and mechanical devices and their uses to produce motion, light, power, technology, and other applications. **Design:** Design techniques, principles, tools, and instruments involved in the production and use of precision technical plans, blueprints, drawings, and models. **Physics:** Physical principles, laws, and applications, including air, water, material dynamics, light, atomic principles, heat, electric theory, earth formations, and meteorological and related natural phenomena. **Public Safety and Security:** Weaponry; public safety; security operations, rules, regulations, precautions, and prevention; and the protection of people, data, and property. **Mechanical Devices:** Machines and tools, including their designs, uses, benefits, repair, and maintenance.

Work Environment: More often outdoors than indoors; noisy; contaminants; hazardous equipment; standing.

Construction Carpenters

* Annual Earnings: $37,660
* Growth: 10.3%
* Annual Job Openings: 223,225
* Percentage of Women: 2.4%

Our sources did not provide separate job openings data for this occupation. The job openings listed here are shared with Rough Carpenters.

Related Apprenticeships—Boatbuilder, Wood (8000 hrs.); Carpenter (8000 hrs.); Carpenter, Interior Systems (5200–8000 hrs., hybrid); Carpenter, Interior Systems (8000 hrs.); Carpenter, Maintenance (8000 hrs.); Carpenter, Mold (2000 hrs.); Carpenter, Ship (8000 hrs.); Casket Assembler (6000 hrs.); Joiner (Ship and Boat Building) (8000 hrs.); Lather (6000 hrs.); Lathing Specialist (3900–6000 hrs., hybrid); Prop Maker (Amusement and Recreation) (8000 hrs.); Residential Carpenter (4000 hrs.); Residential Carpenter Specialist (3900–6000 hrs., hybrid); Shipwright (Ship and Boat) (8000 hrs.).

Construct, erect, install, and repair structures and fixtures of wood, plywood, and wallboard, using carpenter's hand tools and power tools. Measure and mark cutting lines on materials, using ruler, pencil, chalk, and marking gauge. Follow established safety rules and regulations and maintain a safe and clean environment. Verify trueness of structure, using plumb bob and level. Shape or cut materials to specified measurements, using hand tools, machines, or power saw. Study specifications in blueprints, sketches, or building plans to prepare project layout and determine dimensions and materials required. Assemble and fasten materials to make framework or props, using hand tools and wood screws, nails, dowel pins, or glue. Build or repair cabinets, doors, frameworks, floors, and other wooden fixtures used in buildings, using woodworking machines, carpenter's hand tools, and power tools. Erect scaffolding and ladders for assembling structures above ground level. Remove damaged or defective parts or sections of structures and repair or replace, using hand tools. Install structures and fixtures, such as windows, frames, floorings, and trim, or hardware, using carpenter's hand and power tools. Select and order lumber and other required materials. Maintain records, document actions, and present written progress reports. Finish surfaces of woodwork or wallboard in houses and buildings, using paint, hand tools, and paneling. Prepare cost estimates for clients or employers. Arrange for subcontractors to deal with special areas such as heating and electrical wiring work. Inspect ceiling or floor tile, wall coverings, siding, glass, or woodwork to detect broken or damaged structures. Work with or remove hazardous material. Construct forms and chutes for pouring concrete. Cover subfloors with building paper to keep out moisture and lay hardwood, parquet, and wood-strip-block floors by nailing floors to subfloor or cementing them to mastic or asphalt base. Fill cracks and other defects in plaster or plasterboard and sand patch, using patching plaster, trowel, and sanding tool. Perform minor plumbing, welding, or concrete mixing work. Apply shock-absorbing, sound-deadening, and decorative paneling to ceilings and walls.

GOE—Career Cluster/Interest Area: 02. Architecture and Construction. **Work Group:** 02.04. Construction Crafts. **Other Apprenticeable Jobs in This Work Group:** Boilermakers; Brickmasons and Blockmasons; Carpet Installers; Cement Masons and Concrete Finishers; Crane and Tower Operators; Drywall and Ceiling Tile Installers; Electricians; Fence Erectors; Floor Layers, Except Carpet, Wood, and Hard Tiles; Glaziers; Insulation Workers, Floor, Ceiling, and Wall; Insulation Workers, Mechanical; Operating Engineers and Other Construction Equipment Operators; Painters, Construction and Maintenance; Paperhangers; Paving, Surfacing, and Tamping Equipment Operators; Pipe Fitters and Steamfitters; Plasterers and Stucco Masons; Plumbers; Reinforcing Iron and Rebar Workers; Riggers; Roofers; Rough Carpenters; Sheet Metal Workers; Stone Cutters and Carvers, Manufacturing; Stonemasons; Structural Iron and Steel Workers; Tapers; Terrazzo Workers and Finishers; Tile and Marble Setters. **Personality Type:** Realistic. These occupations frequently involve work activities that include practical, hands-on problems and solutions. They often deal with plants; animals; and real-world materials such as wood, tools, and machinery. Many of the occupations require working outside and don't involve a lot of paperwork or working closely with others.

Skills—Management of Personnel Resources; Management of Material Resources; Management of Financial Resources; Repairing; Equipment Maintenance; Quality Control Analysis; Installation; Mathematics.

Education/Training Required (Nonapprenticeship Route): Long-term on-the-job training. **Related Knowledge/Courses—Building and Construction:** Materials, methods, and the appropriate tools to construct objects, structures, and buildings. **Mechanical Devices:** Machines and tools, including their designs, uses, benefits, repair, and maintenance. **Design:** Design techniques, principles, tools, and instruments involved in the production and use of precision technical plans, blueprints, drawings, and models. **Engineering and Technology:** Equipment, tools, and mechanical devices and their uses to produce motion, light, power, technology, and other applications. **Production and Processing:** Inputs, outputs, raw materials, waste, quality control, costs, and techniques for maximizing the manufacture and distribution of goods. **Public Safety and Security:** Weaponry; public safety; security operations, rules, regulations, precautions, and prevention; and the protection of people, data, and property.

Work Environment: Outdoors; noisy; hazardous equipment; standing; walking and running; using hands on objects, tools, or controls.

Further Information: Contact a local joint union-management apprenticeship committee or the nearest office of your state employment service or apprenticeship agency (see Appendix C). To identify the local union office, contact United Brotherhood of Carpenters and Joiners of America, 101 Constitution Avenue NW, Washington, DC 20001. Internet: www.carpenters.org

Construction Laborers

⊛ Annual Earnings: $27,310
⊛ Growth: 10.9%
⊛ Annual Job Openings: 257,407
⊛ Percentage of Women: 3.7%

Related Apprenticeships—Construction Craft Laborer (4000 hrs.); Construction Craft Laborer (8200–10200 hrs., hybrid); Maintenance Technician, Municipal (4000 hrs.); Pointer-Cleaner-Caulker (4500–8000 hrs., hybrid); Tuckpointer, Cleaner, Caulker (6000 hrs.).

Perform tasks involving physical labor at building, highway, and heavy construction projects; tunnel and shaft excavations; and demolition sites. May operate hand and power tools of all types: air hammers, earth tampers, cement mixers, small mechanical hoists, surveying and measuring equipment, and various other types of equipment and instruments. May clean and prepare sites, dig trenches, set braces to support the sides of excavations, erect scaffolding, clean up rubble and debris, and remove asbestos, lead, and other hazardous waste materials. May assist other craft workers. Clean and prepare construction sites to eliminate possible hazards. Read and interpret plans, instructions, and specifications to determine work activities. Control traffic passing near, in, and around work zones. Signal equipment operators to facilitate alignment, movement, and adjustment of machinery, equipment, and materials. Dig ditches or trenches, backfill excavations, and compact and level earth to grade specifications, using picks, shovels, pneumatic tampers, and rakes. Measure, mark, and record openings and distances to lay out areas where construction work will be performed. Position, join, align, and seal structural components such as concrete wall sections and pipes. Load, unload, and identify building materials, machinery, and tools and distribute them to the appropriate locations according to project plans and specifications. Erect and disassemble scaffolding, shoring, braces, traffic barricades, ramps, and other temporary structures. Build and position forms for pouring concrete and dismantle forms after use, using saws, hammers, nails, or bolts. Lubricate, clean, and repair machinery, equipment, and tools. Operate jackhammers and drills to break up concrete or pavement. Smooth and finish freshly poured cement or concrete, using floats, trowels, screeds, or powered cement-finishing tools. Operate, read, and maintain air monitoring and other sampling devices in confined and/or hazardous environments. Install sewer, water, and storm drain pipes, using pipe-laying machinery and laser guidance equipment. Transport and set explosives for tunnel, shaft, and road construction. Provide assistance to craft workers such as carpenters, plasterers, and masons. Tend pumps, compressors, and generators to provide power for tools, machinery, and equipment or to heat and move materials such as asphalt. Mop, brush, or spread paints, cleaning solutions, or other compounds over surfaces to clean them or to provide protection. Place, consolidate, and protect case-in-place concrete or masonry structures. Identify, pack, and transport hazardous and/or radioactive materials. Use computers and other input devices to control robotic pipe cutters and cleaners.

GOE—Career Cluster/Interest Area: 02. Architecture and Construction. **Work Group:** 02.06. Construction Support/Labor. **Other Apprenticeable Jobs in This Work Group:** Helpers—Brickmasons, Blockmasons, Stonemasons, and Tile and Marble Setters; Helpers—Brickmasons,

Blockmasons, Stonemasons, and Tile and Marble Setters; Helpers—Installation, Maintenance, and Repair Workers; Helpers—Installation, Maintenance, and Repair Workers; Plasterers and Stucco Masons. **Personality Type:** Realistic. These occupations frequently involve work activities that include practical, hands-on problems and solutions. They often deal with plants; animals; and real-world materials such as wood, tools, and machinery. Many of the occupations require working outside and don't involve a lot of paperwork or working closely with others.

Skills—Equipment Maintenance; Repairing; Equipment Selection; Installation.

Education/Training Required (Nonapprenticeship Route): Moderate-term on-the-job training. **Related Knowledge/Courses—Building and Construction:** Materials, methods, and the appropriate tools to construct objects, structures, and buildings. **Design:** Design techniques, principles, tools, and instruments involved in the production and use of precision technical plans, blueprints, drawings, and models. **Mechanical Devices:** Machines and tools, including their designs, uses, benefits, repair, and maintenance. **Transportation:** Principles and methods for moving people or goods by air, rail, sea, or road, including their relative costs, advantages, and limitations. **Engineering and Technology:** Equipment, tools, and mechanical devices and their uses to produce motion, light, power, technology, and other applications. **Public Safety and Security:** Weaponry; public safety; security operations, rules, regulations, precautions, and prevention; and the protection of people, data, and property.

Work Environment: Outdoors; noisy; very hot or cold; contaminants; standing; using hands on objects, tools, or controls.

Control and Valve Installers and Repairers, Except Mechanical Door

- ❋ Annual Earnings: $46,140
- ❋ Growth: 0.3%
- ❋ Annual Job Openings: 3,855
- ❋ Percentage of Women: 4.6%

Related Apprenticeships—Electric Meter Installer I (8000 hrs.); Electric Meter Repairer (8000 hrs.); Gas Utility Worker (4000 hrs.); Gas-Meter Mechanic I (6000 hrs.); Gas-Regulator Repairer (6000 hrs.); Meter Repairer (Any Industry) (6000 hrs.).

Install, repair, and maintain mechanical regulating and controlling devices, such as electric meters, gas regulators, thermostats, safety and flow valves, and other mechanical governors. Turn meters on or off to establish or close service. Turn valves to allow measured amounts of air or gas to pass through meters at specified flow rates. Report hazardous field situations and damaged or missing meters. Record meter readings and installation data on meter cards, work orders, or field service orders or enter data into handheld computers. Connect regulators to test stands and turn screw adjustments until gauges indicate that inlet and outlet pressures meet specifications. Disassemble and repair mechanical control devices or valves, such as regulators, thermostats, or hydrants, using power tools, hand tools, and cutting torches. Record maintenance information, including test results, material usage, and repairs made. Disconnect and/or remove defective or unauthorized meters, using hand tools. Lubricate wearing surfaces of mechanical parts, using oils or other lubricants. Test valves and regulators for leaks and accurate temperature and pressure settings, using precision testing equipment. Install regulators and related equipment such as gas meters, odorization units, and gas pressure telemetering equipment. Shut off service and notify repair crews when major repairs are required, such as the replacement of underground pipes or wiring. Examine valves or mechanical control device parts for defects, dents, or loose attachments and mark malfunctioning areas of defective units. Attach air hoses to meter inlets; then plug outlets and observe gauges for pressure losses to test internal seams for leaks. Dismantle meters and replace or adjust defective parts such as cases, shafts, gears, disks, and recording mechanisms, using soldering irons and hand tools. Advise customers on proper installation of valves or regulators and related equipment. Connect hoses from provers to meter inlets and outlets and raise prover bells until prover gauges register zero. Make adjustments to meter components, such as setscrews or timing mechanisms, so that they conform to specifications. Replace defective parts, such as bellows, range springs, and toggle switches, and reassemble units according to blueprints, using cam presses and hand tools.

GOE—Career Cluster/Interest Area: 13. Manufacturing. **Work Group:** 13.13. Machinery Repair. **Other Apprenticeable Jobs in This Work Group:** Home Appliance Repairers; Industrial Machinery Mechanics; Locksmiths and Safe Repairers; Maintenance Workers, Machinery; Mechanical Door Repairers; Millwrights; Signal and Track Switch Repairers. **Personality Type:** Realistic. These occupations frequently involve work activities that include practical, hands-on problems and solutions. They often deal with plants; animals; and real-world materials such as wood, tools, and machinery. Many of the occupations require working outside and don't involve a lot of paperwork or working closely with others.

Skills—Installation; Repairing; Equipment Maintenance; Operation Monitoring; Troubleshooting; Quality Control Analysis; Science; Operation and Control.

Education/Training Required (Nonapprenticeship Route): Moderate-term on-the-job training. **Related Knowledge/Courses— Mechanical Devices:** Machines and tools, including their designs, uses, benefits, repair, and maintenance. **Transportation:** Principles and methods for moving people or goods by air, rail, sea, or road, including their relative costs, advantages, and limitations. **Physics:** Physical principles, laws, and applications, including air, water, material dynamics, light, atomic principles, heat, electric theory, earth formations, and meteorological and related natural phenomena. **Public Safety and Security:** Weaponry; public safety; security operations, rules, regulations, precautions, and prevention; and the protection of people, data, and property. **Design:** Design techniques, principles, tools, and instruments involved in the production and use of precision technical plans, blueprints, drawings, and models. **Chemistry:** The composition, structure, and properties of substances and of the chemical processes and transformations that they undergo. This includes uses of chemicals and their interactions, danger signs, production techniques, and disposal methods.

Work Environment: Outdoors; very hot or cold; very bright or dim lighting; contaminants; cramped work space, awkward positions; hazardous conditions.

Cooks, Institution and Cafeteria

- ❀ Annual Earnings: $21,340
- ❀ Growth: 10.8%
- ❀ Annual Job Openings: 111,898
- ❀ Percentage of Women: 43.4%

Related Apprenticeship—Cook (Any Industry) (4000 hrs.).

Prepare and cook large quantities of food for institutions, such as schools, hospitals, or cafeterias. Clean and inspect galley equipment, kitchen appliances, and work areas to ensure cleanliness and functional operation. Apportion and serve food to facility residents, employees, or patrons. Cook foodstuffs according to menus, special dietary or nutritional restrictions, and numbers of portions to be served. Clean, cut, and cook meat, fish, and poultry. Monitor use of government food commodities to ensure that proper procedures are followed. Wash pots, pans, dishes, utensils, and other cooking equipment. Compile and maintain records of food use and expenditures. Direct activities of one or more workers who assist in preparing and serving meals. Bake breads, rolls, and other pastries. Train new employees. Take inventory of supplies and equipment. Monitor menus and spending to ensure that meals are prepared economically. Plan menus that are varied, nutritionally balanced, and appetizing, taking advantage of foods in season and local availability. Requisition food supplies, kitchen equipment, and appliances based on estimates of future needs. Determine meal prices based on calculations of ingredient prices.

GOE—Career Cluster/Interest Area: 09. Hospitality, Tourism, and Recreation. **Work Group:** 09.04. Food and Beverage Preparation. **Other**

Apprenticeable Jobs in This Work Group: Butchers and Meat Cutters; Chefs and Head Cooks; Cooks, Fast Food; Cooks, Restaurant. **Personality Type:** Realistic. These occupations frequently involve work activities that include practical, hands-on problems and solutions. They often deal with plants; animals; and real-world materials such as wood, tools, and machinery. Many of the occupations require working outside and don't involve a lot of paperwork or working closely with others.

Skills—Equipment Selection; Instructing; Service Orientation.

Education/Training Required (Nonapprenticeship Route): Moderate-term on-the-job training. **Related Knowledge/Courses—Food Production:** Techniques and equipment for planting, growing, and harvesting of food for consumption, including crop-rotation methods, animal husbandry, and food storage/handling techniques. **Public Safety and Security:** Weaponry; public safety; security operations, rules, regulations, precautions, and prevention; and the protection of people, data, and property.

Work Environment: Indoors; very hot or cold; minor burns, cuts, bites, or stings; standing; walking and running; repetitive motions.

Further Information: Contact a local joint union-management apprenticeship committee or the nearest office of your state employment service or apprenticeship agency (see Appendix C). Or contact American Culinary Federation, 180 Center Place Way, St. Augustine, FL 32095. Internet: www.acfchefs.org

Cooks, Restaurant

- ❋ Annual Earnings: $21,220
- ❋ Growth: 11.5%
- ❋ Annual Job Openings: 238,542
- ❋ Percentage of Women: 43.4%

Related Apprenticeships—Cook (Hotel and Restaurant) (4000–6000 hrs., hybrid); Cook (Hotel and Restaurant) (6000 hrs.).

Prepare, season, and cook soups, meats, vegetables, desserts, or other foodstuffs in restaurants. May order supplies, keep records and accounts, price items on menu, or plan menu. Inspect food preparation and serving areas to ensure observance of safe, sanitary food-handling practices. Turn or stir foods to ensure even cooking. Season and cook food according to recipes or personal judgment and experience. Observe and test foods to determine if they have been cooked sufficiently, using methods such as tasting them, smelling them, or piercing them with utensils. Weigh, measure, and mix ingredients according to recipes or personal judgment, using various kitchen utensils and equipment. Portion, arrange, and garnish food and serve food to waiters or patrons. Regulate temperature of ovens, broilers, grills, and roasters. Substitute for or assist other cooks during emergencies or rush periods. Bake, roast, broil, and steam meats, fish, vegetables, and other foods. Wash, peel, cut, and seed fruits and vegetables to prepare them for consumption. Estimate expected food consumption, requisition or purchase supplies, or procure food from storage. Carve and trim meats such as beef, veal, ham, pork, and lamb for hot or cold service or for sandwiches. Coordinate and supervise work of kitchen staff. Consult with supervisory staff to plan menus, taking into consideration factors such as costs and special event needs. Butcher and dress animals, fowl, or shellfish or cut and bone meat prior to cooking. Prepare relishes and hors d'oeuvres. Bake breads, rolls, cakes, and pastries. Keep records and accounts. Plan and price menu items.

GOE—Career Cluster/Interest Area: 09. Hospitality, Tourism, and Recreation. **Work Group:** 09.04. Food and Beverage Preparation. **Other Apprenticeable Jobs in This Work Group:** Butchers and Meat Cutters; Chefs and Head Cooks; Cooks, Fast Food; Cooks, Institution and Cafeteria. **Personality Type:** Realistic. These occupations frequently involve work activities that include practical, hands-on problems and solutions. They often deal with plants; animals; and real-world materials such as wood, tools, and machinery. Many of the occupations require working outside and don't involve a lot of paperwork or working closely with others.

Skill—Equipment Maintenance.

Education/Training Required (Nonapprenticeship Route): Long-term on-the-job training. **Related Knowledge/Courses—Food Production:** Techniques and equipment for planting, growing, and harvesting of food for consumption, including crop-rotation methods, animal husbandry, and food storage/handling techniques. **Production and Processing:** Inputs, outputs, raw materials, waste, quality control, costs, and techniques for maximizing the manufacture and distribution of goods.

Work Environment: Indoors; very hot or cold; minor burns, cuts, bites, or stings; standing; using hands on objects, tools, or controls; repetitive motions.

Further Information: Contact a local joint union-management apprenticeship committee or the nearest office of your state employment service or apprenticeship agency (see Appendix C). Or contact American Culinary Federation, 180 Center Place Way, St. Augustine, FL 32095. Internet: www.acfchefs.org

Correctional Officers and Jailers

* Annual Earnings: $36,970
* Growth: 16.9%
* Annual Job Openings: 56,579
* Percentage of Women: 28.2%

Related Apprenticeship—Correction Officer (2000 hrs.).

Guard inmates in penal or rehabilitative institution in accordance with established regulations and procedures. May guard prisoners in transit between jail, courtroom, prison, or other point. Includes deputy sheriffs and police who spend the majority of their time guarding prisoners in correctional institutions. Conduct head counts to ensure that each prisoner is present. Monitor conduct of prisoners in housing unit or during work or recreational activities according to established policies, regulations, and procedures to prevent escape or violence. Inspect conditions of locks, window bars, grills, doors, and gates at correctional facilities to ensure security and help prevent escapes. Record information such as prisoner identification, charges, and incidences of inmate disturbance and keep daily logs of prisoner activities. Search prisoners and vehicles and conduct shakedowns of cells for valuables and contraband such as weapons or drugs. Use weapons, handcuffs, and physical force to maintain discipline and order among prisoners. Guard facility entrances to screen visitors. Inspect mail for the presence of contraband. Maintain records of prisoners' identification and charges. Process or book convicted individuals into prison. Settle disputes between inmates. Conduct fire, safety, and sanitation inspections. Provide to supervisors oral and written reports of the quality and quantity of work performed by inmates, inmate disturbances and rule violations, and unusual occurrences. Participate in required job training. Take prisoners into custody and escort to locations within and outside of facility such as visiting room, courtroom, or airport. Serve meals, distribute commissary items, and dispense prescribed medication to prisoners. Counsel inmates and respond to legitimate questions, concerns, and requests. Drive passenger vehicles and trucks used to transport inmates to other institutions, courtrooms, hospitals, and work sites. Use nondisciplinary tools and equipment such as a computer. Assign duties to inmates, providing instructions as needed. Investigate crimes that have occurred within an institution or assist police in their investigations of crimes and inmates. Issue clothing, tools, and other authorized items to inmates. Arrange daily schedules for prisoners, including library visits, work assignments, family visits, and counseling appointments. Search for and recapture escapees.

GOE—Career Cluster/Interest Area: 12. Law and Public Safety. **Work Group:** 12.04. Law Enforcement and Public Safety. **Other Apprenticeable Jobs in This Work Group:** Fire Investigators; Police Patrol Officers. **Personality Type:** Realistic. These occupations frequently involve work activities that include practical, hands-on problems and solutions. They often deal with plants; animals; and real-world materials such as wood, tools, and machinery. Many of the occupations require working outside and don't involve a lot of paperwork or working closely with others.

Skills—None met the criteria.

Education/Training Required (Nonapprenticeship Route): Moderate-term on-the-job training. **Related Knowledge/Courses—Public Safety and Security:** Weaponry; public safety; security operations, rules, regulations, precautions, and prevention; and the protection of people, data, and property. **Psychology:** Human behavior and performance, mental processes, psychological research methods, and the assessment and treatment of behavioral and affective disorders. **Therapy and Counseling:** Information and techniques needed to rehabilitate physical and mental ailments and to provide career guidance, including alternative treatments, rehabilitation equipment and its proper use, and methods to evaluate treatment effects. **Law and Government:** Laws, legal codes, court procedures, precedents, government regulations, executive orders, agency rules, and the democratic political process. **Medicine and Dentistry:** The information and techniques needed to diagnose and treat injuries, diseases, and deformities. This includes symptoms, treatment alternatives, drug properties and interactions, and preventive health-care measures. **Sociology and Anthropology:** Group behavior and dynamics; societal trends and influences; and cultures and their history, migrations, ethnicity, and origins.

Work Environment: More often indoors than outdoors; noisy; contaminants; disease or infections; standing.

Crane and Tower Operators

* Annual Earnings: $40,260
* Growth: 2.8%
* Annual Job Openings: 2,626
* Percentage of Women: 1.5%

Related Apprenticeship—Truck Crane Operator (6000 hrs.).

Operate mechanical boom and cable or tower and cable equipment to lift and move materials, machines, or products in many directions. Determine load weights and check them against lifting capacities to prevent overload. Move levers, depress foot pedals, and turn dials to operate cranes, cherry pickers, electromagnets, or other moving equipment for lifting, moving, and placing loads. Inspect cables and grappling devices for wear and install or replace cables as needed. Clean, lubricate, and maintain mechanisms such as cables, pulleys, and grappling devices, making repairs as necessary. Inspect and adjust crane mechanisms and lifting accessories to prevent malfunctions and damage. Direct helpers engaged in placing blocking and outrigging under cranes. Load and unload bundles from trucks and move containers to storage bins, using moving equipment. Weigh bundles, using floor scales, and record weights for company records. Review daily work and delivery schedules to determine orders, sequences of deliveries, and special loading instructions. Direct truck drivers backing vehicles into loading bays and cover, uncover, and secure loads for delivery. Inspect bundle packaging for conformance to regulations and customer requirements and remove and batch packaging tickets.

GOE—Career Cluster/Interest Area: 02. Architecture and Construction. **Work Group:** 02.04. Construction Crafts. **Other Apprenticeable Jobs in This Work Group:** Boilermakers; Brickmasons and Blockmasons; Carpet Installers; Cement Masons and Concrete Finishers; Construction Carpenters; Drywall and Ceiling Tile Installers; Electricians; Fence Erectors; Floor Layers, Except Carpet, Wood, and Hard Tiles; Glaziers; Insulation Workers, Floor, Ceiling, and

Wall; Insulation Workers, Mechanical; Operating Engineers and Other Construction Equipment Operators; Painters, Construction and Maintenance; Paperhangers; Paving, Surfacing, and Tamping Equipment Operators; Pipe Fitters and Steamfitters; Plasterers and Stucco Masons; Plumbers; Reinforcing Iron and Rebar Workers; Riggers; Roofers; Rough Carpenters; Sheet Metal Workers; Stone Cutters and Carvers, Manufacturing; Stonemasons; Structural Iron and Steel Workers; Tapers; Terrazzo Workers and Finishers; Tile and Marble Setters. **Personality Type:** Realistic. These occupations frequently involve work activities that include practical, hands-on problems and solutions. They often deal with plants; animals; and real-world materials such as wood, tools, and machinery. Many of the occupations require working outside and don't involve a lot of paperwork or working closely with others.

Skills—Equipment Maintenance; Operation Monitoring; Operation and Control; Equipment Selection; Repairing; Installation; Technology Design; Troubleshooting.

Education/Training Required (Nonapprenticeship Route): Long-term on-the-job training. **Related Knowledge/Courses—Building and Construction:** Materials, methods, and the appropriate tools to construct objects, structures, and buildings. **Mechanical Devices:** Machines and tools, including their designs, uses, benefits, repair, and maintenance. **Transportation:** Principles and methods for moving people or goods by air, rail, sea, or road, including their relative costs, advantages, and limitations. **Engineering and Technology:** Equipment, tools, and mechanical devices and their uses to produce motion, light, power, technology, and other applications. **Public Safety and Security:** Weaponry; public safety; security operations, rules, regulations, precautions, and prevention; and the protection of people, data, and property. **Design:** Design techniques, principles, tools, and instruments involved in the production and use of precision technical plans, blueprints, drawings, and models.

Work Environment: Noisy; very bright or dim lighting; contaminants; high places; using hands on objects, tools, or controls; repetitive motions.

Data Entry Keyers

- ❋ Annual Earnings: $25,370
- ❋ Growth: –4.7%
- ❋ Annual Job Openings: 79,166
- ❋ Percentage of Women: 81.6%

Related Apprenticeship—Photocomposing-Perforation-Maker (4000 hrs.).

Operate data entry device, such as keyboard or photo-composing perforator. Duties may include verifying data and preparing materials for printing. Read source documents such as canceled checks, sales reports, or bills and enter data in specific data fields or onto tapes or disks for subsequent entry, using keyboards or scanners. Compile, sort, and verify the accuracy of data before it is entered. Compare data with source documents or re-enter data in verification format to detect errors. Store completed documents in appropriate locations. Locate and correct data entry errors or report them to supervisors. Maintain logs of activities and completed work. Select materials needed to complete work assignments. Load machines with required input or output media such as paper, cards, disks, tape, or Braille media. Resolve garbled or indecipherable messages, using cryptographic procedures and equipment.

GOE—Career Cluster/Interest Area: 04. Business and Administration. **Work Group:** 04.08. Clerical Machine Operation. **Other Apprenticeable Jobs in This Work Group:** Mail Clerks and Mail Machine Operators, Except Postal Service; Word Processors and Typists. **Personality Type:** Conventional. These occupations frequently involve following set procedures and routines and can include working with data and details more than with ideas. Usually there is a clear line of authority to follow.

Skills—None met the criteria.

Education/Training Required (Nonapprenticeship Route): Moderate-term on-the-job training. **Related Knowledge/Courses—Clerical Practices:** Administrative and clerical procedures and systems such as word-processing systems, filing and records management systems, stenography and transcription, forms, design principles, and other office procedures and terminology. **Economics and Accounting:** Economic and accounting principles and practices, the financial markets, banking, and the analysis and reporting of financial data. **Computers and Electronics:** Electric circuit boards, processors, chips, and computer hardware and software, including applications and programming. **Customer and Personal Service:** Principles and processes for providing customer and personal services, including needs assessment techniques, quality service standards, alternative delivery systems, and customer satisfaction evaluation techniques.

Work Environment: Indoors; noisy; sitting; using hands on objects, tools, or controls; repetitive motions.

Dental Assistants

* Annual Earnings: $31,550
* Growth: 29.2%
* Annual Job Openings: 29,482
* Percentage of Women: 95.4%

Related Apprenticeship—Dental Assistant (2000 hrs.).

Assist dentist, set up patient and equipment, and keep records. Prepare patient, sterilize and disinfect instruments, set up instrument trays, prepare materials, and assist dentist during dental procedures. Expose dental diagnostic X rays. Record treatment information in patient records. Take and record medical and dental histories and vital signs of patients. Provide postoperative instructions prescribed by dentist. Assist dentist in management of medical and dental emergencies. Pour, trim, and polish study casts. Instruct patients in oral hygiene and plaque control programs. Make preliminary impressions for study casts and occlusal registrations for mounting study casts. Clean and polish removable appliances. Clean teeth, using dental instruments. Apply protective coating of fluoride to teeth. Fabricate temporary restorations and custom impressions from preliminary impressions. Schedule appointments, prepare bills, and receive payment for dental services; complete insurance forms; and maintain records, manually or using computer.

GOE—Career Cluster/Interest Area: 08. Health Science. **Work Group:** 08.03. Dentistry. **Other Apprenticeable Jobs in This Work Group:** No others in group. **Personality Type:** Conventional. These occupations frequently involve following set procedures and routines and can include working with data and details more than with ideas. Usually there is a clear line of authority to follow.

Skills—Equipment Maintenance; Operation and Control; Social Perceptiveness; Management of Material Resources; Operation Monitoring; Equipment Selection; Installation; Repairing.

Education/Training Required (Nonapprenticeship Route): Moderate-term on-the-job training. **Related Knowledge/Courses—Medicine and Dentistry:** The information and techniques needed to diagnose and treat injuries, diseases, and deformities. This includes symptoms, treatment alternatives, drug properties and interactions, and preventive health-care measures. **Chemistry:** The composition, structure, and properties of substances and of the chemical processes and transformations that they undergo. This includes uses of chemicals and their interactions, danger signs, production techniques, and disposal methods. **Clerical Practices:** Administrative and clerical procedures and systems such as word-processing systems, filing and records management systems, stenography and transcription, forms, design principles, and other office procedures and terminology. **Customer and Personal Service:** Principles and processes for providing customer and personal services, including needs assessment techniques, quality service standards, alternative delivery systems, and customer satisfaction evaluation techniques. **Psychology:** Human behavior and performance, mental processes, psychological research methods, and the assessment and treatment of behavioral and affective disorders.

Work Environment: Indoors; contaminants; disease or infections; using hands on objects, tools, or controls; bending or twisting the body; repetitive motions.

Dental Laboratory Technicians

* Annual Earnings: $33,480
* Growth: 3.7%
* Annual Job Openings: 3,479
* Percentage of Women: 50.8%

Related Apprenticeships—Contour Wire Specialist, Denture (8000 hrs.); Dental Ceramist (4000 hrs.); Dental Laboratory Technician (6000 hrs.); Finisher, Denture (2000 hrs.); Orthodontic Technician (4000 hrs.).

Construct and repair full or partial dentures or dental appliances. Read prescriptions or specifications and examine models and impressions to determine the design of dental products to be constructed. Fabricate, alter, and repair dental devices such as dentures, crowns, bridges, inlays, and appliances for straightening teeth. Place tooth models on apparatus that mimics bite and movement of patient's jaw to evaluate functionality of model. Test appliances for conformance to specifications and accuracy of occlusion, using articulators and micrometers. Melt metals or mix plaster, porcelain, or acrylic pastes and pour materials into molds or over frameworks to form dental prostheses or apparatus. Prepare metal surfaces for bonding with porcelain to create artificial teeth, using small hand tools. Remove excess metal or porcelain and polish surfaces of prostheses or frameworks, using polishing machines. Create a model of patient's mouth by pouring plaster into a dental impression and allowing plaster to set. Load newly constructed teeth into porcelain furnaces to bake the porcelain onto the metal framework. Build and shape wax teeth, using small hand instruments and information from observations or dentists' specifications. Apply porcelain paste or wax over prosthesis frameworks or setups, using brushes and spatulas. Fill chipped or low spots in surfaces of devices, using acrylic resins. Prepare wax bite-blocks and impression trays for use. Mold wax over denture set-ups to form the full contours of artificial gums. Train and supervise other dental technicians or dental laboratory bench workers. Rebuild or replace linings, wire sections, and missing teeth to repair dentures. Shape and solder wire and metal frames or bands for dental products, using soldering irons and hand tools.

GOE—Career Cluster/Interest Area: 13. Manufacturing. **Work Group:** 13.06. Production Precision Work. **Other Apprenticeable Jobs in This Work Group:** Bookbinders; Electrical and Electronic Equipment Assemblers; Electromechanical Equipment Assemblers; Engine and Other Machine Assemblers; Gem and Diamond Workers; Jewelers; Medical Appliance Technicians; Molding, Coremaking, and Casting Machine Setters, Operators, and Tenders, Metal and Plastic; Ophthalmic Laboratory Technicians; Precious Metal Workers. **Personality Type:** Realistic. These occupations frequently involve work activities that include practical, hands-on problems and solutions. They often deal with plants; animals; and real-world materials such as wood, tools, and machinery. Many of the occupations require working outside and don't involve a lot of paperwork or working closely with others.

Skills—Equipment Maintenance; Equipment Selection; Management of Material Resources; Repairing; Quality Control Analysis; Operations Analysis; Operation Monitoring; Technology Design.

Education/Training Required (Nonapprenticeship Route): Long-term on-the-job training. **Related Knowledge/Courses—Medicine and Dentistry:** The information and techniques needed to diagnose and treat injuries, diseases, and deformities. This includes symptoms, treatment alternatives, drug properties and interactions, and preventive health-care measures. **Design:** Design techniques, principles, tools, and instruments involved in the production and use of precision technical plans, blueprints, drawings, and models. **Production and Processing:** Inputs, outputs, raw materials, waste, quality control, costs, and techniques for maximizing the manufacture and distribution of goods. **Engineering and Technology:** Equipment, tools, and mechanical devices and their uses to produce motion, light, power, technology, and other applications. **Mechanical Devices:** Machines and tools, including their designs, uses, benefits, repair, and maintenance. **Chemistry:** The composition, structure, and properties of substances and of the chemical processes and transformations that they undergo. This includes uses of chemicals and their interactions, danger signs, production techniques, and disposal methods.

Work Environment: Indoors; noisy; contaminants; sitting; using hands on objects, tools, or controls; repetitive motions.

Desktop Publishers

* Annual Earnings: $35,510
* Growth: 1.0%
* Annual Job Openings: 6,420
* Percentage of Women: 91.2%

Related Apprenticeship—Electronic Prepress System Operator (10000 hrs.).

Format typescript and graphic elements, using computer software to produce publication-ready material. Check preliminary and final proofs for errors and make necessary corrections. Operate desktop publishing software and equipment to design, lay out, and produce camera-ready copy. View monitors for visual representation of work in progress and for instructions and feedback throughout process, making modifications as necessary. Enter text into computer keyboard and select the size and style of type, column width, and appropriate spacing for printed materials. Store copies of publications on paper, magnetic tape, CD, or DVD. Position text and art elements from a variety of databases in a visually appealing way to design print or Web pages, using knowledge of type styles and size and layout patterns. Enter digitized data into electronic prepress system computer memory, using scanner, camera, keyboard, or mouse. Edit graphics and photos, using pixel or bitmap editing, airbrushing, masking, or image retouching. Import text and art elements such as electronic clip art or electronic files from photographs that have been scanned or produced with a digital camera, using computer software. Prepare sample layouts for approval, using computer software. Study layout or other design instructions to determine work to be done and sequence of operations. Load CDs, DVDs, or tapes containing information into system. Convert various types of files for printing or for the Internet, using computer software. Enter data, such as coordinates of images and color specifications, into system to retouch and make color corrections. Select number of colors and determine color separations. Transmit, deliver, or mail publication master to printer for production into film and plates. Collaborate with graphic artists, editors, and writers to produce master copies according to design specifications. Create special effects such as vignettes, mosaics, and image combining and add elements such as sound and animation to electronic publications.

GOE—Career Cluster/Interest Area: 13. Manufacturing. **Work Group:** 13.08. Graphic Arts Production. **Other Apprenticeable Jobs in This Work Group:** Bindery Workers; Etchers and Engravers; Job Printers; Photographic Process Workers; Photographic Processing Machine Operators; Prepress Technicians and Workers; Printing Machine Operators. **Personality Type:** Artistic. These occupations frequently involve working with forms, designs, and patterns. They often require self-expression, and the work can be done without following a clear set of rules.

Skills—Operation and Control; Operations Analysis; Writing; Reading Comprehension; Time Management; Active Listening; Equipment Selection; Service Orientation.

Education/Training Required (Nonapprenticeship Route): Postsecondary vocational training. **Related Knowledge/Courses—Computers and Electronics:** Electric circuit boards, processors, chips, and computer hardware and software, including applications and programming. **Production and Processing:** Inputs, outputs, raw materials, waste, quality control, costs, and techniques for maximizing the manufacture and distribution of goods.

Work Environment: Indoors; sitting; repetitive motions.

Dispatchers, Except Police, Fire, and Ambulance

* Annual Earnings: $33,140
* Growth: 1.5%
* Annual Job Openings: 29,793
* Percentage of Women: 53.4%

Related Apprenticeship—Dispatcher, Service (4000 hrs.).

Schedule and dispatch workers, work crews, equipment, or service vehicles for conveyance of materials, freight, or passengers or for normal installation, service, or emergency repairs rendered outside the place of business. Duties may include using radio, telephone, or computer to transmit assignments and compiling statistics and reports on work progress. Schedule and dispatch workers, work crews, equipment, or service vehicles to appropriate locations according to customer requests, specifications, or needs, using radios or telephones. Arrange for necessary repairs to restore service and schedules. Relay work orders, messages, and information to or from work crews, supervisors, and field inspectors, using telephones or two-way radios. Confer with customers or supervising personnel to address questions, problems, and requests for service or equipment. Prepare daily work and run schedules. Receive or prepare work orders. Oversee all communications within specifically assigned territories. Monitor personnel or equipment locations and utilization to coordinate service and schedules. Record and maintain files and records of customer requests, work or services performed, charges, expenses, inventory, and other dispatch information. Determine types or amounts of equipment, vehicles, materials, or personnel required according to work orders or specifications. Advise personnel about traffic problems such as construction areas, accidents, congestion, weather conditions, and other hazards. Ensure timely and efficient movement of trains according to train orders and schedules. Order supplies and equipment and issue them to personnel.

GOE—Career Cluster/Interest Area: 03. Arts and Communication. **Work Group:** 03.10. Communications Technology. **Other Apprenticeable Jobs in This Work Group:** Air

Traffic Controllers; Airfield Operations Specialists; Police, Fire, and Ambulance Dispatchers. **Personality Type:** Conventional. These occupations frequently involve following set procedures and routines and can include working with data and details more than with ideas. Usually there is a clear line of authority to follow.

Skills—Operations Analysis; Service Orientation; Systems Evaluation; Management of Personnel Resources; Troubleshooting; Systems Analysis; Judgment and Decision Making; Critical Thinking.

Education/Training Required (Nonapprenticeship Route): Moderate-term on-the-job training. **Related Knowledge/Courses—Transportation:** Principles and methods for moving people or goods by air, rail, sea, or road, including their relative costs, advantages, and limitations. **Clerical Practices:** Administrative and clerical procedures and systems such as word-processing systems, filing and records management systems, stenography and transcription, forms, design principles, and other office procedures and terminology. **Public Safety and Security:** Weaponry; public safety; security operations, rules, regulations, precautions, and prevention; and the protection of people, data, and property. **Communications and Media:** Media production, communication, and dissemination techniques and methods, including alternative ways to inform and entertain via written, oral, and visual media.

Work Environment: Indoors; noisy; sitting; using hands on objects, tools, or controls; repetitive motions.

Drywall and Ceiling Tile Installers

❊ Annual Earnings: $36,520
❊ Growth: 7.3%
❊ Annual Job Openings: 30,945
❊ Percentage of Women: 2.9%

Related Apprenticeships—Acoustical Carpenter (8000 hrs.); Carpenter, Acoustical Specialist (3900–6000 hrs., hybrid); Dry-Wall Applicator (4000 hrs.).

Apply plasterboard or other wallboard to ceilings or interior walls of buildings. Apply or mount acoustical tiles or blocks, strips, or sheets of shock-absorbing materials to ceilings and walls of buildings to reduce or reflect sound. Materials may be of decorative quality. Includes lathers who fasten wooden, metal, or rockboard lath to walls, ceilings, or partitions of buildings to provide support base for plaster, fireproofing, or acoustical material. Inspect furrings, mechanical mountings, and masonry surface for plumbness and level, using spirit or water levels. Install metal lath where plaster applications will be exposed to weather or water or for curved or irregular surfaces. Install blanket insulation between studs and tack plastic moisture barriers over insulation. Coordinate work with drywall finishers who cover the seams between drywall panels. Trim rough edges from wallboard to maintain even joints, using knives. Seal joints between ceiling tiles and walls. Scribe and cut edges of tile to fit walls where wall molding is not specified. Read blueprints and other specifications to determine methods of installation, work procedures, and material and tool requirements. Nail channels or wood furring strips to surfaces to provide mounting for tile. Mount tile by using adhesives or by nailing, screwing, stapling, or wire-tying lath directly to structural frameworks. Measure and mark surfaces to lay out work according to blueprints and drawings, using tape measures, straightedges or squares, and marking devices. Hang drywall panels on metal frameworks of walls and ceilings in offices, schools, and other large buildings, using lifts or hoists to adjust panel heights when necessary. Install horizontal and vertical metal or wooden studs to frames so that wallboard can be attached to interior walls. Fasten metal or rockboard lath to the structural framework of walls, ceilings, and partitions of buildings, using nails, screws, staples, or wire-ties. Apply or mount acoustical tile or blocks, strips, or sheets of shock-absorbing materials to ceilings and walls of buildings to reduce reflection of sound or to decorate rooms. Apply cement to backs of tiles and press tiles into place, aligning them with layout marks or joints of previously laid tile. Hang dry lines (stretched string) to wall moldings in order to guide positioning of main runners. Assemble and install metal framing and decorative trim for windows, doorways, and vents. Fit and fasten wallboard or drywall into position on wood or metal frameworks, using glue, nails, or screws.

GOE—Career Cluster/Interest Area: 02. Architecture and Construction. **Work Group:** 02.04. Construction Crafts. **Other Apprenticeable Jobs in This Work Group:** Boilermakers; Brickmasons and Blockmasons; Carpet Installers; Cement Masons and Concrete Finishers; Construction Carpenters; Crane and Tower Operators; Electricians; Fence Erectors; Floor Layers, Except Carpet, Wood, and Hard Tiles; Glaziers; Insulation Workers, Floor, Ceiling, and Wall; Insulation Workers, Mechanical; Operating Engineers and Other Construction Equipment Operators; Painters, Construction and Maintenance; Paperhangers; Paving, Surfacing, and Tamping Equipment Operators; Pipe Fitters and Steamfitters; Plasterers and Stucco Masons; Plumbers; Reinforcing Iron and Rebar Workers; Riggers; Roofers; Rough Carpenters; Sheet Metal Workers; Stone Cutters and Carvers, Manufacturing; Stonemasons; Structural Iron and Steel Workers; Tapers; Terrazzo Workers and Finishers; Tile and Marble Setters. **Personality Type:** Realistic. These occupations frequently involve work activities that include practical, hands-on problems and solutions. They often deal with plants; animals; and real-world materials such as wood, tools, and machinery. Many of the occupations require working outside and don't involve a lot of paperwork or working closely with others.

Skills—Installation; Management of Personnel Resources; Management of Material Resources; Management of Financial Resources; Mathematics; Repairing; Science; Equipment Selection.

Education/Training Required (Nonapprenticeship Route): Moderate-term on-the-job training. **Related Knowledge/Courses—Building and Construction:** Materials, methods, and the appropriate tools to construct objects, structures, and buildings. **Design:** Design techniques, principles, tools, and instruments involved in the production and use of precision technical plans, blueprints, drawings, and models. **Mechanical Devices:** Machines and tools, including their designs, uses, benefits, repair, and maintenance. **Mathematics:** Numbers and their operations and interrelationships, including arithmetic, algebra, geometry, calculus, and statistics and their applications. **Production and Processing:** Inputs, outputs, raw materials, waste, quality control, costs, and techniques for maximizing the manufacture and distribution of goods. **Public Safety and Security:** Weaponry; public safety; security operations, rules, regulations,

precautions, and prevention; and the protection of people, data, and property.

Work Environment: Indoors; contaminants; hazardous equipment; minor burns, cuts, bites, or stings; standing; using hands on objects, tools, or controls.

Earth Drillers, Except Oil and Gas

- ❀ Annual Earnings: $36,310
- ❀ Growth: 6.5%
- ❀ Annual Job Openings: 2,619
- ❀ Percentage of Women: 3.1%

Related Apprenticeship—Well Drill Operator (Construction) (8000 hrs.).

Operate a variety of drills—such as rotary, churn, and pneumatic—to tap sub-surface water and salt deposits, to remove core samples during mineral exploration or soil testing, and to facilitate the use of explosives in mining or construction. May use explosives. Includes horizontal and earth-boring machine operators. Drive or guide truck-mounted equipment into position, level and stabilize rigs, and extend telescoping derricks. Operate hoists to lift power line poles into position. Fabricate well casings. Disinfect, reconstruct, and redevelop contaminated wells and water pumping systems and clean and disinfect new wells in preparation for use. Design well pumping systems. Assemble and position machines, augers, casing pipes, and other equipment, using hand and power tools. Signal crane operators to move equipment. Record drilling progress and geological data. Retrieve lost equipment from bore holes, using retrieval tools and equipment. Review client requirements and proposed locations for drilling operations to determine feasibility and cost estimates. Perform routine maintenance and upgrade work on machines and equipment, such as replacing parts, building up drill bits, and lubricating machinery. Perform pumping tests to assess well performance. Drive trucks, tractors, or truck-mounted drills to and from worksites. Verify depths and alignments of boring positions. Withdraw drill rods from holes and extract core samples. Operate water-well drilling rigs and other equipment to drill, bore, and dig for water wells or for environmental assessment purposes. Drill or bore holes in rock for blasting, grouting, anchoring, or building foundations. Inspect core samples to determine nature of strata or take samples to laboratories for analysis. Monitor drilling operations, checking gauges and listening to equipment to assess drilling conditions and to determine the need to adjust drilling or alter equipment. Observe electronic graph recorders and flow meters that monitor the water used to flush debris from holes. Document geological formations encountered during work. Operate machines to flush earth cuttings or to blow dust from holes. Start, stop, and control drilling speed of machines and insertion of casings into holes. Select the appropriate drill for the job, using knowledge of rock or soil conditions. Operate controls to stabilize machines and to position and align drills. Place and install screens, casings, pumps, and other well fixtures to develop wells. Pour water into wells or pump water or slush into wells to cool drill bits and to remove drillings.

GOE—Career Cluster/Interest Area: 01. Agriculture and Natural Resources. **Work Group:** 01.08. Mining and Drilling. **Other Appprenticeable Jobs in This Work Group:** Excavating and Loading Machine and Dragline Operators; Explosives Workers, Ordnance Handling Experts, and Blasters; Helpers—Extraction Workers; Mine Cutting and Channeling Machine Operators; Rotary Drill Operators, Oil and Gas. **Personality Type:** Realistic. These occupations frequently involve work activities that include practical, hands-on problems and solutions. They often deal with plants; animals; and real-world materials such as wood, tools, and machinery. Many of the occupations require working outside and don't involve a lot of paperwork or working closely with others.

Skills—Repairing; Equipment Maintenance; Operation Monitoring.

Education/Training Required (Nonapprenticeship Route): Moderate-term on-the-job training. **Related Knowledge/Courses Mechanical Devices:** Machines and tools, including their designs, uses, benefits, repair, and maintenance. **Building and Construction:** Materials, methods, and the appropriate tools to construct objects, structures, and buildings. **Chemistry:** The composition, structure, and properties of substances and of the chemical processes and transformations that they undergo. This includes uses of chemicals and their interactions, danger signs, production techniques, and disposal methods. **Engineering and Technology:** Equipment, tools, and mechanical devices and their uses to produce motion, light, power, technology, and other applications. **Public Safety and Security:** Weaponry; public safety; security operations, rules, regulations, precautions, and prevention; and the protection of people, data, and property. **Design:** Design techniques, principles, tools, and instruments involved in the production and use of precision technical plans, blueprints, drawings, and models.

Work Environment: Outdoors; noisy; contaminants; hazardous equipment; standing; using hands on objects, tools, or controls.

Electrical and Electronics Installers and Repairers, Transportation Equipment

❋ Annual Earnings: $43,940
❋ Growth: 4.3%
❋ Annual Job Openings: 1,663
❋ Percentage of Women: 4.6%

Related Apprenticeship—Electrician, Locomotive (8000 hrs.).

Install, adjust, or maintain mobile electronics communication equipment, including sound, sonar, security, navigation, and surveillance systems on trains, watercraft, or other mobile equipment. Inspect and test electrical systems and equipment to locate and diagnose malfunctions by using visual inspections, testing devices, and computer software. Reassemble and test equipment after repairs. Splice wires with knives or cutting pliers and solder connections to fixtures, outlets, and equipment. Install new fuses, electrical cables, or power sources as required. Locate and remove or repair circuit defects such as blown fuses or malfunctioning transistors. Use electrician's tools to adjust, repair, or replace defective wiring and relays in ignition, lighting, air-conditioning, and safety control systems. Refer to schematics and manufacturers' specifications that show connections and provide instructions on how to locate problems. Maintain equipment service records. Cut openings and drill holes for fixtures, outlet boxes, and fuse holders, using electric drills and routers. Use hand tools to measure, cut, and install frameworks and conduit to support and connect wiring, control panels, and junction boxes. Use hand tools to install electrical equipment such as air-conditioning, heating, or ignition systems and components such as generator brushes and commutators. Install fixtures, outlets, terminal boards, switches, and wall boxes with hand tools. Use electrician's tools to repair or rebuild equipment such as starters, generators, distributors, or door controls. Confer with customers to determine nature of malfunctions. Estimate repair costs based on parts and labor requirements.

GOE—Career Cluster/Interest Area: 13. Manufacturing. **Work Group:** 13.12. Electrical and Electronic Repair. **Other Apprenticeable Jobs in This Work Group:** Avionics Technicians; Electric Motor, Power Tool, and Related Repairers; Electrical and Electronics Repairers, Commercial and Industrial Equipment; Electronic Equipment Installers and Repairers, Motor Vehicles; Electronic Home Entertainment Equipment Installers and Repairers; Radio Mechanics. **Personality Type:** Realistic. These occupations frequently involve work activities that include practical, hands-on problems and solutions. They often deal with plants; animals; and real-world materials such as wood, tools, and machinery. Many of the occupations require working outside and don't involve a lot of paperwork or working closely with others.

Skills—Installation; Repairing; Troubleshooting; Equipment Selection; Complex Problem Solving; Operation Monitoring; Equipment Maintenance; Operation and Control.

Education/Training Required (Nonapprenticeship Route): Postsecondary vocational training. **Related Knowledge/Courses— Mechanical Devices:** Machines and tools, including their designs, uses, benefits, repair, and maintenance. **Engineering and Technology:**

Equipment, tools, and mechanical devices and their uses to produce motion, light, power, technology, and other applications. **Building and Construction:** Materials, methods, and the appropriate tools to construct objects, structures, and buildings. **Physics:** Physical principles, laws, and applications, including air, water, material dynamics, light, atomic principles, heat, electric theory, earth formations, and meteorological and related natural phenomena. **Design:** Design techniques, principles, tools, and instruments involved in the production and use of precision technical plans, blueprints, drawings, and models. **Production and Processing:** Inputs, outputs, raw materials, waste, quality control, costs, and techniques for maximizing the manufacture and distribution of goods.

Work Environment: Outdoors; contaminants; hazardous conditions; standing; using hands on objects, tools, or controls; repetitive motions.

Electrical and Electronics Repairers, Commercial and Industrial Equipment

- ❋ Annual Earnings: $47,110
- ❋ Growth: 6.8%
- ❋ Annual Job Openings: 6,607
- ❋ Percentage of Women: 15.2%

Related Apprenticeships—Avionics Technician (8000 hrs.); Control Equipment Electronics Technician (10000 hrs.); Electronic-Sales-and-Service Technician (8000 hrs.); Field Service Engineer (4000 hrs.); Meteorological Equipment Repairer (8000 hrs.); Supervisory Control and Data Acquisition Technician (SCADA) (8000 hrs.); Visual Imagery Intrusion Detection Systems (Maintenance) (2500 hrs. or competency).

Repair, test, adjust, or install electronic equipment, such as industrial controls, transmitters, and antennas. Perform scheduled preventive maintenance tasks, such as checking, cleaning, and repairing equipment, to detect and prevent problems. Examine work orders and converse with equipment operators to detect equipment problems and to ascertain whether mechanical or human errors contributed to the problems. Operate equipment to demonstrate proper use and to analyze malfunctions. Set up and test industrial equipment to ensure that it functions properly. Test faulty equipment to diagnose malfunctions, using test equipment and software and applying knowledge of the functional operation of electronic units and systems. Repair and adjust equipment, machines, and defective components, replacing worn parts such as gaskets and seals in watertight electrical equipment. Calibrate testing instruments and installed or repaired equipment to prescribed specifications. Advise management regarding customer satisfaction, product performance, and suggestions for product improvements. Study blueprints, schematics, manuals, and other specifications to determine installation procedures. Inspect components of industrial equipment for accurate assembly and installation and for defects such as loose connections and frayed wires. Maintain equipment logs that record performance problems, repairs, calibrations, and tests. Coordinate efforts with other workers involved in installing and maintaining equipment or components. Maintain inventory of spare parts. Consult with customers, supervisors, and engineers to plan layout of equipment and to resolve problems in system operation and maintenance. Install repaired equipment in various settings, such as industrial or military establishments. Send defective units to the manufacturer or to a specialized repair shop for repair. Determine feasibility of using standardized equipment and develop specifications for equipment required to perform additional functions. Enter information into computer to copy program or to draw, modify, or store schematics, applying knowledge of software package used. Sign overhaul documents for equipment replaced or repaired. Develop or modify industrial electronic devices, circuits, and equipment according to available specifications.

GOE—Career Cluster/Interest Area: 13. Manufacturing. **Work Group:** 13.12. Electrical and Electronic Repair. **Other Apprenticeable Jobs in This Work Group:** Avionics Technicians; Electric Motor, Power Tool, and Related Repairers; Electrical and Electronics Installers and Repairers, Transportation Equipment; Electronic Equipment Installers and Repairers, Motor Vehicles; Electronic Home Entertainment Equipment Installers and Repairers; Radio Mechanics. **Personality Type:** Realistic. These occupations frequently involve work activities that include practical, hands-on problems and solutions. They often deal with plants; animals; and real-world materials such as wood, tools, and machinery. Many of the occupations require working outside and don't involve a lot of paperwork or working closely with others.

Skills—Installation; Repairing; Operation Monitoring; Troubleshooting; Equipment Maintenance; Operation and Control; Systems Analysis; Science.

Education/Training Required (Nonapprenticeship Route): Postsecondary vocational training. **Related Knowledge/Courses— Mechanical Devices:** Machines and tools, including their designs, uses, benefits, repair, and maintenance. **Computers and Electronics:** Electric circuit boards, processors, chips,

and computer hardware and software, including applications and programming. **Telecommunications:** Transmission, broadcasting, switching, control, and operation of telecommunications systems. **Engineering and Technology:** Equipment, tools, and mechanical devices and their uses to produce motion, light, power, technology, and other applications.

Work Environment: Indoors; noisy; cramped work space, awkward positions; hazardous conditions; standing; using hands on objects, tools, or controls.

Electrical and Electronics Repairers, Powerhouse, Substation, and Relay

* Annual Earnings: $58,970
* Growth: –4.7%
* Annual Job Openings: 1,591
* Percentage of Women: 4.6%

Related Apprenticeships—Corrosion-Control Fitter (8000 hrs.); Electrician, Powerhouse (8000 hrs.); Electrician, Substation (6000 hrs.); Relay Technician (4000 hrs.).

Inspect, test, repair, or maintain electrical equipment in generating stations, substations, and in-service relays. Construct, test, maintain, and repair substation relay and control systems. Inspect and test equipment and circuits to identify malfunctions or defects, using wiring diagrams and testing devices such as ohmmeters, voltmeters, or ammeters. Consult manuals, schematics, wiring diagrams, and engineering personnel to troubleshoot and solve equipment problems and to determine optimum equipment functioning. Notify facility personnel of equipment shutdowns. Open and close switches to isolate defective relays; then perform adjustments or repairs. Prepare and maintain records detailing tests, repairs, and maintenance. Analyze test data to diagnose malfunctions, to determine performance characteristics of systems, and to evaluate effects of system modifications. Test insulators and bushings of equipment by inducing voltage across insulation, testing current, and calculating insulation loss. Repair, replace, and clean equipment and components such as circuit breakers, brushes, and commutators. Disconnect voltage regulators, bolts, and screws and connect replacement regulators to high-voltage lines. Schedule and supervise the construction and testing of special devices and the implementation of unique monitoring or control systems. Run signal quality and connectivity tests for individual cables and record results. Schedule and supervise splicing or termination of cables in color-code order. Test oil in circuit breakers and transformers for dielectric strength, refilling oil periodically. Maintain inventories of spare parts for all equipment, requisitioning parts as necessary. Set forms and pour concrete footings for installation of heavy equipment.

GOE—Career Cluster/Interest Area: 02. Architecture and Construction. **Work Group:** 02.05. Systems and Equipment Installation, Maintenance, and Repair. **Other Apprenticeable Jobs in This Work Group:** Electrical Power-Line Installers and Repairers; Elevator Installers and Repairers; Heating and Air Conditioning Mechanics and Installers; Maintenance and Repair Workers, General; Refrigeration Mechanics and Installers; Telecommunications Equipment Installers and Repairers, Except Line Installers; Telecommunications Line Installers and Repairers. **Personality Type:** Realistic. These occupations frequently involve work activities that include practical, hands-on problems

and solutions. They often deal with plants; animals; and real-world materials such as wood, tools, and machinery. Many of the occupations require working outside and don't involve a lot of paperwork or working closely with others.

Skills—Installation; Repairing; Equipment Maintenance; Troubleshooting; Operation Monitoring; Operation and Control; Science; Operations Analysis.

Education/Training Required (Nonapprenticeship Route): Postsecondary vocational training. **Related Knowledge/Courses—Mechanical Devices:** Machines and tools, including their designs, uses, benefits, repair, and maintenance. **Design:** Design techniques, principles, tools, and instruments involved in the production and use of precision technical plans, blueprints, drawings, and models. **Telecommunications:** Transmission, broadcasting, switching, control, and operation of telecommunications systems. **Physics:** Physical principles, laws, and applications, including air, water, material dynamics, light, atomic principles, heat, electric theory, earth formations, and meteorological and related natural phenomena. **Building and Construction:** Materials, methods, and the appropriate tools to construct objects, structures, and buildings. **Public Safety and Security:** Weaponry; public safety; security operations, rules, regulations, precautions, and prevention; and the protection of people, data, and property.

Work Environment: Outdoors; noisy; very bright or dim lighting; hazardous conditions; standing; using hands on objects, tools, or controls.

Electrical Drafters

* Annual Earnings: $49,250
* Growth: 4.1%
* Annual Job Openings: 4,786
* Percentage of Women: 21.8%

Our sources did not provide separate job openings data for this occupation. The job openings listed here are shared with Electronic Drafters.

Related Apprenticeships—Drafter, Electrical (8000 hrs.); Estimator and Drafter (8000 hrs.).

Develop specifications and instructions for installation of voltage transformers, overhead or underground cables, and related electrical equipment used to conduct electrical energy from transmission lines or high-voltage distribution lines to consumers. Use computer-aided drafting equipment and/or conventional drafting stations; technical handbooks; tables; calculators; and traditional drafting tools such as boards, pencils, protractors, and T-squares. Draft working drawings, wiring diagrams, wiring connection specifications, or cross-sections of underground cables as required for instructions to installation crew. Confer with engineering staff and other personnel to resolve problems. Draw master sketches to scale, showing relation of proposed installations to existing facilities and exact specifications and dimensions. Measure factors that affect installation and arrangement of equipment, such as distances to be spanned by wire and cable. Assemble documentation packages and produce drawing sets, which are then checked by an engineer or an architect. Review completed construction drawings and cost estimates for accuracy and conformity to standards and regulations. Prepare and interpret specifications, calculating weights, volumes, and stress factors. Explain drawings to production or construction teams and provide adjustments as necessary. Supervise and train other technologists, technicians, and drafters. Study work order requests to determine type of service, such as lighting or power, demanded by installation. Visit proposed installation sites and draw rough sketches of location. Determine the order of work and the method of presentation, such as orthographic or isometric drawing. Reproduce working drawings on copy machines or trace drawings in ink. Write technical reports and draw charts that display statistics and data.

GOE—Career Cluster/Interest Area: 15. Scientific Research, Engineering, and Mathematics. **Work Group:** 15.09. Engineering Technology. **Other Apprenticeable Jobs in This Work Group:** Aerospace Engineering and Operations Technicians; Electrical Engineering Technicians; Electro-Mechanical Technicians; Electronic Drafters; Electronics Engineering Technicians; Mapping Technicians; Mechanical Drafters; Mechanical Engineering Technicians; Surveying and Mapping Technicians; Surveying Technicians. **Personality Type:** Realistic. These occupations frequently involve work activities that include practical, hands-on problems and solutions. They often deal with plants; animals; and real-world materials such as wood, tools, and machinery. Many of the occupations require working outside and don't involve a lot of paperwork or working closely with others.

Skills—Mathematics; Installation; Active Learning; Critical Thinking; Quality Control Analysis; Technology Design; Equipment Selection; Operations Analysis.

Education/Training Required (Nonapprenticeship Route): Postsecondary vocational training. **Related Knowledge/Courses—Design:**

Design techniques, principles, tools, and instruments involved in the production and use of precision technical plans, blueprints, drawings, and models. **Engineering and Technology:** Equipment, tools, and mechanical devices and their uses to produce motion, light, power, technology, and other applications. **Building and Construction:** Materials, methods, and the appropriate tools to construct objects, structures, and buildings. **Computers and Electronics:** Electric circuit boards, processors, chips, and computer hardware and software, including applications and programming. **Telecommunications:** Transmission, broadcasting, switching, control, and operation of telecommunications systems. **Clerical Practices:** Administrative and clerical procedures and systems such as word-processing systems, filing and records management systems, stenography and transcription, forms, design principles, and other office procedures and terminology.

Work Environment: Indoors; sitting.

Electrical Engineering Technicians

* Annual Earnings: $52,140
* Growth: 3.6%
* Annual Job Openings: 12,583
* Percentage of Women: 20.6%

Our sources did not provide separate job openings data for this occupation. The job openings listed here are shared with Electronics Engineering Technicians.

Related Apprenticeship—Electrical Technician (8000 hrs.).

Apply electrical theory and related knowledge to test and modify developmental or operational electrical machinery and electrical control equipment and circuitry in industrial or commercial plants and laboratories. Usually work under direction of engineering staff. Assemble electrical and electronic systems and prototypes according to engineering data and knowledge of electrical principles, using hand tools and measuring instruments. Provide technical assistance and resolution when electrical or engineering problems are encountered before, during, and after construction. Install and maintain electrical control systems and solid state equipment. Modify electrical prototypes, parts, assemblies, and systems to correct functional deviations. Set up and operate test equipment to evaluate performance of developmental parts, assemblies, or systems under simulated operating conditions and record results. Collaborate with electrical engineers and other personnel to identify, define, and solve developmental problems. Build, calibrate, maintain, troubleshoot, and repair electrical instruments or testing equipment. Analyze and interpret test information to resolve design-related problems. Write commissioning procedures for electrical installations. Prepare project cost and work-time estimates. Evaluate engineering proposals, shop drawings, and design comments for sound electrical engineering practice and conformance with established safety and design criteria and recommend approval or disapproval. Draw or modify diagrams and write engineering specifications to clarify design details and functional criteria of experimental electronics units. Conduct inspections for quality control and assurance programs, reporting findings and recommendations. Prepare contracts and initiate, review, and coordinate modifications to contract specifications and plans throughout the construction process. Plan, schedule, and monitor work of support personnel to assist supervisor. Review existing electrical engineering criteria to identify necessary revisions, deletions, or amendments to outdated material. Perform supervisory duties such as recommending work assignments, approving leaves, and completing performance evaluations. Plan method and sequence of operations for developing and testing experimental electronic and electrical equipment. Visit construction sites to observe conditions impacting design and to identify solutions to technical design problems involving electrical systems equipment that arise during construction.

GOE—Career Cluster/Interest Area: 15. Scientific Research, Engineering, and Mathematics. **Work Group:** 15.09. Engineering Technology. **Other Apprenticeable Jobs in This Work Group:** Aerospace Engineering and Operations Technicians; Electrical Drafters; Electro-Mechanical Technicians; Electronic Drafters; Electronics Engineering Technicians; Mapping Technicians; Mechanical Drafters; Mechanical Engineering Technicians; Surveying and Mapping Technicians; Surveying Technicians. **Personality Type:** Realistic. These occupations frequently involve work activities that include practical, hands-on problems and solutions. They often deal with plants; animals; and real-world materials such as wood, tools, and machinery. Many of the occupations require working outside and don't involve a lot of paperwork or working closely with others.

Skills—Repairing; Installation; Troubleshooting; Science; Operations Analysis; Technology Design; Mathematics; Equipment Maintenance.

Education/Training Required (Nonapprenticeship Route): Associate degree. **Related Knowledge/Courses—Engineering and Technology:** Equipment, tools, and mechanical devices and their uses to produce motion, light, power, technology, and other applications.

Design: Design techniques, principles, tools, and instruments involved in the production and use of precision technical plans, blueprints, drawings, and models. **Computers and Electronics:** Electric circuit boards, processors, chips, and computer hardware and software, including applications and programming. **Physics:** Physical principles, laws, and applications, including air, water, material dynamics, light, atomic principles, heat, electric theory, earth formations, and meteorological and related natural phenomena. **Mechanical Devices:** Machines and tools, including their designs, uses, benefits, repair, and maintenance. **Telecommunications:** Transmission, broadcasting, switching, control, and operation of telecommunications systems.

Work Environment: Indoors; noisy; sitting; using hands on objects, tools, or controls.

Electrical Power-Line Installers and Repairers

- ❋ Annual Earnings: $52,570
- ❋ Growth: 7.2%
- ❋ Annual Job Openings: 6,401
- ❋ Percentage of Women: 0.9%

Related Apprenticeships—Cable Installer-Repairer (6000 hrs.); Cable Splicer (8000 hrs.); Line Erector (6000 hrs.); Line Maintainer (8000 hrs.); Line Repairer (6000 hrs.); Trouble Shooter II (6000 hrs.).

Install or repair cables or wires used in electrical power or distribution systems. May erect poles and light- or heavy-duty transmission towers. Adhere to safety practices and procedures, such as checking equipment regularly and erecting barriers around work areas. Open switches or attach grounding devices to remove electrical hazards from disturbed or fallen lines or to facilitate repairs. Climb poles or use truck-mounted buckets to access equipment. Place insulating or fireproofing materials over conductors and joints. Install, maintain, and repair electrical distribution and transmission systems, including conduits; cables; wires; and related equipment such as transformers, circuit breakers, and switches. Identify defective sectionalizing devices, circuit breakers, fuses, voltage regulators, transformers, switches, relays, or wiring, using wiring diagrams and electrical-testing instruments. Drive vehicles equipped with tools and materials to job sites. Coordinate work assignment preparation and completion with other workers. String wire conductors and cables between poles, towers, trenches, pylons, and buildings, setting lines in place and using winches to adjust tension. Inspect and test power lines and auxiliary equipment to locate and identify problems, using reading and testing instruments. Test conductors according to electrical diagrams and specifications to identify corresponding conductors and to prevent incorrect connections. Replace damaged poles with new poles and straighten the poles. Install watt-hour meters and connect service drops between power lines and consumers' facilities. Attach crossarms, insulators, and auxiliary equipment to poles prior to installing them. Travel in trucks, helicopters, and airplanes to inspect lines for freedom from obstruction and adequacy of insulation. Dig holes, using augers, and set poles, using cranes and power equipment. Trim trees that could be hazardous to the functioning of cables or wires. Splice or solder cables together or to overhead transmission lines, customer service lines, or street light lines, using hand tools, epoxies, or specialized equipment. Cut and peel lead sheathing and insulation from defective or newly installed cables and conduits prior to splicing.

GOE—Career Cluster/Interest Area: 02. Architecture and Construction. **Work Group:** 02.05. Systems and Equipment Installation, Maintenance, and Repair. **Other Apprenticeable Jobs in This Work Group:** Electrical and Electronics Repairers, Powerhouse, Substation, and Relay; Elevator Installers and Repairers; Heating and Air Conditioning Mechanics and Installers; Maintenance and Repair Workers, General; Refrigeration Mechanics and Installers; Telecommunications Equipment Installers and Repairers, Except Line Installers; Telecommunications Line Installers and Repairers. **Personality Type:** Realistic. These occupations frequently involve work activities that include practical, hands-on problems and solutions. They often deal with plants; animals; and real-world materials such as wood, tools, and machinery. Many of the occupations require working outside and don't involve a lot of paperwork or working closely with others.

Skills—Repairing; Installation; Equipment Maintenance; Operation Monitoring; Troubleshooting; Operation and Control; Equipment Selection; Technology Design.

Education/Training Required (Nonapprenticeship Route): Long-term on-the-job training. **Related Knowledge/Courses—Building and Construction:** Materials, methods, and the appropriate tools to construct objects, structures, and buildings. **Mechanical Devices:** Machines and tools, including their designs, uses, benefits, repair, and maintenance. **Customer and Personal Service:** Principles and processes for providing customer and personal services, including needs assessment techniques, quality service standards, alternative delivery systems, and customer satisfaction evaluation techniques. **Engineering and Technology:** Equipment, tools, and mechanical devices and their uses to produce motion, light, power, technology, and other applications. **Transportation:** Principles and methods for moving people or goods by air, rail, sea, or road, including their relative costs, advantages, and limitations. **Design:** Design techniques, principles, tools, and instruments involved in the production and use of precision technical plans, blueprints, drawings, and models.

Work Environment: Outdoors; very hot or cold; high places; hazardous conditions; hazardous equipment; using hands on objects, tools, or controls.

Electricians

- ❋ Annual Earnings: $44,780
- ❋ Growth: 7.4%
- ❋ Annual Job Openings: 79,083
- ❋ Percentage of Women: 1.9%

Related Apprenticeships—Electrician (8000 hrs.); Electrician (Ship and Boat) (8000 hrs.); Electrician (Water Transportation) (8000 hrs.); Electrician, Maintenance (8000 hrs.); Neon-Sign Servicer (8000 hrs.); Protective-Signal Installer (8000 hrs.); Protective-Signal Repairer (6000 hrs.); Residential Wireman (4800 hrs.); Street-Light Servicer (8000 hrs.).

Install, maintain, and repair electrical wiring, equipment, and fixtures. Ensure that work is in accordance with relevant codes. May install or service street lights, intercom systems, or electrical control systems. Maintain current electrician's license or identification card to meet governmental regulations. Connect wires to circuit breakers, transformers, or other components. Repair or replace wiring, equipment, and fixtures, using hand tools and power tools. Assemble, install, test, and maintain electrical or electronic wiring, equipment, appliances, apparatus, and fixtures, using hand tools and power tools. Test electrical systems and continuity of circuits in electrical wiring, equipment, and fixtures, using testing devices such as ohmmeters, voltmeters, and oscilloscopes, to ensure compatibility and safety of system. Use a variety of tools and equipment such as power construction equipment, measuring devices, power tools, and testing equipment, including oscilloscopes, ammeters, and test lamps. Plan layout and installation of electrical wiring, equipment, and fixtures based on job specifications and local codes. Inspect electrical systems, equipment, and components to identify hazards, defects, and the need for adjustment or repair and to ensure compliance with codes. Direct and train workers to install, maintain, or repair electrical wiring, equipment, and fixtures. Diagnose malfunctioning systems, apparatus, and components, using test equipment and hand tools, to locate the cause of a breakdown and correct the problem. Prepare sketches or follow blueprints to determine the location of wiring and equipment and to ensure conformance to building and safety codes. Install ground leads and connect power cables to equipment such as motors. Work from ladders, scaffolds, and roofs to install, maintain, or repair electrical wiring, equipment, and fixtures. Perform business management duties such as maintaining records and files, preparing reports, and ordering supplies and equipment. Fasten small metal or plastic boxes to walls to house electrical switches or outlets. Place conduit, pipes, or tubing inside designated partitions, walls, or other concealed areas and pull insulated wires or cables through the conduit to complete circuits between boxes. Advise management on whether continued operation of equipment could be hazardous.

GOE—Career Cluster/Interest Area: 02. Architecture and Construction. **Work Group:** 02.04. Construction Crafts. **Other Apprenticeable Jobs in This Work Group:** Boilermakers; Brickmasons and Blockmasons; Carpet Installers; Cement Masons and Concrete Finishers; Construction Carpenters; Crane and Tower Operators; Drywall and Ceiling Tile Installers; Fence Erectors; Floor Layers, Except Carpet, Wood, and Hard Tiles; Glaziers; Insulation Workers, Floor, Ceiling, and Wall; Insulation Workers, Mechanical; Operating Engineers and Other Construction Equipment Operators; Painters, Construction and Maintenance; Paperhangers; Paving, Surfacing, and Tamping Equipment Operators; Pipe Fitters and Steamfitters; Plasterers and Stucco Masons; Plumbers; Reinforcing Iron and Rebar Workers; Riggers; Roofers; Rough Carpenters; Sheet Metal Workers; Stone Cutters and Carvers, Manufacturing; Stonemasons; Structural Iron and Steel Workers; Tapers; Terrazzo Workers and Finishers; Tile and Marble Setters. **Personality Type:** Realistic. These occupations frequently involve work activities that include practical, hands-on problems and solutions. They often deal with plants; animals; and real-world materials such as wood, tools, and machinery. Many of the occupations require working outside and don't involve a lot of paperwork or working closely with others.

Skills—Repairing; Operation Monitoring; Installation; Equipment Maintenance; Troubleshooting; Operation and Control; Quality Control Analysis.

Education/Training Required (Nonapprenticeship Route): Long-term on-the-job training. **Related Knowledge/Courses—Building and Construction:** Materials, methods, and the appropriate tools to construct objects, structures, and buildings. **Mechanical Devices:** Machines and tools, including their designs, uses, benefits, repair, and maintenance. **Design:** Design techniques, principles, tools, and instruments involved in the production and use of precision technical plans, blueprints, drawings, and models. **Physics:** Physical principles, laws, and applications, including air, water, material dynamics, light, atomic principles, heat, electric theory, earth formations, and meteorological and related natural phenomena. **Telecommunications:** Transmission, broadcasting, switching, control, and operation of telecommunications systems. **Engineering and Technology:** Equipment, tools, and mechanical devices and their uses to produce motion, light, power, technology, and other applications.

Work Environment: Outdoors; noisy; minor burns, cuts, bites, or stings; standing; walking and running; using hands on objects, tools, or controls.

Further Information: Contact a local joint union-management apprenticeship committee or the nearest office of your state employment service or apprenticeship agency (see Appendix C). For information about union apprenticeship programs, contact the following:

For information about union apprenticeship and training programs, contact

National Joint Apprenticeship Training Committee, 301 Prince George's Blvd., Upper Marlboro, MD 20774. Internet: www.njatc.org

National Electrical Contractors Association, 3 Metro Center, Suite 1100, Bethesda, MD 20814. Internet: www.necanet.org

International Brotherhood of Electrical Workers, 1125 15th St. NW, Washington, DC 20005.

For information about independent apprenticeship programs, contact

Associated Builders and Contractors, Workforce Development Department, 4250 North Fairfax Dr., 9th Floor, Arlington, VA 22203. Internet: www.trytools.org

Independent Electrical Contractors, Inc., 4401 Ford Ave., Suite 1100, Alexandria, VA 22302. Internet: www.ieci.org

National Association of Home Builders, Home Builders Institute, 1201 15th St. NW, Washington, DC 20005. Internet: www.hbi.org

National Center for Construction Education and Research, 3600 NW 43rd St., Bldg. G, Gainesville, FL 32606. Internet: www.nccer.org

Electro-Mechanical Technicians

* Annual Earnings: $46,610
* Growth: 2.6%
* Annual Job Openings: 1,142
* Percentage of Women: 20.6%

Related Apprenticeships—Assembler, Electromechanical (8000 hrs.); Electromechanical Technician (6000 hrs.).

Operate, test, and maintain unmanned, automated, servo-mechanical, or electromechanical equipment. May operate unmanned submarines, aircraft, or other equipment at worksites, such as oil rigs, deep ocean exploration, or hazardous waste removal. May assist engineers in testing and designing robotics equipment. Test performance of electromechanical assemblies, using test instruments such as oscilloscopes, electronic voltmeters, and bridges. Read blueprints, schematics, diagrams, and technical orders to determine methods and sequences of assembly. Install electrical and electronic parts and hardware in housings or assemblies, using soldering equipment and hand tools.

Align, fit, and assemble component parts, using hand tools, power tools, fixtures, templates, and microscopes. Inspect parts for surface defects. Analyze and record test results and prepare written testing documentation. Verify dimensions and clearances of parts to ensure conformance to specifications, using precision measuring instruments. Operate metalworking machines to fabricate housings, jigs, fittings, and fixtures. Repair, rework, and calibrate hydraulic and pneumatic assemblies and systems to meet operational specifications and tolerances. Train others to install, use, and maintain robots. Develop, test, and program new robots.

GOE—Career Cluster/Interest Area: 15. Scientific Research, Engineering, and Mathematics. **Work Group:** 15.09. Engineering Technology. **Other Apprenticeable Jobs in This Work Group:** Aerospace Engineering and Operations Technicians; Electrical Drafters; Electrical Engineering Technicians; Electronic Drafters; Electronics Engineering Technicians; Mapping Technicians; Mechanical Drafters; Mechanical Engineering Technicians; Surveying and Mapping Technicians; Surveying Technicians. **Personality Type:** Realistic. These occupations frequently involve work activities that include practical, hands-on problems and solutions. They often deal with plants; animals; and real-world materials such as wood, tools, and machinery. Many of the occupations require working outside and don't involve a lot of paperwork or working closely with others.

Skills—Equipment Maintenance; Operation Monitoring; Installation; Quality Control Analysis; Operation and Control; Troubleshooting; Repairing; Science.

Education/Training Required (Nonapprenticeship Route): Associate degree. **Related**

Knowledge/Courses—Mechanical Devices: Machines and tools, including their designs, uses, benefits, repair, and maintenance. **Engineering and Technology:** Equipment, tools, and mechanical devices and their uses to produce motion, light, power, technology, and other applications. **Computers and Electronics:** Electric circuit boards, processors, chips, and computer hardware and software, including applications and programming. **Mathematics:** Numbers and their operations and interrelationships, including arithmetic, algebra, geometry, calculus, and statistics and their applications. **Design:** Design techniques, principles, tools, and instruments involved in the production and use of precision technical plans, blueprints, drawings, and models. **Physics:** Physical principles, laws, and applications, including air, water, material dynamics, light, atomic principles, heat, electric theory, earth formations, and meteorological and related natural phenomena.

Work Environment: Indoors; noisy; contaminants; hazardous equipment; standing; using hands on objects, tools, or controls.

Electronic Drafters

- ❋ Annual Earnings: $49,250
- ❋ Growth: 4.1%
- ❋ Annual Job Openings: 4,786
- ❋ Percentage of Women: 21.8%

Our sources did not provide separate job openings data for this occupation. The job openings listed here are shared with Electrical Drafters.

Related Apprenticeships—Design Drafter, Electromechanical (8000 hrs.); Drafter, Electronic (8000 hrs.).

Draw wiring diagrams, circuit board assembly diagrams, schematics, and layout drawings used for manufacture, installation, and repair of electronic equipment. Draft detail and assembly drawings of design components, circuitry, and printed circuit boards, using computer-assisted equipment or standard drafting techniques and devices. Consult with engineers to discuss and interpret design concepts and determine requirements of detailed working drawings. Locate files relating to specified design project in database library, load program into computer, and record completed job data. Examine electronic schematics and supporting documents to develop, compute, and verify specifications for drafting data, such as configuration of parts, dimensions, and tolerances. Supervise and coordinate work activities of workers engaged in drafting, designing layouts, assembling, and testing printed circuit boards. Compare logic element configuration on display screen with engineering schematics and calculate figures to convert, redesign, and modify element. Review work orders and procedural manuals and confer with vendors and design staff to resolve problems and modify design. Review blueprints to determine customer requirements and consult with assembler regarding schematics, wiring procedures, and conductor paths. Train students to use drafting machines and to prepare schematic diagrams, block diagrams, control drawings, logic diagrams, integrated circuit drawings, and interconnection diagrams. Generate computer tapes of final layout design to produce layered photo masks and photo plotting design onto film. Select drill size to drill test head, according to test design and specifications, and submit guide layout to designated department. Key and program specified commands and engineering specifications into computer system to change

E

functions and test final layout. Copy drawings of printed circuit board fabrication, using print machine or blueprinting procedure. Plot electrical test points on layout sheets and draw schematics for wiring test fixture heads to frames.

GOE—Career Cluster/Interest Area: 15. Scientific Research, Engineering, and Mathematics. **Work Group:** 15.09. Engineering Technology. **Other Apprenticeable Jobs in This Work Group:** Aerospace Engineering and Operations Technicians; Electrical Drafters; Electrical Engineering Technicians; Electro-Mechanical Technicians; Electronics Engineering Technicians; Mapping Technicians; Mechanical Drafters; Mechanical Engineering Technicians; Surveying and Mapping Technicians; Surveying Technicians. **Personality Type:** Conventional. These occupations frequently involve following set procedures and routines and can include working with data and details more than with ideas. Usually there is a clear line of authority to follow.

Skills—Technology Design; Operations Analysis; Installation; Equipment Selection; Mathematics; Coordination; Negotiation; Complex Problem Solving.

Education/Training Required (Nonapprenticeship Route): Postsecondary vocational training. **Related Knowledge/Courses—Design:** Design techniques, principles, tools, and instruments involved in the production and use of precision technical plans, blueprints, drawings, and models. **Engineering and Technology:** Equipment, tools, and mechanical devices and their uses to produce motion, light, power, technology, and other applications. **Mechanical Devices:** Machines and tools, including their designs, uses, benefits, repair, and maintenance. **Physics:** Physical principles, laws, and applications, including air, water, material dynamics,

light, atomic principles, heat, electric theory, earth formations, and meteorological and related natural phenomena. **Telecommunications:** Transmission, broadcasting, switching, control, and operation of telecommunications systems. **Mathematics:** Numbers and their operations and interrelationships, including arithmetic, algebra, geometry, calculus, and statistics and their applications.

Work Environment: Indoors; noisy; sitting; using hands on objects, tools, or controls; repetitive motions.

Electronics Engineering Technicians

- ❋ Annual Earnings: $52,140
- ❋ Growth: 3.6%
- ❋ Annual Job Openings: 12,583
- ❋ Percentage of Women: 20.6%

Our sources did not provide separate job openings data for this occupation. The job openings listed here are shared with Electrical Engineering Technicians.

Related Apprenticeships—Calibration Laboratory Technician (8000 hrs.); Electrical Instrument Repairer (6000 hrs.); Electronics Technician (8000 hrs.); Instrument Mechanic (Any Industry) (8000 hrs.); Instrument Mechanic, Weapons Systems (8000 hrs.); Instrument Repairer (Any Industry) (8000 hrs.); Instrument Technician (Utilities) (8000 hrs.); Instrumentation Technician (8000 hrs.).

Lay out, build, test, troubleshoot, repair, and modify developmental and production electronic components, parts, equipment, and systems, such as computer equipment, missile control instrumentation, electron tubes, test equipment, and machine tool numerical

controls, **applying principles and theories of electronics, electrical circuitry, engineering mathematics, electronic and electrical testing, and physics. Usually work under direction of engineering staff.** Read blueprints, wiring diagrams, schematic drawings, and engineering instructions for assembling electronics units, applying knowledge of electronic theory and components. Test electronics units, using standard test equipment, and analyze results to evaluate performance and determine need for adjustment. Perform preventative maintenance and calibration of equipment and systems. Assemble, test, and maintain circuitry or electronic components according to engineering instructions, technical manuals, and knowledge of electronics, using hand and power tools. Adjust and replace defective or improperly functioning circuitry and electronics components, using hand tools and soldering iron. Write reports and record data on testing techniques, laboratory equipment, and specifications to assist engineers. Identify and resolve equipment malfunctions, working with manufacturers and field representatives as necessary to procure replacement parts. Provide user applications and engineering support and recommendations for new and existing equipment with regard to installation, upgrades, and enhancement. Maintain system logs and manuals to document testing and operation of equipment. Provide customer support and education, working with users to identify needs, determine sources of problems, and provide information on product use. Maintain working knowledge of state-of-the-art tools or software by reading or by attending conferences, workshops, or other training. Build prototypes from rough sketches or plans. Design basic circuitry and draft sketches for clarification of details and design documentation under engineers' direction, using drafting instruments and computer-aided design (CAD) equipment. Procure parts and maintain inventory and related documentation. Research equipment and component needs, sources, competitive prices, delivery times, and ongoing operational costs. Write computer or microprocessor software programs. Fabricate parts such as coils, terminal boards, and chassis, using bench lathes, drills, or other machine tools. Develop and upgrade preventative maintenance procedures for components, equipment, parts, and systems.

GOE—Career Cluster/Interest Area: 15. Scientific Research, Engineering, and Mathematics. **Work Group:** 15.09. Engineering Technology. **Other Apprenticeable Jobs in This Work Group:** Aerospace Engineering and Operations Technicians; Electrical Drafters; Electrical Engineering Technicians; Electro-Mechanical Technicians; Electronic Drafters; Mapping Technicians; Mechanical Drafters; Mechanical Engineering Technicians; Surveying and Mapping Technicians; Surveying Technicians. **Personality Type:** Realistic. These occupations frequently involve work activities that include practical, hands-on problems and solutions. They often deal with plants; animals; and real-world materials such as wood, tools, and machinery. Many of the occupations require working outside and don't involve a lot of paperwork or working closely with others.

Skills—Repairing; Troubleshooting; Operation Monitoring; Equipment Maintenance; Systems Analysis; Quality Control Analysis; Systems Evaluation; Operation and Control.

Education/Training Required (Nonapprenticeship Route): Associate degree. **Related Knowledge/Courses—Telecommunications:** Transmission, broadcasting, switching, control, and operation of telecommunications systems. **Engineering and Technology:** Equipment, tools, and mechanical devices and their uses to produce motion, light, power, technology, and other applications. **Design:** Design techniques, principles, tools, and instruments involved in the production and use of precision technical plans, blueprints, drawings, and models. **Mechanical Devices:** Machines and tools, including their designs, uses, benefits, repair, and maintenance. **Computers and Electronics:** Electric circuit boards, processors, chips, and computer hardware and software, including applications and programming. **Physics:** Physical principles, laws, and applications, including air, water, material dynamics, light, atomic principles, heat, electric theory, earth formations, and meteorological and related natural phenomena.

Work Environment: Indoors; contaminants; hazardous conditions; hazardous equipment; sitting; using hands on objects, tools, or controls.

Elevator Installers and Repairers

- ❀ Annual Earnings: $68,000
- ❀ Growth: 8.8%
- ❀ Annual Job Openings: 2,850
- ❀ Percentage of Women: 3.1%

Related Apprenticeships—Elevator Constructor (8000 hrs.); Elevator Repairer (8000 hrs.).

Assemble, install, repair, or maintain electric or hydraulic freight or passenger elevators, escalators, or dumbwaiters. Assemble, install, repair, and maintain elevators, escalators, moving sidewalks, and dumbwaiters, using hand and power tools and testing devices such as test lamps, ammeters, and voltmeters. Test newly installed equipment to ensure that it meets specifications such as stopping at floors for set amounts of time. Check that safety regulations and building codes are met and complete service reports, verifying conformance to standards. Locate malfunctions in brakes, motors, switches, and signal and control systems, using test equipment. Connect electrical wiring to control panels and electric motors. Read and interpret blueprints to determine the layout of system components, frameworks, and foundations, and to select installation equipment. Adjust safety controls, counterweights, door mechanisms, and components such as valves, ratchets, seals, and brake linings. Inspect wiring connections, control panel hookups, door installations, and alignments and clearances of cars and hoistways to ensure that equipment will operate properly. Disassemble defective units and repair or replace parts such as locks, gears, cables, and electric wiring. Maintain log books that detail all repairs and checks performed. Participate in additional training to keep skills up to date. Attach guide shoes and rollers to minimize the lateral motion of cars as they travel through shafts. Connect car frames to counterweights, using steel cables. Bolt or weld steel rails to the walls of shafts to guide elevators, working from scaffolding or platforms. Assemble elevator cars, installing each car's platform, walls, and doors. Install outer doors and door frames at elevator entrances on each floor of a structure. Install electrical wires and controls by attaching conduit along shaft walls from floor to floor, then pulling plastic-covered wires through the conduit. Cut prefabricated sections of framework, rails, and other components to specified dimensions. Operate elevators to determine power demands and test power consumption to detect overload factors. Assemble electrically powered stairs, steel frameworks, and tracks and install associated motors and electrical wiring.

GOE—**Career Cluster/Interest Area:** 02. Architecture and Construction. **Work Group:** 02.05. Systems and Equipment Installation, Maintenance, and Repair. **Other Apprenticeable Jobs in This Work Group:** Electrical and Electronics Repairers, Powerhouse, Substation, and Relay; Electrical Power-Line Installers and Repairers; Heating and Air Conditioning Mechanics and Installers; Maintenance and Repair Workers, General; Refrigeration Mechanics and Installers; Telecommunications Equipment Installers and Repairers, Except Line Installers; Telecommunications Line Installers and Repairers. **Personality Type:** Realistic. These occupations frequently involve work activities that include practical, hands-on problems and solutions. They often deal with plants; animals; and real-world materials such as wood, tools, and machinery. Many of the occupations require working outside and don't involve a lot of paperwork or working closely with others.

Skills—Installation; Repairing; Equipment Maintenance; Troubleshooting; Quality Control Analysis; Technology Design; Equipment Selection; Science.

Education/Training Required (Nonapprenticeship Route): Long-term on-the-job training. **Related Knowledge/Courses—Building and Construction:** Materials, methods, and the appropriate tools to construct objects, structures, and buildings. **Mechanical Devices:** Machines and tools, including their designs, uses, benefits, repair, and maintenance. **Physics:** Physical principles, laws, and applications, including air, water, material dynamics, light, atomic principles, heat, electric theory, earth formations, and meteorological and related natural phenomena. **Design:** Design techniques, principles, tools, and instruments involved in the production and use of precision technical plans, blueprints, drawings, and models. **Engineering and Technology:** Equipment, tools, and mechanical devices and their uses to produce motion, light, power, technology, and other applications. **Public Safety and Security:** Weaponry; public safety; security operations, rules, regulations, precautions, and prevention; and the protection of people, data, and property.

Work Environment: Contaminants; high places; hazardous conditions; hazardous equipment; standing; using hands on objects, tools, or controls.

Further Information: Contact a local of the International Union of Elevator Constructors, a local joint union-management apprenticeship committee, or the nearest office of your state employment service or apprenticeship agency (see Appendix C).

Embalmers

- Annual Earnings: $36,800
- Growth: 14.3%
- Annual Job Openings: 1,660
- Percentage of Women: 54.1%

Related Apprenticeship—Embalmer (Personal Services) (4000 hrs.).

Prepare bodies for interment in conformity with legal requirements. Conform to laws of health and sanitation and ensure that legal requirements concerning embalming are met. Apply cosmetics to impart lifelike appearance to the deceased. Incise stomach and abdominal walls and probe internal organs, using trocar, to withdraw blood and waste matter from organs. Close incisions, using needles and sutures. Reshape or reconstruct disfigured or maimed bodies when necessary, using derma-surgery techniques and materials such as clay, cotton, plaster of paris, and wax. Make incisions in arms or thighs and drain blood from circulatory system and replace it with embalming fluid, using pump. Dress bodies and place them in caskets. Join lips, using needles and thread or wire. Conduct interviews to arrange for the preparation of obituary notices, to assist with the selection of caskets or urns, and to determine the location and time of burials or cremations. Perform the duties of funeral directors, including coordinating funeral activities. Attach trocar to pump-tube, start pump, and repeat probing to force embalming fluid into organs. Perform special procedures necessary for remains that are to be transported to other states or overseas or where death was caused by infectious disease. Maintain records such as itemized lists of clothing or valuables delivered with body and names of persons embalmed. Insert convex celluloid or cotton between eyeballs and eyelids to prevent slipping and sinking of eyelids. Wash and dry bodies, using germicidal soap and towels or hot air dryers. Arrange for transporting the deceased to another state for interment. Supervise funeral attendants and other funeral home staff. Pack body orifices with cotton saturated with embalming fluid to prevent escape of gases or waste matter. Assist with placing caskets in hearses and organize cemetery processions. Serve as pallbearers, attend visiting rooms, and provide other assistance to the bereaved. Direct casket and floral display placement and arrange guest seating. Arrange funeral home equipment and perform general maintenance. Assist coroners at death scenes or at autopsies, file police reports, and testify at inquests or in court if employed by a coroner.

GOE—Career Cluster/Interest Area: 08. Health Science. **Work Group:** 08.09. Health Protection and Promotion. **Other Apprenticeable Jobs in This Work Group:** No others in group. **Personality Type:** Realistic. These occupations frequently involve work activities that include practical, hands-on problems and solutions. They often deal with plants; animals; and real-world materials such as wood, tools, and machinery. Many of the occupations require working outside and don't involve a lot of paperwork or working closely with others.

Skills—Science; Service Orientation; Management of Financial Resources; Management of Material Resources; Social Perceptiveness; Equipment Maintenance; Operation Monitoring; Equipment Selection.

Education/Training Required (Nonapprenticeship Route): Postsecondary vocational training. **Related Knowledge/Courses— Chemistry:** The composition, structure, and properties of substances and of the chemical processes and transformations that they undergo. This includes uses of chemicals and their interactions, danger signs, production techniques, and disposal methods. **Biology:** Plant and animal living tissue, cells, organisms, and entities, including their functions, interdependencies, and interactions with each other and the environment. **Philosophy and Theology:** Different philosophical systems and religions, including their basic principles, values, ethics, ways of thinking, customs, and practices and their impact on human culture. **Customer and Personal Service:** Principles and processes for providing customer and personal services, including needs assessment techniques, quality service standards, alternative delivery systems, and customer satisfaction evaluation techniques. **Therapy and Counseling:**

Information and techniques needed to rehabilitate physical and mental ailments and to provide career guidance, including alternative treatments, rehabilitation equipment and its proper use, and methods to evaluate treatment effects. **Medicine and Dentistry:** The information and techniques needed to diagnose and treat injuries, diseases, and deformities. This includes symptoms, treatment alternatives, drug properties and interactions, and preventive health-care measures.

Work Environment: Indoors; contaminants; disease or infections; hazardous conditions; standing; using hands on objects, tools, or controls.

Emergency Management Specialists

* Annual Earnings: $48,380
* Growth: 12.3%
* Annual Job Openings: 1,538
* Percentage of Women: 36.7%

Related Apprenticeship—Production Controller (4000 hrs. or competency).

Coordinate disaster response or crisis management activities, provide disaster-preparedness training, and prepare emergency plans and procedures for natural (e.g., hurricanes, floods, earthquakes), wartime, or technological (e.g., nuclear power plant emergencies, hazardous materials spills) disasters or hostage situations. Keep informed of activities or changes that could affect the likelihood of an emergency, as well as those that could affect response efforts and details of plan implementation. Prepare plans that outline operating procedures to be used in response to disasters or emergencies such as hurricanes, nuclear accidents, and terrorist attacks and in recovery from these events. Propose alteration of emergency response procedures based on regulatory changes, technological changes, or knowledge gained from outcomes of previous emergency situations. Maintain and update all resource materials associated with emergency-preparedness plans. Coordinate disaster response or crisis management activities such as ordering evacuations, opening public shelters, and implementing special needs plans and programs. Develop and maintain liaisons with municipalities, county departments, and similar entities in order to facilitate plan development, response effort coordination, and exchanges of personnel and equipment. Keep informed of federal, state, and local regulations affecting emergency plans and ensure that plans adhere to these regulations. Design and administer emergency and disaster-preparedness training courses that teach people how to effectively respond to major emergencies and disasters. Prepare emergency situation status reports that describe response and recovery efforts, needs, and preliminary damage assessments. Inspect facilities and equipment such as emergency management centers and communications equipment to determine their operational and functional capabilities in emergency situations. Consult with officials of local and area governments, schools, hospitals, and other institutions in order to determine their needs and capabilities in the event of a natural disaster or other emergency. Develop and perform tests and evaluations of emergency management plans in accordance with state and federal regulations. Attend meetings, conferences, and workshops related to emergency management to learn new information and to develop working relationships with other emergency management specialists.

GOE—Career Cluster/Interest Area: 12. Law and Public Safety. **Work Group:** 12.01. Managerial Work in Law and Public Safety. **Other Apprenticeable Jobs in This Work Group:** Municipal Fire Fighting and Prevention Supervisors. **Personality Type:** Social. These occupations frequently involve working with, communicating with, and teaching people and often involve helping or providing service to others.

Skills—Management of Material Resources; Service Orientation; Judgment and Decision Making; Complex Problem Solving; Coordination; Operations Analysis; Management of Financial Resources; Writing.

Education/Training Required (Nonapprenticeship Route): Work experience in a related occupation. **Related Knowledge/Courses— Public Safety and Security:** Weaponry; public safety; security operations, rules, regulations, precautions, and prevention; and the protection of people, data, and property. **Customer and Personal Service:** Principles and processes for providing customer and personal services, including needs assessment techniques, quality service standards, alternative delivery systems, and customer satisfaction evaluation techniques. **Education and Training:** Instructional methods and training techniques, including curriculum design principles, learning theory, group and individual teaching techniques, design of individual development plans, and test design principles. **Law and Government:** Laws, legal codes, court procedures, precedents, government regulations, executive orders, agency rules, and the democratic political process. **Physics:** Physical principles, laws, and applications, including air, water, material dynamics, light, atomic principles, heat, electric theory, earth formations, and meteorological and related natural phenomena. **Telecommunications:** Transmission, broadcasting, switching, control, and operation of telecommunications systems.

Work Environment: Indoors; sitting.

Emergency Medical Technicians and Paramedics

* Annual Earnings: $28,400
* Growth: 19.2%
* Annual Job Openings: 19,513
* Percentage of Women: 31.9%

Related Apprenticeships—Emergency Medical Technician (6000 hrs.); Paramedic (4000 hrs.).

Assess injuries, administer emergency medical care, and extricate trapped individuals. Transport injured or sick persons to medical facilities. Administer first-aid treatment and life-support care to sick or injured persons in prehospital setting. Perform emergency diagnostic and treatment procedures, such as stomach suction, airway management, or heart monitoring, during ambulance ride. Observe, record, and report to physician the patient's condition or injury, the treatment provided, and reactions to drugs and treatment. Immobilize patient for placement on stretcher and ambulance transport, using backboard or other spinal immobilization device. Maintain vehicles and medical and communication equipment and replenish first-aid equipment and supplies. Assess nature and extent of illness or injury to establish and prioritize medical procedures. Communicate with dispatchers and treatment center personnel to provide information about situation, to arrange reception of victims, and to receive instructions for further treatment. Comfort and reassure patients. Decontaminate ambulance interior following treatment of patient with infectious disease and report case to proper authorities. Operate equipment such as electrocardiograms (EKGs), external defibrillators, and bag-valve mask resuscitators in advanced life-support environments. Drive mobile intensive care unit to specified location, following instructions from emergency medical dispatcher. Coordinate with treatment center personnel to obtain patients' vital statistics and medical history, to determine the circumstances of the emergency, and to administer emergency treatment. Coordinate work with other emergency medical team members and police and fire department personnel. Attend training classes to maintain certification licensure, keep abreast of new developments in the field, or maintain existing knowledge. Administer drugs orally or by injection and perform intravenous procedures under a physician's direction.

GOE—Career Cluster/Interest Area: 12. Law and Public Safety. **Work Group:** 12.06. Emergency Responding. **Other Apprenticeable Jobs in This Work Group:** Forest Fire Fighters; Municipal Fire Fighters. **Personality Type:** Social. These occupations frequently involve working with, communicating with, and teaching people and often involve helping or providing service to others.

Skills—Operation Monitoring; Operation and Control; Management of Personnel Resources; Systems Analysis; Systems Evaluation; Service Orientation.

Education/Training Required (Nonapprenticeship Route): Postsecondary vocational training. **Related Knowledge/Courses—Medicine and Dentistry:** The information and techniques needed to diagnose and treat injuries, diseases, and deformities. This includes symptoms, treatment alternatives, drug properties and

interactions, and preventive health-care measures. **Customer and Personal Service:** Principles and processes for providing customer and personal services, including needs assessment techniques, quality service standards, alternative delivery systems, and customer satisfaction evaluation techniques. **Therapy and Counseling:** Information and techniques needed to rehabilitate physical and mental ailments and to provide career guidance, including alternative treatments, rehabilitation equipment and its proper use, and methods to evaluate treatment effects. **Psychology:** Human behavior and performance, mental processes, psychological research methods, and the assessment and treatment of behavioral and affective disorders. **Transportation:** Principles and methods for moving people or goods by air, rail, sea, or road, including their relative costs, advantages, and limitations. **Education and Training:** Instructional methods and training techniques, including curriculum design principles, learning theory, group and individual teaching techniques, design of individual development plans, and test design principles.

Work Environment: Outdoors; noisy; very bright or dim lighting; contaminants; cramped work space, awkward positions; disease or infections.

Environmental Science and Protection Technicians, Including Health

❋ Annual Earnings: $39,370
❋ Growth: 28.0%
❋ Annual Job Openings: 8,404
❋ Percentage of Women: 43.3%

Related Apprenticeship—Laboratory Assistant (6000 hrs.).

Perform laboratory and field tests to monitor the environment and investigate sources of pollution, including those that affect health. Under direction of environmental scientists or specialists, may collect samples of gases, soil, water, and other materials for testing and take corrective actions as assigned. Collect samples of gases, soils, water, industrial wastewater, and asbestos products to conduct tests on pollutant levels and identify sources of pollution. Record test data and prepare reports, summaries, and charts that interpret test results. Develop and implement programs for monitoring of environmental pollution and radiation. Discuss test results and analyses with customers. Set up equipment or stations to monitor and collect pollutants from sites such as smokestacks, manufacturing plants, or mechanical equipment. Maintain files, such as hazardous waste databases, chemical usage data, personnel exposure information, and diagrams showing equipment locations. Develop testing procedures or direct activities of workers in laboratory. Prepare samples or photomicrographs for testing and analysis. Calibrate microscopes and test instruments. Examine and analyze material for presence and concentration of contaminants such as asbestos, using variety of microscopes. Calculate amount of pollutant in samples or compute air pollution or gas flow in industrial processes, using chemical and mathematical formulas. Make recommendations to control or eliminate unsafe conditions at workplaces or public facilities. Weigh, analyze, and measure collected sample particles such as lead, coal dust, or rock to determine concentration of pollutants. Provide information and technical and program assistance to government representatives, employers, and the general public on the issues of public health, environmental protection, or workplace safety.

Conduct standardized tests to ensure materials and supplies used throughout power supply systems meet processing and safety specifications. Perform statistical analysis of environmental data. Respond to and investigate hazardous conditions or spills or outbreaks of disease or food poisoning, collecting samples for analysis. Determine amounts and kinds of chemicals to use in destroying harmful organisms and removing impurities from purification systems. Inspect sanitary conditions at public facilities. Inspect workplaces to ensure the absence of health and safety hazards such as high noise levels, radiation, or lighting that is too bright or dim.

GOE—Career Cluster/Interest Area: 01. Agriculture and Natural Resources. **Work Group:** 01.03. Resource Technologies for Plants, Animals, and the Environment. **Other Apprenticeable Jobs in This Work Group:** Geological Sample Test Technicians. **Personality Type:** Investigative. These occupations frequently involve working with ideas and require an extensive amount of thinking. They can involve searching for facts and figuring out problems mentally.

Skills—Quality Control Analysis; Systems Analysis; Systems Evaluation; Operation Monitoring; Operation and Control; Science.

Education/Training Required (Nonapprenticeship Route): Associate degree. **Related Knowledge/Courses—Biology:** Plant and animal living tissue, cells, organisms, and entities, including their functions, interdependencies, and interactions with each other and the environment. **Chemistry:** The composition, structure, and properties of substances and of the chemical processes and transformations that they undergo. This includes uses of chemicals and their interactions, danger signs, production techniques, and disposal methods. **Geography:**

Various methods for describing the location and distribution of land, sea, and air masses, including their physical locations, relationships, and characteristics. **Physics:** Physical principles, laws, and applications, including air, water, material dynamics, light, atomic principles, heat, electric theory, earth formations, and meteorological and related natural phenomena. **Computers and Electronics:** Electric circuit boards, processors, chips, and computer hardware and software, including applications and programming. **Building and Construction:** Materials, methods, and the appropriate tools to construct objects, structures, and buildings.

Work Environment: More often indoors than outdoors; noisy; very hot or cold; contaminants; sitting.

Equal Opportunity Representatives and Officers

* ❋ Annual Earnings: $48,400
* ❋ Growth: 4.9%
* ❋ Annual Job Openings: 15,841
* ❋ Percentage of Women: 54.0%

Our sources did not provide separate job openings data for this occupation. The job openings listed here are shared with Coroners; Environmental Compliance Inspectors; Government Property Inspectors and Investigators; and Licensing Examiners and Inspectors.

Related Apprenticeship—Military Equal Opportunity (MEO) (2000 hrs. or competency).

Monitor and evaluate compliance with equal opportunity laws, guidelines, and policies to ensure that employment practices and contracting arrangements give equal opportunity without regard to race, religion, color, national origin, sex, age, or disability. Investigate employment practices and alleged violations of laws to document and correct discriminatory factors. Interpret civil rights laws and equal opportunity regulations for individuals and employers. Study equal opportunity complaints to clarify issues. Meet with persons involved in equal opportunity complaints to verify case information and to arbitrate and settle disputes. Coordinate, monitor, and revise complaint procedures to ensure timely processing and review of complaints. Prepare reports of selection, survey, and other statistics, and recommendations for corrective action. Conduct surveys and evaluate findings to determine whether systematic discrimination exists. Develop guidelines for nondiscriminatory employment practices and monitor their implementation and impact. Review company contracts to determine actions required to meet governmental equal opportunity provisions. Counsel newly hired members of minority and disadvantaged groups, informing them about details of civil rights laws. Provide information, technical assistance, and training to supervisors, managers, and employees on topics such as employee supervision, hiring, grievance procedures, and staff development. Verify that all job descriptions are submitted for review and approval and that descriptions meet regulatory standards. Act as liaisons between minority placement agencies and employers or between job search committees and other equal opportunity administrators. Consult with community representatives to develop technical assistance agreements in accordance with governmental regulations. Meet with job search committees or coordinators to explain the role of the equal opportunity coordinator, to provide resources for advertising, and to explain expectations for future contacts. Participate in the recruitment of employees through job fairs, career days, and advertising plans.

GOE—Career Cluster/Interest Area: 07. Government and Public Administration. **Work Group:** 07.03. Regulations Enforcement. **Other Apprenticeable Jobs in This Work Group:** Compliance Officers, Except Agriculture, Construction, Health and Safety, and Transportation; Construction and Building Inspectors; Fire Inspectors; Fish and Game Wardens; Government Property Inspectors and Investigators; Nuclear Monitoring Technicians; Transportation Vehicle, Equipment and Systems Inspectors, Except Aviation. **Personality Type:** Social. These occupations frequently involve working with, communicating with, and teaching people and often involve helping or providing service to others.

Skills—Negotiation; Persuasion; Social Perceptiveness; Service Orientation; Complex Problem Solving; Judgment and Decision Making; Active Listening; Writing.

Education/Training Required (Nonapprenticeship Route): Long-term on-the-job training. **Related Knowledge/Courses—Law and Government:** Laws, legal codes, court procedures, precedents, government regulations, executive orders, agency rules, and the democratic political process. **Personnel and Human Resources:** Principles and procedures for personnel recruitment; selection; training; compensation and benefits; labor relations and negotiation; and personnel information systems. **Clerical Practices:** Administrative and clerical procedures and systems such as word-processing systems, filing and records management systems, stenography and transcription, forms, design principles, and other office procedures and terminology. **English Language:** The structure and content of the English language, including the meaning and spelling of words, rules of composition, and grammar. **Customer and Personal Service:** Principles and processes for providing customer and personal services, including needs assessment techniques, quality service standards, alternative delivery systems, and customer satisfaction evaluation techniques. **Administration and Management:** Principles and processes involved in business and organizational planning, coordination, and execution. This includes strategic planning, resource allocation, manpower modeling, leadership techniques, and production methods.

Work Environment: Indoors; sitting; repetitive motions.

Excavating and Loading Machine and Dragline Operators

- ❋ Annual Earnings: $34,050
- ❋ Growth: 8.3%
- ❋ Annual Job Openings: 6,562
- ❋ Percentage of Women: 1.5%

Related Apprenticeship—Dragline Operator (2000 hrs.).

Operate or tend machinery equipped with scoops, shovels, or buckets to excavate and load loose materials. Move levers, depress foot pedals, and turn dials to operate power machinery such as power shovels, stripping shovels, scraper loaders, and backhoes. Set up and inspect equipment prior to operation. Observe hand signals, grade stakes, and other markings when operating machines so that work can be performed to specifications. Become familiar with digging plans, with machine capabilities and limitations, and with efficient and safe digging procedures in a given application. Operate machinery to perform activities such as backfilling excavations, vibrating or breaking rock or concrete, and making winter roads. Lubricate, adjust, and repair machinery and replace parts such as gears, bearings, and bucket teeth. Create and maintain inclines and ramps. Handle slides, mud, and pit cleanings and maintenance. Move materials over short distances, such as around a construction site, factory, or warehouse. Measure and verify levels of rock, gravel, bases, and other excavated material. Receive written or oral instructions regarding material movement or excavation. Adjust dig face angles for varying overburden depths and set lengths. Drive machines to work sites. Perform manual labor, such as shoveling materials by hand, to prepare or finish sites. Direct ground workers engaged in activities such as moving stakes or markers or changing positions of towers. Direct workers engaged in placing blocks and outriggers to prevent capsizing of machines used to lift heavy loads.

GOE—Career Cluster/Interest Area: 01. Agriculture and Natural Resources. **Work Group:** 01.08. Mining and Drilling. **Other Apprenticeable Jobs in This Work Group:** Earth Drillers, Except Oil and Gas; Explosives Workers, Ordnance Handling Experts, and Blasters; Helpers—Extraction Workers; Mine Cutting and Channeling Machine Operators; Rotary Drill Operators, Oil and Gas. **Personality Type:** Realistic. These occupations frequently involve work activities that include practical, hands-on problems and solutions. They often deal with plants; animals; and real-world materials such as wood, tools, and machinery. Many of the occupations require working outside and don't involve a lot of paperwork or working closely with others.

Skills—Repairing; Equipment Maintenance; Operation and Control; Operation Monitoring; Installation; Equipment Selection; Systems Analysis; Technology Design.

Education/Training Required (Nonapprenticeship Route): Moderate-term on-the-job training. **Related Knowledge/Courses—Building and Construction:** Materials, methods, and the appropriate tools to construct objects, structures, and buildings. **Mechanical Devices:** Machines and tools, including their designs, uses, benefits, repair, and maintenance. **Transportation:** Principles and methods for moving people or goods by air, rail, sea, or road, including their relative costs, advantages, and limitations. **Production and Processing:** Inputs, outputs, raw materials, waste, quality control, costs, and techniques for maximizing the manufacture and distribution of goods. **Public Safety and Security:** Weaponry; public safety; security operations, rules, regulations, precautions, and prevention; and the protection of people, data, and property. **Engineering and Technology:** Equipment, tools, and mechanical devices and their uses to produce motion, light, power, technology, and other applications.

Work Environment: Outdoors; noisy; contaminants; whole-body vibration; sitting; using hands on objects, tools, or controls.

Farmers and Ranchers

- ❋ Annual Earnings: $33,360
- ❋ Growth: –8.5%
- ❋ Annual Job Openings: 129,552
- ❋ Percentage of Women: 25.0%

Related Apprenticeships—Beekeeper (8000 hrs.); Farmer, General (Agriculture) (8000 hrs.).

On an ownership or rental basis, operate farms, ranches, greenhouses, nurseries, timber tracts, or other agricultural production establishments that produce crops, horticultural specialties, livestock, poultry, finfish,

shellfish, or animal specialties. May plant, cultivate, harvest, perform post-harvest activities on, and market crops and livestock; may hire, train, and supervise farm workers or supervise a farm labor contractor; may prepare cost, production, and other records. May maintain and operate machinery and perform physical work. Breed and raise stock such as cattle, poultry, and honeybees, using recognized breeding practices to ensure continued improvement in stock. Lubricate, adjust, and make minor repairs to farm equipment, using oilcans, grease guns, and hand tools. Assist in animal births and care for newborn livestock. Assemble, position, and secure structures such as trellises, beehives, or fences, using hand tools. Operate dairy farms that produce bulk milk. Manage and oversee the day-to-day running of farms raising poultry or pigs for the production of meat and breeding stock. Maintain colonies of bees to produce honey and hive byproducts, pollinate crops, and/or produce queens and bees for sale. Keep hens in order to produce table eggs for eating or fertile eggs for breeding. Maintain financial, tax, production, and employee records. Maintain facilities such as fencing, water supplies, and outdoor housing and wind shelters. Hire, train, and direct workers engaged in planting, cultivating, irrigating, harvesting, and marketing crops and in raising livestock. Grow out-of-season or early crops in greenhouses or cold-frame beds or bud and graft plant stock. Herd cattle, using horses or all-terrain vehicles. Buy or sell futures contracts or price products in advance of future sales so that risk is limited and/or profit is increased. Clean and disinfect buildings and yards and remove manure. Transport grain to silos for storage and burn or bale any straw that is left behind. Set up and operate farm machinery to cultivate, harvest, and haul crops. Select

animals for market and provide transportation of livestock to market. Select and purchase supplies and equipment such as seed, fertilizers, and farm machinery. Remove lower-quality or older animals from herds and purchase other livestock to replace culled animals. Purchase and store livestock feed. Control the spread of disease and parasites in herds by using vaccination and medication and by separating sick animals. Clean, grade, and package crops for marketing. Clean and sanitize milking equipment, storage tanks, collection cups, and cows' udders or ensure that procedures are followed to maintain sanitary conditions for handling of milk.

GOE—Career Cluster/Interest Area: 01. Agriculture and Natural Resources. **Work Group:** 01.01. Managerial Work in Agriculture and Natural Resources. **Other Apprenticeable Jobs in This Work Group:** No others in group. **Personality Type:** Realistic. These occupations frequently involve work activities that include practical, hands-on problems and solutions. They often deal with plants; animals; and real-world materials such as wood, tools, and machinery. Many of the occupations require working outside and don't involve a lot of paperwork or working closely with others.

Skills—Repairing; Equipment Maintenance; Management of Financial Resources; Installation; Operation Monitoring; Operation and Control; Management of Material Resources; Troubleshooting.

Education/Training Required (Nonapprenticeship Route): Long-term on-the-job training. **Related Knowledge/Courses—Food Production:** Techniques and equipment for planting, growing, and harvesting of food for consumption, including crop-rotation methods, animal husbandry, and food storage/handling techniques. **Building and Construction:** Materials, methods, and the appropriate tools to construct objects, structures, and buildings. **Biology:** Plant and animal living tissue, cells, organisms, and entities, including their functions, interdependencies, and interactions with each other and the environment. **Mechanical Devices:** Machines and tools, including their designs, uses, benefits, repair, and maintenance. **Sales and Marketing:** Principles and methods involved in showing, promoting, and selling products or services. This includes marketing strategies and tactics, product demonstration and sales techniques, and sales control systems. **Economics and Accounting:** Economic and accounting principles and practices, the financial markets, banking, and the analysis and reporting of financial data.

Work Environment: Outdoors; contaminants; hazardous equipment; minor burns, cuts, bites, or stings; standing; using hands on objects, tools, or controls.

Fashion Designers

- ❀ Annual Earnings: $62,810
- ❀ Growth: 5.0%
- ❀ Annual Job Openings: 1,968
- ❀ Percentage of Women: 55.5%

Related Apprenticeship—Fur Designer (8000 hrs.).

Design clothing and accessories. Create original garments or design garments that follow well-established fashion trends. May develop the line of color and kinds of materials. Examine sample garments on and off models; then modify designs to achieve desired effects. Determine prices for styles. Select materials and production techniques to be used for products. Draw patterns for articles designed; then cut patterns and cut material according to patterns, using measuring instruments and scissors. Design custom clothing and accessories for individuals, retailers, or theatrical, television, or film productions. Attend fashion shows and review garment magazines and manuals to gather information about fashion trends and consumer preferences. Develop a group of products and/or accessories and market them through venues such as boutiques or mail-order catalogs. Test fabrics or oversee testing so that garment-care labels can be created. Visit textile showrooms to keep up to date on the latest fabrics. Sew together sections of material to form mock-ups or samples of garments or articles, using sewing equipment. Research the styles and periods of clothing needed for film or theatrical productions. Direct and coordinate workers involved in drawing and cutting patterns and constructing samples or finished garments. Purchase new or used clothing and accessory items as needed to complete designs. Provide sample garments to agents and sales representatives and arrange for showings of sample garments at sales meetings or fashion shows. Identify target markets for designs, looking at factors such as age, gender, and socioeconomic status. Read scripts and consult directors and other production staff to develop design concepts and plan productions. Confer with sales and management executives or with clients to discuss design ideas. Collaborate with other designers to coordinate special products and designs. Sketch rough and detailed drawings of apparel or accessories and write specifications such as color schemes, construction, material types, and accessory requirements. Adapt other designers' ideas for the mass market.

GOE—Career Cluster/Interest Area: 03. Arts and Communication. **Work Group:** 03.05. Design. **Other Apprenticeable Jobs in This Work Group:** Floral Designers; Interior Designers; Merchandise Displayers and Window Trimmers. **Personality Type:** Artistic. These occupations frequently involve working with forms, designs, and patterns. They often require self-expression, and the work can be done without following a clear set of rules.

Skills—Technology Design; Operations Analysis; Quality Control Analysis; Negotiation; Time Management; Systems Evaluation; Mathematics; Active Learning.

Education/Training Required (Nonapprenticeship Route): Associate degree. **Related Knowledge/Courses—Fine Arts:** Theory and techniques required to produce, compose, and perform works of music, dance, visual arts, drama, and sculpture. **Design:** Design techniques, principles, tools, and instruments involved in the production and use of precision technical plans, blueprints, drawings, and models. **Sales and Marketing:** Principles and methods involved in showing, promoting, and selling products or services. This includes marketing strategies and tactics, product demonstration and sales techniques, and sales control systems. **Production and Processing:** Inputs, outputs, raw materials, waste, quality control, costs, and techniques for maximizing the manufacture and distribution of goods. **Communications and Media:** Media production, communication, and dissemination techniques and methods, including alternative ways to inform and entertain via written, oral, and visual media. **Administration and Management:** Principles and processes involved in business and organizational planning, coordination, and execution. This includes strategic planning, resource allocation, manpower modeling, leadership techniques, and production methods.

Work Environment: Indoors; sitting; using hands on objects, tools, or controls.

Fence Erectors

* Annual Earnings: $26,720
* Growth: 10.6%
* Annual Job Openings: 2,812
* Percentage of Women: 3.1%

Related Apprenticeship—Fence Erector (6000 hrs.).

Erect and repair metal and wooden fences and fence gates around highways, industrial establishments, residences, or farms, using hand and power tools. Insert metal tubing through rail supports. Discuss fencing needs with customers and estimate and quote prices. Weld metal parts together, using portable gas welding equipment. Stretch wire, wire mesh, or chain-link fencing between posts and attach fencing to frames. Set metal or wooden posts in upright positions in postholes. Nail top and bottom rails to fence posts or insert them in slots on posts. Nail pointed slats to rails to construct picket fences. Mix and pour concrete around bases of posts or tamp soil into postholes to embed posts. Blast rock formations and rocky areas with dynamite to facilitate posthole digging. Make rails for fences by sawing lumber or by cutting metal tubing to required lengths. Establish the location for a fence and gather information needed to ensure that there are no electric cables or water lines in the area. Erect alternate panel, basket weave, and louvered fences. Construct and repair barriers, retaining walls, trellises, and other types of fences, walls, and gates. Align posts, using lines or by sighting, and verify vertical alignment of posts, using plumb bobs or spirit levels. Assemble gates and fasten gates into position, using hand tools. Attach fence rail supports to posts, using hammers and pliers. Complete top fence rails of metal fences by connecting tube sections, using metal sleeves. Attach rails or tension wire along bottoms of posts to form fencing frames. Measure and lay out fence lines and mark posthole positions, following instructions, drawings, or specifications. Dig postholes, using spades, posthole diggers, or power-driven augers.

GOE—Career Cluster/Interest Area: 02. Architecture and Construction. **Work Group:** 02.04. Construction Crafts. **Other Apprenticeable Jobs in This Work Group:** Boilermakers; Brickmasons and Blockmasons; Carpet Installers; Cement Masons and Concrete Finishers; Construction Carpenters; Crane and Tower Operators; Drywall and Ceiling Tile Installers; Electricians; Floor Layers, Except Carpet, Wood, and Hard Tiles; Glaziers; Insulation Workers, Floor, Ceiling, and Wall; Insulation Workers, Mechanical; Operating Engineers and Other Construction Equipment Operators; Painters, Construction and Maintenance; Paperhangers; Paving, Surfacing, and Tamping Equipment Operators; Pipe Fitters and Steamfitters; Plasterers and Stucco Masons; Plumbers; Reinforcing Iron and Rebar Workers; Riggers; Roofers; Rough Carpenters; Sheet Metal Workers; Stone Cutters and Carvers, Manufacturing; Stonemasons; Structural Iron and Steel Workers; Tapers; Terrazzo Workers and Finishers; Tile and Marble Setters. **Personality Type:** Realistic. These occupations frequently involve work activities that include practical, hands-on problems and solutions. They often deal with plants; animals; and real-world materials such as wood, tools, and machinery. Many of the occupations require

working outside and don't involve a lot of paperwork or working closely with others.

Skills—Installation; Repairing; Equipment Maintenance; Management of Material Resources; Equipment Selection; Coordination; Management of Personnel Resources; Operation and Control.

Education/Training Required (Nonapprenticeship Route): Moderate-term on-the-job training. **Related Knowledge/Course—Building and Construction:** Materials, methods, and the appropriate tools to construct objects, structures, and buildings.

Work Environment: Outdoors; noisy; minor burns, cuts, bites, or stings; standing; kneeling, crouching, stooping, or crawling; using hands on objects, tools, or controls.

Fiberglass Laminators and Fabricators

- ❀ Annual Earnings: $26,630
- ❀ Growth: 6.2%
- ❀ Annual Job Openings: 7,315
- ❀ Percentage of Women: 30.4%

Related Apprenticeship—Composite Fitter Mechanic (4000 hrs.).

Laminate layers of fiberglass on molds to form boat decks and hulls, bodies for golf carts or automobiles, or other products. Apply lacquers and waxes to surfaces of mold to facilitate assembly and removal of laminated parts. Check all dies, templates, and cutout patterns to be used in the manufacturing process to ensure that they conform to dimensional data, photographs, blueprints, samples, and customer specifications. Check completed products for conformance to specifications and for defects by measuring with rulers or micrometers, by checking them visually, or by tapping them to detect bubbles or dead spots. Cure materials by letting them set at room temperature, placing them under heat lamps, or baking them in ovens. Inspect, clean, and assemble molds before beginning work. Mask off mold areas that are not to be laminated, using cellophane, wax paper, masking tape, or special sprays containing mold-release substances. Mix catalysts into resins and saturate cloth and mats with mixtures, using brushes. Pat or press layers of saturated mat or cloth into place on molds, using brushes or hands, and smooth out wrinkles and air bubbles with hands or squeegees. Release air bubbles and smooth seams, using rollers. Repair or modify damaged or defective glass-fiber parts, checking thicknesses, densities, and contours to ensure a close fit after repair. Select precut fiberglass mats, cloth, and woodbracing materials as required by projects being assembled. Spray chopped fiberglass, resins, and catalysts onto prepared molds or dies, using pneumatic spray guns with chopper attachments. Trim cured materials by sawing them with diamond-impregnated cutoff wheels. Trim excess materials from molds, using hand shears or trimming knives. Bond wood reinforcing strips to decks and cabin structures of watercraft, using resin-saturated fiberglass. Apply layers of plastic resin to mold surfaces prior to placement of fiberglass mats, repeating layers until products have the desired thicknesses and plastics have jelled.

GOE—Career Cluster/Interest Area: 13. Manufacturing. **Work Group:** 13.14. Vehicle and Facility Mechanical Work. **Other Apprenticeable Jobs in This Work Group:** Aircraft Mechanics and Service Technicians; Aircraft Structure, Surfaces, Rigging, and Systems Assemblers; Automotive Body and Related Repairers; Automotive Glass Installers and Repairers; Automotive Master Mechanics; Automotive Specialty Technicians; Bus and Truck Mechanics and Diesel Engine Specialists; Farm Equipment Mechanics; Mobile Heavy Equipment Mechanics, Except Engines; Motorboat Mechanics; Motorcycle Mechanics; Outdoor Power Equipment and Other Small Engine Mechanics; Rail Car Repairers; Recreational Vehicle Service Technicians. **Personality Type:** Realistic. These occupations frequently involve work activities that include practical, hands-on problems and solutions. They often deal with plants; animals; and real-world materials such as wood, tools, and machinery. Many of the occupations require working outside and don't involve a lot of paperwork or working closely with others.

Skills—Repairing; Operation and Control.

Education/Training Required (Nonapprenticeship Route): Moderate-term on-the-job training. **Related Knowledge/Courses—Chemistry:** The composition, structure, and properties of substances and of the chemical processes and transformations that they undergo. This includes uses of chemicals and their interactions, danger signs, production techniques, and disposal methods. **Production and Processing:** Inputs, outputs, raw materials, waste, quality control, costs, and techniques for maximizing the manufacture and distribution of goods. **Building and Construction:** Materials, methods, and the appropriate tools to construct objects, structures, and buildings. **Mechanical Devices:** Machines and tools, including their designs, uses, benefits, repair, and maintenance. **Engineering and Technology:** Equipment, tools, and mechanical devices and their uses to produce motion, light, power, technology, and other applications. **Public Safety and Security:** Weaponry; public safety; security operations, rules, regulations, precautions, and prevention; and the protection of people, data, and property.

Work Environment: No data available.

Fine Artists, Including Painters, Sculptors, and Illustrators

- ❈ Annual Earnings: $42,070
- ❈ Growth: 9.9%
- ❈ Annual Job Openings: 3,830
- ❈ Percentage of Women: 52.4%

Related Apprenticeships—Illustrator (Professional and Kindred) (8000 hrs.); Painter (Professional and Kindred) (2000 hrs.).

Create original artwork, using any of a wide variety of mediums and techniques such as painting and sculpture. Use materials such as pens and ink, watercolors, charcoal, oil, or computer software to create artwork. Integrate and develop visual elements such as line, space, mass, color, and perspective to produce desired effects, such as the illustration of ideas, emotions, or moods. Confer with clients, editors, writers, art directors, and other interested parties regarding the nature and content of artwork to be produced. Submit preliminary or finished artwork or project plans to clients for approval, incorporating changes as necessary. Maintain portfolios of artistic work to demonstrate styles, interests, and abilities. Create finished artwork as decoration or to elucidate or substitute for spoken or written messages. Cut, bend, laminate, arrange, and fasten individual or mixed raw and manufactured materials and products to form works of art. Monitor events, trends, and other circumstances, research specific subject areas, attend art exhibitions, and read art publications to develop ideas and keep current on art-world activities. Study different techniques to learn how to apply them to artistic endeavors. Render drawings, illustrations, and sketches of buildings, manufactured products, or models, working from sketches, blueprints, memory, models, or reference materials. Create sculptures, statues, and other three-dimensional artwork by using abrasives and tools to shape, carve, and fabricate materials such as clay, stone, wood, or metal. Create sketches, profiles, or likenesses of posed subjects or photographs, using any combination of freehand drawing, mechanical assembly kits, and computer imaging. Develop project budgets for approval, estimating time lines and material costs. Study styles, techniques, colors, textures, and materials used in works undergoing restoration to ensure consistency during the restoration process. Shade and fill in sketch outlines and backgrounds, using a variety of media such as water colors, markers, and transparent washes, labeling designated colors when necessary. Collaborate with engineers, mechanics, and other technical experts as necessary to build and install creations.

GOE—Career Cluster/Interest Area: 03. Arts and Communication. **Work Group:** 03.04. Studio Art. **Other Apprenticeable Jobs in This Work Group:** Craft Artists; Potters, Manufacturing. **Personality Type:** Artistic. These occupations frequently involve working with forms, designs, and patterns. They often require self-expression, and the work can be done without following a clear set of rules.

Skills—Management of Financial Resources; Equipment Selection; Operations Analysis; Repairing; Equipment Maintenance; Installation; Complex Problem Solving; Mathematics.

Education/Training Required (Nonapprenticeship Route): Long-term on-the-job training. **Related Knowledge/Courses—Fine Arts:**

Theory and techniques required to produce, compose, and perform works of music, dance, visual arts, drama, and sculpture. **Design:** Design techniques, principles, tools, and instruments involved in the production and use of precision technical plans, blueprints, drawings, and models. **Sales and Marketing:** Principles and methods involved in showing, promoting, and selling products or services. This includes marketing strategies and tactics, product demonstration and sales techniques, and sales control systems. **Production and Processing:** Inputs, outputs, raw materials, waste, quality control, costs, and techniques for maximizing the manufacture and distribution of goods. **Economics and Accounting:** Economic and accounting principles and practices, the financial markets, banking, and the analysis and reporting of financial data. **Communications and Media:** Media production, communication, and dissemination techniques and methods, including alternative ways to inform and entertain via written, oral, and visual media.

Work Environment: Indoors; contaminants; standing; using hands on objects, tools, or controls; repetitive motions.

Fire Inspectors

* Annual Earnings: $50,830
* Growth: 11.0%
* Annual Job Openings: 644
* Percentage of Women: 22.3%

Our sources did not provide separate job openings data for this occupation. The job openings listed here are shared with Fire Investigators.

Related Apprenticeship—Fire Inspector (8000 hrs.).

Inspect buildings and equipment to detect fire hazards and enforce state and local regulations. Inspect buildings to locate hazardous conditions and fire code violations such as accumulations of combustible material, electrical wiring problems, and inadequate or non-functional fire exits. Identify corrective actions necessary to bring properties into compliance with applicable fire codes, laws, regulations, and standards and explain these measures to property owners or their representatives. Conduct inspections and acceptance testing of newly installed fire protection systems. Inspect and test fire protection or fire detection systems to verify that such systems are installed in accordance with appropriate laws, codes, ordinances, regulations, and standards. Conduct fire code compliance follow-ups to ensure that corrective actions have been taken in cases where violations were found. Inspect properties that store, handle, and use hazardous materials to ensure compliance with laws, codes, and regulations; issue hazardous materials permits to facilities found in compliance. Write detailed reports of fire inspections performed, fire code violations observed, and corrective recommendations offered. Review blueprints and plans for new or remodeled buildings to ensure the structures meet fire safety codes. Develop or review fire exit plans. Attend training classes to maintain current knowledge of fire prevention, safety, and firefighting procedures. Present and explain fire code requirements and fire prevention information to architects, contractors, attorneys, engineers, developers, fire service personnel, and the general public. Conduct fire exit drills to monitor and evaluate evacuation procedures. Inspect liquefied petroleum installations, storage containers, and transportation and delivery systems for compliance with fire laws. Search for clues as to the cause of a fire after the fire is completely extinguished. Develop and coordinate fire prevention programs such as false alarm billing, fire inspection reporting, and hazardous materials management. Testify in court regarding fire code and fire safety issues. Recommend changes to fire prevention, inspection, and fire code endorsement procedures.

GOE—Career Cluster/Interest Area: 07. Government and Public Administration. **Work Group:** 07.03. Regulations Enforcement. **Other Apprenticeable Jobs in This Work Group:** Compliance Officers, Except Agriculture, Construction, Health and Safety, and Transportation; Construction and Building Inspectors; Equal Opportunity Representatives and Officers; Fish and Game Wardens; Government Property Inspectors and Investigators; Nuclear Monitoring Technicians; Transportation Vehicle, Equipment and Systems Inspectors, Except Aviation. **Personality Type:** Conventional. These occupations frequently involve following set procedures and routines and can include working with data and details more than with ideas. Usually there is a clear line of authority to follow.

Skills—Science; Persuasion; Operations Analysis; Service Orientation; Negotiation; Operation Monitoring; Writing; Complex Problem Solving.

Education/Training Required (Nonapprenticeship Route): Work experience in a related occupation. **Related Knowledge/Courses— Building and Construction:** Materials, methods, and the appropriate tools to construct objects, structures, and buildings. **Public Safety and Security:** Weaponry; public safety; security operations, rules, regulations, precautions, and prevention; and the protection of people, data, and property. **Physics:** Physical principles, laws, and applications, including air, water, material dynamics, light, atomic principles, heat, electric

theory, earth formations, and meteorological and related natural phenomena. **Customer and Personal Service:** Principles and processes for providing customer and personal services, including needs assessment techniques, quality service standards, alternative delivery systems, and customer satisfaction evaluation techniques. **Law and Government:** Laws, legal codes, court procedures, precedents, government regulations, executive orders, agency rules, and the democratic political process. **Design:** Design techniques, principles, tools, and instruments involved in the production and use of precision technical plans, blueprints, drawings, and models.

Work Environment: More often outdoors than indoors; noisy; very hot or cold; very bright or dim lighting; hazardous equipment.

Fire Investigators

- ❋ Annual Earnings: $50,830
- ❋ Growth: 11.0%
- ❋ Annual Job Openings: 644
- ❋ Percentage of Women: 22.3%

Our sources did not provide separate job openings data for this occupation. The job openings listed here are shared with Fire Inspectors.

Related Apprenticeships—Arson and Bomb Investigator (4000 hrs.); Fire Marshall (4000 hrs.).

Conduct investigations to determine causes of fires and explosions. Package collected pieces of evidence in securely closed containers such as bags, crates, or boxes to protect them. Examine fire sites and collect evidence such as glass, metal fragments, charred wood, and accelerant residue for use in determining the cause of a fire. Instruct children about the dangers of fire. Analyze evidence and other information to determine probable cause of fire or explosion. Photograph damage and evidence related to causes of fires or explosions to document investigation findings. Subpoena and interview witnesses, property owners, and building occupants to obtain information and sworn testimony. Swear out warrants and arrest and process suspected arsonists. Testify in court cases involving fires, suspected arson, and false alarms. Prepare and maintain reports of investigation results and records of convicted arsonists and arson suspects. Test sites and materials to establish facts such as burn patterns and flash points of materials, using test equipment. Conduct internal investigation to determine negligence and violation of laws and regulations by fire department employees. Dust evidence or portions of fire scenes for latent fingerprints.

GOE—Career Cluster/Interest Area: 12. Law and Public Safety. **Work Group:** 12.04. Law Enforcement and Public Safety. **Other Apprenticeable Jobs in This Work Group:** Correctional Officers and Jailers; Police Patrol Officers. **Personality Type:** Investigative. These occupations frequently involve working with ideas and require an extensive amount of thinking. They can involve searching for facts and figuring out problems mentally.

Skills—Science; Equipment Maintenance; Management of Personnel Resources; Operation and Control; Equipment Selection; Repairing; Judgment and Decision Making; Operations Analysis.

Education/Training Required (Nonapprenticeship Route): Work experience in a related occupation. **Related Knowledge/Courses— Building and Construction:** Materials, methods, and the appropriate tools to construct objects, structures, and buildings. **Public Safety and Security:** Weaponry; public safety; security operations, rules, regulations, precautions, and prevention; and the protection of people, data, and property. **Physics:** Physical principles, laws, and applications, including air, water, material dynamics, light, atomic principles, heat, electric theory, earth formations, and meteorological and related natural phenomena. **Chemistry:** The composition, structure, and properties of substances and of the chemical processes and transformations that they undergo. This includes uses of chemicals and their interactions, danger signs, production techniques, and disposal methods. **Mechanical Devices:** Machines and tools, including their designs, uses, benefits, repair, and maintenance. **Law and Government:** Laws, legal codes, court procedures, precedents, government regulations, executive orders, agency rules, and the democratic political process.

Work Environment: Indoors; noisy; contaminants; hazardous conditions; hazardous equipment; using hands on objects, tools, or controls.

First-Line Supervisors/Managers of Housekeeping and Janitorial Workers

- Annual Earnings: $32,850
- Growth: 12.7%
- Annual Job Openings: 30,613
- Percentage of Women: 32.6%

Related Apprenticeship—Manager, Household (Private Residence) (4000 hrs.).

Supervise work activities of cleaning personnel in hotels, hospitals, offices, and other establishments. Direct activities for stopping the spread of infections in facilities such as hospitals. Inspect work performed to ensure that it meets specifications and established standards. Plan and prepare employee work schedules. Perform or assist with cleaning duties as necessary. Investigate complaints about service and equipment and take corrective action. Coordinate activities with other departments to ensure that services are provided in an efficient and timely manner. Check equipment to ensure that it is in working order. Inspect and evaluate the physical condition of facilities to determine the type of work required. Select the most suitable cleaning materials for different types of linens, furniture, flooring, and surfaces. Instruct staff in work policies and procedures and the use and maintenance of equipment. Issue supplies and equipment to workers. Forecast necessary levels of staffing and stock at different times to facilitate effective scheduling and ordering. Inventory stock to ensure that supplies and equipment are available in adequate amounts. Evaluate employee performance and recommend personnel actions such as promotions, transfers, and dismissals. Confer with staff to resolve performance and personnel problems and to discuss company policies. Establish and implement operational standards and procedures for the departments they supervise. Recommend or arrange for additional services such as painting, repair work, renovations, and the replacement of furnishings and equipment. Select and order or purchase new equipment, supplies, and furnishings. Recommend changes that could improve service and increase operational efficiency. Maintain required records of work hours, budgets, payrolls, and other information. Screen job applicants and hire new employees. Supervise in-house services such as laundries, maintenance and repair, dry cleaning, and valet services. Advise managers, desk clerks, or admitting personnel of rooms ready for occupancy. Perform financial tasks such as estimating costs and preparing and managing budgets.

Prepare activity and personnel reports and reports containing information such as occupancy, hours worked, facility usage, work performed, and departmental expenses.

GOE—Career Cluster/Interest Area: 04. Business and Administration. **Work Group:** 04.02. Managerial Work in Business Detail. **Other Apprenticeable Jobs in This Work Group:** No others in group. **Personality Type:** Enterprising. These occupations frequently involve starting up and carrying out projects and can involve leading people and making many decisions. They sometimes require risk taking and often deal with business.

Skills—Management of Personnel Resources; Monitoring; Equipment Maintenance; Equipment Selection; Service Orientation; Writing; Systems Evaluation; Science.

Education/Training Required (Nonapprenticeship Route): Work experience in a related occupation. **Related Knowledge/Courses—Chemistry:** The composition, structure, and properties of substances and of the chemical processes and transformations that they undergo. This includes uses of chemicals and their interactions, danger signs, production techniques, and disposal methods. **Building and Construction:** Materials, methods, and the appropriate tools to construct objects, structures, and buildings. **Public Safety and Security:** Weaponry; public safety; security operations, rules, regulations, precautions, and prevention; and the protection of people, data, and property. **Physics:** Physical principles, laws, and applications, including air, water, material dynamics, light, atomic principles, heat, electric theory, earth formations, and meteorological and related natural phenomena. **Mechanical Devices:** Machines and tools, including their designs, uses, benefits, repair, and maintenance. **Administration and Management:** Principles and processes involved in business and organizational planning, coordination, and execution. This includes strategic planning, resource allocation, manpower modeling, leadership techniques, and production methods.

Work Environment: Indoors; contaminants; disease or infections; standing; walking and running.

First-Line Supervisors/Managers of Retail Sales Workers

* ❋ Annual Earnings: $34,470
* ❋ Growth: 4.2%
* ❋ Annual Job Openings: 221,241
* ❋ Percentage of Women: 41.8%

Related Apprenticeship—Manager, Retail Store (6000 hrs.).

Directly supervise sales workers in a retail establishment or department. Duties may include management functions, such as purchasing, budgeting, accounting, and personnel work, in addition to supervisory duties. Provide customer service by greeting and assisting customers and responding to customer inquiries and complaints. Assign employees to specific duties. Monitor sales activities to ensure that customers receive satisfactory service and quality goods. Direct and supervise employees engaged in sales, inventory-taking, reconciling cash receipts, or performing services for customers. Inventory stock and reorder when inventory drops to a specified level. Keep records of purchases, sales, and requisitions. Enforce safety, health, and security rules. Examine products purchased for resale or received for storage to assess the condition of each product or item. Hire, train, and evaluate personnel in sales or marketing establishments, promoting or firing workers when appropriate. Perform work activities of subordinates, such as cleaning and organizing shelves and displays and selling merchandise. Establish and implement policies, goals, objectives, and procedures for their department. Instruct staff on how to handle difficult and complicated sales. Formulate pricing policies for merchandise according to profitability requirements. Estimate consumer demand and determine the types and amounts of goods to be sold. Examine merchandise to ensure that it is correctly priced and displayed and that it functions as advertised. Plan and prepare work schedules and keep records of employees' work schedules and time cards. Review inventory and sales records to prepare reports for management and budget departments. Plan and coordinate advertising campaigns and sales promotions and prepare merchandise displays and advertising copy. Confer with company officials to develop methods and procedures to increase sales, expand markets, and promote business. Establish credit policies and operating procedures. Plan budgets and authorize payments and merchandise returns.

GOE—Career Cluster/Interest Area: 14. Retail and Wholesale Sales and Service. **Work Group:** 14.01. Managerial Work in Retail/Wholesale Sales and Service. **Other Apprenticeable Jobs in This Work Group:** Funeral Directors. **Personality Type:** Enterprising. These occupations frequently involve starting up and carrying out projects and can involve leading people and making many decisions. They sometimes require risk taking and often deal with business.

Skills—Management of Personnel Resources; Management of Financial Resources; Persuasion; Repairing; Equipment Maintenance; Monitoring; Troubleshooting; Social Perceptiveness.

Education/Training Required (Nonapprenticeship Route): Work experience in a related occupation. **Related Knowledge/Courses—Sales and Marketing:** Principles and methods involved in showing, promoting, and selling products or services. This includes marketing strategies and tactics, product demonstration and sales techniques, and sales control systems. **Personnel and Human Resources:** Principles and procedures for personnel recruitment; selection; training; compensation and benefits; labor relations and negotiation; and personnel information systems. **Administration and Management:** Principles and processes involved in business and organizational planning, coordination, and execution. This includes strategic planning, resource allocation, manpower modeling, leadership techniques, and production methods. **Economics and Accounting:** Economic and accounting principles and practices, the financial markets, banking, and the analysis and reporting of financial data. **Customer and Personal Service:** Principles and processes for providing customer and personal services, including needs assessment techniques, quality service standards, alternative delivery systems, and customer satisfaction evaluation techniques.

Work Environment: Indoors; hazardous equipment; standing; walking and running; using hands on objects, tools, or controls.

Fish and Game Wardens

- ❋ Annual Earnings: $47,830
- ❋ Growth: –0.2%
- ❋ Annual Job Openings: 576
- ❋ Percentage of Women: 22.3%

Related Apprenticeship—Fish and Game Warden (Government Service) (4000 hrs.).

Patrol assigned area to prevent fish and game law violations. Investigate reports of damage to crops or property by wildlife. Compile biological data. Patrol assigned areas by car, boat, airplane, or horse or on foot to enforce game, fish, or boating laws and to manage wildlife programs, lakes, or land. Investigate hunting accidents and reports of fish and game law violations and issue warnings or citations and file reports as necessary. Serve warrants, make arrests, and compile and present evidence for court actions. Protect and preserve native wildlife, plants, and ecosystems. Promote and provide hunter and trapper safety training. Seize equipment used in fish and game law violations and arrange for disposition of fish or game illegally taken or possessed. Provide assistance to other local law enforcement agencies as required. Address schools, civic groups, sporting clubs, and the media to disseminate information concerning wildlife conservation and regulations. Recommend revisions or changes in hunting and trapping regulations or seasons and in animal management programs so that wildlife balances and habitats can be maintained. Inspect commercial operations relating to fish and wildlife, recreation, and protected areas. Collect and report information on populations and conditions of fish and wildlife in their habitats, availability of game food and cover, and suspected pollution. Survey areas and compile figures of bag counts of hunters to determine the effectiveness of control measures. Participate in search-and-rescue operations and in firefighting efforts. Investigate crop, property, or habitat damage or destruction or instances of water pollution to determine causes and to advise property owners of preventive measures. Design and implement control measures to prevent or counteract damage caused by wildlife or people. Document and detail the extent of crop, property, or habitat damage and make financial loss estimates and compensation recommendations. Supervise the activities of seasonal workers. Issue licenses, permits, and other documentation. Provide advice and information to park and reserve visitors. Perform facilities maintenance work such as constructing or repairing structures and controlling weeds and pests.

GOE—Career Cluster/Interest Area: 07. Government and Public Administration. **Work Group:** 07.03. Regulations Enforcement. **Other Apprenticeable Jobs in This Work Group:** Compliance Officers, Except Agriculture, Construction, Health and Safety, and Transportation; Construction and Building Inspectors; Equal Opportunity Representatives and Officers; Fire Inspectors; Government Property Inspectors and Investigators; Nuclear Monitoring Technicians; Transportation Vehicle, Equipment and Systems Inspectors, Except Aviation. **Personality Type:** Realistic. These occupations frequently involve work activities that include practical, hands-on problems and solutions. They often deal with plants; animals; and real-world materials such as wood, tools, and machinery. Many of the occupations require working outside and don't involve a lot of paperwork or working closely with others.

Skills—Equipment Maintenance; Persuasion; Science; Social Perceptiveness; Speaking; Writing; Repairing; Negotiation.

Education/Training Required (Nonapprenticeship Route): Associate degree. **Related Knowledge/Courses—Biology:** Plant and animal living tissue, cells, organisms, and entities, including their functions, interdependencies, and interactions with each other and the environment. **Law and Government:** Laws, legal codes, court procedures, precedents, government

regulations, executive orders, agency rules, and the democratic political process. **Geography:** Various methods for describing the location and distribution of land, sea, and air masses, including their physical locations, relationships, and characteristics. **Public Safety and Security:** Weaponry; public safety; security operations, rules, regulations, precautions, and prevention; and the protection of people, data, and property. **Psychology:** Human behavior and performance, mental processes, psychological research methods, and the assessment and treatment of behavioral and affective disorders. **Sociology and Anthropology:** Group behavior and dynamics; societal trends and influences; and cultures and their history, migrations, ethnicity, and origins.

Work Environment: Outdoors; very hot or cold; very bright or dim lighting; contaminants; hazardous equipment; minor burns, cuts, bites, or stings.

Food Batchmakers

- ❋ Annual Earnings: $23,730
- ❋ Growth: 10.9%
- ❋ Annual Job Openings: 15,704
- ❋ Percentage of Women: 58.6%

Related Apprenticeships—Candy Maker (6000 hrs.); Cheesemaker (4000 hrs.).

Set up and operate equipment that mixes or blends ingredients used in the manufacturing of food products. Includes candy makers and cheese makers. Record production and test data for each food product batch, such as the ingredients used, temperature, test results, and time cycle. Observe gauges and thermometers to determine if the mixing chamber temperature is within specified limits and turn valves to control the temperature. Clean and sterilize vats and factory processing areas. Press switches and turn knobs to start, adjust, and regulate equipment such as beaters, extruders, discharge pipes, and salt pumps. Observe and listen to equipment to detect possible malfunctions, such as leaks or plugging, and report malfunctions or undesirable tastes to supervisors. Set up, operate, and tend equipment that cooks, mixes, blends, or processes ingredients in the manufacturing of food products according to formulas or recipes. Mix or blend ingredients according to recipes by using a paddle or an agitator or by controlling vats that heat and mix ingredients. Select and measure or weigh ingredients, using English or metric measures and balance scales. Follow recipes to produce food products of specified flavor, texture, clarity, bouquet, or color. Turn valve controls to start equipment and to adjust operation to maintain product quality. Determine mixing sequences, based on knowledge of temperature effects and of the solubility of specific ingredients. Fill processing or cooking containers, such as kettles, rotating cookers, pressure cookers, or vats, with ingredients by opening valves, by starting pumps or injectors, or by hand. Give directions to other workers who are assisting in the batchmaking process. Homogenize or pasteurize material to prevent separation or to obtain prescribed butterfat content, using a homogenizing device. Inspect vats after cleaning to ensure that fermentable residue has been removed. Examine, feel, and taste product samples during production to evaluate quality, color, texture, flavor, and bouquet and document the results. Test food product samples for moisture content, acidity level, specific gravity, or butterfat content and continue processing until desired levels are reached. Formulate or modify recipes for specific kinds of food products.

GOE—Career Cluster/Interest Area: 13. Manufacturing. **Work Group:** 13.03. Production Work, Assorted Materials Processing. **Other Apprenticeable Jobs in This Work Group:** Bakers; Chemical Equipment Operators and Tenders; Coating, Painting, and Spraying Machine Setters, Operators, and Tenders; Cooling and Freezing Equipment Operators and Tenders; Cutting and Slicing Machine Setters, Operators, and Tenders; Extruding, Forming, Pressing, and Compacting Machine Setters, Operators, and Tenders; Furnace, Kiln, Oven, Drier, and Kettle Operators and Tenders; Heat Treating Equipment Setters, Operators, and Tenders, Metal and Plastic; Metal-Refining Furnace Operators and Tenders; Mixing and Blending Machine Setters, Operators, and Tenders; Plating and Coating Machine Setters, Operators, and Tenders, Metal and Plastic; Sawing Machine Setters, Operators, and Tenders, Wood; Separating, Filtering, Clarifying, Precipitating, and Still Machine Setters, Operators, and Tenders; Sewing Machine Operators; Slaughterers and Meat Packers; Team Assemblers; Woodworking Machine Setters, Operators, and Tenders, Except Sawing. **Personality Type:** Realistic. These occupations frequently involve work activities that include practical, hands-on problems and solutions. They often deal with plants; animals; and real-world materials such as wood, tools, and machinery. Many of the occupations require working outside and don't involve a lot of paperwork or working closely with others.

Skills—Operation Monitoring; Operation and Control; Equipment Maintenance; Repairing; Quality Control Analysis; Troubleshooting.

Education/Training Required (Nonapprenticeship Route): Short-term on-the-job training. **Related Knowledge/Courses—Production**

and Processing: Inputs, outputs, raw materials, waste, quality control, costs, and techniques for maximizing the manufacture and distribution of goods. **Public Safety and Security:** Weaponry; public safety; security operations, rules, regulations, precautions, and prevention; and the protection of people, data, and property. **Chemistry:** The composition, structure, and properties of substances and of the chemical processes and transformations that they undergo. This includes uses of chemicals and their interactions, danger signs, production techniques, and disposal methods.

Work Environment: Noisy; contaminants; standing; using hands on objects, tools, or controls; bending or twisting the body; repetitive motions.

Food Service Managers

- ❀ Annual Earnings: $44,570
- ❀ Growth: 5.0%
- ❀ Annual Job Openings: 59,302
- ❀ Percentage of Women: 43.2%

Related Apprenticeship—Manager, Food Service (6000 hrs.).

Plan, direct, or coordinate activities of an organization or department that serves food and beverages. Monitor compliance with health and fire regulations regarding food preparation and serving and building maintenance for lodging and dining facilities. Monitor food preparation methods, portion sizes, and garnishing and presentation of food to ensure that food is prepared and presented in an acceptable manner. Count money and make bank deposits. Investigate and resolve complaints regarding food quality, service, or accommodations. Coordinate assignments of cooking personnel to ensure economical use of food and timely preparation. Schedule and receive food and beverage deliveries, checking delivery contents to verify product quality and quantity. Monitor budgets and payroll records and review financial transactions to ensure that expenditures are authorized and budgeted. Schedule staff hours and assign duties. Maintain food and equipment inventories and keep inventory records. Establish standards for personnel performance and customer service. Perform some food preparation or service tasks such as cooking, clearing tables, and serving food and drinks when necessary. Plan menus and food utilization based on anticipated number of guests, nutritional value, palatability, popularity, and costs. Keep records required by government agencies regarding sanitation, and food subsidies when appropriate. Test cooked food by tasting and smelling it to ensure palatability and flavor conformity. Organize and direct worker training programs, resolve personnel problems, hire new staff, and evaluate employee performance in dining and lodging facilities. Order and purchase equipment and supplies. Review work procedures and operational problems to determine ways to improve service, performance, or safety. Assess staffing needs and recruit staff, using methods such as newspaper advertisements or attendance at job fairs. Arrange for equipment maintenance and repairs and coordinate a variety of services such as waste removal and pest control. Record the number, type, and cost of items sold to determine which items may be unpopular or less profitable. Review menus and analyze recipes to determine labor and overhead costs and assign prices to menu items.

GOE—Career Cluster/Interest Area: 09. Hospitality, Tourism, and Recreation. **Work Group:** 09.01. Managerial Work in Hospitality and Tourism. **Other Apprenticeable Jobs**

in This Work Group: No others in group. **Personality Type:** Enterprising. These occupations frequently involve starting up and carrying out projects and can involve leading people and making many decisions. They sometimes require risk taking and often deal with business.

Skills—Management of Financial Resources; Management of Personnel Resources; Systems Evaluation; Management of Material Resources; Systems Analysis; Negotiation; Service Orientation; Persuasion.

Education/Training Required (Nonapprenticeship Route): Work experience in a related occupation. **Related Knowledge/Courses— Food Production:** Techniques and equipment for planting, growing, and harvesting of food for consumption, including crop-rotation methods, animal husbandry, and food storage/handling techniques. **Sales and Marketing:** Principles and methods involved in showing, promoting, and selling products or services. This includes marketing strategies and tactics, product demonstration and sales techniques, and sales control systems. **Personnel and Human Resources:** Principles and procedures for personnel recruitment; selection; training; compensation and benefits; labor relations and negotiation; and personnel information systems. **Production and Processing:** Inputs, outputs, raw materials, waste, quality control, costs, and techniques for maximizing the manufacture and distribution of goods. **Education and Training:** Instructional methods and training techniques, including curriculum design principles, learning theory, group and individual teaching techniques, design of individual development plans, and test design principles. **Administration and Management:** Principles and processes involved in business and organizational planning, coordination, and execution. This includes strategic planning, resource allocation, manpower modeling, leadership techniques, and production methods.

Work Environment: Indoors; very hot or cold; standing; walking and running; using hands on objects, tools, or controls; repetitive motions.

Forest Fire Fighters

* Annual Earnings: $43,170
* Growth: 12.1%
* Annual Job Openings: 18,887
* Percentage of Women: 3.5%

Our sources did not provide separate job openings data for this occupation. The job openings listed here are shared with Municipal Fire Fighters.

Related Apprenticeships—Fire Suppression Technician (4000 hrs.); Wildland Fire Fighter Specialist (2000 hrs.).

Control and suppress fires in forests or vacant public land. Maintain contact with fire dispatchers at all times to notify them of the need for additional firefighters and supplies or to detail any difficulties encountered. Rescue fire victims and administer emergency medical aid. Collaborate with other firefighters as a member of a firefighting crew. Patrol burned areas after fires to locate and eliminate hot spots that may restart fires. Extinguish flames and embers to suppress fires, using shovels or engine- or hand-driven water or chemical pumps. Fell trees, cut and clear brush, and dig trenches to create firelines, using axes, chain saws, or shovels. Maintain knowledge of current firefighting practices by participating in drills and by attending seminars, conventions, and conferences. Operate pumps connected to high-pressure hoses. Participate in physical training to maintain high levels of physical fitness. Establish water supplies, connect hoses, and direct water onto fires. Maintain fire equipment and firehouse living quarters. Inform and educate the public about fire prevention. Take action to contain any hazardous chemicals that could catch fire, leak, or spill. Organize fire caches, positioning equipment for the most effective response. Transport personnel and cargo to and from fire areas. Participate in fire prevention and inspection programs. Perform forest maintenance and improvement tasks such as cutting brush, planting trees, building trails, and marking timber. Test and maintain tools, equipment, jump gear, and parachutes to ensure readiness for fire-suppression activities. Observe forest areas from fire lookout towers to spot potential problems. Orient self in relation to fire, using compass and map, and collect supplies and equipment dropped by parachute. Serve as fully trained lead helicopter crewmember and as helispot manager. Drop weighted paper streamers from aircraft to determine the speed and direction of the wind at fire sites.

GOE—Career Cluster/Interest Area: 12. Law and Public Safety. **Work Group:** 12.06. Emergency Responding. **Other Apprenticeable Jobs in This Work Group:** Emergency Medical Technicians and Paramedics; Municipal Fire Fighters. **Personality Type:** Realistic. These occupations frequently involve work activities that include practical, hands-on problems and solutions. They often deal with plants; animals; and real-world materials such as wood, tools, and machinery. Many of the occupations require working outside and don't involve a lot of paperwork or working closely with others.

Skills—Repairing; Equipment Maintenance; Management of Personnel Resources; Operation Monitoring; Equipment Selection; Operation and Control; Systems Analysis; Operations Analysis.

Education/Training Required (Nonapprenticeship Route): Long-term on-the-job training. **Related Knowledge/Courses—Geography:** Various methods for describing the location and distribution of land, sea, and air masses, including their physical locations, relationships, and characteristics. **Customer and Personal Service:** Principles and processes for providing customer and personal services, including needs assessment techniques, quality service standards, alternative delivery systems, and customer satisfaction evaluation techniques. **Mechanical Devices:** Machines and tools, including their designs, uses, benefits, repair, and maintenance. **Public Safety and Security:** Weaponry; public safety; security operations, rules, regulations, precautions, and prevention; and the protection of people, data, and property. **Education and Training:** Instructional methods and training techniques, including curriculum design principles, learning theory, group and individual teaching techniques, design of individual development plans, and test design principles. **Psychology:** Human behavior and performance, mental processes, psychological research methods, and the assessment and treatment of behavioral and affective disorders.

Work Environment: Outdoors; very hot or cold; contaminants; hazardous conditions; minor burns, cuts, bites, or stings; using hands on objects, tools, or controls.

Funeral Directors

- ❋ Annual Earnings: $50,370
- ❋ Growth: 12.5%
- ❋ Annual Job Openings: 3,939
- ❋ Percentage of Women: 36.7%

Related Apprenticeship—Director, Funeral (4000 hrs.).

Perform various tasks to arrange and direct funeral services, such as coordinating transportation of bodies to mortuaries for embalming, interviewing families or other authorized people to arrange details, selecting pallbearers, procuring officials for religious rites, and providing transportation for mourners. Obtain information needed to complete legal documents such as death certificates and burial permits. Oversee the preparation and care of the remains of people who have died. Consult with families or friends of the deceased to arrange funeral details such as obituary notice wording, casket selection, and plans for services. Plan, schedule, and coordinate funerals, burials, and cremations, arranging details such as floral delivery and the time and place of services. Perform embalming duties as necessary. Arrange for clergy members to perform needed services. Contact cemeteries to schedule the opening and closing of graves. Provide information on funeral service options, products, and merchandise and maintain a casket display area. Close caskets and lead funeral corteges to churches or burial sites. Offer counsel and comfort to bereaved families and friends. Inform survivors of benefits for which they may be eligible. Discuss and negotiate prearranged funerals with clients. Maintain financial records, order merchandise, and prepare accounts. Provide or arrange transportation between sites for the remains, mourners, pallbearers, clergy, and flowers. Plan placement of caskets at funeral sites and place and adjust lights, fixtures, and floral displays. Direct preparations and shipment of bodies for out-of-state burials. Manage funeral home operations, including the hiring, training, and supervision of embalmers, funeral attendants, or other staff. Clean funeral home facilities and grounds. Arrange for pallbearers and inform pallbearers and honorary groups of their duties. Receive and usher people to their seats for services. Participate in community activities for funeral home promotion or other purposes.

GOE—Career Cluster/Interest Area: 14. Retail and Wholesale Sales and Service. **Work Group:** 14.01. Managerial Work in Retail/Wholesale Sales and Service. **Other Apprenticeable Jobs in This Work Group:** First-Line Supervisors/Managers of Retail Sales Workers. **Personality Type:** Enterprising. These occupations frequently involve starting up and carrying out projects and can involve leading people and making many decisions. They sometimes require risk taking and often deal with business.

Skills—Management of Personnel Resources; Social Perceptiveness; Negotiation; Management of Financial Resources; Service Orientation.

Education/Training Required (Nonapprenticeship Route): Associate degree. **Related Knowledge/Courses—Chemistry:** The composition, structure, and properties of substances and of the chemical processes and transformations that they undergo. This includes uses of chemicals and their interactions, danger signs, production techniques, and disposal methods. **Philosophy and Theology:** Different philosophical systems and religions, including their basic principles, values, ethics, ways of thinking, customs, and practices and their impact on human culture. **Therapy and Counseling:** Information and techniques needed to rehabilitate physical and mental ailments and to provide career guidance, including alternative treatments, rehabilitation equipment and its proper use, and methods to evaluate treatment effects. **Customer and Personal Service:** Principles and processes for providing customer and personal services, including needs assessment techniques, quality service standards, alternative delivery systems, and customer satisfaction evaluation techniques. **Biology:** Plant and animal living tissue, cells, organisms, and entities, including their functions, interdependencies, and interactions with each other and the environment. **Sales and Marketing:** Principles and methods involved in showing, promoting, and selling products or services. This includes marketing strategies and tactics, product demonstration and sales techniques, and sales control systems.

Work Environment: More often indoors than outdoors; contaminants; disease or infections; standing.

Gem and Diamond Workers

- ❀ Annual Earnings: $31,200
- ❀ Growth: –2.2%
- ❀ Annual Job Openings: 7,375
- ❀ Percentage of Women: 30.4%

Our sources did not provide separate job openings data for this occupation. The job openings listed here are shared with Jewelers and with Precious Metal Workers.

Related Apprenticeships—Brilliandeer-Lopper (6000 hrs.); Diamond Selector (Jewelry) (8000 hrs.); Gem Cutter (Jewelry) (6000 hrs.).

Fabricate, finish, or evaluate the quality of gems and diamonds used in jewelry or industrial tools. Regulate the speed of revolutions and reciprocating actions of drilling mechanisms. Regrind drill points and advance drill cutting points according to specifications for channel depths and shapes. Measure sizes of stones' bore holes and cuts to ensure adherence to specifications, using precision measuring instruments. Assign grades to stones for their polish, symmetry, and clarity according to established grading systems. Replace, true, and sharpen blades, drills, and plates. Lap girdles on rough diamonds, using diamond-girdling lathes. Locate and mark drilling or cutting positions on stones or dies, using diamond chips and power hand tools. Lap inner walls of channels, using machines that revolve stones and rotate wires or needles in channels. Secure gems or diamonds in holders, chucks, dops, lapidary sticks, or blocks for cutting, polishing, grinding, drilling, or shaping. Select shaping wheels for tasks and mix and apply abrasives, bort, or polishing compounds. Sort rough diamonds into categories based on shape, size, color, and quality. Test accuracy of die holes by pulling specified lengths of wire through dies and measuring their resistance or by taking a series of readings along the lengths of wires, using electronic micrometers. Secure stones in metal mountings, using solder. Immerse stones in prescribed chemical solutions to determine specific gravities and key properties of gemstones or substitutes. Examine gem surfaces and internal structures, using polariscopes, refractometers, microscopes, and other optical instruments to differentiate between stones; to identify rare specimens; or to detect flaws, defects, or peculiarities affecting gem values. Split gems along pre-marked lines to remove imperfections, using blades and jewelers' hammers. Estimate wholesale and retail value of gems, following pricing guides, market fluctuations, and other relevant economic factors.

Grind, drill, and finish jewel bearings for use in precision instruments such as compasses and chronometers. Dismantle lapping, boring, cutting, polishing, and shaping equipment and machinery to clean and lubricate it.

GOE—Career Cluster/Interest Area: 13. Manufacturing. **Work Group:** 13.06. Production Precision Work. **Other Apprenticeable Jobs in This Work Group:** Bookbinders; Dental Laboratory Technicians; Electrical and Electronic Equipment Assemblers; Electromechanical Equipment Assemblers; Engine and Other Machine Assemblers; Jewelers; Medical Appliance Technicians; Molding, Coremaking, and Casting Machine Setters, Operators, and Tenders, Metal and Plastic; Ophthalmic Laboratory Technicians; Precious Metal Workers. **Personality Type:** Realistic. These occupations frequently involve work activities that include practical, hands-on problems and solutions. They often deal with plants; animals; and real-world materials such as wood, tools, and machinery. Many of the occupations require working outside and don't involve a lot of paperwork or working closely with others.

Skills—Management of Material Resources; Management of Financial Resources; Equipment Selection; Judgment and Decision Making; Quality Control Analysis; Equipment Maintenance; Mathematics; Time Management.

Education/Training Required (Nonapprenticeship Route): Postsecondary vocational training. **Related Knowledge/Courses—Production and Processing:** Inputs, outputs, raw materials, waste, quality control, costs, and techniques for maximizing the manufacture and distribution of goods. **Sales and Marketing:** Principles and methods involved in showing, promoting, and selling products or services. This includes marketing strategies and tactics, product demonstration and sales techniques, and sales control systems. **Design:** Design techniques, principles, tools, and instruments involved in the production and use of precision technical plans, blueprints, drawings, and models. **Administration and Management:** Principles and processes involved in business and organizational planning, coordination, and execution. This includes strategic planning, resource allocation, manpower modeling, leadership techniques, and production methods.

Work Environment: Indoors; hazardous equipment; minor burns, cuts, bites, or stings; sitting; using hands on objects, tools, or controls.

Geological Sample Test Technicians

- ❀ Annual Earnings: $50,950
- ❀ Growth: 8.6%
- ❀ Annual Job Openings: 1,895
- ❀ Percentage of Women: 43.3%

Our sources did not provide separate job openings data for this occupation. The job openings listed here are shared with Geophysical Data Technicians.

Related Apprenticeships—Test Engine Operator (4000 hrs.); Tester (Petroleum Refining) (6000 hrs.).

Test and analyze geological samples, crude oil, or petroleum products to detect presence of petroleum, gas, or mineral deposits indicating potential for exploration and production or to determine physical and chemical properties to ensure that products meet quality standards. Test and analyze samples in order to determine their content and characteristics, using laboratory apparatus and testing equipment. Collect and prepare solid and fluid samples for analysis. Assemble, operate, and maintain field and laboratory testing, measuring, and mechanical equipment, working as part of a crew when required. Compile and record testing and operational data for review and further analysis. Adjust and repair testing, electrical, and mechanical equipment and devices. Supervise well exploration and drilling activities and well completions. Inspect engines for wear and defective parts, using equipment and measuring devices. Prepare notes, sketches, geological maps, and cross sections. Participate in geological, geophysical, geochemical, hydrographic, or oceanographic surveys; prospecting field trips; exploratory drilling; well logging; or underground mine survey programs. Plot information from aerial photographs, well logs, section descriptions, and other databases. Assess the environmental impacts of development projects on subsurface materials. Collaborate with hydrogeologists to evaluate groundwater and well circulation. Prepare, transcribe, and/or analyze seismic, gravimetric, well log, or other geophysical and survey data. Participate in the evaluation of possible mining locations.

GOE—Career Cluster/Interest Area: 01. Agriculture and Natural Resources. **Work Group:** 01.03. Resource Technologies for Plants, Animals, and the Environment. **Other Apprenticeable Jobs in This Work Group:** Environmental Science and Protection Technicians, Including Health. **Personality Type:** Realistic. These occupations frequently involve work activities that include practical, hands-on problems and solutions. They often deal with plants; animals; and real-world materials such as wood, tools, and machinery. Many of the occupations require working outside and don't involve a lot of paperwork or working closely with others.

Skills—Science; Equipment Maintenance; Operation Monitoring; Quality Control Analysis; Mathematics; Operations Analysis; Installation; Operation and Control.

Education/Training Required (Nonapprenticeship Route): Associate degree. **Related Knowledge/Courses—Chemistry:** The composition, structure, and properties of substances and of the chemical processes and transformations that they undergo. This includes uses of chemicals and their interactions, danger signs, production techniques, and disposal methods. **Geography:** Various methods for describing the location and distribution of land, sea, and air masses, including their physical locations, relationships, and characteristics. **Physics:** Physical principles, laws, and applications, including air, water, material dynamics, light, atomic principles, heat, electric theory, earth formations, and meteorological and related natural phenomena. **Mechanical Devices:** Machines and tools, including their designs, uses, benefits, repair, and maintenance. **Mathematics:** Numbers and their operations and interrelationships, including arithmetic, algebra, geometry, calculus, and statistics and their applications. **Computers and Electronics:** Electric circuit boards, processors, chips, and computer hardware and software, including applications and programming.

Work Environment: Indoors; noisy; contaminants; more often standing than sitting; using hands on objects, tools, or controls.

Glaziers

- ❀ Annual Earnings: $35,230
- ❀ Growth: 11.9%
- ❀ Annual Job Openings: 6,416
- ❀ Percentage of Women: 3.1%

Related Apprenticeships—Glazier (6000 hrs.); Glazier, Stained Glass (8000 hrs.).

Install glass in windows, skylights, store-fronts, and display cases or on surfaces such as building fronts, interior walls, ceilings, and tabletops. Read and interpret blueprints and specifications to determine size, shape, color, type, and thickness of glass; location of framing; installation procedures; and staging and scaffolding materials required. Determine plumb of walls or ceilings, using plumb-lines and levels. Fabricate and install metal sashes and moldings for glass installation, using aluminum or steel framing. Measure mirrors and dimensions of areas to be covered to determine work procedures. Fasten glass panes into wood sashes or frames with clips, points, or moldings, adding weather seals or putty around pane edges to seal joints. Secure mirrors in position, using mastic cement, putty, bolts, or screws. Cut, fit, install, repair, and replace glass and glass substitutes such as plastic and aluminum in building interiors or exteriors and in furniture or other products. Cut and remove broken glass prior to installing replacement glass. Set glass doors into frames and bolt metal hinges, handles, locks, and other hardware to attach doors to frames and walls. Score glass with cutters' wheels, breaking off excess glass by hand or with notched tools. Cut, assemble, fit, and attach metal-framed glass enclosures for showers, bathtubs, display cases, skylights, solariums, and other structures. Drive trucks to installation sites and unload mirrors, glass equipment, and tools. Install pre-assembled metal or wood frameworks for windows or doors to be fitted with glass panels, using hand tools. Cut and attach mounting strips, metal or wood moldings, rubber gaskets, or metal clips to surfaces in preparation for mirror installation. Assemble, erect, and dismantle scaffolds, rigging, and hoisting equipment. Load and arrange glass and mirrors onto delivery trucks, using suction cups or cranes to lift glass. Measure and mark outlines or patterns on glass to indicate cutting lines. Grind and polish glass, smoothing edges when necessary. Prepare glass for cutting by resting it on rack edges or against cutting tables and by brushing a thin layer of oil along cutting lines or by dipping cutting tools in oil. Pack spaces between moldings and glass with glazing compounds, and trim excess material with glazing knives.

GOE—Career Cluster/Interest Area: 02. Architecture and Construction. **Work Group:** 02.04. Construction Crafts. **Other Apprenticeable Jobs in This Work Group:** Boilermakers; Brickmasons and Blockmasons; Carpet Installers; Cement Masons and Concrete Finishers; Construction Carpenters; Crane and Tower Operators; Drywall and Ceiling Tile Installers; Electricians; Fence Erectors; Floor Layers, Except Carpet, Wood, and Hard Tiles; Insulation Workers, Floor, Ceiling, and Wall; Insulation Workers, Mechanical; Operating Engineers and Other Construction Equipment Operators; Painters, Construction and Maintenance; Paperhangers; Paving, Surfacing, and Tamping Equipment Operators; Pipe Fitters and Steamfitters; Plasterers and Stucco Masons; Plumbers; Reinforcing Iron and Rebar Workers; Riggers; Roofers; Rough Carpenters; Sheet Metal Workers; Stone Cutters and Carvers, Manufacturing; Stonemasons; Structural Iron and Steel Workers; Tapers; Terrazzo Workers and Finishers; Tile and Marble Setters. **Personality Type:** Realistic. These occupations frequently involve work activities that include practical, hands-on problems and solutions. They often deal with plants; animals; and real-world materials such as wood, tools, and machinery. Many of the occupations require working outside and don't involve a lot of paperwork or working closely with others.

Skills—Installation; Mathematics; Repairing.

Education/Training Required (Nonapprenticeship Route): Long-term on-the-job training. **Related Knowledge/Courses—Building and Construction:** Materials, methods, and the appropriate tools to construct objects, structures, and buildings. **Mechanical Devices:** Machines and tools, including their designs, uses, benefits, repair, and maintenance. **Design:** Design techniques, principles, tools, and instruments involved in the production and use of precision technical plans, blueprints, drawings, and models. **Engineering and Technology:** Equipment, tools, and mechanical devices and their uses to produce motion, light, power, technology, and other applications. **Mathematics:** Numbers and their operations and interrelationships, including arithmetic, algebra, geometry, calculus, and statistics and their applications. **Public Safety and Security:** Weaponry; public safety; security operations, rules, regulations, precautions, and prevention; and the protection of people, data, and property.

Work Environment: Outdoors; noisy; very hot or cold; contaminants; standing; using hands on objects, tools, or controls.

Further Information: Contact a local of the International Union of Painters and Allied Trades, a local joint union-management apprenticeship committee, or the nearest office of your state employment service or apprenticeship agency (see Appendix C).

Government Property Inspectors and Investigators

- ✺ Annual Earnings: $48,400
- ✺ Growth: 4.9%
- ✺ Annual Job Openings: 15,841
- ✺ Percentage of Women: 54.0%

Our sources did not provide separate job openings data for this occupation. The job openings listed here are shared with Coroners; Environmental Compliance Inspectors; Equal Opportunity Representatives and Officers; and Licensing Examiners and Inspectors.

Related Apprenticeship—Inspector, Quality Assurance (6000 hrs.).

Investigate or inspect government property to ensure compliance with contract agreements and government regulations. Prepare correspondence, reports of inspections or investigations, and recommendations for action. Inspect government-owned equipment and materials in the possession of private contractors to ensure compliance with contracts and regulations and to prevent misuse. Examine records, reports, and documents to establish facts and detect discrepancies. Inspect manufactured or processed products to ensure compliance with contract specifications and legal requirements. Locate and interview plaintiffs, witnesses, or representatives of business or government to gather facts relevant to inspections or alleged violations. Recommend legal or administrative action to protect government property. Submit samples of products to government laboratories for testing as required. Coordinate with and assist law enforcement agencies in matters of mutual concern. Testify in court or at administrative proceedings concerning findings of investigations. Collect, identify, evaluate, and preserve case evidence. Monitor investigations of suspected offenders to ensure that they are conducted in accordance with constitutional requirements. Investigate applications for special licenses or permits, as well as alleged violations of licenses or permits.

GOE—Career Cluster/Interest Area: 07. Government and Public Administration. **Work Group:** 07.03. Regulations Enforcement. **Other Apprenticeable Jobs in This Work Group:** Compliance Officers, Except Agriculture, Construction, Health and Safety, and Transportation; Construction and Building Inspectors; Equal Opportunity Representatives and Officers; Fire Inspectors; Fish and Game Wardens; Nuclear Monitoring Technicians; Transportation Vehicle, Equipment and Systems Inspectors, Except Aviation. **Personality Type:** Conventional. These occupations frequently involve following set procedures and routines and can include working with data and details more than with ideas. Usually there is a clear line of authority to follow.

Skills—Quality Control Analysis; Technology Design; Science; Troubleshooting; Equipment Selection; Coordination; Operation and Control; Service Orientation.

Education/Training Required (Nonapprenticeship Route): Long-term on-the-job training. **Related Knowledge/Courses—Building and Construction:** Materials, methods, and the appropriate tools to construct objects, structures, and buildings. **Engineering and Technology:** Equipment, tools, and mechanical devices and their uses to produce motion, light, power, technology, and other applications. **Public Safety and Security:** Weaponry; public safety; security operations, rules, regulations, precautions, and prevention; and the protection of people, data, and property. **Mechanical Devices:** Machines and tools, including their designs, uses, benefits,

repair, and maintenance. **Computers and Electronics:** Electric circuit boards, processors, chips, and computer hardware and software, including applications and programming. **Transportation:** Principles and methods for moving people or goods by air, rail, sea, or road, including their relative costs, advantages, and limitations.

Work Environment: Indoors; more often standing than sitting; walking and running; using hands on objects, tools, or controls.

Hairdressers, Hairstylists, and Cosmetologists

- ❋ Annual Earnings: $22,210
- ❋ Growth: 12.4%
- ❋ Annual Job Openings: 73,030
- ❋ Percentage of Women: 93.4%

Related Apprenticeships—Cosmetologist (2000 hrs.); Hair Stylist (2000 hrs.).

Provide beauty services, such as shampooing, cutting, coloring, and styling hair and massaging and treating scalp. May also apply makeup, dress wigs, perform hair removal, and provide nail and skin care services. Keep work stations clean and sanitize tools such as scissors and combs. Cut, trim, and shape hair or hairpieces based on customers' instructions, hair type, and facial features, using clippers, scissors, trimmers, and razors. Analyze patrons' hair and other physical features to determine and recommend beauty treatment or suggest hairstyles. Schedule client appointments. Bleach, dye, or tint hair, using applicator or brush. Update and maintain customer information records, such as beauty services provided. Shampoo, rinse, condition, and dry hair and scalp or hairpieces with water, liquid soap, or other solutions. Operate cash registers to receive payments from patrons.

Demonstrate and sell hair care products and cosmetics. Apply water, setting, straightening, or waving solutions to hair and use curlers, rollers, hot combs, and curling irons to press and curl hair. Develop new styles and techniques. Comb, brush, and spray hair or wigs to set style. Shape eyebrows and remove facial hair, using depilatory cream, tweezers, electrolysis, or wax. Administer therapeutic medication and advise patron to seek medical treatment for chronic or contagious scalp conditions. Massage and treat scalp for hygienic and remedial purposes, using hands, fingers, or vibrating equipment. Shave, trim, and shape beards and moustaches. Train or supervise other hairstylists, hairdressers, and assistants. Recommend and explain the use of cosmetics, lotions, and creams to soften and lubricate skin and enhance and restore natural appearance. Give facials to patrons, using special compounds such as lotions and creams. Clean, shape, and polish fingernails and toenails, using files and nail polish. Apply artificial fingernails. Attach wigs or hairpieces to model heads and dress wigs and hairpieces according to instructions, samples, sketches, or photographs.

GOE—Career Cluster/Interest Area: 09. Hospitality, Tourism, and Recreation. **Work Group:** 09.07. Barber and Beauty Services. **Other Apprenticeable Jobs in This Work Group:** Barbers. **Personality Type:** Artistic. These occupations frequently involve working with forms, designs, and patterns. They often require self-expression, and the work can be done without following a clear set of rules.

Skills—Science; Operations Analysis; Equipment Selection; Management of Financial Resources; Equipment Maintenance; Learning Strategies; Social Perceptiveness; Management of Material Resources.

Education/Training Required (Nonapprenticeship Route): Postsecondary vocational training. **Related Knowledge/Courses— Chemistry:** The composition, structure, and properties of substances and of the chemical processes and transformations that they undergo. This includes uses of chemicals and their interactions, danger signs, production techniques, and disposal methods. **Sales and Marketing:** Principles and methods involved in showing, promoting, and selling products or services. This includes marketing strategies and tactics, product demonstration and sales techniques, and sales control systems. **Customer and Personal Service:** Principles and processes for providing customer and personal services, including needs assessment techniques, quality service standards, alternative delivery systems, and customer satisfaction evaluation techniques.

Work Environment: Indoors; contaminants; minor burns, cuts, bites, or stings; standing; using hands on objects, tools, or controls; repetitive motions.

Heating and Air Conditioning Mechanics and Installers

* Annual Earnings: $38,360
* Growth: 8.7%
* Annual Job Openings: 29,719
* Percentage of Women: 2.7%

Our sources did not provide separate job openings data for this occupation. The job openings listed here are shared with Refrigeration Mechanics and Installers.

Related Apprenticeships—Air and Hydronic Balancing Technician (6000 hrs.); Furnace Installer (6000 hrs.); Furnace Installer and Repairer (8000 hrs.); Heating and Air-

Conditioning Instrument Servicer (6000 hrs.); Oil Burner Servicer and Installer (4000 hrs.).

Install, service, and repair heating and air conditioning systems in residences and commercial establishments. Obtain and maintain required certifications. Comply with all applicable standards, policies, and procedures, including safety procedures and the maintenance of a clean work area. Repair or replace defective equipment, components, or wiring. Test electrical circuits and components for continuity, using electrical test equipment. Reassemble and test equipment following repairs. Inspect and test system to verify system compliance with plans and specifications and to detect and locate malfunctions. Discuss heating-cooling system malfunctions with users to isolate problems or to verify that malfunctions have been corrected. Test pipe or tubing joints and connections for leaks, using pressure gauge or soap-and-water solution. Record and report all faults, deficiencies, and other unusual occurrences, as well as the time and materials expended on work orders. Adjust system controls to setting recommended by manufacturer to balance system, using hand tools. Recommend, develop, and perform preventive and general maintenance procedures such as cleaning, power-washing, and vacuuming equipment; oiling parts; and changing filters. Lay out and connect electrical wiring between controls and equipment according to wiring diagram, using electrician's hand tools. Install auxiliary components to heating-cooling equipment, such as expansion and discharge valves, air ducts, pipes, blowers, dampers, flues, and stokers, following blueprints. Assist with other work in coordination with repair and maintenance teams. Install, connect, and adjust thermostats, humidistats, and timers, using hand tools. Generate work orders that address deficiencies in need of correction. Join pipes or tubing to equipment and to fuel, water, or refrigerant source to form complete circuit. Assemble, position, and mount heating or cooling equipment, following blueprints. Study blueprints, design specifications, and manufacturers' recommendations to ascertain the configuration of heating or cooling equipment components and to ensure the proper installation of components. Cut and drill holes in floors, walls, and roof to install equipment, using power saws and drills.

GOE—Career Cluster/Interest Area: 02. Architecture and Construction. **Work Group:** 02.05. Systems and Equipment Installation, Maintenance, and Repair. **Other Apprenticeable Jobs in This Work Group:** Electrical and Electronics Repairers, Powerhouse, Substation, and Relay; Electrical Power-Line Installers and Repairers; Elevator Installers and Repairers; Maintenance and Repair Workers, General; Refrigeration Mechanics and Installers; Telecommunications Equipment Installers and Repairers, Except Line Installers; Telecommunications Line Installers and Repairers. **Personality Type:** Realistic. These occupations frequently involve work activities that include practical, hands-on problems and solutions. They often deal with plants; animals; and real-world materials such as wood, tools, and machinery. Many of the occupations require working outside and don't involve a lot of paperwork or working closely with others.

Skills—Repairing; Installation; Equipment Maintenance; Troubleshooting; Systems Evaluation; Science; Systems Analysis; Coordination.

Education/Training Required (Nonapprenticeship Route): Long-term on-the-job training. **Related Knowledge/Courses—Mechanical Devices:** Machines and tools, including their designs, uses, benefits, repair, and maintenance. **Building and Construction:** Materials, methods, and the appropriate tools to construct objects, structures, and buildings. **Design:** Design techniques, principles, tools, and instruments involved in the production and use of precision technical plans, blueprints, drawings, and models. **Physics:** Physical principles, laws, and applications, including air, water, material dynamics, light, atomic principles, heat, electric theory, earth formations, and meteorological and related natural phenomena. **Engineering and Technology:** Equipment, tools, and mechanical devices and their uses to produce motion, light, power, technology, and other applications. **Sales and Marketing:** Principles and methods involved in showing, promoting, and selling products or services. This includes marketing strategies and tactics, product demonstration and sales techniques, and sales control systems.

Work Environment: Outdoors; very hot or cold; contaminants; hazardous conditions; minor burns, cuts, bites, or stings; using hands on objects, tools, or controls.

Further Information: Contact a local joint union-management apprenticeship committee, or the nearest office of your state employment service or apprenticeship agency (see Appendix C). Information is also available at some of the organizations linked to www.coolcareers.org/.

Helpers—Brickmasons, Blockmasons, Stonemasons, and Tile and Marble Setters

* Annual Earnings: $26,260
* Growth: 11.0%
* Annual Job Openings: 22,500
* Percentage of Women: 6.2%

Related Apprenticeships—Marble Finisher (3500–4000 hrs., hybrid); Marble Finisher (4000 hrs.); Tile Finisher (3500–4000 hrs., hybrid); Tile Finisher (4000 hrs.).

Help brickmasons, blockmasons, stonemasons, or tile and marble setters by performing duties of lesser skill. Duties include using, supplying, or holding materials or tools and cleaning work area and equipment. Transport materials, tools, and machines to installation sites, manually or using conveyance equipment. Move or position materials such as marble slabs, using cranes, hoists, or dollies. Modify material moving, mixing, grouting, grinding, polishing, or cleaning procedures according to installation or material requirements. Correct surface imperfections or fill chipped, cracked, or broken bricks or tiles, using fillers, adhesives, and grouting materials. Arrange and store materials, machines, tools, and equipment. Apply caulk, sealants, or other agents to installed surfaces. Select or locate and supply materials to masons for installation, following drawings or numbered sequences. Remove excess grout and residue from tile or brick joints, using sponges or trowels. Remove damaged tile, brick, or mortar and clean and prepare surfaces, using pliers, hammers, chisels, drills, wire brushes, and metal wire anchors. Provide assistance in the preparation, installation, repair, and/or rebuilding of tile, brick, or stone surfaces. Mix mortar, plaster, and grout, manually or using machines, according to standard formulas. Erect scaffolding or other installation structures. Cut materials to specified sizes for installation, using power saws or tile cutters. Clean installation surfaces, equipment, tools, work sites, and storage areas, using water, chemical solutions, oxygen lances, or polishing machines. Apply grout between joints of bricks or tiles, using grouting trowels.

GOE—Career Cluster/Interest Area: 02. Architecture and Construction. Work Group: 02.06. Construction Support/Labor. Other Apprenticeable Jobs in This Work Group: Construction Laborers; Helpers—Brickmasons, Blockmasons, Stonemasons, and Tile and Marble Setters; Helpers—Installation, Maintenance, and Repair Workers; Helpers—Installation, Maintenance, and Repair Workers; Plasterers and Stucco Masons. Personality Type: Realistic. These occupations frequently involve work activities that include practical, hands-on problems and solutions. They often deal with plants; animals; and real-world materials such as wood, tools, and machinery. Many of the occupations require working outside and don't involve a lot of paperwork or working closely with others.

Skills—Repairing; Equipment Maintenance; Installation; Management of Material Resources; Operation and Control; Mathematics; Operations Analysis.

Education/Training Required (Nonapprenticeship Route): Short-term on-the-job training. Related Knowledge/Courses—Building and Construction: Materials, methods, and the appropriate tools to construct objects, structures, and buildings. Chemistry: The composition, structure, and properties of substances and of the chemical processes and transformations that they undergo. This includes uses of chemicals and their interactions, danger signs, production techniques, and disposal methods. Transportation: Principles and methods for moving people or goods by air, rail, sea, or road, including their relative costs, advantages, and limitations. Production and Processing: Inputs, outputs, raw materials, waste, quality control, costs, and techniques for maximizing the manufacture and distribution of goods. Mechanical Devices:

Machines and tools, including their designs, uses, benefits, repair, and maintenance. Design: Design techniques, principles, tools, and instruments involved in the production and use of precision technical plans, blueprints, drawings, and models.

Work Environment: Outdoors; standing; walking and running; kneeling, crouching, stooping, or crawling; using hands on objects, tools, or controls; repetitive motions.

Helpers—Installation, Maintenance, and Repair Workers

❋ Annual Earnings: $22,920
❋ Growth: 11.8%
❋ Annual Job Openings: 52,058
❋ Percentage of Women: 4.6%

Related Apprenticeships—Facilities Locator (4000 hrs.); Service Planner (Light, Heat) (8000 hrs.); Service Planner (Light, Heating) (7500–8000 hrs., hybrid).

Help installation, maintenance, and repair workers in maintenance, parts replacement, and repair of vehicles, industrial machinery, and electrical and electronic equipment. Perform duties such as furnishing tools, materials, and supplies to other workers; cleaning work area, machines, and tools; and holding materials or tools for other workers. Tend and observe equipment and machinery to verify efficient and safe operation. Examine and test machinery, equipment, components, and parts for defects and to ensure proper functioning. Adjust, connect, or disconnect wiring, piping, tubing, and other parts, using hand tools or power tools. Install or replace machinery, equipment, and new or replacement parts and instruments, using hand tools or power tools. Clean or lubricate vehicles, machinery, equipment, instruments, tools, work areas, and other objects, using hand tools, power tools, and cleaning equipment. Apply protective materials to equipment, components, and parts to prevent defects and corrosion. Transfer tools, parts, equipment, and supplies to and from workstations and other areas. Disassemble broken or defective equipment in order to facilitate repair; reassemble equipment when repairs are complete. Assemble and maintain physical structures, using hand tools or power tools. Provide assistance to more skilled workers involved in the adjustment, maintenance, part replacement, and repair of tools, equipment, and machines. Position vehicles, machinery, equipment, physical structures, and other objects for assembly or installation, using hand tools, power tools, and moving equipment. Hold or supply tools, parts, equipment, and supplies for other workers. Prepare work stations so mechanics and repairers can conduct work.

GOE—Career Cluster/Interest Area: 02. Architecture and Construction. **Work Group:** 02.06. Construction Support/Labor. **Other Apprenticeable Jobs in This Work Group:** Construction Laborers; Helpers—Brickmasons, Blockmasons, Stonemasons, and Tile and Marble Setters; Helpers—Brickmasons, Blockmasons, Stonemasons, and Tile and Marble Setters; Helpers—Installation, Maintenance, and Repair Workers; Plasterers and Stucco Masons. **Personality Type:** Realistic. These occupations frequently involve work activities that include practical, hands-on problems and solutions. They often deal with plants; animals; and real-world materials such as wood, tools, and machinery. Many of the occupations require working outside and don't involve a lot of paperwork or working closely with others.

Skills—Installation; Operation Monitoring; Repairing; Equipment Maintenance; Troubleshooting; Operations Analysis; Operation and Control; Science.

Education/Training Required (Nonapprenticeship Route): Short-term on-the-job training. **Related Knowledge/Courses—Mechanical Devices:** Machines and tools, including their designs, uses, benefits, repair, and maintenance. **Engineering and Technology:** Equipment, tools, and mechanical devices and their uses to produce motion, light, power, technology, and other applications. **Building and Construction:** Materials, methods, and the appropriate tools to construct objects, structures, and buildings. **Chemistry:** The composition, structure, and properties of substances and of the chemical processes and transformations that they undergo. This includes uses of chemicals and their interactions, danger signs, production techniques, and disposal methods. **Design:** Design techniques, principles, tools, and instruments involved in the production and use of precision technical plans, blueprints, drawings, and models. **Public Safety and Security:** Weaponry; public safety; security operations, rules, regulations, precautions, and prevention; and the protection of people, data, and property.

Work Environment: Noisy; hazardous conditions; hazardous equipment; standing; using hands on objects, tools, or controls; bending or twisting the body.

Home Appliance Repairers

- Annual Earnings: $33,560
- Growth: 1.5%
- Annual Job Openings: 4,243
- Percentage of Women: 1.5%

Related Apprenticeships—Air Conditioner Installer, Window (6000 hrs.); Customer Service Representative (6000 hrs.); Electric Tool Repairer (8000 hrs.); Electrical Appliance Repairer (6000 hrs.); Electrical Appliance Servicer (6000 hrs.); Gas Appliance Servicer (6000 hrs.).

Repair, adjust, or install all types of electric or gas household appliances, such as refrigerators, washers, dryers, and ovens. Clean, lubricate, and touch up minor defects on newly installed or repaired appliances. Observe and test operation of appliances following installation and make any initial installation adjustments that are necessary. Level refrigerators, adjust doors, and connect water lines to water pipes for ice makers and water dispensers, using hand tools. Level washing machines and connect hoses to water pipes, using hand tools. Maintain stocks of parts used in on-site installation, maintenance, and repair of appliances. Instruct customers regarding operation and care of appliances and provide information such as emergency service numbers. Provide repair cost estimates and recommend whether appliance repair or replacement is a better choice. Conserve, recover, and recycle refrigerants used in cooling systems. Contact supervisors or offices to receive repair assignments. Install gas pipes and water lines to connect appliances to existing gas lines or plumbing. Record maintenance and repair work performed on appliances. Respond to emergency calls for problems such as gas leaks. Assemble new or reconditioned appliances. As part of appliance installation, disassemble and reinstall existing kitchen cabinets or assemble and install prefabricated kitchen cabinets and trim. Hang steel supports from beams or joists to hold hoses, vents, and gas pipes in place. Install appliances such as refrigerators, washing machines, and stoves. Set appliance thermostats and check to ensure that they are functioning properly. Refer to schematic drawings, product manuals, and troubleshooting guides to diagnose and repair problems. Clean and reinstall parts. Disassemble appliances so that problems can be diagnosed and repairs can be made. Light and adjust pilot lights on gas stoves and examine valves and burners for gas leakage and specified flame. Test and examine gas pipelines and equipment to locate leaks and faulty connections and to determine the pressure and flow of gas. Take measurements to determine whether appliances will fit in installation locations; perform minor carpentry work when necessary to ensure proper installation. Measure, cut, and thread pipe and connect it to feeder lines and equipment or appliances, using rules and hand tools. Reassemble units after repairs are made, making adjustments and cleaning and lubricating parts as needed.

GOE—Career Cluster/Interest Area: 13. Manufacturing. **Work Group:** 13.13. Machinery Repair. **Other Apprenticeable Jobs in This Work Group:** Control and Valve Installers and Repairers, Except Mechanical Door; Industrial Machinery Mechanics; Locksmiths and Safe Repairers; Maintenance Workers, Machinery; Mechanical Door Repairers; Millwrights; Signal and Track Switch Repairers. **Personality Type:** Realistic. These occupations frequently involve work activities that include practical, hands-on problems and solutions. They often deal with plants; animals; and real-world materials such as wood, tools, and machinery. Many of the occupations require working outside and don't involve a lot of paperwork or working closely with others.

Skills—Repairing; Installation; Troubleshooting; Technology Design; Systems Analysis; Equipment Maintenance; Science; Equipment Selection.

Education/Training Required (Nonapprenticeship Route): Long-term on-the-job training. **Related Knowledge/Courses—Sales and Marketing:** Principles and methods involved in showing, promoting, and selling products or services. This includes marketing strategies and tactics, product demonstration and sales techniques, and sales control systems. **Mechanical Devices:** Machines and tools, including their designs, uses, benefits, repair, and maintenance. **Customer and Personal Service:** Principles and processes for providing customer and personal services, including needs assessment techniques, quality service standards, alternative delivery systems, and customer satisfaction evaluation techniques. **Physics:** Physical principles, laws, and applications, including air, water, material dynamics, light, atomic principles, heat, electric theory, earth formations, and meteorological and related natural phenomena. **Economics and Accounting:** Economic and accounting principles and practices, the financial markets, banking, and the analysis and reporting of financial data. **Engineering and Technology:** Equipment, tools, and mechanical devices and their uses to produce motion, light, power, technology, and other applications.

Work Environment: Indoors; standing; kneeling, crouching, stooping, or crawling; using hands on objects, tools, or controls.

Human Resources Assistants, Except Payroll and Timekeeping

- ❋ Annual Earnings: $34,970
- ❋ Growth: 11.3%
- ❋ Annual Job Openings: 18,647
- ❋ Percentage of Women: 91.9%

Related Apprenticeship—Personnel Systems Management (2000 hrs. or competency).

Compile and keep personnel records. Record data for each employee, such as address, weekly earnings, absences, amount of sales or production, supervisory reports on ability, and date of and reason for termination. Compile and type reports from employment records. File employment records. Search employee files and furnish information to authorized persons. Explain company personnel policies, benefits, and procedures to employees or job applicants. Process, verify, and maintain documentation relating to personnel activities such as staffing, recruitment, training, grievances, performance evaluations, and classifications. Record data for each employee, including such information as addresses, weekly earnings, absences, amount of sales or production, supervisory reports on performance, and dates of and reasons for terminations. Process and review employment applications to evaluate qualifications or eligibility of applicants. Answer questions regarding examinations, eligibility, salaries, benefits, and other pertinent information. Examine employee files to answer inquiries and provide information for personnel actions. Gather personnel records from other departments or employees. Search employee files to obtain information for authorized persons and organizations such as credit bureaus and finance companies. Interview job applicants to obtain and verify information used to screen and evaluate them. Request information from law enforcement officials, previous employers, and other references to determine applicants' employment acceptability. Compile and prepare reports and documents pertaining to personnel activities. Inform job applicants of their acceptance or rejection of employment. Select applicants meeting specified job requirements and refer them to hiring personnel. Arrange for in-house and external training activities. Arrange for advertising or posting of job vacancies and notify eligible workers of position availability. Provide assistance in administering employee benefit programs and worker's compensation plans. Prepare badges, passes, and identification cards and perform other security-related duties. Administer and score applicant and employee aptitude, personality, and interest assessment instruments.

GOE—Career Cluster/Interest Area: 04. Business and Administration. **Work Group:** 04.07. Records and Materials Processing. **Other Apprenticeable Jobs in This Work Group:** Office Clerks, General; Postal Service Clerks; Production, Planning, and Expediting Clerks. **Personality Type:** Conventional. These occupations frequently involve following set procedures and routines and can include working with data and details more than with ideas. Usually there is a clear line of authority to follow.

Skills—Writing; Active Listening; Management of Personnel Resources.

Education/Training Required (Nonapprenticeship Route): Short-term on-the-job training. **Related Knowledge/Courses—Clerical Practices:** Administrative and clerical procedures and systems such as word-processing systems, filing and records management systems, stenography and transcription, forms, design principles, and other office procedures and terminology. **Personnel and Human Resources:** Principles and procedures for personnel recruitment; selection; training; compensation and benefits; labor relations and negotiation; and personnel information systems. **Customer and Personal Service:** Principles and processes for providing customer and personal services, including needs assessment

techniques, quality service standards, alternative delivery systems, and customer satisfaction evaluation techniques. **Computers and Electronics:** Electric circuit boards, processors, chips, and computer hardware and software, including applications and programming. **Economics and Accounting:** Economic and accounting principles and practices, the financial markets, banking, and the analysis and reporting of financial data. **Sociology and Anthropology:** Group behavior and dynamics; societal trends and influences; and cultures and their history, migrations, ethnicity, and origins.

Work Environment: Indoors; noisy; sitting.

Industrial Engineering Technicians

- ❋ Annual Earnings: $47,490
- ❋ Growth: 9.9%
- ❋ Annual Job Openings: 6,172
- ❋ Percentage of Women: 20.6%

Related Apprenticeships—Industrial Engineering Technician (8000 hrs.); Quality Control Technician (4000 hrs.).

Apply engineering theory and principles to problems of industrial layout or manufacturing production, usually under the direction of engineering staff. May study and record time, motion, method, and speed involved in performance of production, maintenance, clerical, and other worker operations for such purposes as establishing standard production rates or improving efficiency. Recommend revision to methods of operation, material handling, equipment layout, or other changes to increase production or improve standards. Study time, motion, methods, and speed involved in maintenance, production, and other operations to establish standard production rate and improve efficiency. Interpret engineering drawings, schematic diagrams, or formulas and confer with management or engineering staff to determine quality and reliability standards. Recommend modifications to existing quality or production standards to achieve optimum quality within limits of equipment capability. Aid in planning work assignments in accordance with worker performance, machine capacity, production schedules, and anticipated delays. Observe workers using equipment to verify that equipment is being operated and maintained according to quality assurance standards. Observe workers operating equipment or performing tasks to determine time involved and fatigue rate, using timing devices. Prepare charts, graphs, and diagrams to illustrate workflow, routing, floor layouts, material handling, and machine utilization. Evaluate data and write reports to validate or indicate deviations from existing standards. Read worker logs, product processing sheets, and specification sheets to verify that records adhere to quality assurance specifications. Prepare graphs or charts of data or enter data into computer for analysis. Record test data, applying statistical quality control procedures. Select products for tests at specified stages in production process and test products for performance characteristics and adherence to specifications. Compile and evaluate statistical data to determine and maintain quality and reliability of products.

GOE—Career Cluster/Interest Area: 04. Business and Administration. **Work Group:** 04.05. Accounting, Auditing, and Analytical Support. **Other Apprenticeable Jobs in This Work Group:** No others in group. **Personality Type:** Investigative. These occupations frequently involve working with ideas and require an extensive amount of thinking. They can involve searching for facts and figuring out problems mentally.

Skills—Operations Analysis; Technology Design; Repairing; Troubleshooting; Systems Evaluation; Systems Analysis; Quality Control Analysis; Mathematics.

Education/Training Required (Nonapprenticeship Route): Associate degree. **Related Knowledge/Courses—Production and Processing:** Inputs, outputs, raw materials, waste, quality control, costs, and techniques for maximizing the manufacture and distribution of goods. **Engineering and Technology:** Equipment, tools, and mechanical devices and their uses to produce motion, light, power, technology, and other applications. **Design:** Design techniques, principles, tools, and instruments involved in the production and use of precision technical plans, blueprints, drawings, and models. **Clerical Practices:** Administrative and clerical procedures and systems such as word-processing systems, filing and records management systems, stenography and transcription, forms, design principles, and other office procedures and terminology. **Mathematics:** Numbers and their operations and interrelationships, including arithmetic, algebra, geometry, calculus, and statistics and their applications. **Mechanical Devices:** Machines and tools, including their designs, uses, benefits, repair, and maintenance.

Work Environment: Indoors; noisy; contaminants; hazardous equipment; standing; walking and running.

Industrial Machinery Mechanics

- ❋ Annual Earnings: $42,350
- ❋ Growth: 9.0%
- ❋ Annual Job Openings: 23,361
- ❋ Percentage of Women: 3.8%

Related Apprenticeships—Auto-Maintenance-Equipment Servicer (8000 hrs.); Aviation Support Equipment Repairer (8000 hrs.); Bakery-Machine Mechanic (6000 hrs.); Canal Equipment Mechanic (4000 hrs.); Composing-Room Machinist (12000 hrs.); Conveyor Maintenance Mechanic (4000 hrs.); Cooling Tower Technician (4000 hrs.); Electric-Product-Line Maintenance Mechanic (2000 hrs.); Forge-Shop-Machine Repairer (6000 hrs.); Fuel System Maintenance Worker (4000 hrs.); Hydraulic Repairer (8000 hrs.); Hydraulic-Press Servicer (Ordinance) (4000 hrs.); Hydroelectric-Machinery Mechanic (6000 hrs.); Industrial Machinery Systems Technician (4000 hrs.); Laundry-Machine Mechanic (6000 hrs.); Machine Fixer (Carpet and Rug) (8000 hrs.); Machine Repairer, Maintenance (8000 hrs.); Machinist, Linotype (8000 hrs.); Maintenance Mechanic (Any Industry) (8000 hrs.); Maintenance Mechanic (Grain and Feed) (4000 hrs.); Maintenance Mechanic, Compgas (8000 hrs.); Overhauler (Textile) (4000 hrs.); Pinsetter Adjuster, Automatic (6000 hrs.); Pneumatic Tool Repairer (8000 hrs.); Pneumatic Tube Repairer (4000 hrs.); Powerhouse Mechanic (8000 hrs.); Pump Erector (Construction) (4000 hrs.); Pump Servicer (6000 hrs.); Repairer I (Chemicals) (8000 hrs.); Repairer, Welding Equipment (4000 hrs.); Repairer, Welding Systems and Equipment (6000 hrs.); Rubberizing Mechanic (8000 hrs.); Scale Mechanic (8000 hrs.); Sewing Machine Repairer (6000 hrs.); Stoker Erector and Servicer (8000 hrs.); Treatment Plant Mechanic (6000 hrs.).

Repair, install, adjust, or maintain industrial production and processing machinery or refinery and pipeline distribution systems. Disassemble machinery and equipment to remove parts and make repairs. Repair and replace broken or malfunctioning components of machinery and equipment. Repair and maintain the operating condition of industrial production and processing machinery and equipment. Examine parts for defects such as breakage and excessive wear. Reassemble equipment after completion of inspections, testing, or repairs. Observe and test the operation of machinery and equipment to diagnose malfunctions, using voltmeters and other testing devices. Operate newly repaired machinery and equipment to verify the adequacy of repairs. Clean, lubricate, and adjust parts, equipment, and machinery. Analyze test results, machine error messages, and information obtained from operators to diagnose equipment problems. Record repairs and maintenance performed. Study blueprints and manufacturers' manuals to determine correct installation and operation of machinery. Record parts and materials used, ordering or requisitioning new parts and materials as necessary. Cut and weld metal to repair broken metal parts, fabricate new parts, and assemble new equipment. Demonstrate equipment functions and features to machine operators. Enter codes and instructions to program computer-controlled machinery.

GOE—Career Cluster/Interest Area: 13. Manufacturing. **Work Group:** 13.13. Machinery Repair. **Other Apprenticeable Jobs in This Work Group:** Control and Valve Installers and Repairers, Except Mechanical Door; Home Appliance Repairers; Locksmiths and Safe Repairers; Maintenance Workers, Machinery; Mechanical Door Repairers; Millwrights; Signal and Track Switch Repairers. **Personality Type:**

Realistic. These occupations frequently involve work activities that include practical, hands-on problems and solutions. They often deal with plants; animals; and real-world materials such as wood, tools, and machinery. Many of the occupations require working outside and don't involve a lot of paperwork or working closely with others.

Skills—Installation; Repairing; Equipment Maintenance; Operation Monitoring; Troubleshooting; Technology Design; Equipment Selection; Operation and Control.

Education/Training Required (Nonapprenticeship Route): Long-term on-the-job training. **Related Knowledge/Courses—Mechanical Devices:** Machines and tools, including their designs, uses, benefits, repair, and maintenance. **Engineering and Technology:** Equipment, tools, and mechanical devices and their uses to produce motion, light, power, technology, and other applications. **Building and Construction:** Materials, methods, and the appropriate tools to construct objects, structures, and buildings. **Design:** Design techniques, principles, tools, and instruments involved in the production and use of precision technical plans, blueprints, drawings, and models. **Chemistry:** The composition, structure, and properties of substances and of the chemical processes and transformations that they undergo. This includes uses of chemicals and their interactions, danger signs, production techniques, and disposal methods. **Physics:** Physical principles, laws, and applications, including air, water, material dynamics, light, atomic principles, heat, electric theory, earth formations, and meteorological and related natural phenomena.

Work Environment: Noisy; contaminants; hazardous conditions; hazardous equipment; standing; using hands on objects, tools, or controls.

Industrial Production Managers

- ❀ Annual Earnings: $80,560
- ❀ Growth: –5.9%
- ❀ Annual Job Openings: 14,889
- ❀ Percentage of Women: 16.4%

Related Apprenticeship—Wine Maker (Vinous Liquor) (4000 hrs.).

Plan, direct, or coordinate the work activities and resources necessary for manufacturing products in accordance with specifications for cost, quality, and quantity. Direct and coordinate production, processing, distribution, and marketing activities of industrial organization. Review processing schedules and production orders to make decisions concerning inventory requirements, staffing requirements, work procedures, and duty assignments, considering budgetary limitations and time constraints. Review operations and confer with technical or administrative staff to resolve production or processing problems. Develop and implement production tracking and quality control systems, analyzing reports on production, quality control, maintenance, and other aspects of operations to detect problems. Hire, train, evaluate, and discharge staff, and resolve personnel grievances. Set and monitor product standards, examining samples of raw products or directing testing during processing, to ensure finished products are of prescribed quality. Prepare and maintain production reports and personnel records. Coordinate and recommend procedures for maintenance or modification of facilities and equipment, including the replacement of machines. Initiate and coordinate inventory and cost control programs.

Institute employee suggestion or involvement programs. Maintain current knowledge of the quality control field, relying on current literature pertaining to materials use, technological advances, and statistical studies. Review plans and confer with research and support staff to develop new products and processes. Develop budgets and approve expenditures for supplies, materials, and human resources, ensuring that materials, labor, and equipment are used efficiently to meet production targets. Negotiate prices of materials with suppliers.

GOE—Career Cluster/Interest Area: 13. Manufacturing. **Work Group:** 13.01. Managerial Work in Manufacturing. **Other Apprenticeable Jobs in This Work Group:** No others in group. **Personality Type:** Enterprising. These occupations frequently involve starting up and carrying out projects and can involve leading people and making many decisions. They sometimes require risk taking and often deal with business.

Skills—Management of Personnel Resources; Systems Analysis; Systems Evaluation; Management of Financial Resources; Management of Material Resources; Negotiation; Operation Monitoring; Monitoring.

Education/Training Required (Nonapprenticeship Route): Work experience in a related occupation. **Related Knowledge/Courses—Production and Processing:** Inputs, outputs, raw materials, waste, quality control, costs, and techniques for maximizing the manufacture and distribution of goods. **Mechanical Devices:** Machines and tools, including their designs, uses, benefits, repair, and maintenance. **Administration and Management:** Principles and processes involved in business and organizational planning, coordination, and execution. This includes strategic planning, resource allocation,

manpower modeling, leadership techniques, and production methods. **Design:** Design techniques, principles, tools, and instruments involved in the production and use of precision technical plans, blueprints, drawings, and models. **Personnel and Human Resources:** Principles and procedures for personnel recruitment; selection; training; compensation and benefits; labor relations and negotiation; and personnel information systems. **Engineering and Technology:** Equipment, tools, and mechanical devices and their uses to produce motion, light, power, technology, and other applications.

Work Environment: Indoors; sitting.

Inspectors, Testers, Sorters, Samplers, and Weighers

- ❋ Annual Earnings: $30,310
- ❋ Growth: –7.0%
- ❋ Annual Job Openings: 75,361
- ❋ Percentage of Women: 38.8%

Related Apprenticeships—Airplane Inspector (6000 hrs.); Automobile Tester (8000 hrs.); Automobile-Repair-Service Estimator (8000 hrs.); Cable Tester (Telephone and Telegraph) (8000 hrs.); Calibrator (Military) (4000 hrs.); Complaint Inspector (8000 hrs.); Diesel Engine Tester (8000 hrs.); Electric Meter Tester (8000 hrs.); Electric-Distribution Checker (4000 hrs.); Electronics Tester (6000 hrs.); Experimental Assembler (4000 hrs.); Grader (Woodworking) (8000 hrs.); Hydrometer Calibrator (4000 hrs.); Inspector, Electromechanic (8000 hrs.); Inspector, Metal Fabricating (8000 hrs.); Inspector, Outside Product (8000 hrs.); Inspector, Precision (4000 hrs.); Inspector, Set-Up and Lay-Out (8000 hrs.); Operational Test Mechanic (6000 hrs.); Quality Control Inspector (4000 hrs.);

Radiographer (8000 hrs.); Relay Tester (8000 hrs.); Rubber Tester (8000 hrs.); Testing and Regulating Technician (8000 hrs.); Thermometer Tester (2000 hrs.); Trouble Locator, Test Desk (4000 hrs.); X-ray Equipment Tester (4000 hrs.).

Inspect, test, sort, sample, or weigh nonagricultural raw materials or processed, machined, fabricated, or assembled parts or products for defects, wear, and deviations from specifications. May use precision measuring instruments and complex test equipment. Discard or reject products, materials, and equipment not meeting specifications. Analyze and interpret blueprints, data, manuals, and other materials to determine specifications, inspection and testing procedures, adjustment and certification methods, formulas, and measuring instruments required. Inspect, test, or measure materials, products, installations, and work for conformance to specifications. Notify supervisors and other personnel of production problems and assist in identifying and correcting these problems. Discuss inspection results with those responsible for products and recommend necessary corrective actions. Record inspection or test data, such as weights, temperatures, grades, or moisture content, and quantities inspected or graded. Mark items with details such as grade and acceptance or rejection status. Observe and monitor production operations and equipment to ensure conformance to specifications and make or order necessary process or assembly adjustments. Measure dimensions of products to verify conformance to specifications, using measuring instruments such as rulers, calipers, gauges, or micrometers. Analyze test data and make computations as necessary to determine test results. Collect or select samples for testing or for use as models. Check arriving materials to ensure that they match purchase orders and submit discrepancy reports when problems are found. Compare colors, shapes, textures, or grades of products or materials with color charts, templates, or samples to verify conformance to standards. Write test and inspection reports describing results, recommendations, and needed repairs. Read dials and meters to verify that equipment is functioning at specified levels. Remove defects, such as chips and burrs, and lap corroded or pitted surfaces. Clean, maintain, repair, and calibrate measuring instruments and test equipment such as dial indicators, fixed gauges, and height gauges. Adjust, clean, or repair products or processing equipment to correct defects found during inspections. Stack and arrange tested products for further processing, shipping, or packaging and transport products to other work stations as necessary.

GOE—Career Cluster/Interest Area: 13. Manufacturing. **Work Group:** 13.07. Production Quality Control. **Other Apprenticeable Jobs in This Work Group:** No others in group. **Personality Type:** Conventional. These occupations frequently involve following set procedures and routines and can include working with data and details more than with ideas. Usually there is a clear line of authority to follow.

Skills—Quality Control Analysis; Operation Monitoring; Operation and Control; Repairing; Systems Evaluation; Troubleshooting.

Education/Training Required (Nonapprenticeship Route): Moderate-term on-the-job training. **Related Knowledge/Course—Production and Processing:** Inputs, outputs, raw materials, waste, quality control, costs, and techniques for maximizing the manufacture and distribution of goods.

Work Environment: Noisy; standing; using hands on objects, tools, or controls; repetitive motions.

Insulation Workers, Floor, Ceiling, and Wall

- ❁ Annual Earnings: $31,280
- ❁ Growth: 8.4%
- ❁ Annual Job Openings: 6,580
- ❁ Percentage of Women: 3.1%

Related Apprenticeships—Cork Insulator, Refrigeration Plant (8000 hrs.); Insulation Worker (8000 hrs.).

Line and cover structures with insulating materials. May work with batt, roll, or blown insulation materials. Distribute insulating materials evenly into small spaces within floors, ceilings, or walls, using blowers and hose attachments or cement mortars. Cover and line structures with blown or rolled forms of materials to insulate against cold, heat, or moisture, using saws, knives, rasps, trowels, blowers, and other tools and implements. Move controls, buttons, or levers to start blowers and regulate flow of materials through nozzles. Remove old insulation such as asbestos, following safety procedures. Read blueprints and select appropriate insulation, based on space characteristics and the heat-retaining or -excluding characteristics of the material. Prepare surfaces for insulation application by brushing or spreading on adhesives, cement, or asphalt or by attaching metal pins to surfaces. Measure and cut insulation for covering surfaces, using tape measures, hand saws, power saws, knives, or scissors. Fit, wrap, staple, or glue insulating materials to structures or surfaces, using hand tools or wires. Fill blower hoppers with insulating materials. Cover, seal, or finish insulated surfaces or access holes with plastic covers, canvas strips, sealants, tape, cement, or asphalt mastic.

GOE—Career Cluster/Interest Area: 02. Architecture and Construction. **Work Group:** 02.04. Construction Crafts. **Other Apprenticeable Jobs in This Work Group:** Boilermakers; Brickmasons and Blockmasons; Carpet Installers; Cement Masons and Concrete Finishers; Construction Carpenters; Crane and Tower Operators; Drywall and Ceiling Tile Installers; Electricians; Fence Erectors; Floor Layers, Except Carpet, Wood, and Hard Tiles; Glaziers; Insulation Workers, Mechanical; Operating Engineers and Other Construction Equipment Operators; Painters, Construction and Maintenance; Paperhangers; Paving, Surfacing, and Tamping Equipment Operators; Pipe Fitters and Steamfitters; Plasterers and Stucco Masons; Plumbers; Reinforcing Iron and Rebar Workers; Riggers; Roofers; Rough Carpenters; Sheet Metal Workers; Stone Cutters and Carvers, Manufacturing; Stonemasons; Structural Iron and Steel Workers; Tapers; Terrazzo Workers and Finishers; Tile and Marble Setters. **Personality Type:** Realistic. These occupations frequently involve work activities that include practical, hands-on problems and solutions. They often deal with plants; animals; and real-world materials such as wood, tools, and machinery. Many of the occupations require working outside and don't involve a lot of paperwork or working closely with others.

Skills—Installation; Repairing; Management of Material Resources; Equipment Maintenance; Mathematics; Equipment Selection.

Education/Training Required (Nonapprenticeship Route): Moderate-term on-the-job training. **Related Knowledge/Courses—Building and Construction:** Materials, methods, and the appropriate tools to construct objects, structures, and buildings. **Production and Processing:** Inputs, outputs, raw materials, waste, quality control, costs, and techniques for maximizing the manufacture and distribution of goods. **Transportation:** Principles and methods for moving people or goods by air, rail, sea, or road, including their relative costs, advantages, and limitations. **Personnel and Human Resources:** Principles and procedures for personnel recruitment; selection; training; compensation and benefits; labor relations and negotiation; and personnel information systems. **Design:** Design techniques, principles, tools, and instruments involved in the production and use of precision technical plans, blueprints, drawings, and models. **Economics and Accounting:** Economic and accounting principles and practices, the financial markets, banking, and the analysis and reporting of financial data.

Work Environment: Indoors; contaminants; standing; using hands on objects, tools, or controls.

Insulation Workers, Mechanical

- ❀ Annual Earnings: $36,570
- ❀ Growth: 8.6%
- ❀ Annual Job Openings: 5,787
- ❀ Percentage of Women: 3.1%

Related Apprenticeship—Pipe Coverer and Insulator (8000 hrs.).

Apply insulating materials to pipes or ductwork or other mechanical systems to help control and maintain temperature. Cover, seal, or finish insulated surfaces or access holes with plastic covers, canvas strips, sealants, tape, cement, or asphalt mastic. Measure and cut insulation for covering surfaces, using tape measures, handsaws, knives, and scissors. Prepare surfaces for insulation application by brushing or spreading on adhesives, cement, or asphalt, or by attaching metal pins to surfaces. Select appropriate insulation such as fiberglass, Styrofoam, or cork, based on the heat-retaining or -excluding characteristics of the material. Read blueprints and specifications to determine job requirements. Install sheet metal around insulated pipes with screws to protect the insulation from weather conditions or physical damage. Determine the amounts and types of insulation needed, and methods of installation, based on factors such as location, surface shape, and equipment use. Apply, remove, and repair insulation on industrial equipment, pipes, ductwork, or other mechanical systems, such as heat exchangers, tanks, and vessels, to help control noise and maintain temperatures. Remove or seal off old asbestos insulation, following safety procedures. Move controls, buttons, or levers to start blowers and to regulate flow of materials through nozzles. Fill blower hoppers with insulating materials. Distribute insulating materials evenly into small spaces within floors, ceilings, or walls, using blowers and hose attachments or cement mortar. Fit insulation around obstructions, and shape insulating materials and protective coverings as required.

GOE—Career Cluster/Interest Area: 02. Architecture and Construction. **Work Group:** 02.04. Construction Crafts. **Other Apprenticeable Jobs in This Work Group:** Boilermakers; Brickmasons and Blockmasons; Carpet Installers; Cement Masons and Concrete Finishers; Construction Carpenters; Crane and Tower Operators; Drywall and Ceiling Tile Installers; Electricians; Fence Erectors; Floor Layers, Except Carpet, Wood, and Hard Tiles; Glaziers; Insulation Workers, Floor, Ceiling, and

Wall; Operating Engineers and Other Construction Equipment Operators; Painters, Construction and Maintenance; Paperhangers; Paving, Surfacing, and Tamping Equipment Operators; Pipe Fitters and Steamfitters; Plasterers and Stucco Masons; Plumbers; Reinforcing Iron and Rebar Workers; Riggers; Roofers; Rough Carpenters; Sheet Metal Workers; Stone Cutters and Carvers, Manufacturing; Stonemasons; Structural Iron and Steel Workers; Tapers; Terrazzo Workers and Finishers; Tile and Marble Setters. **Personality Type:** Realistic. These occupations frequently involve work activities that include practical, hands-on problems and solutions. They often deal with plants; animals; and real-world materials such as wood, tools, and machinery. Many of the occupations require working outside and don't involve a lot of paperwork or working closely with others.

Skills—Installation; Repairing; Mathematics; Coordination; Management of Personnel Resources; Equipment Selection; Management of Material Resources; Equipment Maintenance.

Education/Training Required (Nonapprenticeship Route): Moderate-term on-the-job training. **Related Knowledge/Courses—Building and Construction:** Materials, methods, and the appropriate tools to construct objects, structures, and buildings. **Design:** Design techniques, principles, tools, and instruments involved in the production and use of precision technical plans, blueprints, drawings, and models. **Mechanical Devices:** Machines and tools, including their designs, uses, benefits, repair, and maintenance. **Transportation:** Principles and methods for moving people or goods by air, rail, sea, or road, including their relative costs, advantages, and limitations. **Education and Training:** Instructional methods and training

techniques, including curriculum design principles, learning theory, group and individual teaching techniques, design of individual development plans, and test design principles. **Public Safety and Security:** Weaponry; public safety; security operations, rules, regulations, precautions, and prevention; and the protection of people, data, and property.

Work Environment: Indoors; contaminants; standing; using hands on objects, tools, or controls.

Interior Designers

- ❋ Annual Earnings: $43,970
- ❋ Growth: 19.5%
- ❋ Annual Job Openings: 8,434
- ❋ Percentage of Women: 55.5%

Related Apprenticeship—Interior Designer (4000 hrs.).

Plan, design, and furnish interiors of residential, commercial, or industrial buildings. Formulate design that is practical, aesthetic, and conducive to intended purposes, such as raising productivity, selling merchandise, or improving lifestyle. May specialize in a particular field, style, or phase of interior design. Estimate material requirements and costs and present design to client for approval. Confer with client to determine factors affecting planning interior environments, such as budget, architectural preferences, and purpose and function. Advise client on interior design factors such as space planning, layout, and utilization of furnishings or equipment and color coordination. Select or design and purchase furnishings, artwork, and accessories. Formulate environmental plan to be practical, esthetic, and conducive to intended purposes such as raising productivity or selling merchandise. Subcontract fabrication, installation, and arrangement of carpeting, fixtures, accessories, draperies, paint and wall coverings, artwork, furniture, and related items. Render design ideas in form of paste-ups or drawings. Plan and design interior environments for boats, planes, buses, trains, and other enclosed spaces.

GOE—Career Cluster/Interest Area: 03. Arts and Communication. **Work Group:** 03.05. Design. **Other Apprenticeable Jobs in This Work Group:** Fashion Designers; Floral Designers; Merchandise Displayers and Window Trimmers. **Personality Type:** Artistic. These occupations frequently involve working with forms, designs, and patterns. They often require self-expression, and the work can be done without following a clear set of rules.

Skills—Installation; Management of Financial Resources; Persuasion; Operations Analysis; Negotiation; Active Learning; Mathematics; Speaking.

Education/Training Required (Nonapprenticeship Route): Associate degree. **Related Knowledge/Courses—Design:** Design techniques, principles, tools, and instruments involved in the production and use of precision technical plans, blueprints, drawings, and models. **Sales and Marketing:** Principles and methods involved in showing, promoting, and selling products or services. This includes marketing strategies and tactics, product demonstration and sales techniques, and sales control systems. **Building and Construction:** Materials, methods, and the appropriate tools to construct objects, structures, and buildings. **Clerical Practices:** Administrative and clerical procedures and systems such as word-processing systems, filing and records management

systems, stenography and transcription, forms, design principles, and other office procedures and terminology. **Fine Arts:** Theory and techniques required to produce, compose, and perform works of music, dance, visual arts, drama, and sculpture. **Administration and Management:** Principles and processes involved in business and organizational planning, coordination, and execution. This includes strategic planning, resource allocation, manpower modeling, leadership techniques, and production methods.

Work Environment: Indoors; sitting.

Jewelers

- ❋ Annual Earnings: $31,200
- ❋ Growth: –2.2%
- ❋ Annual Job Openings: 7,375
- ❋ Percentage of Women: 30.4%

Our sources did not provide separate job openings data for this occupation. The job openings listed here are shared with Gem and Diamond Workers and with Precious Metal Workers.

Related Apprenticeships—Bench Hand (Jewelry–Silver) (4000 hrs.); Bracelet and Brooch Maker (8000 hrs.); Caster (Jewelry–Silver) (4000 hrs.); Engine Turner (Jewelry) (4000 hrs.); Jeweler (4000 hrs.); Model Maker II (Jewelry) (8000 hrs.); Mold Maker I (Jewelry) (8000 hrs.); Mold Maker II (Jewelry) (4000 hrs.); Solderer (Jewelry) (6000 hrs.); Stone Setter (Jewelry) (8000 hrs.).

Fabricate and repair jewelry articles. Make models or molds to create jewelry items. Plate articles such as jewelry pieces and watch dials, using silver, gold, nickel, or other metals. Burn grooves or crevices in molds to correct defects, using soldering guns. Immerse gemstones in chemical solutions to determine specific gravity and other key properties necessary for identification and appraisal. Position stones and metal pieces and set, mount, and secure items in place, using setting and hand tools. Pour molten metal alloys or other materials into molds to cast models of jewelry. Remove mold castings from metal or jewelry workpieces and place workpieces in water or on trays to cool. Melt and roll out metal into sheets or bars and stamp out jewelry such as gold and silver chains, using presses or dies. Select and acquire metals and gems for designs. Record the weights and processing times of finished pieces. Press models into clay and build up clay around exposed parts of models to retain plaster. Mark and drill holes in jewelry mountings to center stones according to design specifications. Grade stones based on their color, perfection, and quality of cut. Examine gemstone surfaces and internal structures to evaluate genuineness, quality, and value, using polariscopes, refractometers, and other optical instruments. Determine appraised values of diamonds and other gemstones based on price guides, market fluctuations, and stone grades and rarity. Design and fabricate molds, models, and machine accessories and modify hand tools used to cast metal and jewelry pieces. Smooth soldered joints and rough spots, using hand files and emery paper, and polish smoothed areas with polishing wheels or buffing wire. Compute costs of labor and materials to determine production costs of products and articles. Build sand molds in flasks, following patterns, and heat flasks to dry and harden molds, using furnaces or torches. Alter existing jewelry mountings to reposition jewels or to adjust mountings. Soften metal to be used in designs by heating it with a gas torch and shape it, using hammers and dies. Buy and sell jewelry or serve as agents between buyers and sellers.

GOE—Career Cluster/Interest Area: 13. Manufacturing. **Work Group:** 13.06. Production Precision Work. **Other Apprenticeable Jobs in This Work Group:** Bookbinders; Dental Laboratory Technicians; Electrical and Electronic Equipment Assemblers; Electromechanical Equipment Assemblers; Engine and Other Machine Assemblers; Gem and Diamond Workers; Medical Appliance Technicians; Molding, Coremaking, and Casting Machine Setters, Operators, and Tenders, Metal and Plastic; Ophthalmic Laboratory Technicians; Precious Metal Workers. **Personality Type:** Realistic. These occupations frequently involve work activities that include practical, hands-on problems and solutions. They often deal with plants; animals; and real-world materials such as wood, tools, and machinery. Many of the occupations require working outside and don't involve a lot of paperwork or working closely with others.

Skills—Management of Financial Resources; Repairing; Equipment Selection; Equipment Maintenance; Management of Material Resources; Technology Design; Installation; Operations Analysis.

Education/Training Required (Nonapprenticeship Route): Postsecondary vocational training. **Related Knowledge/Courses—Design:** Design techniques, principles, tools, and instruments involved in the production and use of precision technical plans, blueprints, drawings, and models. **Sales and Marketing:** Principles and methods involved in showing, promoting, and selling products or services. This includes marketing strategies and tactics, product demonstration and sales techniques, and sales control systems. **Production and Processing:** Inputs, outputs, raw materials, waste, quality control, costs, and techniques for maximizing the manufacture and distribution of goods. **Chemistry:** The composition, structure, and properties of substances and of the chemical processes and transformations that they undergo. This includes uses of chemicals and their interactions, danger signs, production techniques, and disposal methods. **Engineering and Technology:** Equipment, tools, and mechanical devices and their uses to produce motion, light, power, technology, and other applications. **Mechanical Devices:** Machines and tools, including their designs, uses, benefits, repair, and maintenance.

Work Environment: Indoors; sitting; using hands on objects, tools, or controls; repetitive motions.

Landscaping and Groundskeeping Workers

- ❋ Annual Earnings: $22,240
- ❋ Growth: 18.1%
- ❋ Annual Job Openings: 307,138
- ❋ Percentage of Women: 6.2%

Related Apprenticeships—Greenskeeper II (4000 hrs.); Landscape Gardener (8000 hrs.); Landscape Management Technician (2000 hrs.); Landscape Technician (4000 hrs.).

Landscape or maintain grounds of property, using hand or power tools or equipment. Workers typically perform a variety of tasks, which may include any combination of the following: sod laying, mowing, trimming, planting, watering, fertilizing, digging, raking, sprinkler installation, and installation of mortarless segmental concrete masonry wall units. Operate powered equipment such as mowers, tractors, twin-axle vehicles, snowblowers, chain saws, electric clippers, sod cutters, and pruning saws. Mow and edge lawns, using power mowers and edgers. Shovel snow from walks, driveways, and parking lots and spread salt in those areas. Care for established lawns by mulching; aerating; weeding; grubbing and removing thatch; and trimming and edging around flower beds, walks, and walls. Use hand tools such as shovels, rakes, pruning saws, saws, hedge and brush trimmers, and axes. Prune and trim trees, shrubs, and hedges, using shears, pruners, or chain saws. Maintain and repair tools; equipment; and structures such as buildings, greenhouses, fences, and benches, using hand and power tools. Gather and remove litter. Mix and spray or spread fertilizers, herbicides, or insecticides onto grass, shrubs, and trees, using hand or automatic sprayers or spreaders. Provide proper upkeep of sidewalks, driveways, parking lots, fountains, planters, burial sites, and other grounds features. Water lawns, trees, and plants, using portable sprinkler systems, hoses, or watering cans. Trim and pick flowers and clean flowerbeds. Rake, mulch, and compost leaves. Plant seeds, bulbs, foliage, flowering plants, grass, ground covers, trees, and shrubs and apply mulch for protection, using gardening tools. Follow planned landscaping designs to determine where to lay sod, sow grass, or plant flowers and foliage. Decorate gardens with stones and plants. Maintain irrigation systems, including winterizing the systems and starting them up in spring. Care for natural turf fields, making sure the underlying soil has the required composition to allow proper drainage and to support the grasses used on the fields. Use irrigation methods to adjust the amount of water consumption and to prevent waste. Haul or spread topsoil and spread straw over seeded soil to hold soil in place. Advise customers on plant selection and care. Care for artificial turf fields, periodically removing the turf and replacing cushioning pads and vacuuming and disinfecting the turf after use to prevent the growth of harmful bacteria.

GOE—Career Cluster/Interest Area: 01. Agriculture and Natural Resources. **Work Group:** 01.05. Nursery, Groundskeeping, and Pest Control. **Other Apprenticeable Jobs in This Work Group:** Pest Control Workers; Pesticide Handlers, Sprayers, and Applicators, Vegetation; Tree Trimmers and Pruners. **Personality Type:** Realistic. These occupations frequently involve work activities that include practical, hands-on problems and solutions. They often deal with plants; animals; and real-world materials such as wood, tools, and machinery. Many of the occupations require working outside and don't involve a lot of paperwork or working closely with others.

Skills—Equipment Maintenance; Repairing; Operation Monitoring; Installation; Equipment Selection.

Education/Training Required (Nonapprenticeship Route): Short-term on-the-job training. **Related Knowledge/Course—Mechanical Devices:** Machines and tools, including their designs, uses, benefits, repair, and maintenance.

Work Environment: Outdoors; noisy; very hot or cold; contaminants; standing; using hands on objects, tools, or controls.

Legal Secretaries

- ❋ Annual Earnings: $38,810
- ❋ Growth: 11.7%
- ❋ Annual Job Openings: 38,682
- ❋ Percentage of Women: 96.9%

Related Apprenticeship—Legal Secretary (2000 hrs.).

Perform secretarial duties, utilizing legal terminology, procedures, and documents.

Prepare legal papers and correspondence, such as summonses, complaints, motions, and subpoenas. May also assist with legal research. Prepare and process legal documents and papers, such as summonses, subpoenas, complaints, appeals, motions, and pretrial agreements. Mail, fax, or arrange for delivery of legal correspondence to clients, witnesses, and court officials. Receive and place telephone calls. Schedule and make appointments. Make photocopies of correspondence, documents, and other printed matter. Organize and maintain law libraries, documents, and case files. Assist attorneys in collecting information such as employment, medical, and other records. Attend legal meetings, such as client interviews, hearings, or depositions, and take notes. Draft and type office memos. Review legal publications and perform database searches to identify laws and court decisions relevant to pending cases. Submit articles and information from searches to attorneys for review and approval for use. Complete various forms such as accident reports, trial and courtroom requests, and applications for clients.

GOE—Career Cluster/Interest Area: 04. Business and Administration. **Work Group:** 04.04. Secretarial Support. **Other Apprenticeable Jobs in This Work Group:** Medical Secretaries; Secretaries, Except Legal, Medical, and Executive. **Personality Type:** Conventional. These occupations frequently involve following set procedures and routines and can include working with data and details more than with ideas. Usually there is a clear line of authority to follow.

Skills—Writing; Reading Comprehension; Time Management; Social Perceptiveness; Judgment and Decision Making; Operation and Control; Active Listening; Speaking.

Education/Training Required (Nonapprenticeship Route): Associate degree. **Related Knowledge/Courses—Clerical Practices:** Administrative and clerical procedures and systems such as word-processing systems, filing and records management systems, stenography and transcription, forms, design principles, and other office procedures and terminology. **Law and Government:** Laws, legal codes, court procedures, precedents, government regulations, executive orders, agency rules, and the democratic political process. **Economics and Accounting:** Economic and accounting principles and practices, the financial markets, banking, and the analysis and reporting of financial data. **Computers and Electronics:** Electric circuit boards, processors, chips, and computer hardware and software, including applications and programming. **Customer and Personal Service:** Principles and processes for providing customer and personal services, including needs assessment techniques, quality service standards, alternative delivery systems, and customer satisfaction evaluation techniques.

Work Environment: Indoors; sitting; repetitive motions.

Licensed Practical and Licensed Vocational Nurses

- ❋ Annual Earnings: $37,940
- ❋ Growth: 14.0%
- ❋ Annual Job Openings: 70,610
- ❋ Percentage of Women: 94.2%

Related Apprenticeship—Nurse, Licensed Practical (2000 hrs.).

Care for ill, injured, convalescent, or disabled persons in hospitals, nursing homes, clinics, private homes, group homes, and similar institutions. **May work under the supervision of a registered nurse. Licensing required.** Administer prescribed medications or start intravenous fluids, recording times and amounts on patients' charts. Observe patients, charting and reporting changes in patients' conditions, such as adverse reactions to medication or treatment, and taking any necessary actions. Provide basic patient care and treatments such as taking temperatures or blood pressures, dressing wounds, treating bedsores, giving enemas or douches, rubbing with alcohol, massaging, or performing catheterizations. Sterilize equipment and supplies, using germicides, sterilizer, or autoclave. Answer patients' calls and determine how to assist them. Work as part of a health-care team to assess patient needs, plan and modify care, and implement interventions. Measure and record patients' vital signs, such as height, weight, temperature, blood pressure, pulse, and respiration. Collect samples such as blood, urine, and sputum from patients and perform routine laboratory tests on samples. Prepare patients for examinations, tests, or treatments and explain procedures. Assemble and use equipment such as catheters, tracheotomy tubes, and oxygen suppliers. Evaluate nursing intervention outcomes, conferring with other health-care team members as necessary. Record food and fluid intake and output. Help patients with bathing, dressing, maintaining personal hygiene, moving in bed, or standing and walking. Apply compresses, ice bags, and hot water bottles. Inventory and requisition supplies and instruments. Clean rooms and make beds. Supervise nurses' aides and assistants. Make appointments, keep records, and perform other clerical duties in doctors' offices and clinics. In private home settings, provide medical treatment and personal care, such as cooking for patients, keeping their rooms orderly, seeing that patients are comfortable and in good spirits, and instructing family members in simple nursing tasks. Set up equipment and prepare medical treatment rooms. Prepare food trays and examine them for conformance to prescribed diet. Wash and dress bodies of deceased persons. Assist in delivery, care, and feeding of infants.

GOE—Career Cluster/Interest Area: 08. Health Science. **Work Group:** 08.08. Patient Care and Assistance. **Other Apprenticeable Jobs in This Work Group:** Home Health Aides; Nursing Aides, Orderlies, and Attendants. **Personality Type:** Social. These occupations frequently involve working with, communicating with, and teaching people and often involve helping or providing service to others.

Skills—Service Orientation; Systems Analysis; Management of Personnel Resources; Social Perceptiveness; Systems Evaluation.

Education/Training Required (Nonapprenticeship Route): Postsecondary vocational training. **Related Knowledge/Courses—Psychology:** Human behavior and performance, mental processes, psychological research methods, and the assessment and treatment of behavioral and affective disorders. **Medicine and Dentistry:** The information and techniques needed to diagnose and treat injuries, diseases, and deformities. This includes symptoms, treatment alternatives, drug properties and interactions, and preventive health-care measures. **Therapy and Counseling:** Information and techniques needed to rehabilitate physical and mental ailments and to provide career guidance, including alternative treatments, rehabilitation equipment and its proper use, and methods to evaluate treatment effects. **Biology:** Plant and animal living tissue, cells, organisms, and entities, including their functions, interdependencies, and interactions with each other and the environment. **Philosophy and Theology:** Different philosophical systems and religions, including their basic principles, values, ethics, ways of thinking, customs, and practices and their impact on human culture. **Customer and Personal Service:** Principles and processes for providing customer and personal services, including needs assessment techniques, quality service standards, alternative delivery systems, and customer satisfaction evaluation techniques.

Work Environment: Indoors; disease or infections; standing; walking and running.

Locksmiths and Safe Repairers

* Annual Earnings: $33,230
* Growth: 22.1%
* Annual Job Openings: 3,545
* Percentage of Women: 13.9%

Related Apprenticeships—Locksmith (8000 hrs.); Safe and Vault Service Mechanic (8000 hrs.).

Repair and open locks, make keys, change locks and safe combinations, and install and repair safes. Cut new or duplicate keys, using keycutting machines. Keep records of company locks and keys. Insert new or repaired tumblers into locks to change combinations. Move picklocks in cylinders to open door locks without keys. Disassemble mechanical or electrical locking devices and repair or replace worn tumblers, springs, and other parts, using hand tools. Repair and adjust safes, vault doors, and vault components, using hand tools, lathes, drill presses, and welding and acetylene cutting apparatus. Install safes, vault doors, and deposit boxes according to blueprints, using equipment such as powered drills, taps, dies, truck cranes, and dollies. Open safe locks by drilling. Remove interior and exterior finishes on safes and vaults and spray on new finishes.

GOE—Career Cluster/Interest Area: 13. Manufacturing. **Work Group:** 13.13. Machinery Repair. **Other Apprenticeable Jobs in This Work Group:** Control and Valve Installers and Repairers, Except Mechanical Door; Home Appliance Repairers; Industrial Machinery Mechanics; Maintenance Workers, Machinery; Mechanical Door Repairers; Millwrights; Signal and Track Switch Repairers. **Personality Type:** Realistic. These occupations frequently involve work activities that include practical, hands-on problems and solutions. They often deal with plants; animals; and real-world materials such as wood, tools, and machinery. Many of the occupations require working outside and don't involve a lot of paperwork or working closely with others.

Skills—Installation; Repairing; Equipment Maintenance; Troubleshooting; Equipment Selection; Service Orientation; Technology Design; Management of Material Resources.

Education/Training Required (Nonapprenticeship Route): Moderate-term on-the-job training. **Related Knowledge/Courses—Sales and Marketing:** Principles and methods involved in showing, promoting, and selling products or services. This includes marketing strategies and tactics, product demonstration and sales techniques, and sales control systems. **Clerical Practices:** Administrative and clerical procedures and systems such as word-processing systems, filing and records management systems, stenography and transcription, forms, design principles, and other office procedures and terminology. **Customer and Personal Service:** Principles and processes for providing customer and personal services, including needs assessment techniques, quality service standards, alternative delivery systems,

and customer satisfaction evaluation techniques. **Administration and Management:** Principles and processes involved in business and organizational planning, coordination, and execution. This includes strategic planning, resource allocation, manpower modeling, leadership techniques, and production methods. **Mechanical Devices:** Machines and tools, including their designs, uses, benefits, repair, and maintenance. **Public Safety and Security:** Weaponry; public safety; security operations, rules, regulations, precautions, and prevention; and the protection of people, data, and property.

Work Environment: More often outdoors than indoors; noisy; very bright or dim lighting; standing; using hands on objects, tools, or controls.

Locomotive Engineers

- ❋ Annual Earnings: $57,520
- ❋ Growth: 2.9%
- ❋ Annual Job Openings: 3,548
- ❋ Percentage of Women: 6.5%

Our sources did not provide separate job openings data for this occupation. The job openings listed here are shared with Locomotive Firers; and with Rail Yard Engineers, Dinkey Operators, and Hostlers.

Related Apprenticeship—Locomotive Engineer (8000 hrs.).

Drive electric, diesel-electric, steam, or gas-turbine-electric locomotives to transport passengers or freight. Interpret train orders, electronic or manual signals, and railroad rules and regulations. Monitor gauges and meters that measure speed, amperage, battery charge, and air pressure in brake lines and in main reservoirs. Observe tracks to detect obstructions. Interpret train orders, signals, and railroad rules and regulations that govern the operation of locomotives. Receive starting signals from conductors; then move controls such as throttles and air brakes to drive electric, diesel-electric, steam, or gas-turbine-electric locomotives. Confer with conductors or traffic control center personnel via radiophones to issue or receive information concerning stops, delays, or oncoming trains. Operate locomotives to transport freight or passengers between stations and to assemble and disassemble trains within rail yards. Respond to emergency conditions or breakdowns, following applicable safety procedures and rules. Check to ensure that brake examination tests are conducted at shunting stations. Call out train signals to assistants to verify meanings. Inspect locomotives to verify adequate fuel, sand, water, and other supplies before each run and to check for mechanical problems. Prepare reports regarding any problems encountered, such as accidents, signaling problems, unscheduled stops, or delays. Check to ensure that documentation, including procedure manuals and logbooks, is in the driver's cab and available for staff use. Inspect locomotives after runs to detect damaged or defective equipment. Drive diesel-electric rail-detector cars to transport rail-flaw-detecting machines over tracks. Monitor train-loading procedures to ensure that freight and rolling stock are loaded or unloaded without damage.

GOE—Career Cluster/Interest Area: 16. Transportation, Distribution, and Logistics. **Work Group:** 16.04. Rail Vehicle Operation. **Other Apprenticeable Jobs in This Work Group:** No others in group. **Personality Type:** Realistic. These occupations frequently involve work activities that include practical, hands-on problems and solutions. They often deal with plants; animals; and real-world materials such as wood, tools, and machinery. Many of the occupations require working outside and don't involve a lot of paperwork or working closely with others.

Skills—Operation Monitoring; Operation and Control; Troubleshooting; Instructing; Active Listening; Equipment Maintenance; Service Orientation; Quality Control Analysis.

Education/Training Required (Nonapprenticeship Route): Moderate-term on-the-job training. **Related Knowledge/Courses—Transportation:** Principles and methods for moving people or goods by air, rail, sea, or road, including their relative costs, advantages, and limitations. **Mechanical Devices:** Machines and tools, including their designs, uses, benefits, repair, and maintenance. **Public Safety and Security:** Weaponry; public safety; security operations, rules, regulations, precautions, and prevention; and the protection of people, data, and property.

Work Environment: Outdoors; noisy; contaminants; hazardous equipment; using hands on objects, tools, or controls; repetitive motions.

Machinists

- ❋ Annual Earnings: $35,230
- ❋ Growth: –3.1%
- ❋ Annual Job Openings: 39,505
- ❋ Percentage of Women: 6.7%

Related Apprenticeships—Fixture Maker (Light Fixtures) (4000 hrs.); Instrument Maker (8000 hrs.); Instrument Maker and Repairer (10000 hrs.); Machinist (8000 hrs.); Machinist, Automotive (8000 hrs.); Machinist, Experimental (8000 hrs.); Machinist, Outside (Ship) (8000 hrs.); Maintenance Machinist (8000 hrs.); NIMS Certified Machinist (5600 hrs. or competency);

Rocket Motor Mechanic (8000 hrs.); Test Technician (Professional and Kindred) (10000 hrs.).

Set up and operate a variety of machine tools to produce precision parts and instruments. Includes precision instrument makers who fabricate, modify, or repair mechanical instruments. May also fabricate and modify parts to make or repair machine tools or maintain industrial machines, applying knowledge of mechanics, shop mathematics, metal properties, layout, and machining procedures. Calculate dimensions and tolerances, using knowledge of mathematics and instruments such as micrometers and vernier calipers. Align and secure holding fixtures, cutting tools, attachments, accessories, and materials onto machines. Select the appropriate tools, machines, and materials to be used in preparation of machinery work. Monitor the feed and speed of machines during the machining process. Machine parts to specifications, using machine tools such as lathes, milling machines, shapers, or grinders. Set up, adjust, and operate all of the basic machine tools and many specialized or advanced variation tools to perform precision machining operations. Measure, examine, and test completed units to detect defects and ensure conformance to specifications, using precision instruments such as micrometers. Set controls to regulate machining or enter commands to retrieve, input, or edit computerized machine control media. Position and fasten work pieces. Maintain industrial machines, applying knowledge of mechanics, shop mathematics, metal properties, layout, and machining procedures. Observe and listen to operating machines or equipment to diagnose machine malfunctions and to determine need for adjustments or repairs. Check work pieces to ensure that they are properly lubricated and cooled. Lay out, measure, and mark metal stock to display placement of cuts. Study sample parts, blueprints, drawings, and engineering information to determine methods and sequences of operations needed to fabricate products and determine product dimensions and tolerances. Confer with engineering, supervisory, and manufacturing personnel to exchange technical information. Program computers and electronic instruments such as numerically controlled machine tools. Operate equipment to verify operational efficiency. Clean and lubricate machines, tools, and equipment to remove grease, rust, stains, and foreign matter. Design fixtures, tooling, and experimental parts to meet special engineering needs. Evaluate experimental procedures and recommend changes or modifications for improved efficiency and adaptability to setup and production.

GOE—Career Cluster/Interest Area: 13. Manufacturing. **Work Group:** 13.05. Production Machining Technology. **Other Apprenticeable Jobs in This Work Group:** Computer-Controlled Machine Tool Operators, Metal and Plastic; Foundry Mold and Coremakers; Lay-Out Workers, Metal and Plastic; Model Makers, Metal and Plastic; Numerical Tool and Process Control Programmers; Patternmakers, Metal and Plastic; Tool and Die Makers; Tool Grinders, Filers, and Sharpeners. **Personality Type:** Realistic. These occupations frequently involve work activities that include practical, hands-on problems and solutions. They often deal with plants; animals; and real-world materials such as wood, tools, and machinery. Many of the occupations require working outside and don't involve a lot of paperwork or working closely with others.

Skills—Operation Monitoring; Repairing; Operation and Control; Quality Control Analysis; Equipment Maintenance; Troubleshooting.

Education/Training Required (Nonapprenticeship Route): Long-term on-the-job training. **Related Knowledge/Courses—Mechanical Devices:** Machines and tools, including their designs, uses, benefits, repair, and maintenance. **Design:** Design techniques, principles, tools, and instruments involved in the production and use of precision technical plans, blueprints, drawings, and models. **Engineering and Technology:** Equipment, tools, and mechanical devices and their uses to produce motion, light, power, technology, and other applications. **Production and Processing:** Inputs, outputs, raw materials, waste, quality control, costs, and techniques for maximizing the manufacture and distribution of goods. **Mathematics:** Numbers and their operations and interrelationships, including arithmetic, algebra, geometry, calculus, and statistics and their applications.

Work Environment: Indoors; noisy; hazardous equipment; standing; using hands on objects, tools, or controls; repetitive motions.

Further Information: Contact a local joint union-management apprenticeship committee, or the nearest office of your state employment service or apprenticeship agency (see Appendix C). Information is also available from the National Institute for Metalworking Skills, 10565 Fairfax Boulevard, Suite 203, Fairfax, VA 22030. Internet: www.nims-skills.org

Maintenance and Repair Workers, General

- ✸ Annual Earnings: $32,570
- ✸ Growth: 10.1%
- ✸ Annual Job Openings: 165,502
- ✸ Percentage of Women: 4.0%

Related Apprenticeships—Maintenance Repairer, Buildings (4000 hrs.); Maintenance Repairer, Industrial (8000 hrs.); Marine Services Technician (6000 hrs.).

Perform work involving the skills of two or more maintenance or craft occupations to keep machines, mechanical equipment, or the structure of an establishment in repair. Duties may involve pipe fitting; boiler making; insulating; welding; machining; carpentry; repairing electrical or mechanical equipment; installing, aligning, and balancing new equipment; and repairing buildings, floors, or stairs. Repair or replace defective equipment parts, using hand tools and power tools, and reassemble equipment. Perform routine preventive maintenance to ensure that machines continue to run smoothly, building systems operate efficiently, and the physical condition of buildings does not deteriorate. Inspect drives, motors, and belts; check fluid levels; replace filters; and perform other maintenance actions, following checklists. Use tools ranging from common hand and power tools, such as hammers, hoists, saws, drills, and wrenches, to precision measuring instruments and electrical and electronic testing devices. Assemble, install, or repair wiring, electrical and electronic components, pipe systems and plumbing, machinery, and equipment. Diagnose mechanical problems and determine how to correct them, checking blueprints, repair manuals, and parts catalogs as necessary. Inspect, operate, and test machinery and equipment to diagnose machine malfunctions. Record maintenance and repair work performed and the costs of the work. Clean and lubricate shafts, bearings, gears, and other parts of machinery. Dismantle devices to gain access to and remove defective parts, using hoists, cranes, hand tools, and power tools. Plan and lay out repair work, using diagrams, drawings, blueprints, maintenance manuals, and schematic diagrams. Adjust functional parts of devices and control instruments, using hand tools, levels, plumb bobs, and straightedges. Order parts, supplies, and equipment from catalogs and suppliers or obtain them from storerooms. Paint and repair roofs, windows, doors, floors, woodwork, plaster, drywall, and other parts of building structures. Operate cutting torches or welding equipment to cut or join metal parts. Align and balance new equipment after installation. Inspect used parts to determine changes in dimensional requirements, using rules, calipers, micrometers, and other measuring instruments. Set up and operate machine tools to repair or fabricate machine parts, jigs and fixtures, and tools. Maintain and repair specialized equipment and machinery found in cafeterias, laundries, hospitals, stores, offices, and factories.

GOE—Career Cluster/Interest Area: 02. Architecture and Construction. **Work Group:** 02.05. Systems and Equipment Installation, Maintenance, and Repair. **Other Apprenticeable Jobs in This Work Group:** Electrical and Electronics Repairers, Powerhouse, Substation, and Relay; Electrical Power-Line Installers and Repairers; Elevator Installers and Repairers; Heating and Air Conditioning Mechanics and Installers; Refrigeration Mechanics and Installers; Telecommunications Equipment Installers and Repairers, Except Line Installers; Telecommunications Line Installers and Repairers. **Personality Type:** Realistic. These occupations frequently involve work activities that include practical, hands-on problems and solutions. They often deal with plants; animals; and real-world materials such as wood, tools, and machinery. Many of the occupations require working

outside and don't involve a lot of paperwork or working closely with others.

Skills—Equipment Maintenance; Installation; Repairing; Troubleshooting; Operation Monitoring; Operation and Control; Equipment Selection; Technology Design.

Education/Training Required (Nonapprenticeship Route): Moderate-term on-the-job training. **Related Knowledge/Courses—Building and Construction:** Materials, methods, and the appropriate tools to construct objects, structures, and buildings. **Mechanical Devices:** Machines and tools, including their designs, uses, benefits, repair, and maintenance. **Design:** Design techniques, principles, tools, and instruments involved in the production and use of precision technical plans, blueprints, drawings, and models. **Physics:** Physical principles, laws, and applications, including air, water, material dynamics, light, atomic principles, heat, electric theory, earth formations, and meteorological and related natural phenomena. **Engineering and Technology:** Equipment, tools, and mechanical devices and their uses to produce motion, light, power, technology, and other applications. **Public Safety and Security:** Weaponry; public safety; security operations, rules, regulations, precautions, and prevention; and the protection of people, data, and property.

Work Environment: Indoors; noisy; minor burns, cuts, bites, or stings; standing; walking and running; using hands on objects, tools, or controls.

Maintenance Workers, Machinery

❋ Annual Earnings: $35,590
❋ Growth: –1.1%
❋ Annual Job Openings: 15,055
❋ Percentage of Women: 3.8%

Related Apprenticeship—Pinsetter Mechanic, Automatic (4000 hrs.).

Lubricate machinery, change parts, or perform other routine machinery maintenance. Reassemble machines after the completion of repair or maintenance work. Start machines and observe mechanical operation to determine efficiency and to detect problems. Inspect or test damaged machine parts and mark defective areas or advise supervisors of repair needs. Lubricate or apply adhesives or other materials to machines, machine parts, or other equipment, according to specified procedures. Install, replace, or change machine parts and attachments, according to production specifications. Dismantle machines and remove parts for repair, using hand tools, chain falls, jacks, cranes, or hoists. Record production, repair, and machine maintenance information. Read work orders and specifications to determine machines and equipment requiring repair or maintenance. Set up and operate machines and adjust controls to regulate operations. Collaborate with other workers to repair or move machines, machine parts, or equipment. Inventory and requisition machine parts, equipment, and other supplies so that stock can be maintained and replenished. Transport machine parts, tools, equipment, and other material between work areas and storage, using cranes, hoists, or dollies. Clean machines and machine parts, using cleaning solvents, cloths, air guns, hoses, vacuums, or other equipment. Collect and discard worn machine parts and other refuse to maintain machinery and work areas. Replace or repair metal, wood, leather, glass, or other lining in machines or in equipment compartments or containers. Remove hardened material from machines or machine parts, using abrasives, power and hand tools, jackhammers, sledgehammers, or other equipment. Measure, mix, prepare, and test chemical solutions used to clean or repair machinery and equipment. Replace, empty, or replenish machine and equipment containers such as gas tanks or boxes.

GOE—Career Cluster/Interest Area: 13. Manufacturing. **Work Group:** 13.13. Machinery Repair. **Other Apprenticeable Jobs in This Work Group:** Control and Valve Installers and Repairers, Except Mechanical Door; Home Appliance Repairers; Industrial Machinery Mechanics; Locksmiths and Safe Repairers; Mechanical Door Repairers; Millwrights; Signal and Track Switch Repairers. **Personality Type:** Realistic. These occupations frequently involve work activities that include practical, hands-on problems and solutions. They often deal with plants; animals; and real-world materials such as wood, tools, and machinery. Many of the occupations require working outside and don't involve a lot of paperwork or working closely with others.

Skills—Installation; Repairing; Equipment Maintenance; Troubleshooting; Operation Monitoring; Operation and Control; Technology Design; Equipment Selection.

Education/Training Required (Nonapprenticeship Route): Moderate-term on-the-job training. **Related Knowledge/Courses—Mechanical Devices:** Machines and tools, including their designs, uses, benefits, repair, and maintenance. **Building and Construction:** Materials, methods, and the appropriate tools to construct objects, structures, and buildings. **Engineering and Technology:** Equipment, tools, and mechanical devices and their uses to produce motion, light, power, technology, and other applications. **Physics:** Physical principles, laws, and applications, including air, water, material dynamics, light, atomic principles, heat, electric theory, earth formations, and meteorological and related natural phenomena. **Chemistry:** The composition, structure, and properties of substances and of the chemical processes and transformations that they undergo. This includes uses of chemicals and their interactions, danger signs, production techniques, and disposal methods. **Design:** Design techniques, principles, tools, and instruments involved in the production and use of precision technical plans, blueprints, drawings, and models.

Work Environment: Noisy; very hot or cold; contaminants; hazardous equipment; standing; using hands on objects, tools, or controls.

Mapping Technicians

- ❋ Annual Earnings: $33,640
- ❋ Growth: 19.4%
- ❋ Annual Job Openings: 8,299
- ❋ Percentage of Women: 9.9%

Our sources did not provide separate job openings data for this occupation. The job openings listed here are shared with Surveying Technicians.

Related Apprenticeships—Geodetic Computator (4000 hrs.); Photogrammetric Technician (6000 hrs.).

Calculate mapmaking information from field notes and draw and verify accuracy of topographical maps. Check all layers of maps to ensure accuracy, identifying and marking errors and making corrections. Determine scales, line sizes, and colors to be used for hard copies of computerized maps, using plotters. Monitor mapping work and the updating of maps to ensure accuracy, the inclusion of new and/or changed information, and compliance with rules and regulations. Identify and compile database information to create maps in response to requests. Produce and update overlay maps to show information boundaries, water locations, and topographic features on various base maps and at different scales. Trace contours and topographic details to generate maps that denote specific land and property locations and geographic attributes. Lay out and match aerial photographs in sequences in which they were taken and identify any areas missing from photographs. Compare topographical features and contour lines with images from aerial photographs, old maps, and other reference materials to verify the accuracy of their identification. Compute and measure scaled distances between reference points to establish relative positions of adjoining prints and enable the creation of photographic mosaics. Research resources such as survey maps and legal descriptions to verify property lines and to obtain information needed for mapping. Form three-dimensional images of aerial photographs taken from different locations, using mathematical techniques and plotting instruments. Enter GPS data, legal deeds, field notes, and land survey reports into GIS workstations so that information can be transformed into graphic land descriptions such as maps and drawings. Analyze aerial photographs to detect and interpret significant military, industrial, resource, or topographical data. Redraw and correct maps, such as revising parcel maps to reflect tax code area changes, using information from official records and surveys. Train staff members in duties such as tax mapping, the use of computerized mapping equipment, and the interpretation of source documents.

GOE—Career Cluster/Interest Area: 15. Scientific Research, Engineering, and Mathematics. **Work Group:** 15.09. Engineering Technology. **Other Apprenticeable Jobs in This Work Group:** Aerospace Engineering and Operations Technicians; Electrical Drafters; Electrical Engineering Technicians; Electro-Mechanical Technicians; Electronic Drafters; Electronics Engineering Technicians; Mechanical Drafters; Mechanical Engineering Technicians; Surveying and Mapping Technicians; Surveying Technicians. **Personality Type:** Conventional. These occupations frequently involve following set procedures and routines and can include working with data and details more than with ideas. Usually there is a clear line of authority to follow.

Skills—Technology Design; Operations Analysis; Programming; Quality Control Analysis; Science; Troubleshooting; Mathematics; Complex Problem Solving.

Education/Training Required (Nonapprenticeship Route): Moderate-term on-the-job training. **Related Knowledge/Courses—Geography:** Various methods for describing the location and distribution of land, sea, and air masses, including their physical locations, relationships, and characteristics. **Design:** Design techniques, principles, tools, and instruments involved in the production and use of precision technical plans, blueprints, drawings, and models. **Computers and Electronics:** Electric circuit boards, processors, chips, and computer hardware and software, including applications and programming. **Engineering and Technology:** Equipment, tools, and mechanical devices and their uses to produce motion, light, power, technology, and other applications. **Mathematics:** Numbers and their operations and interrelationships, including arithmetic, algebra, geometry, calculus, and statistics and their applications. **Clerical Practices:** Administrative and clerical procedures and systems such as word-processing systems, filing and records management systems, stenography and transcription, forms, design principles, and other office procedures and terminology.

Work Environment: Indoors; sitting; using hands on objects, tools, or controls; repetitive motions.

Mates—Ship, Boat, and Barge

- ✳ Annual Earnings: $57,210
- ✳ Growth: 17.9%
- ✳ Annual Job Openings: 2,665
- ✳ Percentage of Women: 14.8%

Our sources did not provide separate job openings data for this occupation. The job openings listed here are shared with Pilots, Ship; and with Ship and Boat Captains.

Related Apprenticeship—Officer In Charge of Navigational Watch (OICNW) (3000 hrs.).

Supervise and coordinate activities of crew aboard ships, boats, barges, or dredges. Determine geographical position of ship, using lorans, azimuths of celestial bodies, or computers, and use this information to determine the course and speed of the ship. Observe water from ship's masthead to advise on navigational direction. Supervise crews in cleaning and maintaining decks, superstructures, and bridges. Supervise crew members in the repair or replacement of defective gear and equipment. Steer vessels, using navigational devices such as compasses and sextants and navigational aids such as lighthouses and buoys. Inspect equipment such as cargo-handling gear, lifesaving equipment, visual-signaling equipment, and fishing, towing, or dredging gear to detect problems. Arrange for ships to be stocked, fueled, and repaired. Assume command of vessel in the event that ship's master becomes incapacitated. Participate in activities related to maintenance of vessel security. Stand watches on vessel during specified periods while vessel is under way. Observe loading and unloading of cargo and equipment to ensure that handling and storage are performed according to specifications.

GOE—Career Cluster/Interest Area: 16. Transportation, Distribution, and Logistics. **Work Group:** 16.05. Water Vehicle Operation. **Other Apprenticeable Jobs in This Work Group:** Dredge Operators; Pilots, Ship; Sailors and Marine Oilers. **Personality Type:** Enterprising. These occupations frequently involve starting up and carrying out projects and can involve leading people and making many decisions. They sometimes require risk taking and often deal with business.

Skills—Equipment Maintenance; Repairing; Operation and Control; Operation Monitoring; Troubleshooting; Installation; Equipment Selection; Judgment and Decision Making.

Education/Training Required (Nonapprenticeship Route): Work experience in a related occupation. **Related Knowledge/Courses—Geography:** Various methods for describing the location and distribution of land, sea, and air masses, including their physical locations, relationships, and characteristics. **Transportation:** Principles and methods for moving people or goods by air, rail, sea, or road, including their relative costs, advantages, and limitations. **Public Safety and Security:** Weaponry; public safety; security operations, rules, regulations,

precautions, and prevention; and the protection of people, data, and property. **Telecommunications:** Transmission, broadcasting, switching, control, and operation of telecommunications systems. **Personnel and Human Resources:** Principles and procedures for personnel recruitment; selection; training; compensation and benefits; labor relations and negotiation; and personnel information systems. **Mechanical Devices:** Machines and tools, including their designs, uses, benefits, repair, and maintenance.

Work Environment: More often outdoors than indoors; very hot or cold; standing; using hands on objects, tools, or controls.

Mechanical Door Repairers

* Annual Earnings: $31,880
* Growth: 14.9%
* Annual Job Openings: 1,706
* Percentage of Women: 4.6%

Related Apprenticeships—Automated Access Systems Technician (3520 hrs.); Door-Closer Mechanic (6000 hrs.).

Install, service, or repair opening and closing mechanisms of automatic doors and hydraulic door closers. Includes garage door mechanics. Adjust doors to open or close with the correct amount of effort and make simple adjustments to electric openers. Wind large springs with upward motion of arm. Inspect job sites, assessing headroom, side room, and other conditions to determine appropriateness of door for a given location. Collect payment upon job completion. Complete required paperwork, such as work orders, according to services performed or required. Fasten angle iron back-hangers to ceilings and tracks, using fasteners or welding equipment. Repair or replace worn or broken door parts, using hand tools. Carry springs to tops of doors, using ladders or scaffolding, and attach springs to tracks in order to install spring systems. Set doors into place or stack hardware sections into openings after rail or track installation. Remove or disassemble defective automatic mechanical door closers, using hand tools. Install door frames, rails, steel rolling curtains, electronic-eye mechanisms, and electric door openers and closers, using power tools, hand tools, and electronic test equipment. Apply hardware to door sections, such as drilling holes to install locks. Assemble and fasten tracks to structures or bucks, using impact wrenches or welding equipment. Run low-voltage wiring on ceiling surfaces, using insulated staples. Cut door stops and angle irons to fit openings. Study blueprints and schematic diagrams to determine appropriate methods of installing and repairing automated door openers. Operate lifts, winches, or chain falls to move heavy curtain doors. Order replacement springs, sections, and slats. Bore and cut holes in flooring as required for installation, using hand tools and power tools. Set in and secure floor treadles for door-activating mechanisms; then connect power packs and electrical panelboards to treadles. Lubricate door closer oil chambers and pack spindles with leather washers. Install dock seals, bumpers, and shelters. Fabricate replacements for worn or broken parts, using welders, lathes, drill presses, and shaping and milling machines. Clean door closer parts, using caustic soda, rotary brushes, and grinding wheels.

GOE—Career Cluster/Interest Area: 13. Manufacturing. **Work Group:** 13.13. Machinery Repair. **Other Apprenticeable Jobs in This Work Group:** Control and Valve Installers and Repairers, Except Mechanical Door; Home Appliance Repairers; Industrial Machinery

Mechanics; Locksmiths and Safe Repairers; Maintenance Workers, Machinery; Millwrights; Signal and Track Switch Repairers. **Personality Type:** Realistic. These occupations frequently involve work activities that include practical, hands-on problems and solutions. They often deal with plants; animals; and real-world materials such as wood, tools, and machinery. Many of the occupations require working outside and don't involve a lot of paperwork or working closely with others.

Skills—Installation; Repairing; Troubleshooting; Equipment Maintenance; Equipment Selection; Time Management; Systems Evaluation; Mathematics.

Education/Training Required (Nonapprenticeship Route): Moderate-term on-the-job training. **Related Knowledge/Courses—Building and Construction:** Materials, methods, and the appropriate tools to construct objects, structures, and buildings. **Mechanical Devices:** Machines and tools, including their designs, uses, benefits, repair, and maintenance. **Engineering and Technology:** Equipment, tools, and mechanical devices and their uses to produce motion, light, power, technology, and other applications. **Sales and Marketing:** Principles and methods involved in showing, promoting, and selling products or services. This includes marketing strategies and tactics, product demonstration and sales techniques, and sales control systems. **Design:** Design techniques, principles, tools, and instruments involved in the production and use of precision technical plans, blueprints, drawings, and models.

Work Environment: Outdoors; very hot or cold; hazardous equipment; standing; climbing ladders, scaffolds, or poles; using hands on objects, tools, or controls.

Mechanical Drafters

⁂ Annual Earnings: $44,740
⁂ Growth: 5.2%
⁂ Annual Job Openings: 10,902
⁂ Percentage of Women: 21.8%

Related Apprenticeships—Detailer (8000 hrs.); Die Designer (8000 hrs.); Drafter, Auto Design Layout (8000 hrs.); Drafter, Automotive Design (8000 hrs.); Drafter, Detail (8000 hrs.); Drafter, Mechanical (8000 hrs.); Drafter, Tool Design (8000 hrs.); Engineering Assistant, Mechanical Equipment (8000 hrs.); Mold Designer (Plastics Industry) (4000 hrs.).

Prepare detailed working diagrams of machinery and mechanical devices, including dimensions, fastening methods, and other engineering information. Develop detailed design drawings and specifications for mechanical equipment, dies, tools, and controls, using computer-assisted drafting (CAD) equipment. Coordinate with and consult other workers to design, lay out, or detail components and systems and to resolve design or other problems. Review and analyze specifications, sketches, drawings, ideas, and related data to assess factors affecting component designs and the procedures and instructions to be followed. Position instructions and comments onto drawings. Compute mathematical formulas to develop and design detailed specifications for components or machinery, using computer-assisted equipment. Modify and revise designs to correct operating deficiencies or to reduce production problems. Design scale or full-size blueprints of specialty items such as furniture and automobile body or chassis components. Check dimensions of materials to be used and assign numbers to the materials. Lay out and draw schematic, orthographic, or angle views to depict functional relationships of components, assemblies, systems, and machines. Confer with customer representatives to review schematics and answer questions pertaining to installation of systems. Draw freehand sketches of designs, trace finished drawings onto designated paper for the reproduction of blueprints, and reproduce working drawings on copy machines. Supervise and train other drafters, technologists, and technicians. Lay out, draw, and reproduce illustrations for reference manuals and technical publications to describe operation and maintenance of mechanical systems. Shade or color drawings to clarify and emphasize details and dimensions or eliminate background, using ink, crayon, airbrush, and overlays.

GOE—Career Cluster/Interest Area: 15. Scientific Research, Engineering, and Mathematics. **Work Group:** 15.09. Engineering Technology. **Other Apprenticeable Jobs in This Work Group:** Aerospace Engineering and Operations Technicians; Electrical Drafters; Electrical Engineering Technicians; Electro-Mechanical Technicians; Electronic Drafters; Electronics Engineering Technicians; Mapping Technicians; Mechanical Engineering Technicians; Surveying and Mapping Technicians; Surveying Technicians. **Personality Type:** Realistic. These occupations frequently involve work activities that include practical, hands-on problems and solutions. They often deal with plants; animals; and real-world materials such as wood, tools, and machinery. Many of the occupations require working outside and don't involve a lot of paperwork or working closely with others.

Skills—Technology Design; Installation; Equipment Selection; Operations Analysis; Quality Control Analysis; Mathematics; Repairing; Science.

Education/Training Required (Nonapprenticeship Route): Postsecondary vocational training. **Related Knowledge/Courses—Design:** Design techniques, principles, tools, and instruments involved in the production and use of precision technical plans, blueprints, drawings, and models. **Engineering and Technology:** Equipment, tools, and mechanical devices and their uses to produce motion, light, power, technology, and other applications. **Building and Construction:** Materials, methods, and the appropriate tools to construct objects, structures, and buildings. **Physics:** Physical principles, laws, and applications, including air, water, material dynamics, light, atomic principles, heat, electric theory, earth formations, and meteorological and related natural phenomena. **Mathematics:** Numbers and their operations and interrelationships, including arithmetic, algebra, geometry, calculus, and statistics and their applications. **English Language:** The structure and content of the English language, including the meaning and spelling of words, rules of composition, and grammar.

Work Environment: Indoors; noisy; sitting; using hands on objects, tools, or controls; repetitive motions.

Mechanical Engineering Technicians

- ❋ Annual Earnings: $47,280
- ❋ Growth: 6.4%
- ❋ Annual Job Openings: 3,710
- ❋ Percentage of Women: 20.6%

Related Apprenticeships—Heat Transfer Technician (8000 hrs.); Mechanical Engineering Technician (8000 hrs.); Optomechanical Technician (8000 hrs.); Tool Design Checker (8000 hrs.).

Apply theory and principles of mechanical engineering to modify, develop, and test machinery and equipment under direction of engineering staff or physical scientists. Prepare parts sketches and write work orders and purchase requests to be furnished by outside contractors. Draft detail drawing or sketch for drafting room completion or to request parts fabrication by machine, sheet, or wood shops. Review project instructions and blueprints to ascertain test specifications, procedures, and objectives and test nature of technical problems such as redesign. Review project instructions and specifications to identify, modify, and plan requirements fabrication, assembly, and testing. Devise, fabricate, and assemble new or modified mechanical components for products such as industrial machinery or equipment and measuring instruments. Discuss changes in design, method of manufacture and assembly, and drafting techniques and procedures with staff and coordinate corrections. Set up and conduct tests of complete units and components under operational conditions to investigate proposals for improving equipment performance. Inspect lines and figures for clarity and return erroneous drawings to designer for correction. Analyze test results in relation to design or rated specifications and test objectives and modify or adjust equipment to meet specifications. Evaluate tool drawing designs by measuring drawing dimensions and comparing with original specifications for form and function, using engineering skills. Confer with technicians and submit reports of test results to engineering department and recommend design or material changes. Calculate required capacities for equipment of proposed system to obtain specified performance and submit data to engineering personnel for approval. Record test procedures and results, numerical and graphical data, and recommendations for changes in product or test methods. Read dials and meters to determine amperage, voltage, and electrical output and input at specific operating temperature to analyze parts performance. Estimate cost factors, including labor and material, for purchased and fabricated parts and costs for assembly, testing, or installing. Set up prototype and test apparatus and operate test-controlling equipment to observe and record prototype test results.

GOE—Career Cluster/Interest Area: 15. Scientific Research, Engineering, and Mathematics. **Work Group:** 15.09. Engineering Technology. **Other Apprenticeable Jobs in This Work Group:** Aerospace Engineering and Operations Technicians; Electrical Drafters; Electrical Engineering Technicians; Electro-Mechanical Technicians; Electronic Drafters; Electronics Engineering Technicians; Mapping Technicians; Mechanical Drafters; Surveying and Mapping Technicians; Surveying Technicians. **Personality Type:** Realistic. These occupations frequently involve work activities that include practical, hands-on problems and solutions. They often deal with plants; animals; and real-world materials such as wood, tools, and machinery. Many of the occupations require working outside and don't involve a lot of paperwork or working closely with others.

Skills—Installation; Troubleshooting; Technology Design; Operations Analysis; Equipment Selection; Science; Mathematics; Systems Evaluation.

Education/Training Required (Nonapprenticeship Route): Associate degree. **Related Knowledge/Courses—Engineering and**

Technology: Equipment, tools, and mechanical devices and their uses to produce motion, light, power, technology, and other applications. **Design:** Design techniques, principles, tools, and instruments involved in the production and use of precision technical plans, blueprints, drawings, and models. **Mechanical Devices:** Machines and tools, including their designs, uses, benefits, repair, and maintenance. **Physics:** Physical principles, laws, and applications, including air, water, material dynamics, light, atomic principles, heat, electric theory, earth formations, and meteorological and related natural phenomena. **Chemistry:** The composition, structure, and properties of substances and of the chemical processes and transformations that they undergo. This includes uses of chemicals and their interactions, danger signs, production techniques, and disposal methods. **Production and Processing:** Inputs, outputs, raw materials, waste, quality control, costs, and techniques for maximizing the manufacture and distribution of goods.

Work Environment: Indoors; noisy; contaminants; hazardous equipment; sitting.

Medical and Clinical Laboratory Technicians

* Annual Earnings: $34,270
* Growth: 15.0%
* Annual Job Openings: 10,866
* Percentage of Women: 78.1%

Related Apprenticeship—Medical-Laboratory Technician (4000 hrs.).

Perform routine medical laboratory tests for the diagnosis, treatment, and prevention of disease. May work under the supervision of a medical technologist. Conduct chemical analyses of bodily fluids, such as blood and urine, using microscope or automatic analyzer to detect abnormalities or diseases, and enter findings into computer. Set up, adjust, maintain, and clean medical laboratory equipment. Analyze the results of tests and experiments to ensure conformity to specifications, using special mechanical and electrical devices. Analyze and record test data to issue reports that use charts, graphs and narratives. Conduct blood tests for transfusion purposes and perform blood counts. Perform medical research to further control and cure disease. Obtain specimens, cultivating, isolating, and identifying microorganisms for analysis. Examine cells stained with dye to locate abnormalities. Collect blood or tissue samples from patients, observing principles of asepsis to obtain blood sample. Consult with a pathologist to determine a final diagnosis when abnormal cells are found. Inoculate fertilized eggs, broths, or other bacteriological media with organisms. Cut, stain, and mount tissue samples for examination by pathologists. Supervise and instruct other technicians and laboratory assistants. Prepare standard volumetric solutions and reagents to be combined with samples, following standardized formulas or experimental procedures. Prepare vaccines and serums by standard laboratory methods, testing for virus inactivity and sterility. Test raw materials, processes, and finished products to determine quality and quantity of materials or characteristics of a substance.

GOE—Career Cluster/Interest Area: 08. Health Science. **Work Group:** 08.06. Medical Technology. **Other Apprenticeable Jobs in This Work Group:** Medical Equipment Preparers; Medical Records and Health Information Technicians; Opticians, Dispensing; Radiologic Technologists. **Personality Type:** Realistic. These occupations frequently involve work activities that include practical, hands-on problems and solutions. They often deal with plants; animals; and real-world materials such as wood, tools, and machinery. Many of the occupations require working outside and don't involve a lot of paperwork or working closely with others.

Skills—Science; Equipment Maintenance; Troubleshooting; Quality Control Analysis; Operation Monitoring; Operation and Control; Monitoring; Installation.

Education/Training Required (Nonapprenticeship Route): Associate degree. **Related Knowledge/Courses—Medicine and Dentistry:** The information and techniques needed to diagnose and treat injuries, diseases, and deformities. This includes symptoms, treatment alternatives, drug properties and interactions, and preventive health-care measures. **Therapy and Counseling:** Information and techniques needed to rehabilitate physical and mental ailments and to provide career guidance, including alternative treatments, rehabilitation equipment and its proper use, and methods to evaluate treatment effects. **Biology:** Plant and animal living tissue, cells, organisms, and entities, including their functions, interdependencies, and interactions with each other and the environment. **Clerical Practices:** Administrative and clerical procedures and systems such as word-processing systems, filing and records management systems, stenography and transcription, forms, design principles, and other office procedures and terminology.

Work Environment: Indoors; disease or infections; standing; walking and running; using hands on objects, tools, or controls.

Medical Appliance Technicians

❈ Annual Earnings: $32,640
❈ Growth: 9.4%
❈ Annual Job Openings: 895
❈ Percentage of Women: 50.8%

Related Apprenticeships—Artificial Plastic Eye Maker (10000 hrs.); Orthotics Technician (2000 hrs.); Prosthetics Technician (8000 hrs.).

Construct, fit, maintain, or repair medical supportive devices, such as braces, artificial limbs, joints, arch supports, and other surgical and medical appliances. Fit appliances onto patients and make any necessary adjustments. Make orthotic/prosthetic devices using materials such as thermoplastic and thermosetting materials, metal alloys and leather, and hand and power tools. Read prescriptions or specifications to determine the type of product or device to be fabricated and the materials and tools that will be required. Repair, modify, and maintain medical supportive devices, such as artificial limbs, braces, and surgical supports, according to specifications. Instruct patients in use of prosthetic or orthotic devices. Take patients' body or limb measurements for use in device construction. Construct or receive casts or impressions of patients' torsos or limbs for use as cutting and fabrication patterns. Bend, form, and shape fabric or material so that it conforms to prescribed contours needed to fabricate structural components. Drill and tap holes for rivets and glue, weld, bolt, and rivet parts together to form prosthetic or orthotic devices. Lay out and mark dimensions of parts, using templates and precision measuring instruments. Test medical supportive devices for proper alignment, movement, and biomechanical stability, using meters and alignment fixtures. Cover or pad metal or plastic structures and devices, using coverings such as rubber, leather, felt, plastic, or fiberglass. Polish artificial limbs, braces, and supports, using grinding and buffing wheels. Service and repair machinery used in the fabrication of appliances. Mix pigments to match patients' skin coloring, according to formulas, and apply mixtures to orthotic or prosthetic devices.

GOE—Career Cluster/Interest Area: 13. Manufacturing. **Work Group:** 13.06. Production Precision Work. **Other Apprenticeable Jobs in This Work Group:** Bookbinders; Dental Laboratory Technicians; Electrical and Electronic Equipment Assemblers; Electromechanical Equipment Assemblers; Engine and Other Machine Assemblers; Gem and Diamond Workers; Jewelers; Molding, Coremaking, and Casting Machine Setters, Operators, and Tenders, Metal and Plastic; Ophthalmic Laboratory Technicians; Precious Metal Workers. **Personality Type:** Realistic. These occupations frequently involve work activities that include practical, hands-on problems and solutions. They often deal with plants; animals; and real-world materials such as wood, tools, and machinery. Many of the occupations require working outside and don't involve a lot of paperwork or working closely with others.

Skills—Technology Design; Repairing; Installation; Quality Control Analysis; Science; Equipment Selection; Active Learning; Equipment Maintenance.

Education/Training Required (Nonapprenticeship Route): Long-term on-the-job training. **Related Knowledge/Courses—Production and Processing:** Inputs, outputs, raw materials, waste, quality control, costs, and techniques for maximizing the manufacture and distribution of goods. **Mechanical Devices:** Machines and tools, including their designs, uses, benefits, repair, and maintenance. **Design:** Design techniques, principles, tools, and instruments involved in the production and use of precision technical plans, blueprints, drawings, and models. **Medicine and Dentistry:** The information and techniques needed to diagnose and treat injuries, diseases, and deformities. This includes symptoms, treatment alternatives, drug properties and interactions, and preventive healthcare measures. **Engineering and Technology:** Equipment, tools, and mechanical devices and their uses to produce motion, light, power, technology, and other applications. **Customer and Personal Service:** Principles and processes for providing customer and personal services, including needs assessment techniques, quality service standards, alternative delivery systems, and customer satisfaction evaluation techniques.

Work Environment: Indoors; noisy; contaminants; disease or infections; hazardous equipment; using hands on objects, tools, or controls.

Medical Assistants

- ❋ Annual Earnings: $27,430
- ❋ Growth: 35.4%
- ❋ Annual Job Openings: 92,977
- ❋ Percentage of Women: 90.4%

Related Apprenticeships—Medical Assistant (4000 hrs.); Podiatric Assistant (4000 hrs.).

Perform administrative and certain clinical duties under the direction of physicians. Administrative duties may include scheduling appointments, maintaining medical records, billing, and coding for insurance purposes. Clinical duties may include taking and recording vital signs and medical histories, preparing patients for examination, **drawing blood, and administering medications as directed by physician.** Record patients' medical history, vital statistics, and information such as test results in medical records. Prepare treatment rooms for patient examinations, keeping the rooms neat and clean. Interview patients to obtain medical information and measure their vital signs, weights, and heights. Authorize drug refills and provide prescription information to pharmacies. Clean and sterilize instruments and dispose of contaminated supplies. Prepare and administer medications as directed by a physician. Show patients to examination rooms and prepare them for the physician. Explain treatment procedures, medications, diets, and physicians' instructions to patients. Help physicians examine and treat patients, handing them instruments and materials or performing such tasks as giving injections or removing sutures. Collect blood, tissue, or other laboratory specimens, log the specimens, and prepare them for testing. Perform routine laboratory tests and sample analyses. Contact medical facilities or departments to schedule patients for tests or admission. Operate X-ray, electrocardiogram (EKG), and other equipment to administer routine diagnostic tests. Change dressings on wounds. Set up medical laboratory equipment. Perform general office duties such as answering telephones, taking dictation, or completing insurance forms. Greet and log in patients arriving at office or clinic. Schedule appointments for patients. Inventory and order medical, lab, or office supplies and equipment. Keep financial records and perform other bookkeeping duties, such as handling credit and collections and mailing monthly statements to patients.

GOE—Career Cluster/Interest Area: 08. Health Science. **Work Group:** 08.02. Medicine and Surgery. **Other Apprenticeable Jobs in**

This Work Group: Medical Transcriptionists; Pharmacy Technicians; Surgical Technologists. **Personality Type:** Social. These occupations frequently involve working with, communicating with, and teaching people and often involve helping or providing service to others.

Skill—Systems Analysis.

Education/Training Required (Nonapprenticeship Route): Moderate-term on-the-job training. **Related Knowledge/Courses—Medicine and Dentistry:** The information and techniques needed to diagnose and treat injuries, diseases, and deformities. This includes symptoms, treatment alternatives, drug properties and interactions, and preventive health-care measures. **Clerical Practices:** Administrative and clerical procedures and systems such as word-processing systems, filing and records management systems, stenography and transcription, forms, design principles, and other office procedures and terminology. **Psychology:** Human behavior and performance, mental processes, psychological research methods, and the assessment and treatment of behavioral and affective disorders. **Therapy and Counseling:** Information and techniques needed to rehabilitate physical and mental ailments and to provide career guidance, including alternative treatments, rehabilitation equipment and its proper use, and methods to evaluate treatment effects. **Customer and Personal Service:** Principles and processes for providing customer and personal services, including needs assessment techniques, quality service standards, alternative delivery systems, and customer satisfaction evaluation techniques. **Public Safety and Security:** Weaponry; public safety; security operations, rules, regulations, precautions, and prevention; and the protection of people, data, and property.

Work Environment: Indoors; disease or infections; standing; walking and running; using hands on objects, tools, or controls.

Medical Equipment Preparers

- ❋ Annual Earnings: $27,040
- ❋ Growth: 14.2%
- ❋ Annual Job Openings: 8,363
- ❋ Percentage of Women: 90.4%

Related Apprenticeship—Central Sterile Processing Technician (2000 hrs.).

Prepare, sterilize, install, or clean laboratory or health-care equipment. May perform routine laboratory tasks and operate or inspect equipment. Organize and assemble routine and specialty surgical instrument trays and other sterilized supplies, filling special requests as needed. Clean instruments to prepare them for sterilization. Operate and maintain steam autoclaves, keeping records of loads completed, items in loads, and maintenance procedures performed. Record sterilizer test results. Disinfect and sterilize equipment such as respirators, hospital beds, and oxygen and dialysis equipment, using sterilizers, aerators, and washers. Start equipment and observe gauges and equipment operation to detect malfunctions and to ensure equipment is operating to prescribed standards. Examine equipment to detect leaks, worn or loose parts, or other indications of disrepair. Report defective equipment to appropriate supervisors or staff. Check sterile supplies to ensure that they are not outdated. Maintain records of inventory and equipment usage. Attend hospital in-service programs related to areas of work specialization. Purge wastes from equipment by connecting equipment to water sources and flushing water through systems. Deliver equipment to specified hospital locations or to patients' residences. Assist hospital staff with patient care duties such as providing transportation or setting up traction. Install and set up medical equipment, using hand tools.

GOE—Career Cluster/Interest Area: 08. Health Science. **Work Group:** 08.06. Medical Technology. **Other Apprenticeable Jobs in This Work Group:** Medical and Clinical Laboratory Technicians; Medical Records and Health Information Technicians; Opticians, Dispensing; Radiologic Technologists. **Personality Type:** Realistic. These occupations frequently involve work activities that include practical, hands-on problems and solutions. They often deal with plants; animals; and real-world materials such as wood, tools, and machinery. Many of the occupations require working outside and don't involve a lot of paperwork or working closely with others.

Skills—Operation Monitoring; Equipment Maintenance; Management of Material Resources; Quality Control Analysis; Operation and Control; Service Orientation; Monitoring; Science.

Education/Training Required (Nonapprenticeship Route): Short-term on-the-job training. **Related Knowledge/Courses—Chemistry:** The composition, structure, and properties of substances and of the chemical processes and transformations that they undergo. This includes uses of chemicals and their interactions, danger signs, production techniques, and disposal methods. **Biology:** Plant and animal living tissue, cells, organisms, and entities, including their functions, interdependencies, and interactions with each other and the environment. **Medicine and Dentistry:** The information and techniques needed to diagnose and treat injuries, diseases,

and deformities. This includes symptoms, treatment alternatives, drug properties and interactions, and preventive health-care measures. **Production and Processing:** Inputs, outputs, raw materials, waste, quality control, costs, and techniques for maximizing the manufacture and distribution of goods. **Education and Training:** Instructional methods and training techniques, including curriculum design principles, learning theory, group and individual teaching techniques, design of individual development plans, and test design principles. **Customer and Personal Service:** Principles and processes for providing customer and personal services, including needs assessment techniques, quality service standards, alternative delivery systems, and customer satisfaction evaluation techniques.

Work Environment: Indoors; contaminants; disease or infections; standing; using hands on objects, tools, or controls; repetitive motions.

Medical Equipment Repairers

- ❋ Annual Earnings: $40,320
- ❋ Growth: 21.7%
- ❋ Annual Job Openings: 2,351
- ❋ Percentage of Women: 13.9%

Related Apprenticeships—Biomedical Equipment Technician (8000 hrs.); Dental-Equipment Installer and Servicer (6000 hrs.); Electromedical Equipment Repairer (4000 hrs.).

Test, adjust, or repair biomedical or electromedical equipment. Inspect and test malfunctioning medical and related equipment following manufacturers' specifications, using test and analysis instruments. Examine medical equipment and facility's structural environment and check for proper use of equipment to protect patients and staff from electrical or mechanical hazards and to ensure compliance with safety regulations. Disassemble malfunctioning equipment and remove, repair, and replace defective parts such as motors, clutches, or transformers. Keep records of maintenance, repair, and required updates of equipment. Perform preventive maintenance or service such as cleaning, lubricating, and adjusting equipment. Test and calibrate components and equipment, following manufacturers' manuals and troubleshooting techniques and using hand tools, power tools, and measuring devices. Explain and demonstrate correct operation and preventive maintenance of medical equipment to personnel. Study technical manuals and attend training sessions provided by equipment manufacturers to maintain current knowledge. Plan and carry out work assignments, using blueprints, schematic drawings, technical manuals, wiring diagrams, and liquid and air flow sheets, following prescribed regulations, directives, and other instructions as required. Solder loose connections, using soldering iron. Test, evaluate, and classify excess or in-use medical equipment and determine serviceability, condition, and disposition in accordance with regulations. Research catalogs and repair part lists to locate sources for repair parts, requisitioning parts and recording their receipt. Evaluate technical specifications to identify equipment and systems best suited for intended use and possible purchase based on specifications, user needs, and technical requirements. Contribute expertise to develop medical maintenance standard operating procedures. Compute power and space requirements for installing medical, dental, or related equipment and install units to manufacturers' specifications. Supervise and advise subordinate personnel. Repair shop equipment, metal furniture, and hospital equipment, including welding broken parts and

replacing missing parts, or bring item into local shop for major repairs.

GOE—Career Cluster/Interest Area: 13. Manufacturing. **Work Group:** 13.15. Medical and Technical Equipment Repair. **Other Apprenticeable Jobs in This Work Group:** Camera and Photographic Equipment Repairers; Watch Repairers. **Personality Type:** Realistic. These occupations frequently involve work activities that include practical, hands-on problems and solutions. They often deal with plants; animals; and real-world materials such as wood, tools, and machinery. Many of the occupations require working outside and don't involve a lot of paperwork or working closely with others.

Skills—Repairing; Installation; Equipment Maintenance; Troubleshooting; Science; Operation Monitoring; Systems Analysis; Quality Control Analysis.

Education/Training Required (Nonapprenticeship Route): Associate degree. **Related Knowledge/Courses—Mechanical Devices:** Machines and tools, including their designs, uses, benefits, repair, and maintenance. **Computers and Electronics:** Electric circuit boards, processors, chips, and computer hardware and software, including applications and programming. **Engineering and Technology:** Equipment, tools, and mechanical devices and their uses to produce motion, light, power, technology, and other applications. **Physics:** Physical principles, laws, and applications, including air, water, material dynamics, light, atomic principles, heat, electric theory, earth formations, and meteorological and related natural phenomena. **Telecommunications:** Transmission, broadcasting, switching, control, and operation of telecommunications systems. **Medicine and Dentistry:** The information and techniques needed to diagnose and treat injuries, diseases, and deformities. This includes symptoms, treatment alternatives, drug properties and interactions, and preventive health-care measures.

Work Environment: Indoors; contaminants; disease or infections; standing; using hands on objects, tools, or controls.

Medical Records and Health Information Technicians

* Annual Earnings: $29,290
* Growth: 17.8%
* Annual Job Openings: 39,048
* Percentage of Women: 92.0%

Related Apprenticeships—Medical Coder (2712 hrs.); Tumor Registrar (4000 hrs.).

Compile, process, and maintain medical records of hospital and clinic patients in a manner consistent with medical, administrative, ethical, legal, and regulatory requirements of the health-care system. Process, maintain, compile, and report patient information for health requirements and standards. Protect the security of medical records to ensure that confidentiality is maintained. Review records for completeness, accuracy, and compliance with regulations. Retrieve patient medical records for physicians, technicians, or other medical personnel. Release information to persons and agencies according to regulations. Plan, develop, maintain, and operate a variety of health record indexes and storage and retrieval systems to collect, classify, store, and analyze information. Enter data such as demographic characteristics, history and extent of disease, diagnostic procedures, and treatment into computer. Process and prepare business and government forms. Compile and maintain patients' medical records to document condition and treatment and to provide data for research or cost control and care improvement efforts. Process patient admission and discharge documents. Assign the patient to diagnosis-related groups (DRGs), using appropriate computer software. Transcribe medical reports. Identify, compile, abstract, and code patient data, using standard classification systems. Resolve or clarify codes and diagnoses with conflicting, missing, or unclear information by consulting with doctors or others or by participating in the coding team's regular meetings. Compile medical care and census data for statistical reports on diseases treated, surgeries performed, or use of hospital beds. Post medical insurance billings. Train medical records staff. Prepare statistical reports, narrative reports, and graphic presentations of information such as tumor registry data for use by hospital staff, researchers, or other users. Manage the department and supervise clerical workers, directing and controlling activities of personnel in the medical records department. Develop in-service educational materials. Consult classification manuals to locate information about disease processes.

GOE—Career Cluster/Interest Area: 08. Health Science. **Work Group:** 08.06. Medical Technology. **Other Apprenticeable Jobs in This Work Group:** Medical and Clinical Laboratory Technicians; Medical Equipment Preparers; Opticians, Dispensing; Radiologic Technologists. **Personality Type:** Conventional. These occupations frequently involve following set procedures and routines and can include working with data and details more than with ideas. Usually there is a clear line of authority to follow.

Skill—Systems Analysis.

Education/Training Required (Nonapprenticeship Route): Associate degree. **Related Knowledge/Courses—Clerical Practices:** Administrative and clerical procedures and systems such as word-processing systems, filing and records management systems, stenography and transcription, forms, design principles, and other office procedures and terminology. **Law and Government:** Laws, legal codes, court procedures, precedents, government regulations, executive orders, agency rules, and the democratic political process. **Customer and Personal Service:** Principles and processes for providing customer and personal services, including needs assessment techniques, quality service standards, alternative delivery systems, and customer satisfaction evaluation techniques.

Work Environment: Indoors; noisy; sitting; using hands on objects, tools, or controls; repetitive motions.

Medical Secretaries

- ✹ Annual Earnings: $28,950
- ✹ Growth: 16.7%
- ✹ Annual Job Openings: 60,659
- ✹ Percentage of Women: 96.9%

Related Apprenticeship—Medical Secretary (2000 hrs.).

Perform secretarial duties, using specific knowledge of medical terminology and hospital, clinical, or laboratory procedures. Duties include scheduling appointments, billing patients, and compiling and recording medical charts, reports, and correspondence. Answer telephones and direct calls to appropriate staff. Schedule and confirm patient diagnostic appointments, surgeries, and medical consultations. Greet visitors, ascertain purpose of visit, and direct them to appropriate staff. Operate office equipment, such as voice mail messaging systems, and use word processing, spreadsheet, and other software applications to prepare reports, invoices, financial statements, letters, case histories, and medical records. Complete insurance and other claim forms. Interview patients to complete documents, case histories, and forms such as intake and insurance forms. Receive and route messages and documents such as laboratory results to appropriate staff. Compile and record medical charts, reports, and correspondence, using typewriter or personal computer. Transmit correspondence and medical records by mail, e-mail, or fax. Maintain medical records, technical library documents, and correspondence files. Perform various clerical and administrative functions, such as ordering and maintaining an inventory of supplies. Perform bookkeeping duties, such as credits and collections, preparing and sending financial statements and bills, and keeping financial records. Transcribe recorded messages and practitioners' diagnoses and recommendations into patients' medical records. Arrange hospital admissions for patients. Prepare correspondence and assist physicians or medical scientists with preparation of reports, speeches, articles, and conference proceedings.

GOE—Career Cluster/Interest Area: 04. Business and Administration. **Work Group:** 04.04. Secretarial Support. **Other Apprenticeable Jobs in This Work Group:** Legal Secretaries; Secretaries, Except Legal, Medical, and Executive. **Personality Type:** Conventional. These occupations frequently involve following set procedures and routines and can include working with data and details more than with ideas. Usually there is a clear line of authority to follow.

Skills—None met the criteria.

Education/Training Required (Nonapprenticeship Route): Moderate-term on-the-job training. **Related Knowledge/Courses—Clerical Practices:** Administrative and clerical procedures and systems such as word-processing systems, filing and records management systems, stenography and transcription, forms, design principles, and other office procedures and terminology. **Medicine and Dentistry:** The information and techniques needed to diagnose and treat injuries, diseases, and deformities. This includes symptoms, treatment alternatives, drug properties and interactions, and preventive health-care measures. **Customer and Personal Service:** Principles and processes for providing customer and personal services, including needs assessment techniques, quality service standards, alternative delivery systems, and customer satisfaction evaluation techniques. **Computers and Electronics:** Electric circuit boards, processors, chips, and computer hardware and software, including applications and programming. **Economics and Accounting:** Economic and accounting principles and practices, the financial markets, banking, and the analysis and reporting of financial data.

Work Environment: Noisy; disease or infections; sitting; using hands on objects, tools, or controls.

Medical Transcriptionists

- ❋ Annual Earnings: $31,250
- ❋ Growth: 13.5%
- ❋ Annual Job Openings: 18,080
- ❋ Percentage of Women: 90.4%

Related Apprenticeship—Medical Transcriptionist (4000 hrs., hybrid).

Use transcribing machines with headset and foot pedal to listen to recordings by physicians and other health-care professionals dictating a variety of medical reports, such as emergency room visits, diagnostic imaging studies, operations, chart reviews, and final summaries. Transcribe dictated reports and translate medical jargon and abbreviations into their expanded forms. Edit as necessary and return reports in either printed or electronic form to the dictator for review and signature or correction. Transcribe dictation for a variety of medical reports such as patient histories, physical examinations, emergency room visits, operations, chart reviews, consultation, or discharge summaries. Review and edit transcribed reports or dictated material for spelling, grammar, clarity, consistency, and proper medical terminology. Distinguish between homonyms and recognize inconsistencies and mistakes in medical terms, referring to dictionaries; drug references; and other sources on anatomy, physiology, and medicine. Return dictated reports in printed or electronic form for physicians' review, signature, and corrections and for inclusion in patients' medical records. Translate medical jargon and abbreviations into their expanded forms to ensure the accuracy of patient and health-care facility records. Take dictation, using either shorthand or a stenotype machine or using headsets and transcribing machines; then convert dictated materials or rough notes to written form. Identify mistakes in reports and check with doctors to obtain the correct information. Perform data entry and data retrieval services, providing data for inclusion in medical records and for transmission to physicians. Produce medical reports, correspondence, records, patient-care information, statistics, medical research, and administrative material. Answer inquiries concerning the progress of medical cases within the limits of confidentiality laws. Set up and maintain medical files and databases, including records such as X-ray, lab, and procedure reports; medical histories; diagnostic workups; admission and discharge summaries; and clinical resumes. Perform a variety of clerical and office tasks, such as handling incoming and outgoing mail, completing and submitting insurance claims, typing, filing, and operating office machines. Decide which information should be included or excluded in reports. Receive patients, schedule appointments, and maintain patient records. Receive and screen telephone calls and visitors.

GOE—Career Cluster/Interest Area: 08. Health Science. **Work Group:** 08.02. Medicine and Surgery. **Other Apprenticeable Jobs in This Work Group:** Medical Assistants; Pharmacy Technicians; Surgical Technologists. **Personality Type:** Conventional. These occupations frequently involve following set procedures and routines and can include working with data and details more than with ideas. Usually there is a clear line of authority to follow.

Skills—Active Listening; Reading Comprehension; Time Management.

Education/Training Required (Nonapprenticeship Route): Postsecondary vocational training. **Related Knowledge/Courses—Clerical Practices:** Administrative and clerical procedures and systems such as word-processing systems, filing and records management systems, stenography and transcription, forms, design principles, and other office procedures and terminology. **English Language:** The structure and content of the English language, including the meaning and spelling of words, rules of composition, and grammar. **Medicine and Dentistry:**

The information and techniques needed to diagnose and treat injuries, diseases, and deformities. This includes symptoms, treatment alternatives, drug properties and interactions, and preventive health-care measures. **Computers and Electronics:** Electric circuit boards, processors, chips, and computer hardware and software, including applications and programming.

Work Environment: Indoors; sitting; using hands on objects, tools, or controls; repetitive motions.

Merchandise Displayers and Window Trimmers

* Annual Earnings: $24,830
* Growth: 10.7%
* Annual Job Openings: 9,103
* Percentage of Women: 55.5%

Related Apprenticeships—Decorator (Any Industry) (8000 hrs.); Displayer, Merchandise (2000 hrs.).

Plan and erect commercial displays, such as those in windows and interiors of retail stores and at trade exhibitions. Take photographs of displays and signage. Plan and erect commercial displays to entice and appeal to customers. Place prices and descriptive signs on backdrops, fixtures, merchandise, or floor. Change or rotate window displays, interior display areas, and signage to reflect changes in inventory or promotion. Obtain plans from display designers or display managers and discuss their implementation with clients or supervisors. Develop ideas or plans for merchandise displays or window decorations. Consult with advertising and sales staff to determine type of merchandise to be featured and time and place for each display. Arrange properties, furniture, merchandise, backdrops, and other accessories as shown in prepared sketches. Construct or assemble displays and display components from fabric, glass, paper, and plastic according to specifications, using hand tools and woodworking power tools. Collaborate with others to obtain products and other display items. Use computers to produce signage. Dress mannequins for displays. Maintain props and mannequins, inspecting them for imperfections and applying preservative coatings as necessary. Select themes, lighting, colors, and props to be used. Attend training sessions and corporate planning meetings to obtain new ideas for product launches. Instruct sales staff in color-coordination of clothing racks and counter displays. Store, pack, and maintain records of props and display items. Prepare sketches, floor plans, or models of proposed displays. Cut out designs on cardboard, hardboard, and plywood according to motif of event. Install booths, exhibits, displays, carpets, and drapes as guided by floor plan of building and specifications. Install decorations such as flags, banners, festive lights, and bunting on or in building, street, exhibit hall, or booth. Create and enhance mannequin faces by mixing and applying paint and attaching measured eyelash strips, using artist's brush, airbrush, pins, ruler, and scissors.

GOE—Career Cluster/Interest Area: 03. Arts and Communication. **Work Group:** 03.05. Design. **Other Apprenticeable Jobs in This Work Group:** Fashion Designers; Floral Designers; Interior Designers. **Personality Type:** Artistic. These occupations frequently involve working with forms, designs, and patterns. They often require self-expression, and the work can be done without following a clear set of rules.

Skills—Persuasion; Negotiation; Management of Personnel Resources.

Education/Training Required (Nonapprenticeship Route): Moderate-term on-the-job training. **Related Knowledge/Courses—Sales and Marketing:** Principles and methods involved in showing, promoting, and selling products or services. This includes marketing strategies and tactics, product demonstration and sales techniques, and sales control systems. **Design:** Design techniques, principles, tools, and instruments involved in the production and use of precision technical plans, blueprints, drawings, and models. **Administration and Management:** Principles and processes involved in business and organizational planning, coordination, and execution. This includes strategic planning, resource allocation, manpower modeling, leadership techniques, and production methods. **Computers and Electronics:** Electric circuit boards, processors, chips, and computer hardware and software, including applications and programming.

Work Environment: Indoors; contaminants; walking and running; using hands on objects, tools, or controls; bending or twisting the body; repetitive motions.

Millwrights

- ❀ Annual Earnings: $46,090
- ❀ Growth: 5.8%
- ❀ Annual Job Openings: 4,758
- ❀ Percentage of Women: 2.9%

Related Apprenticeships—Automated Equipment Engineer-Technician (8000 hrs.); Machine Erector (8000 hrs.); Millwright (5200–8000 hrs., hybrid); Millwright (8000 hrs.).

Install, dismantle, or move machinery and heavy equipment according to layout plans, blueprints, or other drawings. Replace defective parts of machine or adjust clearances and alignment of moving parts. Align machines and equipment, using hoists, jacks, hand tools, squares, rules, micrometers, and plumb bobs. Connect power unit to machines or steam piping to equipment and test unit to evaluate its mechanical operation. Repair and lubricate machines and equipment. Assemble and install equipment, using hand tools and power tools. Position steel beams to support bedplates of machines and equipment, using blueprints and schematic drawings to determine work procedures. Signal crane operator to lower basic assembly units to bedplate and align unit to centerline. Insert shims, adjust tension on nuts and bolts, or position parts, using hand tools and measuring instruments to set specified clearances between moving and stationary parts. Move machinery and equipment, using hoists, dollies, rollers, and trucks. Attach moving parts and subassemblies to basic assembly unit, using hand tools and power tools. Assemble machines and bolt, weld, rivet, or otherwise fasten them to foundation or other structures, using hand tools and power tools. Lay out mounting holes, using measuring instruments, and drill holes with power drill. Bolt parts, such as side and deck plates, jaw plates, and journals, to basic assembly unit. Dismantle machines, using hammers, wrenches, crowbars, and other hand tools. Level bedplate and establish centerline, using straightedge, levels, and transit. Shrink-fit bushings, sleeves, rings, liners, gears, and wheels to specified items, using portable gas heating equipment. Dismantle machinery and equipment for shipment to installation site, usually performing installation and maintenance work as part of team. Construct foundation for machines, using hand tools and building materials such as wood, cement, and steel. Install robot and modify its program, using teach pendant. Operate engine lathe to grind, file, and turn machine parts to dimensional specifications.

GOE—Career Cluster/Interest Area: 13. Manufacturing. **Work Group:** 13.13. Machinery Repair. **Other Apprenticeable Jobs in This Work Group:** Control and Valve Installers and Repairers, Except Mechanical Door; Home Appliance Repairers; Industrial Machinery Mechanics; Locksmiths and Safe Repairers; Maintenance Workers, Machinery; Mechanical Door Repairers; Signal and Track Switch Repairers. **Personality Type:** Realistic. These occupations frequently involve work activities that include practical, hands-on problems and solutions. They often deal with plants; animals; and real-world materials such as wood, tools, and machinery. Many of the occupations require working outside and don't involve a lot of paperwork or working closely with others.

Skills—Installation; Repairing; Troubleshooting; Equipment Maintenance; Equipment Selection; Mathematics; Technology Design; Operation Monitoring.

Education/Training Required (Nonapprenticeship Route): Long-term on-the-job training. **Related Knowledge/Courses—Mechanical Devices:** Machines and tools, including their designs, uses, benefits, repair, and maintenance. **Building and Construction:** Materials, methods, and the appropriate tools to construct objects, structures, and buildings. **Physics:** Physical principles, laws, and applications, including air, water, material dynamics, light, atomic principles, heat, electric theory, earth formations, and meteorological and related natural phenomena. **Engineering and Technology:** Equipment, tools, and mechanical devices and their uses to produce motion, light, power, technology, and other applications. **Design:** Design techniques, principles, tools, and instruments involved in the production and use of precision technical plans, blueprints, drawings, and models. **Public Safety and Security:** Weaponry; public safety; security operations, rules, regulations, precautions, and prevention; and the protection of people, data, and property.

Work Environment: Noisy; very hot or cold; very bright or dim lighting; contaminants; hazardous equipment; using hands on objects, tools, or controls.

Further Information: Contact a local joint union-management apprenticeship committee or the nearest office of your state employment service or apprenticeship agency (see Appendix C). To identify the local union office, contact United Brotherhood of Carpenters and Joiners of America, 101 Constitution Ave. NW, Washington, DC 20001. Internet: www. carpenters.org

Mine Cutting and Channeling Machine Operators

- ✳ Annual Earnings: $39,930
- ✳ Growth: 3.8%
- ✳ Annual Job Openings: 923
- ✳ Percentage of Women: 3.1%

Related Apprenticeship—Drilling-Machine Operator (6000 hrs.).

Operate machinery—such as longwall shears, plows, and cutting machines—to cut or channel along the face or seams of coal mines, stone quarries, or other mining surfaces to facilitate blasting, separating, or removing minerals or materials from mines or from the earth's surface. Position jacks, timbers, or roof supports and install casings to prevent cave-ins. Reposition machines and move controls to make additional holes or cuts. Cut entries between rooms and haulage-ways. Observe indicator lights and gauges and listen to machine operation to detect binding or stoppage of tools or other equipment problems. Replace worn or broken tools and machine bits and parts, using wrenches, pry bars, and other hand tools, and lubricate machines, using grease guns. Press buttons to activate conveyor belts and push or pull chain handles to regulate conveyor movement so that material can be moved or loaded into dinkey cars or dump trucks. Move planer levers to control and adjust the movement of equipment and the speed, height, and depth of cuts and to rotate swivel cutting booms. Cut slots along working faces of coal, salt, or other non-metal deposits to facilitate blasting by moving levers to start the machine and to control the vertical reciprocating drills. Cut and move shale from open pits. Signal that machine plow blades are properly positioned, using electronic buzzers or two-way radios. Drive mobile, truck-mounted, or track-mounted drilling or cutting machine in mines and quarries or on construction sites. Move controls to start and position drill cutters or torches and to advance tools into mines or quarry faces to complete horizontal or vertical cuts. Advance plow blades through coal strata by remote control according to electronic or radio signals from the tailer. Determine locations, boundaries, and depths of holes or channels to be cut. Signal crew members to adjust the speed of equipment to the rate of installation of roof supports and to adjust the speed of conveyors to the volume of coal. Remove debris such as loose shale from channels and planer travel areas. Charge and set off explosives in blasting holes. Signal truck drivers to position their vehicles for receiving shale from planer hoppers. Monitor movement of shale along conveyors from hoppers to trucks or railcars. Guide and assist crews in laying track for machines and resetting planer rails, supports, and blocking, using jacks, shovels, sledges, picks, and pinch bars.

GOE—Career Cluster/Interest Area: 01. Agriculture and Natural Resources. **Work Group:** 01.08. Mining and Drilling. **Other Apprenticeable Jobs in This Work Group:** Earth Drillers, Except Oil and Gas; Excavating and Loading Machine and Dragline Operators; Explosives Workers, Ordnance Handling Experts, and Blasters; Helpers—Extraction Workers; Rotary Drill Operators, Oil and Gas. **Personality Type:** Realistic. These occupations frequently involve work activities that include practical, hands-on problems and solutions. They often deal with plants; animals; and real-world materials such as wood, tools, and machinery. Many of the occupations require working outside and don't involve a lot of paperwork or working closely with others.

Skills—Repairing; Equipment Maintenance; Operation and Control; Operation Monitoring; Coordination; Troubleshooting.

Education/Training Required (Nonapprenticeship Route): Moderate-term on-the-job training. **Related Knowledge/Courses—Mechanical Devices:** Machines and tools, including their designs, uses, benefits, repair, and maintenance. **Physics:** Physical principles, laws, and applications, including air, water, material dynamics, light, atomic principles, heat, electric theory, earth formations, and meteorological and related natural phenomena.

Work Environment: Noisy; contaminants; hazardous conditions; hazardous equipment; using hands on objects, tools, or controls; repetitive motions.

Mixing and Blending Machine Setters, Operators, and Tenders

* Annual Earnings: $30,340
* Growth: –5.1%
* Annual Job Openings: 18,661
* Percentage of Women: 11.2%

Related Apprenticeship—Tinter (Paint and Varnish) (4000 hrs.).

Set up, operate, or tend machines to mix or blend materials such as chemicals, tobacco, liquids, color pigments, or explosive ingredients. Weigh or measure materials, ingredients, and products to ensure conformance to requirements. Test samples of materials or products to ensure compliance with specifications by using test equipment. Start machines to mix or blend ingredients; then allow them to mix for specified times. Dump or pour specified amounts of materials into machinery and equipment. Operate or tend machines to mix or blend any of a wide variety of materials, such as spices, dough batter, tobacco, fruit juices, chemicals, livestock feed, food products, color pigments, or explosive ingredients. Observe production and monitor equipment to ensure safe and efficient operation. Stop mixing or blending machines when specified product qualities are obtained; then open valves and start pumps to transfer mixtures. Collect samples of materials or products for laboratory testing. Use hand tools or other devices to add or mix chemicals and ingredients for processing. Examine materials, ingredients, or products visually or with hands to ensure conformance to established standards. Record operational and production data on specified forms. Transfer materials, supplies, and products between work areas, using moving equipment and hand tools. Tend accessory equipment such as pumps and conveyors to move materials or ingredients through production processes. Read work orders to determine production specifications and information. Compound and process ingredients or dyes according to formulas. Unload mixtures into containers or onto conveyors for further processing. Clean and maintain equipment with hand tools. Dislodge and clear jammed materials or other items from machinery and equipment with hand tools. Open valves to drain slurry from mixers into storage tanks.

GOE—Career Cluster/Interest Area: 13. Manufacturing. **Work Group:** 13.03. Production Work, Assorted Materials Processing. **Other Apprenticeable Jobs in This Work Group:** Bakers; Chemical Equipment Operators and Tenders; Coating, Painting, and Spraying Machine Setters, Operators, and Tenders; Cooling and Freezing Equipment Operators and Tenders; Cutting and Slicing Machine Setters, Operators, and Tenders; Extruding, Forming, Pressing, and Compacting Machine Setters, Operators, and Tenders; Food Batchmakers; Furnace, Kiln, Oven, Drier, and Kettle Operators and Tenders; Heat Treating Equipment Setters, Operators, and Tenders, Metal and Plastic; Metal-Refining Furnace Operators and Tenders; Plating and Coating Machine Setters, Operators, and Tenders, Metal and Plastic; Sawing Machine Setters, Operators, and Tenders, Wood; Separating, Filtering, Clarifying, Precipitating, and Still Machine Setters, Operators, and Tenders; Sewing Machine Operators; Slaughterers and Meat Packers; Team Assemblers; Woodworking Machine Setters, Operators, and Tenders, Except Sawing. **Personality Type:** Realistic. These occupations frequently involve work activities that include practical, hands-on problems and solutions. They often deal with plants; animals; and real-world materials such as wood, tools, and machinery. Many of the occupations require working outside and don't involve a lot of paperwork or working closely with others.

Skills—Operation Monitoring; Operation and Control; Equipment Maintenance; Repairing; Troubleshooting; Technology Design; Quality Control Analysis; Science.

Education/Training Required (Nonapprenticeship Route): Moderate-term on-the-job training. **Related Knowledge/Courses—Production and Processing:** Inputs, outputs, raw materials, waste, quality control, costs, and techniques for maximizing the manufacture and distribution of goods. **Chemistry:** The composition, structure, and properties of substances and of the chemical processes and transformations that they undergo. This includes uses of chemicals and their interactions, danger signs, production techniques, and disposal methods. **Mechanical Devices:** Machines and tools, including their designs, uses, benefits, repair, and maintenance. **Physics:** Physical principles, laws, and applications, including air, water, material dynamics, light, atomic principles, heat, electric theory, earth formations, and meteorological and related natural phenomena. **Mathematics:** Numbers and their operations and interrelationships, including arithmetic, algebra, geometry, calculus, and statistics and their applications. **Public Safety and Security:** Weaponry; public safety; security operations, rules, regulations, precautions, and prevention; and the protection of people, data, and property.

Work Environment: Noisy; contaminants; hazardous conditions; standing; walking and running; using hands on objects, tools, or controls.

Mobile Heavy Equipment Mechanics, Except Engines

❋ Annual Earnings: $41,450
❋ Growth: 12.3%
❋ Annual Job Openings: 11,037
❋ Percentage of Women: 1.4%

Related Apprenticeships—Construction Equipment Mechanic (8000 hrs.); Logging-Equipment Mechanic (8000 hrs.); Mechanic, Endless Track Vehicle (8000 hrs.).

Diagnose, adjust, repair, or overhaul mobile mechanical, hydraulic, and pneumatic equipment, such as cranes, bulldozers, graders, and conveyors, used in construction, logging, and surface mining. Test mechanical products and equipment after repair or assembly to ensure proper performance and compliance with manufacturers' specifications. Repair and replace damaged or worn parts. Diagnose faults or malfunctions to determine required repairs, using engine diagnostic equipment such as computerized test equipment and calibration devices. Operate and inspect machines or heavy equipment to diagnose defects. Dismantle and reassemble heavy equipment, using hoists and hand tools. Clean, lubricate, and perform other routine maintenance work on equipment and vehicles. Examine parts for damage or excessive wear, using micrometers and gauges. Read and understand operating manuals, blueprints, and technical drawings. Schedule maintenance for industrial machines and equipment and keep equipment service records. Overhaul and test machines or equipment to ensure operating efficiency. Assemble gear systems and align frames and gears. Fit bearings to adjust, repair, or overhaul mobile mechanical, hydraulic, and pneumatic equipment. Weld or solder broken parts and structural members, using electric or gas welders and soldering tools. Clean parts by spraying them with grease solvent or immersing them in tanks of solvent. Adjust, maintain, and repair or replace subassemblies, such as transmissions and crawler heads, using hand tools, jacks, and cranes. Adjust and maintain industrial machinery, using control and regulating devices. Fabricate needed parts or items from sheet metal. Direct workers who are assembling or disassembling equipment or cleaning parts.

GOE—Career Cluster/Interest Area: 13. Manufacturing. **Work Group:** 13.14. Vehicle and Facility Mechanical Work. **Other Apprenticeable Jobs in This Work Group:** Aircraft Mechanics and Service Technicians; Aircraft Structure, Surfaces, Rigging, and Systems Assemblers; Automotive Body and Related Repairers; Automotive Glass Installers and Repairers; Automotive Master Mechanics; Automotive Specialty Technicians; Bus and Truck Mechanics and Diesel Engine Specialists; Farm Equipment Mechanics; Fiberglass Laminators and Fabricators; Motorboat Mechanics; Motorcycle Mechanics; Outdoor Power Equipment and Other Small Engine Mechanics; Rail Car Repairers; Recreational Vehicle Service Technicians. **Personality Type:** Realistic. These occupations frequently involve work activities that include practical, hands-on problems and solutions. They often deal with plants; animals; and real-world materials such as wood, tools, and machinery. Many of the occupations require working outside and don't involve a lot of paperwork or working closely with others.

Skills—Installation; Repairing; Equipment Maintenance; Operation Monitoring; Troubleshooting; Operation and Control; Equipment Selection; Technology Design.

Education/Training Required (Nonapprenticeship Route): Long-term on-the-job training. **Related Knowledge/Courses—Mechanical Devices:** Machines and tools, including their designs, uses, benefits, repair, and maintenance. **Engineering and Technology:** Equipment, tools, and mechanical devices and their uses to produce motion, light, power, technology, and other applications. **Physics:** Physical principles, laws, and applications, including air, water, material dynamics, light, atomic principles, heat, electric theory, earth formations, and meteorological and related natural phenomena.

Work Environment: Noisy; contaminants; hazardous equipment; minor burns, cuts, bites, or stings; standing; using hands on objects, tools, or controls.

Motorboat Mechanics

- ❋ Annual Earnings: $34,210
- ❋ Growth: 19.0%
- ❋ Annual Job Openings: 4,326
- ❋ Percentage of Women: 3.4%

Related Apprenticeships—Motorboat Mechanic (6000 hrs.); Outboard-Motor Mechanic (4000 hrs.).

Repair and adjust electrical and mechanical equipment of gasoline or diesel-powered inboard or inboard-outboard boat engines. Disassemble and inspect motors to locate defective parts, using mechanic's hand tools and gauges. Adjust generators and replace faulty wiring, using hand tools and soldering irons. Start motors and monitor performance for signs of malfunctioning such as smoke, excessive vibration, and misfiring. Adjust carburetor mixtures, electrical point settings, and timing while motors are running in water-filled test tanks. Idle motors and observe thermometers to determine the effectiveness of cooling systems. Inspect and repair or adjust propellers and propeller shafts. Mount motors to boats and operate boats at various speeds on waterways to conduct operational tests. Replace parts such as gears, magneto points, piston rings, and spark plugs, and then reassemble engines. Repair or rework parts, using machine tools such as lathes, mills, drills, and grinders. Repair engine mechanical equipment such as power-tilts, bilge pumps, or power take-offs. Set starter locks and align and repair steering or throttle controls, using gauges, screwdrivers, and wrenches. Document inspection and test results, as well as work performed or to be performed.

GOE—Career Cluster/Interest Area: 13. Manufacturing. **Work Group:** 13.14. Vehicle and Facility Mechanical Work. **Other Apprenticeable Jobs in This Work Group:** Aircraft Mechanics and Service Technicians; Aircraft Structure, Surfaces, Rigging, and Systems Assemblers; Automotive Body and Related Repairers; Automotive Glass Installers and Repairers; Automotive Master Mechanics; Automotive Specialty Technicians; Bus and Truck Mechanics and Diesel Engine Specialists; Farm Equipment Mechanics; Fiberglass Laminators and Fabricators; Mobile Heavy Equipment Mechanics, Except Engines; Motorcycle Mechanics; Outdoor Power Equipment and Other Small Engine Mechanics; Rail Car Repairers; Recreational Vehicle Service Technicians. **Personality Type:** Realistic. These occupations frequently involve work activities that include practical, hands-on problems and solutions. They often deal with plants; animals; and real-world materials such as wood, tools, and machinery. Many of the occupations require working outside and don't involve a lot of paperwork or working closely with others.

Skills—Repairing; Installation; Equipment Maintenance; Troubleshooting; Technology Design; Operation Monitoring; Operation and Control; Equipment Selection.

Education/Training Required (Nonapprenticeship Route): Long-term on-the-job training. **Related Knowledge/Courses—Mechanical Devices:** Machines and tools, including their designs, uses, benefits, repair, and maintenance. **Engineering and Technology:** Equipment, tools, and mechanical devices and their uses to produce motion, light, power, technology, and other applications. **Design:** Design techniques, principles, tools, and instruments involved in the production and use of precision technical plans, blueprints, drawings, and models. **Physics:** Physical principles, laws, and applications, including air, water, material dynamics, light, atomic principles, heat, electric theory, earth formations, and meteorological and related natural phenomena. **Chemistry:** The composition, structure, and properties of substances and of the chemical processes and transformations that they undergo. This includes uses of chemicals and their interactions, danger signs, production techniques, and disposal methods. **Transportation:** Principles and methods for moving people or goods by air, rail, sea, or road, including their relative costs, advantages, and limitations.

Work Environment: More often indoors than outdoors; standing; using hands on objects, tools, or controls.

Motorcycle Mechanics

* Annual Earnings: $30,300
* Growth: 12.5%
* Annual Job Openings: 3,564
* Percentage of Women: 3.4%

Related Apprenticeship—Motorcycle Repairer (6000 hrs.).

Diagnose, adjust, repair, or overhaul motorcycles, scooters, mopeds, dirt bikes, or similar motorized vehicles. Repair and adjust motorcycle subassemblies such as forks, transmissions, brakes, and drive chains according to specifications. Replace defective parts, using hand tools, arbor presses, flexible power presses, or power tools. Connect test panels to engines and measure generator output, ignition timing, and other engine performance indicators. Listen to engines, examine vehicle frames, and confer with customers to determine nature and extent of malfunction or damage. Reassemble and test subassembly units. Dismantle engines and repair or replace defective parts, such as magnetos, carburetors, and generators. Remove cylinder heads; grind valves; scrape off carbon; and replace defective valves, pistons, cylinders, and rings, using hand tools and power tools. Repair or replace other parts, such as headlights, horns, handlebar controls, gasoline and oil tanks, starters, and mufflers. Disassemble subassembly units and examine condition, movement, or alignment of parts visually or by using gauges. Hammer out dents and bends in frames, weld tears and breaks, and reassemble frames and reinstall engines.

GOE—Career Cluster/Interest Area: 13. Manufacturing. **Work Group:** 13.14. Vehicle and Facility Mechanical Work. **Other Apprenticeable Jobs in This Work Group:** Aircraft

Mechanics and Service Technicians; Aircraft Structure, Surfaces, Rigging, and Systems Assemblers; Automotive Body and Related Repairers; Automotive Glass Installers and Repairers; Automotive Master Mechanics; Automotive Specialty Technicians; Bus and Truck Mechanics and Diesel Engine Specialists; Farm Equipment Mechanics; Fiberglass Laminators and Fabricators; Mobile Heavy Equipment Mechanics, Except Engines; Motorboat Mechanics; Outdoor Power Equipment and Other Small Engine Mechanics; Rail Car Repairers; Recreational Vehicle Service Technicians. **Personality Type:** Realistic. These occupations frequently involve work activities that include practical, hands-on problems and solutions. They often deal with plants; animals; and real-world materials such as wood, tools, and machinery. Many of the occupations require working outside and don't involve a lot of paperwork or working closely with others.

Skills—Repairing; Installation; Troubleshooting; Equipment Maintenance; Science; Technology Design; Mathematics; Equipment Selection.

Education/Training Required (Nonapprenticeship Route): Long-term on-the-job training. **Related Knowledge/Courses—Mechanical Devices:** Machines and tools, including their designs, uses, benefits, repair, and maintenance. **Design:** Design techniques, principles, tools, and instruments involved in the production and use of precision technical plans, blueprints, drawings, and models. **Engineering and Technology:** Equipment, tools, and mechanical devices and their uses to produce motion, light, power, technology, and other applications. **Physics:** Physical principles, laws, and applications, including air, water, material dynamics, light, atomic principles, heat, electric theory, earth formations, and meteorological and related

natural phenomena. **Transportation:** Principles and methods for moving people or goods by air, rail, sea, or road, including their relative costs, advantages, and limitations. **Chemistry:** The composition, structure, and properties of substances and of the chemical processes and transformations that they undergo. This includes uses of chemicals and their interactions, danger signs, production techniques, and disposal methods.

Work Environment: Indoors; noisy; contaminants; standing; using hands on objects, tools, or controls; bending or twisting the body.

Multiple Machine Tool Setters, Operators, and Tenders, Metal and Plastic

- ✽ Annual Earnings: $30,390
- ✽ Growth: 0.3%
- ✽ Annual Job Openings: 15,709
- ✽ Percentage of Women: 30.4%

Related Apprenticeships—Four-Slide-Machine Setter (4000 hrs.); Gear Hobber Setup Operator (8000 hrs.); Gearcut-Machine Set-Up Operator and Tool Setter (6000 hrs.); Gear-Cutting-Machine Setup Operator (6000 hrs.); Gunsmith (8000 hrs.); Machine Operator I (2000 hrs.); Machine Setter (Any Industry) (8000 hrs.); Machine Setter (Clock) (8000 hrs.); Machine Setter (Machine Shop) (6000 hrs.); Machine Set-Up Operator (4000 hrs.); Machine Tryout Setter (8000 hrs.); Ornamental Metal Worker (8000 hrs.); Spring Maker (8000 hrs.); Spring-Manufacturing Set-Up Technician (8000 hrs.); Tool Machine Set-Up Operator (6000 hrs.).

Set up, operate, or tend more than one type of cutting or forming machine tool or robot. Inspect workpieces for defects and measure workpieces to determine accuracy of machine operation, using rules, templates, or other measuring instruments. Observe machine operation to detect workpiece defects or machine malfunctions; adjust machines as necessary. Read blueprints or job orders to determine product specifications and tooling instructions and to plan operational sequences. Set up and operate machines such as lathes, cutters, shears, borers, millers, grinders, presses, drills, and auxiliary machines to make metallic and plastic workpieces. Position, adjust, and secure stock material or workpieces against stops; on arbors; or in chucks, fixtures, or automatic feeding mechanisms manually or by using hoists. Select, install, and adjust alignment of drills, cutters, dies, guides, and holding devices, using templates, measuring instruments, and hand tools. Change worn machine accessories such as cutting tools and brushes, using hand tools. Make minor electrical and mechanical repairs and adjustments to machines and notify supervisors when major service is required. Start machines and turn handwheels or valves to engage feeding, cooling, and lubricating mechanisms. Perform minor machine maintenance, such as oiling or cleaning machines, dies, or workpieces or adding coolant to machine reservoirs. Select the proper coolants and lubricants and start their flow. Remove burrs, sharp edges, rust, or scale from workpieces, using files, hand grinders, wire brushes, or power tools. Instruct other workers in machine setup and operation. Record operational data such as pressure readings, lengths of strokes, feed rates, and speeds. Extract or lift jammed pieces from machines, using fingers, wire hooks, or lift bars. Set machine stops or guides to specified lengths as indicated by scales, rules, or templates. Move controls or mount gears, cams, or templates in machines to set feed rates and cutting speeds, depths, and angles. Compute data such as gear dimensions and machine settings, applying knowledge of shop mathematics. Align layout marks with dies or blades. Measure and mark reference points and cutting lines on workpieces, using traced templates, compasses, and rules.

GOE—Career Cluster/Interest Area: 13. Manufacturing. **Work Group:** 13.02. Machine Setup and Operation. **Other Apprenticeable Jobs in This Work Group:** Crushing, Grinding, and Polishing Machine Setters, Operators, and Tenders; Cutting, Punching, and Press Machine Setters, Operators, and Tenders, Metal and Plastic; Extruding and Drawing Machine Setters, Operators, and Tenders, Metal and Plastic; Forging Machine Setters, Operators, and Tenders, Metal and Plastic; Grinding, Lapping, Polishing, and Buffing Machine Tool Setters, Operators, and Tenders, Metal and Plastic; Lathe and Turning Machine Tool Setters, Operators, and Tenders, Metal and Plastic; Milling and Planing Machine Setters, Operators, and Tenders, Metal and Plastic; Paper Goods Machine Setters, Operators, and Tenders; Rolling Machine Setters, Operators, and Tenders, Metal and Plastic; Textile Knitting and Weaving Machine Setters, Operators, and Tenders; Textile Winding, Twisting, and Drawing Out Machine Setters, Operators, and Tenders. **Personality Type:** Realistic. These occupations frequently involve work activities that include practical, hands-on problems and solutions. They often deal with plants; animals; and real-world materials such as wood, tools, and machinery. Many of the occupations require working outside and don't involve a lot of paperwork or working closely with others.

Skills—Operation Monitoring; Repairing; Equipment Maintenance; Quality Control Analysis; Operation and Control; Troubleshooting; Installation; Learning Strategies.

Education/Training Required (Nonapprenticeship Route): Moderate-term on-the-job training. **Related Knowledge/Courses—Mechanical Devices:** Machines and tools, including their designs, uses, benefits, repair, and maintenance. **Production and Processing:** Inputs, outputs, raw materials, waste, quality control, costs, and techniques for maximizing the manufacture and distribution of goods. **Design:** Design techniques, principles, tools, and instruments involved in the production and use of precision technical plans, blueprints, drawings, and models. **Engineering and Technology:** Equipment, tools, and mechanical devices and their uses to produce motion, light, power, technology, and other applications.

Work Environment: Noisy; contaminants; hazardous equipment; minor burns, cuts, bites, or stings; standing; using hands on objects, tools, or controls.

Municipal Fire Fighters

- ❋ Annual Earnings: $43,170
- ❋ Growth: 12.1%
- ❋ Annual Job Openings: 18,887
- ❋ Percentage of Women: 3.5%

Our sources did not provide separate job openings data for this occupation. The job openings listed here are shared with Forest Fire Fighters.

Related Apprenticeships—Fire Apparatus Engineer (6000 hrs.); Fire Engineer (2000 hrs.); Fire Fighter (6000 hrs.); Fire Fighter Diver (7000 hrs.); Fire Fighter Paramedic (8000 hrs.); Fire Fighter, Crash, Fire (2000 hrs.); Fire Medic (6000 hrs.).

Control and extinguish municipal fires, protect life and property, and conduct rescue efforts. Administer first aid and cardiopulmonary resuscitation to injured persons. Rescue victims from burning buildings and accident sites. Search burning buildings to locate fire victims. Drive and operate fire fighting vehicles and equipment. Move toward the source of a fire, using knowledge of types of fires, construction design, building materials, and physical layout of properties. Dress with equipment such as fire-resistant clothing and breathing apparatus. Position and climb ladders to gain access to upper levels of buildings or to rescue individuals from burning structures. Take action to contain hazardous chemicals that might catch fire, leak, or spill. Assess fires and situations and report conditions to superiors to receive instructions, using two-way radios. Respond to fire alarms and other calls for assistance, such as automobile and industrial accidents. Operate pumps connected to high-pressure hoses. Select and attach hose nozzles, depending on fire type, and direct streams of water or chemicals onto fires. Create openings in buildings for ventilation or entrance, using axes, chisels, crowbars, electric saws, or core cutters. Inspect fire sites after flames have been extinguished to ensure that there is no further danger. Lay hose lines and connect them to water supplies. Protect property from water and smoke, using waterproof salvage covers, smoke ejectors, and deodorants. Participate in physical training activities to maintain a high level of physical fitness. Salvage property by removing broken glass, pumping out water, and ventilating buildings to remove smoke. Participate in fire drills and demonstrations of fire fighting techniques. Clean and maintain fire stations and fire fighting equipment and apparatus. Collaborate with police to respond to accidents, disasters, and arson investigation calls. Establish firelines to prevent unauthorized persons from entering areas near fires. Inform and educate the public on fire prevention. Inspect buildings for fire hazards and compliance with fire prevention ordinances, testing and checking smoke alarms and fire suppression equipment as necessary.

GOE—Career Cluster/Interest Area: 12. Law and Public Safety. **Work Group:** 12.06. Emergency Responding. **Other Apprenticeable Jobs in This Work Group:** Emergency Medical Technicians and Paramedics; Forest Fire Fighters. **Personality Type:** Realistic. These occupations frequently involve work activities that include practical, hands-on problems and solutions. They often deal with plants; animals; and real-world materials such as wood, tools, and machinery. Many of the occupations require working outside and don't involve a lot of paperwork or working closely with others.

Skills—Equipment Maintenance; Equipment Selection; Service Orientation; Operation Monitoring; Science; Social Perceptiveness; Coordination; Complex Problem Solving.

Education/Training Required (Nonapprenticeship Route): Long-term on-the-job training. **Related Knowledge/Courses—Medicine and Dentistry:** The information and techniques needed to diagnose and treat injuries, diseases, and deformities. This includes symptoms, treatment alternatives, drug properties and interactions, and preventive health-care measures. **Physics:** Physical principles, laws, and applications, including air, water, material dynamics, light, atomic principles, heat, electric theory, earth formations, and meteorological and related natural phenomena. **Customer and Personal Service:** Principles and processes for providing customer and personal services, including needs assessment techniques, quality service standards, alternative delivery systems, and customer

satisfaction evaluation techniques. **Building and Construction:** Materials, methods, and the appropriate tools to construct objects, structures, and buildings. **Chemistry:** The composition, structure, and properties of substances and of the chemical processes and transformations that they undergo. This includes uses of chemicals and their interactions, danger signs, production techniques, and disposal methods. **Public Safety and Security:** Weaponry; public safety; security operations, rules, regulations, precautions, and prevention; and the protection of people, data, and property.

Work Environment: More often outdoors than indoors; noisy; contaminants; disease or infections; hazardous equipment.

Municipal Fire Fighting and Prevention Supervisors

- ❋ Annual Earnings: $65,040
- ❋ Growth: 11.5%
- ❋ Annual Job Openings: 3,771
- ❋ Percentage of Women: 7.2%

Our sources did not provide separate job openings data for this occupation. The job openings listed here are shared with Forest Fire Fighting and Prevention Supervisors.

Related Apprenticeships—Fire Captain (6000 hrs.); Fire Prevention Officer (4000 hrs.).

Supervise fire fighters who control and extinguish municipal fires, protect life and property, and conduct rescue efforts. Assign firefighters to jobs at strategic locations to facilitate rescue of persons and maximize application of extinguishing agents. Provide emergency medical services as required and perform light to heavy rescue functions at emergencies. Assess nature and extent of fire, condition of building, danger to adjacent buildings, and water supply status to determine crew or company requirements. Instruct and drill fire department personnel in assigned duties, including firefighting, medical care, hazardous materials response, fire prevention, and related subjects. Evaluate the performance of assigned firefighting personnel. Direct the training of firefighters, assigning of instructors to training classes, and providing of supervisors with reports on training progress and status. Prepare activity reports listing fire call locations, actions taken, fire types and probable causes, damage estimates, and situation dispositions. Maintain required maps and records. Attend in-service training classes to remain current in knowledge of codes, laws, ordinances, and regulations. Evaluate fire station procedures to ensure efficiency and enforcement of departmental regulations. Direct firefighters in station maintenance duties and participate in these duties. Compile and maintain equipment and personnel records, including accident reports. Direct investigation of cases of suspected arson, hazards, and false alarms and submit reports outlining findings. Recommend personnel actions related to disciplinary procedures, performance, leaves of absence, and grievances. Supervise and participate in the inspection of properties to ensure that they are in compliance with applicable fire codes, ordinances, laws, regulations, and standards. Write and submit proposals for repair, modification, or replacement of firefighting equipment. Coordinate the distribution of fire prevention promotional materials. Identify corrective actions needed to bring properties into compliance with applicable fire codes and ordinances and conduct follow-up inspections to see if corrective actions have been taken. Participate in creating fire safety guidelines and evacuation schemes for non-residential buildings.

GOE—Career Cluster/Interest Area: 12. Law and Public Safety. **Work Group:** 12.01. Managerial Work in Law and Public Safety. **Other Apprenticeable Jobs in This Work Group:** Emergency Management Specialists. **Personality Type:** Enterprising. These occupations frequently involve starting up and carrying out projects and can involve leading people and making many decisions. They sometimes require risk taking and often deal with business.

Skills—Equipment Maintenance; Management of Personnel Resources; Service Orientation; Operation Monitoring; Management of Material Resources; Coordination; Operation and Control; Equipment Selection.

Education/Training Required (Nonapprenticeship Route): Work experience in a related occupation. **Related Knowledge/Courses—Public Safety and Security:** Weaponry; public safety; security operations, rules, regulations, precautions, and prevention; and the protection of people, data, and property. **Building and Construction:** Materials, methods, and the appropriate tools to construct objects, structures, and buildings. **Medicine and Dentistry:** The information and techniques needed to diagnose and treat injuries, diseases, and deformities. This includes symptoms, treatment alternatives, drug properties and interactions, and preventive health-care measures. **Education and Training:** Instructional methods and training techniques, including curriculum design principles, learning theory, group and individual teaching techniques, design of individual development plans, and test design principles. **Mechanical Devices:** Machines and tools, including their designs, uses, benefits, repair, and maintenance. **Therapy and Counseling:** Information and techniques needed to rehabilitate physical and mental ailments and to provide career guidance, including alternative treatments, rehabilitation equipment and its proper use, and methods to evaluate treatment effects.

Work Environment: More often outdoors than indoors; noisy; contaminants; disease or infections; hazardous equipment.

Nuclear Monitoring Technicians

* ❋ Annual Earnings: $66,140
* ❋ Growth: 6.7%
* ❋ Annual Job Openings: 1,021
* ❋ Percentage of Women: 43.3%

Our sources did not provide separate job openings data for this occupation. The job openings listed here are shared with Nuclear Equipment Operation Technicians.

Related Apprenticeship—Radiation Monitor (8000 hrs.).

Collect and test samples to monitor results of nuclear experiments and contamination of humans, facilities, and environment. Calculate safe radiation exposure times for personnel, using plant contamination readings and prescribed safe levels of radiation. Provide initial response to abnormal events and to alarms from radiation monitoring equipment. Monitor personnel in order to determine the amounts and intensities of radiation exposure. Inform supervisors when individual exposures or area radiation levels approach maximum permissible limits. Instruct personnel in radiation safety procedures and demonstrate use of protective clothing and equipment. Determine intensities and types of radiation in work areas, equipment, and materials, using radiation detectors and other instruments. Collect samples of air, water, gases, and solids to determine radioactivity levels of contamination. Set up equipment that automatically detects area radiation deviations and test detection equipment to ensure its accuracy. Determine or recommend radioactive decontamination procedures according to the size and nature of equipment and the degree of contamination. Decontaminate objects by cleaning with soap or solvents or by abrading with wire brushes, buffing wheels, or sandblasting machines. Place radioactive waste, such as sweepings and broken sample bottles, into containers for disposal. Calibrate and maintain chemical instrumentation sensing elements and sampling system equipment, using calibration instruments and hand tools. Place irradiated nuclear fuel materials in environmental chambers for testing and observe reactions through cell windows. Enter data into computers in order to record characteristics of nuclear events and locating coordinates of particles. Operate manipulators from outside cells to move specimens into and out of shielded containers, to remove specimens from cells, or to place specimens on benches or equipment workstations. Prepare reports describing contamination tests, material and equipment decontaminated, and methods used in decontamination processes. Confer with scientists directing projects to determine significant events to monitor during tests. Immerse samples in chemical compounds to prepare them for testing.

GOE—Career Cluster/Interest Area: 07. Government and Public Administration. **Work Group:** 07.03. Regulations Enforcement. **Other Apprenticeable Jobs in This Work Group:** Compliance Officers, Except Agriculture, Construction, Health and Safety, and Transportation; Construction and Building Inspectors; Equal Opportunity Representatives and Officers; Fire Inspectors; Fish and Game Wardens; Government Property Inspectors and Investigators;

Transportation Vehicle, Equipment and Systems Inspectors, Except Aviation. **Personality Type:** Realistic. These occupations frequently involve work activities that include practical, hands-on problems and solutions. They often deal with plants; animals; and real-world materials such as wood, tools, and machinery. Many of the occupations require working outside and don't involve a lot of paperwork or working closely with others.

Skills—Science; Operation Monitoring; Equipment Maintenance; Mathematics; Operation and Control; Equipment Selection; Technology Design; Systems Analysis.

Education/Training Required (Nonapprenticeship Route): Associate degree. **Related Knowledge/Courses—Physics:** Physical principles, laws, and applications, including air, water, material dynamics, light, atomic principles, heat, electric theory, earth formations, and meteorological and related natural phenomena. **Chemistry:** The composition, structure, and properties of substances and of the chemical processes and transformations that they undergo. This includes uses of chemicals and their interactions, danger signs, production techniques, and disposal methods. **Public Safety and Security:** Weaponry; public safety; security operations, rules, regulations, precautions, and prevention; and the protection of people, data, and property. **Engineering and Technology:** Equipment, tools, and mechanical devices and their uses to produce motion, light, power, technology, and other applications. **Biology:** Plant and animal living tissue, cells, organisms, and entities, including their functions, interdependencies, and interactions with each other and the environment. **Design:** Design techniques, principles, tools, and instruments involved in the production and use of precision technical plans, blueprints, drawings, and models.

Work Environment: Indoors; noisy; very hot or cold; contaminants; radiation; hazardous conditions.

Nursing Aides, Orderlies, and Attendants

- ❀ Annual Earnings: $23,160
- ❀ Growth: 18.2%
- ❀ Annual Job Openings: 321,036
- ❀ Percentage of Women: 88.9%

Related Apprenticeships—Certified Nursing Assistant (Medication Aide Specialty) (700–1200 hrs. or competency); Nurse Assistant (2000 hrs.); Nurse Assistant, Certified/CNA/Level 1 (300–600 hrs. or competency); Nurse Assistant, Certified/CNA/Level 2 (Advanced) (300–600 hrs. or competency); Nurse Assistant, Certified/CNA/Level 3 (Dementia Specialty) (1000 hrs. or competency); Nurse Assistant, Certified/CNA/Level 3 (Geriatric Specialty) (1000 hrs. or competency); Nurse Assistant, Certified/CNA/Level 3 (Restorative Specialty) (1000 hrs. or competency); Nurse Assistant, Certified/CNA/Level 4 (Mentor Specialty) (1000 hrs. or competency); Nursing Assistant, Certified (6000 hrs. or competency).

Provide basic patient care under direction of nursing staffs. Perform duties such as feeding, bathing, dressing, grooming, or moving patients or changing linens. Answer patients' call signals. Turn and reposition bedridden patients, alone or with assistance, to prevent bedsores. Observe patients' conditions, measuring and recording food and liquid intake and output and vital signs, reporting changes to professionals. Feed patients who are unable to feed themselves. Provide patients with help walking, exercising, and moving in and out of bed. Provide patient care by supplying and emptying bed pans, applying dressings, and supervising exercise routines. Bathe, groom, shave, dress, or drape patients to prepare them for surgery, treatment, or examination. Transport patients to treatment units, using a wheelchair or stretcher. Clean rooms and change linens. Collect specimens such as urine, feces, or sputum. Prepare, serve, and collect food trays. Deliver messages, documents, and specimens. Answer phones and direct visitors. Restrain patients if necessary. Set up equipment such as oxygen tents, portable X-ray machines, and overhead irrigation bottles. Explain medical instructions to patients and family members. Work as part of a medical team that examines and treats clinic outpatients. Maintain inventories by storing, preparing, sterilizing, and issuing supplies such as dressing packs and treatment trays. Administer medications and treatments such as catheterizations, suppositories, irrigations, enemas, massages, and douches as directed by a physician or nurse. Perform clerical duties such as processing documents and scheduling appointments.

GOE—Career Cluster/Interest Area: 08. Health Science. **Work Group:** 08.08. Patient Care and Assistance. **Other Apprenticeable Jobs in This Work Group:** Home Health Aides; Licensed Practical and Licensed Vocational Nurses. **Personality Type:** Social. These occupations frequently involve working with, communicating with, and teaching people and often involve helping or providing service to others.

Skills—None met the criteria.

Education/Training Required (Nonapprenticeship Route): Postsecondary vocational training. **Related Knowledge/Courses—Medicine and Dentistry:** The information and techniques needed to diagnose and treat injuries, diseases, and deformities. This includes symptoms, treatment alternatives, drug properties and interactions, and preventive health-care measures. **Psychology:** Human behavior and performance, mental processes, psychological research methods, and the assessment and treatment of behavioral and affective disorders. **Therapy and Counseling:** Information and techniques needed to rehabilitate physical and mental ailments and to provide career guidance, including alternative treatments, rehabilitation equipment and its proper use, and methods to evaluate treatment effects. **Customer and Personal Service:** Principles and processes for providing customer and personal services, including needs assessment techniques, quality service standards, alternative delivery systems, and customer satisfaction evaluation techniques.

Work Environment: Indoors; disease or infections; standing; walking and running; using hands on objects, tools, or controls; bending or twisting the body.

Office Clerks, General

* Annual Earnings: $24,460
* Growth: 12.6%
* Annual Job Openings: 765,803
* Percentage of Women: 81.9%

Related Apprenticeship—Health Unit Coordinator (2000 hrs.).

Perform duties too varied and diverse to be classified in any specific office clerical occupation requiring limited knowledge of office management systems and procedures. Clerical duties may be assigned in accordance

with the office procedures of individual establishments and may include a combination of answering telephones, bookkeeping, typing or word processing, stenography, office machine operation, and filing. Collect, count, and disburse money; do basic bookkeeping; and complete banking transactions. Communicate with customers, employees, and other individuals to answer questions, disseminate or explain information, take orders, and address complaints. Answer telephones, direct calls, and take messages. Compile, copy, sort, and file records of office activities, business transactions, and other activities. Complete and mail bills, contracts, policies, invoices, or checks. Operate office machines such as photocopiers and scanners, facsimile machines, voice mail systems, and personal computers. Compute, record, and proofread data and other information, such as records or reports. Maintain and update filing, inventory, mailing, and database systems, either manually or using a computer. Open, sort, and route incoming mail; answer correspondence; and prepare outgoing mail. Review files, records, and other documents to obtain information to respond to requests. Deliver messages and run errands. Inventory and order materials, supplies, and services. Complete work schedules, manage calendars, and arrange appointments. Process and prepare documents such as business or government forms and expense reports. Monitor and direct the work of lower-level clerks. Type, format, proofread, and edit correspondence and other documents from notes or dictating machines, using computers or typewriters. Count, weigh, measure, or organize materials. Train other staff members to perform work activities, such as using computer applications. Prepare meeting agendas, attend meetings, and record and transcribe minutes. Troubleshoot problems involving office equipment, such as computer hardware and software. Make travel arrangements for office personnel.

GOE—Career Cluster/Interest Area: 04. Business and Administration. **Work Group:** 04.07. Records and Materials Processing. **Other Apprenticeable Jobs in This Work Group:** Human Resources Assistants, Except Payroll and Timekeeping; Postal Service Clerks; Production, Planning, and Expediting Clerks. **Personality Type:** Conventional. These occupations frequently involve following set procedures and routines and can include working with data and details more than with ideas. Usually there is a clear line of authority to follow.

Skills—None met the criteria.

Education/Training Required (Nonapprenticeship Route): Short-term on-the-job training. **Related Knowledge/Courses—Clerical Practices:** Administrative and clerical procedures and systems such as word-processing systems, filing and records management systems, stenography and transcription, forms, design principles, and other office procedures and terminology. **Economics and Accounting:** Economic and accounting principles and practices, the financial markets, banking, and the analysis and reporting of financial data. **Customer and Personal Service:** Principles and processes for providing customer and personal services, including needs assessment techniques, quality service standards, alternative delivery systems, and customer satisfaction evaluation techniques. **Personnel and Human Resources:** Principles and procedures for personnel recruitment; selection; training; compensation and benefits; labor relations and negotiation; and personnel information systems. **Mathematics:** Numbers and their operations and interrelationships, including arithmetic, algebra, geometry, calculus, and statistics and their applications. **Computers and Electronics:** Electric circuit boards, processors, chips, and computer hardware and software, including applications and programming.

Work Environment: Indoors; sitting; using hands on objects, tools, or controls.

Operating Engineers and Other Construction Equipment Operators

* Annual Earnings: $38,130
* Growth: 8.4%
* Annual Job Openings: 55,468
* Percentage of Women: 1.7%

Related Apprenticeships—Elevating-Grader Operator (4000 hrs.); Motor-Grader Operator (6000 hrs.); Operating Engineer (6000 hrs.); Operating Engineer (Grade and Paving Equipment Operator) (4000–6000 hrs., hybrid); Operating Engineer (Heavy Duty Repairer) (4000–6000 hrs., hybrid); Operating Engineer (Plant Equipment Operator) (4000–6000 hrs., hybrid); Operating Engineer (Universal-Equipment Operator) (4000–6000 hrs., hybrid).

Operate one or several types of power construction equipment, such as motor graders, bulldozers, scrapers, compressors, pumps, derricks, shovels, tractors, or front-end loaders, to excavate, move, and grade earth; erect structures; or pour concrete or other hard-surface pavement. May repair and maintain equipment in addition to other duties. Learn and follow safety regulations. Take actions to avoid potential hazards and obstructions such as utility lines, other equipment, other workers, and falling objects. Adjust handwheels and depress pedals to control attachments such as blades, buckets, scrapers, and swing booms. Start

engines; move throttles, switches, and levers; and depress pedals to operate machines such as bulldozers, trench excavators, road graders, and backhoes. Locate underground services, such as pipes and wires, prior to beginning work. Monitor operations to ensure that health and safety standards are met. Align machines, cutterheads, or depth gauge makers with reference stakes and guidelines or ground or position equipment by following hand signals of other workers. Load and move dirt, rocks, equipment, and materials, using trucks, crawler tractors, power cranes, shovels, graders, and related equipment. Drive and maneuver equipment equipped with blades in successive passes over working areas to remove topsoil, vegetation, and rocks and to distribute and level earth or terrain. Coordinate machine actions with other activities, positioning or moving loads in response to hand or audio signals from crew members. Operate tractors and bulldozers to perform such tasks as clearing land, mixing sludge, trimming backfills, and building roadways and parking lots. Repair and maintain equipment, making emergency adjustments or assisting with major repairs as necessary. Check fuel supplies at sites to ensure adequate availability. Connect hydraulic hoses, belts, mechanical linkages, or power takeoff shafts to tractors. Operate loaders to pull out stumps, rip asphalt or concrete, rough-grade properties, bury refuse, or perform general cleanup. Select and fasten bulldozer blades or other attachments to tractors, using hitches. Test atmosphere for adequate oxygen and explosive conditions when working in confined spaces. Operate compactors, scrapers, and rollers to level, compact, and cover refuse at disposal grounds. Talk to clients and study instructions, plans, and diagrams to establish work requirements.

GOE—Career Cluster/Interest Area: 02. Architecture and Construction. **Work Group:** 02.04. Construction Crafts. **Other Apprenticeable Jobs in This Work Group:** Boilermakers; Brickmasons and Blockmasons; Carpet Installers; Cement Masons and Concrete Finishers; Construction Carpenters; Crane and Tower Operators; Drywall and Ceiling Tile Installers; Electricians; Fence Erectors; Floor Layers, Except Carpet, Wood, and Hard Tiles; Glaziers; Insulation Workers, Floor, Ceiling, and Wall; Insulation Workers, Mechanical; Painters, Construction and Maintenance; Paperhangers; Paving, Surfacing, and Tamping Equipment Operators; Pipe Fitters and Steamfitters; Plasterers and Stucco Masons; Plumbers; Reinforcing Iron and Rebar Workers; Riggers; Roofers; Rough Carpenters; Sheet Metal Workers; Stone Cutters and Carvers, Manufacturing; Stonemasons; Structural Iron and Steel Workers; Tapers; Terrazzo Workers and Finishers; Tile and Marble Setters. **Personality Type:** Realistic. These occupations frequently involve work activities that include practical, hands-on problems and solutions. They often deal with plants; animals; and real-world materials such as wood, tools, and machinery. Many of the occupations require working outside and don't involve a lot of paperwork or working closely with others.

Skills—Equipment Maintenance; Installation; Operation and Control; Operation Monitoring; Repairing; Equipment Selection; Management of Financial Resources; Management of Material Resources.

Education/Training Required (Nonapprenticeship Route): Moderate-term on-the-job training. **Related Knowledge/Courses—Building and Construction:** Materials, methods, and the appropriate tools to construct objects, structures, and buildings. **Mechanical Devices:** Machines and tools, including their designs, uses, benefits, repair, and maintenance. **Engineering and Technology:** Equipment, tools, and mechanical devices and their uses to produce motion, light, power, technology, and other applications. **Design:** Design techniques, principles, tools, and instruments involved in the production and use of precision technical plans, blueprints, drawings, and models. **Production and Processing:** Inputs, outputs, raw materials, waste, quality control, costs, and techniques for maximizing the manufacture and distribution of goods. **Public Safety and Security:** Weaponry; public safety; security operations, rules, regulations, precautions, and prevention; and the protection of people, data, and property.

Work Environment: Outdoors; noisy; very hot or cold; contaminants; whole-body vibration; using hands on objects, tools, or controls.

Further Information: Contact a local joint union-management apprenticeship committee, or the nearest office of your state employment service or apprenticeship agency (see Appendix C). Information is also available from the International Union of Operating Engineers, 1125 17th St. NW, Washington, DC 20036. Internet: www.iuoe.org

Opticians, Dispensing

* Annual Earnings: $31,430
* Growth: 8.7%
* Annual Job Openings: 3,143
* Percentage of Women: 73.4%

Related Apprenticeship—Optician, Dispensing (4000 hrs.).

Design, measure, fit, and adapt lenses and frames for client according to written optical

prescription or specification. Assist client with selecting frames. Measure customer for size of eyeglasses and coordinate frames with facial and eye measurements and optical prescription. Prepare work order for optical laboratory containing instructions for grinding and mounting lenses in frames. Verify exactness of finished lens spectacles. Adjust frame and lens position to fit client. May shape or reshape frames. Measure clients' bridge and eye size, temple length, vertex distance, pupillary distance, and optical centers of eyes, using measuring devices. Verify that finished lenses are ground to specifications. Prepare work orders and instructions for grinding lenses and fabricating eyeglasses. Assist clients in selecting frames according to style and color and ensure that frames are coordinated with facial and eye measurements and optical prescriptions. Maintain records of customer prescriptions, work orders, and payments. Perform administrative duties such as tracking inventory and sales, submitting patient insurance information, and performing simple bookkeeping. Recommend specific lenses, lens coatings, and frames to suit client needs. Sell goods such as contact lenses, spectacles, sunglasses, and other goods related to eyes in general. Heat, shape, or bend plastic or metal frames to adjust eyeglasses to fit clients, using pliers and hands. Evaluate prescriptions in conjunction with clients' vocational and avocational visual requirements. Instruct clients in how to wear and care for eyeglasses. Determine clients' current lens prescriptions, when necessary, using lensometers or lens analyzers and clients' eyeglasses. Show customers how to insert, remove, and care for their contact lenses. Repair damaged frames. Obtain a customer's previous record or verify a prescription with the examining optometrist or ophthalmologist. Arrange and maintain displays of optical merchandise. Fabricate lenses to meet prescription specifications. Grind lens edges or apply coatings to lenses. Assemble eyeglasses by cutting and edging lenses and fitting the lenses into frames. Supervise the training of student opticians.

GOE—Career Cluster/Interest Area: 08. Health Science. **Work Group:** 08.06. Medical Technology. **Other Apprenticeable Jobs in This Work Group:** Medical and Clinical Laboratory Technicians; Medical Equipment Preparers; Medical Records and Health Information Technicians; Radiologic Technologists. **Personality Type:** Enterprising. These occupations frequently involve starting up and carrying out projects and can involve leading people and making many decisions. They sometimes require risk taking and often deal with business.

Skills—Persuasion; Technology Design; Service Orientation; Equipment Selection; Science; Speaking; Mathematics; Management of Financial Resources.

Education/Training Required (Nonapprenticeship Route): Long-term on-the-job training. **Related Knowledge/Courses—Sales and Marketing:** Principles and methods involved in showing, promoting, and selling products or services. This includes marketing strategies and tactics, product demonstration and sales techniques, and sales control systems. **Customer and Personal Service:** Principles and processes for providing customer and personal services, including needs assessment techniques, quality service standards, alternative delivery systems, and customer satisfaction evaluation techniques. **Production and Processing:** Inputs, outputs, raw materials, waste, quality control, costs, and techniques for maximizing the manufacture and distribution of goods. **Clerical Practices:** Administrative and clerical procedures and systems such as word-processing systems, filing and records management systems, stenography and transcription, forms, design principles, and other office procedures and terminology. **Economics and Accounting:** Economic and accounting principles and practices, the financial markets, banking, and the analysis and reporting of financial data. **Psychology:** Human behavior and performance, mental processes, psychological research methods, and the assessment and treatment of behavioral and affective disorders.

Work Environment: Indoors; standing; using hands on objects, tools, or controls.

Painters, Construction and Maintenance

- ❋ Annual Earnings: $32,080
- ❋ Growth: 11.8%
- ❋ Annual Job Openings: 101,140
- ❋ Percentage of Women: 7.7%

Related Apprenticeships—Architectural, Coatings Finisher (6000 hrs.); Painter (Construction) (6000 hrs.); Painter, Shipyard (6000 hrs.); Pavement Striper (4000 hrs.).

Paint walls, equipment, buildings, bridges, and other structural surfaces with brushes, rollers, and spray guns. May remove old paint to prepare surfaces before painting. May mix colors or oils to obtain desired color or consistencies. Cover surfaces with dropcloths or masking tape and paper to protect surfaces during painting. Fill cracks, holes, and joints with caulk, putty, plaster, or other fillers, using caulking guns or putty knives. Apply primers or sealers to prepare new surfaces such as bare wood or metal for finish coats. Apply paint, stain, varnish, enamel, and other finishes to equipment, buildings, bridges, and/or other structures, using brushes, spray guns, or rollers. Calculate amounts of required materials and estimate costs, based on surface measurements and/or work orders. Read work orders or receive instructions from supervisors or homeowners to determine work requirements. Erect scaffolding and swing gates, or set up ladders, to work above ground level. Remove fixtures such as pictures, door knobs, lamps, and electric switch covers prior to painting. Wash and treat surfaces with oil, turpentine, mildew remover, or other preparations, and sand rough spots to ensure that finishes will adhere properly. Mix and match colors of paint, stain, or varnish with oil and thinning and drying additives to obtain desired colors and consistencies. Remove old finishes by stripping, sanding, wire brushing, burning, or using water and/or abrasive blasting. Select and purchase tools and finishes for surfaces to be covered, considering durability, ease of handling, methods of application, and customers' wishes. Smooth surfaces, using sandpaper, scrapers, brushes, steel wool, and/or sanding machines. Polish final coats to specified finishes. Use special finishing techniques such as sponging, ragging, layering, or faux finishing. Waterproof buildings, using waterproofers and caulking. Cut stencils, and brush and spray lettering and decorations on surfaces. Spray or brush hot plastics or pitch onto surfaces. Bake finishes on painted and enameled articles, using baking ovens.

GOE—Career Cluster/Interest Area: 02. Architecture and Construction. **Work Group:** 02.04. Construction Crafts. **Other Apprenticeable Jobs in This Work Group:** Boilermakers; Brickmasons and Blockmasons; Carpet Installers; Cement Masons and Concrete Finishers; Construction Carpenters; Crane and Tower Operators; Drywall and Ceiling Tile Installers; Electricians; Fence Erectors; Floor Layers, Except

Carpet, Wood, and Hard Tiles; Glaziers; Insulation Workers, Floor, Ceiling, and Wall; Insulation Workers, Mechanical; Operating Engineers and Other Construction Equipment Operators; Paperhangers; Paving, Surfacing, and Tamping Equipment Operators; Pipe Fitters and Steamfitters; Plasterers and Stucco Masons; Plumbers; Reinforcing Iron and Rebar Workers; Riggers; Roofers; Rough Carpenters; Sheet Metal Workers; Stone Cutters and Carvers, Manufacturing; Stonemasons; Structural Iron and Steel Workers; Tapers; Terrazzo Workers and Finishers; Tile and Marble Setters. **Personality Type:** Realistic. These occupations frequently involve work activities that include practical, hands-on problems and solutions. They often deal with plants; animals; and real-world materials such as wood, tools, and machinery. Many of the occupations require working outside and don't involve a lot of paperwork or working closely with others.

Skills—Equipment Maintenance; Management of Material Resources; Equipment Selection; Repairing; Management of Personnel Resources; Monitoring; Coordination.

Education/Training Required (Nonapprenticeship Route): Moderate-term on-the-job training. **Related Knowledge/Courses—Building and Construction:** Materials, methods, and the appropriate tools to construct objects, structures, and buildings. **Design:** Design techniques, principles, tools, and instruments involved in the production and use of precision technical plans, blueprints, drawings, and models. **Transportation:** Principles and methods for moving people or goods by air, rail, sea, or road, including their relative costs, advantages, and limitations. **Customer and Personal Service:** Principles and processes for providing customer and personal services, including needs assessment techniques, quality service standards, alternative delivery systems, and customer satisfaction evaluation techniques. **Production and Processing:** Inputs, outputs, raw materials, waste, quality control, costs, and techniques for maximizing the manufacture and distribution of goods. **Administration and Management:** Principles and processes involved in business and organizational planning, coordination, and execution. This includes strategic planning, resource allocation, manpower modeling, leadership techniques, and production methods.

Work Environment: Contaminants; standing; climbing ladders, scaffolds, or poles; using hands on objects, tools, or controls; bending or twisting the body; repetitive motions.

Painters, Transportation Equipment

- ❀ Annual Earnings: $36,000
- ❀ Growth: 8.4%
- ❀ Annual Job Openings: 3,268
- ❀ Percentage of Women: 16.6%

Related Apprenticeship—Painter, Transportation Equipment (6000 hrs.).

Operate or tend painting machines to paint surfaces of transportation equipment, such as automobiles, buses, trucks, trains, boats, and airplanes. Dispose of hazardous waste in an appropriate manner. Select paint according to company requirements and match colors of paint following specified color charts. Mix paints to match color specifications or vehicles' original colors; then stir and thin the paints, using spatulas or power mixing equipment. Remove grease, dirt, paint, and rust from vehicle surfaces in preparation for paint application, using abrasives, solvents, brushes, blowtorches, washing tanks, or sandblasters. Pour paint into spray guns and adjust nozzles and paint mixes to get the proper paint flow and coating thickness. Monitor painting operations to identify flaws such as blisters and streaks so that their causes can be corrected. Sand vehicle surfaces between coats of paint or primer to remove flaws and enhance adhesion for subsequent coats. Disassemble, clean, and reassemble sprayers and power equipment, using solvents, wire brushes, and cloths for cleaning duties. Remove accessories from vehicles, such as chrome or mirrors, and mask other surfaces with tape or paper to protect them from paint. Spray prepared surfaces with specified amounts of primers and decorative or finish coatings. Allow the sprayed product to dry and then touch up any spots that may have been missed. Apply rust-resistant undercoats and caulk and seal seams. Select the correct spray gun system for the material being applied. Apply primer over any repairs made to vehicle surfaces. Adjust controls on infrared ovens, heat lamps, portable ventilators, and exhaust units to speed the drying of vehicles between coats. Fill small dents and scratches with body fillers and smooth surfaces to prepare vehicles for painting. Apply designs, lettering, or other identifying or decorative items to finished products, using paint brushes or paint sprayers. Paint by hand areas that cannot be reached with a spray gun or those that need retouching, using brushes. Sand the final finish and apply sealer once a vehicle has dried properly. Buff and wax the finished paintwork. Lay out logos, symbols, or designs on painted surfaces according to blueprint specifications, using measuring instruments, stencils, and patterns.

GOE—Career Cluster/Interest Area: 13. Manufacturing. **Work Group:** 13.09. Hands-On Work, Assorted Materials. **Other Apprenticeable Jobs in This Work Group:** Cutters and Trimmers, Hand; Fabric and Apparel Patternmakers; Glass Blowers, Molders, Benders, and Finishers; Molding and Casting Workers; Painting, Coating, and Decorating Workers. **Personality Type:** Realistic. These occupations frequently involve work activities that include practical, hands-on problems and solutions. They often deal with plants; animals; and real-world materials such as wood, tools, and machinery. Many of the occupations require working outside and don't involve a lot of paperwork or working closely with others.

Skills—Repairing; Equipment Maintenance; Monitoring; Operation and Control; Technology Design; Science; Equipment Selection; Quality Control Analysis.

Education/Training Required (Nonapprenticeship Route): Moderate-term on-the-job training. **Related Knowledge/Courses—Chemistry:** The composition, structure, and properties of substances and of the chemical processes and transformations that they undergo. This includes uses of chemicals and their interactions, danger signs, production techniques, and disposal methods. **Production and Processing:** Inputs, outputs, raw materials, waste, quality control, costs, and techniques for maximizing the manufacture and distribution of goods. **Mechanical Devices:** Machines and tools, including their designs, uses, benefits, repair, and maintenance.

Work Environment: Noisy; contaminants; hazardous conditions; standing; using hands on objects, tools, or controls; repetitive motions.

Paralegals and Legal Assistants

* Annual Earnings: $44,990
* Growth: 22.2%
* Annual Job Openings: 22,756
* Percentage of Women: 89.1%

Related Apprenticeship—Paralegal (6000 hrs.).

Assist lawyers by researching legal precedent, investigating facts, or preparing legal documents. Conduct research to support a legal proceeding, to formulate a defense, or to initiate legal action. Prepare legal documents, including briefs, pleadings, appeals, wills, contracts, and real estate closing statements. Prepare affidavits or other documents, maintain document file, and file pleadings with court clerk. Gather and analyze research data, such as statutes; decisions; and legal articles, codes, and documents. Investigate facts and law of cases to determine causes of action and to prepare cases. Call upon witnesses to testify at hearing. Direct and coordinate law office activity, including delivery of subpoenas. Arbitrate disputes between parties and assist in real estate closing process. Keep and monitor legal volumes to ensure that law library is up to date. Appraise and inventory real and personal property for estate planning.

GOE—Career Cluster/Interest Area: 12. Law and Public Safety. **Work Group:** 12.03. Legal Support. **Other Apprenticeable Jobs in This Work Group:** No others in group. **Personality Type:** Conventional. These occupations frequently involve following set procedures and routines and can include working with data and details more than with ideas. Usually there is a clear line of authority to follow.

Skills—Writing; Active Listening; Speaking; Time Management; Reading Comprehension; Monitoring.

Education/Training Required (Nonapprenticeship Route): Associate degree. **Related Knowledge/Courses—Clerical Practices:** Administrative and clerical procedures and systems such as word-processing systems, filing and records management systems, stenography and transcription, forms, design principles, and other office procedures and terminology. **Law and Government:** Laws, legal codes, court procedures, precedents, government regulations, executive orders, agency rules, and the democratic political process. **Computers and Electronics:** Electric circuit boards, processors, chips, and computer hardware and software, including applications and programming. **Personnel and Human Resources:** Principles and procedures for personnel recruitment; selection; training; compensation and benefits; labor relations and negotiation; and personnel information systems. **English Language:** The structure and content of the English language, including the meaning and spelling of words, rules of composition, and grammar. **Customer and Personal Service:** Principles and processes for providing customer and personal services, including needs assessment techniques, quality service standards, alternative delivery systems, and customer satisfaction evaluation techniques.

Work Environment: Indoors; sitting; repetitive motions.

Parts Salespersons

- ❋ Annual Earnings: $28,130
- ❋ Growth: −2.2%
- ❋ Annual Job Openings: 52,414
- ❋ Percentage of Women: 16.3%

Related Apprenticeship—Salesperson, Parts (4000 hrs.).

Sell spare and replacement parts and equipment in repair shop or parts store. Read catalogs, microfiche viewers, or computer displays to determine replacement part stock numbers and prices. Determine replacement parts required according to inspections of old parts, customer requests, or customers' descriptions of malfunctions. Receive and fill telephone orders for parts. Fill customer orders from stock. Prepare sales slips or sales contracts. Receive payment or obtain credit authorization. Take inventory of stock. Advise customers on substitution or modification of parts when identical replacements are not available. Examine returned parts for defects and exchange defective parts or refund money. Mark and store parts in stockrooms according to prearranged systems. Discuss use and features of various parts, based on knowledge of machines or equipment. Demonstrate equipment to customers and explain functioning of equipment. Place new merchandise on display. Measure parts, using precision measuring instruments, to determine whether similar parts may be machined to required sizes. Repair parts or equipment.

GOE—Career Cluster/Interest Area: 14. Retail and Wholesale Sales and Service. **Work Group:** 14.03. General Sales. **Other Apprenticeable Jobs in This Work Group:** No others in group. **Personality Type:** Enterprising. These occupations frequently involve starting up and carrying out projects and can involve leading people and making many decisions. They sometimes require risk taking and often deal with business.

Skills—Service Orientation; Management of Personnel Resources; Negotiation; Equipment Selection; Operations Analysis; Management of Financial Resources; Social Perceptiveness; Persuasion.

Education/Training Required (Nonapprenticeship Route): Moderate-term on-the-job training. **Related Knowledge/Courses—Sales and Marketing:** Principles and methods involved in showing, promoting, and selling products or services. This includes marketing strategies and tactics, product demonstration and sales techniques, and sales control systems. **Customer and Personal Service:** Principles and processes for providing customer and personal services, including needs assessment techniques, quality service standards, alternative delivery systems, and customer satisfaction evaluation techniques. **Mechanical Devices:** Machines and tools, including their designs, uses, benefits, repair, and maintenance. **Computers and Electronics:** Electric circuit boards, processors, chips, and computer hardware and software, including applications and programming. **Production and Processing:** Inputs, outputs, raw materials, waste, quality control, costs, and techniques for maximizing the manufacture and distribution of goods. **Mathematics:** Numbers and their operations and interrelationships, including arithmetic, algebra, geometry, calculus, and statistics and their applications.

Work Environment: Indoors; noisy; contaminants; standing; repetitive motions.

Paving, Surfacing, and Tamping Equipment Operators

* Annual Earnings: $32,360
* Growth: 9.0%
* Annual Job Openings: 3,471
* Percentage of Women: 1.7%

Related Apprenticeship—Asphalt Paving Machine Operator (6000 hrs.).

Operate equipment used for applying concrete, asphalt, or other materials to road beds, parking lots, or airport runways and taxiways or equipment used for tamping gravel, dirt, or other materials. Includes concrete and asphalt paving machine operators,

form tampers, tamping machine operators, and stone spreader operators. Start machine, engage clutch, and push and move levers to guide machine along forms or guidelines and to control the operation of machine attachments. Operate machines to spread, smooth, level, or steel-reinforce stone, concrete, or asphalt on road beds. Inspect, clean, maintain, and repair equipment, using mechanics' hand tools, or report malfunctions to supervisors. Operate oil distributors, loaders, chip spreaders, dump trucks, and snowplows. Coordinate truck dumping. Set up and tear down equipment. Operate tamping machines or manually roll surfaces to compact earth fills, foundation forms, and finished road materials according to grade specifications. Shovel blacktop. Drive machines onto truck trailers and drive trucks to transport machines and material to and from job sites. Observe distribution of paving material to adjust machine settings or material flow and indicate low spots for workers to add material. Light burners or start heating units of machines and regulate screed temperatures and asphalt flow rates. Control paving machines to push dump trucks and to maintain a constant flow of asphalt or other material into hoppers or screeds. Set up forms and lay out guidelines for curbs according to written specifications, using string, spray paint, and concrete/water mixes. Fill tanks, hoppers, or machines with paving materials. Drive and operate curbing machines to extrude concrete or asphalt curbing. Cut or break up pavement and drive guardrail posts, using machines equipped with interchangeable hammers. Install dies, cutters, and extensions to screeds onto machines, using hand tools. Operate machines that clean or cut expansion joints in concrete or asphalt and that rout out cracks in pavement. Place strips of material such as cork, asphalt, or steel into joints or place rolls of expansion-joint material on machines that automatically insert material.

GOE—Career Cluster/Interest Area: 02. Architecture and Construction. **Work Group:** 02.04. Construction Crafts. **Other Apprenticeable Jobs in This Work Group:** Boilermakers; Brickmasons and Blockmasons; Carpet Installers; Cement Masons and Concrete Finishers; Construction Carpenters; Crane and Tower Operators; Drywall and Ceiling Tile Installers; Electricians; Fence Erectors; Floor Layers, Except Carpet, Wood, and Hard Tiles; Glaziers; Insulation Workers, Floor, Ceiling, and Wall; Insulation Workers, Mechanical; Operating Engineers and Other Construction Equipment Operators; Painters, Construction and Maintenance; Paperhangers; Pipe Fitters and Steamfitters; Plasterers and Stucco Masons; Plumbers; Reinforcing Iron and Rebar Workers; Riggers; Roofers; Rough Carpenters; Sheet Metal Workers; Stone Cutters and Carvers, Manufacturing; Stonemasons; Structural Iron and Steel Workers; Tapers; Terrazzo Workers and Finishers; Tile and Marble Setters. **Personality Type:** Realistic. These occupations frequently involve work activities that include practical, hands-on problems and solutions. They often deal with plants; animals; and real-world materials such as wood, tools, and machinery. Many of the occupations require working outside and don't involve a lot of paperwork or working closely with others.

Skills—Operation Monitoring; Equipment Maintenance; Operation and Control; Repairing; Equipment Selection; Installation; Troubleshooting; Technology Design.

Education/Training Required (Nonapprenticeship Route): Moderate-term on-the-job training. **Related Knowledge/Courses—Building and Construction:** Materials, methods, and the appropriate tools to construct objects, structures, and buildings. **Mechanical Devices:** Machines and tools, including their designs, uses, benefits, repair, and maintenance. **Transportation:** Principles and methods for moving people or goods by air, rail, sea, or road, including their relative costs, advantages, and limitations. **Engineering and Technology:** Equipment, tools, and mechanical devices and their uses to produce motion, light, power, technology, and other applications. **Public Safety and Security:** Weaponry; public safety; security operations, rules, regulations, precautions, and prevention; and the protection of people, data, and property.

Work Environment: Outdoors; noisy; very hot or cold; contaminants; hazardous equipment; using hands on objects, tools, or controls.

Payroll and Timekeeping Clerks

❋ Annual Earnings: $33,810
❋ Growth: 3.1%
❋ Annual Job Openings: 18,544
❋ Percentage of Women: 92.4%

Related Apprenticeship—Financial Management (2000 hrs. or competency).

Compile and post employee time and payroll data. May compute employees' time worked, production, and commission. May compute and post wages and deductions. May prepare paychecks. Process and issue employee paychecks and statements of earnings and deductions. Compute wages and deductions and enter data into computers. Compile employee time, production, and payroll data from time sheets and other records. Review time sheets, work charts, wage computation, and other information to detect and reconcile payroll discrepancies. Verify attendance, hours worked, and pay adjustments and post information onto designated records. Record employee information, such as exemptions, transfers, and resignations, to maintain and update payroll records. Keep informed about changes in tax and deduction laws that apply to the payroll process. Issue and record adjustments to pay related to previous errors or retroactive increases. Provide information to employees and managers on payroll matters, tax issues, benefit plans, and collective agreement provisions. Complete time sheets showing employees' arrival and departure times. Post relevant work hours to client files to bill clients properly. Distribute and collect timecards each pay period. Complete, verify, and process forms and documentation for administration of benefits such as pension plans and unemployment and medical insurance. Prepare and balance period-end reports and reconcile issued payrolls to bank statements. Compile statistical reports, statements, and summaries related to pay and benefits accounts and submit them to appropriate departments. Coordinate special programs, such as United Way campaigns, that involve payroll deductions.

GOE—Career Cluster/Interest Area: 04. Business and Administration. **Work Group:** 04.06. Mathematical Clerical Support. **Other Apprenticeable Jobs in This Work Group:** Bookkeeping, Accounting, and Auditing Clerks. **Personality Type:** Conventional. These occupations frequently involve following set procedures and routines and can include working with data and details more than with ideas. Usually there is a clear line of authority to follow.

Skills—Mathematics; Time Management; Writing; Active Listening; Judgment and Decision Making; Speaking; Learning Strategies; Reading Comprehension.

P

Education/Training Required (Nonapprenticeship Route): Moderate-term on-the-job training. **Related Knowledge/Courses—Clerical Practices:** Administrative and clerical procedures and systems such as word-processing systems, filing and records management systems, stenography and transcription, forms, design principles, and other office procedures and terminology. **Economics and Accounting:** Economic and accounting principles and practices, the financial markets, banking, and the analysis and reporting of financial data. **Mathematics:** Numbers and their operations and interrelationships, including arithmetic, algebra, geometry, calculus, and statistics and their applications. **Administration and Management:** Principles and processes involved in business and organizational planning, coordination, and execution. This includes strategic planning, resource allocation, manpower modeling, leadership techniques, and production methods. **Personnel and Human Resources:** Principles and procedures for personnel recruitment; selection; training; compensation and benefits; labor relations and negotiation; and personnel information systems. **Computers and Electronics:** Electric circuit boards, processors, chips, and computer hardware and software, including applications and programming.

Work Environment: Indoors; noisy; sitting; repetitive motions.

Pest Control Workers

- ❀ Annual Earnings: $29,030
- ❀ Growth: 15.5%
- ❀ Annual Job Openings: 6,006
- ❀ Percentage of Women: 2.2%

Related Apprenticeship—Exterminator, Termite (4000 hrs.).

Spray or release chemical solutions or toxic gases and set traps to kill pests and vermin, such as mice, termites, and roaches, that infest buildings and surrounding areas. Record work activities performed. Inspect premises to identify infestation source and extent of damage to property, wall and roof porosity, and access to infested locations. Spray or dust chemical solutions, powders, or gases into rooms; onto clothing, furnishings, or wood; and over marshlands, ditches, and catch-basins. Clean work site after completion of job. Direct or assist other workers in treatment and extermination processes to eliminate and control rodents, insects, and weeds. Drive truck equipped with power spraying equipment. Measure area dimensions requiring treatment, using rule; calculate fumigant requirements; and estimate cost for service. Post warning signs and lock building doors to secure area to be fumigated. Cut or bore openings in building or surrounding concrete, access infested areas, insert nozzle, and inject pesticide to impregnate ground. Study preliminary reports and diagrams of infested area and determine treatment type required to eliminate and prevent recurrence of infestation. Dig up and burn or spray weeds with herbicides. Set mechanical traps and place poisonous paste or bait in sewers, burrows, and ditches. Clean and remove blockages from infested areas to facilitate spraying procedure and provide drainage, using broom, mop, shovel, and rake. Position and fasten edges of tarpaulins over building and tape vents to ensure airtight environment and check for leaks.

GOE—Career Cluster/Interest Area: 01. Agriculture and Natural Resources. **Work Group:** 01.05. Nursery, Groundskeeping, and

Pest Control. **Other Apprenticeable Jobs in This Work Group:** Landscaping and Groundskeeping Workers; Pesticide Handlers, Sprayers, and Applicators, Vegetation; Tree Trimmers and Pruners. **Personality Type:** Realistic. These occupations frequently involve work activities that include practical, hands-on problems and solutions. They often deal with plants; animals; and real-world materials such as wood, tools, and machinery. Many of the occupations require working outside and don't involve a lot of paperwork or working closely with others.

Skills—Equipment Selection; Persuasion; Service Orientation; Social Perceptiveness; Management of Material Resources; Active Learning; Equipment Maintenance; Coordination.

Education/Training Required (Nonapprenticeship Route): Moderate-term on-the-job training. **Related Knowledge/Courses—Sales and Marketing:** Principles and methods involved in showing, promoting, and selling products or services. This includes marketing strategies and tactics, product demonstration and sales techniques, and sales control systems. **Biology:** Plant and animal living tissue, cells, organisms, and entities, including their functions, interdependencies, and interactions with each other and the environment. **Chemistry:** The composition, structure, and properties of substances and of the chemical processes and transformations that they undergo. This includes uses of chemicals and their interactions, danger signs, production techniques, and disposal methods. **Customer and Personal Service:** Principles and processes for providing customer and personal services, including needs assessment techniques, quality service standards, alternative delivery systems, and customer satisfaction evaluation techniques. **Building and Construction:** Materials, methods, and the appropriate tools to construct objects, structures,

and buildings. **Law and Government:** Laws, legal codes, court procedures, precedents, government regulations, executive orders, agency rules, and the democratic political process.

Work Environment: More often outdoors than indoors; very hot or cold; contaminants; hazardous conditions; using hands on objects, tools, or controls.

Pesticide Handlers, Sprayers, and Applicators, Vegetation

* Annual Earnings: $28,560
* Growth: 14.0%
* Annual Job Openings: 7,443
* Percentage of Women: 6.2%

Related Apprenticeship—Agricultural Service Worker (4000 hrs.).

Mix or apply pesticides, herbicides, fungicides, or insecticides through sprays, dusts, vapors, soil incorporation, or chemical application on trees, shrubs, lawns, or botanical crops. Usually requires specific training and state or federal certification. Fill sprayer tanks with water and chemicals, according to formulas. Mix pesticides, herbicides, and fungicides for application to trees, shrubs, lawns, or botanical crops. Cover areas to specified depths with pesticides, applying knowledge of weather conditions, droplet sizes, elevation-to-distance ratios, and obstructions. Lift, push, and swing nozzles, hoses, and tubes to direct spray over designated areas. Start motors and engage machinery such as sprayer agitators and pumps or portable spray equipment. Connect hoses and nozzles selected according to terrain, distribution pattern requirements, types of infestations, and velocities. Clean and service machinery to ensure operating efficiency, using water, gasoline, lubricants, and/or hand tools. Provide driving instructions to truck drivers to ensure complete coverage of designated areas, using hand and horn signals. Plant grass with seed spreaders and operate straw blowers to cover seeded areas with mixtures of asphalt and straw.

GOE—Career Cluster/Interest Area: 01. Agriculture and Natural Resources. **Work Group:** 01.05. Nursery, Groundskeeping, and Pest Control. **Other Apprenticeable Jobs in This Work Group:** Landscaping and Groundskeeping Workers; Pest Control Workers; Tree Trimmers and Pruners. **Personality Type:** Realistic. These occupations frequently involve work activities that include practical, hands-on problems and solutions. They often deal with plants; animals; and real-world materials such as wood, tools, and machinery. Many of the occupations require working outside and don't involve a lot of paperwork or working closely with others.

Skills—Repairing; Equipment Maintenance; Operation Monitoring; Management of Material Resources; Installation; Operation and Control; Quality Control Analysis; Science.

Education/Training Required (Nonapprenticeship Route): Moderate-term on-the-job training. **Related Knowledge/Courses—Biology:** Plant and animal living tissue, cells, organisms, and entities, including their functions, interdependencies, and interactions with each other and the environment. **Chemistry:** The composition, structure, and properties of substances and of the chemical processes and transformations that they undergo. This includes uses of chemicals and their interactions, danger signs, production techniques, and disposal methods. **Mechanical Devices:** Machines and tools, including their designs, uses, benefits, repair, and maintenance. **Transportation:** Principles and methods for moving people or goods by air, rail, sea, or road, including their relative costs, advantages, and limitations. **Customer and Personal Service:** Principles and processes for providing customer and personal services, including needs assessment techniques, quality service standards, alternative delivery systems, and customer satisfaction evaluation techniques. **Public Safety and Security:** Weaponry; public safety; security operations, rules, regulations, precautions, and prevention; and the protection of people, data, and property.

Work Environment: Outdoors; noisy; contaminants; hazardous conditions; using hands on objects, tools, or controls; repetitive motions.

Petroleum Pump System Operators, Refinery Operators, and Gaugers

- ❋ Annual Earnings: $53,010
- ❋ Growth: –13.4%
- ❋ Annual Job Openings: 4,477
- ❋ Percentage of Women: 30.4%

Related Apprenticeships—Gauger (Petroleum Products) (4000 hrs.); Refinery Operator (6000 hrs.).

Control the operation of petroleum-refining or -processing units. May specialize in controlling manifold and pumping systems, gauging or testing oil in storage tanks, or regulating the flow of oil into pipelines. Calculate test result values, using standard formulas. Clamp seals around valves to secure tanks. Signal other workers by telephone or radio to operate pumps, open and close valves, and check temperatures. Start pumps and open valves or use automated equipment to regulate the flow of oil in pipelines and into and out of tanks. Synchronize activities with other pumphouses to ensure a continuous flow of products and a minimum of contamination between products. Verify that incoming and outgoing products are moving through the correct meters and that meters are working properly. Prepare calculations for receipts and deliveries of oil and oil products. Read automatic gauges at specified intervals to determine the flow rate of oil into or from tanks and the amount of oil in tanks. Record and compile operating data, instrument readings, documentation, and results of laboratory analyses. Control or operate manifold and pumping systems to circulate liquids through a petroleum refinery. Monitor process indicators, instruments, gauges, and meters to detect and report any possible problems. Clean interiors of processing units by circulating chemicals and solvents within units. Operate control panels to coordinate and regulate process variables such as temperature and pressure and to direct product flow rate according to process schedules. Read and analyze specifications, schedules, logs, test results, and laboratory recommendations to determine how to set equipment controls to produce the required qualities and quantities of products. Perform tests to check the qualities and grades of products, such as assessing levels of bottom sediment, water, and foreign materials in oil samples, using centrifugal testers. Collect product samples by turning bleeder valves or by lowering containers into tanks to obtain oil samples. Patrol units to monitor the amount of oil in storage tanks and to verify that activities and operations are safe, efficient, and in compliance with regulations. Operate auxiliary equipment and control multiple processing units during distilling or treating operations, moving controls that regulate valves, pumps, compressors, and auxiliary equipment.

GOE—Career Cluster/Interest Area: 13. Manufacturing. **Work Group:** 13.16. Utility Operation and Energy Distribution. **Other Apprenticeable Jobs in This Work Group:** Chemical Plant and System Operators; Power Distributors and Dispatchers; Power Plant Operators; Stationary Engineers and Boiler Operators; Water and Liquid Waste Treatment Plant and System Operators. **Personality Type:** Realistic. These occupations frequently involve work activities that include practical, hands-on problems and solutions. They often deal with plants; animals; and real-world materials such as wood, tools, and machinery. Many of the occupations require working outside and don't involve a lot of paperwork or working closely with others.

Skills—Operation Monitoring; Operation and Control; Science; Troubleshooting; Repairing; Equipment Maintenance; Quality Control Analysis; Installation.

Education/Training Required (Nonapprenticeship Route): Long-term on-the-job training. **Related Knowledge/Courses—Mechanical Devices:** Machines and tools, including their designs, uses, benefits, repair, and maintenance. **Chemistry:** The composition, structure, and properties of substances and of the chemical processes and transformations that they undergo. This includes uses of chemicals and their interactions, danger signs, production techniques, and disposal methods. **Engineering and Technology:** Equipment, tools, and mechanical devices and their uses to produce motion, light, power, technology, and other applications. **Public Safety and Security:** Weaponry; public safety; security operations, rules, regulations, precautions, and prevention; and the protection of people, data, and property. **Production and Processing:** Inputs, outputs, raw materials, waste, quality control, costs, and techniques for maximizing the manufacture and distribution of goods. **Education and Training:** Instructional methods and training techniques, including curriculum design principles, learning theory, group and individual teaching techniques, design of individual development plans, and test design principles.

Work Environment: Indoors; contaminants; hazardous conditions; standing; using hands on objects, tools, or controls.

Pharmacy Technicians

* Annual Earnings: $26,720
* Growth: 32.0%
* Annual Job Openings: 54,453
* Percentage of Women: 80.1%

Related Apprenticeships—Pharmacist Assistant (2000 hrs.); Pharmacy Technician (2000–2500 hrs. or competency).

Prepare medications under the direction of a pharmacist. May measure, mix, count out, label, and record amounts and dosages of medications. Receive written prescription or refill requests and verify that information is complete and accurate. Maintain proper storage and security conditions for drugs. Answer telephones, responding to questions or requests. Fill bottles with prescribed medications and type and affix labels. Assist customers by answering simple questions, locating items, or referring them to the pharmacist for medication information. Price and file prescriptions that have been filled. Clean and help maintain equipment and work areas and sterilize glassware according to prescribed methods. Establish and maintain patient profiles, including lists of medications taken by individual patients. Order, label, and count stock of medications, chemicals, and supplies and enter inventory data into computer. Receive and store incoming supplies, verify quantities against invoices, and inform supervisors of stock needs and shortages. Transfer medication from vials to the appropriate number of sterile disposable syringes, using aseptic techniques. Under pharmacist supervision, add measured drugs or nutrients to intravenous solutions under sterile conditions to prepare intravenous (IV) packs. Supply and monitor robotic machines that dispense medicine into containers and label the containers. Prepare and process medical insurance claim forms and records. Mix pharmaceutical preparations according to written prescriptions. Operate cash registers to accept payment from customers. Compute charges for medication and equipment dispensed to hospital patients and enter data in computer. Deliver medications and pharmaceutical supplies to patients, nursing stations, or surgery. Price stock and mark items for sale. Maintain and merchandise home healthcare products and services.

GOE—Career Cluster/Interest Area: 08. Health Science. **Work Group:** 08.02. Medicine and Surgery. **Other Apprenticeable Jobs in This Work Group:** Medical Assistants; Medical Transcriptionists; Surgical Technologists. **Personality Type:** Conventional. These occupations frequently involve following set procedures and routines and can include working with data and details more than with ideas. Usually there is a clear line of authority to follow.

Skills—Service Orientation; Active Listening; Instructing; Mathematics; Speaking; Active Learning; Troubleshooting; Writing.

Education/Training Required (Nonapprenticeship Route): Moderate-term on-the-job training. **Related Knowledge/Courses—Medicine and Dentistry:** The information and techniques needed to diagnose and treat injuries, diseases, and deformities. This includes symptoms, treatment alternatives, drug properties and interactions, and preventive health-care measures. **Chemistry:** The composition, structure, and properties of substances and of the chemical processes and transformations that they undergo. This includes uses of chemicals and their interactions, danger signs, production techniques, and disposal methods. **Customer and Personal Service:** Principles and processes for providing customer and personal services, including needs assessment techniques, quality service standards, alternative delivery systems, and customer satisfaction evaluation techniques. **Mathematics:** Numbers and their operations and interrelationships, including arithmetic, algebra, geometry, calculus, and statistics and their applications. **Clerical Practices:** Administrative and clerical procedures and systems such as word-processing systems, filing and records management systems, stenography and transcription, forms, design principles, and other office procedures and terminology.

Work Environment: Indoors; standing; using hands on objects, tools, or controls; repetitive motions.

Photographers

- ❋ Annual Earnings: $27,720
- ❋ Growth: 10.3%
- ❋ Annual Job Openings: 16,100
- ❋ Percentage of Women: 43.3%

Related Apprenticeship—Photographer, Still (6000 hrs.).

Photograph persons, subjects, merchandise, or other commercial products. May develop negatives and produce finished prints. Take pictures of individuals, families, and small groups, either in studio or on location. Adjust apertures, shutter speeds, and camera focus based on a combination of factors such as lighting, field depth, subject motion, film type, and film speed. Use traditional or digital cameras, along with a variety of equipment such as tripods, filters, and flash attachments. Create artificial light, using flashes and reflectors. Determine desired images and picture composition; select and adjust subjects, equipment, and lighting to achieve desired effects. Scan photographs into computers for editing, storage, and electronic transmission. Test equipment prior to use to ensure that it is in good working order. Review sets of photographs to select the best work. Estimate or measure light levels, distances, and numbers of exposures needed, using measuring devices and formulas. Manipulate and enhance scanned or digital images to create desired effects, using computers and specialized software. Perform maintenance tasks necessary to keep equipment working properly. Perform general office duties such as scheduling appointments, keeping books, and ordering supplies. Consult with clients or advertising staff and study assignments to determine project goals, locations, and equipment needs. Select and assemble equipment and required background properties according to subjects, materials, and conditions. Enhance, retouch, and resize photographs and negatives, using airbrushing and other techniques. Set up, mount, or install photographic equipment and cameras. Produce computer-readable digital images from film, using flatbed scanners and photofinishing laboratories. Develop and print exposed film, using chemicals, touchup tools, and developing and printing equipment, or send film to photofinishing laboratories for processing. Direct activities of workers who are setting up photographic equipment. Employ a variety of specialized photographic materials and techniques, including infrared and ultraviolet films, macro-photography, photogrammetry, and sensitometry. Engage in research to develop new photographic procedures and materials.

GOE—Career Cluster/Interest Area: 03. Arts and Communication. **Work Group:** 03.09. Media Technology. **Other Apprenticeable Jobs in This Work Group:** Audio and Video Equipment Technicians; Broadcast Technicians; Camera Operators, Television, Video, and Motion Picture; Radio Operators; Sound Engineering Technicians. **Personality Type:** Artistic. These occupations frequently involve working with forms, designs, and patterns. They often require self-expression, and the work can be done without following a clear set of rules.

Skills—Persuasion; Equipment Maintenance; Management of Financial Resources; Operation Monitoring; Service Orientation; Equipment Selection; Technology Design; Operations Analysis.

Education/Training Required (Nonapprenticeship Route): Long-term on-the-job training. **Related Knowledge/Courses—Sales and Marketing:** Principles and methods involved in showing, promoting, and selling products or services. This includes marketing strategies and tactics, product demonstration and sales techniques, and sales control systems. **Fine Arts:** Theory and techniques required to produce, compose, and perform works of music, dance, visual arts, drama, and sculpture. **Clerical Practices:** Administrative and clerical procedures and systems such as word-processing systems, filing and records management systems, stenography and transcription, forms, design principles, and other office procedures and terminology. **Customer and Personal Service:** Principles and processes for providing customer and personal services, including needs assessment techniques, quality service standards, alternative delivery systems, and customer satisfaction evaluation techniques. **Communications and Media:** Media production, communication, and dissemination techniques and methods, including alternative ways to inform and entertain via written, oral, and visual media. **Production and Processing:** Inputs, outputs, raw materials, waste, quality control, costs, and techniques for maximizing the manufacture and distribution of goods.

Work Environment: More often indoors than outdoors; sitting; using hands on objects, tools, or controls.

Pilots, Ship

❋ Annual Earnings: $57,210
❋ Growth: 17.9%
❋ Annual Job Openings: 2,665
❋ Percentage of Women: 14.8%

Our sources did not provide separate job openings data for this occupation. The job openings listed here are shared with Mates—Ship, Boat, and Barge and with Ship and Boat Captains.

Related Apprenticeship—Pilot, Ship (3000 hrs.).

Command ships to steer them into and out of harbors, estuaries, straits, and sounds and on rivers, lakes, and bays. Must be licensed by U.S. Coast Guard with limitations indicating class and tonnage of vessels for which licenses are valid and routes and waters that may be piloted. Maintain and repair boats and equipment. Give directions to crew members who are steering ships. Make nautical maps. Set ships' courses to avoid reefs, outlying shoals, and other hazards, using navigational aids such as lighthouses and buoys. Report to appropriate authorities any violations of federal or state pilotage laws. Relieve crew members on tugs and launches. Provide assistance to vessels approaching or leaving seacoasts, navigating harbors, and docking and undocking. Provide assistance in maritime rescue operations. Prevent ships from engaging in unsafe operations. Operate amphibious craft during troop landings. Maintain ships' logs. Learn to operate new technology systems and procedures, through the use of instruction, simulators, and models. Advise ships' masters on harbor rules and customs procedures. Steer ships into and out of berths, or signal tugboat captains to berth and unberth ships. Serve as vessel's docking master upon arrival at a port and when at a berth. Operate ship-to-shore radios to exchange information needed for ship operations. Consult maps, charts, weather reports, and navigation equipment to determine and direct ship movements. Direct course and speeds of ship, based on specialized knowledge of local winds, weather, water depths, tides, currents, and hazards. Oversee cargo storage on or below decks.

GOE—Career Cluster/Interest Area: 16. Transportation, Distribution, and Logistics. **Work Group:** 16.05. Water Vehicle Operation. **Other Apprenticeable Jobs in This Work Group:** Dredge Operators; Mates—Ship, Boat, and Barge; Sailors and Marine Oilers. **Personality Type:** Realistic. These occupations frequently involve work activities that include practical, hands-on problems and solutions. They often deal with plants; animals; and real-world materials such as wood, tools, and machinery. Many of the occupations require working outside and don't involve a lot of paperwork or working closely with others.

Skills—Operation and Control; Operation Monitoring; Judgment and Decision Making; Management of Personnel Resources; Troubleshooting; Equipment Maintenance; Negotiation; Coordination.

Education/Training Required (Nonapprenticeship Route): Work experience in a related occupation. **Related Knowledge/Courses— Transportation:** Principles and methods for moving people or goods by air, rail, sea, or road, including their relative costs, advantages, and limitations. **Geography:** Various methods for describing the location and distribution of land, sea, and air masses, including their physical locations, relationships, and characteristics. **Public Safety and Security:** Weaponry; public safety; security operations, rules, regulations, precautions, and prevention; and the protection of people, data, and property. **Telecommunications:** Transmission, broadcasting, switching, control, and operation of telecommunications systems. **Mechanical Devices:** Machines and tools, including their designs, uses, benefits, repair, and maintenance. **Law and Government:** Laws, legal codes, court procedures, precedents, government regulations, executive orders, agency rules, and the democratic political process.

Work Environment: More often indoors than outdoors; more often standing than sitting; keeping or regaining balance; using hands on objects, tools, or controls.

Pipe Fitters and Steamfitters

- ✷ Annual Earnings: $44,090
- ✷ Growth: 10.6%
- ✷ Annual Job Openings: 68,643
- ✷ Percentage of Women: 1.8%

Our sources did not provide separate job openings data for this occupation. The job openings listed here are shared with Plumbers.

Related Apprenticeships—Coppersmith (Ship and Boat) (8000 hrs.); Gas-Main Fitter (8000 hrs.); Pipe Fitter–Sprinkler Fitter (8000 hrs.); Pipe Fitter (Construction) (8000 hrs.); Pipe Fitter (Ship and Boat) (8000 hrs.); Steam Service Inspector (8000 hrs.).

Lay out, assemble, install, and maintain pipe systems, pipe supports, and related hydraulic and pneumatic equipment for steam, hot water, heating, cooling, lubricating, sprinkling, and industrial production and processing systems. Cut, thread, and hammer pipe to specifications, using tools such as saws, cutting torches, and pipe threaders and benders. Assemble and secure pipes, tubes, fittings, and related equipment according to specifications by welding, brazing, cementing, soldering, and threading joints. Attach pipes to walls, structures, and fixtures, such as radiators or tanks, using brackets, clamps, tools, or welding equipment. Inspect, examine, and test installed systems and pipelines, using pressure gauge, hydrostatic testing, observation, or other methods. Measure and mark pipes for cutting and threading. Lay out full scale drawings of pipe systems, supports, and related equipment, following blueprints. Plan pipe system layout, installation, or repair according to specifications. Select pipe sizes and types and related materials, such as supports, hangers, and hydraulic cylinders, according to specifications. Cut and bore holes in structures such as bulkheads, decks, walls, and mains prior to pipe installation, using hand and power tools. Modify, clean, and maintain pipe systems, units, fittings, and related machines and equipment, following specifications and using hand and power tools. Install automatic controls used to regulate pipe systems. Turn valves to shut off steam, water, or other gases or liquids from pipe sections, using valve keys or wrenches. Remove and replace worn components. Prepare cost estimates for clients. Inspect work sites for obstructions and to ensure that holes will not cause structural weakness. Operate motorized pumps to remove water from flooded manholes, basements, or facility floors. Dip nonferrous piping materials in a mixture of molten tin and lead to obtain a coating that prevents erosion or galvanic and electrolytic action.

GOE—Career Cluster/Interest Area: 02. Architecture and Construction. **Work Group:** 02.04. Construction Crafts. **Other Apprenticeable Jobs in This Work Group:** Boilermakers; Brickmasons and Blockmasons; Carpet Installers; Cement Masons and Concrete Finishers; Construction Carpenters; Crane and Tower Operators; Drywall and Ceiling Tile Installers; Electricians; Fence Erectors; Floor Layers, Except Carpet, Wood, and Hard Tiles; Glaziers; Insulation Workers, Floor, Ceiling, and Wall; Insulation Workers, Mechanical; Operating Engineers and Other Construction Equipment Operators; Painters, Construction and Maintenance; Paperhangers; Paving, Surfacing, and Tamping Equipment Operators; Plasterers and Stucco Masons; Plumbers; Reinforcing Iron and Rebar Workers; Riggers; Roofers; Rough Carpenters; Sheet Metal Workers; Stone Cutters and Carvers, Manufacturing; Stonemasons; Structural Iron and Steel Workers; Tapers; Terrazzo Workers and Finishers; Tile and Marble Setters. **Personality Type:** Realistic. These occupations frequently involve work activities that include practical, hands-on problems and solutions. They often deal with plants; animals; and real-world materials such as wood, tools, and machinery. Many of the occupations require working outside and don't involve a lot of paperwork or working closely with others.

Skills—Installation; Repairing; Systems Analysis; Management of Personnel Resources; Equipment Maintenance; Operation Monitoring; Operation and Control; Technology Design.

Education/Training Required (Nonapprenticeship Route): Long-term on-the-job training. **Related Knowledge/Courses—Building and Construction:** Materials, methods, and the appropriate tools to construct objects, structures, and buildings. **Design:** Design techniques, principles, tools, and instruments involved in the production and use of precision technical plans, blueprints, drawings, and models. **Mechanical Devices:** Machines and tools, including their designs, uses, benefits, repair, and maintenance. **Engineering and Technology:** Equipment, tools, and mechanical devices and their uses to produce motion, light, power, technology, and other applications. **Economics and Accounting:** Economic and accounting principles and practices, the financial markets, banking, and the analysis and reporting of financial data. **Transportation:** Principles and methods for moving people or goods by air, rail, sea, or road, including their relative costs, advantages, and limitations.

Work Environment: Outdoors; hazardous equipment; minor burns, cuts, bites, or stings; standing; using hands on objects, tools, or controls; repetitive motions.

Further Information: Contact a local joint union-management apprenticeship committee, or the nearest office of your state employment service or apprenticeship agency (see Appendix C). Information is also available from the United Association of Journeymen and Apprentices of the Plumbing and Pipefitting Industry, 901 Massachusetts Ave. NW, Washington, DC 20001. Internet: www.ua.org

Plasterers and Stucco Masons

- ❋ Annual Earnings: $36,430
- ❋ Growth: 8.1%
- ❋ Annual Job Openings: 4,509
- ❋ Percentage of Women: 3.1%

Related Apprenticeships—Plasterer (4000 hrs.); Plasterer (4500–8000 hrs., hybrid).

Apply interior or exterior plaster, cement, stucco, or similar materials. May also set ornamental plaster. Apply coats of plaster or stucco to walls, ceilings, or partitions of buildings, using trowels, brushes, or spray guns. Mix mortar and plaster to desired consistency or direct workers who perform mixing. Create decorative textures in finish coat, using brushes or trowels, sand, pebbles, or stones. Apply insulation to building exteriors by installing prefabricated insulation systems over existing walls or by covering the outer wall with insulation board, reinforcing mesh, and a base coat. Cure freshly plastered surfaces. Clean and prepare surfaces for applications of plaster, cement, stucco, or similar materials, such as by drywall taping. Rough the undercoat surface with a scratcher so the finish coat will adhere. Apply weatherproof decorative coverings to exterior surfaces of buildings, such as troweling or spraying on coats of stucco. Install guide wires on exterior surfaces of buildings to indicate thickness of plaster or stucco and nail wire mesh, lath, or similar materials to the outside surface to hold stucco in place. Spray acoustic materials or texture finish over walls and ceilings. Mold and install ornamental plaster pieces, panels, and trim.

GOE—Career Cluster/Interest Area: 02. Architecture and Construction. **Work Group:** 02.04. Construction Crafts. **Other Apprenticeable Jobs in This Work Group:** Boilermakers; Brickmasons and Blockmasons; Carpet Installers; Cement Masons and Concrete Finishers; Construction Carpenters; Crane and Tower Operators; Drywall and Ceiling Tile Installers; Electricians; Fence Erectors; Floor Layers, Except Carpet, Wood, and Hard Tiles; Glaziers; Insulation Workers, Floor, Ceiling, and Wall; Insulation Workers, Mechanical; Operating Engineers and Other Construction Equipment Operators; Painters, Construction and Maintenance; Paperhangers; Paving, Surfacing, and Tamping Equipment Operators; Pipe Fitters and Steamfitters; Plumbers; Reinforcing Iron and Rebar Workers; Riggers; Roofers; Rough Carpenters; Sheet Metal Workers; Stone Cutters and Carvers, Manufacturing; Stonemasons; Structural Iron and Steel Workers; Tapers; Terrazzo Workers and Finishers; Tile and Marble Setters. **Personality Type:** Realistic. These occupations frequently involve work activities that include practical, hands-on problems and solutions. They often deal with plants; animals; and real-world materials such as wood, tools, and machinery. Many of the occupations require working outside and don't involve a lot of paperwork or working closely with others.

Skills—Management of Material Resources; Repairing; Installation; Technology Design; Equipment Maintenance; Management of Financial Resources; Equipment Selection; Operations Analysis.

Education/Training Required (Nonapprenticeship Route): Long-term on-the-job training. **Related Knowledge/Courses—Building and Construction:** Materials, methods, and the appropriate tools to construct objects, structures, and buildings. **Public Safety and Security:** Weaponry; public safety; security operations, rules, regulations, precautions, and prevention; and the protection of people, data, and property.

Work Environment: High places; standing; walking and running; using hands on objects, tools, or controls; bending or twisting the body; repetitive motions.

Further Information: Contact a local joint union-management apprenticeship committee or the nearest office of your state employment service or apprenticeship agency (see Appendix C). To identify the local union office, contact International Union of Bricklayers and Allied Craftworkers, International Masonry Institute, The James Brice House, 42 East St., Annapolis, MD 21401. Internet: www.imiweb.org

Plumbers

- ❀ Annual Earnings: $44,090
- ❀ Growth: 10.6%
- ❀ Annual Job Openings: 68,643
- ❀ Percentage of Women: 1.8%

Our sources did not provide separate job openings data for this occupation. The job openings listed here are shared with Pipe Fitters and Steamfitters.

Related Apprenticeship—Plumber (8000 hrs.).

Assemble, install, and repair pipes, fittings, and fixtures of heating, water, and drainage systems according to specifications and plumbing codes. Measure, cut, thread, and bend pipe to required angles, using hand and power tools or machines such as pipe cutters, pipe-threading machines, and pipe-bending machines. Study building plans and inspect structures to assess material and equipment needs to establish the sequence of pipe installations and to plan installation around obstructions such as electrical wiring. Locate and mark the position of pipe installations, connections, passage holes, and fixtures in structures, using measuring instruments such as rulers and levels. Assemble pipe sections, tubing, and fittings, using couplings, clamps, screws, bolts, cement, plastic solvent, caulking, or soldering, brazing, and welding equipment. Fill pipes or plumbing fixtures with water or air and observe pressure gauges to detect and locate leaks. Install pipe assemblies, fittings, valves, appliances such as dishwashers and water heaters, and fixtures such as sinks and toilets, using hand and power tools. Direct workers engaged in pipe cutting and preassembly and installation of plumbing systems and components. Cut openings in structures to accommodate pipes and pipe fittings, using hand and power tools. Review blueprints and building codes and specifications to determine work details and procedures. Install underground storm, sanitary, and water piping systems and extend piping to connect fixtures and plumbing to these systems. Repair and maintain plumbing, replacing defective washers, replacing or mending broken pipes, and opening clogged drains. Keep records of assignments and produce detailed work reports. Hang steel supports from ceiling joists to hold pipes in place. Perform complex calculations and planning for special or very large jobs. Clear away debris in renovations. Install oxygen and medical gas in hospitals. Prepare written work cost estimates and negotiate contracts. Use specialized techniques, equipment, or materials, such as performing computer-assisted welding of small pipes or working with the special piping used in microchip fabrication.

GOE—Career Cluster/Interest Area: 02. Architecture and Construction. **Work Group:** 02.04. Construction Crafts. **Other Apprenticeable Jobs in This Work Group:** Boilermakers; Brickmasons and Blockmasons; Carpet Installers; Cement Masons and Concrete Finishers; Construction Carpenters; Crane and Tower Operators; Drywall and Ceiling Tile Installers; Electricians; Fence Erectors; Floor Layers, Except Carpet, Wood, and Hard Tiles; Glaziers; Insulation Workers, Floor, Ceiling, and Wall; Insulation Workers, Mechanical; Operating Engineers and Other Construction Equipment Operators; Painters, Construction and Maintenance; Paperhangers; Paving, Surfacing, and Tamping Equipment Operators; Pipe Fitters and Steamfitters; Plasterers and Stucco Masons; Reinforcing Iron and Rebar Workers; Riggers; Roofers; Rough Carpenters; Sheet Metal Workers; Stone Cutters and Carvers, Manufacturing; Stonemasons; Structural Iron and Steel Workers; Tapers; Terrazzo Workers and Finishers; Tile and Marble Setters. **Personality Type:** Realistic. These occupations frequently involve work activities that include practical, hands-on problems and solutions. They often deal with plants; animals; and real-world materials such as wood, tools, and machinery. Many of the occupations require working outside and don't involve a lot of paperwork or working closely with others.

Skills—Installation; Quality Control Analysis; Repairing; Operation and Control; Operation Monitoring; Mathematics; Systems Analysis.

Education/Training Required (Nonapprenticeship Route): Long-term on-the-job training. **Related Knowledge/Courses—Building and Construction:** Materials, methods, and the appropriate tools to construct objects, structures, and buildings. **Physics:** Physical principles, laws, and applications, including air, water, material dynamics, light, atomic principles, heat, electric theory, earth formations, and meteorological and related natural phenomena. **Mechanical Devices:** Machines and tools, including their designs, uses, benefits, repair, and maintenance. **Design:** Design techniques, principles, tools, and instruments involved in the production and use of precision technical plans, blueprints, drawings, and models. **Engineering and Technology:** Equipment, tools, and mechanical devices and their uses to produce motion, light, power, technology, and other applications. **Customer and Personal Service:** Principles and processes for providing customer and personal services, including needs assessment techniques, quality service standards, alternative delivery systems, and customer satisfaction evaluation techniques.

Work Environment: Outdoors; contaminants; cramped work space, awkward positions; hazardous equipment; minor burns, cuts, bites, or stings; using hands on objects, tools, or controls.

Further Information: Contact a local joint union-management apprenticeship committee, or the nearest office of your state employment service or apprenticeship agency (see Appendix C). Information is also available from the United Association of Journeymen and Apprentices of the Plumbing and Pipefitting Industry, 901 Massachusetts Ave. NW, Washington, DC 20001. Internet: www.ua.org

Police Patrol Officers

- ❋ Annual Earnings: $49,630
- ❋ Growth: 10.8%
- ❋ Annual Job Openings: 37,842
- ❋ Percentage of Women: 12.8%

Our sources did not provide separate job openings data for this occupation. The job openings listed here are shared with Sheriffs and Deputy Sheriffs.

Related Apprenticeship—Police Officer I (4000 hrs.).

Patrol assigned areas to enforce laws and ordinances, regulate traffic, control crowds, prevent crime, and arrest violators. Provide for public safety by maintaining order, responding to emergencies, protecting people and property, enforcing motor vehicle and criminal laws, and promoting good community relations. Monitor, note, report, and investigate suspicious persons and situations, safety hazards, and unusual or illegal activity in patrol area. Record facts to prepare reports that document incidents and activities. Identify, pursue, and arrest suspects and perpetrators of criminal acts. Patrol specific areas on foot, horseback, or motorized conveyance, responding promptly to calls for assistance. Review facts of incidents to determine whether criminal acts or statute violations were involved. Investigate traffic accidents and other accidents to determine causes and to determine whether crimes have been committed. Render aid to accident victims and other persons requiring first aid for physical injuries. Testify in court to present evidence or act as witness in traffic and criminal cases. Photograph or draw diagrams of crime or accident scenes and interview principals and eyewitnesses. Relay complaint and emergency-request information to appropriate agency dispatchers. Evaluate complaint and emergency-request information to determine response requirements. Process prisoners and prepare and maintain records of prisoner bookings and prisoner statuses during booking and pre-trial processes. Monitor traffic to ensure motorists observe traffic regulations and exhibit safe driving procedures. Issue citations or warnings to violators of motor vehicle ordinances. Direct traffic flow and reroute traffic during emergencies. Inform citizens of community services and recommend options to facilitate longer-term problem resolution. Provide road information to assist motorists. Inspect public establishments to ensure compliance with rules and regulations. Act as official escorts at times, such as when leading funeral processions or firefighters.

GOE—Career Cluster/Interest Area: 12. Law and Public Safety. **Work Group:** 12.04. Law Enforcement and Public Safety. **Other Apprenticeable Jobs in This Work Group:** Correctional Officers and Jailers; Fire Investigators. **Personality Type:** Realistic. These occupations frequently involve work activities that include practical, hands-on problems and solutions. They often deal with plants; animals; and real-world materials such as wood, tools, and machinery. Many of the occupations require working outside and don't involve a lot of paperwork or working closely with others.

Skills—Negotiation; Service Orientation; Management of Personnel Resources; Systems Analysis; Systems Evaluation.

Education/Training Required (Nonapprenticeship Route): Long-term on-the-job training. **Related Knowledge/Courses—Psychology:** Human behavior and performance, mental processes, psychological research methods, and the assessment and treatment of behavioral and affective disorders. **Public Safety and Security:** Weaponry; public safety; security operations, rules, regulations, precautions, and prevention; and the protection of people, data, and property. **Law and Government:** Laws, legal codes, court procedures, precedents, government regulations, executive orders, agency rules, and the democratic political process. **Customer and Personal**

Service: Principles and processes for providing customer and personal services, including needs assessment techniques, quality service standards, alternative delivery systems, and customer satisfaction evaluation techniques. **Therapy and Counseling:** Information and techniques needed to rehabilitate physical and mental ailments and to provide career guidance, including alternative treatments, rehabilitation equipment and its proper use, and methods to evaluate treatment effects. **Sociology and Anthropology:** Group behavior and dynamics; societal trends and influences; and cultures and their history, migrations, ethnicity, and origins.

Work Environment: Outdoors; noisy; very hot or cold; contaminants; hazardous equipment; using hands on objects, tools, or controls.

Police, Fire, and Ambulance Dispatchers

- ❋ Annual Earnings: $32,660
- ❋ Growth: 13.6%
- ❋ Annual Job Openings: 17,628
- ❋ Percentage of Women: 53.4%

Related Apprenticeships—Alarm Operator (Government Service) (2000 hrs.); Telecommunicator (8000 hrs.).

Receive complaints from public concerning crimes and police emergencies. Broadcast orders to police patrol units in vicinity of complaint to investigate. Operate radio, telephone, or computer equipment to receive reports of fires and medical emergencies and relay information or orders to proper officials. Question callers about their locations and the nature of their problems to determine types of response needed. Receive incoming telephone or alarm system calls regarding emergency and nonemergency police and fire service, emergency ambulance service, information, and after-hours calls for departments within a city. Determine response requirements and relative priorities of situations and dispatch units in accordance with established procedures. Record details of calls, dispatches, and messages. Enter, update, and retrieve information from teletype networks and computerized data systems regarding such things as wanted persons, stolen property, vehicle registration, and stolen vehicles. Maintain access to and security of highly sensitive materials. Relay information and messages to and from emergency sites, to law enforcement agencies, and to all other individuals or groups requiring notification. Scan status charts and computer screens and contact emergency response field units to determine emergency units available for dispatch. Observe alarm registers and scan maps to determine whether a specific emergency is in the dispatch service area. Maintain files of information relating to emergency calls such as personnel rosters, and emergency call-out and pager files. Monitor various radio frequencies such as those used by public works departments, school security, and civil defense to keep apprised of developing situations. Learn material and pass required tests for certification. Read and effectively interpret small-scale maps and information from a computer screen to determine locations and provide directions. Answer routine inquiries and refer calls not requiring dispatches to appropriate departments and agencies. Test and adjust communication and alarm systems and report malfunctions to maintenance units. Provide emergency medical instructions to callers. Monitor alarm systems to detect emergencies such as fires and illegal entry into establishments. Operate and maintain mobile dispatch vehicles and equipment.

GOE—Career Cluster/Interest Area: 03. Arts and Communication. **Work Group:** 03.10. Communications Technology. **Other Apprenticeable Jobs in This Work Group:** Air Traffic Controllers; Airfield Operations Specialists; Dispatchers, Except Police, Fire, and Ambulance. **Personality Type:** Conventional. These occupations frequently involve following set procedures and routines and can include working with data and details more than with ideas. Usually there is a clear line of authority to follow.

Skills—Negotiation; Operation Monitoring.

Education/Training Required (Nonapprenticeship Route): Moderate-term on-the-job training. **Related Knowledge/Courses—Telecommunications:** Transmission, broadcasting, switching, control, and operation of telecommunications systems. **Customer and Personal Service:** Principles and processes for providing customer and personal services, including needs assessment techniques, quality service standards, alternative delivery systems, and customer satisfaction evaluation techniques. **Clerical Practices:** Administrative and clerical procedures and systems such as word-processing systems, filing and records management systems, stenography and transcription, forms, design principles, and other office procedures and terminology. **Law and Government:** Laws, legal codes, court procedures, precedents, government regulations, executive orders, agency rules, and the democratic political process. **Psychology:** Human behavior and performance, mental processes, psychological research methods, and the assessment and treatment of behavioral and affective disorders. **Public Safety and Security:** Weaponry; public safety; security operations, rules, regulations, precautions, and prevention; and the protection of people, data, and property.

Work Environment: Indoors; noisy; sitting; using hands on objects, tools, or controls; repetitive motions.

Postal Service Clerks

- ✾ Annual Earnings: $45,050
- ✾ Growth: 1.2%
- ✾ Annual Job Openings: 3,703
- ✾ Percentage of Women: 49.5%

Related Apprenticeship—Post Office Clerk (4000 hrs.).

Perform any combination of tasks in a post office, such as receiving letters and parcels; selling postage and revenue stamps, postal cards, and stamped envelopes; filling out and selling money orders; placing mail in pigeonholes of mail rack or in bags according to state, address, or other scheme; and examining mail for correct postage. Keep money drawers in order and record and balance daily transactions. Weigh letters and parcels; compute mailing costs based on type, weight, and destination; and affix correct postage. Obtain signatures from recipients of registered or special-delivery mail. Register, certify, and insure letters and parcels. Sell and collect payment for products such as stamps, prepaid mail envelopes, and money orders. Check mail to ensure correct postage and that packages and letters are in proper condition for mailing. Answer questions regarding mail regulations and procedures, postage rates, and post-office boxes. Complete forms regarding address changes, theft or loss of mail, or special services such as registered or priority mail. Provide assistance to the public in complying with federal regulations of U.S. Postal Service and other federal agencies. Sort incoming and outgoing mail according to type and destination by hand or by operating electronic mail-sorting and scanning devices. Cash money orders. Rent post-office boxes to customers. Put undelivered parcels away, retrieve them when customers come to claim them, and complete any related documentation. Provide customers with assistance in filing claims for mail theft or lost or damaged mail. Respond to complaints regarding mail theft, delivery problems, and lost or damaged mail, filling out forms and making appropriate referrals for investigation. Receive letters and parcels and place mail into bags. Feed mail into postage-canceling devices or hand-stamp mail to cancel postage. Transport mail from one workstation to another. Set postage meters and calibrate them to ensure correct operation. Post announcements or government information on public bulletin boards.

GOE—Career Cluster/Interest Area: 04. Business and Administration. **Work Group:** 04.07. Records and Materials Processing. **Other Apprenticeable Jobs in This Work Group:** Human Resources Assistants, Except Payroll and Timekeeping; Office Clerks, General; Production, Planning, and Expediting Clerks. **Personality Type:** Conventional. These occupations frequently involve following set procedures and routines and can include working with data and details more than with ideas. Usually there is a clear line of authority to follow.

Skills—None met the criteria.

Education/Training Required (Nonapprenticeship Route): Short-term on-the-job training. **Related Knowledge/Courses—Sales and Marketing:** Principles and methods involved in showing, promoting, and selling products or services. This includes marketing strategies and tactics, product demonstration and sales techniques, and sales control systems. **Transportation:**

Principles and methods for moving people or goods by air, rail, sea, or road, including their relative costs, advantages, and limitations. **Clerical Practices:** Administrative and clerical procedures and systems such as word-processing systems, filing and records management systems, stenography and transcription, forms, design principles, and other office procedures and terminology. **Public Safety and Security:** Weaponry; public safety; security operations, rules, regulations, precautions, and prevention; and the protection of people, data, and property.

Work Environment: Indoors; noisy; contaminants; standing; bending or twisting the body; repetitive motions.

Power Plant Operators

- ✵ Annual Earnings: $56,640
- ✵ Growth: 2.7%
- ✵ Annual Job Openings: 1,796
- ✵ Percentage of Women: 2.3%

Related Apprenticeships—Hydroelectric-Station Operator (6000 hrs.); Power-Plant Operator (8000 hrs.); Turbine Operator (8000 hrs.).

Control, operate, or maintain machinery to generate electric power. Includes auxiliary equipment operators. Monitor and inspect power plant equipment and indicators to detect evidence of operating problems. Adjust controls to generate specified electrical power or to regulate flow of power between generating stations and substations. Operate or control power-generating equipment, including boilers, turbines, generators, and reactors, via control boards or semi-automatic equipment. Regulate equipment operations and conditions such as water levels based on data from recording and indicating instruments or from computers. Take readings from charts, meters, and gauges at established intervals and take corrective steps as necessary. Inspect records and logbook entries and communicate with other plant personnel to assess equipment operating status. Start or stop generators, auxiliary pumping equipment, turbines, and other power plant equipment; connect or disconnect equipment from circuits. Control and maintain auxiliary equipment, such as pumps, fans, compressors, condensers, feedwater heaters, filters, and chlorinators, to supply water, fuel, lubricants, air, and auxiliary power. Clean, lubricate, and maintain equipment such as generators, turbines, pumps, and compressors to prevent equipment failure or deterioration. Communicate with systems operators to regulate and coordinate transmission loads and frequencies and line voltages. Record and compile operational data, completing and maintaining forms, logs, and reports. Open and close valves and switches in sequence on signals from other workers to start or shut down auxiliary units. Collect oil, water, and electrolyte samples for laboratory analysis. Make adjustments or minor repairs, such as tightening leaking gland and pipe joints; report any needs for major repairs. Control generator output to match phase, frequency, and voltage of electricity supplied to panels. Place standby emergency electrical generators on line in emergencies and monitor system's temperature, output, and lubrication. Receive outage calls and call in necessary personnel during power outages and emergencies.

GOE—Career Cluster/Interest Area: 13. Manufacturing. **Work Group:** 13.16. Utility Operation and Energy Distribution. **Other Apprenticeable Jobs in This Work Group:** Chemical Plant and System Operators; Petroleum Pump System Operators, Refinery Operators, and Gaugers; Power Distributors and

Dispatchers; Stationary Engineers and Boiler Operators; Water and Liquid Waste Treatment Plant and System Operators. **Personality Type:** Realistic. These occupations frequently involve work activities that include practical, hands-on problems and solutions. They often deal with plants; animals; and real-world materials such as wood, tools, and machinery. Many of the occupations require working outside and don't involve a lot of paperwork or working closely with others.

Skills—Operation Monitoring; Equipment Maintenance; Operation and Control; Technology Design; Systems Evaluation; Science; Equipment Selection; Coordination.

Education/Training Required (Nonapprenticeship Route): Long-term on-the-job training. **Related Knowledge/Courses—Physics:** Physical principles, laws, and applications, including air, water, material dynamics, light, atomic principles, heat, electric theory, earth formations, and meteorological and related natural phenomena. **Mechanical Devices:** Machines and tools, including their designs, uses, benefits, repair, and maintenance. **Chemistry:** The composition, structure, and properties of substances and of the chemical processes and transformations that they undergo. This includes uses of chemicals and their interactions, danger signs, production techniques, and disposal methods. **Engineering and Technology:** Equipment, tools, and mechanical devices and their uses to produce motion, light, power, technology, and other applications. **Public Safety and Security:** Weaponry; public safety; security operations, rules, regulations, precautions, and prevention; and the protection of people, data, and property. **Computers and Electronics:** Electric circuit boards, processors, chips, and computer hardware and software, including applications and programming.

Work Environment: Indoors; noisy; very hot or cold; contaminants; high places; hazardous conditions.

Precious Metal Workers

- ✳ Annual Earnings: $31,200
- ✳ Growth: –2.2%
- ✳ Annual Job Openings: 7,375
- ✳ Percentage of Women: 30.4%

Our sources did not provide separate job openings data for this occupation. The job openings listed here are shared with Jewelers and with Gem and Diamond Workers.

Related Apprenticeships—Chaser (Jewelry-Silver) (8000 hrs.); Pewter Caster (6000 hrs.); Pewter Fabricator (8000 hrs.); Pewter Finisher (4000 hrs.); Pewterer (4000 hrs.); Silversmith II (6000 hrs.).

Cast, anneal, solder, hammer, or shape gold, silver, pewter, or other metals to form jewelry or other metal items such as goblets or candlesticks. Weigh completed items to determine weights and record any deviations. Shape and straighten damaged or twisted articles by hand or using pliers. Solder parts together or fill holes and cracks with metal solder, using gas torches. Strike articles with small tools or punch them with hammers to indent them or restore embossing. Trim gates and sharp points from cast parts, using band saws. Verify that bottom edges of articles are level by using straightedges or by rocking them back and forth on flat surfaces. Weigh and mix alloy ingredients, using formulas and knowledge of ingredients' chemical properties. Wire parts such as legs, spouts, and handles to article bodies in preparation for soldering. Strike molds to separate dried castings from molds. Carry castings or finished items to storage areas or to different workstations. Rout out locations where parts are to be joined to items, using routing machines. Secure molded items in chucks of lathes and activate lathes to finish inner and outer surfaces of items. Sand interior mold parts to remove glaze residue, apply new glaze to molds, and allow it to dry for mold assembly. Design silver articles such as jewelry and serving pieces. Design and fabricate models of new casting molds and chipping and turning tools used to finish product surfaces. Research reference materials, analyze production data, and consult with interested parties to develop ideas for new products. Assemble molds, wrap molds in heat-resistant cloth, and ladle molten alloy into mold openings, repeating casting processes as necessary to produce specified numbers of parts. Glue plastic separators to handles of coffeepots and teapots. Rotate molds to distribute alloys and to prevent formation of air pockets. Anneal precious metal objects such as coffeepots, tea sets, and trays in gas ovens for prescribed times to soften metal for reworking. Cut and file pieces of jewelry such as rings, brooches, bracelets, and lockets. Determine placement of auxiliary parts, such as handles and spouts, and mark locations of parts. Engrave decorative lines on items, using engraving tools.

GOE—Career Cluster/Interest Area: 13. Manufacturing. **Work Group:** 13.06. Production Precision Work. **Other Apprenticeable Jobs in This Work Group:** Bookbinders; Dental Laboratory Technicians; Electrical and Electronic Equipment Assemblers; Electromechanical Equipment Assemblers; Engine and Other Machine Assemblers; Gem and Diamond Workers; Jewelers; Medical Appliance Technicians; Molding, Coremaking, and Casting Machine Setters, Operators, and Tenders, Metal and Plastic; Ophthalmic Laboratory Technicians. **Personality Type:** Realistic. These occupations frequently involve work activities that include practical, hands-on problems and solutions. They often deal with plants; animals; and real-world materials such as wood, tools, and machinery. Many of the occupations require working outside and don't involve a lot of paperwork or working closely with others.

Skills—Repairing; Management of Material Resources; Operations Analysis; Quality Control Analysis; Equipment Maintenance; Technology Design; Troubleshooting; Operation Monitoring.

Education/Training Required (Nonapprenticeship Route): Postsecondary vocational training. **Related Knowledge/Courses—Production and Processing:** Inputs, outputs, raw materials, waste, quality control, costs, and techniques for maximizing the manufacture and distribution of goods. **Mechanical Devices:** Machines and tools, including their designs, uses, benefits, repair, and maintenance. **Chemistry:** The composition, structure, and properties of substances and of the chemical processes and transformations that they undergo. This includes uses of chemicals and their interactions, danger signs, production techniques, and disposal methods. **Design:** Design techniques, principles, tools, and instruments involved in the production and use of precision technical plans, blueprints, drawings, and models. **Engineering and Technology:** Equipment, tools, and mechanical devices and their uses to produce motion, light, power, technology, and other applications. **Sales and Marketing:** Principles and methods involved in showing, promoting, and selling products or services. This includes marketing strategies and tactics, product demonstration and sales techniques, and sales control systems.

Work Environment: Indoors; very hot or cold; hazardous equipment; minor burns, cuts, bites, or stings; standing; using hands on objects, tools, or controls.

Prepress Technicians and Workers

- ❁ Annual Earnings: $33,990
- ❁ Growth: –21.1%
- ❁ Annual Job Openings: 10,002
- ❁ Percentage of Women: 30.4%

Related Apprenticeships—Compositor (8000 hrs.); Dot Etcher (10000 hrs.); Electrotyper (10000 hrs.); Etcher, Hand (Printing and Publishing) (10000 hrs.); Etcher, Photoengraving (8000 hrs.); Linotype Operator (Printing and Publishing) (10000 hrs.); Lithographic Plate-maker (8000 hrs.); Monotype-Keyboard Operator (6000 hrs.); Paste-Up Artist (6000 hrs.); Photoengraver (10000 hrs.); Photoengraving Finisher (10000 hrs.); Photoengraving Printer (10000 hrs.); Photoengraving Proofer (10000 hrs.); Photographer, Lithographic (10000 hrs.); Photographer, Photoengraving (12000 hrs.); Photographic-Plate Maker (8000 hrs.); Plate Finisher (Printing and Publishing) (12000 hrs.); Proofsheet Corrector (Printing) (8000 hrs.); Retoucher, Photoengraving (10000 hrs.); Scanner Operator (4000 hrs.); Stereotyper (2000 hrs.); Stripper (Printing and Publishing) (10000 hrs.); Stripper, Lithographic II (8000 hrs.).

Set up and prepare material for printing presses. Enter, store, and retrieve information on computer-aided equipment. Enter, position, and alter text size, using computers, to make up and arrange pages so that printed materials can be produced. Maintain, adjust, and clean equipment and perform minor repairs. Operate and maintain laser plate-making equipment that converts electronic data to plates without the use of film. Examine photographic images for obvious imperfections prior to platemaking. Operate presses to print proofs of plates, monitoring printing quality to ensure that it is adequate. Monitor contact between cover glass and masks inside vacuum frames to prevent flaws resulting from overexposure or light reflection. Transfer images from master plates to unexposed plates and immerse plates in developing solutions to develop images. Examine unexposed photographic plates to detect flaws or foreign particles prior to printing. Lower vacuum frames onto plate-film assemblies, activate vacuums to establish contact between film and plates, and set timers to activate ultraviolet lights that expose plates. Examine finished plates to detect flaws, verify conformity with master plates, and measure dot sizes and centers, using light-boxes and microscopes. Perform close alignment or registration of double and single flats to sensitized plates prior to exposure to produce composite images. Remove plate-film assemblies from vacuum frames and place exposed plates in automatic processors to develop images and dry plates. Position and angle screens for proper exposure. Inspect developed film for specified results and quality, using magnifying glasses and scopes; forward acceptable negatives or positives to other workers or to customers. Punch holes in light-sensitive plates and insert pins in holes to prepare plates for contact with positive or negative film. Unload exposed film from scanners and place film in automatic processors to develop images. Place masking paper on areas of plates not covered by positives or negatives to prevent exposure. Mount negatives and plates in cameras, set exposure controls, and expose plates to light through negatives to transfer images onto plates.

GOE—Career Cluster/Interest Area: 13. Manufacturing. **Work Group:** 13.08. Graphic Arts Production. **Other Apprenticeable Jobs in This Work Group:** Bindery Workers; Desktop Publishers; Etchers and Engravers; Job Printers; Photographic Process Workers; Photographic Processing Machine Operators; Printing Machine Operators. **Personality Type:** Realistic. These occupations frequently involve work activities that include practical, hands-on problems and solutions. They often deal with plants; animals; and real-world materials such as wood, tools, and machinery. Many of the occupations require working outside and don't involve a lot of paperwork or working closely with others.

Skills—Troubleshooting; Equipment Selection; Installation; Equipment Maintenance; Operations Analysis; Operation and Control; Repairing; Technology Design.

Education/Training Required (Nonapprenticeship Route): Postsecondary vocational training. **Related Knowledge/Courses—Computers and Electronics:** Electric circuit boards, processors, chips, and computer hardware and software, including applications and programming. **Communications and Media:** Media production, communication, and dissemination techniques and methods, including alternative ways to inform and entertain via written, oral, and visual media. **English Language:** The structure and content of the English language, including the meaning and spelling of words, rules of composition, and grammar. **Design:** Design techniques, principles, tools, and instruments involved in the production and use of precision technical plans, blueprints, drawings, and models. **Production and Processing:** Inputs, outputs, raw materials, waste, quality control, costs, and techniques for maximizing the manufacture

and distribution of goods. **Clerical Practices:** Administrative and clerical procedures and systems such as word-processing systems, filing and records management systems, stenography and transcription, forms, design principles, and other office procedures and terminology.

Work Environment: Indoors; noisy; contaminants; sitting; using hands on objects, tools, or controls; repetitive motions.

Printing Machine Operators

- ❋ Annual Earnings: $31,490
- ❋ Growth: –5.7%
- ❋ Annual Job Openings: 12,274
- ❋ Percentage of Women: 22.2%

Related Apprenticeships—Assistant Press Operator (4000 hrs.); Ben-Day Artist (12000 hrs.); Cylinder Press Operator (8000 hrs.); Embosser (4000 hrs.); Embossing-Press Operator (8000 hrs.); Engraver, Machine (8000 hrs.); Engraving Press Operator (6000 hrs.); Letterer (Professional and Kindred) (4000 hrs.); Lithograph Press Operator (1000–4000 hrs. or competency); Lithograph-Press Operator, Tin (8000 hrs.); Offset-Press Operator I (8000 hrs.); Platen-Press Operator (8000 hrs.); Printer, Plastic (8000 hrs.); Printer-Slotter Operator (8000 hrs.); Proof-Press Operator (10000 hrs.); Rotogravure-Press Operator (8000 hrs.); Sketch Maker I (Printing and Publishing) (10000 hrs.); Steel-Die Printer (8000 hrs.); Wallpaper Printer I (8000 hrs.); Webpress Operator (8000 hrs.).

Set up or operate various types of printing machines, such as offset, letterset, intaglio, or gravure presses or screen printers, to produce print on paper or other materials. Inspect and examine printed products for print clarity, color accuracy, conformance to specifications, and external defects. Push buttons, turn handles, or move controls and levers to start and control printing machines. Reposition printing plates, adjust pressure rolls, or otherwise adjust machines to improve print quality, using knobs, handwheels, or hand tools. Set and adjust speed, temperature, ink flow, and positions and pressure tolerances of equipment. Examine job orders to determine details such as quantities to be printed, production times, stock specifications, colors, and color sequences. Select and install printing plates, rollers, feed guides, gauges, screens, stencils, type, dies, and cylinders in machines according to specifications, using hand tools. Monitor feeding, printing, and racking processes of presses to maintain specified operating levels and to detect malfunctions; make any necessary adjustments. Operate equipment at slow speed to ensure proper ink coverage, alignment, and registration. Load, position, and adjust unprinted materials on holding fixtures or in equipment loading and feeding mechanisms. Pour or spread paint, ink, color compounds, and other materials into reservoirs, troughs, hoppers, or color holders of printing units, making measurements and adjustments to control color and viscosity. Repair, maintain, or adjust equipment. Blend and test paint, inks, stains, and solvents according to types of material being printed and work order specifications. Clean and lubricate printing machines and components, using oil, solvents, brushes, rags, and hoses. Remove printed materials from presses, using handtrucks, electric lifts, or hoists, and transport them to drying, storage, or finishing areas. Input instructions to program automated machinery, using a computer keyboard. Place printed items in ovens to dry or set ink. Squeeze or spread ink on plates, pads, or rollers, using putty knives, brushes, or sponges. Measure screens and use measurements to center and align screens in proper positions and sequences on machines, using gauges and hand tools.

GOE—Career Cluster/Interest Area: 13. Manufacturing. **Work Group:** 13.08. Graphic Arts Production. **Other Apprenticeable Jobs in This Work Group:** Bindery Workers; Desktop Publishers; Etchers and Engravers; Job Printers; Photographic Process Workers; Photographic Processing Machine Operators; Prepress Technicians and Workers. **Personality Type:** Realistic. These occupations frequently involve work activities that include practical, hands-on problems and solutions. They often deal with plants; animals; and real-world materials such as wood, tools, and machinery. Many of the occupations require working outside and don't involve a lot of paperwork or working closely with others.

Skills—Operation Monitoring; Operation and Control; Equipment Maintenance; Repairing; Quality Control Analysis; Troubleshooting; Equipment Selection; Technology Design.

Education/Training Required (Nonapprenticeship Route): Moderate-term on-the-job training. **Related Knowledge/Courses—Mechanical Devices:** Machines and tools, including their designs, uses, benefits, repair, and maintenance. **Production and Processing:** Inputs, outputs, raw materials, waste, quality control, costs, and techniques for maximizing the manufacture and distribution of goods. **Chemistry:** The composition, structure, and properties of substances and of the chemical processes and transformations that they undergo. This includes uses of chemicals and their interactions, danger signs, production techniques, and disposal methods.

Work Environment: Noisy; contaminants; hazardous conditions; hazardous equipment; standing; using hands on objects, tools, or controls.

Private Detectives and Investigators

- ❀ Annual Earnings: $37,640
- ❀ Growth: 18.2%
- ❀ Annual Job Openings: 7,329
- ❀ Percentage of Women: 38.2%

Related Apprenticeship—Investigator, Private (2000 hrs.).

Detect occurrences of unlawful acts or infractions of rules in private establishments or seek, examine, and compile information for clients. Question persons to obtain evidence for cases of divorce, child custody, or missing persons or information about an individual's character or financial status. Conduct private investigations on a paid basis. Confer with establishment officials, security departments, police, or postal officials to identify problems, provide information, and receive instructions. Observe and document activities of individuals to detect unlawful acts or to obtain evidence for cases, using binoculars and still or video cameras. Investigate companies' financial standings or locate funds stolen by embezzlers, using accounting skills. Monitor industrial or commercial properties to enforce conformance to establishment rules and to protect people or property. Search computer databases, credit reports, public records, tax and legal filings, and other resources to locate persons or to compile information for investigations. Write reports and case summaries to document investigations. Count cash and review transactions, sales checks, and register tapes to verify amounts and to identify shortages. Perform undercover operations such as evaluating employee performance and honesty by posing as customers or employees. Expose fraudulent insurance claims or stolen funds. Alert appropriate personnel to suspects'

locations. Conduct background investigations of individuals, such as pre-employment checks, to obtain information about each individual's character, financial status, or personal history. Testify at hearings and court trials to present evidence. Warn troublemakers causing problems on establishment premises and eject them from premises when necessary. Obtain and analyze information on suspects, crimes, and disturbances to solve cases, identify criminal activity, and gather information for court cases. Apprehend suspects and release them to law-enforcement authorities or security personnel.

GOE—Career Cluster/Interest Area: 12. Law and Public Safety. **Work Group:** 12.05. Safety and Security. **Other Apprenticeable Jobs in This Work Group:** Security Guards. **Personality Type:** Enterprising. These occupations frequently involve starting up and carrying out projects and can involve leading people and making many decisions. They sometimes require risk taking and often deal with business.

Skills—Management of Financial Resources; Persuasion; Time Management; Writing; Service Orientation; Technology Design; Speaking; Judgment and Decision Making.

Education/Training Required (Nonapprenticeship Route): Work experience in a related occupation. **Related Knowledge/Courses—Clerical Practices:** Administrative and clerical procedures and systems such as word-processing systems, filing and records management systems, stenography and transcription, forms, design principles, and other office procedures and terminology. **Law and Government:** Laws, legal codes, court procedures, precedents, government regulations, executive orders, agency rules, and the democratic political process. **Customer and Personal Service:** Principles and processes for providing customer and personal services, including needs assessment techniques, quality service standards, alternative delivery systems, and customer satisfaction evaluation techniques. **Computers and Electronics:** Electric circuit boards, processors, chips, and computer hardware and software, including applications and programming. **Sales and Marketing:** Principles and methods involved in showing, promoting, and selling products or services. This includes marketing strategies and tactics, product demonstration and sales techniques, and sales control systems. **Mathematics:** Numbers and their operations and interrelationships, including arithmetic, algebra, geometry, calculus, and statistics and their applications.

Work Environment: More often indoors than outdoors; standing; walking and running.

Production, Planning, and Expediting Clerks

* Annual Earnings: $39,690
* Growth: 4.2%
* Annual Job Openings: 52,735
* Percentage of Women: 56.8%

Related Apprenticeships—Material Coordinator (4000 hrs.); Supercargo (Water Transportation) (4000 hrs.).

Coordinate and expedite the flow of work and materials within or between departments of an establishment according to production schedules. Examine documents, materials, and products, and monitor work processes to assess completeness, accuracy, and conformance to standards and specifications. Review documents such as production schedules, work orders, and staffing tables to determine personnel and materials requirements, and material priorities. Revise production schedules when required due to design changes, labor or material shortages, backlogs, or other interruptions, collaborating with management, marketing, sales, production, and engineering. Confer with department supervisors and other personnel to assess progress and discuss needed changes. Confer with establishment personnel, vendors, and customers to coordinate production and shipping activities, and to resolve complaints or eliminate delays. Record production data, including volume produced, consumption of raw materials, and quality control measures. Requisition and maintain inventories of materials and supplies necessary to meet production demands. Calculate figures such as required amounts of labor and materials, manufacturing costs, and wages, using pricing schedules, adding machines, calculators, or computers. Distribute production schedules and work orders to departments. Compile information such as production rates and progress, materials inventories, materials used, and customer information, so that status reports can be completed. Arrange for delivery, assembly, and distribution of supplies and parts to expedite flow of materials and meet production schedules. Contact suppliers to verify shipment details. Maintain files such as maintenance records, bills of lading, and cost reports. Plan production commitments and timetables for business units, specific programs, and/or jobs, using sales forecasts. Establish and prepare product construction directions and locations; information on required tools, materials, and equipment; numbers of workers needed; and cost projections. Compile and prepare documentation related to production sequences, transportation, personnel schedules, and purchase, maintenance, and repair orders. Provide documentation and information to account for delays, difficulties, and changes to cost estimates.

GOE—Career Cluster/Interest Area: 04. Business and Administration. **Work Group:** 04.07. Records and Materials Processing. **Other Apprenticeable Jobs in This Work Group:** Human Resources Assistants, Except Payroll and Timekeeping; Office Clerks, General; Postal Service Clerks. **Personality Type:** Conventional. These occupations frequently involve following set procedures and routines and can include working with data and details more than with ideas. Usually there is a clear line of authority to follow.

Skills—Management of Material Resources; Operations Analysis; Management of Financial Resources; Systems Evaluation; Negotiation; Mathematics; Coordination; Persuasion.

Education/Training Required (Nonapprenticeship Route): Moderate-term on-the-job training. **Related Knowledge/Courses—Production and Processing:** Inputs, outputs, raw materials, waste, quality control, costs, and techniques for maximizing the manufacture and distribution of goods. **Clerical Practices:** Administrative and clerical procedures and systems such as word-processing systems, filing and records management systems, stenography and transcription, forms, design principles, and other office procedures and terminology. **Computers and Electronics:** Electric circuit boards, processors, chips, and computer hardware and software, including applications and programming. **Administration and Management:** Principles and processes involved in business and organizational planning, coordination, and execution. This includes strategic planning, resource allocation, manpower modeling, leadership techniques, and production methods. **Mathematics:** Numbers and their operations and interrelationships, including arithmetic, algebra, geometry, calculus, and statistics and their applications.

Customer and Personal Service: Principles and processes for providing customer and personal services, including needs assessment techniques, quality service standards, alternative delivery systems, and customer satisfaction evaluation techniques.

Work Environment: Indoors; noisy; contaminants; sitting.

Purchasing Agents, Except Wholesale, Retail, and Farm Products

* Annual Earnings: $52,460
* Growth: 0.1%
* Annual Job Openings: 22,349
* Percentage of Women: 51.1%

Related Apprenticeships—Purchasing Agent (8000 hrs.); Subcontract Administrator (4000 hrs. or competency); Subcontract Administrator Associate (4000 hrs. or competency).

Purchase machinery, equipment, tools, parts, supplies, or services necessary for the operation of an establishment. Purchase raw or semi-finished materials for manufacturing. Purchase the highest-quality merchandise at the lowest possible price and in correct amounts. Prepare purchase orders, solicit bid proposals, and review requisitions for goods and services. Research and evaluate suppliers based on price, quality, selection, service, support, availability, reliability, production and distribution capabilities, and the supplier's reputation and history. Analyze price proposals, financial reports, and other data and information to determine reasonable prices. Monitor and follow applicable laws and regulations. Negotiate, or renegotiate, and administer contracts with suppliers, vendors, and other representatives. Monitor shipments to ensure that goods come in on time and trace shipments and follow up undelivered goods in the event of problems. Confer with staff, users, and vendors to discuss defective or unacceptable goods or services and determine corrective action. Evaluate and monitor contract performance to ensure compliance with contractual obligations and to determine need for changes. Maintain and review computerized or manual records of items purchased, costs, delivery, product performance, and inventories. Review catalogs, industry periodicals, directories, trade journals, and Internet sites and consult with other department personnel to locate necessary goods and services. Study sales records and inventory levels of current stock to develop strategic purchasing programs that facilitate employee access to supplies. Interview vendors and visit suppliers' plants and distribution centers to examine and learn about products, services, and prices. Arrange the payment of duty and freight charges. Hire, train, and/or supervise purchasing clerks, buyers, and expediters. Write and review product specifications, maintaining a working technical knowledge of the goods or services to be purchased. Monitor changes affecting supply and demand, tracking market conditions, price trends, or futures markets. Formulate policies and procedures for bid proposals and procurement of goods and services. Attend meetings, trade shows, conferences, conventions, and seminars to network with people in other purchasing departments.

GOE—Career Cluster/Interest Area: 14. Retail and Wholesale Sales and Service. **Work Group:** 14.05. Purchasing. **Other Apprenticeable Jobs in This Work Group:** No others in group. **Personality Type:** Conventional. These occupations frequently involve following set procedures and routines and can include working with data and details more than with ideas. Usually there is a clear line of authority to follow.

Skills—Operations Analysis; Management of Financial Resources; Management of Material Resources; Mathematics; Writing; Management of Personnel Resources; Speaking; Judgment and Decision Making.

Education/Training Required (Nonapprenticeship Route): Long-term on-the-job training. **Related Knowledge/Courses—Clerical Practices:** Administrative and clerical procedures and systems such as word-processing systems, filing and records management systems, stenography and transcription, forms, design principles, and other office procedures and terminology. **Economics and Accounting:** Economic and accounting principles and practices, the financial markets, banking, and the analysis and reporting of financial data. **Production and Processing:** Inputs, outputs, raw materials, waste, quality control, costs, and techniques for maximizing the manufacture and distribution of goods. **Administration and Management:** Principles and processes involved in business and organizational planning, coordination, and execution. This includes strategic planning, resource allocation, manpower modeling, leadership techniques, and production methods. **Computers and Electronics:** Electric circuit boards, processors, chips, and computer hardware and software, including applications and programming. **Communications and Media:** Media production, communication, and dissemination techniques and methods, including alternative ways to inform and entertain via written, oral, and visual media.

Work Environment: Indoors; sitting; using hands on objects, tools, or controls; repetitive motions.

Radiologic Technologists

* Annual Earnings: $50,260
* Growth: 15.1%
* Annual Job Openings: 12,836
* Percentage of Women: 72.9%

Our sources did not provide separate job openings data for this occupation. The job openings listed here are shared with Radiologic Technicians.

Related Apprenticeships—Computed Tomography (CT) Technologist (1838 hrs.); Diagnostic Imaging Specialty (2500 hrs. or competency); Magnetic Resonance Imaging (MRI) Technologist (1856 hrs.); Mammography Technologist (1856 hrs.).

Take X rays and Computerized Axial Tomography (CAT or CT) scans or administer nonradioactive materials into patient's bloodstream for diagnostic purposes. Includes technologists who specialize in other modalities such as computed tomography, ultrasound, and magnetic resonance. Use radiation safety measures and protection devices to comply with government regulations and to ensure safety of patients and staff. Review and evaluate developed X rays, videotape, or computer-generated information to determine if images are satisfactory for diagnostic purposes. Position imaging equipment and adjust controls to set exposure times and distances, according to specification of examinations. Explain procedures and observe patients to ensure safety and comfort during scans. Key commands and data into computers to document and specify scan sequences, adjust transmitters and receivers, or photograph certain images. Operate or oversee operation of radiologic and magnetic imaging equipment to produce images of the body for diagnostic purposes. Position and immobilize patients on examining tables. Record, process, and maintain patient data and treatment records, and prepare reports. Take thorough and accurate patient medical histories. Remove and process film. Set up examination rooms, ensuring that all necessary equipment is ready. Monitor patients' conditions and reactions, reporting abnormal signs to physicians. Coordinate work with clerical personnel or other technologists. Provide assistance in dressing or changing seriously ill, injured, or disabled patients. Demonstrate new equipment, procedures, and techniques to staff and provide technical assistance. Collaborate with other medical team members such as physicians and nurses to conduct angiography or special vascular procedures. Prepare and administer oral or injected contrast media to patients. Monitor video displays of areas being scanned and adjust density or contrast to improve picture quality. Operate fluoroscope to aid physicians to view and guide wires or catheters through blood vessels to areas of interest. Assign duties to radiologic staffs to maintain patient flows and achieve production goals. Perform scheduled maintenance and minor emergency repairs on radiographic equipment. Perform administrative duties such as developing departmental operating budgets, coordinating purchases of supplies and equipment, and preparing work schedules.

GOE—Career Cluster/Interest Area: 08. Health Science. **Work Group:** 08.06. Medical Technology. **Other Apprenticeable Jobs in This Work Group:** Medical and Clinical Laboratory Technicians; Medical Equipment Preparers; Medical Records and Health Information Technicians; Opticians, Dispensing. **Personality Type:** Realistic. These occupations frequently involve work activities that include practical, hands-on problems and solutions. They often deal with plants; animals; and real-world materials such as wood, tools, and machinery. Many of the occupations require working outside and don't involve a lot of paperwork or working closely with others.

Skills—Operation Monitoring; Operation and Control.

Education/Training Required (Nonapprenticeship Route): Associate degree. **Related Knowledge/Courses—Medicine and Dentistry:** The information and techniques needed to diagnose and treat injuries, diseases, and deformities. This includes symptoms, treatment alternatives, drug properties and interactions, and preventive health-care measures. **Physics:** Physical principles, laws, and applications, including air, water, material dynamics, light, atomic principles, heat, electric theory, earth formations, and meteorological and related natural phenomena. **Customer and Personal Service:** Principles and processes for providing customer and personal services, including needs assessment techniques, quality service standards, alternative delivery systems, and customer satisfaction evaluation techniques. **Biology:** Plant and animal living tissue, cells, organisms, and entities, including their functions, interdependencies, and interactions with each other and the environment. **Psychology:** Human behavior and performance, mental processes, psychological research methods, and the assessment and treatment of behavioral and affective disorders. **Chemistry:** The composition, structure, and properties of substances and of the chemical processes and transformations that they undergo. This includes uses of chemicals and their interactions, danger signs, production techniques, and disposal methods.

Work Environment: Indoors; disease or infections; standing; walking and running; using hands on objects, tools, or controls; repetitive motions.

Rail Car Repairers

- Annual Earnings: $44,970
- Growth: 5.1%
- Annual Job Openings: 1,989
- Percentage of Women: 1.4%

Related Apprenticeships—Car Repairer (Railroad Equipment) (8000 hrs.); Mechanical-Unit Repairer (8000 hrs.); Mine-Car Repairer (4000 hrs.).

Diagnose, adjust, repair, or overhaul railroad rolling stock, mine cars, or mass-transit rail cars. Repair or replace defective or worn parts such as bearings, pistons, and gears, using hand tools, torque wrenches, power tools, and welding equipment. Test units for operability before and after repairs. Remove locomotives, car mechanical units, or other components, using pneumatic hoists and jacks, pinch bars, hand tools, and cutting torches. Record conditions of cars and repair and maintenance work performed or to be performed. Inspect components such as bearings, seals, gaskets, wheels, and coupler assemblies to determine if repairs are needed. Inspect the interior and exterior of rail cars coming into rail yards to identify defects and to determine the extent of wear and damage. Adjust repaired or replaced units as needed to ensure proper operation. Perform scheduled maintenance and clean units and components. Repair and maintain electrical and electronic controls for propulsion and braking systems. Repair, fabricate, and install steel or wood fittings, using blueprints, shop sketches, and instruction manuals. Disassemble units such as water pumps, control valves, and compressors so that repairs can be made. Align car sides for installation of car ends and crossties, using width gauges, turnbuckles, and wrenches. Measure diameters of axle wheel seats, using micrometers, and mark dimensions on axles so that wheels can be bored to specified dimensions. Replace defective wiring and insulation and tighten electrical connections, using hand tools. Test electrical systems of cars by operating systems and using testing equipment such as ammeters. Install and repair interior flooring, fixtures, walls, plumbing, steps, and platforms. Examine car roofs for wear and damage and repair defective sections, using roofing material, cement, nails, and waterproof paint. Paint car exteriors, interiors, and fixtures. Repair car upholstery. Repair window sash frames, attach weather stripping and channels to frames, and replace window glass, using hand tools.

GOE—Career Cluster/Interest Area: 13. Manufacturing. **Work Group:** 13.14. Vehicle and Facility Mechanical Work. **Other Apprenticeable Jobs in This Work Group:** Aircraft Mechanics and Service Technicians; Aircraft Structure, Surfaces, Rigging, and Systems Assemblers; Automotive Body and Related Repairers; Automotive Glass Installers and Repairers; Automotive Master Mechanics; Automotive Specialty Technicians; Bus and Truck Mechanics and Diesel Engine Specialists; Farm Equipment Mechanics; Fiberglass Laminators and Fabricators; Mobile Heavy Equipment Mechanics, Except Engines; Motorboat Mechanics; Motorcycle Mechanics; Outdoor Power Equipment and Other Small Engine Mechanics; Recreational Vehicle Service Technicians. **Personality Type:** Realistic. These occupations frequently involve work activities that include practical, hands-on problems and solutions. They often deal with plants; animals; and real-world materials such as wood, tools, and machinery. Many of the occupations require

working outside and don't involve a lot of paperwork or working closely with others.

Skills—Repairing; Installation; Equipment Maintenance; Troubleshooting; Operation Monitoring; Technology Design; Operation and Control; Systems Analysis.

Education/Training Required (Nonapprenticeship Route): Long-term on-the-job training. **Related Knowledge/Courses—Mechanical Devices:** Machines and tools, including their designs, uses, benefits, repair, and maintenance. **Public Safety and Security:** Weaponry; public safety; security operations, rules, regulations, precautions, and prevention; and the protection of people, data, and property. **Production and Processing:** Inputs, outputs, raw materials, waste, quality control, costs, and techniques for maximizing the manufacture and distribution of goods.

Work Environment: Outdoors; noisy; very hot or cold; contaminants; standing; using hands on objects, tools, or controls.

Recreational Vehicle Service Technicians

* Annual Earnings: $31,760
* Growth: 18.2%
* Annual Job Openings: 2,442
* Percentage of Women: 4.6%

Related Apprenticeship—Repairer, Recreational Vehicles (8000 hrs.).

Diagnose, inspect, adjust, repair, or overhaul recreational vehicles, including travel trailers. May specialize in maintaining gas, electrical, hydraulic, plumbing, or chassis/towing systems as well as repairing generators, appliances, and interior components. Examine or test operation of parts or systems that have been repaired to ensure completeness of repairs. Repair plumbing and propane gas lines, using caulking compounds and plastic or copper pipe. Inspect recreational vehicles to diagnose problems; then perform necessary adjustment, repair, or overhaul. Locate and repair frayed wiring, broken connections, or incorrect wiring, using ohmmeters, soldering irons, tape, and hand tools. Confer with customers, read work orders, and examine vehicles needing repair to determine the nature and extent of damage. List parts needed, estimate costs, and plan work procedures, using parts lists, technical manuals, and diagrams. Connect electrical systems to outside power sources and activate switches to test the operation of appliances and light fixtures. Connect water hoses to inlet pipes of plumbing systems and test operation of toilets and sinks. Remove damaged exterior panels and repair and replace structural frame members. Open and close doors, windows, and drawers to test their operation, trimming edges to fit as necessary. Repair leaks with caulking compound or replace pipes, using pipe wrenches. Refinish wood surfaces on cabinets, doors, moldings, and floors, using power sanders, putty, spray equipment, brushes, paints, or varnishes. Reset hardware, using chisels, mallets, and screwdrivers. Seal open sides of modular units to prepare them for shipment, using polyethylene sheets, nails, and hammers.

GOE—Career Cluster/Interest Area: 13. Manufacturing. **Work Group:** 13.14. Vehicle and Facility Mechanical Work. **Other Apprenticeable Jobs in This Work Group:** Aircraft Mechanics and Service Technicians; Aircraft Structure, Surfaces, Rigging, and Systems Assemblers; Automotive Body and Related Repairers; Automotive Glass Installers and Repairers; Automotive Master Mechanics; Automotive Specialty Technicians; Bus and Truck Mechanics and Diesel Engine Specialists; Farm Equipment Mechanics; Fiberglass Laminators and Fabricators; Mobile Heavy Equipment Mechanics, Except Engines; Motorboat Mechanics; Motorcycle Mechanics; Outdoor Power Equipment and Other Small Engine Mechanics; Rail Car Repairers. **Personality Type:** Realistic. These occupations frequently involve work activities that include practical, hands-on problems and solutions. They often deal with plants; animals; and real-world materials such as wood, tools, and machinery. Many of the occupations require working outside and don't involve a lot of paperwork or working closely with others.

Skills—Repairing; Installation; Troubleshooting; Equipment Maintenance; Technology Design; Operation Monitoring; Equipment Selection; Systems Evaluation.

Education/Training Required (Nonapprenticeship Route): Long-term on-the-job training. **Related Knowledge/Courses—Mechanical Devices:** Machines and tools, including their designs, uses, benefits, repair, and maintenance. **Building and Construction:** Materials, methods, and the appropriate tools to construct objects, structures, and buildings. **Chemistry:** The composition, structure, and properties of substances and of the chemical processes and transformations that they undergo. This includes uses of chemicals and their interactions, danger signs, production techniques, and disposal methods. **Physics:** Physical principles, laws, and applications, including air, water, material dynamics, light, atomic principles, heat, electric theory, earth formations, and meteorological and related natural phenomena. **Engineering and Technology:** Equipment, tools, and mechanical devices and their uses to produce motion, light, power, technology, and other applications. **Design:**

Design techniques, principles, tools, and instruments involved in the production and use of precision technical plans, blueprints, drawings, and models.

Work Environment: Noisy; contaminants; cramped work space, awkward positions; hazardous equipment; standing; using hands on objects, tools, or controls.

Refrigeration Mechanics and Installers

- ✳ Annual Earnings: $38,360
- ✳ Growth: 8.7%
- ✳ Annual Job Openings: 29,719
- ✳ Percentage of Women: 2.7%

Our sources did not provide separate job openings data for this occupation. The job openings listed here are shared with Heating and Air Conditioning Mechanics and Installers.

Related Apprenticeships—Refrigeration Mechanic (Any Industry) (6000 hrs.); Refrigeration Unit Repairer (6000 hrs.).

Install and repair industrial and commercial refrigerating systems. Braze or solder parts to repair defective joints and leaks. Observe and test system operation, using gauges and instruments. Test lines, components, and connections for leaks. Dismantle malfunctioning systems and test components, using electrical, mechanical, and pneumatic testing equipment. Adjust or replace worn or defective mechanisms and parts and reassemble repaired systems. Read blueprints to determine location, size, capacity, and type of components needed to build refrigeration system. Supervise and instruct assistants. Perform mechanical overhauls and refrigerant reclaiming. Install wiring to connect components to an electric power source. Cut, bend, thread, and connect pipe to functional components and water, power, or refrigeration system. Adjust valves according to specifications and charge system with proper type of refrigerant by pumping the specified gas or fluid into the system. Estimate, order, pick up, deliver, and install materials and supplies needed to maintain equipment in good working condition. Install expansion and control valves, using acetylene torches and wrenches. Mount compressor, condenser, and other components in specified locations on frames, using hand tools and acetylene welding equipment. Keep records of repairs and replacements made and causes of malfunctions. Schedule work with customers and initiate work orders, house requisitions, and orders from stock. Lay out reference points for installation of structural and functional components, using measuring instruments. Fabricate and assemble structural and functional components of refrigeration system, using hand tools, power tools, and welding equipment. Lift and align components into position, using hoist or block and tackle. Drill holes and install mounting brackets and hangers into floor and walls of building. Insulate shells and cabinets of systems.

GOE—Career Cluster/Interest Area: 02. Architecture and Construction. **Work Group:** 02.05. Systems and Equipment Installation, Maintenance, and Repair. **Other Apprenticeable Jobs in This Work Group:** Electrical and Electronics Repairers, Powerhouse, Substation, and Relay; Electrical Power-Line Installers and Repairers; Elevator Installers and Repairers; Heating and Air Conditioning Mechanics and Installers; Maintenance and Repair Workers, General; Telecommunications Equipment Installers and Repairers, Except Line Installers; Telecommunications Line Installers and

Repairers. **Personality Type:** Realistic. These occupations frequently involve work activities that include practical, hands-on problems and solutions. They often deal with plants; animals; and real-world materials such as wood, tools, and machinery. Many of the occupations require working outside and don't involve a lot of paperwork or working closely with others.

Skills—Installation; Repairing; Equipment Maintenance; Operation Monitoring; Science; Systems Evaluation; Systems Analysis; Troubleshooting.

Education/Training Required (Nonapprenticeship Route): Long-term on-the-job training. **Related Knowledge/Courses—Building and Construction:** Materials, methods, and the appropriate tools to construct objects, structures, and buildings. **Mechanical Devices:** Machines and tools, including their designs, uses, benefits, repair, and maintenance. **Engineering and Technology:** Equipment, tools, and mechanical devices and their uses to produce motion, light, power, technology, and other applications. **Physics:** Physical principles, laws, and applications, including air, water, material dynamics, light, atomic principles, heat, electric theory, earth formations, and meteorological and related natural phenomena. **Chemistry:** The composition, structure, and properties of substances and of the chemical processes and transformations that they undergo. This includes uses of chemicals and their interactions, danger signs, production techniques, and disposal methods. **Design:** Design techniques, principles, tools, and instruments involved in the production and use of precision technical plans, blueprints, drawings, and models.

Work Environment: Outdoors; very hot or cold; cramped work space, awkward positions;

minor burns, cuts, bites, or stings; standing; using hands on objects, tools, or controls.

Reinforcing Iron and Rebar Workers

* Annual Earnings: $37,890
* Growth: 11.5%
* Annual Job Openings: 4,502
* Percentage of Women: 2.2%

Related Apprenticeships—Reinforcing Ironworker, Concrete (6000–8000 hrs., hybrid); Reinforcing Metal Worker (6000 hrs.).

Position and secure steel bars or mesh in concrete forms to reinforce concrete. Use a variety of fasteners, rod-bending machines, blowtorches, and hand tools. Cut rods to required lengths, using metal shears, hacksaws, bar cutters, or acetylene torches. Determine quantities, sizes, shapes, and locations of reinforcing rods from blueprints, sketches, or oral instructions. Space and fasten together rods in forms according to blueprints, using wire and pliers. Place blocks under rebar to hold the bars off the deck when reinforcing floors. Bend steel rods with hand tools and rod-bending machines and weld them with arc-welding equipment. Cut and fit wire mesh or fabric, using hooked rods, and position fabric or mesh in concrete to reinforce concrete. Position and secure steel bars, rods, cables, or mesh in concrete forms, using fasteners, rod-bending machines, blowtorches, and hand tools.

GOE—Career Cluster/Interest Area: 02. Architecture and Construction. **Work Group:** 02.04. Construction Crafts. **Other Apprenticeable Jobs in This Work Group:** Boilermakers; Brickmasons and Blockmasons; Carpet Installers; Cement Masons and Concrete Finishers; Construction Carpenters; Crane and Tower

Operators; Drywall and Ceiling Tile Installers; Electricians; Fence Erectors; Floor Layers, Except Carpet, Wood, and Hard Tiles; Glaziers; Insulation Workers, Floor, Ceiling, and Wall; Insulation Workers, Mechanical; Operating Engineers and Other Construction Equipment Operators; Painters, Construction and Maintenance; Paperhangers; Paving, Surfacing, and Tamping Equipment Operators; Pipe Fitters and Steamfitters; Plasterers and Stucco Masons; Plumbers; Riggers; Roofers; Rough Carpenters; Sheet Metal Workers; Stone Cutters and Carvers, Manufacturing; Stonemasons; Structural Iron and Steel Workers; Tapers; Terrazzo Workers and Finishers; Tile and Marble Setters. **Personality Type:** Realistic. These occupations frequently involve work activities that include practical, hands-on problems and solutions. They often deal with plants; animals; and real-world materials such as wood, tools, and machinery. Many of the occupations require working outside and don't involve a lot of paperwork or working closely with others.

Skills—Installation; Equipment Selection; Coordination; Management of Material Resources; Mathematics; Operation and Control; Monitoring; Management of Personnel Resources.

Education/Training Required (Nonapprenticeship Route): Long-term on-the-job training. **Related Knowledge/Courses—Building and Construction:** Materials, methods, and the appropriate tools to construct objects, structures, and buildings. **Mechanical Devices:** Machines and tools, including their designs, uses, benefits, repair, and maintenance. **Public Safety and Security:** Weaponry; public safety; security operations, rules, regulations, precautions, and prevention; and the protection of people, data, and property. **Transportation:** Principles and methods for moving people or goods by air, rail, sea, or road, including their relative costs, advantages, and limitations.

Work Environment: Outdoors; noisy; contaminants; minor burns, cuts, bites, or stings; standing; using hands on objects, tools, or controls.

Further Information: Contact a local joint union-management apprenticeship committee, or the nearest office of your state employment service or apprenticeship agency (see Appendix C). International Association of Bridge, Structural, Ornamental, and Reinforcing Iron Workers, Apprenticeship Department, 1750 New York Ave. NW, Suite 400, Washington, DC 20006. Internet: www.ironworkers.org

Residential Advisors

- ❀ Annual Earnings: $23,050
- ❀ Growth: 18.5%
- ❀ Annual Job Openings: 8,053
- ❀ Percentage of Women: 69.0%

Related Apprenticeship—Public Affairs (2500 hrs. or competency).

Coordinate activities for residents of boarding schools, college fraternities or sororities, college dormitories, or similar establishments. Order supplies and determine need for maintenance, repairs, and furnishings. May maintain household records and assign rooms. May refer residents to counseling resources if needed. Enforce rules and regulations to ensure the smooth and orderly operation of dormitory programs. Provide emergency first aid and summon medical assistance when necessary. Mediate interpersonal problems between residents. Administer, coordinate, or recommend disciplinary and corrective actions. Communicate with other staff to resolve problems with individual students. Counsel students in the handling of issues such as family, financial, and educational problems. Make regular rounds to ensure that residents and areas are safe and secure. Observe students to detect and report unusual behavior. Determine the need for facility maintenance and repair and notify appropriate personnel. Collaborate with counselors to develop counseling programs that address the needs of individual students. Develop program plans for individuals or assist in plan development. Hold regular meetings with each assigned unit. Direct and participate in on- and off-campus recreational activities for residents of institutions, boarding schools, fraternities or sororities, children's homes, or similar establishments. Assign rooms to students. Provide requested information on students' progress and the development of case plans. Confer with medical personnel to better understand the backgrounds and needs of individual residents. Answer telephones and route calls or deliver messages. Supervise participants in work-study programs. Process contract cancellations for students who are unable to follow residence hall policies and procedures. Sort and distribute mail. Supervise the activities of housekeeping personnel. Order supplies for facilities. Supervise students' housekeeping work to ensure that it is done properly. Chaperone group-sponsored trips and social functions. Compile information such as residents' daily activities and the quantities of supplies used to prepare required reports. Accompany and supervise students during meals. Provide transportation or escort for expeditions such as shopping trips or visits to doctors or dentists. Inventory, pack, and remove items left behind by former residents.

GOE—Career Cluster/Interest Area: 10. Human Service. **Work Group:** 10.01. Counseling and Social Work. **Other Apprenticeable**

Jobs in This Work Group: Social and Human Service Assistants. **Personality Type:** Social. These occupations frequently involve working with, communicating with, and teaching people and often involve helping or providing service to others.

Skills—Social Perceptiveness; Monitoring; Management of Personnel Resources; Time Management; Persuasion; Service Orientation; Management of Financial Resources; Negotiation.

Education/Training Required (Nonapprenticeship Route): Short-term on-the-job training. **Related Knowledge/Courses—Therapy and Counseling:** Information and techniques needed to rehabilitate physical and mental ailments and to provide career guidance, including alternative treatments, rehabilitation equipment and its proper use, and methods to evaluate treatment effects. **Philosophy and Theology:** Different philosophical systems and religions, including their basic principles, values, ethics, ways of thinking, customs, and practices and their impact on human culture. **Sociology and Anthropology:** Group behavior and dynamics; societal trends and influences; and cultures and their history, migrations, ethnicity, and origins. **Psychology:** Human behavior and performance, mental processes, psychological research methods, and the assessment and treatment of behavioral and affective disorders. **Personnel and Human Resources:** Principles and procedures for personnel recruitment; selection; training; compensation and benefits; labor relations and negotiation; and personnel information systems. **Public Safety and Security:** Weaponry; public safety; security operations, rules, regulations, precautions, and prevention; and the protection of people, data, and property.

Work Environment: Indoors; noisy; sitting.

Roofers

* Annual Earnings: $33,240
* Growth: 14.3%
* Annual Job Openings: 38,398
* Percentage of Women: 1.1%

Related Apprenticeship—Roofer (4000 hrs.).

Cover roofs of structures with shingles, slate, asphalt, aluminum, wood, and related materials. May spray roofs, sidings, and walls with material to bind, seal, insulate, or soundproof sections of structures. Install, repair, or replace single-ply roofing systems, using waterproof sheet materials such as modified plastics, elastomeric coatings, or other asphaltic compositions. Apply alternate layers of hot asphalt or tar and roofing paper to roofs, according to specification. Apply gravel or pebbles over top layers of roofs, using rakes or stiff-bristled brooms. Cement or nail flashing strips of metal or shingle over joints to make them watertight. Punch holes in slate, tile, terra cotta, or wooden shingles, using punches and hammers. Hammer and chisel away rough spots or remove them with rubbing bricks to prepare surfaces for waterproofing. Align roofing materials with edges of roofs. Mop or pour hot asphalt or tar onto roof bases. Apply plastic coatings and membranes, fiberglass, or felt over sloped roofs before applying shingles. Install vapor barriers and/or layers of insulation on the roof decks of flat roofs and seal the seams. Install partially overlapping layers of material over roof insulation surfaces, determining distance of roofing material overlap using chalk lines, gauges on shingling hatchets, or lines on shingles. Inspect problem roofs to determine the best procedures for repairing them. Glaze top layers to make a smooth finish, or embed gravel in the bitumen for rough surfaces. Cut roofing paper to size, using knives, and nail or staple roofing paper to roofs in overlapping strips to form bases for other materials. Cut felt, shingles, and strips of flashing and fit them into angles formed by walls, vents, and intersecting roof surfaces. Cover roofs and exterior walls of structures with slate, asphalt, aluminum, wood, gravel, gypsum, and/or related materials, using brushes, knives, punches, hammers, and other tools. Clean and maintain equipment. Cover exposed nailheads with roofing cement or caulking to prevent water leakage and rust. Waterproof and damp-proof walls, floors, roofs, foundations, and basements by painting or spraying surfaces with waterproof coatings or by attaching waterproofing membranes to surfaces. Spray roofs, sidings, and walls with material to bind, seal, insulate, or soundproof sections of structures, using spray guns, air compressors, and heaters.

GOE—Career Cluster/Interest Area: 02. Architecture and Construction. **Work Group:** 02.04. Construction Crafts. **Other Apprenticeable Jobs in This Work Group:** Boilermakers; Brickmasons and Blockmasons; Carpet Installers; Cement Masons and Concrete Finishers; Construction Carpenters; Crane and Tower Operators; Drywall and Ceiling Tile Installers; Electricians; Fence Erectors; Floor Layers, Except Carpet, Wood, and Hard Tiles; Glaziers; Insulation Workers, Floor, Ceiling, and Wall; Insulation Workers, Mechanical; Operating Engineers and Other Construction Equipment Operators; Painters, Construction and Maintenance; Paperhangers; Paving, Surfacing, and Tamping Equipment Operators; Pipe Fitters and Steamfitters; Plasterers and Stucco Masons; Plumbers; Reinforcing Iron and Rebar Workers; Riggers; Rough Carpenters; Sheet Metal Workers; Stone Cutters and Carvers, Manufacturing;

Stonemasons; Structural Iron and Steel Workers; Tapers; Terrazzo Workers and Finishers; Tile and Marble Setters. **Personality Type:** Realistic. These occupations frequently involve work activities that include practical, hands-on problems and solutions. They often deal with plants; animals; and real-world materials such as wood, tools, and machinery. Many of the occupations require working outside and don't involve a lot of paperwork or working closely with others.

Skills—Repairing; Installation; Equipment Maintenance; Operations Analysis; Technology Design; Mathematics; Management of Personnel Resources; Coordination.

Education/Training Required (Nonapprenticeship Route): Moderate-term on-the-job training. **Related Knowledge/Courses—Building and Construction:** Materials, methods, and the appropriate tools to construct objects, structures, and buildings. **Design:** Design techniques, principles, tools, and instruments involved in the production and use of precision technical plans, blueprints, drawings, and models. **Engineering and Technology:** Equipment, tools, and mechanical devices and their uses to produce motion, light, power, technology, and other applications. **Transportation:** Principles and methods for moving people or goods by air, rail, sea, or road, including their relative costs, advantages, and limitations.

Work Environment: Outdoors; high places; minor burns, cuts, bites, or stings; kneeling, crouching, stooping, or crawling; keeping or regaining balance; using hands on objects, tools, or controls.

Rotary Drill Operators, Oil and Gas

- ❀ Annual Earnings: $43,480
- ❀ Growth: –5.4%
- ❀ Annual Job Openings: 2,145
- ❀ Percentage of Women: 3.1%

Related Apprenticeship—Prospecting Driller (Petroleum) (4000 hrs.).

Set up or operate a variety of drills to remove petroleum products from the earth and to find and remove core samples for testing during oil and gas exploration. Train crews and introduce procedures to make drill work more safe and effective. Observe pressure gauge and move throttles and levers to control the speed of rotary tables and to regulate pressure of tools at bottoms of boreholes. Count sections of drill rod to determine depths of boreholes. Push levers and brake pedals to control gasoline, diesel, electric, or steam draw works that lower and raise drill pipes and casings in and out of wells. Connect sections of drill pipe, using hand tools and powered wrenches and tongs. Maintain records of footage drilled, location and nature of strata penetrated, materials and tools used, services rendered, and time required. Maintain and adjust machinery to ensure proper performance. Start and examine operation of slush pumps to ensure circulation and consistency of drilling fluid or mud in well. Locate and recover lost or broken bits, casings, and drill pipes from wells, using special tools. Weigh clay and mix with water and chemicals to make drilling mud. Direct rig crews in drilling and other activities, such as setting up rigs and completing or servicing wells. Monitor progress of drilling operations and select and change drill bits according to the nature of strata, using hand tools. Repair or replace defective parts of machinery, such as rotary drill rigs, water trucks, air compressors, and pumps, using hand tools. Clean and oil pulleys, blocks, and cables. Bolt together pump and engine parts and connect tanks and flow lines. Remove core samples during drilling to determine the nature of the strata being drilled. Cap wells with packers or turn valves to regulate outflow of oil from wells. Line drilled holes with pipes and install all necessary hardware to prepare new wells. Position and prepare truck-mounted derricks at drilling areas that are specified on field maps. Plug observation wells and restore sites. Lower and explode charges in boreholes to start flow of oil from wells. Dig holes, set forms, and mix and pour concrete for foundations of steel or wooden derricks.

GOE—Career Cluster/Interest Area: 01. Agriculture and Natural Resources. **Work Group:** 01.08. Mining and Drilling. **Other Apprenticeable Jobs in This Work Group:** Earth Drillers, Except Oil and Gas; Excavating and Loading Machine and Dragline Operators; Explosives Workers, Ordnance Handling Experts, and Blasters; Helpers—Extraction Workers; Mine Cutting and Channeling Machine Operators. **Personality Type:** Realistic. These occupations frequently involve work activities that include practical, hands-on problems and solutions. They often deal with plants; animals; and real-world materials such as wood, tools, and machinery. Many of the occupations require working outside and don't involve a lot of paperwork or working closely with others.

Skills—Repairing; Equipment Maintenance; Operation Monitoring; Operation and Control; Installation; Operations Analysis; Troubleshooting; Systems Analysis.

Education/Training Required (Nonapprenticeship Route): Moderate-term on-the-job training. **Related Knowledge/Courses—Mechanical Devices:** Machines and tools, including their designs, uses, benefits, repair, and maintenance. **Chemistry:** The composition, structure, and properties of substances and of the chemical processes and transformations that they undergo. This includes uses of chemicals and their interactions, danger signs, production techniques, and disposal methods. **Personnel and Human Resources:** Principles and procedures for personnel recruitment; selection; training; compensation and benefits; labor relations and negotiation; and personnel information systems. **Transportation:** Principles and methods for moving people or goods by air, rail, sea, or road, including their relative costs, advantages, and limitations. **Physics:** Physical principles, laws, and applications, including air, water, material dynamics, light, atomic principles, heat, electric theory, earth formations, and meteorological and related natural phenomena. **Mathematics:** Numbers and their operations and interrelationships, including arithmetic, algebra, geometry, calculus, and statistics and their applications.

Work Environment: Outdoors; noisy; very hot or cold; contaminants; hazardous equipment; using hands on objects, tools, or controls.

Rough Carpenters

* Annual Earnings: $37,660
* Growth: 10.3%
* Annual Job Openings: 223,225
* Percentage of Women: 2.4%

Our sources did not provide separate job openings data for this occupation. The job openings listed here are shared with Construction Carpenters.

Related Apprenticeships—Carpenter, Piledriver (8000 hrs.); Carpenter, Rough (8000 hrs.); Form Builder (Construction) (3350–4600 hrs., hybrid); Form Builder (Construction) (4000 hrs.); Timber Framer (5000–6000 hrs., hybrid).

Build rough wooden structures, such as concrete forms, scaffolds, tunnel, bridge, or sewer supports, billboard signs, and temporary frame shelters, according to sketches, blueprints, or oral instructions. Study blueprints and diagrams to determine dimensions of structure or form to be constructed. Measure materials or distances, using square, measuring tape, or rule to lay out work. Cut or saw boards, timbers, or plywood to required size, using handsaw, power saw, or woodworking machine. Assemble and fasten material together to construct wood or metal framework of structure, using bolts, nails, or screws. Anchor and brace forms and other structures in place, using nails, bolts, anchor rods, steel cables, planks, wedges, and timbers. Mark cutting lines on materials, using pencil and scriber. Erect forms, framework, scaffolds, hoists, roof supports, or chutes, using hand tools, plumb rule, and level. Install rough door and window frames, subflooring, fixtures, or temporary supports in structures undergoing construction or repair. Examine structural timbers and supports to detect decay and replace timbers as required, using hand tools, nuts, and bolts. Bore boltholes in timber, masonry, or concrete walls, using power drill. Fabricate parts, using woodworking and metalworking machines. Dig or direct digging of post holes and set poles to support structures. Build sleds from logs and timbers for use in hauling camp buildings and machinery through wooded areas. Build chutes for pouring concrete.

GOE—Career Cluster/Interest Area: 02. Architecture and Construction. **Work Group:** 02.04. Construction Crafts. **Other Apprenticeable Jobs in This Work Group:** Boilermakers; Brickmasons and Blockmasons; Carpet Installers; Cement Masons and Concrete Finishers; Construction Carpenters; Crane and Tower Operators; Drywall and Ceiling Tile Installers; Electricians; Fence Erectors; Floor Layers, Except Carpet, Wood, and Hard Tiles; Glaziers; Insulation Workers, Floor, Ceiling, and Wall; Insulation Workers, Mechanical; Operating Engineers and Other Construction Equipment Operators; Painters, Construction and Maintenance; Paperhangers; Paving, Surfacing, and Tamping Equipment Operators; Pipe Fitters and Steamfitters; Plasterers and Stucco Masons; Plumbers; Reinforcing Iron and Rebar Workers; Riggers; Roofers; Sheet Metal Workers; Stone Cutters and Carvers, Manufacturing; Stonemasons; Structural Iron and Steel Workers; Tapers; Terrazzo Workers and Finishers; Tile and Marble Setters. **Personality Type:** Realistic. These occupations frequently involve work activities that include practical, hands-on problems and solutions. They often deal with plants; animals; and real-world materials such as wood, tools, and machinery. Many of the occupations require working outside and don't involve a lot of paperwork or working closely with others.

Skills—Repairing; Installation; Management of Personnel Resources; Equipment Selection; Mathematics; Technology Design; Equipment Maintenance; Coordination.

Education/Training Required (Nonapprenticeship Route): Long-term on-the-job training. **Related Knowledge/Courses—Building and Construction:** Materials, methods, and the appropriate tools to construct objects, structures, and buildings. **Design:** Design techniques, principles, tools, and instruments involved in the production and use of precision technical plans, blueprints, drawings, and models. **Engineering and Technology:** Equipment, tools, and mechanical devices and their uses to produce motion, light, power, technology, and other applications. **Mechanical Devices:** Machines and tools, including their designs, uses, benefits, repair, and maintenance. **Production and Processing:** Inputs, outputs, raw materials, waste, quality control, costs, and techniques for maximizing the manufacture and distribution of goods. **Physics:** Physical principles, laws, and applications, including air, water, material dynamics, light, atomic principles, heat, electric theory, earth formations, and meteorological and related natural phenomena.

Work Environment: Outdoors; noisy; very hot or cold; contaminants; standing; using hands on objects, tools, or controls.

Further Information: Contact a local joint union-management apprenticeship committee or the nearest office of your state employment service or apprenticeship agency (see Appendix C). To identify the local union office, contact United Brotherhood of Carpenters and Joiners of America, 101 Constitution Avenue NW, Washington, DC 20001. Internet: www.carpenters.org

Sailors and Marine Oilers

- ❋ Annual Earnings: $32,570
- ❋ Growth: 15.7%
- ❋ Annual Job Openings: 8,600
- ❋ Percentage of Women: 14.8%

Related Apprenticeship—Able Seaman (2760 hrs.).

Stand watch to look for obstructions in path of vessels; measure water depths; turn wheels on bridges; or use emergency equipment as directed by captains, mates, or pilots. Break out, rig, overhaul, and store cargo-handling gear, stationary rigging, and running gear. Perform a variety of maintenance tasks to preserve the painted surface of ships and to maintain line and ship equipment. Must hold government-issued certification and tankerman certification when working aboard liquid-carrying vessels. Provide engineers with assistance in repairing and adjusting machinery. Attach hoses and operate pumps to transfer substances to and from liquid cargo tanks. Give directions to crew members engaged in cleaning wheelhouses and quarterdecks. Load or unload materials from vessels. Lower and man lifeboats when emergencies occur. Participate in shore patrols. Read pressure and temperature gauges or displays and record data in engineering logs. Record in ships' logs data such as weather conditions and distances traveled. Stand by wheels when ships are on automatic pilot and verify accuracy of courses, using magnetic compasses. Steer ships under the direction of commanders or navigating officers or direct helmsmen to steer, following designated courses. Chip and clean rust spots on decks, superstructures, and sides of ships, using wire brushes and hand or air chipping machines. Relay specified signals to other ships, using visual signaling devices such as blinker lights and semaphores. Splice and repair ropes, wire cables, and cordage, using marlinespikes, wirecutters, twine, and hand tools. Paint or varnish decks, superstructures, lifeboats, or sides of ships. Overhaul lifeboats and lifeboat gear and lower or raise lifeboats with winches or falls. Operate, maintain, and repair ship equipment such as winches, cranes, derricks, and weapons systems. Measure depths of water in shallow or unfamiliar waters, using leadlines, and telephone or shout depth information to vessel bridges. Maintain ships' engines under direction of ships' engineering officers. Lubricate machinery, equipment, and engine parts such as gears, shafts, and bearings. Handle lines to moor vessels to wharfs, to tie up vessels to other vessels, or to rig towing lines. Examine machinery to verify specified pressures and lubricant flows. Clean and polish wood trim, brass, and other metal parts. Break out, rig, and stow cargo-handling gear, stationary rigging, and running gear. Stand gangway watches to prevent unauthorized persons from boarding ships in port. Tie barges together into tow units for tugboats to handle, inspecting barges periodically during voyages and disconnecting them when destinations are reached.

GOE—Career Cluster/Interest Area: 16. Transportation, Distribution, and Logistics. **Work Group:** 16.05. Water Vehicle Operation. **Other Apprenticeable Jobs in This Work Group:** Dredge Operators; Mates—Ship, Boat, and Barge; Pilots, Ship. **Personality Type:** Realistic. These occupations frequently involve work activities that include practical, hands-on problems and solutions. They often deal with plants; animals; and real-world materials such as wood, tools, and machinery. Many of the occupations require working outside and don't involve a lot of paperwork or working closely with others.

Skills—Repairing; Equipment Maintenance.

Education/Training Required (Nonapprenticeship Route): Short-term on-the-job training. **Related Knowledge/Courses—Mechanical Devices:** Machines and tools, including their designs, uses, benefits, repair, and maintenance. **Transportation:** Principles and methods for moving people or goods by air, rail, sea, or road, including their relative costs, advantages, and limitations. **Engineering and Technology:** Equipment, tools, and mechanical devices and their uses to produce motion, light, power, technology, and other applications. **Public Safety and Security:** Weaponry; public safety; security operations, rules, regulations, precautions, and prevention; and the protection of people, data, and property. **Geography:** Various methods for describing the location and distribution of land, sea, and air masses, including their physical locations, relationships, and characteristics. **Production and Processing:** Inputs, outputs, raw materials, waste, quality control, costs, and techniques for maximizing the manufacture and distribution of goods.

Work Environment: Outdoors; minor burns, cuts, bites, or stings; standing; keeping or regaining balance; using hands on objects, tools, or controls; bending or twisting the body.

Secretaries, Except Legal, Medical, and Executive

- ❋ Annual Earnings: $28,220
- ❋ Growth: 1.2%
- ❋ Annual Job Openings: 239,630
- ❋ Percentage of Women: 96.9%

Related Apprenticeship—Script Supervisor (2000 hrs.).

Perform routine clerical and administrative functions such as drafting correspondence, scheduling appointments, organizing and maintaining paper and electronic files, or providing information to callers. Operate office equipment such as fax machines, copiers, and phone systems and use computers for spreadsheet, word-processing, database management, and other applications. Answer telephones and give information to callers, take messages, or transfer calls to appropriate individuals. Greet visitors and callers, handle their inquiries, and direct them to the appropriate persons according to their needs. Set up and maintain paper and electronic filing systems for records, correspondence, and other material. Locate and attach appropriate files to incoming correspondence requiring replies. Open, read, route, and distribute incoming mail and other material and prepare answers to routine letters. Complete forms in accordance with company procedures. Make copies of correspondence and other printed material. Review work done by others to check for correct spelling and grammar, ensure that company format policies are followed, and recommend revisions. Compose, type, and distribute meeting notes, routine correspondence, and reports. Learn to operate new office technologies as they are developed and implemented. Maintain scheduling and event calendars. Schedule and confirm appointments for clients, customers, or supervisors. Manage projects and contribute to committee and team work. Mail newsletters, promotional material, and other information. Order and dispense supplies. Conduct searches to find needed information, using such sources as the Internet. Provide services to customers, such as order placement and account information. Collect and disburse funds from cash accounts and keep records of collections and disbursements. Prepare and mail checks. Establish work procedures and schedules and keep track of the daily work of clerical staff. Coordinate conferences and meetings. Take dictation in shorthand or by machine and transcribe information. Arrange conferences, meetings, and travel reservations for office personnel. Operate electronic mail systems and coordinate the flow of information both internally and with other

organizations. Supervise other clerical staff and provide training and orientation to new staff.

GOE—Career Cluster/Interest Area: 04. Business and Administration. **Work Group:** 04.04. Secretarial Support. **Other Apprenticeable Jobs in This Work Group:** Legal Secretaries; Medical Secretaries. **Personality Type:** Conventional. These occupations frequently involve following set procedures and routines and can include working with data and details more than with ideas. Usually there is a clear line of authority to follow.

Skill—Writing.

Education/Training Required (Nonapprenticeship Route): Moderate-term on-the-job training. **Related Knowledge/Courses—Clerical Practices:** Administrative and clerical procedures and systems such as word-processing systems, filing and records management systems, stenography and transcription, forms, design principles, and other office procedures and terminology. **Customer and Personal Service:** Principles and processes for providing customer and personal services, including needs assessment techniques, quality service standards, alternative delivery systems, and customer satisfaction evaluation techniques. **Computers and Electronics:** Electric circuit boards, processors, chips, and computer hardware and software, including applications and programming. **Economics and Accounting:** Economic and accounting principles and practices, the financial markets, banking, and the analysis and reporting of financial data. **English Language:** The structure and content of the English language, including the meaning and spelling of words, rules of composition, and grammar. **Personnel and Human Resources:** Principles and procedures for personnel recruitment; selection; training; compensation and benefits; labor relations and negotiation; and personnel information systems.

Work Environment: Indoors; sitting; repetitive motions.

Security Guards

- ❀ Annual Earnings: $22,570
- ❀ Growth: 16.9%
- ❀ Annual Job Openings: 222,085
- ❀ Percentage of Women: 23.0%

Related Apprenticeship—Guard, Security (3000–6000 hrs., hybrid).

Guard, patrol, or monitor premises to prevent theft, violence, or infractions of rules. Monitor and authorize entrance and departure of employees, visitors, and other persons to guard against theft and maintain security of premises. Write reports of daily activities and irregularities, such as equipment or property damage, theft, presence of unauthorized persons, or unusual occurrences. Call police or fire departments in cases of emergency, such as fire or presence of unauthorized persons. Answer alarms and investigate disturbances. Circulate among visitors, patrons, or employees to preserve order and protect property. Patrol industrial or commercial premises to prevent and detect signs of intrusion and ensure security of doors, windows, and gates. Escort or drive motor vehicle to transport individuals to specified locations or to provide personal protection. Operate detecting devices to screen individuals and prevent passage of prohibited articles into restricted areas. Answer telephone calls to take messages, answer questions, and provide information during nonbusiness hours or when switchboard is closed. Warn persons of rule infractions or violations and apprehend or evict violators from premises, using force when necessary. Inspect and adjust security systems, equipment, or machinery to ensure operational use and to detect evidence of tampering. Monitor and adjust controls that regulate building systems, such as air conditioning, furnace, or boiler.

GOE—Career Cluster/Interest Area: 12. Law and Public Safety. **Work Group:** 12.05. Safety and Security. **Other Apprenticeable Jobs in This Work Group:** Private Detectives and Investigators. **Personality Type:** Realistic. These occupations frequently involve work activities that include practical, hands-on problems and solutions. They often deal with plants; animals; and real-world materials such as wood, tools, and machinery. Many of the occupations require working outside and don't involve a lot of paperwork or working closely with others.

Skills—None met the criteria.

Education/Training Required (Nonapprenticeship Route): Short-term on-the-job training. **Related Knowledge/Course—Public Safety and Security:** Weaponry; public safety; security operations, rules, regulations, precautions, and prevention; and the protection of people, data, and property.

Work Environment: More often outdoors than indoors; noisy; very hot or cold; more often sitting than standing.

Sheet Metal Workers

- ❀ Annual Earnings: $39,210
- ❀ Growth: 6.7%
- ❀ Annual Job Openings: 31,677
- ❀ Percentage of Women: 3.1%

Related Apprenticeships—Sheet Metal Worker (8000 hrs.); Sheet Metal Worker (8000–10000 hrs., hybrid).

Fabricate, assemble, install, and repair sheet metal products and equipment, such as ducts, control boxes, drainpipes, and furnace casings. Work may involve any of the following: setting up and operating fabricating machines to cut, bend, and straighten sheet metal; shaping metal over anvils, blocks, or forms, using hammer; operating soldering and welding equipment to join sheet metal parts; and inspecting, assembling, and smoothing seams and joints of burred surfaces. Determine project requirements, including scope, assembly sequences, and required methods and materials, according to blueprints, drawings, and written or verbal instructions. Lay out, measure, and mark dimensions and reference lines on material such as roofing panels according to drawings or templates, using calculators, scribes, dividers, squares, and rulers. Maneuver completed units into position for installation and anchor the units. Convert blueprints into shop drawings to be followed in the construction and assembly of sheet metal products. Install assemblies such as flashing, pipes, tubes, heating and air conditioning ducts, furnace casings, rain gutters, and downspouts in supportive frameworks. Select gauges and types of sheet metal or non-metallic material according to product specifications. Drill and punch holes in metal for screws, bolts, and rivets. Fasten seams and joints together with welds, bolts, cement, rivets, solder, caulks, metal drive clips, and bonds to assemble components into products or to repair sheet metal items. Fabricate or alter parts at construction sites, using shears, hammers, punches, and drills. Finish parts, using hacksaws and hand, rotary, or squaring shears. Trim, file, grind, deburr, buff, and smooth surfaces, seams, and joints of assembled parts, using hand tools and portable power tools. Maintain equipment, making repairs and modifications when necessary. Shape metal material over anvils, blocks, or other forms, using hand tools. Transport prefabricated parts to construction sites for assembly and installation. Develop and lay out patterns that use materials most efficiently, using computerized metalworking equipment to experiment with different layouts. Inspect individual parts, assemblies, and installations for conformance to specifications and building codes, using measuring instruments such as calipers, scales, and micrometers. Secure metal roof panels in place and interlock and fasten grooved panel edges. Fasten roof panel edges and machine-made molding to structures, nailing or welding pieces into place.

GOE—Career Cluster/Interest Area: 02. Architecture and Construction. **Work Group:** 02.04. Construction Crafts. **Other Apprenticeable Jobs in This Work Group:** Boilermakers; Brickmasons and Blockmasons; Carpet Installers; Cement Masons and Concrete Finishers; Construction Carpenters; Crane and Tower Operators; Drywall and Ceiling Tile Installers; Electricians; Fence Erectors; Floor Layers, Except Carpet, Wood, and Hard Tiles; Glaziers; Insulation Workers, Floor, Ceiling, and Wall; Insulation Workers, Mechanical; Operating Engineers and Other Construction Equipment Operators; Painters, Construction and Maintenance; Paperhangers; Paving, Surfacing, and Tamping Equipment Operators; Pipe Fitters and Steamfitters; Plasterers and Stucco Masons; Plumbers; Reinforcing Iron and Rebar Workers; Riggers; Roofers; Rough Carpenters; Stone Cutters and Carvers, Manufacturing; Stonemasons; Structural Iron and Steel Workers; Tapers; Terrazzo Workers and Finishers; Tile and Marble Setters. **Personality Type:** Realistic. These occupations frequently involve work activities that include practical, hands-on problems and solutions. They often deal with plants; animals; and real-world materials such as wood, tools, and machinery. Many of the occupations require working outside and don't involve a lot of paperwork or working closely with others.

Skills—Installation; Repairing; Equipment Maintenance; Mathematics; Technology Design; Equipment Selection; Troubleshooting; Coordination.

Education/Training Required (Nonapprenticeship Route): Long-term on-the-job training. **Related Knowledge/Courses—Building and Construction:** Materials, methods, and the appropriate tools to construct objects, structures, and buildings. **Mechanical Devices:** Machines and tools, including their designs, uses, benefits, repair, and maintenance. **Physics:** Physical principles, laws, and applications, including air, water, material dynamics, light, atomic principles, heat, electric theory, earth formations, and meteorological and related natural phenomena. **Design:** Design techniques, principles, tools, and instruments involved in the production and use of precision technical plans, blueprints, drawings, and models. **Production and Processing:** Inputs, outputs, raw materials, waste, quality control, costs, and techniques for maximizing the manufacture and distribution of goods. **Mathematics:** Numbers and their operations and interrelationships, including arithmetic, algebra, geometry, calculus, and statistics and their applications.

Work Environment: Noisy; contaminants; hazardous equipment; minor burns, cuts, bites, or stings; standing; using hands on objects, tools, or controls.

Further Information: Contact a local joint union-management apprenticeship committee or the nearest office of your state employment service or apprenticeship agency (see Appendix C). To identify the local union office, contact Sheet Metal Workers International Association, 1750 New York Ave. NW, Washington, DC 20006. Internet: www.smwia.org; or Sheet Metal and Air-Conditioning Contractors' National Association, 4201 Lafayette Center Dr., Chantilly, VA 20151. Internet: www.smacna.org

Slaughterers and Meat Packers

- ✳ Annual Earnings: $22,500
- ✳ Growth: 12.7%
- ✳ Annual Job Openings: 15,511
- ✳ Percentage of Women: 30.4%

Related Apprenticeship—Butcher, All-Around (6000 hrs.).

Work in slaughtering, meat packing, or wholesale establishments performing precision functions involving the preparation of meat. Work may include specialized slaughtering tasks, cutting standard or premium cuts of meat for marketing, making sausage, or wrapping meat. Skin sections of animals or whole animals. Trim, clean, and/or cure animal hides. Cut, trim, skin, sort, and wash viscera of slaughtered animals to separate edible portions from offal. Shackle hind legs of animals to raise them for slaughtering or skinning. Slaughter animals in accordance with religious laws, and determine that carcasses meet specified religious standards. Wrap dressed carcasses and/or meat cuts. Trim head meat and sever or remove parts of animals' heads or skulls. Stun animals prior to slaughtering. Slit open, eviscerate, and trim carcasses of slaughtered animals.

Shave or singe and defeather carcasses and wash them in preparation for further processing or packaging. Sever jugular veins to drain blood and facilitate slaughtering. Saw, split, or scribe carcasses into smaller portions to facilitate handling. Remove bones and cut meat into standard cuts in preparation for marketing. Grind meat into hamburger and into trimmings used to prepare sausages, luncheon meats, and other meat products. Tend assembly lines, performing a few of the many cuts needed to process carcasses.

GOE—Career Cluster/Interest Area: 13. Manufacturing. **Work Group:** 13.03. Production Work, Assorted Materials Processing. **Other Apprenticeable Jobs in This Work Group:** Bakers; Chemical Equipment Operators and Tenders; Coating, Painting, and Spraying Machine Setters, Operators, and Tenders; Cooling and Freezing Equipment Operators and Tenders; Cutting and Slicing Machine Setters, Operators, and Tenders; Extruding, Forming, Pressing, and Compacting Machine Setters, Operators, and Tenders; Food Batchmakers; Furnace, Kiln, Oven, Drier, and Kettle Operators and Tenders; Heat Treating Equipment Setters, Operators, and Tenders, Metal and Plastic; Metal-Refining Furnace Operators and Tenders; Mixing and Blending Machine Setters, Operators, and Tenders; Plating and Coating Machine Setters, Operators, and Tenders, Metal and Plastic; Sawing Machine Setters, Operators, and Tenders, Wood; Separating, Filtering, Clarifying, Precipitating, and Still Machine Setters, Operators, and Tenders; Sewing Machine Operators; Team Assemblers; Woodworking Machine Setters, Operators, and Tenders, Except Sawing. **Personality Type:** Realistic. These occupations frequently involve work activities that include practical, hands-on problems and solutions. They often deal with plants; animals; and real-world materials such as wood, tools, and machinery. Many of the occupations require working outside and don't involve a lot of paperwork or working closely with others.

Skills—Operation and Control; Operation Monitoring; Equipment Maintenance; Quality Control Analysis; Repairing; Service Orientation; Monitoring; Management of Material Resources.

Education/Training Required (Nonapprenticeship Route): Moderate-term on-the-job training. **Related Knowledge/Courses—Food Production:** Techniques and equipment for planting, growing, and harvesting of food for consumption, including crop-rotation methods, animal husbandry, and food storage/handling techniques. **Chemistry:** The composition, structure, and properties of substances and of the chemical processes and transformations that they undergo. This includes uses of chemicals and their interactions, danger signs, production techniques, and disposal methods. **Mechanical Devices:** Machines and tools, including their designs, uses, benefits, repair, and maintenance. **Production and Processing:** Inputs, outputs, raw materials, waste, quality control, costs, and techniques for maximizing the manufacture and distribution of goods.

Work Environment: Indoors; contaminants; minor burns, cuts, bites, or stings; standing; using hands on objects, tools, or controls; repetitive motions.

Social and Human Service Assistants

❉ Annual Earnings: $26,630
❉ Growth: 33.6%
❉ Annual Job Openings: 80,142
❉ Percentage of Women: 70.5%

Related Apprenticeship—Direct Support Specialist (3000 hrs. or competency).

Assist professionals from a wide variety of fields such as psychology, rehabilitation, or social work to provide client services, as well as support for families. May assist clients in identifying available benefits and social and community services and help clients obtain them. May assist social workers with developing, organizing, and conducting programs to prevent and resolve problems relevant to substance abuse, human relationships, rehabilitation, or adult daycare. Keep records and prepare reports for owner or management concerning visits with clients. Submit reports and review reports or problems with superior. Interview individuals and family members to compile information on social, educational, criminal, institutional, or drug histories. Provide information and refer individuals to public or private agencies or community services for assistance. Consult with supervisors concerning programs for individual families. Advise clients regarding food stamps, child care, food, money management, sanitation, or housekeeping. Oversee day-to-day group activities of residents in institution. Visit individuals in homes or attend group meetings to provide information on agency services, requirements, and procedures. Monitor free, supplementary meal program to ensure cleanliness of facility and that eligibility guidelines are met for persons receiving meals. Meet with youth groups to acquaint them with consequences of delinquent acts. Assist in planning of food budgets, using charts and sample budgets. Transport and accompany clients to shopping areas or to appointments, using automobiles. Assist in locating housing for displaced individuals. Observe and discuss meal preparation and suggest alternate methods of food preparation. Observe clients' food selections and recommend alternative economical and nutritional food choices. Explain rules established by owner or management, such as sanitation and maintenance requirements or parking regulations. Care for children in clients' homes during clients' appointments. Inform tenants of facilities such as laundries and playgrounds. Assist clients with preparation of forms such as tax or rent forms. Demonstrate use and care of equipment for tenants' use.

GOE—Career Cluster/Interest Area: 10. Human Service. **Work Group:** 10.01. Counseling and Social Work. **Other Apprenticeable Jobs in This Work Group:** Residential Advisors. **Personality Type:** Conventional. These occupations frequently involve following set procedures and routines and can include working with data and details more than with ideas. Usually there is a clear line of authority to follow.

Skill—Negotiation.

Education/Training Required (Nonapprenticeship Route): Moderate-term on-the-job training. **Related Knowledge/Courses—Therapy and Counseling:** Information and techniques needed to rehabilitate physical and mental ailments and to provide career guidance, including alternative treatments, rehabilitation equipment and its proper use, and methods to evaluate treatment effects. **Philosophy and Theology:** Different philosophical systems and religions, including their basic principles, values, ethics, ways of thinking, customs, and practices and their impact on human culture. **Psychology:** Human behavior and performance, mental processes, psychological research methods, and the assessment and treatment of behavioral and affective disorders. **Customer and Personal Service:** Principles and processes for providing customer and personal services, including needs assessment techniques, quality service standards, alternative delivery systems, and customer satisfaction evaluation techniques. **Sociology and Anthropology:** Group behavior and dynamics; societal trends and influences; and cultures and their history, migrations, ethnicity, and origins. **Clerical Practices:** Administrative and clerical procedures and systems such as word-processing systems, filing and records management systems, stenography and transcription, forms, design principles, and other office procedures and terminology.

Work Environment: Indoors; noisy; sitting.

Sound Engineering Technicians

- ❋ Annual Earnings: $46,550
- ❋ Growth: 9.1%
- ❋ Annual Job Openings: 1,194
- ❋ Percentage of Women: 15.6%

Related Apprenticeships—Recording Engineer (4000 hrs.); Sound Mixer (8000 hrs.).

Operate machines and equipment to record, synchronize, mix, or reproduce music, voices, or sound effects in sporting arenas, theater productions, recording studios, or movie and video productions. Confer with producers, performers, and others in order to determine and achieve the desired sound for a production such as a musical recording or a film. Set up, test, and adjust recording equipment for recording sessions and live performances; tear down equipment after event completion. Regulate volume level and sound quality during recording sessions, using control consoles. Prepare for recording sessions by performing activities such as selecting and setting up microphones. Report equipment problems and ensure that required repairs are made. Mix and edit voices, music, and taped sound effects for live performances and for prerecorded events, using sound mixing boards. Synchronize and equalize prerecorded dialogue, music, and sound effects with visual action of motion pictures or television productions, using control consoles. Record speech, music, and other sounds on recording media, using recording equipment. Reproduce and duplicate sound recordings from original recording media, using sound editing and duplication equipment. Separate instruments, vocals, and other sounds; then combine sounds later during the mixing or post-production stage. Keep logs of recordings. Create musical instrument digital interface programs for music projects, commercials, or film post-production.

GOE—Career Cluster/Interest Area: 03. Arts and Communication. **Work Group:** 03.09. Media Technology. **Other Apprenticeable Jobs in This Work Group:** Audio and Video Equipment Technicians; Broadcast Technicians; Camera Operators, Television, Video, and Motion Picture; Photographers; Radio Operators. **Personality Type:** Realistic. These occupations frequently involve work activities that include practical, hands-on problems and solutions. They often deal with plants; animals; and real-world materials such as wood, tools, and machinery. Many of the occupations require working outside and don't involve a lot of paperwork or working closely with others.

Skills—Technology Design; Operation and Control; Operation Monitoring; Installation; Equipment Maintenance; Troubleshooting; Management of Material Resources; Social Perceptiveness.

Education/Training Required (Nonapprenticeship Route): Postsecondary vocational training. **Related Knowledge/Courses—Fine Arts:** Theory and techniques required to produce, compose, and perform works of music, dance, visual arts, drama, and sculpture. **Communications and Media:** Media production, communication, and dissemination techniques and methods, including alternative ways to inform and entertain via written, oral, and visual media. **Telecommunications:** Transmission, broadcasting, switching, control, and operation of telecommunications systems. **Computers and Electronics:** Electric circuit boards, processors, chips, and computer hardware and software, including applications and programming. **Customer and Personal Service:** Principles and processes for providing customer and personal services, including needs assessment techniques, quality service standards, alternative delivery systems, and customer satisfaction evaluation techniques. **Production and Processing:** Inputs, outputs, raw materials, waste, quality control, costs, and techniques for maximizing the manufacture and distribution of goods.

Work Environment: Indoors; noisy; sitting; using hands on objects, tools, or controls; repetitive motions.

Stationary Engineers and Boiler Operators

* Annual Earnings: $47,640
* Growth: 3.4%
* Annual Job Openings: 1,892
* Percentage of Women: 2.3%

Related Apprenticeships—Boiler Operator (8000 hrs.); Firer, Marine (2115.5 hrs.); Stationary Engineer (8000 hrs.).

Operate or maintain stationary engines, boilers, or other mechanical equipment to provide utilities for buildings or industrial processes. Operate equipment such as steam engines, generators, motors, turbines, and steam boilers. Operate or tend stationary engines; boilers; and auxiliary equipment such as pumps, compressors and air-conditioning equipment to supply and maintain steam or heat for buildings, marine vessels, or pneumatic tools. Observe and interpret readings on gauges, meters, and charts registering various aspects of boiler operation to ensure that boilers are operating properly. Test boiler water quality or arrange for testing and take any necessary corrective action, such as adding chemicals to prevent corrosion and harmful deposits. Activate valves to maintain required amounts of water in boilers, to adjust supplies of combustion air, and to control the flow of fuel into burners. Monitor boiler water, chemical, and fuel levels and make adjustments to maintain required levels. Fire coal furnaces by hand or with stokers and gas- or oil-fed boilers, using automatic gas feeds or oil pumps. Monitor and inspect equipment, computer terminals, switches, valves, gauges, alarms, safety devices, and meters to detect leaks or malfunctions and to ensure that equipment is operating efficiently and safely. Analyze problems and take appropriate action to ensure continuous and reliable operation of equipment and systems. Maintain daily logs of operation, maintenance, and safety activities, including test results, instrument readings, and details of equipment malfunctions and maintenance work. Adjust controls or valves on equipment to provide power and to regulate and set operations of system or industrial processes. Switch from automatic controls to manual controls and isolate equipment mechanically and electrically to allow for safe inspection and repair work. Clean and lubricate boilers and auxiliary equipment and make minor adjustments as needed, using hand tools. Check the air quality of ventilation systems and make adjustments to ensure compliance with mandated safety codes. Perform or arrange for repairs, such as complete overhauls; replacement of defective valves, gaskets, or bearings; or fabrication of new parts. Weigh, measure, and record fuel used.

GOE—Career Cluster/Interest Area: 13. Manufacturing. **Work Group:** 13.16. Utility Operation and Energy Distribution. **Other Apprenticeable Jobs in This Work Group:** Chemical Plant and System Operators; Petroleum Pump System Operators, Refinery Operators, and Gaugers; Power Distributors and Dispatchers; Power Plant Operators; Water and Liquid Waste Treatment Plant and System Operators. **Personality Type:** Realistic. These occupations frequently involve work activities that include practical, hands-on problems and solutions. They often deal with plants; animals; and real-world materials such as wood, tools, and machinery. Many of the occupations require working outside and don't involve a lot of paperwork or working closely with others.

Skills—Repairing; Equipment Maintenance; Operation Monitoring; Installation; Operation

and Control; Systems Analysis; Operations Analysis; Troubleshooting.

Education/Training Required (Nonapprenticeship Route): Long-term on-the-job training. **Related Knowledge/Courses—Mechanical Devices:** Machines and tools, including their designs, uses, benefits, repair, and maintenance. **Building and Construction:** Materials, methods, and the appropriate tools to construct objects, structures, and buildings. **Chemistry:** The composition, structure, and properties of substances and of the chemical processes and transformations that they undergo. This includes uses of chemicals and their interactions, danger signs, production techniques, and disposal methods. **Physics:** Physical principles, laws, and applications, including air, water, material dynamics, light, atomic principles, heat, electric theory, earth formations, and meteorological and related natural phenomena. **Engineering and Technology:** Equipment, tools, and mechanical devices and their uses to produce motion, light, power, technology, and other applications. **Design:** Design techniques, principles, tools, and instruments involved in the production and use of precision technical plans, blueprints, drawings, and models.

Work Environment: Noisy; very hot or cold; very bright or dim lighting; contaminants; hazardous conditions; hazardous equipment.

Stonemasons

- ❋ Annual Earnings: $36,950
- ❋ Growth: 10.0%
- ❋ Annual Job Openings: 2,657
- ❋ Percentage of Women: 1.6%

Related Apprenticeships—Marble Setter (4500–8000 hrs., hybrid); Marble Setter (6000 hrs.); Monument Setter (Construction) (8000 hrs.); Stonemason (4500–8000 hrs., hybrid); Stonemason (6000 hrs.).

Build stone structures, such as piers, walls, and abutments. Lay walks; curbstones; or special types of masonry for vats, tanks, and floors. Lay out wall patterns or foundations, using straight edge, rule, or staked lines. Shape, trim, face, and cut marble or stone preparatory to setting, using power saws, cutting equipment, and hand tools. Set vertical and horizontal alignment of structures, using plumb bob, gauge line, and level. Mix mortar or grout and pour or spread mortar or grout on marble slabs, stone, or foundation. Remove wedges; fill joints between stones; finish joints between stones, using a trowel; and smooth the mortar to an attractive finish, using a tuckpointer. Clean excess mortar or grout from surface of marble, stone, or monument, using sponge, brush, water, or acid. Set stone or marble in place according to layout or pattern. Lay brick to build shells of chimneys and smokestacks or to line or reline industrial furnaces, kilns, boilers, and similar installations. Replace broken or missing masonry units in walls or floors. Smooth, polish, and bevel surfaces, using hand tools and power tools. Drill holes in marble or ornamental stone and anchor brackets in holes. Repair cracked or chipped areas of stone or marble, using blowtorch and mastic, and remove rough or defective spots from concrete, using power grinder or chisel and hammer. Remove sections of monument from truck bed and guide stone onto foundation, using skids, hoist, or truck crane. Construct and install prefabricated masonry units. Dig trench for foundation of monument, using pick and shovel. Position mold along guidelines of wall, press mold in place, and remove mold and paper from wall. Line interiors of molds with treated paper and fill molds with composition-stone mixture.

GOE—Career Cluster/Interest Area: 02. Architecture and Construction. **Work Group:** 02.04. Construction Crafts. **Other Apprenticeable Jobs in This Work Group:** Boilermakers; Brickmasons and Blockmasons; Carpet Installers; Cement Masons and Concrete Finishers; Construction Carpenters; Crane and Tower Operators; Drywall and Ceiling Tile Installers; Electricians; Fence Erectors; Floor Layers, Except Carpet, Wood, and Hard Tiles; Glaziers; Insulation Workers, Floor, Ceiling, and Wall; Insulation Workers, Mechanical; Operating Engineers and Other Construction Equipment Operators; Painters, Construction and Maintenance; Paperhangers; Paving, Surfacing, and Tamping Equipment Operators; Pipe Fitters and Steamfitters; Plasterers and Stucco Masons; Plumbers; Reinforcing Iron and Rebar Workers; Riggers; Roofers; Rough Carpenters; Sheet Metal Workers; Stone Cutters and Carvers, Manufacturing; Structural Iron and Steel Workers; Tapers; Terrazzo Workers and Finishers; Tile and Marble Setters. **Personality Type:** Realistic. These occupations frequently involve work activities that include practical, hands-on problems and solutions. They often deal with plants; animals; and real-world materials such as wood, tools, and machinery. Many of the occupations require working outside and don't involve a lot of paperwork or working closely with others.

Skills—Installation; Management of Personnel Resources; Equipment Selection; Repairing; Equipment Maintenance; Mathematics; Management of Material Resources; Technology Design.

Education/Training Required (Nonapprenticeship Route): Long-term on-the-job training.

Related Knowledge/Courses—Building and Construction: Materials, methods, and the appropriate tools to construct objects, structures, and buildings. **Mechanical Devices:** Machines and tools, including their designs, uses, benefits, repair, and maintenance. **Design:** Design techniques, principles, tools, and instruments involved in the production and use of precision technical plans, blueprints, drawings, and models. **Mathematics:** Numbers and their operations and interrelationships, including arithmetic, algebra, geometry, calculus, and statistics and their applications. **Public Safety and Security:** Weaponry; public safety; security operations, rules, regulations, precautions, and prevention; and the protection of people, data, and property. **Education and Training:** Instructional methods and training techniques, including curriculum design principles, learning theory, group and individual teaching techniques, design of individual development plans, and test design principles.

Work Environment: Outdoors; standing; walking and running; kneeling, crouching, stooping, or crawling; using hands on objects, tools, or controls; bending or twisting the body.

Structural Iron and Steel Workers

- ❋ Annual Earnings: $42,130
- ❋ Growth: 6.0%
- ❋ Annual Job Openings: 6,969
- ❋ Percentage of Women: 2.2%

Related Apprenticeships—Assembler, Metal Building (4000 hrs.); Structural Ironworker (6000–8000 hrs., hybrid); Structural Steel/Ironworker (6000–8000 hrs., hybrid); Structural-Steel Worker (6000 hrs.); Tank Setter (Petroleum Products) (4000 hrs.).

Raise, place, and unite iron or steel girders, columns, and other structural members to form completed structures or structural frameworks. May erect metal storage tanks and assemble prefabricated metal buildings. Read specifications and blueprints to determine the locations, quantities, and sizes of materials required. Verify vertical and horizontal alignment of structural-steel members, using plumb bobs, laser equipment, transits, and/or levels. Connect columns, beams, and girders with bolts, following blueprints and instructions from supervisors. Hoist steel beams, girders, and columns into place, using cranes, or signal hoisting equipment operators to lift and position structural-steel members. Bolt aligned structural-steel members in position for permanent riveting, bolting, or welding into place. Ride on girders or other structural-steel members to position them or use rope to guide them into position. Fabricate metal parts, such as steel frames, columns, beams, and girders, according to blueprints or instructions from supervisors. Pull, push, or pry structural-steel members into approximate positions for bolting into place. Cut, bend, and weld steel pieces, using metal shears, torches, and welding equipment. Fasten structural-steel members to hoist cables, using chains, cables, or rope. Assemble hoisting equipment and rigging such as cables, pulleys, and hooks to move heavy equipment and materials. Force structural-steel members into final positions, using turnbuckles, crowbars, jacks, and hand tools. Erect metal and precast concrete components for structures such as buildings, bridges, dams, towers, storage tanks, fences, and highway guard rails. Unload and position prefabricated steel units for hoisting as needed. Drive drift pins through rivet holes to align rivet holes in structural-steel members with corresponding holes in previously placed members. Dismantle structures and equipment. Insert sealing strips, wiring, insulating material, ladders, flanges, gauges, and valves, depending on types of structures being assembled. Catch hot rivets in buckets and insert rivets in holes, using tongs. Place blocks under reinforcing bars used to reinforce floors. Hold rivets while riveters use air-hammers to form heads on rivets.

GOE—Career Cluster/Interest Area: 02. Architecture and Construction. **Work Group:** 02.04. Construction Crafts. **Other Apprenticeable Jobs in This Work Group:** Boilermakers; Brickmasons and Blockmasons; Carpet Installers; Cement Masons and Concrete Finishers; Construction Carpenters; Crane and Tower Operators; Drywall and Ceiling Tile Installers; Electricians; Fence Erectors; Floor Layers, Except Carpet, Wood, and Hard Tiles; Glaziers; Insulation Workers, Floor, Ceiling, and Wall; Insulation Workers, Mechanical; Operating Engineers and Other Construction Equipment Operators; Painters, Construction and Maintenance; Paperhangers; Paving, Surfacing, and Tamping Equipment Operators; Pipe Fitters and Steamfitters; Plasterers and Stucco Masons; Plumbers; Reinforcing Iron and Rebar Workers; Riggers; Roofers; Rough Carpenters; Sheet Metal Workers; Stone Cutters and Carvers, Manufacturing; Stonemasons; Tapers; Terrazzo Workers and Finishers; Tile and Marble Setters. **Personality Type:** Realistic. These occupations frequently involve work activities that include practical, hands-on problems and solutions. They often deal with plants; animals; and real-world materials such as wood, tools, and machinery. Many of the occupations require working outside and don't involve a lot of paperwork or working closely with others.

Skills—Equipment Maintenance; Installation; Troubleshooting; Equipment Selection; Coordination; Technology Design; Operation Monitoring; Repairing.

Education/Training Required (Nonapprenticeship Route): Long-term on-the-job training. **Related Knowledge/Courses—Building and Construction:** Materials, methods, and the appropriate tools to construct objects, structures, and buildings. **Engineering and Technology:** Equipment, tools, and mechanical devices and their uses to produce motion, light, power, technology, and other applications. **Mechanical Devices:** Machines and tools, including their designs, uses, benefits, repair, and maintenance. **Production and Processing:** Inputs, outputs, raw materials, waste, quality control, costs, and techniques for maximizing the manufacture and distribution of goods. **Design:** Design techniques, principles, tools, and instruments involved in the production and use of precision technical plans, blueprints, drawings, and models. **Physics:** Physical principles, laws, and applications, including air, water, material dynamics, light, atomic principles, heat, electric theory, earth formations, and meteorological and related natural phenomena.

Work Environment: Outdoors; noisy; very hot or cold; high places; hazardous equipment; using hands on objects, tools, or controls.

Further Information: Contact a local joint union-management apprenticeship committee, or the nearest office of your state employment service or apprenticeship agency (see Appendix C). International Association of Bridge, Structural, Ornamental, and Reinforcing Iron Workers, Apprenticeship Department, 1750 New York Ave. NW, Suite 400, Washington, DC 20006. Internet: www.ironworkers.org

Structural Metal Fabricators and Fitters

❀ Annual Earnings: $31,030
❀ Growth: –0.2%
❀ Annual Job Openings: 20,746
❀ Percentage of Women: 30.4%

Related Apprenticeships—Fabricator-Assembler, Metal Products (8000 hrs.); Fitter (Machine Shop) (4000 hrs.); Fitter I (Any Industry) (6000 hrs.); Former, Hand (Any Industry) (4000 hrs.); Metal Fabricator (8000 hrs.); Ship Propeller Finisher (6000 hrs.).

Fabricate, lay out, position, align, and fit parts of structural metal products. Position, align, fit, and weld parts to form complete units or subunits, following blueprints and layout specifications and using jigs, welding torches, and hand tools. Verify conformance of workpieces to specifications, using squares, rulers, and measuring tapes. Tack-weld fitted parts together. Lay out and examine metal stock or workpieces to be processed to ensure that specifications are met. Align and fit parts according to specifications, using jacks, turnbuckles, wedges, drift pins, pry bars, and hammers. Locate and mark workpiece bending and cutting lines, allowing for stock thickness, machine and welding shrinkage, and other component specifications. Position or tighten braces, jacks, clamps, ropes, or bolt straps or bolt parts in position for welding or riveting. Study engineering drawings and blueprints to determine materials requirements and task sequences. Move parts into position manually or by using hoists or cranes. Set up and operate fabricating machines such as brakes, rolls, shears, flame cutters, grinders, and drill presses to bend, cut, form, punch, drill, or otherwise form and assemble metal components. Hammer, chip, and grind workpieces to cut, bend, and straighten metal. Smooth workpiece edges and fix taps, tubes, and valves. Design and construct templates and fixtures, using hand tools. Straighten warped or bent parts, using sledges, hand torches, straightening presses, or bulldozers. Mark reference points onto floors or face blocks and transpose them to workpieces, using measuring devices, squares, chalk, and soapstone. Set up face blocks, jigs, and fixtures. Remove high spots and cut bevels, using hand files, portable grinders, and cutting torches. Direct welders to build up low spots or short pieces with weld. Lift or move materials and finished products, using large cranes. Heat-treat parts, using acetylene torches. Preheat workpieces to make them malleable, using hand torches or furnaces. Install boilers, containers, and other structures. Erect ladders and scaffolding to fit together large assemblies.

GOE—Career Cluster/Interest Area: 13. Manufacturing. **Work Group:** 13.04. Welding, Brazing, and Soldering. **Other Apprenticeable Jobs in This Work Group:** Welders, Cutters, and Welder Fitters; Welding, Soldering, and Brazing Machine Setters, Operators, and Tenders. **Personality Type:** Realistic. These occupations frequently involve work activities that include practical, hands-on problems and solutions. They often deal with plants; animals; and real-world materials such as wood, tools, and machinery. Many of the occupations require working outside and don't involve a lot of paperwork or working closely with others.

Skills—Quality Control Analysis; Operation Monitoring; Equipment Maintenance; Installation; Repairing; Operation and Control; Technology Design; Equipment Selection.

Education/Training Required (Nonapprenticeship Route): Moderate-term on-the-job training. **Related Knowledge/Courses—Design:** Design techniques, principles, tools, and instruments involved in the production and use of precision technical plans, blueprints, drawings, and models. **Building and Construction:** Materials, methods, and the appropriate tools to construct objects, structures, and buildings. **Mechanical Devices:** Machines and tools, including their designs, uses, benefits, repair, and maintenance. **Production and Processing:** Inputs, outputs, raw materials, waste, quality control, costs, and techniques for maximizing the manufacture and distribution of goods.

Work Environment: Noisy; contaminants; hazardous equipment; minor burns, cuts, bites, or stings; standing; using hands on objects, tools, or controls.

Surgical Technologists

- ❋ Annual Earnings: $37,540
- ❋ Growth: 24.5%
- ❋ Annual Job Openings: 15,365
- ❋ Percentage of Women: 80.1%

Related Apprenticeship—Surgical Technologist (4000 hrs. or competency).

Assist in operations under the supervision of surgeons, registered nurses, or other surgical personnel. May help set up operating rooms; prepare and transport patients for surgery; adjust lights and equipment; pass instruments and other supplies to surgeons and surgeons' assistants; hold retractors; cut sutures; and help count sponges, needles, supplies, and instruments. Count sponges, needles, and instruments before and after operations. Maintain a proper sterile field during surgical procedures. Hand instruments and supplies to surgeons and surgeons' assistants, hold retractors and cut sutures, and perform other tasks as directed by surgeons during operations. Prepare patients for surgery, including positioning patients on operating tables and covering them with sterile surgical drapes to prevent exposure. Scrub arms and hands and assist surgical teams to scrub and put on gloves, masks, and surgical clothing. Wash and sterilize equipment, using germicides and sterilizers. Monitor and continually assess operating room conditions, including needs of the patient and surgical team. Prepare dressings or bandages and apply or assist with their application following surgeries. Clean and restock operating rooms, gathering and placing equipment and supplies and arranging instruments according to instructions such as those found on a preference card. Operate, assemble, adjust, or monitor sterilizers, lights, suction machines, and diagnostic equipment to ensure proper operation. Prepare, care for, and dispose of tissue specimens taken for laboratory analysis. Provide technical assistance to surgeons, surgical nurses, and anesthesiologists. Maintain supply of fluids such as plasma, saline, blood, and glucose for use during operations. Maintain files and records of surgical procedures. Observe patients' vital signs to assess physical condition. Order surgical supplies.

GOE—Career Cluster/Interest Area: 08. Health Science. **Work Group:** 08.02. Medicine and Surgery. **Other Apprenticeable Jobs in This Work Group:** Medical Assistants; Medical Transcriptionists; Pharmacy Technicians. **Personality Type:** Realistic. These occupations frequently involve work activities that include practical, hands-on problems and solutions. They often deal with plants; animals; and real-world materials such as wood, tools, and machinery. Many of the occupations require working outside and don't involve a lot of paperwork or working closely with others.

Skills—Operation Monitoring; Quality Control Analysis.

Education/Training Required (Nonapprenticeship Route): Postsecondary vocational training. **Related Knowledge/Courses—Medicine and Dentistry:** The information and techniques needed to diagnose and treat injuries, diseases, and deformities. This includes symptoms, treatment alternatives, drug properties and interactions, and preventive health-care measures. **Biology:** Plant and animal living tissue, cells, organisms, and entities, including their functions, interdependencies, and interactions with each other and the environment. **Psychology:** Human behavior and performance, mental processes, psychological research methods, and the assessment and treatment of behavioral and affective disorders. **Chemistry:** The composition, structure, and properties of substances and of the chemical processes and transformations that they undergo. This includes uses of chemicals and their interactions, danger signs, production techniques, and disposal methods. **Therapy and Counseling:** Information and techniques needed to rehabilitate physical and mental ailments and to provide career guidance, including alternative treatments, rehabilitation equipment and its proper use, and methods to evaluate treatment effects. **Customer and Personal Service:** Principles and processes for providing customer and personal services, including needs assessment techniques, quality service standards, alternative delivery systems, and customer satisfaction evaluation techniques.

Work Environment: Indoors; contaminants; disease or infections; hazardous conditions; standing; using hands on objects, tools, or controls.

Surveying Technicians

- ❊ Annual Earnings: $33,640
- ❊ Growth: 19.4%
- ❊ Annual Job Openings: 8,299
- ❊ Percentage of Women: 9.9%

Our sources did not provide separate job openings data for this occupation. The job openings listed here are shared with Mapping Technicians.

Related Apprenticeship—Surveyor Assistant, Instruments (4000 hrs.).

Adjust and operate surveying instruments such as theodolite and electronic distance-measuring equipment and compile notes, make sketches, and enter data into computers. Perform calculations to determine Earth curvature corrections, atmospheric impacts on measurements, traverse closures and adjustments, azimuths, level runs, and placement of markers. Record survey measurements and descriptive data using notes, drawings, sketches, and inked tracings. Search for section corners, property irons, and survey points. Position and hold the vertical rods, or targets, that theodolite operators use for sighting to measure angles, distances, and elevations. Lay out grids and determine horizontal and vertical controls. Compare survey computations with applicable standards to determine adequacy of data. Set out and recover stakes, marks, and other monumentation. Conduct surveys to ascertain the locations of natural features and man-made structures on Earth's surface, underground, and underwater, using electronic distance-measuring equipment and other surveying instruments. Direct and supervise work of subordinate members of surveying parties.

Compile information necessary to stake projects for construction, using engineering plans. Prepare topographic and contour maps of land surveyed, including site features and other relevant information, such as charts, drawings, and survey notes. Place and hold measuring tapes when electronic distance-measuring equipment is not used. Collect information needed to carry out new surveys using source maps, previous survey data, photographs, computer records, and other relevant information. Operate and manage land-information computer systems, performing tasks such as storing data, making inquiries, and producing plots and reports. Run rods for benches and cross-section elevations. Perform manual labor, such as cutting brush for lines, carrying stakes, rebar, and other heavy items, and stacking rods. Maintain equipment and vehicles used by surveying crews. Provide assistance in the development of methods and procedures for conducting field surveys.

GOE—Career Cluster/Interest Area: 15. Scientific Research, Engineering, and Mathematics. **Work Group:** 15.09. Engineering Technology. **Other Apprenticeable Jobs in This Work Group:** Aerospace Engineering and Operations Technicians; Electrical Drafters; Electrical Engineering Technicians; Electro-Mechanical Technicians; Electronic Drafters; Electronics Engineering Technicians; Mapping Technicians; Mechanical Drafters; Mechanical Engineering Technicians; Surveying and Mapping Technicians. **Personality Type:** Realistic. These occupations frequently involve work activities that include practical, hands-on problems and solutions. They often deal with plants; animals; and real-world materials such as wood, tools, and machinery. Many of the occupations require working outside and don't involve a lot of paperwork or working closely with others.

Skills—Mathematics; Operation and Control; Management of Personnel Resources; Operation Monitoring; Systems Analysis.

Education/Training Required (Nonapprenticeship Route): Moderate-term on-the-job training. **Related Knowledge/Courses—Geography:** Various methods for describing the location and distribution of land, sea, and air masses, including their physical locations, relationships, and characteristics. **Design:** Design techniques, principles, tools, and instruments involved in the production and use of precision technical plans, blueprints, drawings, and models. **Building and Construction:** Materials, methods, and the appropriate tools to construct objects, structures, and buildings. **Mathematics:** Numbers and their operations and interrelationships, including arithmetic, algebra, geometry, calculus, and statistics and their applications. **Law and Government:** Laws, legal codes, court procedures, precedents, government regulations, executive orders, agency rules, and the democratic political process. **Engineering and Technology:** Equipment, tools, and mechanical devices and their uses to produce motion, light, power, technology, and other applications.

Work Environment: Outdoors; very hot or cold; very bright or dim lighting; hazardous equipment; minor burns, cuts, bites, or stings; using hands on objects, tools, or controls.

Tank Car, Truck, and Ship Loaders

* Annual Earnings: $33,140
* Growth: 9.2%
* Annual Job Openings: 4,519
* Percentage of Women: 16.9%

Related Apprenticeship—Pumper-Gauger (6000 hrs.).

Load and unload chemicals and bulk solids such as coal, sand, and grain into or from tank cars, trucks, or ships by using material-moving equipment. May perform various other tasks relating to shipment of products. May gauge or sample shipping tanks and test them for leaks. Verify numbers of tank cars, barges, or truck loads to ensure car placement accuracy based on written or verbal instructions. Observe positions of cars passing loading spouts and swing spouts into correct positions at appropriate times. Operate ship loading and unloading equipment, conveyors, hoists, and other specialized material-handling equipment such as railroad tank car unloading equipment. Monitor product movement to and from storage tanks, coordinating activities with other workers to ensure constant product flow. Record operating data such as products and quantities pumped, gauge readings, and operating times manually or by using computers. Check vessel conditions and weights to ensure cleanliness and compliance with loading procedures. Operate industrial trucks, tractors, loaders, and other equipment to transport materials to and from transportation vehicles and loading docks and to store and retrieve materials in warehouses. Connect ground cables to carry off static electricity when unloading tanker cars. Seal outlet valves on tank cars, barges, and trucks. Test samples for specific gravity with hydrometers or send samples to laboratories for testing. Remove and replace tank car dome caps or direct other workers in their removal and replacement. Lower gauge rods into tanks or read meters to verify contents, temperatures, and volumes of liquid loads. Clean interiors of tank cars or tank trucks with mechanical spray nozzles. Operate conveyors and equipment to transfer grain or other materials from transportation vehicles. Test vessels for leaks, damage,

and defects and repair or replace defective parts as necessary. Unload cars containing liquids by connecting hoses to outlet plugs and pumping compressed air into cars to force liquids into storage tanks. Copy and attach load specifications to loaded tanks. Start pumps and adjust valves or cables to regulate flow of products to vessels, utilizing knowledge of loading procedures.

GOE—Career Cluster/Interest Area: 13. Manufacturing. **Work Group:** 13.17. Loading, Moving, Hoisting, and Conveying. **Other Apprenticeable Jobs in This Work Group:** Conveyor Operators and Tenders. **Personality Type:** Realistic. These occupations frequently involve work activities that include practical, hands-on problems and solutions. They often deal with plants; animals; and real-world materials such as wood, tools, and machinery. Many of the occupations require working outside and don't involve a lot of paperwork or working closely with others.

Skills—Operation Monitoring; Operation and Control; Troubleshooting; Repairing; Equipment Maintenance.

Education/Training Required (Nonapprenticeship Route): Moderate-term on-the-job training. **Related Knowledge/Courses—Production and Processing:** Inputs, outputs, raw materials, waste, quality control, costs, and techniques for maximizing the manufacture and distribution of goods. **Transportation:** Principles and methods for moving people or goods by air, rail, sea, or road, including their relative costs, advantages, and limitations. **Mechanical Devices:** Machines and tools, including their designs, uses, benefits, repair, and maintenance. **Public Safety and Security:** Weaponry; public safety; security operations, rules, regulations, precautions, and prevention; and the protection of people, data, and property. **Building and Construction:** Materials, methods, and the appropriate tools to construct objects, structures, and buildings. **Chemistry:** The composition, structure, and properties of substances and of the chemical processes and transformations that they undergo. This includes uses of chemicals and their interactions, danger signs, production techniques, and disposal methods.

Work Environment: Outdoors; noisy; very hot or cold; contaminants; high places; hazardous equipment.

Tapers

- ✲ Annual Earnings: $42,050
- ✲ Growth: 7.1%
- ✲ Annual Job Openings: 9,026
- ✲ Percentage of Women: 2.9%

Related Apprenticeship—Taper (4000 hrs.).

Seal joints between sheets of plasterboard or other wallboard to prepare wall surfaces for painting or papering. Sand rough spots of dried cement between applications of compounds. Remove extra compound after surfaces have been covered sufficiently. Press paper tape over joints to embed tape into sealing compound and to seal joints. Mix sealing compounds by hand or with portable electric mixers. Install metal molding at wall corners to secure wallboards. Check adhesives to ensure that they will work and will remain durable. Apply texturizing compounds and primers to walls and ceilings before final finishing, using trowels, brushes, rollers, or spray guns. Sand or patch nicks or cracks in plasterboard or wallboard. Apply additional coats to fill in holes and make surfaces smooth. Use mechanical applicators that spread compounds and embed tape in one operation. Spread sealing compound between boards or panels and over cracks, holes, and nail and screw heads, using trowels, broadknives, or spatulas. Spread and smooth cementing material over tape, using trowels or floating machines to blend joints with wall surfaces. Select the correct sealing compound or tape. Countersink nails or screws below surfaces of walls before applying sealing compounds, using hammers or screwdrivers.

GOE—Career Cluster/Interest Area: 02. Architecture and Construction. **Work Group:** 02.04. Construction Crafts. **Other Apprenticeable Jobs in This Work Group:** Boilermakers; Brickmasons and Blockmasons; Carpet Installers; Cement Masons and Concrete Finishers; Construction Carpenters; Crane and Tower Operators; Drywall and Ceiling Tile Installers; Electricians; Fence Erectors; Floor Layers, Except Carpet, Wood, and Hard Tiles; Glaziers; Insulation Workers, Floor, Ceiling, and Wall; Insulation Workers, Mechanical; Operating Engineers and Other Construction Equipment Operators; Painters, Construction and Maintenance; Paperhangers; Paving, Surfacing, and Tamping Equipment Operators; Pipe Fitters and Steamfitters; Plasterers and Stucco Masons; Plumbers; Reinforcing Iron and Rebar Workers; Riggers; Roofers; Rough Carpenters; Sheet Metal Workers; Stone Cutters and Carvers, Manufacturing; Stonemasons; Structural Iron and Steel Workers; Terrazzo Workers and Finishers; Tile and Marble Setters. **Personality Type:** Realistic. These occupations frequently involve work activities that include practical, hands-on problems and solutions. They often deal with plants; animals; and real-world materials such as wood, tools, and machinery. Many of the occupations require working outside and don't involve a lot of paperwork or working closely with others.

Skills—Installation; Management of Personnel Resources; Management of Material Resources; Repairing; Equipment Selection; Equipment Maintenance.

Education/Training Required (Nonapprenticeship Route): Moderate-term on-the-job training. **Related Knowledge/Courses—Building and Construction:** Materials, methods, and the appropriate tools to construct objects, structures, and buildings. **Design:** Design techniques, principles, tools, and instruments involved in the production and use of precision technical plans, blueprints, drawings, and models. **Public Safety and Security:** Weaponry; public safety; security operations, rules, regulations, precautions, and prevention; and the protection of people, data, and property.

Work Environment: Indoors; contaminants; minor burns, cuts, bites, or stings; standing; using hands on objects, tools, or controls; bending or twisting the body.

Teacher Assistants

- ❋ Annual Earnings: $21,580
- ❋ Growth: 10.4%
- ❋ Annual Job Openings: 193,986
- ❋ Percentage of Women: 92.3%

Related Apprenticeship—Teacher Aide I (4000 hrs.).

Perform duties that are instructional in nature or deliver direct services to students or parents. Serve in a position for which a teacher or another professional has ultimate responsibility for the design and implementation of educational programs and services. Provide extra assistance to students with special needs, such as non-English-speaking students or those with physical and mental disabilities. Tutor and assist children individually or in small groups to help them master assignments and to reinforce learning concepts presented by teachers. Supervise students in classrooms, halls, cafeterias, school yards, and gymnasiums or on field trips. Enforce administration policies and rules governing students. Observe students' performance and record relevant data to assess progress. Discuss assigned duties with classroom teachers to coordinate instructional efforts. Instruct and monitor students in the use and care of equipment and materials to prevent injuries and damage. Present subject matter to students under the direction and guidance of teachers, using lectures, discussions, or supervised role-playing methods. Organize and label materials and display students' work in a manner appropriate for their eye levels and perceptual skills. Distribute tests and homework assignments and collect them when they are completed. Type, file, and duplicate materials. Distribute teaching materials such as textbooks, workbooks, papers, and pencils to students. Use computers, audiovisual aids, and other equipment and materials to supplement presentations. Attend staff meetings and serve on committees as required. Prepare lesson materials, bulletin board displays, exhibits, equipment, and demonstrations. Carry out therapeutic regimens such as behavior modification and personal development programs under the supervision of special education instructors, psychologists, or speech-language pathologists. Provide disabled students with assistive devices, supportive technology, and assistance accessing facilities such as restrooms. Assist in bus loading and unloading. Take class attendance and maintain attendance records. Grade homework and tests, and compute and record results, using answer sheets or electronic marking devices. Organize and supervise games and other recreational activities to promote physical, mental, and social development.

GOE—Career Cluster/Interest Area: 05. Education and Training. **Work Group:** 05.02. Preschool, Elementary, and Secondary Teaching and Instructing. **Other Apprenticeable Jobs in This Work Group:** No others in group. **Personality Type:** Social. These occupations frequently involve working with, communicating with, and teaching people and often involve helping or providing service to others.

Skills—Social Perceptiveness; Learning Strategies; Instructing; Active Listening; Persuasion; Negotiation; Service Orientation; Writing.

Education/Training Required (Nonapprenticeship Route): Short-term on-the-job training. **Related Knowledge/Courses—Geography:** Various methods for describing the location and distribution of land, sea, and air masses, including their physical locations, relationships, and characteristics. **History and Archeology:** Historical events and their causes, indicators, and impact on particular civilizations and cultures. **Psychology:** Human behavior and performance, mental processes, psychological research methods, and the assessment and treatment of behavioral and affective disorders. **Therapy and Counseling:** Information and techniques needed to rehabilitate physical and mental ailments and to provide career guidance, including alternative treatments, rehabilitation equipment and its proper use, and methods to evaluate treatment effects. **Sociology and Anthropology:** Group behavior and dynamics; societal trends and influences; and cultures and their history, migrations, ethnicity, and origins. **English Language:** The structure and content of the English language, including the meaning and spelling of words, rules of composition, and grammar.

Work Environment: Indoors; noisy; standing.

Team Assemblers

- ❋ Annual Earnings: $24,630
- ❋ Growth: 0.1%
- ❋ Annual Job Openings: 264,135
- ❋ Percentage of Women: 30.4%

Related Apprenticeship—Production Technologist (competency).

Work as part of a team having responsibility for assembling an entire product or component of a product. Team assemblers can perform all tasks conducted by the team in the assembly process and rotate through all or most of them rather than being assigned to a specific task on a permanent basis. May participate in making management decisions affecting the work. Team leaders who work as part of the team should be included. Rotate through all the tasks required in a particular production process. Determine work assignments and procedures. Shovel and sweep work areas. Operate heavy equipment such as forklifts. Provide assistance in the production of wiring assemblies.

GOE—Career Cluster/Interest Area: 13. Manufacturing. **Work Group:** 13.03. Production Work, Assorted Materials Processing. **Other Apprenticeable Jobs in This Work Group:** Bakers; Chemical Equipment Operators and Tenders; Coating, Painting, and Spraying Machine Setters, Operators, and Tenders; Cooling and Freezing Equipment Operators and Tenders; Cutting and Slicing Machine Setters, Operators, and Tenders; Extruding, Forming, Pressing, and Compacting Machine Setters, Operators, and Tenders; Food Batchmakers; Furnace, Kiln, Oven, Drier, and Kettle Operators and Tenders; Heat Treating Equipment Setters, Operators, and Tenders, Metal and Plastic; Metal-Refining Furnace Operators and Tenders; Mixing and Blending Machine Setters, Operators, and Tenders; Plating and Coating Machine Setters, Operators, and Tenders, Metal and Plastic; Sawing Machine Setters, Operators, and Tenders, Wood; Separating, Filtering, Clarifying, Precipitating, and Still Machine Setters, Operators, and Tenders; Sewing Machine Operators; Slaughterers and Meat Packers; Woodworking Machine Setters, Operators, and Tenders, Except Sawing. **Personality Type:** Realistic. These occupations frequently involve work activities that include practical, hands-on problems and solutions. They often deal with plants; animals; and real-world materials such as wood, tools, and machinery. Many of the occupations require working outside and don't involve a lot of paperwork or working closely with others.

Skills—Operation Monitoring; Installation; Quality Control Analysis; Equipment Maintenance; Technology Design; Equipment Selection; Repairing; Operation and Control.

Education/Training Required (Nonapprenticeship Route): Moderate-term on-the-job training. **Related Knowledge/Courses—Production and Processing:** Inputs, outputs, raw materials, waste, quality control, costs, and techniques for maximizing the manufacture and distribution of goods. **Mechanical Devices:** Machines and tools, including their designs, uses, benefits, repair, and maintenance.

Work Environment: Indoors; noisy; contaminants; standing; using hands on objects, tools, or controls; repetitive motions.

Telecommunications Equipment Installers and Repairers, Except Line Installers

* Annual Earnings: $54,070
* Growth: 2.5%
* Annual Job Openings: 13,541
* Percentage of Women: 15.2%

Related Apprenticeships—Automatic-Equipment Technician (8000 hrs.); Central-Office Installer (8000 hrs.); Central-Office Repairer (8000 hrs.); Electronic Systems Technician (8000 hrs.); Equipment Installer (Telephone and Telegraph) (8000 hrs.); Maintenance Mechanic, Telephone (6000 hrs.); Private-Branch-Exchange Repairer (8000 hrs.); Private-Branch-Exchange Installer (8000 hrs.); Sound Technician (6000 hrs.); Station Installer and Repairer (8000 hrs.); Technician, Submarine Cable (4000 hrs.); Telecommunications Technician (8000 hrs.).

Set up, rearrange, or remove switching and dialing equipment used in central offices. Service or repair telephones and other communication equipment on customers' properties. May install equipment in new locations or install wiring and telephone jacks in buildings under construction. Note differences in wire and cable colors so that work can be performed correctly. Test circuits and components of malfunctioning telecommunications equipment to isolate sources of malfunctions, using test meters, circuit diagrams, polarity probes, and other hand tools. Test repaired, newly installed, or updated equipment to ensure that it functions properly and conforms to specifications, using test equipment and observation. Drive crew trucks to and from work areas. Inspect equipment on a regular basis to ensure proper functioning. Repair or replace faulty equipment such as defective and damaged telephones, wires, switching system components, and associated equipment. Remove and remake connections to change circuit layouts, following work orders or diagrams. Demonstrate equipment to customers, explain how it is to be used, and respond to any inquiries or complaints. Analyze test readings, computer printouts, and trouble reports to determine equipment repair needs and required repair methods. Adjust or modify equipment to enhance equipment performance or to respond to customer requests. Remove loose wires and other debris after work is completed. Request support from technical service centers when on-site procedures fail to solve installation or maintenance problems. Communicate with bases, using telephones or two-way radios, to receive instructions or technical advice or to report equipment status. Assemble and install communication equipment such as data and telephone communication lines, wiring, switching equipment, wiring frames, power apparatus, computer systems, and networks. Collaborate with other workers to locate and correct malfunctions. Review manufacturers' instructions, manuals, technical specifications, building permits, and ordinances to determine communication equipment requirements and procedures. Test connections to ensure that power supplies are adequate and that communications links function. Refer to manufacturers' manuals to obtain maintenance instructions pertaining to specific malfunctions. Climb poles and ladders, use truck-mounted booms, and enter areas such as manholes and cable vaults to install, maintain, or inspect equipment.

GOE—Career Cluster/Interest Area: 02. Architecture and Construction. **Work Group:** 02.05. Systems and Equipment Installation, Maintenance, and Repair. **Other Apprenticeable**

Jobs in This Work Group: Electrical and Electronics Repairers, Powerhouse, Substation, and Relay; Electrical Power-Line Installers and Repairers; Elevator Installers and Repairers; Heating and Air Conditioning Mechanics and Installers; Maintenance and Repair Workers, General; Refrigeration Mechanics and Installers; Telecommunications Line Installers and Repairers. **Personality Type:** Realistic. These occupations frequently involve work activities that include practical, hands-on problems and solutions. They often deal with plants; animals; and real-world materials such as wood, tools, and machinery. Many of the occupations require working outside and don't involve a lot of paperwork or working closely with others.

Skills—Installation; Repairing; Troubleshooting; Technology Design; Equipment Selection; Systems Analysis; Quality Control Analysis; Equipment Maintenance.

Education/Training Required (Nonapprenticeship Route): Postsecondary vocational training. **Related Knowledge/Courses—Telecommunications:** Transmission, broadcasting, switching, control, and operation of telecommunications systems. **Mechanical Devices:** Machines and tools, including their designs, uses, benefits, repair, and maintenance. **Computers and Electronics:** Electric circuit boards, processors, chips, and computer hardware and software, including applications and programming. **Engineering and Technology:** Equipment, tools, and mechanical devices and their uses to produce motion, light, power, technology, and other applications. **Design:** Design techniques, principles, tools, and instruments involved in the production and use of precision technical plans, blueprints, drawings, and models. **Public Safety and Security:** Weaponry; public safety; security operations, rules, regulations, precautions, and prevention; and the protection of people, data, and property.

Work Environment: Outdoors; noisy; very hot or cold; contaminants; cramped work space, awkward positions; using hands on objects, tools, or controls.

Telecommunications Line Installers and Repairers

* Annual Earnings: $47,220
* Growth: 4.6%
* Annual Job Openings: 14,719
* Percentage of Women: 8.6%

Related Apprenticeships—Cable Television Installer (2000 hrs.); Line Installer-Repairer (8000 hrs.).

String and repair telephone and television cable, including fiber optics and other equipment for transmitting messages or television programming. Travel to customers' premises to install, maintain, and repair audio and visual electronic reception equipment and accessories. Inspect and test lines and cables, recording and analyzing test results, to assess transmission characteristics and locate faults and malfunctions. Splice cables, using hand tools, epoxy, or mechanical equipment. Measure signal strength at utility poles, using electronic test equipment. Set up service for customers, installing, connecting, testing, and adjusting equipment. Place insulation over conductors and seal splices with moisture-proof covering. Access specific areas to string lines and install terminal boxes, auxiliary equipment, and appliances, using bucket trucks, or by climbing poles and ladders or entering tunnels, trenches, or crawl spaces. String cables between structures and lines from poles, towers, or trenches and pull lines to proper tension.

Install equipment such as amplifiers and repeaters to maintain the strength of communications transmissions. Lay underground cable directly in trenches or string it through conduits running through trenches. Pull up cable by hand from large reels mounted on trucks; then pull lines through ducts by hand or with winches. Clean and maintain tools and test equipment. Explain cable service to subscribers after installation and collect any installation fees that are due. Compute impedance of wires from poles to houses to determine additional resistance needed for reducing signals to desired levels. Use a variety of construction equipment to complete installations, including digger derricks, trenchers, and cable plows. Dig trenches for underground wires and cables. Dig holes for power poles, using power augers or shovels, set poles in place with cranes, and hoist poles upright, using winches. Fill and tamp holes, using cement, earth, and tamping devices. Participate in the construction and removal of telecommunication towers and associated support structures.

GOE—Career Cluster/Interest Area: 02. Architecture and Construction. **Work Group:** 02.05. Systems and Equipment Installation, Maintenance, and Repair. **Other Apprenticeable Jobs in This Work Group:** Electrical and Electronics Repairers, Powerhouse, Substation, and Relay; Electrical Power-Line Installers and Repairers; Elevator Installers and Repairers; Heating and Air Conditioning Mechanics and Installers; Maintenance and Repair Workers, General; Refrigeration Mechanics and Installers; Telecommunications Equipment Installers and Repairers, Except Line Installers. **Personality Type:** Realistic. These occupations frequently involve work activities that include practical, hands-on problems and solutions. They often deal with plants; animals; and real-world materials such as wood, tools, and machinery. Many of the occupations require working outside and don't involve a lot of paperwork or working closely with others.

Skills—Installation; Troubleshooting; Repairing; Equipment Maintenance; Programming; Technology Design; Quality Control Analysis; Equipment Selection.

Education/Training Required (Nonapprenticeship Route): Long-term on-the-job training. **Related Knowledge/Courses—Telecommunications:** Transmission, broadcasting, switching, control, and operation of telecommunications systems. **Engineering and Technology:** Equipment, tools, and mechanical devices and their uses to produce motion, light, power, technology, and other applications. **Building and Construction:** Materials, methods, and the appropriate tools to construct objects, structures, and buildings. **Customer and Personal Service:** Principles and processes for providing customer and personal services, including needs assessment techniques, quality service standards, alternative delivery systems, and customer satisfaction evaluation techniques. **Design:** Design techniques, principles, tools, and instruments involved in the production and use of precision technical plans, blueprints, drawings, and models. **Mechanical Devices:** Machines and tools, including their designs, uses, benefits, repair, and maintenance.

Work Environment: Outdoors; very hot or cold; contaminants; cramped work space, awkward positions; hazardous equipment; using hands on objects, tools, or controls.

Further Information: Contact a local joint union-management apprenticeship committee, or the nearest office of your state employment service or apprenticeship agency (see Appendix C). Information is also available from the National Joint Apprenticeship and Training Center (NJATC), 301 Prince Georges Blvd., Suite D, Upper Marlboro, MD 20774. Internet: www.njatc.org

Tellers

- ❋ Annual Earnings: $22,920
- ❋ Growth: 13.5%
- ❋ Annual Job Openings: 146,077
- ❋ Percentage of Women: 84.8%

Related Apprenticeship—Teller (Financial) (2000 hrs.).

Receive and pay out money. Keep records of money and negotiable instruments involved in a financial institution's various transactions. Balance currency, coin, and checks in cash drawers at ends of shifts and calculate daily transactions, using computers, calculators, or adding machines. Cash checks and pay out money after verifying that signatures are correct, that written and numerical amounts agree, and that accounts have sufficient funds. Receive checks and cash for deposit, verify amounts, and check accuracy of deposit slips. Examine checks for endorsements and to verify other information such as dates, bank names, identification of the persons receiving payments, and the legality of the documents. Enter customers' transactions into computers to record transactions and issue computer-generated receipts. Count currency, coins, and checks received, by hand or using currency-counting machine, to prepare them for deposit or shipment to branch banks or the Federal Reserve Bank. Identify transaction mistakes when debits and credits do not balance. Prepare and verify cashier's checks. Arrange monies received in cash boxes and coin dispensers according to denomination. Process transactions such as term deposits, retirement savings plan contributions, automated teller transactions, night deposits, and mail deposits. Receive mortgage, loan, or public utility bill payments, verifying payment dates and amounts due. Resolve problems or discrepancies concerning customers' accounts. Explain, promote, or sell products or services such as travelers' checks, savings bonds, money orders, and cashier's checks, using computerized information about customers to tailor recommendations. Perform clerical tasks such as typing, filing, and microfilm photography. Monitor bank vaults to ensure cash balances are correct. Order a supply of cash to meet daily needs. Sort and file deposit slips and checks. Receive and count daily inventories of cash, drafts, and travelers' checks. Process and maintain records of customer loans. Count, verify, and post armored car deposits. Carry out special services for customers, such as ordering bank cards and checks. Compute financial fees, interest, and service charges. Obtain and process information required for the provision of services, such as opening accounts, savings plans, and purchasing bonds.

GOE—Career Cluster/Interest Area: 06. Finance and Insurance. **Work Group:** 06.04. Finance/Insurance Customer Service. **Other Apprenticeable Jobs in This Work Group:** No others in group. **Personality Type:** Conventional. These occupations frequently involve following set procedures and routines and can include working with data and details more than with ideas. Usually there is a clear line of authority to follow.

Skills—Service Orientation; Mathematics.

Education/Training Required (Nonapprenticeship Route): Short-term on-the-job training. **Related Knowledge/Courses—Customer and Personal Service:** Principles and processes for providing customer and personal services, including needs assessment techniques, quality service standards, alternative delivery systems, and customer satisfaction evaluation techniques. **Sales and Marketing:** Principles and methods involved in showing, promoting, and selling products or services. This includes marketing strategies and tactics, product demonstration and sales techniques, and sales control systems. **English Language:** The structure and content of the English language, including the meaning and spelling of words, rules of composition, and grammar. **Clerical Practices:** Administrative and clerical procedures and systems such as word-processing systems, filing and records management systems, stenography and transcription, forms, design principles, and other office procedures and terminology.

Work Environment: Indoors; more often standing than sitting; using hands on objects, tools, or controls; repetitive motions.

Terrazzo Workers and Finishers

* Annual Earnings: $34,390
* Growth: 10.9%
* Annual Job Openings: 1,052
* Percentage of Women: 0.7%

Related Apprenticeships—Terrazzo Finisher (3500–4000 hrs., hybrid); Terrazzo Finisher (4000 hrs.); Terrazzo Worker (4500–8000 hrs., hybrid); Terrazzo Worker (6000 hrs.).

Apply a mixture of cement, sand, pigment, or marble chips to floors, stairways, and cabinet fixtures to fashion durable and decorative surfaces. Blend marble chip mixtures and place into panels; then push a roller over the surface to embed the chips. Cut metal division strips and press them into the terrazzo base wherever there is to be a joint or change of color, to form desired designs or patterns, and to help prevent cracks. Measure designated amounts of ingredients for terrazzo or grout according to standard formulas and specifications, using graduated containers and scale and load ingredients into portable mixer. Mold expansion joints and edges, using edging tools, jointers, and straightedges. Spread, level, and smooth concrete and terrazzo mixtures to form bases and finished surfaces, using rakes, shovels, hand or power trowels, hand or power screeds, and floats. Grind curved surfaces and areas inaccessible to surfacing machine, such as stairways and cabinet tops, with portable hand grinder. Grind surfaces with a power grinder and polish surfaces with polishing or surfacing machines. Position and secure moisture membrane and wire mesh prior to pouring base materials for terrazzo installation. Modify mixing, grouting, grinding, and cleaning procedures according to type of installation or material used. Wash polished terrazzo surface, using cleaner and water, and apply sealer and curing agent according to manufacturer's specifications, using brush or sprayer. Mix cement, sand, and water to produce concrete, grout, or slurry, using hoe, trowel, tamper, scraper, or concrete-mixing machine. Sprinkle colored marble or stone chips, powdered steel, or coloring powder over surface to produce prescribed finish. Wet surface to prepare for bonding, fill holes and cracks with grout or slurry, and smooth, using trowel. Cut out damaged areas, drill holes for reinforcing rods, and position reinforcing rods to repair concrete, using power saw and drill. Clean installation site, mixing and storage areas, tools, machines, and equipment and store materials and equipment. Fill slight depressions left by grinding with a matching grout material and then hand-trowel for a smooth, uniform surface. Chip, scrape, and grind high spots, ridges, and rough projections to finish concrete, using pneumatic chisel, hand chisel, or other hand tools.

GOE—Career Cluster/Interest Area: 02. Architecture and Construction. **Work Group:** 02.04. Construction Crafts. **Other Apprenticeable Jobs in This Work Group:** Boilermakers; Brickmasons and Blockmasons; Carpet Installers; Cement Masons and Concrete Finishers; Construction Carpenters; Crane and Tower Operators; Drywall and Ceiling Tile Installers; Electricians; Fence Erectors; Floor Layers, Except Carpet, Wood, and Hard Tiles; Glaziers; Insulation Workers, Floor, Ceiling, and Wall; Insulation Workers, Mechanical; Operating Engineers and Other Construction Equipment Operators; Painters, Construction and Maintenance; Paperhangers; Paving, Surfacing, and Tamping Equipment Operators; Pipe Fitters and Steamfitters; Plasterers and Stucco Masons; Plumbers; Reinforcing Iron and Rebar Workers; Riggers; Roofers; Rough Carpenters; Sheet Metal Workers; Stone Cutters and Carvers, Manufacturing; Stonemasons; Structural Iron and Steel Workers; Tapers; Tile and Marble Setters. **Personality Type:** Realistic. These occupations frequently involve work activities that include practical, hands-on problems and solutions. They often deal with plants; animals; and real-world materials such as wood, tools, and machinery. Many of the occupations require working outside and don't involve a lot of paperwork or working closely with others.

Skills—Installation; Equipment Maintenance; Repairing; Coordination; Equipment Selection; Mathematics; Operation and Control; Troubleshooting.

Education/Training Required (Nonapprenticeship Route): Long-term on-the-job training. **Related Knowledge/Courses—Building**

and Construction: Materials, methods, and the appropriate tools to construct objects, structures, and buildings. **Mechanical Devices:** Machines and tools, including their designs, uses, benefits, repair, and maintenance. **Production and Processing:** Inputs, outputs, raw materials, waste, quality control, costs, and techniques for maximizing the manufacture and distribution of goods. **Design:** Design techniques, principles, tools, and instruments involved in the production and use of precision technical plans, blueprints, drawings, and models. **Engineering and Technology:** Equipment, tools, and mechanical devices and their uses to produce motion, light, power, technology, and other applications.

Work Environment: Noisy; contaminants; standing; walking and running; using hands on objects, tools, or controls; repetitive motions.

Tile and Marble Setters

* Annual Earnings: $38,720
* Growth: 15.4%
* Annual Job Openings: 9,066
* Percentage of Women: 2.4%

Related Apprenticeships—Mosaic Worker (4500–8000 hrs., hybrid); Mosaic Worker (6000 hrs.); Tile Setter (4500–8000 hrs., hybrid); Tile Setter (6000 hrs.).

Apply hard tile, marble, and wood tile to walls, floors, ceilings, and roof decks. Align and straighten tile, using levels, squares, and straightedges. Determine and implement the best layout to achieve a desired pattern. Cut and shape tile to fit around obstacles and into odd spaces and corners, using hand- and power-cutting tools. Finish and dress the joints and wipe excess grout from between tiles, using damp sponge. Apply mortar to tile back, position the tile, and press or tap with trowel handle to affix tile to base. Mix, apply, and spread plaster, concrete, mortar, cement, mastic, glue, or other adhesives to form a bed for the tiles, using brush, trowel, and screed. Prepare cost and labor estimates based on calculations of time and materials needed for project. Measure and mark surfaces to be tiled, following blueprints. Level concrete and allow to dry. Build underbeds and install anchor bolts, wires, and brackets. Prepare surfaces for tiling by attaching lath or waterproof paper or by applying a cement mortar coat onto a metal screen. Study blueprints and examine surface to be covered to determine amount of material needed. Cut, surface, polish, and install marble and granite or install pre-cast terrazzo, granite, or marble units. Install and anchor fixtures in designated positions, using hand tools. Cut tile backing to required size, using shears. Remove any old tile, grout, and adhesive, using chisels and scrapers, and clean the surface carefully. Lay and set mosaic tiles to create decorative wall, mural, and floor designs. Assist customers in selection of tile and grout. Remove and replace cracked or damaged tile. Measure and cut metal lath to size for walls and ceilings, using tin snips. Select and order tile and other items to be installed, such as bathroom accessories, walls, panels, and cabinets, according to specifications. Mix and apply mortar or cement to edges and ends of drain tiles to seal halves and joints. Spread mastic or other adhesive base on roof deck to form base for promenade tile, using serrated spreader. Apply a sealer to make grout stain- and water-resistant. Brush glue onto manila paper on which design has been drawn and position tiles, finished side down, onto paper.

GOE—Career Cluster/Interest Area: 02. Architecture and Construction. **Work Group:** 02.04. Construction Crafts. **Other**

Apprenticeable Jobs in This Work Group: Boilermakers; Brickmasons and Blockmasons; Carpet Installers; Cement Masons and Concrete Finishers; Construction Carpenters; Crane and Tower Operators; Drywall and Ceiling Tile Installers; Electricians; Fence Erectors; Floor Layers, Except Carpet, Wood, and Hard Tiles; Glaziers; Insulation Workers, Floor, Ceiling, and Wall; Insulation Workers, Mechanical; Operating Engineers and Other Construction Equipment Operators; Painters, Construction and Maintenance; Paperhangers; Paving, Surfacing, and Tamping Equipment Operators; Pipe Fitters and Steamfitters; Plasterers and Stucco Masons; Plumbers; Reinforcing Iron and Rebar Workers; Riggers; Roofers; Rough Carpenters; Sheet Metal Workers; Stone Cutters and Carvers, Manufacturing; Stonemasons; Structural Iron and Steel Workers; Tapers; Terrazzo Workers and Finishers. **Personality Type:** Realistic. These occupations frequently involve work activities that include practical, hands-on problems and solutions. They often deal with plants; animals; and real-world materials such as wood, tools, and machinery. Many of the occupations require working outside and don't involve a lot of paperwork or working closely with others.

Skills—Installation; Management of Financial Resources; Mathematics; Equipment Selection; Technology Design; Management of Material Resources; Social Perceptiveness; Equipment Maintenance.

Education/Training Required (Nonapprenticeship Route): Long-term on-the-job training. **Related Knowledge/Courses—Building and Construction:** Materials, methods, and the appropriate tools to construct objects, structures, and buildings. **Design:** Design techniques, principles, tools, and instruments involved in the production and use of precision technical plans, blueprints, drawings, and models. **Production and Processing:** Inputs, outputs, raw materials, waste, quality control, costs, and techniques for maximizing the manufacture and distribution of goods. **Economics and Accounting:** Economic and accounting principles and practices, the financial markets, banking, and the analysis and reporting of financial data. **Administration and Management:** Principles and processes involved in business and organizational planning, coordination, and execution. This includes strategic planning, resource allocation, manpower modeling, leadership techniques, and production methods. **Transportation:** Principles and methods for moving people or goods by air, rail, sea, or road, including their relative costs, advantages, and limitations.

Work Environment: Noisy; contaminants; cramped work space, awkward positions; standing; using hands on objects, tools, or controls; bending or twisting the body.

Tool and Die Makers

* Annual Earnings: $45,090
* Growth: –9.6%
* Annual Job Openings: 5,286
* Percentage of Women: 0.9%

Related Apprenticeships—Die Finisher (8000 hrs.); Die Maker (Jewelry-Silver) (8000 hrs.); Die Maker (Paper Goods) (8000 hrs.); Die Maker, Bench, Stamping (8000 hrs.); Die Maker, Stamping (6000 hrs.); Die Maker, Trim (8000 hrs.); Die Maker, Wire Drawing (6000 hrs.); Die Sinker (8000 hrs.); Mold Maker, Die-Cast and Plastic (8000 hrs.); Plastic Fixture Builder (8000 hrs.); Plastic Tool Maker (8000 hrs.); Saw Maker (Cutlery and Tools) (6000 hrs.); Tap and

Die Maker Technician (8000 hrs.); Tool and Die Maker (8000 hrs.); Tool Maker (8000 hrs.); Tool Maker, Bench (8000 hrs.).

Analyze specifications, lay out metal stock, set up and operate machine tools, and fit and assemble parts to make and repair dies, cutting tools, jigs, fixtures, gauges, and machinists' hand tools. Study blueprints, sketches, models, or specifications to plan sequences of operations for fabricating tools, dies, or assemblies. Verify dimensions, alignments, and clearances of finished parts for conformance to specifications, using measuring instruments such as calipers, gauge blocks, micrometers, and dial indicators. Visualize and compute dimensions, sizes, shapes, and tolerances of assemblies, based on specifications. Set up and operate conventional or computer numerically controlled machine tools such as lathes, milling machines, and grinders to cut, bore, grind, or otherwise shape parts to prescribed dimensions and finishes. File, grind, shim, and adjust different parts to properly fit them together. Fit and assemble parts to make, repair, or modify dies, jigs, gauges, and tools, using machine tools and hand tools. Conduct test runs with completed tools or dies to ensure that parts meet specifications; make adjustments as necessary. Inspect finished dies for smoothness, contour conformity, and defects. Smooth and polish flat and contoured surfaces of parts or tools, using scrapers, abrasive stones, files, emery cloths, or power grinders. Lift, position, and secure machined parts on surface plates or worktables, using hoists, vises, v-blocks, or angle plates. Measure, mark, and scribe metal or plastic stock to lay out machining, using instruments such as protractors, micrometers, scribes, and rulers. Cut, shape, and trim blanks or blocks to specified lengths or shapes, using power saws, power shears, rules,

and hand tools. Select metals to be used from a range of metals and alloys, based on properties such as hardness and heat tolerance. Design jigs, fixtures, and templates for use as work aids in the fabrication of parts or products. Set up and operate drill presses to drill and tap holes in parts for assembly. Develop and design new tools and dies, using computer-aided design software. Set pyrometer controls of heat-treating furnaces and feed or place parts, tools, or assemblies into furnaces to harden.

GOE—Career Cluster/Interest Area: 13. Manufacturing. **Work Group:** 13.05. Production Machining Technology. **Other Apprenticeable Jobs in This Work Group:** Computer-Controlled Machine Tool Operators, Metal and Plastic; Foundry Mold and Coremakers; Lay-Out Workers, Metal and Plastic; Machinists; Model Makers, Metal and Plastic; Numerical Tool and Process Control Programmers; Patternmakers, Metal and Plastic; Tool Grinders, Filers, and Sharpeners. **Personality Type:** Realistic. These occupations frequently involve work activities that include practical, hands-on problems and solutions. They often deal with plants; animals; and real-world materials such as wood, tools, and machinery. Many of the occupations require working outside and don't involve a lot of paperwork or working closely with others.

Skills—Repairing; Mathematics; Troubleshooting; Technology Design; Equipment Selection; Installation; Equipment Maintenance; Operation and Control.

Education/Training Required (Nonapprenticeship Route): Long-term on-the-job training. **Related Knowledge/Courses—Mechanical Devices:** Machines and tools, including their designs, uses, benefits, repair, and maintenance. **Design:** Design techniques, principles, tools, and instruments involved in the production and use of precision technical plans, blueprints, drawings, and models. **Engineering and Technology:** Equipment, tools, and mechanical devices and their uses to produce motion, light, power, technology, and other applications. **Production and Processing:** Inputs, outputs, raw materials, waste, quality control, costs, and techniques for maximizing the manufacture and distribution of goods. **Mathematics:** Numbers and their operations and interrelationships, including arithmetic, algebra, geometry, calculus, and statistics and their applications. **Public Safety and Security:** Weaponry; public safety; security operations, rules, regulations, precautions, and prevention; and the protection of people, data, and property.

Work Environment: Noisy; contaminants; hazardous equipment; minor burns, cuts, bites, or stings; standing; using hands on objects, tools, or controls.

Further Information: Contact a local joint union-management apprenticeship committee, or the nearest office of your state employment service or apprenticeship agency (see Appendix C). Information is also available from the National Institute for Metalworking Skills, 10565 Fairfax Boulevard, Suite 203, Fairfax, VA 22030. Internet: www.nims-skills.org

Transportation Vehicle, Equipment, and Systems Inspectors, Except Aviation

- ❋ Annual Earnings: $51,440
- ❋ Growth: 16.4%
- ❋ Annual Job Openings: 2,122
- ❋ Percentage of Women: 14.8%

Our sources did not provide separate job openings data for this occupation. The job openings listed here are shared with Aviation Inspectors; and with Freight and Cargo Inspectors.

Related Apprenticeship—Inspector, Motor Vehicles (4000 hrs.).

Inspect and monitor transportation equipment, vehicles, or systems to ensure compliance with regulations and safety standards. Conduct vehicle or transportation equipment tests, using diagnostic equipment. Investigate and make recommendations on carrier requests for waiver of federal standards. Prepare reports on investigations or inspections and actions taken. Issue notices and recommend corrective actions when infractions or problems are found. Investigate incidents or violations such as delays, accidents, and equipment failures. Investigate complaints regarding safety violations. Inspect repairs to transportation vehicles and equipment to ensure that repair work was performed properly. Examine transportation vehicles, equipment, or systems to detect damage, wear, or malfunction. Inspect vehicles and other equipment for evidence of abuse, damage, or mechanical malfunction. Examine carrier operating rules, employee qualification guidelines, and carrier training and testing programs for compliance with regulations or safety standards. Inspect vehicles or equipment to ensure compliance with rules, standards, or regulations.

GOE—Career Cluster/Interest Area: 07. Government and Public Administration. **Work Group:** 07.03. Regulations Enforcement. **Other Apprenticeable Jobs in This Work Group:** Compliance Officers, Except Agriculture, Construction, Health and Safety, and Transportation; Construction and Building Inspectors; Equal Opportunity Representatives and Officers;

Fire Inspectors; Fish and Game Wardens; Government Property Inspectors and Investigators; Nuclear Monitoring Technicians. **Personality Type:** Realistic. These occupations frequently involve work activities that include practical, hands-on problems and solutions. They often deal with plants; animals; and real-world materials such as wood, tools, and machinery. Many of the occupations require working outside and don't involve a lot of paperwork or working closely with others.

Skills—Repairing; Equipment Maintenance; Troubleshooting; Installation; Quality Control Analysis; Operation Monitoring; Systems Analysis; Systems Evaluation.

Education/Training Required (Nonapprenticeship Route): Work experience in a related occupation. **Related Knowledge/Courses— Mechanical Devices:** Machines and tools, including their designs, uses, benefits, repair, and maintenance. **Transportation:** Principles and methods for moving people or goods by air, rail, sea, or road, including their relative costs, advantages, and limitations. **Public Safety and Security:** Weaponry; public safety; security operations, rules, regulations, precautions, and prevention; and the protection of people, data, and property. **Engineering and Technology:** Equipment, tools, and mechanical devices and their uses to produce motion, light, power, technology, and other applications. **Administration and Management:** Principles and processes involved in business and organizational planning, coordination, and execution. This includes strategic planning, resource allocation, manpower modeling, leadership techniques, and production methods. **Physics:** Physical principles, laws, and applications, including air, water, material dynamics, light, atomic principles, heat, electric theory, earth formations, and meteorological and related natural phenomena.

Work Environment: Outdoors; standing; using hands on objects, tools, or controls.

Tree Trimmers and Pruners

- ❋ Annual Earnings: $29,800
- ❋ Growth: 11.1%
- ❋ Annual Job Openings: 9,621
- ❋ Percentage of Women: 6.2%

Related Apprenticeships—Tree Surgeon (6000 hrs.); Tree Trimmer (Line Clear) (4000 hrs.).

Cut away dead or excess branches from trees or shrubs to maintain right-of-way for roads, sidewalks, or utilities or to improve appearance, health, and value of trees. Prune or treat trees or shrubs, using handsaws, pruning hooks, shears, and clippers. May use truck-mounted lifts and power pruners. May fill cavities in trees to promote healing and prevent deterioration. Supervise others engaged in tree trimming work and train lower-level employees. Transplant and remove trees and shrubs and prepare trees for moving. Operate shredding and chipping equipment and feed limbs and brush into the machines. Remove broken limbs from wires, using hooked extension poles. Prune, cut down, fertilize, and spray trees as directed by tree surgeons. Spray trees to treat diseased or unhealthy trees, including mixing chemicals and calibrating spray equipment. Clean, sharpen, and lubricate tools and equipment. Clear sites, streets, and grounds of woody and herbaceous materials such as tree stumps and fallen trees and limbs. Load debris and refuse onto trucks and haul it away for disposal. Inspect trees to determine whether they have diseases or pest problems.

Cut away dead and excess branches from trees or clear branches around power lines, using climbing equipment or buckets of extended truck booms, and/or chainsaws, hooks, handsaws, shears, and clippers. Collect debris and refuse from tree trimming and removal operations into piles, using shovels, rakes, or other tools. Operate boom trucks, loaders, stump chippers, brush chippers, tractors, power saws, trucks, sprayers, and other equipment and tools. Apply tar or other protective substances to cut surfaces to seal surfaces and to protect them from fungi and insects. Climb trees, using climbing hooks and belts, or climb ladders to gain access to work areas. Split logs or wooden blocks into bolts, pickets, posts, or stakes, using hand tools such as ax wedges, sledgehammers, and mallets. Cable, brace, tie, bolt, stake, and guy trees and branches to provide support. Trim jagged stumps, using saws or pruning shears. Trim, top, and reshape trees to achieve attractive shapes or to remove low-hanging branches. Water, root-feed, and fertilize trees. Harvest tanbark by cutting rings and slits in bark and stripping bark from trees, using spuds or axes. Install lightning protection on trees. Plan and develop budgets for tree work and estimate the monetary value of trees. Provide information to the public regarding trees, such as advice on tree care.

GOE—Career Cluster/Interest Area: 01. Agriculture and Natural Resources. **Work Group:** 01.05. Nursery, Groundskeeping, and Pest Control. **Other Apprenticeable Jobs in This Work Group:** Landscaping and Groundskeeping Workers; Pest Control Workers; Pesticide Handlers, Sprayers, and Applicators, Vegetation. **Personality Type:** Realistic. These occupations frequently involve work activities that include practical, hands-on problems and solutions. They often deal with plants; animals; and real-world materials such as wood, tools, and machinery. Many of the occupations require working outside and don't involve a lot of paperwork or working closely with others.

Skills—Equipment Maintenance; Equipment Selection; Repairing; Operation and Control; Management of Personnel Resources; Science; Operation Monitoring; Installation.

Education/Training Required (Nonapprenticeship Route): Short-term on-the-job training. **Related Knowledge/Courses—Biology:** Plant and animal living tissue, cells, organisms, and entities, including their functions, interdependencies, and interactions with each other and the environment. **Mechanical Devices:** Machines and tools, including their designs, uses, benefits, repair, and maintenance. **Transportation:** Principles and methods for moving people or goods by air, rail, sea, or road, including their relative costs, advantages, and limitations. **Physics:** Physical principles, laws, and applications, including air, water, material dynamics, light, atomic principles, heat, electric theory, earth formations, and meteorological and related natural phenomena. **Public Safety and Security:** Weaponry; public safety; security operations, rules, regulations, precautions, and prevention; and the protection of people, data, and property. **Sales and Marketing:** Principles and methods involved in showing, promoting, and selling products or services. This includes marketing strategies and tactics, product demonstration and sales techniques, and sales control systems.

Work Environment: Outdoors; high places; minor burns, cuts, bites, or stings; standing; climbing ladders, scaffolds, or poles; using hands on objects, tools, or controls.

Truck Drivers, Heavy and Tractor-Trailer

- ❋ Annual Earnings: $36,220
- ❋ Growth: 10.4%
- ❋ Annual Job Openings: 279,032
- ❋ Percentage of Women: 5.2%

Related Apprenticeships—Construction Driver (2400 hrs.); Truck Driver, Heavy (2000 hrs.); Truck Driver, Heavy (3000–4560 hrs., hybrid).

Drive a tractor-trailer combination or a truck with a capacity of at least 26,000 GVW to transport and deliver goods, livestock, or materials in liquid, loose, or packaged form. May be required to unload truck. May require use of automated routing equipment. Requires commercial drivers' license. Follow appropriate safety procedures when transporting dangerous goods. Check vehicles before driving them to ensure that mechanical, safety, and emergency equipment is in good working order. Maintain logs of working hours and of vehicle service and repair status, following applicable state and federal regulations. Obtain receipts or signatures when loads are delivered and collect payment for services when required. Check all load-related documentation to ensure that it is complete and accurate. Maneuver trucks into loading or unloading positions, following signals from loading crew as needed; check that vehicle position is correct and any special loading equipment is properly positioned. Drive trucks with capacities greater than 3 tons, including tractor-trailer combinations, to transport and deliver products, livestock, or other materials. Secure cargo for transport, using ropes, blocks, chain, binders, or covers. Read bills of lading to determine assignment details. Report vehicle defects, accidents, traffic violations, or damage to the vehicles. Read and interpret maps to determine vehicle routes. Couple and uncouple trailers by changing trailer jack positions, connecting or disconnecting air and electrical lines, and manipulating fifth-wheel locks. Collect delivery instructions from appropriate sources, verifying instructions and routes. Drive trucks to weigh stations before and after loading and along routes to document weights and to comply with state regulations. Operate equipment such as truck cab computers, CB radios, and telephones to exchange necessary information with bases, supervisors, or other drivers. Check conditions of trailers after contents have been unloaded to ensure that there has been no damage. Crank trailer landing gear up and down to safely secure vehicles. Wrap goods, using pads, packing paper, and containers, and secure loads to trailer walls, using straps. Perform basic vehicle maintenance tasks such as adding oil, fuel, and radiator fluid or performing minor repairs. Load and unload trucks or help others with loading and unloading, operating any special loading-related equipment on vehicles and using other equipment as necessary.

GOE—Career Cluster/Interest Area: 16. Transportation, Distribution, and Logistics. **Work Group:** 16.03. Truck Driving. **Other Apprenticeable Jobs in This Work Group:** No others in group. **Personality Type:** Realistic. These occupations frequently involve work activities that include practical, hands-on problems and solutions. They often deal with plants; animals; and real-world materials such as wood, tools, and machinery. Many of the occupations require working outside and don't involve a lot of paperwork or working closely with others.

Skills—Equipment Maintenance; Repairing; Operation Monitoring; Troubleshooting; Operation and Control.

Education/Training Required (Nonapprenticeship Route): Moderate-term on-the-job training. **Related Knowledge/Courses—Transportation:** Principles and methods for moving people or goods by air, rail, sea, or road, including their relative costs, advantages, and limitations. **Geography:** Various methods for describing the location and distribution of land, sea, and air masses, including their physical locations, relationships, and characteristics. **Public Safety and Security:** Weaponry; public safety; security operations, rules, regulations, precautions, and prevention; and the protection of people, data, and property. **Law and Government:** Laws, legal codes, court procedures, precedents, government regulations, executive orders, agency rules, and the democratic political process. **Mechanical Devices:** Machines and tools, including their designs, uses, benefits, repair, and maintenance.

Work Environment: Outdoors; very hot or cold; contaminants; sitting; using hands on objects, tools, or controls; repetitive motions.

Water and Liquid Waste Treatment Plant and System Operators

- ❋ Annual Earnings: $37,090
- ❋ Growth: 13.8%
- ❋ Annual Job Openings: 9,575
- ❋ Percentage of Women: 4.0%

Related Apprenticeships—Clarifying-Plant Operator (Text) (2000 hrs.); Waste Treatment Operator (4000 hrs.); Wastewater-Treatment-Plant Operator (4000 hrs.); Water Treatment Plant Operator (6000 hrs.).

Operate or control an entire process or system of machines, often through the use of control boards, to transfer or treat water or liquid waste. Add chemicals such as ammonia, chlorine, or lime to disinfect and deodorize water and other liquids. Operate and adjust controls on equipment to purify and clarify water, process or dispose of sewage, and generate power. Inspect equipment or monitor operating conditions, meters, and gauges to determine load requirements and detect malfunctions. Collect and test water and sewage samples, using test equipment and color analysis standards. Record operational data, personnel attendance, or meter and gauge readings on specified forms. Maintain, repair, and lubricate equipment, using hand tools and power tools. Clean and maintain tanks and filter beds, using hand tools and power tools. Direct and coordinate plant workers engaged in routine operations and maintenance activities.

GOE—Career Cluster/Interest Area: 13. Manufacturing. **Work Group:** 13.16. Utility Operation and Energy Distribution. **Other Apprenticeable Jobs in This Work Group:** Chemical Plant and System Operators; Petroleum Pump System Operators, Refinery Operators, and Gaugers; Power Distributors and Dispatchers; Power Plant Operators; Stationary Engineers and Boiler Operators. **Personality Type:** Realistic. These occupations frequently involve work activities that include practical, hands-on problems and solutions. They often deal with plants; animals; and real-world materials such as wood, tools, and machinery. Many of the occupations require working outside and don't involve a lot of paperwork or working closely with others.

Skills—Operation Monitoring; Operation and Control; Installation; Troubleshooting; Operations Analysis; Management of Material Resources; Equipment Maintenance; Science.

W

Education/Training Required (Nonapprenticeship Route): Long-term on-the-job training. **Related Knowledge/Courses—Biology:** Plant and animal living tissue, cells, organisms, and entities, including their functions, interdependencies, and interactions with each other and the environment. **Chemistry:** The composition, structure, and properties of substances and of the chemical processes and transformations that they undergo. This includes uses of chemicals and their interactions, danger signs, production techniques, and disposal methods. **Physics:** Physical principles, laws, and applications, including air, water, material dynamics, light, atomic principles, heat, electric theory, earth formations, and meteorological and related natural phenomena. **Public Safety and Security:** Weaponry; public safety; security operations, rules, regulations, precautions, and prevention; and the protection of people, data, and property. **Mechanical Devices:** Machines and tools, including their designs, uses, benefits, repair, and maintenance. **Law and Government:** Laws, legal codes, court procedures, precedents, government regulations, executive orders, agency rules, and the democratic political process.

Work Environment: More often outdoors than indoors; noisy; very hot or cold; contaminants; minor burns, cuts, bites, or stings.

Welders, Cutters, and Welder Fitters

* Annual Earnings: $32,270
* Growth: 5.1%
* Annual Job Openings: 61,125
* Percentage of Women: 5.9%

Our sources did not provide separate job openings data for this occupation. The job openings listed here are shared with Solderers and Brazers.

Related Apprenticeships—Lead Burner (8000 hrs.); Welder, Arc (8000 hrs.); Welder, Combination (6000 hrs.); Welder-Fitter (8000 hrs.).

Use hand-welding or flame-cutting equipment to weld or join metal components or to fill holes, indentations, or seams of fabricated metal products. Operate safety equipment and use safe work habits. Weld components in flat, vertical, or overhead positions. Ignite torches or start power supplies and strike arcs by touching electrodes to metals being welded, completing electrical circuits. Clamp, hold, tack-weld, heat-bend, grind, or bolt component parts to obtain required configurations and positions for welding. Detect faulty operation of equipment or defective materials and notify supervisors. Operate manual or semi-automatic welding equipment to fuse metal segments, using processes such as gas tungsten arc, gas metal arc, flux-cored arc, plasma arc, shielded metal arc, resistance welding, and submerged arc welding. Monitor the fitting, burning, and welding processes to avoid overheating of parts or warping, shrinking, distortion, or expansion of material. Examine workpieces for defects and measure workpieces with straightedges or templates to ensure conformance with specifications. Recognize, set up, and operate hand and power tools common to the welding trade, such as shielded metal arc and gas metal arc welding equipment. Lay out, position, align, and secure parts and assemblies prior to assembly, using straightedges, combination squares, calipers, and rulers. Chip or grind off excess weld, slag, or spatter, using hand scrapers or power chippers, portable grinders, or arc-cutting equipment. Analyze engineering drawings, blueprints, specifications, sketches, work orders, and material safety data sheets to plan layout, assembly, and welding operations. Connect and turn regulator valves to activate and adjust gas flow and pressure so that desired flames are obtained. Weld separately or in combination, using aluminum, stainless steel, cast iron, and other alloys. Determine required equipment and welding methods, applying knowledge of metallurgy, geometry, and welding techniques. Mark or tag material with proper job number, piece marks, and other identifying marks as required. Prepare all material surfaces to be welded, ensuring that there is no loose or thick scale, slag, rust, moisture, grease, or other foreign matter.

GOE—Career Cluster/Interest Area: 13. Manufacturing. **Work Group:** 13.04. Welding, Brazing, and Soldering. **Other Apprenticeable Jobs in This Work Group:** Structural Metal Fabricators and Fitters; Welding, Soldering, and Brazing Machine Setters, Operators, and Tenders. **Personality Type:** Realistic. These occupations frequently involve work activities that include practical, hands-on problems and solutions. They often deal with plants; animals; and real-world materials such as wood, tools, and machinery. Many of the occupations require working outside and don't involve a lot of paperwork or working closely with others.

Skills—Repairing; Equipment Maintenance; Installation; Equipment Selection; Operation and Control; Quality Control Analysis.

Education/Training Required (Nonapprenticeship Route): Postsecondary vocational training. **Related Knowledge/Courses—Building and Construction:** Materials, methods, and the appropriate tools to construct objects, structures, and buildings. **Mechanical Devices:** Machines and tools, including their designs, uses, benefits,

repair, and maintenance. **Design:** Design techniques, principles, tools, and instruments involved in the production and use of precision technical plans, blueprints, drawings, and models. **Engineering and Technology:** Equipment, tools, and mechanical devices and their uses to produce motion, light, power, technology, and other applications.

Work Environment: Noisy; contaminants; minor burns, cuts, bites, or stings; standing; using hands on objects, tools, or controls; repetitive motions.

Welding, Soldering, and Brazing Machine Setters, Operators, and Tenders

* Annual Earnings: $30,980
* Growth: 3.0%
* Annual Job Openings: 7,707
* Percentage of Women: 5.9%

Related Apprenticeship—Welding Machine Operator, Arc (6000 hrs.).

Set up, operate, or tend welding, soldering, or brazing machines or robots that weld, braze, solder, or heat-treat metal products, components, or assemblies. Turn and press knobs and buttons or enter operating instructions into computers to adjust and start welding machines. Set up, operate, and tend welding machines that join or bond components to fabricate metal products or assemblies. Load or feed workpieces into welding machines to join or bond components. Correct problems by adjusting controls or by stopping machines and opening holding devices. Give directions to other workers regarding machine setup and use. Inspect, measure, or test completed metal workpieces to ensure conformance to specifications, using measuring and testing devices. Record operational information on specified production reports. Start, monitor, and adjust robotic welding production lines. Read blueprints, work orders, and production schedules to determine product or job instructions and specifications. Assemble, align, and clamp workpieces into holding fixtures to bond, heat-treat, or solder fabricated metal components. Lay out, fit, or connect parts to be bonded, calculating production measurements as necessary. Conduct trial runs before welding, soldering or brazing; make necessary adjustments to equipment. Dress electrodes, using tip dressers, files, emery cloths, or dressing wheels. Remove workpieces and parts from machinery after work is complete, using hand tools. Observe meters, gauges, and machine operations to ensure that soldering or brazing processes meet specifications. Select, position, align, and bolt jigs, holding fixtures, guides, and stops onto machines, using measuring instruments and hand tools. Compute and record settings for new work, applying knowledge of metal properties, principles of welding, and shop mathematics. Select torch tips, alloys, flux, coil, tubing, and wire according to metal types and thicknesses, data charts, and records. Clean, lubricate, maintain, and adjust equipment to maintain efficient operation, using air hoses, cleaning fluids, and hand tools. Prepare metal surfaces and workpieces, using hand-operated equipment such as grinders, cutters, or drills. Set dials and timing controls to regulate electrical current, gas flow pressure, heating and cooling cycles, and shutoff.

GOE—Career Cluster/Interest Area: 13. Manufacturing. **Work Group:** 13.04. Welding, Brazing, and Soldering. **Other Apprenticeable Jobs in This Work Group:** Structural Metal Fabricators and Fitters; Welders, Cutters,

and Welder Fitters. **Personality Type:** Realistic. These occupations frequently involve work activities that include practical, hands-on problems and solutions. They often deal with plants; animals; and real-world materials such as wood, tools, and machinery. Many of the occupations require working outside and don't involve a lot of paperwork or working closely with others.

Skills—Equipment Maintenance; Operation and Control; Operation Monitoring; Repairing; Installation; Troubleshooting; Quality Control Analysis; Equipment Selection.

Education/Training Required (Nonapprenticeship Route): Postsecondary vocational training. **Related Knowledge/Courses—Production and Processing:** Inputs, outputs, raw materials, waste, quality control, costs, and techniques for maximizing the manufacture and distribution of goods. **Mechanical Devices:** Machines and tools, including their designs, uses, benefits, repair, and maintenance. **Engineering and Technology:** Equipment, tools, and mechanical devices and their uses to produce motion, light, power, technology, and other applications. **Design:** Design techniques, principles, tools, and instruments involved in the production and use of precision technical plans, blueprints, drawings, and models. **Public Safety and Security:** Weaponry; public safety; security operations, rules, regulations, precautions, and prevention; and the protection of people, data, and property. **Personnel and Human Resources:** Principles and procedures for personnel recruitment; selection; training; compensation and benefits; labor relations and negotiation; and personnel information systems.

Work Environment: Noisy; contaminants; standing; using hands on objects, tools, or controls; bending or twisting the body; repetitive motions.

Woodworking Machine Setters, Operators, and Tenders, Except Sawing

* Annual Earnings: $24,190
* Growth: 6.4%
* Annual Job Openings: 11,860
* Percentage of Women: 30.4%

Related Apprenticeships—Machine Setter (Woodwork) (8000 hrs.); Wood-turning Lathe Operator (2000 hrs.).

Set up, operate, or tend woodworking machines, such as drill presses, lathes, shapers, routers, sanders, planers, and wood-nailing machines. Start machines, adjust controls, and make trial cuts to ensure that machinery operates properly. Determine product specifications and materials, work methods, and machine setup requirements according to blueprints, oral or written instructions, drawings, or work orders. Feed stock through feed mechanisms or conveyors into planing, shaping, boring, mortising, or sanding machines to produce desired components. Adjust machine tables or cutting devices and set controls on machines to produce specified cuts or operations. Set up, program, operate, or tend computerized or manual woodworking machines, such as drill presses, lathes, shapers, routers, sanders, planers, and wood-nailing machines. Monitor operation of machines and make adjustments to correct problems and ensure conformance to specifications. Select knives, saws, blades, cutter heads, cams, bits, or belts according to workpiece, machine functions, and product specifications. Examine finished workpieces for smoothness, shape, angle, depth of cut, and conformity to specifications and verify dimensions visually and by using hands, rules, calipers, templates, or gauges. Install and adjust blades, cutterheads, boring bits, or sanding belts by using hand tools and rules. Inspect and mark completed workpieces and stack them on pallets, in boxes, or on conveyors so that they can be moved to next workstation. Push or hold workpieces against, under, or through cutting, boring, or shaping mechanisms. With hand tools, change alignment and adjustment of sanding, cutting, or boring machine guides to prevent defects in finished products. Inspect pulleys, drive belts, guards, and fences on machines to ensure that machines operate safely. Remove and replace worn parts, bits, belts, sandpaper, and shaping tools. Secure woodstock against guide or in holding device, place woodstock on a conveyor, or dump woodstock in a hopper to feed woodstock into machines. Clean and maintain products, machines, and work areas. Use hand tools to attach and adjust guides, stops, clamps, chucks, and feed mechanisms. Examine raw woodstock for defects and to ensure conformity to size and other specification standards.

GOE—Career Cluster/Interest Area: 13. Manufacturing. **Work Group:** 13.03. Production Work, Assorted Materials Processing. **Other Apprenticeable Jobs in This Work Group:** Bakers; Chemical Equipment Operators and Tenders; Coating, Painting, and Spraying Machine Setters, Operators, and Tenders; Cooling and Freezing Equipment Operators and Tenders; Cutting and Slicing Machine Setters, Operators, and Tenders; Extruding, Forming, Pressing, and Compacting Machine Setters, Operators, and Tenders; Food Batchmakers; Furnace, Kiln, Oven, Drier, and Kettle Operators and Tenders; Heat Treating Equipment Setters, Operators, and Tenders, Metal and Plastic;

W

Metal-Refining Furnace Operators and Tenders; Mixing and Blending Machine Setters, Operators, and Tenders; Plating and Coating Machine Setters, Operators, and Tenders, Metal and Plastic; Sawing Machine Setters, Operators, and Tenders, Wood; Separating, Filtering, Clarifying, Precipitating, and Still Machine Setters, Operators, and Tenders; Sewing Machine Operators; Slaughterers and Meat Packers; Team Assemblers. **Personality Type:** Realistic. These occupations frequently involve work activities that include practical, hands-on problems and solutions. They often deal with plants; animals; and real-world materials such as wood, tools, and machinery. Many of the occupations require working outside and don't involve a lot of paperwork or working closely with others.

Skills—Equipment Maintenance; Repairing; Operation and Control; Operation Monitoring; Troubleshooting; Equipment Selection; Quality Control Analysis.

Education/Training Required (Nonapprenticeship Route): Moderate-term on-the-job training. **Related Knowledge/Courses—Production and Processing:** Inputs, outputs, raw materials, waste, quality control, costs, and techniques for maximizing the manufacture and distribution of goods. **Mechanical Devices:** Machines and tools, including their designs, uses, benefits, repair, and maintenance. **Design:** Design techniques, principles, tools, and instruments involved in the production and use of precision technical plans, blueprints, drawings, and models. **Mathematics:** Numbers and their operations and interrelationships, including arithmetic, algebra, geometry, calculus, and statistics and their applications.

Work Environment: Noisy; contaminants; hazardous equipment; standing; using hands on objects, tools, or controls; repetitive motions.

Word Processors and Typists

- ✹ Annual Earnings: $30,380
- ✹ Growth: –11.6%
- ✹ Annual Job Openings: 32,279
- ✹ Percentage of Women: 91.2%

Related Apprenticeships—Information Management (Word Processing) (2000 hrs. or competency); Telegraphic-Typewriter Operator (6000 hrs.).

Use word processor/computer or typewriter to type letters, reports, forms, or other material from rough draft, corrected copy, or voice recording. May perform other clerical duties as assigned. Check completed work for spelling, grammar, punctuation, and format. Perform other clerical duties such as answering telephone, sorting and distributing mail, running errands, or sending faxes. Gather, register, and arrange the material to be typed, following instructions. File and store completed documents on computer hard drive or disk and maintain a computer filing system to store, retrieve, update, and delete documents. Type correspondence, reports, text, and other written material from rough drafts, corrected copies, voice recordings, dictation, or previous versions, using a computer, word processor, or typewriter. Print and make copies of work. Keep records of work performed. Compute and verify totals on report forms, requisitions, or bills, using adding machine or calculator. Collate pages of reports and other documents prepared. Electronically sort and compile text and numerical data, retrieving, updating, and merging documents as required. Reformat documents, moving paragraphs or columns. Search for specific sets of stored, typed characters in order to make changes. Adjust settings for format, page layout, line spacing, and other style requirements. Address envelopes or prepare envelope labels, using typewriter or computer. Operate and resupply printers and computers, changing print wheels or fluid cartridges; adding paper; and loading blank tapes, cards, or disks into equipment. Transmit work electronically to other locations. Work with technical material, preparing statistical reports, planning and typing statistical tables, and combining and rearranging material from different sources. Use data entry devices, such as optical scanners, to input data into computers for revision or editing. Transcribe stenotyped notes of court proceedings.

GOE—Career Cluster/Interest Area: 04. Business and Administration. **Work Group:** 04.08. Clerical Machine Operation. **Other Appreceable Jobs in This Work Group:** Data Entry Keyers; Mail Clerks and Mail Machine Operators, Except Postal Service. **Personality Type:** Conventional. These occupations frequently involve following set procedures and routines and can include working with data and details more than with ideas. Usually there is a clear line of authority to follow.

Skills—Installation; Equipment Selection; Social Perceptiveness; Writing.

Education/Training Required (Nonapprenticeship Route): Moderate-term on-the-job training. **Related Knowledge/Courses—Clerical Practices:** Administrative and clerical procedures and systems such as word-processing systems, filing and records management systems, stenography and transcription, forms, design principles, and other office procedures and terminology. **Computers and Electronics:** Electric circuit boards, processors, chips, and computer hardware and software, including applications and programming. **Customer and Personal Service:** Principles and processes for providing customer and personal services, including needs assessment techniques, quality service standards, alternative delivery systems, and customer satisfaction evaluation techniques. **English Language:** The structure and content of the English language, including the meaning and spelling of words, rules of composition, and grammar.

Work Environment: Indoors; sitting.

APPENDIX A

How to Read an Apprenticeship Standards Document

All registered apprenticeships must be governed by a standards agreement that meets certain requirements of the responsible state and/or federal agency. A typical apprenticeship standards document registered with the U.S. Department of Labor's Office of Apprenticeship contains the headings listed below. (The headings within any particular apprenticeship agreement may be ordered differently or, in some cases, combined or divided.) Under each heading you'll find some commentary about what the text of the standards document may specify.

Part I. Definition

Apprenticeship standards usually begin with definitions of key terms, especially "employer" and "apprentice," because these are the parties whose agreement is governed by these standards.

Part II. The Apprenticeship Committee

This section defines the membership of the apprenticeship committee (for example, it may consist of equal numbers of representatives of management and labor) and the committee's responsibilities: for example, establishing the standards for the apprenticeship program, screening and selecting apprentices, determining their progress, communicating with them about their progress or their complaints, maintaining records, monitoring the school where related classroom instruction is given, and issuing certificates to apprentices who have completed the program. The employer of the apprentice may also be required to appoint someone to act as a liaison with the committee.

Part III. Equal Opportunity in Apprenticeship

Usually there is a statement that the apprentices will be recruited, selected, employed, and trained without discrimination on the basis of race, color, religion, national origin, gender, sexual orientation, marital or familial status, disability, lawful political affiliation, or other factors unrelated to ability to do the job. There may also be a statement about affirmative action goals and/or a commitment to provide reasonable accommodation for apprentices with disabilities, although the particulars about these topics are often put into an appendix.

Part IV. Qualifications and Selection of Apprentices

This section defines the minimum requirements for people applying to become apprentices— for example, a minimum age, amount of education, measure of physical fitness, and access to transportation. It may also specify additional measures that are used to differentiate between the minimally qualified applicants and those who are highly qualified: for example, an aptitude test, a selection of relevant courses, a resume, and an interview. It may describe a point system by which you receive a certain number of points depending on how well you meet those requirements. Sometimes the specifics of the selection process are covered in an appendix rather than here.

Part V. Apprenticeship Agreement

This section mentions that the apprentice and the sponsor must sign an agreement, which in turn references this standards document.

Part VI. Obligations of the Employer and Apprentice

This is a general statement of the employer's agreement to provide employment and training (to the extent possible) to the apprentice and the apprentice's agreement to make satisfactory progress toward completion of the training. More specific commitments are to be found in the following sections.

Part VII. Supervision of Apprentices

In this section, the sponsor assures that apprentices will work and learn occupational skills under the supervision of a competent journey worker at all times, or at least until the last phases of the program.

Part VIII. Ratio of Apprentices to Journey Workers

Here you can see the maximum number of apprentices who can be assigned to any one journey worker. Obviously a low number is better. (The national average is probably about eight.)

Part IX. Term of Apprenticeship

This section specifies exactly how many hours of on-the-job training are included in the apprenticeship (for example, 8,000 hours, which is equivalent to four years). It may specify a certain number of calendar years in which these hours must be completed. Usually the work processes that are to be learned are specified in a separate document or an appendix rather than here.

Part X. Credit for Previous Experience

This section states how many hours of prior experience (for example, in military training) or education can be counted toward your apprenticeship commitments and how to apply for recognition of these achievements.

Part XI. Probationary Period

Here you can see the length (in hours) of the period during which the committee can terminate your apprenticeship without having to show cause. These hours, although probationary, typically do count toward your total training period.

Part XII. Related Instruction

This section specifies the number of hours of related instruction that you must complete, but the actual subjects that must be studied are often listed on a separate document or in an appendix. The standards for passing course work (for example, achieving the 80 percent level) may also be specified elsewhere.

Part XIII. Safety and Health Training

This part of the document states that apprentices will learn about safe and healthful work practices in both on-the-job training and related instruction. It affirms the importance of accident prevention skills.

Part XIV. Hours of Work

This statement usually says that you will work the same hours as a journey worker. This protects you from being assigned to a shift that might be atypical of the trade and on which you might not get enough supervision from journey workers. It also protects you from being required to work an abnormally long work week, which would cut into the time available for your night classes.

Part XV. Continuity of Employment

Here the employer or apprenticeship committee promises to provide you with continuous employment during your apprenticeship. Although an escape clause is usually included that allows the employer to lay you off in the event of a lockout, loss of business, and so forth, the statement should affirm that you will be able to resume your apprenticeship as soon as work can be found. The apprenticeship committee may reserve the right to transfer you from one employer to another, with your consent, in order to ensure continuous employment or experience in all aspects of the occupation.

Part XVI. Wages of Apprentices

This section states the arrangement by which you will be awarded steady increases in your pay as you accumulate hours of experience or (in a competency-based program) demonstrate levels of competency. Usually wages are expressed in terms of percentages of a journey worker's wages, and there is a commitment by the employer to determine the average journey worker's wages on a periodic basis. Sometimes the specific pay levels are itemized in the apprenticeship agreement or in an appendix rather than here. In some programs, apprentices who make exceptional progress may be promoted to the next-higher wage level before the number of hours normally required.

Part XVII. Complaint Procedures

This section spells out the procedures for resolving disagreements between the apprentice and the employer. Usually the procedure is designed to avoid a lawsuit to the extent possible. Typically there are separate procedures for complaints regarding discrimination or sexual harassment.

Part XVIII. Registration

Here the committee states that it will register this standards document with a state and/or federal agency and is aware that this registration may be lost if the committee fails to uphold the standards. Registration is good for you, the apprentice, because it requires the committee to include specific standards in this document that protect you, and it also means that your journey worker status will be recognized everywhere. Usually the committee maintains the ability to withdraw from registration voluntarily, but doing so is likely to make their program much less attractive to would-be apprentices.

Part XIX. Records and Certification

This section of the document assures that the apprenticeship committee will keep records of the apprentice's accomplishments and will keep the registration agency informed of any change in the apprentice's status, including completion of all requirements. It also promises that the committee will issue a certificate when the apprentice has completed the program. Apprentices may be required to keep their own set of records.

Part XX. Amendments or Modifications

In this section the committee promises not to change the terms of the apprenticeship without notifying the state and/or federal agency with which the apprenticeship is registered. For your protection, there should also be a statement that the committee cannot change the terms of their agreement with you, the apprentice, without your approval.

Part XXI. Compliance Assurance

Here, as in many contracts, is a statement that nothing in the agreement should be construed as permitting violation of the law.

Part XXII. Signature Page

Here you will find the signatures of the apprenticeship committee's officials and of the state and/or federal administrators with whom the apprenticeship is registered.

Part XXIII. Appendix/Attachments

The appendix or attachments section is usually reserved for specifics that may need to be changed at a future date, such as the following:

❋ Work processes (all the phases of the job that you will learn through on-the-job training)

❋ Wage structure (the level of pay you will earn at each phase of the apprenticeship)

❋ Subjects covered in related instruction (together with the number of hours devoted to each subject)

❋ Examinations that must be passed

❋ The apprenticeship agreement form

❋ The employer's affirmative action plan

APPENDIX B

Excerpts from Standards Documents

Part I. National Standards for the Electrician Apprenticeship (RAIS Code 0159)

On-the-Job Training	
UNIT	APPROXIMATE HOURS

1. Preliminary Work 600
   a. Learning the names and uses of the equipment used in the trade, such as kind, size, and use of cable, wire, boxes, conduits, and fittings, switches, receptacles, service switches, cutouts, etc.
   b. Learning names and uses of the various tools used in assembling this material, care of these tools, and other instructions necessary to familiarize the apprentice with the material and tools of the trade.
   c. Safety.

2. Residential and Commercial Rough Wiring 2,500
   a. Assisting in getting the material from stockroom.
   b. Loading truck and unloading material and equipment on the job.
   c. Laying out the various outlets, switches, receptacles, and other details of the job from blueprints or by direction of the Superintendent of construction.

On-the-Job Training

UNIT	APPROXIMATE HOURS

   d. Laying out the system with materials to be used, where they are to be placed, and other details as to how they shall be run.

   e. Cutting wires, cables, conduit, and raceway; threading and reaming conduit, boring and cutting chases under the direction of the journeyperson.

   f. Installing various kinds of wires, cables, and conduits in accordance with requirements.

   g. Assisting journeyperson in pulling wires, attaching wires to fishtape, and keeping wires from kinds of abrasions.

   h. Connecting conductors to switches, receptacles, or appliances with proper methods of splicing, soldering, and typing.

   i. Installing service switches or load center and subfeeders and fastening up these parts, running raceways, and pulling in conductors under the direction of journeyperson electricians.

   j. Assisting in preparing lists of materials used, including names, number of pieces, or number of feet, etc., for office records.

   k. Loading unused material and cleaning up job area.

3. Residential and Commercial Finish Work 1,500

   a. Connecting and setting switches, receptacles, plates, etc.

   b. Installing proper size and types of fuses for each circuit.

   c. Installing and connecting various kinds of fixtures.

   d. Tracing and polarity of conductors and devices.

   e. Testing the circuit for grounds and shorts and locating and correcting job defects.

   f. Assisting journeyperson in installing and completion of the National Board of Fire Underwriters and special local regulations—proper sizes of wires, services, conduits, etc.

4. Industrial Lighting and Service Installation 2,000

   a. Installing rigid conduit, electric metallic tubing, BX armored cable, and wiremolds on all types of heavy electrical equipment and major-size service entrance installation.

   b. Wiring all types (gas, oil, stoker, etc.) of heating equipment.

   c. Installing wiring and controls for air conditioning.

5. Troubleshooting... 1,000

   a. Repairing all kinds of electrical work.

   b. Checking out trouble and making repairs under supervision of electrician.

   c. Checking out trouble and making repairs without supervision.

(continued)

(continued)

On-the-Job Training	
UNIT	APPROXIMATE HOURS
6. Motor Installation and Control 400	
a. Installing overcurrent devices.	
b. Checking for proper installation and rotation.	
c. Installing replacement motors.	
d. Analyzing motor circuits and troubleshooting.	
e. Installing emergency generators and controls.	
f. Installing pushbuttons, pilot lights, relays, timing devices, and interlocking controls.	
TOTAL 8,000	

Related Instruction

The apprentice shall receive theoretical related instruction for a minimum of 144 hours per year, for each year of their apprenticeship, in all aspects of the trade listed below:

FIRST YEAR

Safety instruction

History

Present and future of the trade

Trade jargon

Tools and equipment

Mathematics

Applied science

Introduction to electricity and electronics

Blueprint reading and specifications

SECOND YEAR

Mathematics for electricians

Electrical wiring, residential

Residential blueprint reading

D.C. fundamentals and circuits

Technical communications

THIRD YEAR

Geometry and trigonometry

Applied physics

Mathematics for electricians II

Motors and generators

Commercial and industrial blueprint reading

Electrical wiring, commercial

FOURTH YEAR

Electrical wiring, industrial

Transformers

Electrical drafting

Applied electronics for industry

Electrical machinery

Analysis and repair

Social economics

Advanced blueprint reading and layout

Part II. National Standards for the Dental Assistant Apprenticeship (RAIS Code 0101)

On-the-Job Training	
UNIT	APPROXIMATE HOURS

1. Ethics and Personal Appearance (proper vocabulary, grammar) 50
2. Care of Dental Equipment and Office (ordering supplies, cleaning, lubricating, maintenance, sterilization of fixed equipment) 50
3. Chair-side Assisting (adopting routine of dentist checklist)....................800
   a. Seat and prepare patients
   b. Arrange instruments
   c. Dental charting
   d. Dental history
   e. Instrument passing
   f. Assist with high-velocity suction
   g. Passing medication prior to filling
   h. Mixing filling material
   i. Releasing patient
   j. Cleanup after patient leaves
   k. Set up for new patient
   l. Greeting new patient

4. Dental Office Management...100
   a. Good organization
   b. Orderliness
   c. No idle gossip or distracting talk—must include patient in conversation
   d. Making appointments over telephone
   e. Use of pegboard bookkeeping
   f. Operation of telephone recorder
   g. Maintain professional dignity

(continued)

(continued)

On-the-Job Training

UNIT	APPROXIMATE HOURS

5. Dental Anatomy 50
   - a. Tooth eruption
   - b. Proper identification
   - c. Know abbreviations for charting
   - d. Know dental anatomy pathology

6. Dental Pathology 200
   - a. Includes all soft tissue, intra- and extra-oral
   - b. Observe all external face features
   - c. Note swellings
   - d. Note scars
   - e. Note pupils of eyes
   - f. Note fingernail beds
   - g. Note distended vessels
   - h. Note blood pressure
   - i. Note texture and color of skin

7. Bacteriology and Sterilization 100
   - a. Autoclave procedure
   - b. Cold sterilization
   - c. Cleaning of instruments
   - d. Use of special chemicals

8. Anesthesia...50
   - a. Preparation of syringe-local
   - b. Correct temperature
   - c. Advice to patient to prevent self-injury
   - d. Observe for any hyper-reactions

9. Dental Roentgenology 100
   - a. Periapical film procedure
   - b. Panolipse film procedure
   - c. Developing film procedure

On-the-Job Training

UNIT	APPROXIMATE HOURS

    d. Proper mounting of film

    e. Basic X-ray interpretation—able to recognize and correct mistakes

10. Oral Hygiene of Pedondontra 100

    a. Toothbrush instructions

    b. Communications and psychological entertainment of patient

    c. Demonstration of instruments

11. Diet and Nutrition 50

    a. Be able to supply patients with diet information

    b. Know carbohydrate chemistry and explain

12. Orthodontra 50

    a. Recognize predisposing factors

    b. Suggest corrections

    c. Inform and illustrate

13. Pharmacology 50

    a. Recognize basic dental drugs

    b. Know side effects

14. Treatment of Emergencies 100

    a. Acquire professional assistance

    b. Know basic life support systems

    c. Know CPR basics

15. Impression Material and Models 150

    a. Assist in impression taking

    b. Mix all impression material

    c. Pour models

    TOTAL 2,000

Related Instruction

UNIT	HOURS
1. Sterilization Procedures, Sanitation, and Personal Hygiene	24
2. Care of Dental Equipment	24
Recordkeeping and Charting	
X-ray Technique and Safety	
Dental Prophylaxis and Oral Health	
Periodontics	
3. Care of Dental Equipment and Supplies	24
Use of Equipment	
4. Operative Dentistry	24
5. Diagnosis and Armamentarium	24
6. Dental Specialties and Instruments	24
TOTAL	144

Part III. From National Standards for Pipe Fitter—Sprinkler Fitter (RAIS Code 0414A)

Apprentice Wage Structure

1st 6 months	50 percent of journey worker's rate
2nd 6 months	55 percent of journey worker's rate
3rd 6 months	60 percent of journey worker's rate
4th 6 months	70 percent of journey worker's rate
5th 6 months	75 percent of journey worker's rate
6th 6 months	80 percent of journey worker's rate
7th 6 months	85 percent of journey worker's rate
8th 6 months	90 percent of journey worker's rate

APPENDIX C

State Apprenticeship Offices

The offices listed here are, for the most part, offices of State Apprenticeship Councils. For states and territories that lack a SAC office, the office listed is that of the Bureau of Apprenticeship and Training. ("USDOL/ETA/OA" stands for "United States Department of Labor; Employment and Training Administration; Office of Apprenticeship"). The Web site listed for each state is not necessarily maintained by the office listed; for example, some are maintained by groups of unions that offer apprenticeships in the state.

Alabama
Gregory Collins
State Director
USDOL/ETA/OA
Medical Forum Bldg., Room 648
950 22nd St. N
Birmingham, AL 35203
(205) 731-1308
E-mail: collins.gregory@dol.gov

Alaska
John Hakala
State Director
USDOL/ETA/OA
Room G-30
605 W. 4th Ave.
Anchorage, AK 99501
(907) 269-3729
E-mail: hakala.john@dol.gov
http://www.ajcn.state.ak.us/apprentice/

Arizona
Dennis Cahill
Director, Apprenticeship Services
Arizona Department of Commerce
1700 W. Washington, Suite 220
Phoenix, AZ 85007
(602) 771-1183
Fax: (602) 771-1205
E-mail: dennisc@azcommerce.com
http://www.azcommerce.com/
    Workforce/Apprenticeships/
    Home.htm

Arkansas

Kenneth Lamkin
State Director
USDOL/ETA/OA
Federal Building—Room 3507
700 W. Capitol St.
Little Rock, AR 72201
(501) 324-5415
E-mail: lamkin.kenneth@dol.gov
http://dwe.arkansas.gov/
   Apprenticeship/
   apprenticeshipindex.html

California

Patricia Garcia
Acting State Director
USDOL/ETA/OA
Suite 1090-N
1301 Clay St.
Oakland, CA 94612-5217
(415) 975-4007
E-mail: garcia.patricia@dol.gov
http://www.dir.ca.gov/
   apprenticeship.html

Colorado

Louis Nagel
State Director
USDOL/ETA/OA
U.S. Custom House
721 19th St., Room 465
Denver, CO 80202
(303) 844-4794
E-mail: nagel.louis@dol.gov
http://www.coworkforce.com/SJH/
   Apprenticeships.asp

Connecticut

Jack M. Guerrera
Apprenticeship Program Manager
Connecticut Labor Department
Office of Apprenticeship & Training
200 Folly Brook Blvd.
Wethersfield, CT 06109-1114
(860) 263-6085
Fax: (860) 263-6088
E-mail: jack.guerrera@ct.gov
http://www.ctdol.state.ct.us/progsupt/
   appren/appren.htm

Delaware

Kevin Calio
Manager
Apprenticeship and Training Section
225 Corporate Blvd.
Suite 104
Newark, DE 19702
(302) 451-3419
Fax: (302) 368-6604
E-mail: kevin.calio@state.de.us

District of Columbia

Lewis Brown
Director
D.C. Apprenticeship Council
609 H St. NE
4th Floor, Room 401
Washington, DC 20002
(202) 698-5099
Fax: (202) 698-5721
E-mail: lewis.brown@dc.gov
http://does.dc.gov/does/cwp/
   view,a,1232,q,618747.asp

Florida

Steven Campora
Director of Apprenticeship
Florida Department of Education
325 W. Gaines St. #754
Tallahassee, FL 32399-0400
(850) 245-0454
Fax: (850) 245-9010
E-mail: steve.campora@fldoe.org
http://www.fldoe.org/workforce/
apprenticeship/

Georgia

Earnest Fowler
Acting State Director
USDOL/ETA/OA
Room 6T80
61 Forsyth St. SW
Atlanta, GA 30303
(404) 302-5895
E-mail: fowler.earnest@dol.gov
http://sdvs.georgia.gov/00/channel_
title/0,2094,26646926_
26882339,00.html
http://www.doe.k12.ga.us/ci_
cta.aspx?PageReq=CICTAYouth

Guam

Ms. Terry L. Barnhart
Program Specialist
Apprenticeship and Training Division
Guam Community College
P.O. Box 23069, GMF
Guam, M.I. 96921
(671) 735-5571
http://guamdol.net/content/view/227
http://www.guamcc.net/admissions/
4_Cert_Degree2002.pdf

Hawaii

Elaine Young
Administrator
Workforce Development Division
Department of Labor and Industrial
Relations
830 Punchbowl St., Room 329
Honolulu, HI 96813
(808) 586-8877
Fax: (808) 586-8822
E-mail: eyoung@dlir.state.hi.us
http://hawaii.gov/labor/wddold/PDF/
construction_apprenticeship_
prog.pdf

Idaho

William Kober
State Director
USDOL/ETA/OA
Suite 204
1150 North Curtis Rd.
Boise, ID 83706-1234
(208) 321-2972
E-mail: kober.william@dol.gov
http://www.idahoworks.org/
http://www.pte.idaho.gov/

Illinois

David Wyatt
State Director
USDOL/ETA/OA
Room 656
230 S. Dearborn St.
Chicago, IL 60604
(312) 596-5508
E-mail: wyatt.david@dol.gov
http://www.ides.state.il.us/
apprenticeship/default.asp

Indiana

John Delgado
State Director
USDOL/ETA/OA
Federal Building and U.S. Courthouse
46 E. Ohio St., Room 528
Indianapolis, IN 46204
(317) 226-7001
E-mail: delgado.john@dol.gov
http://www.learnmoreindiana.org/
needtoknow/knowyouroptions/
Pages/Apprenticeships.aspx

Iowa

Greer Sisson
State Director
USDOL/ETA/OA
210 Walnut St., Room 715
Des Moines, IA 50309
(515) 284-4690
E-mail: sisson.greer@dol.gov
http://www.iowaworkforce.org/
region9/apprenticeship.htm

Kansas

Loretta Shelley
Director
Kansas Department of Commerce
Apprenticeship Program
1000 SW Jackson St., Suite 100
Topeka, KS 66612-1354
(785) 296-4161
Fax: (785) 291-3512
E-mail: lshelley@kansascommerce.
com
http://www.kansasapprenticeship.org

Kentucky

Jim Zimmerman
Director
Kentucky Department of Labor
Division of Employment Standards,
Apprenticeship, and Training
1047 U.S. Highway 127 S., Suite 4
Frankfort, KY 40601
(502) 564-3070
Fax: (502) 564-2248
E-mail: jim.zimmerman@ky.gov
http://www.labor.ky.gov/
ows/employmentstandards/
apprenticeshiptraining/

Louisiana

Heather Stefan
Director, Apprenticeship Division
Louisiana Department of Labor
P.O. Box 94094
Baton Rouge, LA 70804-9094
(225) 342-7820
Fax: (225) 342-2717
E-mail: HStefan@ldol.state.la.us
http://www.laworks.net/Workers.asp

Maine

Gene Ellis
Director of Apprenticeship Standards
Department of Labor
Bureau of Employment Services
55 State House Station
Augusta, ME 04333-0055
(207) 624-6390
Fax: (207) 624-6499
E-mail: gene.a.ellis@maine.gov
http://maine.gov/labor/apprenticeship/
index.htm

Maryland

Roger M. Lash, Jr.
Maryland Apprenticeship & Training
  Program
Division of Workforce Development
1100 N. Eutaw St., Room 201
Baltimore, MD 21201
(410) 767-2246
Fax: (410) 767-2220
E-mail: rlash@dllr.state.md.us
http://www.dllr.state.md.us/labor/
  appr.html

Massachusetts

David Wallace
Director
Division of Apprentice Training
Department of Workforce
  Development
P.O. Box 146759
19 Staniford St.
Boston, MA 02114
(617) 626-5407
Fax: (617) 626-5427
E-mail: dwallace@detma.org
http://www.state.ma.us/dat/Pages/
  WhoWeAre.htm

Michigan

Glenn Bivins
State Director
USDOL/ETA/OAELS-BAT
315 W. Allegan, Room 209
Lansing, MI 48933
(517) 377-1746
E-mail: bivins.glenn@dol.gov
http://www.michigan.gov/
  careers/0,1607,7-170-23461-166992--,
  00.html

Minnesota

Roslyn Wade
Director
Minnesota Department of Labor and
  Industry
Apprenticeship Unit
443 Lafayette Rd.
St. Paul, MN 55155-4303
(651) 284-5090
Fax: (651) 284-5740
E-mail: roslyn.wade@state.mn.us
http://www.doli.state.mn.us/appr.html

Mississippi

Fred Westcott
State Director
USDOL/ETA/OA
Federal Building, Suite 515
100 W. Capitol St.
Jackson, MS 39269
(601) 965-4346
E-mail: westcott.fred@dol.gov
http://www.ngms.state.ms.us/edu/
  Apprentice.htm

Missouri

Neil Perry
State Director
USDOL/ETA/OA
1222 Spruce St., Room 9.102E
Robert A. Young Federal Building
St. Louis, MO 63103
(314) 539-2522
E-mail: perry.neil@dol.gov
http://www.ded.mo.gov/WFD/
  Job%20Seeker%20ServicesSkill%20
  Development/Apprenticeship%20
  Information.aspx

Montana

Mark S. Maki
Supervisor
Apprenticeship and Training Program
Montana Department of Labor &
  Industries
P.O. Box 1728
Helena, MT 59624-1728
(406) 444-3556
Fax: (406) 444-3037
E-mail: mmaki@mt.gov
http://wsd.dli.mt.gov/apprenticeship/
  apprentice.asp

Nebraska

Rick Davis
Acting State Director
USDOL/ETA/OA
Suite C-49
111 S. 18th Plaza
Omaha, NE 68102-1322
(402) 221-3281
E-mail: davis.richard@dol.gov
http://www.workforce.state.ne.us/bat/
  default.htm

Nevada

Lleta Brown
Apprenticeship Training
  Representative
State Apprenticeship Council
c/o Office of the Nevada Labor
  Commissioner
555 E. Washington Ave., Suite 4100
Las Vegas, NV 89101
(702) 486-2738
Fax: (702) 486-2660
E-mail: lbrown@laborcommissioner.
  com
http://www.laborcommissioner.com/
  sac/sac.htm

New Hampshire

Patricia Tormey
Apprenticeship Coordinator/Related
  Instruction
NH Department of Education
Apprenticeship Office
21 South Fruit St., Suite 20
Concord, NH 03301
(603) 271-3893
Fax: (603) 271-4079
E-mail: ptormey@ed.state.nh.us
http://www.labor.state.nh.us/
  apprenticeships.asp

New Jersey

Dennis Fitzgerald
State Director
USDOL/ETA/OA
485 Route 1 S.
Building E, 3rd Floor
Iselin, NJ 08830
(732) 750-9191
E-mail: fitzgerald.dennis@dol.gov
http://lwd.dol.state.nj.us/labor/
  employer/training/Apprenticeship.
  html

New Mexico

Chris Romero
Director of Apprenticeship
New Mexico Department of
  Workforce Solutions
501 Mountain Road NE
Albuquerque, NM 87102
(505) 222-4674
Fax: (505) 222-4676
E-mail: chris.romero1@state.nm.us
http://www.dws.state.nm.us/
  careersolutions/CSS-Apprint.html

New York

Yue Yee
Director
Apprenticeship Training Unit
New York State Department of Labor
State Office Building Campus
    Building #12, Room 436
Albany, NY 12240
(518) 457-6820
Fax: (518) 457-7154
E-mail: yue.yee@labor.state.ny.us
http://www.labor.state.ny.us/
    apprenticeship/appindex.shtm

North Carolina

Brenda Saunders
Bureau Chief
Apprenticeship and Training Bureau
1101 Mail Service Center
4 West Edenton St.
Raleigh, NC 27699-1101
(919) 733-7533
Fax: (919) 715-0398
E-mail: brenda.saunders@nclabor.com
http://www.nclabor.com/appren/
    appindex.htm

North Dakota

Barry Dutton
State Director
USDOL/ETA/OA
304 Broadway
Room 332
Bismarck, ND 58501-5900
(701) 250-4700
E-mail: dutton.barry@dol.gov
http://www.jobsnd.com/seekers/
    train_wia_ojt.html

Ohio

Jean L. Sickles
Director
Ohio State Apprenticeship Council
P.O. Box 1618
Columbus, OH 43216-1618
(614) 644-0202
Fax: (614) 466-7912
E-mail: SICKLJ@odjfs.state.oh.us
http://jfs.ohio.gov/apprenticeship/

Oklahoma

Cynthia McLain
State Director
USDOL/ETA/OA
215 Dean A McGee Ave.
Suite 346
Oklahoma City, OK 73102
(405) 231-4338
E-mail: mclain.cynthia@dol.gov
http://www.oesc.state.ok.us/
http://www.oklahomachoices.com/
    how6.html

Oregon

Stephen Simms
Director
Apprenticeship and Training Division
Oregon State Bureau of Labor and
    Industries
800 NE Oregon St., Suite 1045
Portland, OR 97232
(971) 673-0760
Fax: (971) 673-0768
E-mail: steve.simms@state.or.us
http://www.oregon.gov/BOLI/ATD/
    index.shtml

Pennsylvania

A. Robert Risaliti
Director
Bureau of Labor Law Compliance
PA Department of Labor and Industry
1301 Labor and Industry Building
7th and Forster St.
Harrisburg, PA 17120
(800) 932-0665
Fax: (717) 787-0517
E-mail: arisaliti@state.pa.us
http://www.apprentice.org/

Puerto Rico

Ana Villa
Director
Bureau of Employment Security
P.O. Box 190840
San Juan, PR 00919-0840
(787) 993-9564

Rhode Island

Harold "Buddy" Ekno
Supervisor of Apprenticeship Training
    Programs
RI Department of Labor and Training
Division of Professional Regulation
1511 Pontiac Ave., Building 70
P.O. Box 20247
Cranston, RI 02920-0943
(401) 462-8580
Fax: (401) 462-8528
E-mail: bekno@dlt.state.ri.us
http://www.dlt.ri.gov/apprenticeship/

South Carolina

Ronald Johnson
State Director
USDOL/ETA/OA
Strom Thurmond Federal Building
1835 Assembly St., Room 838
Columbia, SC 29201
(803) 765-5547
E-mail: johnson.ronald@dol.gov
http://www.sctechsystem.com/
    ApprenticeshipCarolina/whatis.htm

South Dakota

Donald Reese
State Director
USDOL/ETA/OA
Room 103
4804 S. Minnesota
Sioux Falls, SD 57108
(605) 330-2566
E-mail: reese.donald@dol.gov
http://www.state.sd.us/applications/
    LD01DOL/

Tennessee

Nathaniel Brown
State Director
USDOL/ETA/OA
Airport Executive Plaza
1321 Murfreesboro Rd., Suite 541
Nashville, TN 37210
(615) 781-5318
E-mail: brown.nat@dol.gov
http://www.tennessee.gov/labor-wfd/

Texas

Dennis Goodson
State Director
USDOL/ETA/OA
300 East 8th St.
Suite 914
Austin, TX 78701
(512) 916-5435
E-mail: goodson.dennis@dol.gov
http://www.twc.state.tx.us/svcs/
    apprentice.html

Utah

Juan Pelaez-Gary
State Director
USDOL/ETA/OA
125 S. State St.
Room 2412
Salt Lake City, UT 84138
(801) 524-5450
E-mail: pelaez-gary.juan@dol.gov
http://www.utahtraining.org/

Vermont

Patricia Nagy
Director
Vermont Department of Labor
Apprenticeship Division
5 Green Mountain Dr.
P.O. Box 488
Montpelier, VT 05601-0488
(802) 828-5082
Fax: (802) 828-4374
E-mail: pnagy@labor.state.vt.us
http://labor.vermont.gov/
    Default.aspx?tabid=214

Virgin Islands

Arah Lockhart
Assistant Commissioner Employment
    and Training
Virgin Islands Department of Labor
2203 Church Street
Christiansted, St. Croix 00820
(340) 776-3700
Fax: (340) 773-0094
E-mail: aclockhart@vidol.gov

Virginia

Beverley Donati
Director
Division of Registered Apprenticeship
Virginia Department of Labor and
    Industry
13 S. Thirteenth St.
Richmond, VA 23219
(804) 225-4362
Fax: (804) 786-8418
E-mail: bev.donati@doli.virginia.gov
http://www.dli.state.va.us/whatwedo/
    apprenticeship/apprenticeship_
    p1.html

Washington

Elizabeth Smith
Apprenticeship Program Manager
Department of Labor and Industries
P.O. Box 44530
Olympia, WA 98504-4530
(360) 902-5320
Fax: (360) 902-4248
E-mail: smel235@lni.wa.gov
http://www.lni.wa.gov/scs/
    apprenticeship/

West Virginia

Kenneth Milnes
State Director
USDOL/ETA/OA
405 Capitol St., Suite 409
Charleston, WV 25301
(304) 347-5794
E-mail: milnes.kenneth@dol.gov
http://www.wvapprenticeships.com/

Wisconsin

Karen Morgan
Bureau Director
State of Wisconsin
Department of Workforce
  Development
Bureau of Apprenticeship Standards
P.O. Box 7972
Madison, WI 53707
(608) 266-3133
Fax: (608) 266-0766
E-mail: Karen.morgan@dwd.state.
  wi.us
http://dwd.wisconsin.gov/
  apprenticeship/default.htm

Wyoming

Karen J. Swindells
State Director
USDOL/ETA/OA
American National Bank Building
1912 Capitol Ave., Room 508
Cheyenne, WY 82001-3661
(307) 772-2448
E-mail: swindells.karen@dol.gov
http://www.wyomingtrades.org/

APPENDIX D

Skills Used in This Book

In each of the descriptions of the best apprenticeable jobs found in Part IV, we've included a listing of the most important skills required for each job. This table contains specific definitions of each skill. Use it as a key to gathering more information about the jobs that interest you.

Explanation of Skills	
Skill	**Definition**
Basic Skills	**Developed capacities that facilitate learning or the more rapid acquisition of knowledge.**
Active Learning	Understanding the implications of new information for both current and future problem-solving and decision-making.
Active Listening	Giving full attention to what other people are saying, taking time to understand the points being made, asking questions as appropriate, and not interrupting at inappropriate times.
Critical Thinking	Using logic and reasoning to identify the strengths and weaknesses of alternative solutions, conclusions, or approaches to problems.
Learning Strategies	Selecting and using training/instructional methods and procedures appropriate for the situation when learning or teaching new things.
Mathematics	Using mathematics to solve problems.
Monitoring	Monitoring/assessing your performance or that of other individuals or organizations to make improvements or take corrective action.
Reading Comprehension	Understanding written sentences and paragraphs in work-related documents.
Science	Using scientific rules and methods to solve problems.
Speaking	Talking to others to convey information effectively.
Writing	Communicating effectively in writing as appropriate for the needs of the audience.

(continued)

(continued)

Explanation of Skills

Skill	Definition
Resource Management Skills	**Developed capacities used to allocate resources efficiently**
Management of Financial Resources	Determining how money will be spent to get the work done and accounting for these expenditures.
Management of Material Resources	Obtaining and seeing to the appropriate use of equipment, facilities, and materials needed to do certain work.
Management of Personnel Resources	Motivating, developing, and directing people as they work; identifying the best people for the job.
Social Skills	**Developed capacities used to work with people to achieve goals**
Coordination	Adjusting actions in relation to others' actions.
Instructing	Teaching others how to do something.
Negotiation	Bringing others together and trying to reconcile differences.
Persuasion	Persuading others to change their minds or behavior.
Service Orientation	Actively looking for ways to help people.
Social Perceptiveness	Being aware of others' reactions and understanding why they react as they do.
Systems Skills	**Developed capacities used to understand, monitor, and improve socio-technical systems**
Judgment and Decision Making	Considering the relative costs and benefits of potential actions to choose the most appropriate one.
Systems Analysis	Determining how a system should work and how changes in conditions, operations, and the environment will affect outcomes.
Systems Evaluation	Identifying measures or indicators of system performance and the actions needed to improve or correct performance relative to the goals of the system.
Technical Skills	**Developed capacities used to design, set up, operate, and correct malfunctions involving application of machines or technological systems**
Operations Analysis	Analyzing needs and product requirements to create a design.
Technology Design	Generating or adapting equipment and technology to serve user needs.
Equipment Selection	Determining the kind of tools and equipment needed to do a job.
Installation	Installing equipment, machines, wiring, or programs to meet specifications.
Programming	Writing computer programs for various purposes.
Operation Monitoring	Watching gauges, dials, or other indicators to make sure a machine is working properly.
Operation and Control	Controlling operations of equipment or systems.

Explanation of Skills

Skill	Definition
Equipment Maintenance	Performing routine maintenance on equipment and determining when and what kind of maintenance is needed.
Troubleshooting	Determining causes of operating errors and deciding what to do about them.
Repairing	Repairing machines or systems, using the needed tools.
Quality Control Analysis	Conducting tests and inspections of products, services, or processes to evaluate quality or performance.

APPENDIX E

The GOE Interest Areas and Work Groups

As Part II explains, the GOE organizes the world of work into large interest areas and more-specific work groups containing jobs with a lot in common. Part II defines the 16 GOE interest areas, but Part III also lists the work groups for each job described. We thought you would want to see the complete GOE taxonomy so you would understand how any job that interests you fits into this structure.

Interest areas have two-digit code numbers; work groups have four-digit code numbers beginning with the code number for the interest area in which they are classified. These are the 16 GOE interest areas and work groups:

01 Agriculture and Natural Resources

    01.01 Managerial Work in Agriculture and Natural Resources

    01.02 Resource Science/Engineering for Plants, Animals, and the Environment

    01.03 Resource Technologies for Plants, Animals, and the Environment

    01.04 General Farming

    01.05 Nursery, Groundskeeping, and Pest Control

    01.06 Forestry and Logging

    01.07 Hunting and Fishing

    01.08 Mining and Drilling

02 Architecture and Construction

    02.01 Managerial Work in Architecture and Construction

    02.02 Architectural Design

    02.03 Architecture/Construction Engineering Technologies

02.04 Construction Crafts

02.05 Systems and Equipment Installation, Maintenance, and Repair

02.06 Construction Support/Labor

03 Arts and Communication

03.01 Managerial Work in Arts and Communication

03.02 Writing and Editing

03.03 News, Broadcasting, and Public Relations

03.04 Studio Art

03.05 Design

03.06 Drama

03.07 Music

03.08 Dance

03.09 Media Technology

03.10 Communications Technology

03.11 Musical Instrument Repair

04 Business and Administration

04.01 Managerial Work in General Business

04.02 Managerial Work in Business Detail

04.03 Human Resources Support

04.04 Secretarial Support

04.05 Accounting, Auditing, and Analytical Support

04.06 Mathematical Clerical Support

04.07 Records and Materials Processing

04.08 Clerical Machine Operation

05 Education and Training

05.01 Managerial Work in Education

05.02 Preschool, Elementary, and Secondary Teaching and Instructing

05.03 Postsecondary and Adult Teaching and Instructing

05.04 Library Services

05.05 Archival and Museum Services

05.06 Counseling, Health, and Fitness Education

06 Finance and Insurance

06.01 Managerial Work in Finance and Insurance

06.02 Finance/Insurance Investigation and Analysis

06.03 Finance/Insurance Records Processing

06.04 Finance/Insurance Customer Service

06.05 Finance/Insurance Sales and Support

07 Government and Public Administration

07.01 Managerial Work in Government and Public Administration

07.02 Public Planning

07.03 Regulations Enforcement

07.04 Public Administration Clerical Support

08 Health Science

08.01 Managerial Work in Medical and Health Services

08.02 Medicine and Surgery

08.03 Dentistry

08.04 Health Specialties

08.05 Animal Care

08.06 Medical Technology

08.07 Medical Therapy

08.08 Patient Care and Assistance

08.09 Health Protection and Promotion

09 Hospitality, Tourism, and Recreation

09.01 Managerial Work in Hospitality and Tourism

09.02 Recreational Services

09.03 Hospitality and Travel Services

09.04 Food and Beverage Preparation

09.05 Food and Beverage Service

09.06 Sports

09.07 Barber and Beauty Services

10 Human Service

10.01 Counseling and Social Work

10.02 Religious Work

10.03 Child/Personal Care and Services

10.04 Client Interviewing

11 Information Technology

11.01 Managerial Work in Information Technology

11.02 Information Technology Specialties

11.03 Digital Equipment Repair

12 Law and Public Safety

        12.01 Managerial Work in Law and Public Safety

        12.02 Legal Practice and Justice Administration

        12.03 Legal Support

        12.04 Law Enforcement and Public Safety

        12.05 Safety and Security

        12.06 Emergency Responding

        12.07 Military

13 Manufacturing

        13.01 Managerial Work in Manufacturing

        13.02 Machine Setup and Operation

        13.03 Production Work, Assorted Materials Processing

        13.04 Welding, Brazing, and Soldering

        13.05 Production Machining Technology

        13.06 Production Precision Work

        13.07 Production Quality Control

        13.08 Graphic Arts Production

        13.09 Hands-On Work, Assorted Materials

        13.10 Woodworking Technology

        13.11 Apparel, Shoes, Leather, and Fabric Care

        13.12 Electrical and Electronic Repair

        13.13 Machinery Repair

        13.14 Vehicle and Facility Mechanical Work

        13.15 Medical and Technical Equipment Repair

        13.16 Utility Operation and Energy Distribution

        13.17 Loading, Moving, Hoisting, and Conveying

14 Retail and Wholesale Sales and Service

        14.01 Managerial Work in Retail/Wholesale Sales and Service

        14.02 Technical Sales

        14.03 General Sales

        14.04 Personal Soliciting

        14.05 Purchasing

        14.06 Customer Service

15 Scientific Research, Engineering, and Mathematics

      15.01 Managerial Work in Scientific Research, Engineering, and Mathematics

      15.02 Physical Sciences

      15.03 Life Sciences

      15.04 Social Sciences

      15.05 Physical Science Laboratory Technology

      15.06 Mathematics and Data Analysis

      15.07 Research and Design Engineering

      15.08 Industrial and Safety Engineering

      15.09 Engineering Technology

16 Transportation, Distribution, and Logistics

      16.01 Managerial Work in Transportation

      16.02 Air Vehicle Operation

      16.03 Truck Driving

      16.04 Rail Vehicle Operation

      16.05 Water Vehicle Operation

      16.06 Other Services Requiring Driving

      16.07 Transportation Support Work

Index

D

M

N

T

455